GLOBAL JOURNEYS
IN METRO DETROIT

GLOBAL JOURNEYS IN METRO DETROIT

Copyright © 1999

•

•

ISBN 0-9673379-0-9

GLOBAL JOURNEYS
IN METRO DETROIT

ITINERARY

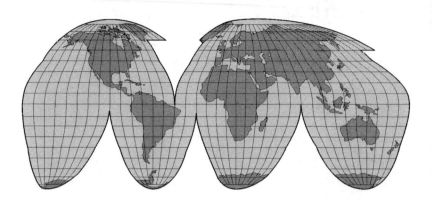

HOW THIS BOOK CAME ABOUT

The idea for this book was sparked halfway around the world as I journeyed to New Zealand. With the help of an itinerary-style guidebook, I was able not only to find my way around that beautiful country in the South Pacific, but also to experience the flavor and culture of its people.

As I returned home, however, I realized that I now knew more about New Zealand's attractions than I did about some in my own hometown. For example, I could better direct someone to art galleries in Auckland than I could to ethnic restaurants in Hamtramck.

This thought motivated me to learn more about the cultural attractions Detroit has to offer the hometown and out-of-town tourist. Detroit's cosmopolitan image came into focus as I found restaurants, markets and boutiques, cultural exhibits and events representing many nationalities and ethnic groups. I discovered that without going far from home, anyone could travel "around the world" right within the Detroit area.

It wasn't, however, until my colleague, Marcia Danner, became aware of my research that the idea for the guidebook began to take form. As a travel writer and editor specializing in Michigan tourism, she, too, was interested in showcasing Detroit's treasures and discovering its little known gems. Marcia introduced me to Patricia Banker Peart, a magazine editor and graphic designer, who was

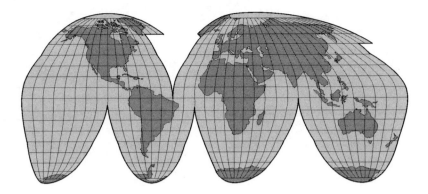

tuned into the cultural pulse of the metro region. One of Pat's editorial interests was writing about the ethnic heritage of Detroit's population and the influence it has on the community.

As we shared our concern that the city needed a guide that could take people easily and safely into its diverse neighborhoods and suburbs, we began to envision an itinerary guidebook. During a two-year period of research and exploration, we came up with more than 50 tours and a thousand listings highlighting many of the cultural groups with a visible presence in the area. Pat researched the cuisine, cultural arts and customs of each country or ethnic group and designed a format to give the reader geographic and cultural background. Marcia searched out local ethnic communities and connected with community leaders and writers from many nationalities to tell the story of immigration to Detroit, the efforts to preserve cultural traditions, and the entertainment and enrichment opportunities for residents and visitors.

As a result of bringing together many representatives of the various racial and ethnic groups in this area, our vision grew into this multicultural guide to Detroit that we call Global Journeys. Profits from book sales will benefit the cultural exchange programs of the New Detroit Coalition and other community-based organizations.

Helen B. Love

PREFACE: DISCOVERING DETROIT'S RICH DIVERSITY

When the Reverend Jesse Jackson compared America to a quilt—a country woven together with common thread from patches of fabric in every shape, size and color—it was easy to see our nation, not as a bland melting pot of immigrants from around the world, but as a rich mixture of culturally diverse people with similar hopes and dreams.

Detroit's patch on that quilt represents a microcosm of America. A city rich with color and vibrant in style. One whose fabric reflects our history of people coming here from around the world to build a better future. A city which struggled for survival, yet always retained the hope that the common thread holding it together would be strong enough for tomorrow.

Global Journeys is a celebration of Detroit's rich heritage and cultural diversity. More than a simple travel guide, it is a multicultural manual with the potential of bringing the people of metro Detroit closer together. Our hope is that it opens your heart and mind—your very spirit—to venture out and experience the world of cultures abundant here in Metro Detroit. We hope it will open the invisible fences that too often separate our neighborhoods and help you build new friends among people you may not have understood. We hope it will help you see the similarities of all humankind while expanding your appreciation and acceptance of our cultural differences.

Those who travel outside the United States often say you can go halfway around the world and feel as if you have not left the country. With *Global Journeys,* we want you to experience the world without ever leaving Metro Detroit. We want you to see and feel the deep legacy of our ethnic and cultural diversity here in this great city.

With the help of *Global Journeys,* you can visit Poland this weekend and Africa the next. You can take a journey to the Far East or the Middle East; Latin America or Europe. You can discover each country's history, traditions, foods, entertainment and so much more. Whether you are a parent looking for creative ways to spend time with your children, a school teacher interested in a fresh approach to studying different cultures, an individual planning a fun outing for a group of friends, or a young adult searching for a greater understanding of Detroit's history, *Global Journeys* is for you.

Welcome to the world of Metro Detroit—enjoy your journey!

Dennis W. Archer
Mayor
City of Detroit

X

SPONSORS

•

GLOBAL TRAVELER
Ford Motor Company

•

AMBASSADORS
Eastman Kodak Company

Masco Corporation

•

ADVENTURERS
Blue Cross Blue Shield of Michigan

Ghafari Associates, Inc.

Al Long Ford
Tarik & Helen Daoud

The Wellness Plan

•

TRAVELING COMPANIONS
Detroit Edison Foundation

IBM Corporation

Kmart

Metropolitan Detroit Convention & Visitors Bureau

•

ARMCHAIR TRAVELERS
Comerica

DaimlerChrysler Corporation

Eastern Market Merchants Association with
Michigan Food & Beverage Association

ELDA, Inc.

Helen B. Love

New Echelon, Inc.

SelectCare

Frank D. Stella

Walbridge Aldinger

ACKNOWLEDGMENTS

With any project of this nature, there are many to thank for making our vision a reality. We are grateful to Ford Motor Company, not only for its commitment to attract and retain talented men and women from a variety of cultures, but also for its significant contribution toward publication of this book. For Ford, the book was always a gift to the city of Detroit.

Eastman Kodak's regional representative offered corporate assistance to jumpstart the book's production when it was only an idea; and when the book was near completion, Masco Corporation fueled our final efforts. And throughout the entire project, ELDA, Inc. provided office space and services; and valuable production management came from our printer, New Echelon, Inc.—a true partner in this project.

We also salute the organizations that shared our goals and vision. In particular, New Detroit, Inc. helped us launch this project as a program of its Racial Justice and Cultural Collaboration Focus Area.

The contributors list recognizes individuals from various cultural groups, who shared their knowledge of multicultural Detroit by serving as advisors and consultants. Many others answered inquiries and returned questionnaires.

A team of writers, representing various ethnic groups and cultural interests, provided much of the preliminary research. From this base, the editors launched an extensive study of each cultural group.

Over the three-year duration of this project, various individuals and company staffs aided in the massive job of compiling listings, verifying information, proofreading copy and reviewing chapters. We thank AAA Michigan, ACCESS, Ameritech and the Ford Communications Network for their assistance.

The final result of this collaborative effort is a volume that showcases the cultural treasures of metro Detroit and the strength and vibrancy that come from its diversity.

CREDITS

Publishing Team:
   Marcia Danner
   Helen B. Love
   Patricia Banker Peart

Editors: Marcia Danner, Patricia Banker Peart

Graphic Design: Patricia Banker Peart

Cover Design: Richard Selonke

Associate Editor: Ellen Piligian

Writers/Researchers: JoAnn Amicangelo, Mary Ball, Thurman Bear, Linda Lyles Daniels, Jennifer Delle Monache, Anahid Derbabian, Martha Garcia, Natalia Krawec Hanks, Carol Hopkins, Lisa Lagerkvist Johnson, Ruth Mossok Johnston, Judith Kiefer, Elizabeth Chiu King, Francine Levine, Jennifer McLeod, Sonia Mishra, Dianne O'Connor, Christine Zia Oram, Sheetal Patel, Bill Semion, Louise Thomas, Khristi Zimmeth

Researchers: Joy Fern, Michaela Garlett, Sarah May, Rosalind Caldwell Jones, Ingerid Parrish, Patricia Hill Welch, Don Samull

Reviewers/Proofreaders: Becky M. Bach, Ann Bright, Amanda L. Brodkin, Susan Char, Lydia Cisaruk, Linda M. Di Pietro, Hunter Downey, Curtrise Garner, Dawn Hounshell, Mike Imirie, Nati Jenks, Debbie Keith, Gilda Keith, Maria Kovac, Edda la Framboise, Margaret Mellott, Suzanne Mittelstadt, Randal Peart, Ingerid Parrish, Sastry Putcha, Scott Renas, Doris Rhea, Steve Roy, Sue Hamilton Smith, Bonnie Townsend

Editorial/Production Assistance: Julie Cantwell, Sue Cavallaro, Michelangelo Cicerone, Julie Hyde-Edwards, Rebecca Kavanaugh

ORGANIZATIONS

The following organizations assisted in the publication of this book by sharing their knowledge, insight and ideas.

City of Detroit
> Office of the Mayor
>> David Smydra
>
> Cultural Affairs Department
>> Marilyn Wheaton, James Hart
>
> Public Information Department
>> Sherrie Farrell, Rose Love
>
> Detroit Recreation Department
>> Ernest W. Burkeen, Jr., Shirley Harbin

Detroit Institute of Arts
> Laurie Barnes, Isabella Basombrio, Amy Parrent

Detroit Upbeat
> Jill DeMaris

International Institute of Metropolitan Detroit
> Mary Ball, Rosemary Bannon, Nada Dalgamouni

International Vistors Council of Metropolitan Detroit
> Julie Oldani

Michigan Council for the Arts
> Betty Boone, Ed Nelson

Michigan Department of Agriculture
> Market Development Division

Michigan Ethnic Heritage Studies Center
> Otto Feinstein, Germaine Strobel

Metropolitan Detroit Visitors & Convention Bureau
> Renee Monforton

National Conference for Community and Justice
> Daniel Krichbaum, Barbara Gray

New Detroit, Inc.
> Horacio Vargas

The Olive Press
> Francine Levine

Travel Michigan
> Cynthia Snyder

University Cultural Center Association
> Connie Mullett

West Bloomfield Schools
> Marcia Tucker

CONTRIBUTORS

AMERICAS

AMERICANA
Linda Lyles Daniels, Sarah May, Wendy Metros, Bill Semion, Molly Zink

AFRICAN AMERICAN HERITAGE
Lila Cabbil, Kimberly Camp, Marguerite Carlton, Linda Lyles Daniels, Charles "MoJo" Johnson, Ron Jackson, Rosalind Caldwell Jones, Debbie Keith, Gilda Keith, Llenda Jackson Leslie, Georgella Muirhead, Robyn Myrick, David Rambeau, Dwight Smith, Cassandra Spratling, Joann Watson, Patricia Hill Welch, Margo Williams, Natalynne Stringer Williams, Shirley Woodson, Nkenge Zola. *Music Consultants:* Jim Dulzo, Mitch Genoa, Wendell Harrison, Amy Davis Jackson, Robert Jones, Arthur LaBrew, Willis Patterson, Khadejah Shelby, Deborah Smith Pollard, James Tatum

CARIBBEAN
Julio Bateau, Vincent Carr, Linda Lyles Daniels, Thomas Sertima, Mavis Spencer, Roland Wiener

JEWISH HERITAGE
Rabbi Marla Feldman, Allan Gale, Ruth Mossok Johnston, Francine Levine, Diana Lieberman, Nancy Gad-Harf

NATIVE AMERICAN HERITAGE
Thurman Bear, Janis Fairbanks, Alveretta Kalebaba, Eva Kennedy, William A. LeBlanc, Jennifer McLeod, Nancy Ragsdale, S. Kay Young

LATIN AMERICA
Martha Garcia, Carol Padilla, Sally Rendon, Ozzie Rivera, Maria Elena Rodriguez, Horacio Vargas, Kathy Wendler

EUROPE

ARMENIA
Hagop Asadurian, Anahid Derbabian, Dickran Toumajan

EASTERN EUROPE
Judith Kiefer, Michael Krolewski

FRANCE
Harriet Berg, Bill Bostick, Lisa Mower Gandelot,
Carol Hopkins, Didet McPhail, James Hansen

GERMANY
Sophie Ellis, Roswitha Koch, Helen Hodge, Adam Medel,
Eugene Carl Strobel, Robert Uhelski

GREAT BRITAIN
Patricia Pilling

GREECE
Mary Ball, Carol Hopkins, Sandy Koukoulas

HUNGARY
Eva Boicourt, Barbara House, Judith Kiefer, Shirley Rakoczy
Przywara, Zolton Sandor

IRELAND
Jack Derrig, Michael Kerwin, Rollande Krandall,
Kathleen O'Neil, Margaret Noonan, Tom Sullivan, Jr.

ITALY
Lisa Bica Grodsky, Jennifer Delle Monache,
Andrea DiTommaso, Carol Hopkins, Severio Mancina

POLAND
Greg Biestek, Joan Bittner, Eva Boicourt, Michael Krolewski,
Pawell Krol, Marcia Lewandowski, Don Samull,
Noreen Smialek-Sinclair, Helen Suchara, David Trioano

SCANDINAVIA
Art Elander, Lisa Lagerkvist Johnson, Betty Holmbo,
Lillian Lagerkvist, Ingerid Parrish, Kathy Usitalo

UKRAINE
Natalia Krawec Hanks, Bohdan Fedorak, Lydia Wroblewski

AFRICA/MIDDLE EAST

AFRICA
Linda Lyles Daniels, Efion Eniang, Beauty Onomake

ARAB WORLD
Ismael Ahmed, Eiman Aziz, Lina Beydoun, Haifa Fakhouri,
Diane Denaro Frank, Kathy Kakish, Rola Nashef, Phyllis Noda,
Louise Thomas, Annette Vanover

CHALDEAN HERITAGE
Christine Zia Oram, Rt. Rev. Sarhad Y. Jammo,
Rev. Manuel Y. Boji, Yacoub Mansour, Jane Shallal,
Mary Kay Sengstock

ASIA

CHINA
Elizabeth Chiu King, Marisa Ming, Jen Yuan Her,
Winnie Wong

JAPAN
Anita Bretzner, Lise Ann Gouin, Mary Kamidoi,
Judith Kiefer, Melissa Kimura, Maki Rann, Toshi Shimoura,
Izumi Suzuki, Valerie Yoshimura

KOREA
Jae Bang, Jeff Galloway, Benjamin Kim, Seungsoon Konarska,
Dianne O'Connor, H. Sook Wilkinson, Moon Ja Yoon

SOUTHEAST ASIA
Antoine Giosoco, Judith Kiefer, Peter Kue, Lucita O'Campo,
Delaila Lapid

INDIA
Sunita Bhama, Raju Dhoop, Ash Hedap, Sonia Mishra,
Sam Narayan, Sheetal Patel

MULTICULTURAL DETROIT

Nada Dalgamouni, Nati Jenks, Judith Kiefer, Khristi Zimmeth

HOW TO NAVIGATE YOUR WAY THROUGH *GLOBAL JOURNEYS*

MAKING THE MOST OF THIS GUIDEBOOK

HOW TO NAVIGATE YOUR WAY THROUGH *GLOBAL JOURNEYS*

On the surface, *Global Journeys* is a travel guide that invites you to explore the rich mixture of cultures in metro Detroit. On a deeper level, it is a book that can help you better understand and appreciate the variety of people living here.

Global Journeys is a book that will take you around the world without ever boarding a plane. From the Americas to Europe, from Africa to the Middle East to Asia, this book will lead you on a fascinating road of cultural discovery. Each chapter is a "visit" to a different country or ethnic heritage, complete with historical and cultural background information, "guided" tours, maps and directions, listings of restaurants, specialty shops, social clubs, historical buildings, cultural events, and more.

WHAT KIND OF TRAVELER DID WE HAVE IN MIND?

Global Journeys is designed for everyone who has an open mind and a sense of adventure.

It is for long-time metro Detroiters who want to make new discoveries about the people who make up this area. It is for visitors who wants to get a glimpse of this historic town. It is for teachers who wants to give students a real-life view of various cultures. It is for parents who want their children to understand their own ethnic heritage or want to expose them to other cultures right in their own backyard. It is for those who may not be able to afford to travel around the world, but would still love to experience the flavor of various cultures. It is for social or religious group organizers who want to plan meaningful field trips or social outings. It is for friends looking for weekend entertainment or an evening out.

CONSIDER THE WORLD OF POSSIBILITIES

Natives of metro Detroit as well as visitors to the city…groups, families and those on their own…teachers and students…will all find this guidebook packed with adventure and the possibility for personal growth. We hope it will provide creative inspiration and encourage involvement as you embark on each journey.

Go ahead and begin by exploring your own ethnic heritage, but don't stop there. Make a commitment to explore other cultures on a regular basis. Perhaps you would like to organize a monthly travel group among your friends or co-workers. Pick a country to explore and then set off to experience its cultural sights and sounds as represented here in metro Detroit. Or plan a party with friends and let a selected country be the party's theme. Festive decorations and ethnic music could set the scene for party-goers dressed in ethnic garb.

If you're a parent looking for outings to broaden the family's world view, you might begin your journey by viewing a video about the country you plan to visit. To further set the scene, you could listen to an audio tape of ethnic music as you travel to and from your destination. To make the experience that much more memorable, collect ideas from each country's holidays and add something new to your family's celebrations.

If you're on your own, consider taking a class to learn folk dancing, the bagpipe or Tai Chi. It's a great way to meet new people while you explore cultural diversity. And for dating couples, the restaurants, performances, exhibitions and events listed will open up new ideas for places to go.

Church, school and social groups will find this book full of opportunities to get better acquainted with cultures around the world. A series of outings for children and adults alike could be based on tours in the book. Or, the world can come to you. Your group could host a multicultural fair and have booths selling the crafts and cuisine of different countries. You could hire performers or invite cultural organization leaders to speak to your group. This introduction could inspire you to venture out for a closer look at the culture.

The possibilities really are limitless when you open your mind to new adventures and open your heart to the people you'll find.

HOW TO USE THIS GUIDEBOOK

We've designed *Global Journeys* to make it easy for you to jump on board any of 50 tours included in the book. Sections devoted to each continent of the world contain specific chapters on countries that have a presence in the metro Detroit area. The format allows you to quickly get a glimpse of the country and its culture and to chart your course for discovery.

● **Background Information:** Each chapter begins with a brief introduction to the history and geography of the featured country, along with an overview of the immigration patterns of the people who have come to Detroit. You might begin your journey by reading this background information to give you a foundation from which to start.

Of course, an entire book could have been written in place of each chapter, so if you're looking for a more in-depth study of a particular culture, take advantage of your local library, consult the web sites listed or call one of the cultural centers listed for a closer look.

● **Tours:** Next are the "guided" tours which are designed for those with either a little time or a lot. Some tours are designed for specific days of the week, others for an afternoon, and still others will fill an entire day and night. Many of the places on the tours are spread out all over the Motor City, which encompasses a good deal of territory. In most cases you won't be able to park your car in one central location and walk through an entire tour. That's why we've included step-by-step directions to take you quickly and safely from one place to another.

→ **Each tour has a code at the beginning, corresponding to its geographic region on the map on pages XXIV and XXV.**

● **Special Listings:** Each chapter includes a listing of some restaurants, markets and shops, historic buildings, cultural arts and exhibits, annual events, social clubs and cultural organizations, local performers, educational opportunities, churches, and media sources. This sampling is designed to provide opportunities for exploring the uniqueness of each culture. Space limitations restrict more extensive listings.

You may also want to peruse Detroit's daily newspapers, the weekly *Metro Times, Hour Detroit* magazine, web sites and radio stations for the latest information on restaurants, cultural arts, entertainment and events. Or, if you're planning ahead, obtain a copy of the special newsletters and publications offered by the various cultural organizations for the scoop on what's happening in their corner of the city.

● **Cultural Sidebars:** Interspersed with the listings are sidebars that highlight cultural aspects of each country. Here you will gain insight about the cuisine, art, music, holidays and customs.

TRAVELING TIPS

● **Call Ahead:** If you have no time to waste, call the places you plan to visit in advance to confirm their hours, admission prices, if any, and whether or not they're still in business at all. With the help of those who compiled the information for each chapter, we have tried to be as accurate and up-to-date as possible. However, since things can change quickly, we encourage you to call ahead.

● **Border Crossing Regulations:** Some of the tours in this guide entail crossing a *real* international border—Canada. If you have any questions concerning immigration, currency exchange or import duty, call the Windsor Convention and Visitors Bureau at 1-800-256-3633.

● **Language Barriers:** As you visit these "countries," you may experience different languages or dialects. Be patient and creative as you attempt to communicate with people whose speech patterns differ from yours.

● **Make notes:** Use the blank pages provided in each section for additions and updates.

TAKE NOTE:

● **Dining:** In our listing of restaurants for each country, we've simply included those deemed authentic by cultural "natives." They are neither rated, nor necessarily recommended. The choices range from formal four-star restaurants to casual small diners. Reading the regional cuisine information provided for each country should reduce any anxiety you might have about trying new foods. If you're a visitor to the city, your hotel concierge can help you make a good selection. And, since we've not included pricing information, you may want to call ahead to get an idea of the restaurant's prices, as well as payment and reservations policies.

● **Restaurants and Shops:** While some establishments have a long history in the Detroit area, others come and go. Restaurants, in particular, frequently change ownership. As new ones open, others go out of business.

● **Media:** There are several radio stations in the Detroit area that feature some ethnic programming. But with ownership and format changes occurring often in the radio industry, there is no guarantee that current programming, schedules or phone numbers will stay the same. Likewise, TV stations and cable offerings change.

● **Exhibits:** Be aware that certain museum exhibits may not always be on view. Collections are often rotated and sometimes displaced for traveling shows or gallery renovation. Becoming a member or "friend" of your favorite museum and getting the organization's newsletter is a good way to stay up-to-date.

● **Events:** Due to the two-to-three-year publishing schedule of this guide-book, specific dates for annual events have not been given, and even the month listed is subject to change. Please check with the sponsoring organization for current information.

● **Organizations:** Phone numbers listed for groups often belong to volunteers. Since many of these contacts are serving a limited term of office, they may no longer be the current officer or chairperson.

● **Religious Centers:** Places of worship serve both the spiritual and cultural needs of the ethnic community. The churches, temples, synagogues and mosques listed in *Global Journeys* represent only a sampling of the ethnic congregations in metro Detroit. For a more complete listing, contact the Christian Communications Council of Metro Detroit Churches at (313) 962-0340. To order the directory published by the Council, send $18 to 1300 Mutual Building, 28 West Adams St., Detroit 48226.

● **Phone Numbers:** Despite a concerted effort by a team of volunteers to verify over a thousand phone numbers listed in this book, there may still be some inaccuracies. Please use the mail-back postcard or e-mail address to correct errors.

● **Work With Us:** Let us know if we've left out something that should have been included in the book. Tell us if a place has gone out of business or if a new shop or restaurant has opened. You can use the form found in this book, e-mail us or visit our web site (**www.globaldetroit.com**) where we'll keep you informed of the latest updates.

As you will discover, the metro-Detroit area has a wealth of diverse cultures for you to explore and people to get to know. Our hope is that *Global Journeys* will inspire you to reach out and experience all this great city has to offer.

May your journeys be memorable.

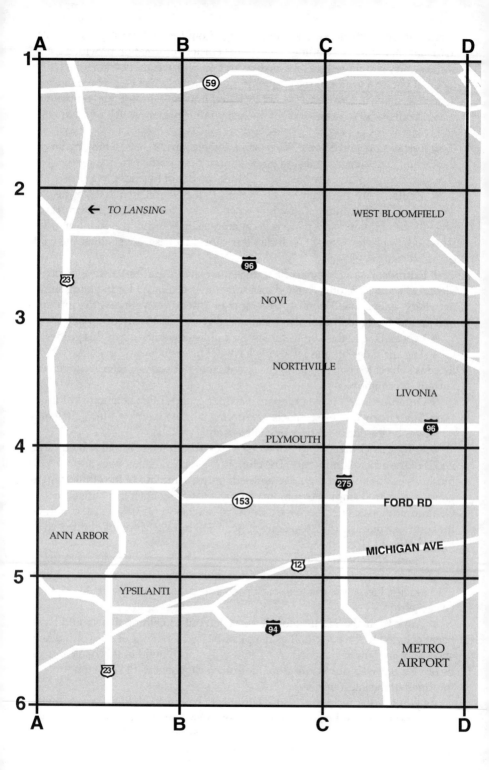

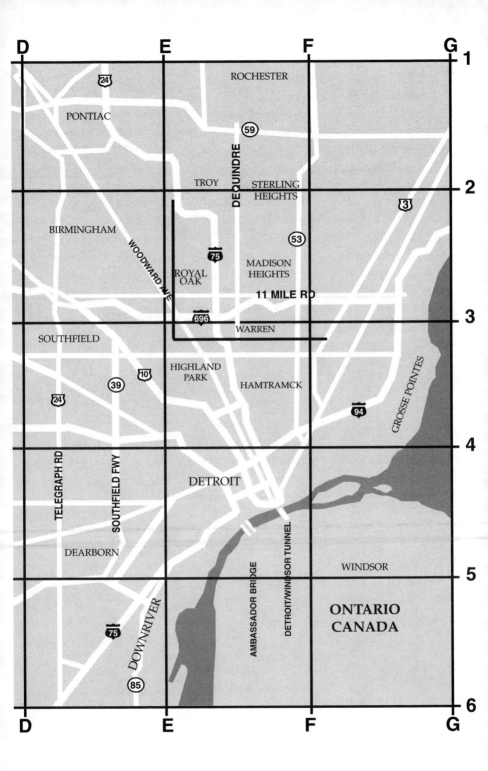

NOTES

GLOBAL JOURNEYS
IN METRO DETROIT

THE AMERICAS

NOTES

HOME SWEET HOME

★★★★★★

Aa Bb Cc Dd Ee Ff Hh Ii Jj Kk Ll Mm Nn
Oo Pp Qq Rr Ss Tt Uu Vv Ww Xx Yy Zz

★★★

1 2 3 4 5 6 7 8 9 0

Samplers were strips of fabric embroidered with examples of different stitches. Although the earliest dated sampler was made in 1598, the sampler's greatest popularity was in the 17th to the 19th centuries, until the advent of the sewing machine. Valued as an exhibition of the maker's skill, these samplers were often framed and hung as artworks. Samplers eventually were used principally to teach girls their stitches, in addition to the alphabet and numerals, which came to form part of a design that often included mottoes or famous quotations. Floral motifs and other pictorial elements gradually became common, and genealogical information was sometimes included.

This chapter is meant to be just a "sampler" of some of the uniquely American culture that has emerged since Colonial times, from cider mills to Cajun cooking, bluegrass banjo to the last drive-in theater.

★★★★★★★★★★★★★★★★★★★★★★★★★★★★★★

THREE CENTURIES OF AMERICANA IN DEARBORN

There can't be anything that says "Americana" more than Henry Ford Museum and Greenfield Village in Dearborn. What has become the world's largest indoor-outdoor museum was developed by auto pioneer Henry Ford in 1929 as a way of showing the sweeping changes that transformed America from a rural, agrarian society to a highly industrialized nation.

Greenfield Village celebrates nearly every aspect of the growth of America, from the homes and workshops where hand-worked crafts were made to the laboratories where inventions were conceived that changed the world. As a testament to America's tradition of innovation, ingenuity and resourcefulness, **Henry Ford Museum** focuses on the tools and products of industrialization. The suggested day-long tours that follow take you through three centuries of Americana as you explore the 81-acre village and 12-acre museum.

[D-E/4-5] *Henry Ford Museum and Greenfield Village are located in Dearborn, west of Southfield (M-39), between Michigan Avenue and Oakwood Blvd.*

From the Southfield Freeway (M-39): *Exit southbound at Michigan Avenue (west) and follow the Southfield service route to the entrance at Village Rd. From northbound Southfield, take Rotunda Drive west to Oakwood Blvd. and turn right. Follow Oakwood to the entrance at Village Rd.*

From I-94: *Exit northbound on Oakwood Blvd. (Exit #206), drive three miles northwest.*

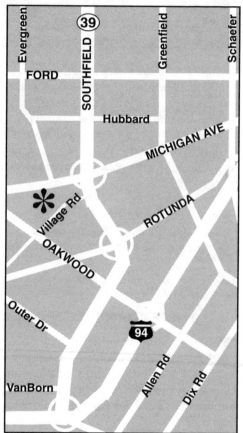

Hours: *Daily 9:00 a.m.- 5:00 p.m. Closed Thanksgiving and Christmas.*

Admission: The Village and Museum charge an admission comparable to other world-class attractions. A number of options are available, including a two-day combination ticket, an annual ticket and family membership. Since each facility has a separate admission and plenty to occupy the visitor, select the ticket option that best suits your plans for a single or multiple visits.

Daily Museum: Adult $12.50, Seniors 62 and over $11.50, Ages 5-12 $6.25.

Daily Village: Adult $12.50, Seniors 62 and over $11.50, Ages 5-12 $6.25.

Two-Day Combination: Adult $22, Ages 5-12 $11.

School Field Trip Group Rate: $5 per person. (Call 313-982-6001 for reservations.)

Annual Ticket: Adults $28, Ages 5-12 $14.
Memberships: Individual $45, Family $90.

History surrounds you as you head through the gates at Dearborn's Greenfield Village. A Model-A shuttle bus putts along narrow roads, past the homes and shops of immigrants and sons of immigrants who helped put America on wheels and in the air. In the distance, the wail of the whistle from a steam-powered locomotive echoes through the trees, between the even more shrill sound of the steamboat Suwanee taking visitors on a Mark Twain-style ride.

Step through the gates of Greenfield Village and board the train for a circle tour of the complex. Or, start your trip back in time on foot by heading west to the farm and craft demonstration areas. **Firestone Farm,** the boyhood home of tire magnate Harvey Firestone on the southwest side of the Village, is the scene of 19th-century farm life demonstrations, including Fall Harvest Days in October and Spring Farm Days in April. Several streets nearby feature mills, workshops and studios, including a **glass shop** where blowers fashion pitchers, vases, holiday ornaments and the like. Stop in at the **Armington & Sims** machine shop and make your own brass candle holder to take home for just $3. Or, visit **Plymouth Carding Mill** to see how pioneers readied wool for weaving at places like the nearby **Textiles Shop.**

In the Village Green area, visit the 1880s **J.R. General Store,** where you can still buy rock candy at 65 cents a box. Hungry? Head next door to the **Eagle Tavern,** a real 1800s stagecoach stop from Clinton, Michigan. Enjoy hearty meals in an 1850s atmosphere as tavern employees greet you as if you'd just stepped off the Detroit-to-Chicago stagecoach. (Another restaurant, **A Taste of History,** offers self-serve lunches and snacks from the past. During the summer season, refreshment stands are open throughout the Village.)

On the east side of the Village Green are the **Logan County Courthouse** where Abraham Lincoln practiced law, the **George Washington Carver Memorial, McGuffey Schoolhouse** and the **Hermitage Slave House.** The loop east also leads to the **Suwanee amusement area**, with the popular carousel ride, and past the homes of famous Americans: **Stephen Foster, Luther Burbank, Robert Frost** and **Noah Webster.**

The facades of Henry Ford Museum are replicas of Philadelphia's Independence Hall, Congress Hall, and Old City Hall.

Some of the earliest structures, dating to the 1600s, are at the east end, such as the **Cotswold Forge** and the **Cape Cod Windmill** located near the **Daggett Farmhouse.**

Continue past the **Susquehanna Plantation** and through the covered bridge to reach the famed **Menlo Park (N.J.) Laboratory** complex of Michigan-born Thomas Edison. Raised in the Port Huron area, to which Edison's family moved from the Netherlands, he created many of his 1,093 patented inventions, including his most famous, the electric light bulb, in this lab. Edison's chair remains just as he left it on the 50th anniversary of electric light.

Nearby is the **Wright Brothers'** home and cycle shop. The Wright family moved from England and eventually to Dayton, Ohio, where the brothers designed and built their famed aircraft that took America into the skies. Across the street is the home of ketchup magnate **H.J. Heinz.** The son of a German immigrant, he began the food empire that bears his name by bottling horseradish in 1869 at—aptly enough—Sharpsburg, Pa.

On your way back to the main gate, stop in to see the boyhood home and shop of the man who helped put America on wheels with the Model T. **Henry Ford's** family moved from Cork County, Ireland, and settled in Dearborn, not far from Greenfield Village. His original workshop was moved from 58 Bagley in Detroit.

Back by the entrance, the air-conditioned **Greenfield Village Store** sells hand-crafted products, books, gifts and souvenirs.

★★★★★★★★★★★★★★★★★★★★★★★★★★★★★★★★★★

TOUR	HENRY FORD MUSEUM

For an indoor experience, explore Henry Ford Museum in the 12-acre building resembling Philadelphia's Independence Hall. From the front galleries containing the museum's collection of **decorative arts** to the huge exhibit hall in the rear devoted to **transportation, communications, lighting, industry, agriculture** and **domestic life,** the exhibits provide a three-dimensional view of American history, culture and technology.

Historical displays in the central concourse and plaza areas feature George Washington's camp bed from the American Revolution and the chair Abraham Lincoln was sitting in when he was assassinated at Ford's Theater in 1865. The presidential collection also includes a parade of limousines used in office by Theodore and Franklin Roosevelt, Eisenhower and Reagan, as well as the vehicle John F. Kennedy was riding in when he was assassinated on Nov. 22, 1963.

One of the most impressive exhibits is the **"Automobile in American**

Life," an apropos display for the house built by Ford. All manner of Fords, from the original to one of the all-time favorites, the first Mustang off the assembly line, are nestled amidst automotive memorabilia. The exhibit not only documents the evolution of the automobile and its industry, but also its cultural impact and how the American landscape changed with the roadside businesses and entertainment that emerged.

At the perimeter of the automotive displays are other **Transportation Exhibits** dedicated to aviation and the age of steam railroads. The mammoth 600-ton Chesapeake & Ohio steam locomotive and Admiral Byrd's 1925 Fokker Trimotor, the first plane to fly over the North Pole, tower over the collection.

Hands-on exhibits in the concourse and plaza areas include "**Innovation Station,**" where visitors team up to solve problems. At one station, for example, participants feed balls into a system by pedaling bicycles, while other team members control the flow of balls to different stations and communicate with others to keep the whole operation running smoothly.

"**Made in America,**" located just to the south of the central concourse, pays homage to the products that are synonymous with American ingenuity. The permanent exhibit showcases more than 1,500 items and is a great spot for kids to ogle at all the activity. Overhead, a conveyor carries an array of American-made products, from the ubiquitous shopping cart and an airplane propeller, to the proverbial kitchen sink. In another section, a robot painter simulates painting a tractor body and car parts moving on the conveyor. Kids can operate a robot in another area and peer into microscopes to see the heart of a computer. To provide historical background, videos concentrate on the national and cultural origins of migrant and immigrant workers who swelled America's work force between 1880 and 1920.

The area on the south side of "Made in America" is devoted to "**Home Arts.**" The collection includes a section that traces the development of the American kitchen and appliances through the decades.

The Museum also mounts special exhibits, and an Imax theater is scheduled to open by the end of 1999.

Both the north and south side of the museum have gift shops and food service. The cafeteria-style restaurant has been refurbished and is now called the **Michigan Cafe**, offering an interesting selection of regional dishes.

*Henry Ford Museum &
Greenfield Village host a
variety of events each
year. For details, call
(313) 982-6150.*

February
BLACK HISTORY MONTH Activities and exhibits focus on the Emancipation, the Great Northern Migration, the Harlem Renaissance and the Civil Rights Movement.

March
WOMEN IN AMERICA *(late March)* Celebrates two centuries of women's lives at work, home and play.

April
SPRING FARM DAYS *(late April)* Costumed presenters in the Village plow and plant fields, shear sheep and tend to other chores at 18th, 19th and 20th century farms. Visitors are encouraged to pitch in and lend a hand.

May
CIVIL WAR REMEMBRANCE Memorial Day observance of the men who wore the blue and gray and the families who kept the home fires burning.

June
MOTOR MUSTER *(mid-June)* Parade of favorite cars of the 1930s, '40s, '50s and '60s, as well as bicycles, motorcycles and vintage commercial vehicles.

COLONIAL LIFE *(late June)* 18th century American life is recreated with Revolutionary War battlefield, urban and rural homesteads and Native American encampment.

July
SALUTE TO AMERICA Fourth of July weekend celebration includes fireworks and open-air concerts by Detroit Symphony Orchestra.

A TASTE OF HISTORY *(mid-July)* A sampling of the culinary artistry of the past at the giant tasting tent and cooking demonstrations. Extended evening hours.

August
CELEBRATION OF EMANCIPATION *(early August)* Special exhibits and reenactments feature traditional African-American music and storytelling.

September
OLD CAR FESTIVAL *(early Sept.)* Collectors from across the nation gather in the Village with vintage vehicles (1932 and earlier) for a car show.

RAILROAD DAYS *(late Sept.)* Vintage and modern train cars and locomotives, model trains, "hobo camp" entertainment and hands-on activities.

October
FALL HARVEST DAYS *(early-mid Oct.)* Harvest-time activities at historic farms of the 18th-through early 20th centuries.

November-December
TRADITIONS OF THE SEASON *From Thanksgiving through the first week in January,* the Museum and Village are decked out in holiday splendor. In the Village, visitors can sing carols in the Town Hall or take an old-fashioned sleigh ride, weather permitting. Seasonal displays in the museum include a gingerbread village and model train sets.

LIVING HISTORY ATTRACTIONS

GREENFIELD VILLAGE/HENRY FORD MUSEUM
20900 Oakwood Blvd., Dearborn
(313) 271-1620
Daily 9am-5pm except Thanksgiving and Christmas. (See tour information.)

CROSSROADS VILLAGE AND HUCKLEBERRY RAILROAD
6140 Bray Rd., (I-475 Exit 13), Flint
(810) 736-7100 or 800-648-7275
Mon-Fri 10am-5:30pm, Sat-Sun/holidays 11am-6:30pm. Attractions in Genesee Recreation Area include restored 1860-80 village and narrow-gauge railroad. Operating blacksmith shop, cider mill, sawmill, grist mill, general store and church are among 28 historic structures. Steam-powered locomotive pulling antique passenger cars departs from Crossroads Depot for 35-minute trip. Carrousel, Ferris wheel and wagon rides also available.

GREENMEAD HISTORICAL PARK
2051 Newburgh Rd., Livonia
(248) 477-7375
Grounds open dawn-dusk May-October and December. Guided tours Sun 1-4pm. Historical village with buildings from 1850s, including general store, church, schoolhouse. Hill House Museum exhibits period furnishings and displays depicting Livonia's earliest settlers. Picnicking facilities on 103-acre farm site.

MILL RACE VICTORIAN VILLAGE
Griswold N. of Main, Northville
(248) 348-1845
Guided tours June-Oct Sun 1-4pm. Historic buildings moved from original sites include the Wash Oak School (1873), New School Church (1845), Hunter House (1851), Yerkes House (1868) and The Cottage House and Blacksmith Shop (1890s).

OAKLAND COUNTY PIONEER AND HISTORICAL SOCIETY
405 Oakland Ave., Pontiac
(248) 338-6732
Office hours Mon-Fri 9am-4pm. Tours by appointment. Pine Grove Historical Museum, the Gov. Moses Wisner Historic House and Grounds and the Drayton Plains one-room schoolhouse are maintained by the Society. National and state historic site features carriage house, working root cellar and restored summer kitchen.

TROY VILLAGE GREEN AND HISTORICAL MUSEUM
60 W. Wattles Rd. at Livernois, Troy
(248) 524-3579
Tue-Sat 9am-5:30pm, Sun 1-5pm. Village includes Caswell House (1832), log cabin (1820s), Poppleton School (1877) and wagon repair shop (1890). Historical exhibits, craft workshops and special events throughout the year.

MUSEUMS AND HISTORIC PLACES

DETROIT
DETROIT FIRE DEPT. HISTORICAL MUSEUM
2737 Gratiot, Detroit
(013) 224-2035
Open Mon-Fri 9am-5pm by appointment only. Detroit fire service history traced from days of early horse-drawn vehicles to present state-of-the-art. Antique fire apparatus, artifacts and pictures.

DETROIT GARDEN CENTER HISTORIC MOROSS HOUSE
1460 E. Jefferson, Detroit
(313) 259-6363
Tue, Wed, Thu, 9:30am-3:30pm. Non-profit volunteer organization offers tours of the home known as the oldest brick house in Detroit. Also offers use of horticultural library, features special events, speakers and workshops.

DETROIT HISTORICAL MUSEUM
5401 Woodward, Detroit
(313) 833-9721
Wed-Sun, 9:30am-5pm. Museum in the Cultural Center focuses on the history of the City of Detroit and its people from 1701 to the present. "Streets of Old Detroit" is a favorite. Workshops, special activities and other programs are ongoing.

DOSSIN GREAT LAKES MUSEUM
100 Strand, Belle Isle, Detroit
(313) 267-6440
Wed-Sun, 10am-5pm. Closed Mon,Tue, & holidays. A unique presentation of ship models, artwork and special exhibits featuring the commercial navigation of the Great Lakes.

MARINER'S CHURCH OF DETROIT
170 E. Jefferson Ave., Detroit (next to Tunnel to Canada)
(313) 259-2206
Sun service at 8:30am & 11am; tours Tue-Sat 10am-3pm. Detroit's earliest Gothic Church, built when Detroit's life centered around the river, is dedicated to sailors on the Great Lakes.

SIBLEY HOUSE
976 E. Jefferson, Detroit
(313) 881-0040
Built in1848, this Greek-Revival landmark was the home of Judge Solomon Sibley, former Detroit mayor. Renovated and used for offices of the Detroit Junior League.

U.S. DISTRICT COURT HOUSE
231 W. Lafayette, Detroit
(313) 226-4969
Mon-Fri 8:30am-5pm. Observe and discuss federal court procedure with a judge. Early 1900s reconstructed court room (previously located in old Federal Building).

ELMWOOD CEMETERY
1200 Elmwood Ave., Detroit
(between Vernor and Lafayette)
Interesting and beautifully-landscaped cemetery with graves of many of Michigan's most famous citizens, including 12 governors. Various self-guided tour booklets are available at the front gate office. Adjacent to **Mt. Elliott,** an historic Catholic cemetery.

SUBURBS
Many local communities have historic homes or small museums showing life as it was around the time of the founding. Historical societies and Chambers of Commerce can provide information. Below are a few examples:

CLAWSON HISTORICAL MUSEUM
41 Fisher, Clawson
(248) 588-9169
Sun, Wed 1-4pm. Group tours by appointment. Historic home contains furnishings of the 1920s and photos from Clawson's early days.

CROCKER HOUSE
15 Union St, Mt. Clemens
(810) 465-2488
Tue-Thu, 10am-4pm; first Sun of month 1-4pm. Closed Jan & holidays. A Victorian home with completely furnished rooms in the manner of the 1870's.

DEARBORN HISTORICAL MUSEUM
915 Brady St., Dearborn
(313) 565-3000
Closed Sun & holidays; Mon-Sat (May-Oct) 9am-5pm; (Nov-Apr) 1pm-5pm.
Two buildings feature period-furnished rooms with exhibits: **The McFadden-Ross House** and **The Commandant's Quarters.** The third building features an agricultural exhibit and early craft shop. The annual colonial festival is held on the grounds in early June, featuring Indian story-telling and dancing, craft demonstrations, folk music, encampments, mock battles and more.

PLYMOUTH HISTORICAL MUSEUM
155 South Main St., Plymouth
(734) 455-8940
Thu, Sat, Sun, 1-4pm. History of Plymouth captured in exhibits and archives. Also offers Plymouth city tours.

WYANDOTTE MUSEUM
2610 Biddle Ave., Wyandotte
(734) 246-4520
First Sun of month 2pm-5pm, Tue, Wed, Thurs 1-4pm.
A Queen Anne Victorian mansion, restored to its natural state. Christmas Open House, Heritage Days, Fall Festival.

THE ARTS & CRAFTS MOVEMENT

Pewabic Pottery, in Detroit, is the oldest art pottery in continuous operation in the United States. Currently, the pottery operates as a ceramic arts learning center, museum and gallery. It was founded in 1903 in conjunction with the "Arts and Crafts" philosophy, an international movement begun at the turn-of-the-century in reaction to the aesthetic decay caused by the industrial revolution. The Arts and Crafts ideal of combining utility and beauty in everyday objects was fully realized in the handmade architectural tiles Pewabic produced. Pewabic earned a national reputation for its famous iridescent glazes, and its tiles became an important feature of many homes and institutions around the country. Among local commissions were Christ Church Cranbrook, Detroit's Guardian Building, the Main Branch of the Detroit Public Library, Detroit Institute of Arts, Holy Redeemer Church and Meadow Brook Hall.

The exhibition schedule at the Pottery provides a forum for the highest quality ceramic art, featuring works that range from traditional to experimental. International leaders in the field, as well as promising emerging artists, are represented.

The museum and archives serve as a research center for the study of the ceramic collection of founder Mary Chase Stratton and historical documents dating from the turn-of-the-century.

See also "Multicultural Detroit" chapter for more on Center for Creative Studies (formerly called Society of Arts and Crafts) and "Great Britain" chapter for more about Cranbrook.

PEWABIC POTTERY

10125 E. Jefferson, Detroit
(at Cadillac across from Waterworks Park)
(313) 822-0954

Mon-Sat 10am-6pm. Ceramics studio, gift shop, research center and exhibition gallery dedicated to Arts and Crafts Movement. A multifaceted education curriculum includes classes and workshops for adults and children. Ongoing exhibits feature ceramic artists of national reputation.

ARTS & CRAFTS RESOURCES

AMERICAN CRAFTSMAN
(248) 548-3513
Cutters Art Glass
814 W. 11 Mile, Royal Oak
Group of local artists and craftsmen devoted to reviving the Arts & Crafts style. Call for exhibit information.

THE MICHIGAN MODERNISM EXPOSITION
Southfield Civic Center, Southfield,
(810) 465-9441
Exposition and sale of 20th century design usually held last weekend in April. Ranked by many as one of the top two Modernism events in the nation; 100 exhibitors.

CRANBROOK ART MUSEUM GIFT SHOP
1221 N. Woodward Ave., Bloomfield Hills
(248) 645-3325
Wed, Fri, Sat 10am-5pm, Thu 10am-9pm.
Sun noon-5pm. Pewabic pottery, books
about Arts & Crafts Movement, note cards.

CAROL GRANT & ANN DUKE
DECORATIVE ARTS
256 N. Saginaw, Pontiac; (248) 745-0999
Wed-Sat noon-6pm. Modern Age, a down-
town Pontiac gallery devoted to 20th century
decorative arts, rents space to Grant and
Duke, who specialize in the Art and Crafts
Movement.

OUR MISSION ANTIQUES
525 Hidden Pines Trail, Holly
(248) 634-7612
By appointment only.
Deals in arts and crafts, metals, pottery and
furniture from early 20th century.

★★★★★★★★★★★★★★★★★★★★★★★★★★★★★★

CRUISIN'

WOODWARD DREAM CRUISE

Annually, this mid-August weekend relives the '60s "cruisin' Woodward" ritual for car lovers in the Motor City. From Pontiac at the north end to Detroit at the south, the stretch became an impromptu, informal place for romance, racing, and the slow cruise through the drive-in.

In the '70s and '80s, cruising died out as gasoline prices soared and muscle cars faded away. But now, thousands of enthusiasts gather for one weekend a year to watch street rods, antiques, classics and hot rods cruise again. Communities along the way sponsor related events, including classic car shows, concerts and street fairs. For information, call the hotline (1-888-493-2196) and listen to spokesperson Tom Force, of Oldies 104.3 WOMC, tell about upcoming plans. The hotline also provides a direct connection to recordings from each participating community: Ferndale, Pleasant Ridge, Huntington Woods, Berkley, Royal Oak, Birmingham and Pontiac.

WOODWARD DREAM CRUISE, INC.
P.O. Box 7066, Huntington Woods 48070; 1-888-493-2196
Organizing committee maintains toll-free hotline about Dream Cruise Weekend events, memberships, merchandise orders and sponsorships.

★★★

DRIVE-IN MOVIES

FORD-WYOMING DRIVE-IN THEATRE
10400 Ford Road, Dearborn; (313) 846-6910
Built in 1951, one of the best—and last—of an All-American institution, has nine screens and holds 3,000 cars. Open year round (with in-car heaters). Customize sound to your car stereo system.

BIG EVENTS

AMERICA'S THANKSGIVING DAY PARADE

Thanksgiving is an all-American holiday and Detroit has been celebrating it on a grand scale since 1926 when the first parade proceeded down Woodward Avenue.

Over 6,000 volunteers put in many hours to stage this spectacle of dozens of floats, marching bands, celebrity clowns and Santa.

The parade begins Thanksgiving Day at 9 a.m. on Woodward near Canfield and heads south to Jefferson. It is broadcast on WDIV (Channel 4) and WJR-AM.

Behind-the-scenes tours of the Parade Company studios are offered year-round by Detroit Upbeat. Call (313) 341-6810.

FRIENDS OF THE PARADE ASSOCIATION (FOPA)
(313) 923-3672
Volunteer opportunities for everything from float-building to marching. Organization sells *Traditions*, a cookbook of local family recipes, for a fundraiser.
Web site for updates: www.theparade.org

MICHIGAN STATE FAIR

Originating in 1849, the Michigan State Fair has the distinction of being our country's first gathering of its kind. Prior to settling at its permanent location at Woodward Avenue and Eight Mile Road in 1905, the State Fair tried out nine different sites across the state. It was Joseph Hudson, founder of

the department store, and several others, who were responsible for bringing the fair to its current site within the city limits of Detroit.

The original purpose of the fair was to foster communication between rural agriculture and urban industry so that farmers could learn of the benefits of new machinery and city dwellers could learn where their food came from and how it was produced. Over the years the exposition evolved into a blend of education, recreation and entertainment.

In addition to the livestock, agricultural and handicraft exhibits, the fair features midway rides and games and special events daily throughout its two-week run in August through Labor Day. Contests range from pig races to clowning competitions and rodeo riding. Parades, performance by the Detroit Mounted Police precision drill team, children's theater productions and family entertainment are part of the daily lineup. Free band shell concerts are held nightly.

MICHIGAN STATE FAIR
1120 W. State Fair, Detroit
(Woodward, south of 8 Mile)
(313) 369-8250 or 369-8300
Runs for two weeks from late August through Labor Day. Features livestock, agriculture and handicraft exhibits; miracle of life birthing center; midway games and rides; free band shell concerts at night; and various contests, demonstrations and performances daily.

AMERICANA **39**

RURAL HERITAGE

ANTIQUE APPLES
Christmas Cove Farm
11573 Kilcherman
Rd., Northport
(616) 386-5637
Over 200 varieties of
apples grown including "antiques" from the
17th to early 19th centuries that are very
difficult to come by. Gift boxes with samples
and history of each apple available for
Christmas, shipped anywhere in the U.S.

SHEEPSTUFF
Mt. Bruce Station
6640 Bordman Rd., Romeo
(810) 798-2660
A Centennial Farm, recently restored to its
Victorian glory by Yvonne and Peter
Uhlianuk, is now primarily dedicated to raising small flocks of New Zealand sheep.
Hands-on demonstrations, workshops,
crafters, music, food, entertainment, are just
part of the annual **Sheep and Wool Festival**
the last weekend in September. The former
caretaker's house has been converted to a
shop selling only the finest quality handmade sweaters, felts, blankets and other
woolens, many by local artisans. Peter
Uhlianuk, and his brother Lee, are popular
figures at the Royal Oak Farmer's Market,
where, along with other family members, they
offer unusual
perennials, herbs,
dried arrangements
and hand-crafted
twig furniture and gar-
den accents.

FARMERS' MARKETS

*For additional information about farm-
ers' markets, as well as U-pick
orchards and berry farms throughout
Michigan, call your local Michigan
State University extension office and
ask for a copy of the Farm Market/
U-Pick Directory.*

Oakland County: (248) 858-0880
Macomb County: (810) 469- 5180
Wayne County: (313) 494-3006

ANN ARBOR FARMERS' MARKET
407 N. Fifth Ave., Ann Arbor
(734) 761-1078
*May-Dec: Wed & Sat 7am-3pm; Jan-April:
Sat 8am-3pm.* Produce stalls at Kerrytown
are next to specialty shops in three renovated historical buildings.

EASTERN MARKET
2934 Russell at Gratiot, Detroit
(313) 833-1560
Year-round: Sat 5am-5pm. Hub of Detroit's
wholesale food industry is open to public on
Saturdays. More than 4,000 growers are
registered to sell fruits and vegetables, bedding plants, flowers, shrubs, Christmas
trees in season, poultry, eggs and other
farm products. (See "Multicultural Detroit.")

FARMINGTON FARMERS' MARKET
Downtown Farmington
(248) 473-7276
April-Oct: Sat 9am-2pm. Fresh produce and
flowers from local growers.

MT. CLEMENS FARMERS' MARKET
Main Street (Downtown)
(810) 463-1528
May- Nov: Fri-Sat 7am-2pm. Fresh produce, seasonal demonstrations.

OAKLAND COUNTY FARMERS' MARKET
2350 Pontiac Lake Rd., Waterford
(l/3 mile W of Telegraph)
(248) 858-5495
*May-Christmas: Tue, Thu & Sat 6:30am-
2pm; Dec. 26-April: Sat only.* Over 100 farmers sell fruits, vegetables, eggs, honey,
baked goods, flowers, plants and crafts.

ROYAL OAK FARMERS' MARKET
316 E. Eleven Mile (2 blks E of Main)
(248) 548-8822
*May-Oct: Tue, Fri & Sat 7am-1pm; Nov.-
Christmas: Fri-Sat 7am-1pm.* 127 stalls with
fresh produce, spring bedding plants, cut
flowers, handicrafts and collectibles.

YPSILANTI FARMERS' MARKET
Railroad Freighthouse at Depot Town
Cross and Rice Streets, Ypsilanti
(734) 483-1480
Year-round: Wed & Sat 7am-3pm. Locally
grown fruits and vegetables in season, spring
bedding plants, full-line citrus produce, baked
goods and other food specialties. *(Exit I-94 at
Huron, 2 miles to Cross St.)*

METROPARKS

🦆🦆🦆 Throughout the year, southeastern Michigan's 13 Huron Clinton Metroparks provide a wealth of ways to explore our heritage. From making maple syrup and other Native American activities to grinding grain at Wolcott Mill, there are numerous workshops, interpretive tours, antique shows and hands-on experiences. A new mobile learning center makes visits to schools.

For newsletter, program and events information, send your name and address to HCMA Newsletter, P.O. Box 2001, Brighton, MI 48116.
Call 1-800-47-PARKS.

QUILTS

The patchwork quilt reached its highest artistic development in the United States. As a result of scarce sewing materials and a need for artistic expression, pioneer women lavished great attention on ingenious geometrical designs fashioned from scraps. Many quilts were signed and dated. Quiltmakers regularly exhibited their work in fairs and international expositions; prizes were awarded for craftsmanship and innovations in design and color.

By 1883, handmade quilts were on three-quarters of the beds in the country. With the advent of inexpensive machine-made bed coverings, however, quiltmaking declined in the early years of the 20th century, except in rural areas. In the 1960s, interest in quilting—both as a handicraft and as an art form—revived. By the mid-1980s quilting had become the most popular form of needlework and antique "heirloom" quilts highly treasured.

(Also see "Slave Quilts" in African American Heritage Chapter.

"TO WARM YOUR HEART"
Village Barn, Franklin; (248) 851-7877
Annually, first week in Feb. Amish and Mennonite quilt show and sale features over 120 quilts from four states. Visitors are asked to bring clean, used blankets to donate to the Salvation Army.

"AMERICA'S ORIGINAL CRAFT—QUILTING"
Wolcott Mill Metro Park, Romeo
1-800-477-3175
Annually in early Oct. Demonstrations, hands-on displays, hand-outs, and more in the interesting restored mill.

GUILDCRAFTERS
2718 W. 12 Mile Rd., Berkley
(248) 541-8545,
10am to 6pm daily; closed Sun. Offers lessons, supplies, and schedule of upcoming quilt shows throughout the metro area.

LAURA SHELBY GROUP, INC.
1-800-58-FIBER
Workshops, classes, shows in traditional African American fiber arts.

THE QUILTING SISTERS
Hartford Memorial Church
18799 James Couzens, Detroit
(313) 861-1399
Coordinator: Pearl Cook. Meets every Wednesday at 5pm in Room 106 and 108.

QUILTING WEB SITE
www.albany.net/ %7eoldquilt/qhl.htm

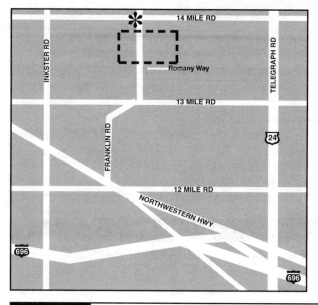

[D-E/2-3] *Franklin Village is located west of Telegraph Road between 13 and 14 Mile Roads in Oakland County. The historic district runs along Franklin Road from 14 Mile south to Romany Way and east to Meadowdale. The Franklin Cider Mill occupies the northwest corner of Franklin Road and 14 Mile.*

TOUR — A TRIP BACK IN TIME

FRANKLIN

Called "The Town Time Forgot," Franklin is a three-square-mile northwestern suburb with an historic district reminiscent of an early American village. Since railroad officials and early highway builders bypassed the town, Franklin was unaffected by Detroit's urban sprawl and retained its 19th century charm.

It was the opening of the Erie Canal in 1825 that brought settlers from New York and New England to the Michigan territory. When growth in Oakland County reached the point that an official post office was to be established in the township in 1828, Dr. Ebeneezer Raynale, physician and appointed postmaster, selected the name Franklin. (Many towns were named after Ben Franklin, who among other distinctions was the first American postmaster.)

Many of the settlers were skilled tradesmen and craftsmen from the east, who replaced log cabins with well-built frame and brick structures that are still standing today. The original business district included Congelton Buggy Works (now the **Village Barn** gift shop), Broughton House (Village Office and Police Department) and Van Every Gristmill **(Franklin Cider Mill)**, as well as taverns, distilleries and two churches. In keeping with the town's early American character, **Franklin Community Church** was built in 1956 in the colonial style with a village green.

The mill on the Rouge River at Franklin and 14 Mile dates back to 1837, the year Michigan became a state. The Van Every Gristmill was converted to a cider mill and became a family destination for Sunday drives starting in the

1920s. A 19th century press from Europe is still used and holds 120 bushels of apples at one time.

To tour Franklin, take a walk down main street, starting at the Cider Mill at 14 Mile and proceed south on Franklin Road to the village green at Franklin Community Church. Along the way are shops and vintage houses.

CIDER MILL TRADITION

ORCHARDS & CIDER MILLS

An outing to pick apples and sample fresh cider and warm homemade donuts is an American tradition. Outlying areas of Detroit offer many routes for viewing the fall color show and visiting cider mills, apple orchards and pumpkin patches.

At some cider mills, visitors can watch the water wheel turn to produce power, and if the timing is right, the pressing and bottling operations. Orchard locations often offer farm market and bakery products, hayrides, a petting zoo and/or autumn festivities.

OAKLAND COUNTY
ASHTON ORCHARDS & CIDER MILL
3925 Seymour Lake Rd, Ortonville
(248) 627-6671
Mon-Sat noon-5:30pm, Sun noon-6 pm (Aug 1-March 30). Farm market, apple cinnamon donuts, pies, breads, gift baskets. Picnic tables, tours. *(I-75 to Sashabaw Rd, 5 miles N to Seymour Lake Rd.)*

DIEHL'S ORCHARD & CIDER MILL
1479 Ranch Rd, Holly; (248) 634-8981
Aug-Oct, daily 9 am-6 pm, Nov-Dec daily 9 am-5 pm. Apples, pears, plums, donuts, pies, jams, gift baskets. Picnic tables, hayrides, tours. *(Follow Milford Rd to E. Rose Center Rd, to Ranch Rd.)*

ERWIN ORCHARDS & COUNTRY STORE
61019 Silver Lake Rd., South Lyon
(248) 437-4704
Daily 9 am-6 pm (April - Dec. 24) Hours vary. Hayride to apple picking area. Cider, donuts and baked goods, seasonal produce, gifts. Halloween events. *(1 mile S of I-96 and Kensington Metro Park- Exit 153)*

FRANKLIN CIDER MILL
7450 Franklin Rd at 14 Mile Rd,
Bloomfield Twp; (248) 626-2968
Mon-Fri 7am-6pm, Sat-Sun 8am-6pm (Aug 31-Nov 30). Donuts, apples, seasonal treats. Hickory Farms beef sticks, cheeses and mustard. Press operations can be viewed at the north end of the building and the water wheel from the rear.

GOODISON CIDER MILL
4295 Orion Rd. at Hilltop Rd., Rochester
(248) 652-8450
Mon-Fri 11am-6 pm, Sat-Sun 9 am-6 pm, until Dec 31. Different from the water-wheel mills, this one-story building is an all-electric operation. Market carries syrups, jams, honey, teas, spices, caramel apples, candies and home-baked pies. Custom pressing.

LONG FAMILY ORCHARD & FARM
1342 Commerce Rd, Commerce Twp.
(248) 360-3774
Specific seasons and hours vary. Call hotline. U-pick apples, pumpkins and other produce. Apples and cider for sale through Christmas. Weekend hayrides, school field trips by appointment. *(at Commerce and Bogie Lake Rd, 5 miles E of Milford, 4 miles S of M-59)*

PAINT CREEK CIDER MILL
4480 Orion Rd, Rochester
(248) 651-8361
Hours vary by season. Restaurant Tue-Sun year-round. Cider made on a 350-ton press, fried cakes, apples, specialty foods, gifts. Hike-bike-ski along 10.4-mile Paint Creek Trail *(3 miles NW of downtown Rochester).*

YATES CIDER MILL
1990 East Avon Rd, Rochester Hills
(248) 651-8300/0135
Daily 9 am-7 pm Sept-Dec. 1863 gristmill on Clinton-Kalamazoo Canal uses original water wheel for power to produce 300 gallons of cider per hour. Donuts, breads and other concessions, including apple shop (weekends). Scheduled tours. Hiking trails at Rochester-Utica State Recreation Area across the street. *(23 Mile and Dequindre)*

MACOMB COUNTY

BLAKE'S ORCHARD & CIDER MILL
17985 Armada Center Rd., Armada
(810) 784-5343
and

BLAKE'S BIG APPLE
1 mile S. of downtown Armada
at North Ave.; (810) 784-9710
Daily 8 am-6 pm. U-pick apples, pears, pumpkins and other produce in season. Dwarf fruit trees, train rides, petting farm, pony rides, fall fairs. *(3 miles W of Armada)*

COON CREEK ORCHARD & CIDER MILL
78777 Coon Creek Rd., Armada
(810) 784-5062
Daily 8 am-6 pm June-Nov. U-pick apples pumpkins, berries; farm animals, gift shop, hayrides. *(4 miles NW of Armada)*

HY'S CIDER MILL
6350 37 Mile Rd., Romeo; (810) 798-3611
Daily 11am-6pm Early Sept-Early Nov. Cider and donuts, apple butter, caramel apples, preserves. U-pick or buy. *(From Van Dyke N, turn right. From Van Dyke S, turn left.)*

MILLER'S BIG RED ORCHARDS
4900 West 32 Mile Rd., Romeo
(810) 752-7888
Daily 9 am-6 pm May-Nov. Cider mill and store with donuts, homemade pies, jams and jellies, dried flowers. U-pick apples and other produce, including pumpkin patch. Tours available. *(3 miles W of Romeo)*

RAPP ORCHARDS
63545 Van Dyke, Romeo; (810) 752-2117
Daily 7:30am-7pm. Produce, deli, preserves, dairy products and cider. U-pick cherries and pumpkins. *(between 29 and 30 Mile Rds.)*

VAN HOUTTE FARM MARKET
69475 Romeo Plank Rd., Romeo
(810) 752-5671
Daily 9 am-7 pm. Apples, cider, pumpkins, squash, gourds, Indian corn in Oct. *(3 miles E of Romeo)*

VERELLEN ORCHARDS & CIDER MILL
63260 Van Dyke, Romeo; (810) 752-2989
Daily 7am-7pm. Cider, pies, donuts, apples, jams and jellies and farm market produce. *(3 miles S of Romeo)*

WESTVIEW ORCHARDS
Van Dyke Rd. at 30 Mile Rd., Romeo
(810) 752-3123
Daily 8am-7pm Aug-March. Ready-picked fruit, cider, produce, syrup, honey, jams, cooking items, gift boxes, farm bakery. School group tours include one-room school-house, hayride. *(2 miles S of Romeo)*

WAYNE COUNTY

APPLE CHARLIE'S SOUTH HURON ORCHARDS & CIDER MILL
38035 South Huron Rd., New Boston
(734) 753-9380
Daily 8am-dark July 1- Oct 31, 9am-dark, Nov-Dec 31. Apples, cider, donuts, breads. Farm animals. *(I-275 S of I-94, exit 11B)*

DAVIES ORCHARD & CIDER MILL
40426 Willow Rd., New Boston
(734) 654-8893 or 654-6019
9am-7pm Mid-Sept-Nov. U-pick and buy apples, plums, pumpkins, honey. *(I-275 to exit 8, W 1/4 mile to Waltz Rd., N 2 miles to Willow Rd., W on Willow 1-1/4 mile)*

LIVINGSTON COUNTY

SPICER ORCHARDS & CIDER MILL
Clyde Road, Hartland; (810) 632-7692
Daily 9am-6pm. Market, donuts, honey, preserves, gift shop, bakery, buy or U-pick fruits. Children's farm, hay fort, pony rides and hayrides. *(US-23 3 miles N of M-59 to Clyde Rd. Exit east, 1/4 mile)*

WASHTENAW COUNTY

OBSTBAUM ORCHARDS & CIDER MILL
9252 Currie, Northville; (248) 349-5569
Sat-Sun only 10am-6pm Labor Day-Thanksgiving. Apples, donuts, caramel apples, pumpkins, pies, cakes, and other food items. Handwoven baskets, dried flowers. Indoor-outdoor seating. *(Beck Rd exit from I-96 or M-14, 4 miles W of Beck Rd between Seven and Eight Mile Rds.)*

WIARD'S ORCHARDS, INC.
5565 Merritt Rd., Ypsilanti; (734) 482-7744
Year-round, 10 am-6 pm. U-pick apples, pumpkins and other fruits. Baked goods, cider, market. Wagon rides, weekend country fair, pony rides, fire engine rides, fall craft fair, live music, animal petting farm, haunted barns. *(I-94 to Huron St, exit 183, S 4 miles)*

WINDY RIDGE ORCHARD & CIDER MILL
9375 Saline-Milan Rd., Saline
(734) 429-7111
Mon-Sat 10 am-6 pm, Sun 11 am-6 pm Mid-Sept-Nov. Cider, donuts, apples. Hayrides, petting corral, pumpkins. Cut-your-own Christmas trees in Dec. *(Intersection of US-12 and Ann Arbor Rd, S 1 mile to farm.)*

CONTRA DANCING

An evening that includes contra dancing might be called a **Contra Dance,** an **Old-Time Country Dance,** or perhaps a **Barn Dance.** A caller, working with a group of live musicians, guides new and experienced dancers alike through a variety of dances.

People of all ages and lifestyles, including children, are welcome. Dancers often go out to a restaurant after the dance, have a potluck before or during the dance, or hang out with musicians in jam sessions and song circles. First-time dancers will likely find experienced dancers extremely friendly and helpful. At most dance events, dancers have a different partner for each dance, although dates who attend together and significant others might dance with each other more than once. Contra Dancing is neither line dancing, nor square dancing, and no particular costumes or dress are required.

For information and updates about all types of folk dancing, call CDS (Country Dance Society) Hotline: (248) 968-3565.

CONTRA DANCES

LOVETT HALL CONTRA DANCE
Greenfield Village, Dearborn
(313) 271-1620 ext. 635
First Sundays, Oct-Dec, Feb- June. Dance, 1:30 pm.

OAKLAND COUNTY TRADITIONAL DANCE SOCIETY
All Saints Episcopal Church, Pontiac
SE corner Williams & Pike
(248) 851-0463, (248) 569-7573
Second Sundays, Sept-May. Instruction: 1pm, Dance: 1:30pm. Fourth Saturdays. Dance, 8pm.

DETROIT CDS CONTRA & SQUARE DANCE
St. John's Fellowship Hall
11 Mile at Woodward, Royal Oak
(248) 968-3565
Third Saturdays. Dance, 8pm.

COUNTRY WESTERN DANCING

*The Country Western dance floor is divided into concentric lanes, moving counter-clockwise around stationary dancers in the center. Traditional styles of dress include: **Country Ballroom:** matching outfits, fringe, rhinestones, skirts for the ladies. **Western Style:** jeans, boots for both sexes; outfits usually do not match.*

DIAMONDS & SPURS
25 S. Saginaw, Pontiac; (248) 334-4409
Tues-Sun 6pm-close. Dance classes nightly, various levels on different days.

EASTPOINTE EAGLES
14855 E. 8 Mile, Eastpointe; (810) 796-3868
Thursdays. Partner & couple dances 6:30-7:30pm, line dancing 7:30-9pm, practice and dancing 9-11pm. Classes available.

WOLVERINE SILVERSPUR DANCERS
Italian American Cultural Center
28111 Imperial, Warren
(313) 526-9432 or (313) 573-4993
Second Saturdays. Dance 7:30pm. Non-profit, social country western dance club.

SWING DANCING

Some say swing dancing originated with the *Texas Tommy,* others say it's a combination of the *Two-Step* and the *Charleston.* Other dances that influenced it are *Black Bottom,* the *Big Apple,* the *Varsity Drag,* the *Lindy Hop* and *Jitterbug.* Regardless of its origins, this dance style is a true American Original that peaked in the 1930s and 40s and is currently enjoying a resurgence of popularity, particularly among athletic younger people. There are a number of variations of Swing dance styles, including "West Coast" which often is part of Country Western events. Many dance clubs, YMCAs and local recreation departments offer lessons. *(Check the local media and dance instruction listings in Multicultural Detroit.)*

BLUE GRASS, COUNTRY & FOLK MUSIC RESOURCES

THE ARK
316 S. Main, Ann Arbor; (734) 761-1451
Coffee house and folk music club, founded in 1965 to keep the American musical traditions of folk and bluegrass alive, produces nearly 250 concerts a year.

KENTUCKIANS OF MICHIGAN
Meets third weekend of month to enjoy Bluegrass music, food and dance. All interested people are welcome to participate. Call Charles Reeves (734) 453-6615 or Carlotta Lowe (810) 756-2239.

PAINT CREEK FOLKLORE SOCIETY
Shares folk and traditional music during monthly meetings that include a workshop, a song swap and jam sessions. Presents four house concerts per year and one major concert (the Tin Whistle, in Nov.), one dance (Starry Night for a Ramble, in Feb.) and one mini-festival (May Playday). Call Shirley Worth (810) 986-0166 for information.

THE CENTENNIAL FARM

Program was begun by the Michigan Historical Commission in 1948 with support from Detroit Edison Company, Consumers Energy, local electrical cooperatives and farm groups. It is intended to recognize farms that have remained in the same family for one hundred years or more and highlight the family farm's contributions to Michigan's development.

For more information about the Centennial Farm Program, contact the Michigan Department of State, Michigan Historical Center, State Historic Preservation Office, 717 W. Allegan Street, Lansing, MI 48918-1800; or call (517) 373-1667.

MEDIA

PRINT

THE COUNTRY REGISTER
3790 Manistee Rd., Saginaw 48603-3143
(517) 793-4211
Free bi-monthly covering Country, Victorian and antique shops. Available at advertiser's stores and Michigan Welcome Centers.

MICHIGAN HISTORY MAGAZINE
717 Allegan, Lansing 48918-1805
1-800-366-3707
(See media listing in "Multicultural Detroit" chapter.)

MAGAZINE OF COUNTRY MUSIC
P.O. Box 1412, Warren MI 48090
(810) 755-0471
Free monthly available at record stores and restaurants. Events listings, interviews.

RADIO

WDET 101.9 FM Detroit
(313) 557-4146
Folks Like Us, *Sat noon-3pm.* Host Matt Watroba presents traditional and modern folk music; guests performing live; and updates on concerts, events and performances in American folk music and dance (local).
and
Arkansas Traveler, *Sat. 3-5pm.* Larry McDaniel plays Bluegrass and traditional acoustic music (local).
and
Mountain Stage, *Sat. 5-7pm.* Larry Groce pesents live concerts featuring folk, blues, acoustic (PRI).

WUOM 91.7 Ann Arbor
American Routes, Sun 4-6pm & Sat 8-10pm. "Roots music" encompases new and old from Rock to Reggae.

DETROIT COUNTRY; WWWW 106.7FM
(313) 259-4323
Country music all day; hotline for updates on concert information (313) 259-W4W4. Sponsors annual **Downtown Hoedown** each May in Hart Plaza, Detroit.

YOUNG COUNTRY; WYCD 99.5 FM
(248) 799-0600
Country music all day; hotline for updates on concert information (810) 788-6599.

WEB SITES
Americana Smorgasbord
www.nic.com/~circa/index.html

American Heritage & American Legacy Magazines
www.americanheritage.com

In colonial America the term **Créole** originally applied to American-born descendants of European-born settlers. The term has since acquired varying meanings in different regions. In Latin America, for instance, the term may refer either to persons of direct Spanish heritage or to members of families whose ancestry goes back to the colonial period. In the United States, in the state of Louisiana, Créoles are the descendants of the early French and/or Spanish settlers, possessing a unique culture and customs. Most are Roman Catholic and speak a French-based language known as Louisiana Créole.

Cajuns are descendants of the 4,000 French Canadians expelled by the British from the captured French colony of **Acadia** (now Nova Scotia, New Brunswick and Prince Edward Island) in 1755. They still maintain communities in the Louisiana bayous and along the Gulf of Mexico. Cajuns have a mixed African, European and Native American ancestry, reflected in their hybrid language. Their hearty, spicy food and lively music are world-famous.

Despite popular misconception, New Orleans is not a Cajun city, though many Cajuns live there. The people, culture and cuisine of New Orleans are Créole, and have a long and distinguished history dating to its founding. New Orleans has managed to combine distinct cultures—history, people, architecture, food, music and traditions—and come up with cooking styles and music emulated around the world.

CRÉOLE & CAJUN COOKING

Both Créoles and Cajuns take food seriously—perhaps even more so than the Chinese, who are likely to greet you with: "Have you eaten well today?" Créoles and Cajuns want to know not only what you have eaten, but what you are planning to eat through the next day. Then they will tell you what they have eaten and plan to eat.

They will gladly share a meal with anyone, having adopted the Spanish "my house is your house" philosophy. The difference between Créole and Cajun cooking perhaps lies in the fact that many Créoles were rich planters who aspired to *grande cuisine* from France or Spain as did their chefs, who combined classic European techniques with local foodstuffs.

The Acadians (later contracted to *Cajun*) were a resilient people used to living under strenuous conditions. They tended to serve strong country food prepared from locally available ingredients—pungent, peppery and practical—all cooked in a single pot.

Both Créole and Cajun chefs usually start a dish by making a *roux* of oil and flour. In addition to the staple rice, there are many common ingredients such as crab, river shrimp, lake shrimp, oysters, crawfish, freshwater and saltwater fish, plus squirrel, wild turkey, duck, frog, turtle, pork, homemade sausage, beans, tomatoes, okra, yams, pecans, oranges and wine, liqueur and brandy. It is an individual, variable and creative cuisine, making written recipes hard to come by.

RESTAURANTS

ALABAZAM!
1515 Ottawa St. (just east of Tunnel), Windsor; (519) 252-8264
Mon-Sat 11:30am-11pm, Sun 3-9pm. Mostly Créole cuisine prepared in an "open performance" kitchen. Live jazz Tuesday and Sunday evenings.

CAJUN EXPRESS
630 Woodward Ave., Detroit
(313) 961-6332
Mon-Fri 11am-3pm. The "real taste" of New Orleans cuisine in downtown Detroit.

FISHBONE'S RHYTHM KITCHEN CAFE
400 Monroe, Detroit (Greektown)
(313) 965-4600
Mon-Thu 6:30am-midnight, Fri-Sat 6:30am-2am, Sun 10:30am-midnight.
and
23722 Jefferson, St. Clair Shores
(810) 498-3000
Wed-Sat 11am-2am, Mon-Tues 11am-2pm, Sun 10:30am-midnight.
and
29244 Northwestern Hwy., Southfield
(248) 351-2925
Sun-Thu 11am-midnight, Fri-Sat 11am-2am. Cajun or Créole feasts in high-spirited sounds and sights of New Orleans.

HOWE'S BAYOU
22848 Woodward (just north of 9 Mile) Ferndale; (248) 691-7145
Mon-Fri 11am-2am, Sat-Sun 5pm-2am. Classic Louisiana fare plus such innovations as Voodoo BBQ Shrimp and Gator Balls. Over 20 brands of Bourbon.

LOUIE'S ON WOODWARD
630 Woodward, Detroit
(313) 963-8424
Sun-Fri 11:30am-9pm, Sat 6-9pm. Try chef Louie Finnan's tangy red beans and rice or blackened red fish.

LOUISIANA CREOLE GUMBO
2053 Gratiot, Detroit (at St. Aubin)
(313) 446-9639
Mon-Sat 11am-10pm, Sun 1-7pm. Pork chops, rib-tip dinners; gumbo and jambalaya. Has dining-in booths; mainly carryout.

MAC'S
104 E. Michigan Ave, Ann Arbor
(734) 944-6227
Daily 11am-11pm. Deep fried alligator, and other Cajun specialities.

MUSIC MENU CAFE
511 Monroe, Detroit (Greektown)
(313) 964-6368
Mon-Fri 11am-2am, Sat 3pm-2am, Sun 4pm-2am. Zydeco shrimp, gumbo, Po'boys and blackened specialities.

FOOD TERMS

Andouille: Spicy country sausage used in gumbo and other Cajun dishes.

Beignet: Doughnuts, square-shaped and minus the hole, sprinkled with powdered sugar.

Boudin: Spicy pork, onions, rice, herbs, sausage.

Café Au Lait: Coffee and chicory with milk; usually a half-and-half mixture of hot coffee and hot milk.

Cafe Brulot: After-dinner brew of hot coffee, spices, orange peel and liqueurs; ignited, then served in special cups.

Crawfish: Sometimes spelled "crayfish" but always pronounced *craw*fish. Resembling little lobsters, they're known locally as "mud-bugs" because they live in the mud of fresh water bayous. Served in a variety of ways, including simply boiled.

Dirty Rice: Pan-fried leftover cooked rice sautéed with green peppers, onion, celery, stock, liver, giblets and many other ingredients.

Étoufée: A succulent, tangy tomato-based sauce; literally means "smothered."

File: Ground sassafras leaves used to season, among other things, gumbo.

Grits: Coarsely ground wheat or corn, cooked down in water; served with salt and butter.

Gumbo: Thick, robust soup with thousands of variations.

Jambalaya: Chefs "sweep up the kitchen" and toss just about everything into the pot. Could include tomatoes and cooked rice, plus ham, shrimp, chicken, celery, onions, and seasonings.

King Cake: A ring-shaped oval pastry, decorated with colored sugar in traditional Mardi Gras colors—purple, green, and gold—which represent justice, faith, and power. A small plastic baby is hidden inside the cake. Tradition requires that whoever gets the baby in their piece must provide the next King Cake.

Po-Boy: Huge sandwich. There are fried oyster po-boys, roast beef and gravy po-boys, softshell crab po-boys and others, all served on crispy-crusted loaf bread.

Red Beans & Rice: Kidney beans cooked in seasonings and spices, usually with chunks of sausage and ham; served over a bed of rice. Traditionally eaten on Monday.

OTHER WORDS

Bayou: The outlet of a lake or one of the delta streams of a river, usually sluggish and marshy.

Lagniappe: An unexpected, nice, surprise. Cajun for "something extra," like the extra doughnut in a baker's dozen.

The Big Easy: Nickname for New Orleans, meaning to "take it easy" or "easy living."

French Quarter: The 100-block area originally settled by the French. The architecture, however, is credited to the Spanish.

Fais do do: The name for a party where traditional Cajun dance is performed. Although this phrase literally means "to make sleep," these parties are the liveliest of occasions.

Jazz: New Orleans is one of, if not *the*, birthplace of this popular style of music. *(See African American Heritage.)*

LET THE GOOD TIMES ROLL!

Music is as much a part of daily life as good food, and saying *"Laissez les bons temps rouler!"* (Let the good times roll!) The Cajuns developed their own form of music, similar to American country music in many ways, but usually sung in French.

Cajun music is a blend of German, Spanish, Scottish, Irish, Anglo-American, Afro-Caribbean, and American Indian influences with a base of western French and French Acadian folk tradition. Traditional Cajun music uses the fiddle, accordion and triangle to create a unique style of music. The name *Zydeco* is a Cajun phonetization from "les haricots" (beans). Zydeco is a rich and lively "bean stew" emanating from the Créole culture and from an earlier music form called "La-la," which combined the accordian-fiddle-washboard in comparably less melodic arrangements. Clifton Chenier (1925-1987), the undisputed king of Zydeco, recorded over 100 albums. Another luminary, Buckwheat Zydeco, makes frequent appearances in the metro area.

(Also see "Americana" chapter.)

FESTIVALS

FROG ISLAND MUSIC FESTIVAL
Depot Town, Ypsilanti; (734) 487-2229
Mid-June, Fri & Sat on banks of Huron River. New Orleans night features nation's top Cajun and Zydeco musicians.

MARDI GRAS IN FERNDALE
Magic Bag, 22918 Woodward, Ferndale (248) 544-3030
Zydeco is just part of the fun during these out-of-season festivities.

MEDIA

WEB SITES
ACADIAN, CREOLE & CAJUN LINKS
www.chezsurette.com/ ACADIAN.HTM

CAJUN
www.rbmulti.nb.ca/ cadienne/cajun

GUMBO PAGES
www.gumbopages.com

MARDI GRAS

The **Carnival season** officially begins January 6 (Twelfth Night, or Epiphany), marking the end of the Christmas season and the beginning of the countdown to Lent. Two official celebrations kick off Carnival: *The Bal Masque of the Twelfth Night Revelers* and the *Ride of the Phunny Phorty Phellows* along St. Charles Avenue in New Orleans. From January 6 until three weeks before Mardi Gras, Carnival organizations host parties, dances and balls. Then the parades begin. From the second weekend before Mardi Gras until Fat Tuesday, there is at least one parade each night in the New Orleans metro area. The celebration culminates on **Fat Tuesday,** with the entire city taking the day off work to eat, drink, parade and party. Carnival ends promptly at midnight on Fat Tuesday, when the police begin clearing the streets of the French Quarter. Mardi Gras officially closes with the convening of the courts of Rex and Comus at the ball of the *Mystick Krewe of Comus.*
Many metro Detroit restaurants feature Mardi Gras specials.

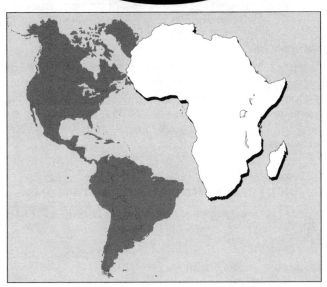

African Americans, this country's principal non-European group, number 30 million and constitute about 12 percent of the U.S. population. According to the 1990 census, Detroit's 777,916 African Americans made up 75.7 percent of the city's population. Their arrival to the city mirrors the movement of people of color across the northern United States.

By the 1830s, some African Americans had settled in the eastern outskirts of Detroit in a largely French and German farm area. That area, near what is now Lafayette Park, was called **Black Bottom** because of the rich, dark soil on which early settlers farmed. In 1839, the first school for black children opened in Detroit.

The city's black population of about 5,000 in 1910 swelled to 120,000 in just 20 years. Many were attracted by the opportunity to work in defense plants during World War I and the awesome $5 a day that Henry Ford paid auto workers. Others succeeded as entrepreneurs. Black-owned newspapers, groceries, restaurants, hotels and other businesses thrived in the '30s and '40s in an area of Black Bottom known as **Paradise Valley.** This economic, social and cultural corridor roughly was bounded by Brush, Gratiot, Hastings and Vernor. Here, 17 nightclubs hosted the country's best "colored" entertainers and racially integrated audiences—a unique combination at the time. (The lone survivor is the 606 Horse Shoe Lounge at 1907 St. Antoine.)

African Americans constituted 9.3 percent (149,119) of Detroit's population in 1940, 28.8 percent (482,223) in 1960 and 63 percent (758,939) in 1980. A significant factor in the population growth was employment offered by the auto industry and advancements nurtured by civil rights organizations, churches, labor union activists and laws.

However, the postwar federal policy of industrial decentralization and urban renewal led to the swift building of superhighways. When construction of I-75 destroyed Paradise Valley, many African Americans resettled north around 12th Street—buying a great deal of property from the Jewish population. In fact, black churches such as Clinton Street Greater Bethlehem Temple, Lighthouse Cathedral and New Mount Zion Missionary Baptist Church were originally synagogues.

After the 1967 civil disturbances in Detroit, some African Americans moved beyond the city's center as housing and loan discrimination eased. According to the 1990 U.S. Census, the tri-county cities with the highest numbers of African American residents (in descending order) are Pontiac, Southfield, Inkster, Highland Park, Oak Park, Romulus, Ecorse, River Rouge and Mount Clemens.

UNDERGROUND RAILROAD STATIONS

There are numerous sites of depots in southern Michigan. Pontiac Trail, in Oakland County, was a well-traveled route for fugitives. Here are a few:

First Quaker meeting site, south side of Grand River, one block west of Farmington Road and Longacre House, 12345 Farmington Road, between 10 and 11 Mile, Farmington.

Franklin Village Green, west side of Franklin Road between Carol and Wellington Streets, Franklin

Finney House Barn site, northeast corner of State and Griswold, Detroit

Second Baptist Church, northwest corner of Monroe and Beaubien, Detroit

George de Baptiste Home site, southwest corner of Larned and Beaubien, Detroit

William Lambert Home site, northeast corner of Larned and St. Aubin, Detroit

Sandwich Baptist Church, northwest of Peter and Watkins Streets, Windsor

John Freeman Walls Log Cabin, northwest of Highway 401 and Puce Road, Maidstone Township, Ontario

More than 40 years before the Civil War there was a highly organized system to help escaped slaves reach places of safety in the North and in Canada. It was called the *Underground Railroad* because of its necessary secrecy and because railway terms were used in order to disguise the real nature of the operation.

The freed slaves were called "freight," routes were called "lines," stopping places were "stations," and those who helped the slaves along the way were "conductors." Slaves were helped from one transfer place to another until they reached safety.

Michigan played an important role on the line, particularly around the Quaker settlement in Farmington and the cross-over to Windsor. After 1850, most slaves headed to Canada because the Revised Fugitive Slave Law made northern states no longer safe for any former slave.

Those who were most active in helping slaves to escape by way of the "railroad" were Northern abolitionists and other antislavery groups, including members of several Protestant denominations, especially Quakers, Methodists, and Mennonites.

Some former slaves were also active in the system. One of these was **Harriet Tubman.** Estimates of the total number of slaves who reached freedom by way of the Underground Railroad vary between 40,000 and 100,000. With the help of more than 180,000 African American soldiers and spies, Union forces were victorious over the Confederacy in 1865 and the necessity for underground activities ceased.

● Some spiritual songs such as "Swing Low, Sweet Chariot," "Steal Away to Jesus," and "Go Down Moses" carried coded messages related to escape. Quilt patterns often carried secret messages as well.

● Since runaways were virtually on their own and underground railways rarely began in the South, the North Star occasionally directed the flight. On dark or cloudy nights, moss, which grows on the north side of tree trunks, served as a guide.

● Disguises gave further protection. Females might dress as males and vice-versa. Fair-skinned African Americans passed as whites; and others pretended to be making deliveries for their masters. **Frederick Douglass** posed as a sailor during his escape from Maryland to New York.

● The stations were generally 10-30 miles apart. They offered food and shelter, often in secret rooms, attics and cellars. When no "station" was available, runaways took shelter in caves, woods and swamps during the day.

● A brightly lit candle in a window or a shimmering lantern, strategically placed, was often a signal that the home or church or meeting house was a station.

TOUR RESOURCES

Guided tours, maps and information are provided by the follwing groups.

BLACK HISTORICAL SITES COMMITTEE
Detroit Historical Museum
(313) 833-1805
Half- to full-day escorted tours for groups highlight the African American experience in Detroit. One packaged tour, for example, explores "The Great Migration and Paradise Valley." Publications available include *Black Historic Sites in Detroit* and *Doorway to Freedom - Underground Railroad*.

BLACK HISTORY TOUR OF DETROIT
(313) 922-1990
Guide Stewart McMillin hosts annual tour.

DETROIT UPBEAT TOURS
(313) 341-6808
Half-day to three-day custom tours arranged for groups to explore Underground Railroad route, Motown music, African art and Southern cuisine.

CONVENTION AND VISITORS BUREAU OF WINDSOR, ESSEX COUNTY AND PELEE ISLAND
(519) 255-6530 or 1-800-265-3633
The brochure "*The Road That Led to Freedom*" outlines an Underground Railroad tour from Windsor to Chatham.

METROPOLITAN DETROIT CONVENTION AND VISITORS BUREAU
(313) 259-4333 or 1-800-338-7648
Request the brochure "*Legacy of the Northern Star: A Visitor's Guide to Detroit's African American Community*" or the video "*Detroit: The Northern Star.*"

HISTORIC MARKERS

Whether "on tour" or just walking around downtown, read a bit of history on state markers at these official Michigan landmarks and historic sites in Detroit (see map opposite):

▲ ELMWOOD CEMETERY
1200 Elmwood
Contains 14 graves of the 102nd U.S. Colored Troops (similar to the men in the 54th Massachusetts Colored Infantry immortalized in the film "Glory"). Other notable African Americans resting here: George de Baptiste and William Lambert.

▲ HOME OF DR. OSSIAN SWEET
2905 Garland
In 1925, Dr. Sweet was charged with the murder of a neighbor who was killed when a group of white residents attacked the Sweet home in an attempt to keep African Americans from integrating the neighborhood. Dr. Sweet was defended successfully by Clarence Darrow in a landmark legal battle that was led by the NAACP and its Detroit branch.

▲ ORCHESTRA HALL
3711 Woodward (at Parsons)
(313) 833-3362
From 1941 to 1951, the name of this site was Paradise Theatre, one of the most famous stages in America for African American entertainers, including Lionel Hampton, Duke Ellington, Count Basie, Billie Holiday and Dizzy Gillespie.

▲ SECOND BAPTIST CHURCH
Greektown (northwest corner of Beaubien and Monroe)
Detroit's oldest African American church, founded by Rev. William C. Monroe.

▲ SOLDIERS & SAILORS MONUMENT
Woodward and Campus Martius (Kennedy Square)
Memorializes local troops who fought in the Civil War. The figure of "Emancipation" is rumored to have been Sojourner Truth, a 19th century abolitionist and feminist who lived in the area at the time.

▲ FREDERICK DOUGLASS-JOHN BROWN MEETING MARKER
Congress and St. Antoine
On March 12, 1859, Frederick Douglass and John Brown met with several black residents of Detroit at the home of William Webb to discuss methods for abolishing slavery.

TOUR — HISTORIC DOWNTOWN

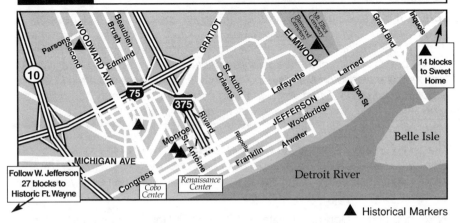

▲ Historical Markers

Note: This tour can be combined with one of the other tours in this chapter to make a full day. Check listings for other museums, restaurants or points of interest you may wish to include.

[E-F/4-5] The best place to start tracing local parts of the **Underground Railroad** is **Second Baptist Church** *on Monroe in Greektown (see map).* Founded in 1836 by 13 former slaves, the church was the first in the Midwest to be founded by blacks. The first seven pastors were Underground Railroad "managers." Tours of the beautifully preserved historic site are offered year-round. As you sit in the **Harriet Tubman Waiting Room,** through which more than 5,000 escaping slaves passed, a well-versed historian will describe Detroiters' roles in the passage to freedom. Call ahead *(313-961-0920)* to make arrangements.

Next go *one block south to Lafayette and head east to Elmwood (about 2 miles). Turn left, then right into* Elmwood Cemetery. Open year-round, the beautiful grounds are the final resting place of many historic African Americans. Pick up a map and guide at the office and drive/stroll through. If it's time for lunch, several great African-American restaurants are in the immediate area, including **East Franklin, I-Hop, Ja-Da, Cafe Mahogany** and **Miss Jo's.** *(See listings.)*

Now get back on *Westbound Jefferson (at Cobo Center it gets tricky, so follow the signs)* to Historic Fort Wayne and the **Tuskegee Airmen National Museum.** The challenges and triumphs of the military's first African American pilots are an inspiration to everyone. Call ahead to check on hours.

During warm weather months, continue your journey by visiting the **John Freeman Walls Historic Site and Underground Railroad Museum,** a Canadian endpoint to the secret route of some slaves. It's about a half-hour from Windsor in Maidstone Township. *(Take eastbound Highway 401 about eight miles. At Exit 28, go north one mile on Puce Road to the historic site.)* Allow about an hour to relive the journey of escaping slaves who found freedom at a log cabin built in 1846. The four-acre site on 25 acres of farmland is open to individuals and groups from May through October by appointment only. A dinner theater can be added to group tours. *(Call 519-256-6253 or 971-7790 for details.)*

AFRICAN AMERICAN HERITAGE **55**

[E-F/4-5} *Set aside a full day for this African American tour of galleries and nearby eateries, or make a really full day by including the Midtown tour or the History tour and having dinner at one of the nearby restaurants—then take in a play or club. Some of the art establishments offer consulting services. Many galleries are closed on Monday and Tuesday and don't open til after 11 a.m., so plan accordingly. Often, individual or group gallery tours may be arranged. See "Africa" and "Caribbean" chapters for additional stops to add to this tour, if you wish. Refer to map on preceding page.*

Start with an early lunch at the exquisite **East Franklin** *(1440 Franklin, between Riopelle and Rivard, two blocks east of Chrysler Fwy. (I-375), two blocks south of Jefferson).* Indulge in the homemade fare (especially the peach cobbler)—you'll walk it off later.

Next, head up to **Donna D Designs** *(210 Iron St.)* for museum-quality African beads, jewelry and crafts. *(Go east on Franklin to Riopelle, turn left; then right on to Jefferson, about a mile to Iron St. Turn right and you're there.)*

Continue east on Jefferson to the Indian Village area. On the left *(8445 and 8469),* you'll see two restored mansions, **Harper Galleries** and **Villa Domain Interiors.** Limited parking is available in their drives. James Valentine, director of Harper, will knowledgeably show you their eclectic collection of antiques. Next door, Gloria Robinson will graciously guide you through the beautiful collections in Villa Domain, including paintings by Donald Calloway. And don't miss **Cultural Accents** in the same location.

Then it's back down Jefferson to the **Metropolitan Center for Creative Arts** (if you've made an appointment). *Turn right on E. Grand Blvd., then left on E. Lafayette for about 500 feet to 6911.* A little over a mile down Lafayette is **Creative Arts-n-Frames** *(1539)* where you can shop for original arts and crafts, most by local artists.

To visit the next group of art galleries, you'll want to park at **Millender Center.** *To get there, continue along Lafayette and turn left onto Beaubien for two blocks; turn right onto Congress and enter the Millender Center deck on the left.* You'll need to walk a few blocks to the next stop, but you'll be back at Millender Center at the end of this tour.

Head west on Congress to Randolph. Turn right (north) on Randolph and take it to the intersection where Randolph, Broadway and Gratiot merge. Cross Gratiot, then go right a few steps to rejoin Randolph. Go left on Randolph to **Harmonie Park.** *Walk one block to the* **Dell Pryor Galleries** (1542 Randolph), where you'll find decorative and fine arts, jewelry and antiques from many cultures and time periods.

Cross the street to **Cafe Mahogany** *(1465 Centre)* for a refreshment break. *Trace your steps back to Gratiot; turn right, then walk two blocks. Turn right onto Library for one block to the* **Sherry Washington Gallery** *(1274 Library, corner of Grand River)* for an inspiring look at the works of contemporary

African American artists. *Cross Grand River and take an immediate left to the* **A.C.T. Gallery** *(29 E. Grand River)* to view up-and-coming artists *(open weekends noon to 5 p.m.).*

The next part of the tour takes you on an elevated journey via the **People Mover.** *Head south one block on Library to Gratiot.* Cross the street, get on at **Cadillac Square** *(station 11).* Hop off, but don't exit, at **Broadway** *(station 12)* for an up-close view of "The Blue Nile," by **Charles McGee.** The only true painting in any of the stations, it has a Noah's Ark theme in an African style. At **Grand Circus Park** *(station 13),* don't miss the extraordinarily lifelike sculpture of a commuter reading a newspaper by **J. Seward Johnson Jr.**

A full-color brochure, with map, explaining all the artwork at the People Mover stations is available from the People Mover office at 150 Michigan Ave., 2nd floor. Call 1-800-541-7245 for information.

Ride two more stops to **Michigan Avenue** *(station 2)* to see the tile mural "Voyage" by **Allie McGhee,** which, in his words, reflects "the diverse energies in our environment: image, rhythm, light and motion."

Reboard the People Mover, then ride to **Cobo Center** *(station 4)* to see tributes to the "Brown Bomber," **Joe Louis Barrow.** You can't miss the 12-foot statue in the first floor atrium near Cobo Center's main entrance *(Washington Boulevard).* Behind it is a display case containing the glove that Louis wore when he knocked out Max Schmeling in 1938. You'll need to make an appointment to visit the **Joe Louis Video Memorial Room,** *on the second floor in Room 0234. (Call 313-222-0594).* Take the People Mover back to **Millender Center** *(station 7).* On the way there, look out the window at Woodward and Jefferson; you'll see sculptor Robert Graham's 24-foot-long sculpture titled **"The Fist,"** another tribute to Joe Louis.

You might want to leave the People Mover to take in these two special spots: *Greektown station,* for **Djenne Beads & Art** *(1045 Beaubien),* featuring exotic jewelry, kente, kuba and mud cloth and *Bricktown station,* for **Spirit in the Park** *(635 Beaubien)* gallery, boutique and bookstore, with many pieces created by artist/owner Joie Coelho.

Before heading for your car, view the tile art in the People Mover station entitled **"Detroit: New Morning,"** a masterpiece of subtle cool colors, iridescent glazes and geometrical details by Alvin Loving Jr.

Dining: If you're ready for dinner try: **Ja Da** *(546 E. Larned, near Millender)* for hot ribs and cool jazz. **Edmund Place** *(69 Edmund, east of Woodward, four blocks north of I-75)* for a Southern or traditional meal in an elegant Victorian setting. **East Franklin** *(1440 Franklin, south of Jefferson, three blocks east of Rivard)* for a Rivertown atmosphere offering Southern cooking and contemporary art by locals for sale on the brick walls. **Soul Food Café,** *(1040 Randolph in Greektown)* for healthy regional cooking in Detroit's newest, first-class soul food restaurant.

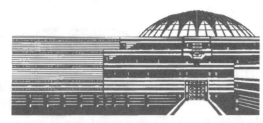

The first contact for visitors arriving at the Charles H. Wright Museum of African American History, as well as for people driving past on E. Warren, is an African mask design above the entrance doors.

The latest jewel in Detroit's Cultural Center is the Charles H. Wright Museum of African American History at Warren and Brush. Founded in 1965 by Detroiter Charles H. Wright, M.D., the museum's first building was on West Grand Blvd., followed by a facility on Frederick Douglass. Exhibits explore the rich legacy and heritage of African Americans in the arts, sciences, literature, politics, labor and philosophy.

The permanent exhibit, which chronicles 400 years of history and culture, is the largest space ever created in this nation for an exhibition devoted to African American people. National traveling exhibits, relating to art, history and technology, round out the museum's mission.

Serious visitors can spend the better part of a day here — three to four hours at the core exhibit, plus time in the changing galleries, museum shop and cafe. Museum hours are Tuesday-Sunday 9:30 a.m.-5 p.m. Admission is $3 for adults and $2 for children 12 and under. Phone: (313) 494-5800.

Directions: *(See Cultural Center in Multicultural Detroit chapter for detailed map.) From I-75 take Warren exit, from I-94 take the John R/Woodward exit or from US-10 (Lodge) take W. Forest. Parking is available in the lot next to the Science Center on John R and in a new lot behind the Museum of African American History between Farnsworth and Frederick Douglass.*

The tour begins with the building itself. Its striking, contemporary architecture encompasses a distinctive African design. The main entrances each have an African mask hung high over textured bronze doors. Sculptural columns on both the exterior and the public interior are based on a traditional African rope motif.

Once inside, start your exploration in the Ford Freedom Rotunda lobby by viewing the colorful flags of the African diaspora and the bold terrazzo floor depicting African and African-American experiences. Called "Genealogy," the colorful design was created by local artist Hubert Massey. Follow its border all the way around the circle to see how many of the names of famous African Americans engraved on bronze tiles you recognize. Look up at the glass dome to see the contemporary pattern which reflects the traditional African Hut form.

The facility is intended to be a gathering place for community events, educational programs, concerts, meetings and private parties and weddings. Carved wood doors with surrounds, based on African art and culture, serve as the entrances to the auditorium and multipurpose rooms. The Louise Lovett Wright Library, named for the founder's first wife, houses historically significant books and periodicals.

You'll want to devote most of your time to the 16,000-square-foot core exhibition, called "Of the People: The African American Experience." It surveys the 400-year legacy and heritage, with Detroit's history woven into the ongoing story.

Upon entering, walk up the ramp of the **Prologue Theater** to cross through a section of a **Middle Passage** ship that brought Africans to America. Cast figures of 50 students from the Detroit community depict the crowded conditions and shackles in the slave ship's hold.

Then begin the progression of eight historical stations that consist of images, quotes, text, artifacts, audio and multi-media displays:

1) **African Memory** links the origin and history on the African continent to African-American culture.

2) **The Crime** focuses on the slave trade, told by those who endured it.

3) **Survival of the Spirit** looks at life as an enslaved American and the escape route through the Underground Railroad.

4) **The Imperfect Union,** about the struggle against slavery, calls for the nation to live up to the ideals of the Declaration of Independence.

5) **Freedom and Betrayal** covers the post-civil war period and the achievements and failures of Reconstruction.

6) **Urban Struggles/Urban Splendor** looks at the Great Migration to northern urban centers and how the jazz sound became the sensation of a new age.

7) **Struggle for Emancipation** is about the 20th century civil rights movement — the legal and legislative means for empowerment, grassroots activism, and the role of investment, education and self-expression.

8) **Becoming the Future** features images of African-descended people throughout the world, and explores political solidarity and cultural connections, including African influence on the English language.

Listening Rooms near stations six and seven showcase the diversity of African American music and the classics of spoken art (folk tales, poetry, drama, sermons and oratory). Also notice the **African American history timeline** on the vertical columns throughout the core exhibit and the display area near the entrance devoted to **achievements and contributions of African Americans.**

Before going through the galleries housing **changing exhibits**, you might want to have lunch or refreshments at the **Lewis Latimer Cafe** on the lower level. Named for the African American inventor of the filament in light bulbs, the cafeteria offers American, African and Caribbean food and has indoor and outdoor plaza seating.

Before you leave, stop in at the **Museum Shop**. The merchandise represents the best of African and African American cultures. Many of the hand-crafted items were selected by a museum official during a trip to Ghana. Carved boxes, dolls, frames, king's staffs, decorative pins, fabric, baskets, masks, statues, books, embroidered dresses, kente purses, shoes and jewelry, as well as affordable souvenirs for children to buy, are among the selection. The mixture of African cultures and crafts represented in the merchandise encompasses the people of Haiti and other nations, as well.

[E-F/4-5] *Spend half a day exploring cultural treasures in the heart of Detroit—from Fisher Building art galleries to the Motown Museum. To make a full day of it, combine with one of the other tours in this chapter or museums in the Cultural Center (see listings on following pages).*

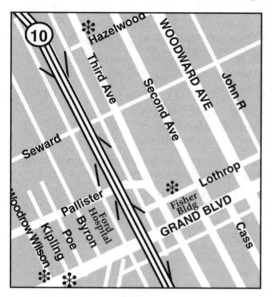

From downtown take Woodward north to Grand Boulevard and go west one block to Second Ave. and the Fisher Building, which has its own parking lot. From the north, take either the Lodge or I-75 to New Center/W. Grand Blvd. exit. On the first floor, you'll find the **Poster Gallery** which carries artwork, Caribbean instruments, cards and woven throws—all with African American themes.

Upstairs, the **National Conference of Artists– Michigan Gallery** features works of local and internation-al artists of African descent in a warm and personal setting. There you can get an audio- or videotape to take home.

For Ethiopian coffee, teas, sandwiches, soup or dessert, exit the Fisher Building's north entrance, turn left and stroll less than a block to **736 JAVA,** a cozy coffeehouse on Lothrop.

To visit the **Motown Historical Museum,** *from the Fisher Building turn right (west) on Grand Boulevard and proceed to 2648 W. Grand Blvd. on the other side of the Lodge Freeway.* You'll find the legendary **Studio A,** authentically reproduced right down to the worn hardwood floor. **The Shop Around** gift shop offers cassettes, CDs, shirts, bags, books, educational packages and more.

Right across Grand Blvd. is the **Institute of American Black Arts.** Dr. Leno Jackson, director, features exhibits and performances by local artists as well as the world-renowned Leroy Foster.

On your way home, pick up a meal and perhaps a famous five-layer coconut cake from **Mr. FoFo's** *(8902 Second),* one of Detroit's long-time favorite carryout kitchens.

[D-E/4-5] Part of Henry Ford's original plan for Greenfield Village in his home-town of Dearborn was to have a group of buildings dedicated to African American history. The Hermitage Slave Houses, Mattox farmhouse and the George Washington Carver log cabin, situated just east of the Village Green, focus on family life and culture of six or seven generations of African Americans. They present a portrait of resilience, progress and triumph over adversity.

The two, 16-foot square **Hermitage Slave Houses** (circa 1820) come from an industrial plantation just north of Savannah, Ga., where about 200 slave workers lived in 52 such buildings arranged in a square. At various times the plantation operated a steam saw mill, an iron foundry, a rice mill, a rice manufactory, brick works and a building construction company. The Hermitage was famous for the superior bricks, known as Savannah Gray Brick, made by its slave workers. Using West African planting, cultivation and processing methods, the slave workers also made rice a highly profitable crop at the plantation.

The **Mattox House** was built in the 1880s in Georgia by descendants of a Whitehall Plantation slave worker after the Emancipation. The home was occupied by members of the Morel-Mattox family until the 1940s, when Henry Ford purchased it as part of his plan to document the history of African Americans.

Next, visit the **George Washington Carver Memorial,** a log cabin Henry Ford had built as a tribute to the agricultural chemist and famous teacher at Tuskegee Institute. It is a replica of the Missouri slave cabin where Carver was born in the 1860s just before the Emancipation. Inside, the exhibit focuses on Carver as an innovator and teacher of various agricultural methods that improved the crops of Southern farmers. He discovered and popularized hundreds of uses for crops such as peanuts, soybeans, sweet potatoes and greens.

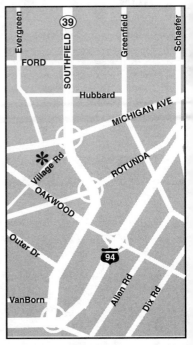

Greenfield Village hosts a number of special events during the year, including **Black History Month** in February, when activities and exhibits focus on the Civil Rights Movement. The **Celebration of Emancipation** in early August features reenactments and traditional African American music and storytelling. *(See listings for "Holidays & Annual Events.")*

Henry Ford Museum & Greenfield Village are in Dearborn west of the Southfield Freeway (M-39) between Michigan Avenue and Oakwood Boulevard. The Village and Museum are open daily 9 a.m. to 5 p.m., except Thanksgiving and Christmas. Interiors of some Village buildings are closed during winter. For admission prices and exhibit and special events schedules, call (313) 271-1620. (Also see "Greenfield Village" in Americana Chapter.)

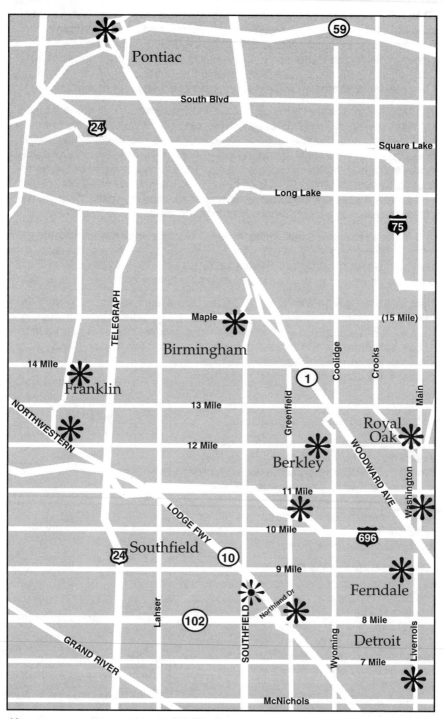

[D-E/1-4] Begin in northwest Detroit in the University of Detroit District (Livernois between 7 Mile and McNichols). For breakfast, try **Mama's Place** (15250 W. Seven Mile) or perhaps **Celebration Cake Boutique** (13330 W. Seven Mile) for cobbler to take with you.

Now stroll along Livernois to find a number of unique shops featuring food, clothes and fun. Be sure not to miss **Abibiman Treasure** (18443), with traditional African artifacts; **art on the ave** (19132) with African, African-American and African Diaspora fine art and artifacts; and **Terry's Enchanted Garden** (19338) with specialty florals as well as Afro-centric designs and black Lladro figurines.

Drive up Livernois to Nine Mile in Ferndale. Turn right to find **Linda's Frameworks** (180 W. Nine Mile; two blocks west of Woodward) and see or perhaps purchase pieces from the collection of dolls by Miss Martha's, Sarah's Attic and Daddy's Long Legs. If you have time, stroll around Ferndale—it's an up-and-coming city with new shops and restaurants opening frequently.

.Go back west on Nine Mile to Greenfield. Turn right. Just north of Lincoln (10 1/2 Mile) in Lincoln Shopping Center is **Book Beat,** one of the few remaining independent and locally owned bookstores which offers exhibits of original African and African American art, books, records, tapes and more.

Go back south on Greenfield to Northland Drive, turn right to find **Umoja Fine Arts** (16250, Suite 104, in the Crossroads Building), the largest publisher and distributor of African-American art in the Midwest. Take Northland Drive into Northland Center to **The Truth Bookstore** (#476). Owner Nefertiti has created an Afrocentric cultural center where everyone feels welcome.

Time for lunch! Take the Lodge Freeway north to I-696, to Northwestern Hwy. to **Beans & Cornbread.** In the Sunset Strip plaza (north of 12 Mile on the east side), this very popular restaurant is southern, soulful, sophisticated, stylish and the fare is highly rated by food critics.

Next, go back on Northwestern to Franklin Rd. Take it to the village of Franklin, where the **Village Green** (west side of Franklin Road) was the site of an Underground Railroad station. Take Franklin Road north to Maple (15 Mile) and go east to Birmingham. Here you can browse these galleries: **Gallery Shaantia** (361 E. Maple), which features furniture, gifts, accessories and tribal art; **G.R. N'Namdi Gallery** (616 Townsend), which specializes in African and African American fine art; and **Mooro Afrioan Gallery** (304 I lamilton flow), which carries sculpture, paintings and artifacts from Zimbabwe, Malawi, South Africa, Zambia and Mozambique.

Time to head up Woodward to **Pontiac** where you can visit **Anderson Gallery** (7 N. Saginaw) to see textiles, special exhibits and presentations on a variety of African arts. Other galleries on Saginaw also feature African Ameican artists.

Backtrack down Woodward. Turn right on 12 Mile to the **Nile Gallery** (3475 Robina, just off 12 Mile, west of Coolidge) to shop for works of local African American artists, as well as antiques and imports.

Now head back east on 12 Mile to see one of Michigan's most recently placed Historical Markers at the **Royal Oak Cemetery.** Go just past Main Street and turn right through the gate. The small graveyard, which adjoins St. Mary's cemetery, is bounded by the intersections of Crooks, Main Street and Rochester Roads. Members of the Hamer family, who were among Royal Oak's first settlers (via the Underground Railroad), are buried here. Park and walk to read the

Historic Marker and view the interesting headstones. Rubbings are permitted if done carefully. Hours are 7 a.m.-9 p.m. daily.

By now it should be supper time (and you should have walked off that lunch!). *Exit the cemetery on Rochester Road and turn right, then left on to Main Street south to* **Memphis Smoke** *(100 S. Main St., at 11 Mile).* If you get there by 6 p.m., parking is pretty easy to find at the rear of the building. Enjoy Southern-style barbecue, ribs, greens, catfish and red beans & rice. Late-evening live entertainment varies from blues to jazz to alternative to zydeco. Rooftop dining in season.

Royal Oak also has a number of other places of special African-American interest, including **Fifth Avenue** *(215 W. Fifth)* music and billiards club, and **Off the Record** *(corner of Fourth and Washington),* a record store with a huge selection of blues, jazz, world and Caribbean music.

RESTAURANTS

SOUL FOOD

ABSOLUT TIFFANY'S
440 Clinton, Detroit; (313) 964-8900
Tue-Wed 11am-midnight, Thurs 11am-1am, Fri 11am-2am, Sat 5pm-2am. Lunch 11am-4pm, dinner 4-11pm. Bar menu 11 pm until one hour before closing. Live entertainment Fri and Sat 9pm-1am at this upscale restaurant that serves seafood, steak, pasta and rotating chef's selections.

BEANS & CORN BREAD
29508 Northwestern Hwy, Southfield (248) 208-1680
Tue-Fri 11am-3pm, Fri-Sat 5pm-10pm, Sun 4pm-9pm, closed Mon. A sophisticated combination of soul food classics from meatloaf to Harlem burritoes, to filet mignon with grilled mushrooms, served with traditional side orders—all with a healthy twist, such as turkey instead of pork for seasoning.

DEARING LOUNGE & BANQUET CENTER
11234 McNichols, Detroit; (313) 371-2034
Daily 2pm-2am. African, barbeque and Cajun cuisine served in upscale environment.

EAST FRANKLIN
1440 Franklin, Detroit; (313) 393-0018
Tue-Thu 11am-9pm, Fri 11am-10pm, Sat noon-10pm, Sun noon-9pm. Meat loaf, chicken-fried steak, black-eyed peas, Southern country-style dishes from varied menu.

FLOOD'S BAR & GRILLE
731 St. Antoine, Detroit; (313) 963-1090
Food and drink Mon 4pm-midnight, Tue-Fri 3pm-2:30am, Sat-Sun 7;m-2:30am. Bar menu 3pm-1:30am. Owner Mike Byrd serves up live entertainment plus seafood, soul food, sandwiches and desserts.

JA•DA
546 E. Larned, Detroit; (313) 965-1700
Mon-Thu 11am-9pm, Fri 11am-2am, Sat 1pm-2am. Restaurant shares its name with the tangy barbecue sauce developed by owners Armanda and Bill Herbert. The upscale downtown spot offers cool jazz, hot ribs and a lively good time.

JUANITA'S KITCHEN
20510 Livernois, Detroit; (313) 345-6300
Sun-Thurs 11am-midnight, Fri-Sat 11am-1:30am. Soul food served with a good portion of music in Detroit's legendary jazz club.

LIL' CHAMPS
18338 Plymouth Rd., Detroit (313) 837-8940
Daily 7:30am-11:30pm. Chicken 'n dressing, oxtails, barbecued pig feet, ham hocks, greens, cakes and cobblers on menu.

MAMA'S PLACE
15228 W. Seven Mile, Detroit (313) 342-6120
Tue-Sun 9am-9pm. Soul food eatery features home-style Southern cooking, including liver and onions and salmon croquettes.

MILT'S GOURMET BAR "B" QUE
10223 Whittier, Detroit; (313) 521-5959
Tues-Thu 11am-8pm, Fri-Sat 11am-10pm. closed Sun-Mon. Ribs and great desserts are very popular with many people, including some local sports figures.

MISS JO'S RIBS 'N' THINGS
20181 Van Dyke, Detroit; (313) 892-0648
Mon-Thu noon-9pm, Fri-Sat noon-11pm, Sun noon-8pm. Home-style Southern cooking featuring ribs, chicken, greens, black-eyed peas, fried corn, potato salad, puddings, cakes and cobblers. Catering and carryout.

"DOWN HOME" COOKING

Soul food emerged in the mid-'60s as a term for traditional, savory food of Southern black Americans. Some items, such as okra and sesame seeds, were brought from Africa by slaves. Others were crops or plantation owners' "castoffs" that slaves creatively prepared for themselves to supplement rationed food. All are well-seasoned, often with African-derived spices.

Dinner staples include greens with ham hocks, cornbread, fried corn, rice, sweet potatoes and pork from neck bones to pigs' feet. Breakfast favorites are biscuits, grits and sausage or fried chicken. Dessert specialties include bread pudding, sweet potato pie and fruit cobblers.

Evolving from African customs is a love of cooking lavishly for family and friends in the home, especially at holidays. Often, a family's way of preparing favorites is passed down from generation to generation—with smell, taste, touch and appearance overriding written recipes, if any.

Like old-fashioned European cuisine, soul food may be good for your soul, but it can be bad for your heart. Contemporary recipes cut the original amount of salt, sugar and fat. Substitutes include turkey instead of pork, honey in place of sugar and baking rather than frying.

"We offer classes in how to cook a delicious, vegetarian 'soul' menu," says **Thelma Raziya Curtis,** founder of Detroit's Healing Support Network Inc. There are no animal products in her macrobiotic recipes for collard greens, black-eyed peas, cornbread and no-bake sweet potato pies.

In his 1995 book, *African American Cookery,* Howard Paige of Southfield suggests we avoid the term "soul food." He says it reflects a narrow view of the important culinary contributions made by people of African descent over hundreds of years.

Paige's 190-page book covers "Big House Cooks" as well as 19th-century East Coast caterers, wagon-train chefs, Creole specialists and the luxury-train gourmets of the '40s. Authentic recipes are updated for healthy eating. The book also profiles culinary scientists such as Lloyd Augustus Hall, who pioneered food-sterilization methods.

SOUL FOOD CAFE
1040 Randolph (across from the Old County Bldg.), Detroit; (313) 965-6880
Mon-Thu 11am-9pm, Fri-Sat 11am-1am, Sun noon-6pm. New eatery offers healthy, yet authentic dining surrounded by works of local black artists and sports memorabilia in an urban Bistro setting. Live entertainment.

THE SOUTHERN CONNECTION
18641 Wyoming, Detroit; (313) 861-1857
Mon-Wed 11am-8pm, Thu-Sat 11am-9pm. Home cooking: catfish, meat loaf, baked chicken and dressing, peach cobbler, triple chocolate cake.

STEVE'S SOUL FOOD
8443 Grand River, Detroit; (313) 894-3464
Daily 11am-9pm.

and
15680 J.L. Hudson Drive, Southfield
(248) 559-5010
Sun-Thu 11am-9pm, Fri-Sat 11am-10pm. Longtime favorite of many Detroiters; reasonable prices for authentic home-style cooking.

WOODWARD VILLAGE CAFE
4200 Woodward Ave., Detroit
(313) 832-3000
Mon-Fri 7 am-9 pm, Sat 9 am-9 pm, Sun 10 am-5 pm. Delicatessen and vegetarian delights, garden burgers, salmon, Amish chicken, turkey and corned beef plus espresso, cappuccino and flavored coffees and fruit drinks.

VEGETARIAN
AKNARTOON'S EATERY
10310 Woodward (at Calvert), Detroit
(313) 867-3102
Mon-Sun 11am-midnight. Healthy, hearty vegetarian and meat dishes (no pork). Popular cabbage soup. Dine in or carryout. A trip next door to the Health Store rounds out this nutritional experience.

THE PANDA DELI & RESTAURANT
7720 W. McNichols, Detroit; (313) 863-8405
Tue-Sat noon-7:30pm, Sun noon-5pm. Favorites include vegetarian Swiss steak, greens with yams, millet cream du jour. All food is prepared with only natural ingredients. Entrées span West African, Oriental, Italian and American cuisines.

OTHER
BROWN BAG EATERY
15070 Hamilton, Highland Park
(313) 869-6668
Orders taken Mon-Fri 11am-4pm. Specializes in catering elegant, unforgettable cuisine, including gumbo and other Creole choices, soul food dishes cooked with smoked turkey, homemade desserts and rolls, hot entrees, fruits and salads.

CAFE MAHOGANY
1465 Centre, Detroit; (313) 235-2233
Sun-Thu 6pm-midnight, Fri 11am-6am, Sat noon-6am. Harmonie Park café and bar features nightly entertainment, light meals and cappuccino.

EDMUND PLACE
69 Edmund, Detroit; (313) 831-5757
Tue-Thu 11am-9pm, Fri 11am-11pm, Sat 1-11pm, Sun noon-9pm. Originally opened as a soul food restaurant, recently remodeled with expanded menu including Creole, French and American cuisine. Elegant atmosphere with piano bar in 1882 brick and stone house in historic Brush Park district.

FOOD O' LOVE CATERING
839 S. Crooks (YMCA), Clawson
1-877-366-3658 (toll free)
Owner Jada Dunwoody-Brent uses her grandmother's recipes for real Southern style dishes and soul food, including sweet potato pie and corn pudding.

HARMONIE GARDEN CAFE
242 John R (south of Madison), Detroit

(313) 961-7255
Mon-Sat 8am-7pm, Sun 11am-5pm. Menu blends African American and Arab dishes at very reasonable prices.

INTERNATIONAL HOUSE OF PANCAKES
2701 E. Jefferson, Detroit; (313) 393-2400
Daily 6am-10pm. Music fills the air and Motown memorabilia abounds. Landlord Walter Bridgeforth displays wife Anita Baker's platinum records.

736 JAVA
736 Lothrop, Detroit; (313) 875-5282
Tue-Thu 7:30-11pm, Fri 7:30pm-2am, Sat noon-2am. Freda G. Sampson beckons friends to meet for coffee, pastries or sandwiches in her cozy coffee house. Live music on weekends. Call for scheduled coffee tastings, poetry readings and book signings.

LOUIE'S ON WOODWARD
630 Woodward, Detroit
(313) 963-8424
Tues-Fri 11:30am-10pm, Mon 11:30am-4pm, Sat 6pm-10pm, Sun. brunch. Offers Creole and Cajun specialties, catering and carryout. Regular entertainment and special Gospel music brunch on Sundays.

MEMPHIS SMOKE
100 S. Main St. at 11 Mile, Royal Oak
(248) 543-4300
Mon-Sat 11:30am-2am, Sun noon-2am. Southern-style barbecue, greens, catfish, red beans and rice. Live entertainment evenings varies from blues to jazz to alternative.

MR. FOFO'S
8902 Second (at Hazelwood), Detroit
(313) 873-4450
Daily 24 hours. Closed some holidays. Home of the "world's largest corned beef sandwich." Homemade desserts, including pound cake, cobblers and five-layer cakes. Supplies sweet potato pie nationally to Kentucky Fried Chicken. Often crowded, but worth the wait.

VICKI'S BARBECUE
3845 W. Warren, Detroit; (313) 894-9906
Sun, Wed 4pm-midnight, Thu noon-midnight, Fri-Sat noon-2am. Takeout eatery noted for shrimp and barbeque chicken.

*Also see **Flood's Bar & Grille** under Jazz Clubs and **Soup Kitchen Saloon** under Blues Clubs.*

GROCERIES

GOURMET FOOD CENTER
15724 W. Seven Mile, Detroit
(313) 838-9588
Mon-Sat 10am-5pm. Cleaned and ready-to-cook chitterlings, or "chitlins;" hog maws; and greens.

BAKERIES

BENA'S HOMEMADE CAKES
3315 Puritan, Detroit; (313) 862-4372
Mon-Fri 9am-5pm, Sat 9am-3pm. Rubena Burch offers "made from scratch" pound cake in a number of flavors daily and fruit-laden Kwanzaa cake in season. Her pound cake is on Hudson's menu at its Northland Mall deli and at its Michigan and Indiana restaurants.

CELEBRATION CAKE BOUTIQUE
13330 W. Seven Mile, Detroit
(313) 342-0400
Tue-Sat 9am-6pm. Unforgettable pound cake, sweet potato pies, fruit cobblers, croissants and cookies line the shelves.

HOLLIE'S SWEETS & BALLOONS
18955 Livernois, Detroit; (313) 862-6540
Mon-Thu 10am-6pm, Fri 10am-7pm, Sat 9am-5pm. Among the wide variety of delicacies are the popular yellow and chocolate layer cakes and the castle cake, a 24-part wedding creation with water fountains.

KRISTIN'S COBBLERS AND CAKES
18980 Schaefer (S of Seven Mile), Detroit
(313) 341-2253
Tue-Fri 6am-6pm, Sat-Sun 8am-4pm. Specialties of this full-service bakery are wedding cakes and a variety of breads, including exceptional rolls. Owners restored property that had been vacant 15 years.

PEOPLE'S BAKERY
2765 S. Fort St., Detroit
(between Outer Drive and Schaefer)
(313) 383-9090
Mon-Sat 7am-5:30pm. Sweet potato pie is among the most popular items at this shop, one of Detroit's long-standing African American businesses. Other goodies include several types of pies, German chocolate and other cakes, doughnuts and dinner rolls.

SWEET POTATO SENSATIONS
17346 Lahser (N of Grand River), Detroit
(313) 532-7996
Tue-Fri 10am-6pm, Sat 10am-4pm. Groceries in Detroit and Flint carry Cassandra Thomas' creations, which include cheesecake, cookies and pies—all made from sweet potatoes.

SHOPS

(Also see "Africa" chapter.)

ABIBIMAN TREASURE
18443 Livernois, Detroit; (313) 861-1510
Call for hours. Traditional African artifacts.

ART ON THE AVE
19132 Livernois, Detroit; (313) 863-4278
Mon-Sat 10am-8pm, Sun 1-6pm. African, African-American and African Diaspora fine art and artifacts.

CREATIVE ARTS-N-FRAMES
1539 E. Lafayette, Detroit
(Lafayette Orleans mini-mall)
(313) 567-0520
Tue-Sat 11am-7pm. Artist James McKissic Sr. makes matte design and cutting an art at his full-service, specialty framing shop. Original art by mostly local artists also is here, along with small artifacts and figurines. Reclamation artist La Vern Homan, shop manager, offers hand-painted furniture and other pieces.

CULTURAL EXPRESSIONS
1032 N. Crooks, Suite C., Clawson
(248) 288-9275
By appointment only. African textiles, wood and bronze statues, masks, traditional and oontemporary African artifacts

DJENNE BEADS & ART
1045 Beaubien, Detroit; (313) 965-6620
Mon-Thu 11am-9pm, Fri-Sat 11am-10pm. Detroit's largest collection of African trade

QUILTS *made by slaves often served as signals on the Underground Railroad to identify "safe houses."* ● *For quilting resources, see "Americana."*

beads let you design your own jewelry; also oils and incense, arts and crafts.

DONNA D DESIGNS
201 Iron St., Detroit; (313) 417-7633
Wed-Fri 11am-6pm, Sat 10am-4pm.
Handcrafted one-of-a-kind and limited edition jewelry features Bauole Brass, vintage African masks, trade beads and charms.

MY SISTAH'S PLACE
11000 W. McNichols, Ste. 226, Detroit
(313) 345-3110
Mon-Fri 9am-5pm. Afrocentric gifts and accessories.

REGAL BRIDE
1823 Burns, Detroit; (313) 822-1455
Call for hours. Owner/designer Andrea Adeo Brown creates African-inspired wedding gowns embellished with embroidered or hand-painted African symbols. She also designs vests, bowties and cummerbunds for men, plus headdresses.

TERRY'S ENCHANTED GARDEN
19338 Livernois; (313) 342-3758
Mon-Fri 9am-5:30pm, Sat 9am-4pm.
Specialty party and wedding floral arrangements, including creative Afrocentric and tropical designs. Clothing boutique. Also stocks black porcelain Lladro figurines.

TRUTH BOOKSTORE
21500 Northwestern Hwy.
(Northland Mall)
Southfield; (248) 557-4824
Mall hours. African American bookstore, gift shop. and cultural center.

TRUTH BOUTIQUE
18000 Vernier (Easland Mall #823)
Harper Woods; (313) 371-2225
Mall hours. Afrocentric gifts and collectibles.

CHURCHES
A LEGACY OF SOCIAL ACTION

From the time of slavery, organized religion has been an important part of African American culture. Many historic benchmarks have occurred in Detroit. The Midwest's first African American congregation was organized at Second Baptist Church in Detroit in 1836. It became a major depot of the Underground Railroad, giving safe haven to 5,000 to 6,000 fugitive slaves.

Detroit's first African Methodist Episcopal church, Bethel AME, was founded in 1839. Historian Charles Blockson found that most AME churches built before the Civil War were stops on the Underground Railroad. The AME church was the nation's first autonomous black institution with a nationwide reach.

According to the book *Heritage of Faith: Detroit's Religious Communities*, "Methodists and Episcopalians outnumbered other denominations in Detroit's African American community in the 19th century. However, following World War I, the situation rapidly changed as newcomers from the South arrived and organized numerous Baptist and Pentecostal congregations."

In 1934, a new denomination was founded in Detroit: Elijah Muhammad organized the first mosque of the Nation of Islam.

Today, hundreds of local churches, large and small, serve African American congregations. Detroit's Council of Baptist Pastors alone has a membership of 400. The largest is Hartford Memorial Baptist Church's congregation of 8,000. Generations of its pastors have shared a deep commitment to social activism.

GALLERIES

DOWNTOWN DETROIT

A.C.T. GALLERY
29 E. Grand River., Detroit; (313) 961-4336
Fri-Sat noon-5pm. Artists' cooperative for
local artists highlights diversity of Detroit's art
community by displaying a variety of media.

ARTS EXTENDED
David Whitney Bldg.,
1553 Woodward, Detroit; (313) 961-5036
Wed-Sat Noon-5pm. Founded in 1958 by a
group of Detroit Public Schools art teachers.

CULTURAL ACCENTS
8468 E. Jefferson (Indian Village), Detroit
(313) 823-8813
Mon-Fri 10am-6pm, Sat 11am-5pm. Fine
collectible dolls by noted artists, such as
Philip Heath, Lulu Tatum, Fayzah Spanos and
Lee Middleton. Figurine lines include Daddy's
Long Legs, All God's Children, Thomas
Blackshear and All that Jazz. Also multicultur-
al greeting cards and jewelry.

DELL PRYOR GALLERIES
1452 Randolph (Harmonie Park), Detroit
(313) 963-5977
Tue-Sat 11am-5pm. Decorative and fine arts
from many cultures and time periods, including fiber design, pottery, art-glass lamps, jewelry and gift items.

HARPER GALLERIES
8445 E. Jefferson (Indian Village), Detroit
(313) 821-1952
Wed-Sat 10am-6pm, Sun noon-9pm. Fine old
furniture and antiques in historic mansion.

JOHANSON CHARLES
1345 Division (Eastern Mkt.)
Detroit; (313) 567-8638
Call for hours. Owners Chris Turner and
Kevin Hanson.

JRAINEY GALLERY
1440 Gratiot (across from Eastern Mkt.)
Detroit; (313) 259-2257
Wed-Sat noon-6pm. New gallery features
African American as well as other local talent.

METROPOLITAN CENTER
FOR CREATIVE ARTS
6911 E. Lafayette, Detroit; (313) 259-2400
By appointment. Alternative space gallery.

SHERRY WASHINGTON GALLERY

1274 Library St., Detroit; (313) 961-4500
Tue-Fri 10am-5pm, Sat noon-5pm.
Contemporary paintings, sculpture and prints
by emerging and established African
American artists.

SPIRIT IN THE PARK
635 Beaubien, Detroit
(between Greektown & Jefferson)
(313) 965-4919
Tues-Sat 10am-6pm. Gallery and boutique
features paintings, clothing, books baskets
and more.

VILLA DOMAIN INTERIORS
8469 E. Jefferson (Indian Village), Detroit
(313) 824-4600
*Wed-Sat 11am-7pm, Sun noon-5pm. Closed
Mon-Tue.* Restored mansion features original
works by African American artists, gifts, collectibles, antiques and furniture. Gallery may
be rented for special events including weddings.

MIDTOWN DETROIT

INSTITUTE OF AMERICAN BLACK ARTISTS
2641 W. Grand Blvd, Detroit
(across from Motown Museum)
(313) 872-0332
Mon-Sun 10am-6pm. Permanent exhibit of
Leroy Foster's portraits of Paul Robeson and
Fredrick Douglass, plus regular shows by
other black artists. Performances, workshops,
and tours for all ages. The community is
encouraged to take advantage of the facility
to promote their own creative endeavors and
new ideas are welcome.

NATIONAL CONFERENCE
OF ARTISTS–MICHIGAN GALLERY
216 Fisher Bldg., Detroit
(313) 875-0923
Tues, Thurs 11am-5pm. Features works of
local and international artists of African
descent. Prices range from a few dollars to
thousands. Books, videos, signed posters and
cards plus the work of art masters.

POSTER GALLERY
110 Fisher Building, Detroit
(313) 875-5211
Mon-Fri 10am-6pm, Sat 11am-5pm. In addition to posters and prints offers many gift
items, cards, toys and games with African
American theme.

NORTH

ANDERSON GALLERY

7 N. Saginaw, Pontiac
(248) 335-4611
Tue-Sat 11am-4pm, Fri 11am-6pm.
Specializes in textiles; offers exhibits and presentations on a variety of African arts. Historic textiles and contemporary fiber art.

GALLERY SHAANTIA
361 E. Maple, Birmingham
(248) 647-9202
Mon, Tues, Wed, Fri 10:30am-5pm; Thu 10:30am-8pm; Sat 10:30am-6pm. Furniture, gifts, accessories, tribal art.

LINDA'S FRAMEWORKS
180 W. Nine Mile Rd., Ferndale
(2 blocks W of Woodward)
(248) 546-0987
Tues-Fri 10am-6pm, Sat 11am-5pm.
Selection of African American collectibles includes Daddy's Long Legs and Sarah's Attic.

MOORE AFRICAN GALLERY
304 Hamilton Row, Birmingham
(248) 647-4662
Mon-Sat 10am-6pm, Sun 12:30-5:30pm.
Sculpture, painting and artifacts from Zimbabwe, Malawi, South Africa, Zambia and Mozambique.

G.R. N'NAMDI GALLERY
161 Townsend, Birmingham

DUNBAR MEMORIAL HOSPITAL Until the late 1920s black doctors were not allowed to practice in hospitals operated by whites. A Victorian mansion at 580 Frederick Douglass served as Detroit's first black hospital and nursing school until 1928. The hospital has been preserved and is on the National Registry of Historic Places. It may be toured. by appointment. Call (313) 831-1111.

(248) 642-2700
Tue-Sat 11am-5:30pm. African and African American fine art includes pieces by Ed Clark, Nanette Carter, Herbert Gentry, Richard Hunt, Jacob Lawrence, Al Loving Jr., and Howardena Pindell.

NILE GALLERY
3475 Robina, Berkley; (248) 548-8881
Tue-Sat 10am-6pm. Custom-designed clothes; many works by local African American artists.

SMITH WATSON GALLERY OF DOLLS & TRAINS
26600 Southfield Rd., Lathrup Village
(S of 11 Mile)
(248) 569-1007
Mon-Fri 10am-5pm, Sat 10am-6pm.
Portrait dolls and other toy collectibles.

UMOJA FINE ARTS
16250 Northland Drive, Suite 104
(Crossroads Bldg.), Southfield
(248) 552-1070; (800) 469-8701
Tues-Sat, noon-5pm; Thu noon-7pm. Largest publisher and distributor of African-American art in the Midwest. Lithographs, posters and sculptures. Offers series on black masters of the blues and legendary players of the Negro Baseball League.

ANN ARBOR
KWANZAA HOUSE GALLERY
122 S. Main St. (2nd floor), Ann Arbor
(734) 213-1900
Fri-Sat noon-7pm and by appointment.
Original paintings, prints, masks, sculpture, Kente and kuba weavings, mud paintings and cloth.

MUSEUMS
CHARLES H. WRIGHT MUSEUM OF AFRICAN AMERICAN HISTORY
315 Warren, Detroit; (313) 494-5800
Tue-Sun 9:30am-5pm. Admission: $3 adults, $2 children 12 and under. Museum documents the history, life and culture of African Americans and serves as a resource center for enhancing knowledge and understanding about African Americans. Educational programming for all ages includes families, teachers and artisans with exhibition-related lecture series, guided tours, school and senior outreach programs, after-school programs, weekend workshops and a theatrical arts program. Well-stocked

museum shop. Call for calendar of events and classes. *(See Museum Tour.)*

CHILDREN'S MUSEUM
67 E. Kirby, Detroit; (313) 494-1210
Mon-Fri 1-4pm, Sat 9am-4pm. Cultural exhibits often include African heritage. Special activities on Saturdays and vacation days. Many programs for school field trips. Teachers and students may borrow museum resources, including photos.

DETROIT HISTORICAL MUSEUM
5401 Woodward, Detroit ; (313) 833-1805
Wed-Fri 9:30am-5pm, Sat-Sun 10am-5pm. The permanent "Doorway to Freedom" exhibit celebrates Detroit's important role in the Underground Railroad. Educational activities include interactive workshops. The Museum Shop includes African American paper dolls, books, figurines and "*Pathways to Michigan,*" a black heritage pamphlet. Annual Black Historic Sites Tour and African American Family Day in February.

DETROIT INSTITUTE OF ARTS
5200 Woodward, Detroit; (313) 833-7900
Wed-Fri 11am-4pm, Sat-Sun 11am-5pm. Celebrated collections of African American works are among the DIA's treasures. Self-guided and group tours. Special programs in February when traditional African American dishes are on the Kresge Court café menu.

GRAYSTONE INTERNATIONAL JAZZ MUSEUM AND HALL OF FAME
Book Bldg., Ste. 201
1249 Washington Blvd.
Detroit; (313) 963-3813
Tues-Fri 11am-4:30pm; open to groups on weekends. Displays feature international jazz stars of all races and many artifacts donated by them. A 20-minute video traces Detroit's jazz history.

HENRY FORD MUSEUM & GREENFIELD VILLAGE
20900 Oakwood Blvd., Dearborn
(313) 271-1620
Daily 9 am-5pm. From April to December, the village's Hermitage Slave Houses take you back more than 100 years, and the Mattox House to the 1930s.

JOE LOUIS MEMORIAL VIDEO ROOM
Cobo Center, Downtown Detroit
(313) 222-0594

By appointment only. Rare photos and equipment used by the world heavyweight champion. Groups may arrange to see a half-hour Emmy-Award-winning video on Louis' career or a one-hour documentary.

JOHN FREEMAN WALLS HISTORIC SITE/ UNDERGROUND RAILROAD MUSEUM
Maidstone Twp., Ontario
(519) 258-6253 or 971-7790
Canadian endpoint of the Underground Railroad (about half hour from Windsor) has log cabin where escaping slaves found freedom.

MOTOWN HISTORICAL MUSEUM
2648 W. Grand Blvd., Detroit
(313) 875-2264
Tue-Sat 10am-5pm, Sun-Mon noon-5pm. Two side-by-side houses and a tiny garage are restored to the way they looked in the '60s when they were home to Berry Gordy's family, Motown Records headquarters and the legendary Studio A. Cassettes, CDs, shirts, bags, books and educational packages available at the Shop Around gift shop.

TUSKEGEE AIRMEN NATIONAL MUSEUM
Historic Fort Wayne
6325 W. Jefferson, Detroit;
(313) 843-8849
Daily 10am-3pm April-Oct; by reservation only Nov-March. The exhibit traces the challenges and triumphs of the military's first African American pilots. Their success helped pave the way for integration of the U.S. Air Force. Photos of overseas missions, scale models of aircraft, authentic equipment and uniforms. Alumni include former Detroit Mayor Coleman A. Young. Group tours led by an airman may be arranged with Richard Jennings at (313) 345-6122 or Wardell Polk at (313) 834-2043.

VISUAL ARTS

ART CHEES DOLLS INC.
(248) 569-7139
African tribal and African American personality dolls, each hand-crafted and researched for authentic attire and physical traits. Presentations on the dolls' history and activities for participants.

BROOM DESIGNS INC.
(313) 863-6158
Mon-Fri 9am-5pm. Founded in 1970, this was the first mass-production card company to feature a black image. Now the family-run business ships its full line of African American greeting cards nationwide. Local sellers include Farmer Jack supermarkets. Wholesale quantities for fund-raising are available to groups.

CLARISSA'S FINE ARTS CREATIONS
(313) 341-7762
Detroit artist Clarissa Johnson's paintings re-create touching scenes of African American life, reproduced in her own line of greeting cards, carried at select shops and galleries.

KRI-ANGELS
(248) 355-3746
Afrocentric angels, six to 32 inches tall, individually handcrafted of raffia and abaca.

BROWN SUGAR AND SPICE
(734) 729-0501
Mon-Thu 9am-5pm. Book displays, T-shirts and other items to give children positive images of black people and cultures. Multicultural children's programs for elementary schools and libraries; workshops available to educators; multicultural books for children and adults specializing in African American, Caribbean and African literature (catalog available).

MY SISTERS & I (AND OUR FRIENDS)
(313) 864-0366
Valerie Miller's line of humorous African American greeting cards.

TOUCH OF COLOR DOLL & ART SHOW
Mt. Morris (near Flint)
(810) 789-2727
Annually in early Nov. Showcases dolls, African American designed jewelry, pottery clothing.

THEATER

BLACK THEATRE PROGRAM
Wayne State University
Studio Theatre
4743 Cass Ave. at Hancock, Detroit
(313) 577-7960 or 577-3010
Performances take place in an intimate 112-seat theatre on the lower level of the Hilberry Theater. One performance a year at the Bonstelle Theatre (3424 Woodward, south of Mack). The Black Theatre touring company performs throughout southeastern Michigan.

THE BILLIARD GALLERY COMPANY
47 E. Adams, Detroit
(313) 963-7665
Sat-Mon in February: The Oscar Micheaux Cinema presents films from the African diaspora during Black History Month.

DETROIT CULTURAL RENAISSANCE ANNUAL SUMMER CAMP
(313) 538-3306
Tillis Butler directs four-week program for minority students, from elementary through high school, at various locations in Detroit. Performance tour showcases the music theory, dance and vocal skills that participants have learned.

HARMONIE PARK PLAYHOUSE
230 E. Grand River, Detroit
(313) 965-2480
Resident African American professional theater company.

PLOWSHARES THEATRE COMPANY
2870 E. Grand Blvd, Detroit
(313) 872-0279
Call for schedules and locations. Gary Anderson directs the company's fall-through-spring drama series. The annual "New Voices" summer festival debuts works by African American playwrights. Many of the company's productions are staged at the Paul Robeson Theatre in Detroit's Northwest Activities Center, 18100 Meyers Rd.

ENTERTAINMENT

BEA'S COMEDY KITCHEN
541 E. Larned, Detroit: (313) 961-2581
Entertainment and dinners nightly.

MUSIC MENU
511 Monroe, Detroit; (313) 964-6368
Sat-Sun nights. Live music from Latin Jazz to Acid Soul.

DETROIT WEST CLUB
14400 Wyoming, Detroit; (313) 834-3233
(at Lyndon)
Dance club with DJ.

THE LIMITED
15535 W. Eight Mile, Detroit
(313) 341-8000
Caters to the "over 30" crowd with live music on weekends.

CULTURAL ARTS

AFRICAN AMERICAN ARTS AND CULTURAL SOCIETY
(313) 861-2700
The performing group presents mostly dance and theater productions.

ART SPECTRUM; (313) 869-9385
By appointment only. With a focus on music and dance, the organization promotes the preservation of classic African American dance forms, such as the cakewalk.

CREATIVE ARTS CENTER
47 Williams, Pontiac; (248) 333-7849
Performing and visual arts workshops and classes for all ages.

DETROIT ASSOCIATION OF BLACK STORYTELLERS
(313) 883-7413 or (313) 345-6625
The multicultural group promotes and perpetuates the ancient art of storytelling using the knowledge and wisdom of African folklore, ancestral stories and the African American experience.

INSTITUTE OF AMERICAN BLACK ARTISTS
2641 W. Grand Blvd, Detroit; (313) 872-0332
Mon-Sun 10am-6pm. Performances, workshops and classes for all ages in all the arts.

ARTS LEAGUE OF MICHIGAN
(313) 964-1670
Presents emerging and renowned artists in a variety of venues to diverse audiences. Promotes arts organizations and individual artists and strengthens their ties to the community. Publishes a directory of metro-area minority artists.

UJAMAA ASSOCIATES
13336 Wade St., Detroit; (313) 526-8284
Helps organizations plan and conduct "edu-cultural" programs for children and adults that feature cultural arts, crafts and games.

CLASSES AND WORKSHOPS

ART

KINDRED SOULS ART INCUBATOR
(313) 868-2914
Women of Color Fine Arts Collective plans to resume workshops with visiting artists and fine-arts and crafts classes for youth and adults when facility becomes available.

NATIONAL CONFERENCE OF ARTISTS–MICHIGAN GALLERY
216 Fisher Bldg., Detroit
(313) 875-0923
Mon-Fri 11am-5pm, Sat 11am-4pm. Seminars, workshops and revolving exhibits educate participants about art from the African diaspora.

NILE GALLERY
3475 Robina, Berkley; (248) 548-8881
Tue-Sat 10am-6pm. Regular classes in bead-making, fiber arts and more.

THE LAURA SHELBY GROUP INC.
P.O. Box 32757
Detroit, MI 48232-0757
1-800-58FIBER
Co-founders J. Alicia Elster and Norma Fuqua present a fiber arts conference called "Affirmation." Lectures, workshops and vendor exhibits feature fiber artists from around the world. Crafts include African American folk art quilting, doll-making, embroidery, beading, basketry, weaving and fabric dyeing.

DANCE

ARTISTRY IN MOTION
24500 Southfield Rd., Southfield
(at 10 Mile)
(248) 557-9320
Ballet, jazz and tap. Call for class information.

THE ART OF MOTION DANCE THEATRE
111 E. Kirby, Detroit; (313) 834-9501
Founder/Director Karen Prall offers classes at the International Institute.

BLACK FOLKS ART INC.
(313) 865-4546
Dancer Sophia Tekani leads dance and percussion classes and presents demonstrations.

CENTER FOR CREATIVE STUDIES
Institute of Music and Dance
200 E. Kirby, Detroit; (313) 872-3118

In addition to classes in ballet, modern, tap, jazz and world traditional dance, offers African workshop in dance and drumming rhythms.

DANCE THEATRE OF HARLEM RESIDENCY PROGRAM
Music Hall for the Performing Arts
350 Madison, Detroit; (313) 963-7622
Month-long program changes from year to year. Call for details.

DETROIT-WINDSOR DANCE ACADEMY
1529 Broadway, Detroit; (313) 963-0050
Classes for kids include modern, ballet, tap, ethnic and spiritual "Praise" dance at local churches. Adult classes include beginning and intermediate modern and tap. Artistic director Debra White-Hunt teaches advanced and professional company classes.

DETROIT DANCE CENTER, INC.
820 W. Baltimore, Ste. 210; Detroit
(313) 87DANCE
Artistic Director Carole Morisseau leads a school for children and adults on beginner through advanced levels "where the focus is on versatility" through study of ballet, modern, African, jazz and tap dance.

DETROIT RECREATION DEPARTMENT
Adams-Butzel Recreation Center
10500 Lyndon, Detroit; (313) 935-3119
Youth dance programs. Adult and youth African dance programs.

PEMAJJU SCHOOL OF DANCE AND RELATED ARTS
2751 E. Jefferson, Ste. 450; Detroit
(313) 396-5666
Penny Godboldo directs a program for children and adults in an array of classes, including classical ballet and authentic New York jazz. Her modern dance program is endorsed by legendary black dance pioneer Katherine Dunham. The affiliated professional Writhm Dance Company and Children's Workshop Company of Detroit present recitals and lecture demonstrations for schools.

MUSIC
BLUES FOR SCHOOLS
(313) 838-0507
Music educator Robert Jones, of radio station WDET 101.9 FM, presents to assemblies and conducts classroom workshops tailored to elementary through high school students.

PEOPLE'S CREATIVE ENSEMBLE
11000 W. McNichols, Ste. B-1, Detroit
(313) 862-2900
Offers year-round drama, vocal and choreography programs, including a six-week summer enrichment workshop, for youths, ages 7 - 19. Director and musician Ron Jackson also presents motivational and self-esteem concerts as well as lectures and demonstrations in schools on topics including the history of jazz, music styles, mechanics and instrument families.

REBIRTH INC.
81 Chandler, Detroit; (313) 875-0289
E-mail: wenhajazz@aol.com
Jazz Master Wendell Harrison and other knowledgeable musicians conduct workshops tailored to students' ages, interests and instruments. Educational programs include "Discovering Jazz," "From Be Bop to Hip Hop," "Jazz Improvisation" and "Afro Cuban and American Jazz Music."

NATIONAL TAP DANCE DAY

Tap dancing is considered an indigenous American dance form. Its roots are traced to a combination of rhythmic African improvisations and spirited Irish and English jigs and clog dances. In the 1930s, innovative performer Bill "Bojangles" Robinson earned the title "King of Tapology" and helped create a nationwide tap dance craze. **National Tap Dance Day** in May is sponsored locally by the Center for Creative Studies Institute for Music and Dance. Call (313) 872-3118.

STRAIGHT AHEAD; (313) 868-6007
The all-female jazz ensemble presents concerts in schools as part of the Omni Arts in Education program. Bassist Marion Hayden, drummer Gayelynn McKinney, pianist Eileen Orr and saxophonist Sabrina LaMarr are all accomplished musicians.

JAZZ WITH TEDDY HARRIS
(313) 883-7920
Jazz master Teddy Harris teaches jazz on keyboards and woodwind instruments in his home and as an artist-in-residence at Highland Park High School.

THE STORYTELLERS; (313) 884-2780
Program Director Robert Allison arranges highly musical lecture-demonstrations of African American, Caribbean, Indian, Brazilian and Native American folklore.

MISCELLANEOUS
WAYNE COUNTY
COMMUNITY COLLEGE
Campuses in Detroit and Taylor
(313) 496-2777
Fall, winter and summer semesters. The Community Education Department's hair-braiding class covers cornrows, zillions and the Goddess style. An Afrocentric "box hat" is among the designs taught in hat making.

WELLNESS
Healing Support Network Inc.
(313) 837-2414
Holistic Wellness Counselor Thelma Raziya Curtis offers a six-week series of group or individual classes on healthy cooking at east- and west-side locations (see "African American Cooking"). Menus include vegetarian, soul and holiday menus. A quick-start, two-hour food preparation class ending with a party for friends can be hosted at the student's home. Children's classes and other workshops also offered.

CULTURAL ORGANIZATIONS

BROADSIDE PRESS
1301 W. Lafayette, #102
Detroit
(313) 963-8526
One of the oldest black-owned book publishing companies in America was founded in 1965 by librarian Dudley Randall. He later was named Detroit's poet laureate for his outstanding contributions to literature. The organization has published more than 200 poets, including Gwendolyn Brooks and Nikki Giovanni. On the third Sunday of every month, the organization hosts a 2pm workshop for poets, followed by readings at 3pm. During summers, Broadside and the Detroit Public Library co-sponsor a "Poet in Residence" series for adults and children at city and suburban locations.

DETROIT BLACK WRITERS GUILD
5601 W. Warren, Detroit
(313) 897-2551
Founded by Peggy A. Moore, the guild offers youth classes, workshops and a contest for amateur writers.

INTERNATIONAL AFRICAN CULTURAL ARTS EXCHANGE CENTER INC.
Director Ali Abdullah seeks to enrich public understanding of African life, its arts and culture through his performing workshop of dancers, musicians and singers. He teaches dance at the Adams-Butzel (313-935-3119) and Joseph Walker Williams (313-224-6582) Recreation Centers and at Wayne County Community College (313-496-2777).

THE SOCIETIE
OF CULTURALLY CONCERNED
(313) 864-2337
Annually sponsors a series of events, including the Detroit Jazz Heritage Reunion (formerly known as the Bluebird Reunion).

FRED HART WILLIAMS GENEALOGICAL SOCIETY
Detroit Public Library
5201 Woodward, Detroit
(313) 833-1000
Burton Historical Collection contains African American genealogical records.

YOUR HERITAGE HOUSE
110 E. Ferry, Detroit
(313) 871-1667
Mon-Fri 11am-5pm, Sat-Sun by appointment. The stately Victorian mansion is a museum and fine arts center for children. Special activities and rotating exhibits are scheduled year-round.

PERFORMING ARTISTS

"It has been said that Detroit boasts more musicians per capita than any other city its size," writes music researcher and pianist Arthur R. La Brew in *Vignettes of Black Musicians in Detroit and Its Surrounding Area: 1900-1988.* "Not only are they talented in one phase of music but easily borrow from other phases to round out their musicality."

People of African descent have created much of America's music. The following pages briefly define major African American styles.
(See also "Africa," "Caribbean" and "Creole and Cajun.")

To explore these styles in depth, visit the **E. Azalia Hackley Memorial Collection** at the main branch of the Detroit Public Library. Call the curator to access the research collection of more than 250,000 items related to African American performing artists, including rare books, manuscripts, news articles, programs and playbills, and recordings.

The site was established in 1943 by the Detroit chapter of the National Association of Negro Musicians, and the library was named in honor of Emma Azalia Smith Hackley (1867-1922), an excellent classical musician who raised public appreciation for black music. She toured the world to study, perform and inspire black students, promoted black folk festivals and raised money for music scholarships. Hackley also was Detroit's second black public schoolteacher. The site's original mission was to collect documents about Detroit musicians, but it later was expanded to include all black performing artists.

The Detroit Public Library is at 5201 Woodward Ave., Detroit; call (313) 833-1460. Open Tue, Thu-Sat 9:30 a.m.-5:30 p.m.; Wed 1-9 p.m.

RADIO HITS

When it went on the air November 7, 1956, WCHB AM 1200 in Detroit was the nation's third black-owned radio station. The call letters are the initials of the station's founders, Hamtramck dentists Wendell Cox and Haley Bell, who were the first minorities to build a station from the ground up. WCHB started with a daytime-only license. Four years later, the founders built a sister FM station, mainly to keep the company on the air after sundown. The FM station originally was called WCHD, then for years was WJZZ, a jazz broadcast pioneer. In September 1996 the station's format changed to urban contemporary, and it became WCHB 105.9 FM. Today, the WCHB stations, WGPR 107.5 FM and WQBH AM 1400, are still owned by African Americans.

BLUES

BLUES lyrics are sometimes joyful, but usually they tell a story of heartbreak, poverty or racism. The music is intense, though structurally simple in its classic form. Rooted in American slave songs, blues was widespread in the South by the late 19th century. Traditional **country blues** singers accompany themselves on acoustic guitar or harmonica. The musical style was popularized by the 1912 publication *Memphis Blues* by W.C. Handy (1873-1958), dubbed the "Father of Blues."

Soon after, **city blues** evolved. **Bessie Smith** (1894-1937) and others typically sang with a jazz band or piano. Solo piano players created **boogie-woogie**—a style with heavy, repetitive bass notes. In Detroit, that style was mastered by **Frank "Sugar Chile" Robinson,** a child prodigy in the early '50s who reportedly earned thousands of dollars a week at the height of his career.

Though it overlapped with jazz, at times almost indistinguishably, blues also developed independently. In the '40s, an **urban blues** style emerged as singers performed with big bands or ensembles of electric guitar or organ, acoustic string bass, drums and saxophones. They included **Alberta Adams,** affectionately known as "Detroit's Queen of the Blues" through the '60s.

After 1950, improved electric guitars and louder, electric basses backed up **B.B. King, Ray Charles** and others. Record companies coined the term *Rhythm and Blues* (R&B) and later, *soul,* for both blues and non-blues styles. Detroit guitarist **John Lee Hooker** is nationally known for his classic style. Blues artists sharing the spotlight include the Delta-sounding **Butler Twins,** the R&B-influenced **Chisel Brothers** and funk-infused **Mudpuppy.**

The following listing of festivals and clubs only begins to scratch the surface of Detroit's Blues scene. More extensive listings and performance updates can be found on the Blues radio programs, the daily newspapers and the Metro Times. *Also check out:*

DETROIT BLUES SOCIETY HOTLINE
(248) 262-6890
Weekly events and performances, calendar and updates.

DETROT BLUES MAGAZINE
(313) 872-BLUES
Bi-Monthly. Call for subscription info.

BLUES FACTORY RECORDS
2911 Elmhurst , Royal Oak; (248) 280-0363

Develops, promotes and records local Blues talent. Call for catalog and artists' info.

DEARBORN MUSIC
2000 Michigan, Dearborn; (313) 561-1000
and
42679 Ford Rd., Canton; (734) 981-7530
Huge selection of Blues and Jazz recordings, local artists on consignment..

OFF THE RECORD
405 S. Washington, Royal Oak
398-4436
Mon-Thu 10am-9pm, Fri-Sat 10am-10pm, Sun 11am-6pm. Area's largest selection of Blues music, magazines and books. Live music every Friday at 7pm.

BLUES FESTIVALS

WINTER
DEEP FREEZE BLUES FESTIVAL
Magic Bag
229218 Woodward, Ferndale
(248) 544-3030
Annually the first weekend in Jan. Warm up with the music of local and national acts.

BLUES IN MONROE
River Raisin Centre for the Arts
114 S. Monroe St., Monroe
1-800-462-2050
Two days in mid-Feb.

JUNE
FROG ISLAND MUSIC FESTIVAL
Depot Town, Ypsilanti; (734) 487-2229
Fri-Sat in mid-June. Features some of the most respected names in blues at site along Huron River.

AUGUST
TAYLOR BLUES FESTIVAL
Heritage Park, Taylor
(on Pardee Rd. between Goddard and Northline)
(313) 278-5340
Mid-Aug weekend. Local and national artists showcase various styles of blues.

DOG DAYS OF SUMMER BLUES FESTIVAL
Magic Bag
22920 Woodward, Ferndale
(248) 544-3030
Annually in Aug. Formerly the Detroit Blues Festival, local artists and national headliners entertain for two days.

SEPTEMBER
ANN ARBOR BLUES & JAZZ FESTIVAL
(734) 747-9955
Weekend after Labor Day. Dance-till-you-drop musical celebration, featuring the top national artists in blues, jazz, roots, gospel and soul. Held at Gallup Park, Michigan Theater and The Bird of Paradise.

BLUES CLUBS

ATTIC BAR
11667 Joseph Campau, Hamtramck
(313) 365-4194
Sun-Sat 4pm-2am. Known as the "Detroit Delta," local blues artists perform daily in a friendly atmosphere.

BEALE ST. BLUES
8 N. Saginaw, Pontiac; (248) 334-7900
Fri-Sat nights. Blues, barbeque, ribs with a Memphis flavor.

FIFTH AVENUE
215 W. Fifth Ave., Royal Oak
(248) 542-9922
Sun-Sat nights. Local and national Blues performers nightly. Voted "Best in Detroit" by *Metro Times.*

LOWERTOWN GRILL
195 W. Liberty, Plymouth
(734) 451-1213
10pm-1am Fri-Sat. Big name live blues.

SOUP KITCHEN
1585 Franklin, Detroit; (313) 259-1374
Tue-Thu, Sun 11am-11pm, Fri -Sat 11am-2am,. Rivertown restaurant and night spot has entertainment in Blues Room weekends starting at 9 pm and other times.

BLUES RADIO

WEMU 89.1 FM
(734) 487-2229
"Jazz, news and blues" station on Eastern Michigan University's campus in Ypsilanti dedicates about 20 percent of its airtime to blues, the most in metropolitan Detroit. Heaviest blues programming is on Sunday: "Big City Blues Cruise," 3-6pm. "The Bone Conduction Music Show," 7-11pm. "Blues on the Mellow Side," 11pm-2am.

WCSX 94.7 FM
(248) 398-7600
"Motor City Blues Project" with Mark Pasman, Sun 8-10pm.

WDET 101.9 FM
(313) 577-4146
"Blues and Music After Hours," with Tim Pulice, Sat-Sun 2am-7am.
"Blues From the Lowlands," with Robert Jones, Sat 10am-noon.
"The Gene Elzy Program," Sat 7-10pm, features "the jazzy side of blues and the blues-y side of jazz."

WQBH AM 1400
(313) 965-4500
"Blues With a Feeling," hosted by Raymone Henderson, Mon-Fri 4-9pm.

GOSPEL

GOSPEL music grew out of a creative mix of white and black hymns, the moans and wails of the blues, and the percussive, dynamic sounds of the turn-of-the-century black "folk church"—mainly Pentecostal, Holiness and Baptist. The diverse styles were merged first by **Thomas A. Dorsey** (1899-1993), a Baptist preacher's son and a jazz and blues pianist/composer. He organized the world's first gospel choir in 1931. More than 500 titles are attributed to him, including **"Precious Lord, Take My Hand"** (1932), which universally is embraced as one of gospel's greatest songs.

Gospel lyrics emotionally tell of a singer's relationship with God. Often, gospel is performed without instrumental accompaniment, but most soloists, groups and choirs choose to be accompanied by a range of instruments, which may include acoustic or electronic piano, organ, drums, tambourines, hand clapping and even strings and brass, depending on whether the style is traditional, contemporary or urban contemporary.

Detroit's place as a center of gospel music is due, in part, to Dorsey's visits here to organize choirs, teach music and create interest in the new form of sacred music. Also, residents warmly received Golden Age (1945-1960) gospel stars such as **Mahalia Jackson** (1912-1972) and the **Clara Ward Singers**. Another factor was the national prominence of Detroit ministers who favored gospel. They included the **Rev. C.L. Franklin** (1915-1984), father of "Queen of Soul" **Aretha Franklin,** and a singer and recording artist in his own right.

Numerous major gospel artists and musicians have come from Detroit. Many of them are part of the Church of God in Christ, the most influential denomination in gospel during the past 40 years. They include **Mattie Moss Clark** (1925-1994), a music department president at the church, who created youth choirs across the country and recorded hundreds of titles on more than 30 albums. She molded a new generation of artists, including her five highly acclaimed daughters, **The Clark Sisters.**

Aretha Franklin returned to her gospel roots to record "**Amazing Grace,**" widely considered her crowning achievement, in Detroit. One of her musical mentors was the **Rev. James Cleveland** (1931-1991), revered as the "King of Gospel." He selected Detroit as the 1967 birthplace of the **Gospel Music Workshop of America Inc.**, now gospel's largest convention. Other influential Detroit gospel artists include the Grammy Award-winning **Winans Family**, minister **Thomas Whitfield** (1954-1992), **Vanessa Bell Armstrong** and **Commissioned.**

GOSPEL RADIO

Among Detroit's earliest broadcasts to feature gospel and jubilee quartets was "Ship of Joy." It debuted in the '30s on WMBC AM, a forerunner of WJLB FM 98, with the Rev. James Murray as host. When he left the program in 1943, sponsors Paul and Joseph Deutch took over and renamed it "Paul's Ship of Joy." For the next 50 years, the Jewish pharmacists featured hundreds of live and recorded performances of gospel musicians. Today, gospel music lovers can dial in a variety of stations. Martha Jean "The Queen" Steinberg, a celebrity in the Black Radio Hall of Fame, broadcasts "Inspiration Time" weekdays 11am-2pm on **WQBH AM 1400.** **WMUZ FM 103** offers "The Gospel Connection with Darryl Ford" weeknights. Numerous programs are on **WMKM 1440 AM,** a 24-hour gospel outlet. "Strong Inspirations with Deborah Smith Pollard" airs Sunday mornings on **WJLB FM 98.**

GOSPEL FESTIVALS

GOSPEL FESTIVAL
Maidstone, Ontario
(519) 258-6253 or (519) 971-7790
First Sat in Aug from about noon-6pm.
Festival at John Freeman Walls Historic Site and Underground Railroad Museum features Canadian and American gospel artists.

THE FARMER JACK PRAISEFEST FEATURING THE MCDONALD'S GOSPELFEST
Hart Plaza, Detroit
(734) 459-6969
Typically in June. Free family event showcases traditional to contemporary gospel music.

GOSPEL RESOURCES

COACHMAN'S RECORDS
6340 Charlevoix, Detroit
(at Mt. Elliott)
(313) 571-2222
Mon-Thu 11am-6pm, Fri-Sat 11am-7:30pm. New gospel and blues releases, plus oldies are sold by Famous Coachman, a Detroit radio personality for decades.

GOD'S WORLD
13533 W. Seven Mile, Detroit
(at Schaefer)
(313) 862-8220
Mon-Sat 10am-7pm, Sun 1-5pm. Offers one of the country's largest selection of gospel CDs, tapes and videos. Every year or two, owner Larry Robinson presents "Be Ye Exalted," one of the region's major concerts of top national and local contemporary gospel artists.

● *Also see page 66, Louie's on Woodward Gospel brunch.*

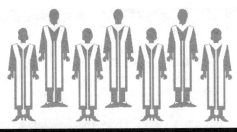

SPIRITUALS

Detroiter Khadejah Shelby traces the history of Spirituals in liner notes for "Hush! Somebody's Calling My Name," a compact disk of 18 spirituals recorded in 1994 by Detroit's Brazeal Dennard Chorale:

"Spirituals evolved from the anguished cries of slaves as they suffered the trials and tribulations of slavery. Eventually, those utterances evolved into elongated sounds which became melodies, thus making slaves the first African-American composers.

"Although spirituals were primarily expressions of religious beliefs, they also filled psychological and political needs. They were used to express a variety of emotions—grief and sorrow, hope for a better life, the yearning to be free—and as a communication tool, especially for escapes. Music was one of the few resources available to the slaves and they took full advantage of the owners' paternalistic notion that their slaves were singing because they were happy.

"Through the years, the unaccompanied choral music with its heavy African influences has had an enormous impact around the world. Once regarded as simple folksongs, spirituals are performed regularly by many of the world's major choral organizations and they also provide thematic material for major oratories and symphonies.

"The spiritual continues to be involved in the political arena. A great deal of the success of Dr. Martin Luther King, Jr.'s non-violent protest was due to the singing of spirituals at protest meetings, voter registration drives and on picket lines. 'We Shall Overcome,' hallmark of the Civil Rights movement, is now the anthem of protest all over the world."

● Though the Brazeal Dennard Chorale performs a variety of music, every one of its recitals includes spirituals. In a commitment to preserving the art form, spirituals are always half of the Chorale's annual Holiday Concert, presented the first Sunday in December at Detroit's Orchestra Hall. *See "Classical Performances" listing.*

JAZZ has been called the only true American art form. The primarily improvised music is rooted in the mingled musical traditions of American blacks. These include West African music, black folk music and later popular music forms influenced by black music or produced by black composers.

Jazz has branched out into so many styles that scholars have not agreed upon one definition. It encompasses a wide array of styles, including ragtime, swing, be-bop, modern, post-bop, progressive and acid. Most jazz is based on the principle that an infinite number of melodies can fit the chord progressions of any song. Performers improvise within the conventions of their chosen style. Written scores, if used at all, are merely guides.

Arts Midwest bestows the prestigious Jazz Master title on only three Midwest musicians a year in its nine-state region. Six Detroiters have earned that award for exceptional musical contributions for 25 years or more: Marcus Belgrave, Roy Brooks, Teddy Harris, Wendell Harrison, Harold McKinney and Donald Walden.

● GRAYSTONE INTERNATIONAL JAZZ MUSEUM AND HALL OF FAME
Book Bldg., Ste. 201
1249 Washington Blvd., Detroit
(313) 963-3813
Mon-Fri 11am-4:30pm; open to groups on weekends. Displays feature international jazz stars of all races and many artifacts donated by them. A 20-minute video traces Detroit's jazz history. The world's only privately owned jazz museum was founded by retired Detroit bus driver James Jenkins. The museum opened in 1974 soon after the death of Edward Kennedy "Duke" Ellington—widely considered the country's greatest all-around musician—and was founded in honor of him and other jazz greats. Ellington wrote nearly 2,000 pieces, ranging from short instrumental works to motion-picture scores.

Other nationally known Detroit jazz artists include Betty Carter, noted for her extraordinary vocal technique. Dorothy Ashby won the Downbeat Magazine Award in 1962 as the "first jazz harpist worthy of the judges' vote." Musicians gaining attention include the groundbreaking female jazz group, Straight Ahead. Pianist James Tatum pioneered the performance of jazz in a religious context with his composition "Contemporary Jazz Mass." Its 1975 premiere at St. Cecilia Church in Detroit was the first time in the United States that a jazz mass was celebrated by Catholic priests.

JAZZ FESTIVALS

FROG ISLAND MUSIC FESTIVAL
Depot Town, Ypsilanti
(734) 487-2229
Fri-Sat in mid-June. The best in local and national jazz is presented in an airy tent on the banks of the Huron River.

BLUE MONDAYS
Hart Plaza Pyramid Theatre, Detroit
(313) 963-3813
Mon 6:30-8:30pm, late June-early Aug. Artists include international and local jazz stars. The series is produced by the Graystone International Jazz Museum in memory of the Graystone Ballroom, one of the Midwest's most fabulous venues. In the days of segregation, blacks were admitted only on Monday nights.

MICHIGAN JAZZ FESTIVAL
Botsford Inn
2800 Grand River, Farmington
(248) 474-4800
Held on a Sunday in July. Features 30 bands.

JAZZ IN THE STREETS
Detroit Historical Museum
5401 Woodward , Detroit; (313) 833-9721
Certain Thursday evenings through June.
Local stars perform for the after-work crowd
in the museum's "Streets of Old Detroit" on
lower level.

JAZZ ON THE BEACH
Belle Isle Beach and Band Shell
(313) 267-7115 or 267-7116
Weekends, late June to Labor Day.

JAZZ & ALTERNATIVE MUSIC
Harmonie Park, Detroit; (313) 877-8077
Mid-summer Wed, 6:30-8pm. Concerts fea-
ture local artists, hosted by the Detroit
Recreation Department.

MONTREUX DETROIT JAZZ FESTIVAL
Hart Plaza, Detroit; (313) 963-7622
Labor Day weekend. North America's largest
free jazz event includes local and international stars, top Michigan student bands, kids'
shows, clinics and jam sessions. Detroit public radio station WDET 101.9 FM usually
broadcasts the festival live.

ANN ARBOR BLUES & JAZZ FESTIVAL
(734) 747-9955
Weekend after Labor Day. Summer's final
funky musical celebration features jazz at the
Bird of Paradise.

DUKE ELLINGTON SACRED
MUSIC CONCERT
St. Paul Episcopal Church
1249 Woodward Ave., Detroit
(313) 963-3813
Annually in Nov. Musical genius Edward
Kennedy "Duke" Ellington wrote three spectacular religious works, designed to fill cav-
ernous cathedrals.

JAZZ CLUBS

Listed here are a few of the majors.
For more on such clubs, check out Detroit
Jazz Monthly magazine, which covers metro
Detroit's thriving jazz scene, including an up-
to-date list of the artists appearing at dozens
of clubs and restaurants. For subscription
information, call (248) 524-2729.

JAZZ NIGHT TOURS
1-800-521-0711
Kirby Tours offers a package, featuring one or
two clubs.

BAKER'S KEYBOARD LOUNGE
20510 Livernois, Detroit; (313) 345-6300
Mon-Sat 11am-2am, Sun 2pm-2am.
R&B, blues, jazz and popular music.

BERT'S MARKET PLACE
2727 Russell, Detroit; (313) 567-2030
Mon-Thu 11am-midnight, Fri-Sat 11am-4am.

BERT'S JAZZ ON THE RIVER
Muse Road, Belle Isle, Detroit
(313) 823-8000
Open seasonally and for special events.
When closed, call its sister location, **Bert's**
Market Place, (313) 567-2030.

BIRD OF PARADISE
207 S. Ashley, Ann Arbor
(734) 930-1723
Daily 7pm-2am. Bassist Ron Brooks owns
metro Detroit's only club to offer jazz seven
nights a week.

BOMAC'S LOUNGE
281 Gratiot Ave., Detroit; (313) 961-5152
Mon, Thu-Sat noon-2am. Sun 8pm-midnight.
Jazz rules five nights a week, plus a Jazz
Jam every Thursday.

FLOOD'S BAR & GRILL
731 St. Antoine, Detroit; (313) 963-1090
Mon 4pm-midnight, Tue-Fri 3pm-2am, Sat-
Sun 7pm-2am. Downtown club features live
jazz and R&B; light meals.

JAZZ RADIO

The widest variety of jazz is on metro
Detroit's public radio stations.

WDET 101.9 FM Detroit
Airs jazz programs daily from 7-10pm. "The
Ed Love Program" Mon-Fri; "The Tim Pulice
Program" Sat; Kim Herron's "Destination Out"
Sun evening.

WEMU 89.1 FM Ypsilanti
Airs avant-garde, be-bop, swing, big band,
'50s and '60s styles seven days a week.

WUOM 91.7 FM Ann Arbor
Plays jazz Saturday nights.

WVMV 98.7 FM Detroit
Syndicated commercial station plays nonstop
"smooth jazz."

CBC 89.9 FM Windsor
Devotes nearly every hour to jazz Sunday-
Thursday nights.

Black symphonic music is classified in two categories. There are traditional European pieces by black composers, such as pioneer **Chevalier de Saint-Georges** (1739-1799). The second category, black-stream music, is influenced by the composer's ethnic background. An example is contemporary composer Anthony Davis' integration of jazz, popular and classical idioms in *Notes From the Underground.* The Harvard University professor's piece was recorded by the Detroit Symphony Orchestra for broadcast in 1997 as part of its national radio series.

Appreciation for classical pieces by African Americans continues to grow. One of the top-selling compact discs by the DSO is *Still, Symphony No. 1,* released in 1993. The CD's title piece by African American composer William Grant Still (1895-1978) is followed by a suite from *The River* by Duke Ellington.

Several African Americans have become part of the **Detroit Symphony Orchestra**. Among them, native Detroiter **Joseph Striplin,** who has been a DSO violinist since 1972.

A long list of professional musicians—including pop stars—started out in the **Detroit Community Symphony,** founded and conducted in the '60s by Anderson White while he was a Detroit Public Schools teacher. Another pioneering educator is noted voice instructor **Willis C. Patterson,** Ph.D., associate dean at the University of Michigan School of Music. Patterson, whose own voice has won numerous awards, was musical director and a performer for *Black American Artsongs,* a U-M recording.

Choral Works:

Deeply committed to the rediscovery and performance of significant choral works by African American composers, the **Brazeal Dennard Chorale** was founded by its namesake in 1972. Native Detroiter Dennard now teaches music at Wayne State University, following a career in the Detroit Public Schools and serving as president of numerous organizations, including the National Association of Negro Musicians. The Chorale and the DSO jointly perform works by African American composers in an annual concert, **Classical Roots.**

One of opera's current stars is tenor **George Shirley,** who grew up in Detroit and earned a music degree at Wayne State University. A few years after Shirley joined New York's celebrated **Metropolitan Opera** in 1961, the concert piece *Attitudes* was written for him by black composer Coleridge-Taylor Perkinson.

Handel's *Messiah* is perhaps the best-known oratorio, a form of classical music in which scriptural text is set to music. Its **"Hallelujah Chorus"** is traditionally performed in churches at Christmas or Easter. Some African American choirs present a jazzy arrangement of this piece by Quincy Jones.

CLASSICAL PERFORMANCES

BRAZEAL DENNARD CHORALE
(313) 331-0378
The Chorale performs works by African-American composers at many events throughout the year, including the Classical Roots concert with the Detroit Symphony Orchestra at Orchestra Hall in February.

JAMES TATUM FOUNDATION JAZZ/ CLASSICAL CONCERT
Detroit Symphony Orchestra Hall
(313) 255-9015

Annually in October. Classical works are performed by Michigan's child prodigies discovered by the James Tatum Foundation for the Arts Inc. The benefit concert also features professional jazz artists.

THE JAMES TOPP SINGERS
(313) 584-6468
Patriotic songs are performed by this men's choir that's been around for 20 years. The group travels the United States performing mostly classical and spiritual choral music and some pop.

HOLIDAYS & ANNUAL EVENTS

Detroit's African American community celebrates its heritage throughout the year, with a variety of annual events commemorating a number of special occasions, people and dates.
Below is just a sampling. For current information on these and other events, check with individual institutions listed in this chapter.

JANUARY 15
MARTIN LUTHER KING BIRTHDAY CELEBRATION
National holiday. A statewide listing of events is available at AAA Michigan branches. Call (313) 336-1500. Website: www.aaamich.com

FEBRUARY
AFRICAN AMERICAN HERITAGE MONTH
Detroit celebrates the traditional Black History Month with a wealth of activities at virtually every cultural institution.The Detroit Public Library publishes a free annual guide. Check local media for events.

CLASSICAL ROOTS
Orchestra Hall; (313) 331-0378
The Brazeal Dennard Chorale and the Detroit Symphony Orchestra perform classical works by African Americans.

MOTOWN HISTORICAL MUSEUM
ANNUAL GALA; (313) 875-2264
Tribute to Motown's legendary artists.

MARTIN LUTHER KING JR. (1929-1968), American clergyman and Nobel Prize winner, was one of the principal leaders of the American Civil Rights Movement and a prominent advocate of nonviolent protest.
King's challenges to segregation and racial discrimination in the 1950s and '60s helped convince many white Americans to support the cause of civil rights in the United States. In 1963, he led a massive demonstration down Woodward Avenue in Detroit when he premiered his "I Have a Dream" speech. After his assassination in 1968, King became a symbol of protest in the struggle for racial justice. On January 15, his birthday —a national holiday—is commemorated in various ways throughout metro Detroit.

MARCH
SALUTE TO DISTINGUISHED WARRIORS
(313) 832-4600
Each year, the Detroit Urban League honors several individuals who have made outstanding contributions to the cause of human and civil rights.

MOTOWN

MOTOWN RECORDS—one of the largest and most successful African American businesses in history—was founded in Detroit in 1959 by **Berry Gordy Jr.** The native Detroiter has had a storybook career—from professional boxer, autoworker, record-store owner, songwriter and producer to media mogul. The Motown team fused gospel and pop into a technologically innovative sound that had unprecedented appeal to black and white listeners.

The first million-seller, **"Shop Around"** (1961), was written by Detroiter **William "Smokey" Robinson** with fine-tuning by Gordy. It was the first of 20 years of hits for Smokey Robinson and the Miracles.

In addition to his business drive and musical skills, Gordy had a gift for spotting singers, many of whom were Detroiters, with superstar potential. They were propelled to stardom by Gordy and his talented team, including writer–producers **Brian** and **Eddie Holland** and **Lamont Dozier** plus **Nick Ashford** and **Valerie Simpson.** Outstanding studio musicians and elaborate costumes also were important, as was precise choreography by **Cholly Atkins,** artist development by **Maxine Powell,** Motown Review performances orchestrated by **Thomas "Dr. Beans" Bowles** and the administrative role of **Esther Gordy Edwards.**

By the end of 1967, Motown stars included **The Four Tops, Marvin Gaye and Tammi Terrell, The Isley Brothers, Gladys Knight and the Pips, Martha Reeves and the Vandellas, The Spinners, The Temptations, Junior Walker and the All Stars, Kim Weston** and child prodigy **"Little Stevie Wonder." The Supremes** (Florence Ballard, Diana Ross and Mary Wilson) recorded five straight number-one hits.

In 1971 Gordy moved Motown to Los Angeles, where the company's recording momentum slowed as it moved into areas such as movie making. But it still produced hits, including releases by Stevie Wonder, who was maturing into a musical genius. **The Jackson Five** had 13 consecutive top 20 singles during their 1969-1975 involvement with Motown.

In 1988 Gordy sold Motown Records to a consortium headed by MCA. A new superstar group emerged: **Boyz II Men.** In 1993 PolyGram Holdings purchased Motown Records from MCA for $325 million, according to *Business Week.* Motown's newest president, Andre Harrell, aims to rebuild the company as a multimedia entertainment empire, based in New York City.

Meanwhile, Motown "golden oldies" are still selling. They account for about 40 percent of the company's annual $100 million sales. Gordy and a number of the original Motown acts have been inducted into the Rock and Roll Hall of Fame in Cleveland.

● **MOTOWN HISTORICAL MUSEUM**
2648 W. Grand Blvd., Detroit
(313) 875-2264
Tue-Sat 10am-5pm, Sun-Mon noon-5pm. Two side-by-side houses and a tiny garage are restored to the way they looked in the '60s when they were home to Berry Gordy's family, Motown Records headquarters and the legendary Studio A. Cassettes, CDs, shirts, bags, books and educational packages available at the Shop Around gift shop.

SPRING
NAACP FREEDOM FUND DINNER
(313) 871-2087
Close to 10,000 people gather annually to make this event the largest fund-raising dinner in the world. Nationally renowned leaders are among the speakers.

BAL AFRICAIN
Detroit Institute of Arts
5200 Woodward, Detroit; (313) 833-0247
Black-tie gala; major fund-raiser for DIA's Friends of African & African American Art.

JULY
AFRO-AMERICAN MUSIC FESTIVAL
Hart Plaza, Detroit
(Woodward and Jefferson)
(313) 863-5554
Third weekend in July. Three days of continuous entertainment spanning traditional and contemporary African American music forms including jazz, blues, gospel and hip-hop. The Metropolitan Arts Complex Inc. sponsors the event, which features food and an array of Afrocentric items.

AUGUST
CELEBRATION OF EMANCIPATION
Greenfield Village
20900 Oakwood Blvd., Dearborn
(313) 271-1620
Early August weekend. Exhibits and reenactments featuring traditional music and storytelling depict struggles and triumphs.

AFRICAN WORLD FESTIVAL
Hart Plaza, Detroit
(Woodward and Jefferson)
(313) 833-9800
Mid-August weekend. Detroit's largest special event celebrates cultures of all people of African descent. Sponsored by the Museum of African American History, it includes children's activities, a film series, entertainment, food, artisans and vendors from around the world.

BUFFALO SOLDIERS ANNUAL PICNIC
(313) 537-7148
Third or fourth Sunday in August. Family outing hosted by local members of the Buffalo Soldiers; pony and hay rides, games and food during this fun outing for families. Call for park location.

OCTOBER
ANCESTOR'S NIGHT
Museum of African American History
(313) 833-9800
Tied to the African Yam Harvest Festivals, the observance commemorates the living, the deceased and those yet to be born. (Many community organizations recognize Ancestor's Night in lieu of Halloween.) Celebrated in the African tradition with costuming, storytelling, dancing, feasting and the pouring of libations.

DECEMBER
HARLEM NUTCRACKER
(313) 964-1670
Presented by the Arts League of Michigan in collaboration with the University Musical Society and Detroit Opera House first time in Detroit in 1998.

"PRAISE" CONCERT
(313) 963-0050
Presented annually in December by the Detroit-Windsor Dance Company.

BUFFALO SOLDIERS

In uniform, the Detroit Calico Troop reenacts the roles of the African American members of the U.S. cavalry in the 19th century. To arrange lectures and demonstrations for school groups, parade appearances and visits to community sites, call (313) 537-7148.

ORGANIZATIONS

NATIONAL ASSOCIATION FOR THE ADVANCEMENT OF COLORED PEOPLE
Detroit Branch; 2990 E. Grand Blvd.
(313) 871-2087
Nationally, seeks to eliminate racial prejudice and secure for African Americans their rights as citizens, justice in the courts and equal opportunity in economic, social and political endeavors. Detroit branch annually hosts fund-raising dinner for nearly 10,000 guests each April.

DETROIT URBAN LEAGUE
208 Mack Ave., Detroit
(313) 832-4600
Group devoted to social service programs with a focus on youth. Honors unsung heroes in Salute to Distinguished Warriors each March.

DETROIT ASSOCIATION OF BLACK ORGANIZATIONS
12048 Grand River, Detroit
(313) 491-0003
Non-profit, charitable federation of business, labor, law enforcement, community and religious groups across Detroit and environs addresses the area's major problems and joins with others in building bridges and interracial broad-based coalitions.

ROSA AND RAYMOND PARKS INSTITUTE
65 Cadillac Square, Ste. 2200, Detroit
(313) 965-0606
Civil rights educational organization sponsors Freedom Tour and other programs.

KWANZAA

KWANZAA is celebrated December 26 through January 1 to acknowledge the participants' African heritage, give thanks for family, reflect on the ending year and rejuvenate the spirit for the coming year.

Introduced in 1966 by Dr. Maulana Karenga, the concept is based on the African tradition of festively celebrating each year's first harvest and expressing thanksgiving. It is not linked to any religious or political organization. Kwanzaa is intended to promote a greater sense of unity, independence and purpose among participants.

To reinforce the connection to Africa, the holiday, its principles of living and its symbols have Swahili names. *Kwanzaa* means "first fruit." Its seven principles, or *nguzo saba*, are unity *(umoja),* self-determination *(kujichagulia),* collective work and responsibility *(ujima),* cooperative economics *(ujamaa),* purpose *(nia),* creativity *(kuumba)* and faith *(imani).* One principle is celebrated each day of Kwanzaa.

Detroiters' books on the celebration include Detroit teacher Dorothy Winbush Riley's "The Complete Book of Kwanzaa: Celebrating Our Cultural Harvest" (1995), available at local outlets including the Shrine of the Black Madonna Bookstore (see Media Outlets listing). "How to Celebrate Kwanzaa," published in 1988 by the Detroit Black Writers' Guild, is on shelves at a dozen Detroit Public Library branches.

For online information, visit the Kwanzaa Information Center at www.new.melanet.com/kwanzaa.

MEDIA

PRINT

CITY VIEW
11000 W. McNichols, Ste. 227; Detroit
(313) 964-3222
Monthly publication with African American news, comment, culture and entertainment.

THE MICHIGAN CITIZEN
211 Glendale, Highland Park
(313) 869-0033
Weekly statewide progressive black publication.

THE MICHIGAN CHRONICLE
479 Ledyard, Detroit
(313) 963-5522
Weekly award-winning African American newspaper. Founded in 1936 by publisher John H. Sengstacke, it is the oldest black newspaper continuously published in Michigan.

SEEDS
(313) 393-0931
The journal of poetry and fiction is published by Sisters of Color, a literature group.

MEDIA OUTLETS

APPLE BOOK CENTER
7900 W. Outer Drive, Detroit
(313) 255-5221
Mon-Sat 10am-7pm, Sun 10am-5pm. A large variety of Afrocentric books as well as regular special events

BOOK BEAT
26010 Greenfield, Oak Park
(in Lincoln Shopping Center)
(248) 968-1190
Mon-Sat 10am-9pm, Sun 11am-6pm. Multicultural books and gifts.

OAK PARK BOOK CENTER
23029 Coolidge, Oak Park
(248) 399-2255
Mon-Sat 9:30am-7pm, Sun 10am-3pm.

SHRINE OF THE BLACK MADONNA
Cultural Center Bookstore
13535 Livernois (N of Davidson), Detroit
(313) 491-0777
Tue-Thu 11am-6pm, Fri-Sun 11am-7pm.

WEB SITES

AFRICA-AMERICAN MOSAIC
Library of Congress reviews 500 years of black history, culture and contributions. lcweb.loc.gov/exhibits/Africa. American/intro

AFRICAN AMERICAN GENEALOGY
www.msstate.edu/archives/history/afrigen

BLACK INFORMATION NETWORK
www.bin.com

BLACK HISTORY AS TOLD BY ARTISTS
wwbighorn.trra.net/artonline/aol/history

THE BLACK CINEMA NETWORK
Covers films from 1920 to the present. nforamp.net/ashleyma/blakcine

BLACK ENTERPRISE MAGAZINE
www.blackenterprise.com

HERITAGE APPAREL
Source for quality apparel and merchandise which honors and celebrates African American history and heritage, including Buffalo Soldiers and Tuskeegee Airmen. www.heritageapparel.com

MUSEUM OF AFRICAN AMERICAN HISTORY
www.ipl.org/exhibit/maah

SOUTHERN FOLKLIFE COLLECTION
Biographies of gospel singers such as Mahalia Jackson and Shirley Caesar. http://ils.unc.eduHHHbarba/sfc.htmi

THE UNIVERSAL BLACK PAGES
Links to African American sites and resources on the internet. www.gatech.edu/bgsa/black pages

RADIO

WCHB 105.9 FM, Detroit
(313) 278-1440

WGPR 107.5 FM, Detroit
(313) 259-8862

(Also see "Music" listings.)

TELEVISION

WTVS CHANNEL 56
"American Black Journal With Darryl Wood," a local weekly series, examines issues, events and newsmakers from an African American perspective. Check local TV listings for times.

The Star of David (Magen David), a six-pointed star made from two equilateral triangles, has been the symbol of Judaism since the 17th century. Blue on a white field, it is the central motif on the flag of Israel and, since 1897, the emblem of Zionism.

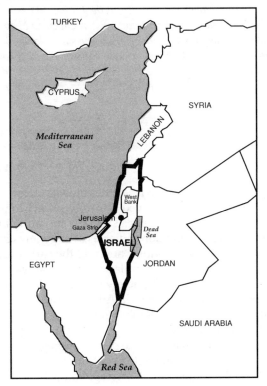

The kingdom of Israel reached the height of its existence and included the most territory under the reign of King David (1000-961 B.C.). Its borders stretched far beyond present-day Israeli borders and included parts of what is now Lebanon, Syria, Jordan and Egypt.

Sandwiched in northern Mesopotamia among the powerful Hittite, Egyptian and Babylonian Empires was a small group of nomadic people believed to have been called Hapiru or Habiru (Hebrews). More is known about the Hebrews than many other early Middle Eastern peoples because of the Bible, which is a recounting of Israelite history, beliefs and literature, and is written in the Hebrew language. Hebrews eventually settled in Canaan, later known as Judah and Israel. They established a kingdom under Saul, then later David of Bethlehem, whose son Solomon ruled over Israel at its height (965-925 B.C.). A great temple was built at Jerusalem that became a focal point of the Israelite religion.

The term Jew stems from the Hebrew yehudi, meaning "a member of the tribe of Judah," the ancient territory later organized as the Roman province of Judaea in A.D. 6. The English word Jew is from the Latin Judaeus, meaning "an inhabitant of Judaea."

Jews trace their ancestry to Abraham, who was the first leader to adopt a monotheistic belief system. Modern Jews are members of a separate ethnic community that, despite severe persecution, has maintained its identity for nearly 4,000 years, from ancient Canaan to the establishment of the modern state of Israel in 1948.

The first Jewish community in the United States was founded by Sephardic Jews from Portugal in 1654 in New Amsterdam (now New York). Jews have been immigrating to the U.S. ever since, from Russia, Poland, Germany—virtually every country—bringing with them a unique cultural blend of homeland and religion. Today, America has the largest Jewish population in the world, and the contributions Jews have made to education, ethics, arts and sciences are immeasurable.

JEWS IN DETROIT

The first known Jewish settler in Detroit was German-born Chapman Abraham, who arrived in Detroit from Montreal, Canada, in 1762. As a trader of goods, Chapman's stay was sporadic, and he later returned to Canada. Documentation indicates solitary Jews found their way to Detroit at the end of the 18th century and into the early decades of the 19th century.

In 1850, the Jewish population of Detroit was about 60. That year, the first meeting of the **Beth El Society** took place at the home of Sarah and Isaac Cozens, on Congress and St. Antoine Streets, becoming the first Jewish congregation in the state. Rabbi Samuel Marcus served many functions: cantor (official singer), teacher and the Mohel (the rabbi who performs the circumcisions on male babies). The small congregation bought one half-acre on Champlain (later Lafayette Street) for the first Jewish cemetery.

In 1861, 17 men from Congregation Beth El formed the Orthodox congregation **Shaarey Zedek.** By 1864, the membership at Shaarey Zedek was up to 64. Large numbers of Jews came later, during the Eastern European migrations of the late 1800s and early 1900s. A Detroit-Yiddish directory in 1907 listed the names, addresses and occupations of more than 2,300 Jews. The center of the earliest Jewish settlement (the Jewish Quarter) in Detroit was on Hastings Street, near the present day Renaissance Center. Although there was a mixture of ethnic cultures, this area remained the hub of the Jewish district and was occupied mostly by Eastern European Jews. The demographics didn't change much for the next 20 years, with the exception of a large influx of Jews fleeing Hitler's regime in the 1930s and '40s.

In 1951, after meeting for several years in the auditorium of the Detroit Institute of Arts, the members of **Temple Israel**, an offshoot of Temple Beth El, commissioned William Kapp, architect of Meadow Brook Hall, to design a remarkable art deco-influenced structure at 17400 Manderson in Detroit.

Gradually, the Jewish community moved northwest of the city, with major institutions and businesses locating on or near major streets. Congregations that started in Detroit bought property in the suburbs. Shaarey Zedek moved to Southfield in 1962, Temple Beth El to Bloomfield Hills in 1973 and Temple Israel to West Bloomfield in 1980.

In the 1980s, another influx of Russian Jews migrated to the Detroit (primarily Oak Park) area, due in part to the relaxation in the Soviet Union's travel restrictions in 1988 and the union's final breakup.

Metropolitan Detroit is now home to 96,000 Jewish Americans. Of this number, about 75 percent live in southern Oakland County. The Orthodox community resides mostly in the Oak Park area, and a large grouping in Southfield, within walking distance of their synagogues. Other Jews live in outlying communities. Currently, the core Jewish community is in Oak Park, Huntington Woods, Southfield, Farmington Hills and West Bloomfield.

ALBERT KAHN'S LEGACY

Much of Detroit's skyline is the creation of premier industrial architect, Albert Kahn, who was internationally renowned at the time of his death in 1942. Among his prolific works are *The Detroit News* and *Free Press* Buildings, the General Motors Building and the Fisher Building, as well as Hill Auditorium and Angel Hall at the University of Michigan. He also designed Cranbrook House in Bloomfield Hills and more than 1,000 industrial buildings for Ford Motor Company. His own home is now the headquarters of the Detroit Urban League (208 Mack Ave.). Kahn was given the opportunity to use his genius as an expression of his heritage in designing these impressive structures:

Temple Beth El (1922), 8801 Woodward Ave., Detroit.
Now the Lighthouse Cathedral, it is monumental in every way. (Beth El's earlier home was designed by Kahn & Mason at 3424 Woodward Ave. and is now the Bonstelle Theater. The current location of Temple Beth El is in Bloomfield Hills at Telegraph and 14 Mile.)

Shaarey Zedek Synagogue (1932), 900 W. Chicago Blvd., Detroit.
The impressive Romanesque Revival building, sensitively preserved and now Clinton Street Greater Bethlehem Temple, stands as a testimony to the success and religious commitment of Jews—and later of African Americans—in Detroit.

◀ **Current home of Shaarey Zedek (1962)**, 27375 Bell Road, Southfield. The synagogue, designed by Albert Kahn Associates and Percival Goodman, looms dramatically over major freeways into Detroit.

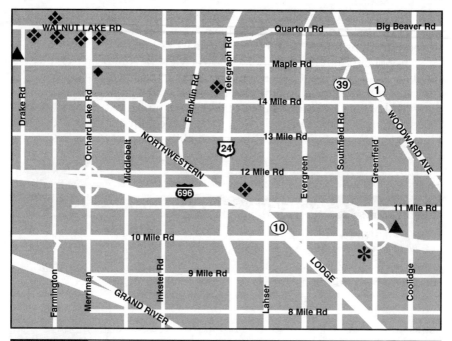

TOUR   FROM OAK PARK TO WEST BLOOMFIELD

[CE/2-4] Start your Jewish journey at Royal Plaza in Oak Park *on Greenfield Road just south of I-696.* Stop in at **Zeman's Bakery** *at 25258 Greenfield Road* to pick up some fresh *challah, mandel* bread (similar to *biscotti*) and sour cream coffee cake. Next door you'll find **Lakewood Kosher Foods** and **New York Bagel.** Be sure to shake off the crumbs before entering the next store, **Borenstein's Books and Gifts** *(25242 Greenfield).* In addition to the latest in books and music, the Judaica and Hebraica merchandise there includes religious artifacts, Israeli giftware, cards and Kosher wines.

For a look at metro Detroit's largest temples and synagogues, *head northwest on I-696 for the express route, or take Greenfield north to Eleven Mile and follow it west for a close-up view of* **Congregation Shaarey Zedek** *at the northwest corner of Bell and Eleven Mile roads in Southfield. (From the expressway, you'll see the imposing structure on the north side before you exit at Telegraph.)*

Turn north on Telegraph and head for 14 Mile Road, just north, on the left, is **Temple Beth El,** a tent-like building designed in 1973 by Minoru Yamasaki. The sanctuary was modeled on the biblical "Tent of Meeting." Inside the temple library is a display of miniature "scale-model" synagogues. Artwork and Judaic artifacts are displayed throughout the building and atrium.

For lunch, proceed to West Bloomfield and the **Stage Deli** *(6873 Orchard Lake Road),* where you can enjoy a lean corned beef sandwich and a piece of *babka* (a bready, tall European coffee cake) as well as the Hollywood-star decor. *To get there, take Telegraph north to Maple and go west four miles. Turn left at Orchard Lake Road* and look for the deli in a strip mall across from the Americana West Movie Theater.

If you *continue west on Maple past Orchard Lake and Farmington roads,* you'll come to the main campus of the **Jewish Community Center (JCC)** *at Drake Road.* There you can visit the **Holocaust Memorial Center** and the **Janice Charach Epstein Gallery.** The library at the center contains some of the best current and historical literature in the area. Children can take part in activities at the **Jewish Discovery Center** (call 248-661-1000 for hours). Also check the performance schedule of the **Jewish Ensemble Theatre** and activities calendar for evening entertainment. On Tuesday evenings, for example, you can join the energetic crowd for Israeli folk dancing at the West Bloomfield center (or at the Oak Park JCC at *Ten Mile between Greenfield and Coolidge).* Before leaving, take a break at **Elijah's Cup** for a coffee and another bakery treat.

If you return to Orchard Lake Road via Walnut Lake Road to the north of the JCC, you'll see the **Temple Israel** complex (5725 Walnut Lake Road), just east of Drake Road. As you continue east, you'll pass **Temple Kol Ami** (5088 Walnut Lake) and **Shaarey Zedek B'nai Israel Center** (4200 Walnut Lake Rd.). One of the area's newest congregations, **Temple Shir Shalom**, is on the *southeast corner of Orchard Lake Road at 3999 Walnut Lake Road.*

Hungry again? This time, *head back to Northwestern Highway (becomes the Lodge/Route 10) going east; exit at 10 Mile Road. Turn left to Southfield Road and left again.* You will see, in a small strip mall *on the northeast corner of Southfield and 10 Mile Roads,* the blue awning announcing **Jerusalem Pizza.** Pick up a delicious and unusual kosher specialty pizza for dinner or a snack.

BRANCHES OF JUDAISM

● **ORTHODOX:** Orthodox Jews interpret Jewish law literally. Like many other Orthodox religious sects, they obey God's law as it is stated. They believe in covering their heads before God, keeping kosher, observing the laws of the Sabbath and following their traditions completely.

● **CONSERVATIVE:** Conservative Jews follow the laws of the Torah with modifications in their observance. They fall in between Orthodox and Reform. While they may observe the Sabbath in part, they do drive to synagogue, and may or may not keep kosher. Their religious services are housed in Synagogues. The use of Hebrew is prevalent throughout the religious services and prayers.

● **REFORM:** Reform Jews believe in the Torah as a divinely inspired work. While they follow the holidays, they interpret tradition within the guidelines of the Reform movement, in which Jewish laws are followed in a modern context. Their religious services are housed in Temples. Less Hebrew is used in the services, depending on the particular temple. Many Reform temples have incorporated more English into the services and prayers.

● **HUMANIST:** Humanistic Judaism is a nontheistic alternative in contemporary Jewish life. This national movement was established by Rabbi Sherwin T. Wine in 1963 in Detroit.

● **RECONSTRUCTIONIST:** The Reconstructionist movement, founded earlier this century, views Judaism as a way of life and considers "tradition" and culture as important as religion.

TRADITIONAL FOODS

Jewish cuisine is not necessarily kosher. Jewish foods have their roots in Central and Eastern Europe, Spain, Africa, the Middle East and just about anywhere Jews lived or migrated. Most of us think of Eastern European food when we think of Jewish cooking—beef brisket, chopped chicken liver, chicken soup, kugel, blintzes, corned beef, pastrami, smoked fish, and boiled chicken in a pot. Traditional foods are served on holidays and *Shabbat* (Sabbath).

Shabbat (also called *Shabbos*) begins at sunset on Friday evening, with the woman of the house ushering in the celebration with the blessing over candles. The table is set with the best china and linen. Dishes that require no last-minute preparation are made ready—a pot might be put on to cook slowly all night, ready for the Saturday afternoon meal, since the laws of the Sabbath prohibit doing work on that day. It is customary to invite guests who might otherwise be alone.

Most *seder* foods (*see Passover*) are traditional for each family, and traditional in either Ashkenazi (Eastern European) or Sephardic (Mediterrean) roots. Passover has its own dietary rules. Since only unleavened bread is allowed, matzo is served.

Kosher wine is served for Jewish holidays and celebrations.

Blintz: A thick crêpe, filled with cheese, jam, fish, fruit or potatoes, then folded and possibly topped with hot blueberries, applesauce, sour cream, or sometimes sprinkled with powdered sugar.

Cabbage Borscht: Soup made with cabbage, beef or beef bones, tomato and sometimes beets—can be made sweet or sweet and sour.

Challah: Traditional egg bread served on Sabbath and assumes different shapes for different holidays.

Gefilte Fish: A combination of fish (usually three types) with eggs, matzoh meal and seasonings; cooked slowly in a fish stock, then cooled and served chilled with horseradish.

Kishke: Stuffing in a casing, with or without gravy. Generally served as a side dish.

Kneidlach: (Matzo Balls) Ball-shaped dumplings added to chicken soup, made primarily from matzoh meal.

Knish: A piece of dough (baking powder or yeast) that encloses a filling of shredded meat, cheese or potato mixture.

Kreplach: "Jewish wontons" (usually half-moon shaped) stuffed with ground or shredded meat and spices.

Kugel: A sweet or savory noodle pudding. Usually served as a side dish with meat, it makes a great luncheon entrée or buffet item.

Latkes: Potato pancakes often served with applesauce, and/or sour cream.

Lox: Smoked salmon sliced thin and served as an appetizer or on a bagel with cream cheese, sliced tomato and raw onion.

Matzo (or Matzoh): A thin, brittle, unleavened bread (much like a cracker). Matzo is also ground and used in matzo balls, breading and pancakes.

Tsimmes: Fruit compote with sweet potatoes.

RESTAURANTS & CATERING

*Note: a **K** at the end of the listing indicates that the food is kosher.*

OAK PARK

BREAD BASKET DELI
26052 Greenfield, Oak Park
(Lincoln Shopping Center)
(248) 968-0022
Tue-Sat 10am-9:45pm, Sun 10am-8:45pm. Very popular spot known for blintzes, potato pancakes, chicken in a pot.

NEW YORK PIZZA WORLD
15280 Lincoln, Oak Park; (248) 968-2102
Mon-Wed, Thu & Sun 11:30am-8pm, Fri 11:30am-3pm, Sat half-hour after sundown to 1am. Varied menu includes pizza, fish & chips, assorted pitas, salads and sides. **K**

TASTE OF CLASS
25254 Greenfield, Oak Park; (248) 967-6020
Sun-Fri 10am-8:30pm, (Fri adjust according to sunset). Jewish and Middle Eastern cuisine. **K**

UNIQUE KOSHER CARRYOUT
25270 Greenfield, Oak Park; (248) 967-1161
Mon-Thu 10am-7pm, Fri 8:30am-4pm (adjust according to sunset). Sun 10am-6pm. Mostly carryout. Glatt kosher. Complete meals, dinners, soups, salads, and sandwiches. **K**

SOUTHFIELD

GATEWAY DELI AND GOURMET RESTAURANT
21754 W. 11 Mile (Harvard Row)
Southfield; (248) 352-4940
Mon-Sat 7am-8pm.. Sandwiches and deli fare, dinners account for the "gourmet."

JERUSALEM PIZZA
25050 Southfield Rd., Southfield
(248) 552-0088 or 1-800-581-1212
Sun-Thu 11am-10pm, Fri 11am to 2 hours before Shabbos (the Sabbath), Sat 1 hour after Shabbos to 1:30am. Kosher pizzas for takeout or small sit-down area. Specialty pizzas include salmon, feta with dill. Will ship pizza anywhere in the United States. **K**

QUALITY KOSHER CATERING, INC.
27375 Bell Rd., Southfield; (248) 352-7758
Mon-Thu 9am-5pm. Unique cuisine—will even prepare kosher game. Caters events from hayrides to Bar/Bat Mitzvahs, serving one to 2,000. Glatt kosher catering to events in hotels and restaurants. **K**

STAR DELI
24555 W.12 Mile Rd., Southfield
(just W of Telegraph); (248) 352-7377
Mon-Sat 7am-9:30pm, Sun 7am-8pm. Take-out only; hand-cut lox.

CLAWSON/ROYAL OAK/TROY

MATI'S DELI
3634 Rochester Rd., Troy; (248) 740-3535
(in Century Plaza
Mon-Fri 10am-6pm, Sat 10am-3pm. New branch of Dearborn location. Kosher-style sandwiches, soups, salads, desserts.

RAY'S ICE CREAM
4233 Coolidge, Royal Oak; (248) 549-5256
Hours vary by season. Premium homemade ice cream. **K**

SAMUEL HOFFMAN'S NEW YORK DELI
1213 W. 14 Mile Rd. (Clawson Center)
Clawson; (248) 280-3817
Daily 7am-9pm. New York-style fare, dine in or take out, catering.

FARMINGTON HILLS

BLOOM'S KITCHEN
32418 Northwestern Hwy., (between 14 Mile and Middlebelt), Farmington Hills
(248) 855-9463
Mon-Thu 8am-8pm, Fri 8am-sundown, Sun 10am-5pm. Mostly carryout but lots of catering and some sit-down.

BREAD BASKET DELI
27740 Grand River, Farmington Hills
(248) 442-4800
Mon-Sat 9am-9pm, Sun 11am-6pm. Full line of Jewish-style deli sandwiches.

BROTHERS BAGEL & DELI
32431 Northwestern Hwy.
Farmington Hills; (248) 626-4400
Mon-Sat 6am-4pm. Limited seating, mostly takeout.

THE DELI

In German, "delikatessen" means an abundance of delicacies. German Jews brought them to us (changing the *k* to *c*) in the late 19th century. Delicatessen food (or "deli") is traditionally carryout, but more and more places offer dining-in as well. Supermarkets and produce markets have added deli departments over the last decade, many offering the same types of Jewish-style cuisine. New York is still considered home to the "true Jewish Deli."

There, the noise level must be high, pickles must be on the tables, sandwiches must be huge and the waiters must be surly. Here, we'd probably agree with everything but the waiters, but we sometimes get those anyway. All delis do carryout in a big way— for home meals, catering for parties, and trays for sitting *Shiva* (the Jewish mourning period).

WEST BLOOMFIELD

ELIJAH'S CUP
6600 W. Maple, W. Bloomfield
(at the Jewish Community Center)
(248) 788-5603
Mon-Thu 7:30am-7pm, Fri 7:30am-3pm, Sat 1-6pm, Sun 8am-5pm. The place to meet and eat baked goods before or after a visit to the Epstein Gallery or Holocaust Museum.

DELI UNIQUE
6724 Orchard Lake Rd. (S of Maple)
W. Bloomfield; (248) 737-3890
Mon-Thu 11am-10pm, Fri 11am-11pm, Sat 9am-11pm, Sun 9am-9pm. Extensive menu, including julienne salad, sour cream coffee cake and famous vegetarian "chopped liver."

JEWEL KOSHER CATERING, INC.
5642 W. Maple Rd., W. Bloomfield
(248) 661-4050
By appointment only. Glatt kosher catering for two or 2,500. **K**

LA DIFFERENCE
7295 Orchard Lake Rd.,
W. Bloomfield
(248) 932-8934
Mon-Fri 11am-2pm, 4-9pm; Sun 11am-2pm, 4-9pm; Sat (in winter only) opens one hour after sundown. Kosher restaurant offering elegance with affordability. **K**

PLAZA DELI
29145 Northwestern Hwy.,Southfield
(near 12 Mile Rd.)
(248) 356-2310
Sit-down, but mostly carryout. Known for sandwiches and fast service.

STAGE & CO.
6873 Orchard Lake Rd., W. Bloomfield
(248) 855-6622
Tue-Thu 10am-10pm, Fri 10am-11pm, Sat 9am-12am, Sun 9am-10pm. Sandwiches named after Broadway shows; classic chicken soup with rice, matzoh ball or kreplach; chopped liver. Big carryout department.

SPERBER'S NORTH
6600 Maple Rd., W. Bloomfield
(at the Jewish Community Center)
(248) 661-5151
Mon, Wed, Thu 10am-3pm, Fri 10am-2pm, Tue 5-8pm. Glatt kosher specialties include homemade challah. **K**

BLOOMFIELD HILLS/BINGHAM FARMS

DELI UNIQUE
30100 Telegraph, Bingham Farms
(between 12 and 13 Mile Rds.)
(248) 645-5288
and
1475 N. Woodward Ave., Bloomfield Hills
(at the Kingsley Inn)
(248) 646-7923
Mon-Thu 11am-9pm, Fri 11am-10pm, Sat

9am-10pm, Sun 9am-9pm. Known for julienne salad, sour cream coffee cake, and vegetarian "chopped liver."

EMBER'S DELI
3598 W. Maple Rd. (at Lahser)
Bloomfield Hills; (248) 645-1033
Mon-Sat 7am-9pm, Sun 8am-3pm. The place to meet and greet first thing in the morning. Known for inexpensive breakfast specials and thick french fries.

STEVE'S DELI
6646 Telegraph, Bloomfield Hills
(Bloomfield Plaza)
(248) 932-0800
Mon-Fri 10am-8pm, Sat-Sun 9am-8pm. Seating and carryout, homemade soups and Romanik Brownies. Fast service.

BISCAYNE BAGEL & DELI
660 Woodward, Detroit; (313) 964-4003
Mon-Fri 7am-5pm. This newcomer to the bagel world has deli sandwiches, ethnic foods, five homemade soups daily.

MATI'S DELI
1842 Monroe (at Outer Dr.), Dearborn
(313) 277-3253
Mon-Fri 10am-6pm, Sat 10am-3pm.. Offbeat sit-down deli in a 1926 gas station near Dearborn's historic district. Deli sandwiches on double-baked, crusty rye; soups, cream cheese brownies, good prices, fast and friendly.

WHAT'S KOSHER?

You can buy kosher hamburger and you can buy kosher cheese, but you can't make a kosher cheeseburger. Why not? Because eating meat and dairy together just isn't kosher.

Buying kosher and "keeping kosher" *(kashruth)* are different. Many non-Jewish people, who are concerned about purity, quality and even animal rights, like to buy kosher products, especially meats. To be labeled kosher, meat must be handled meticulously by certified butchers, who perform a quick and painless slaughter and use no preservatives, additives or fillers. Kosher processing of chicken, for instance, is the safest there is, but these practices stem from ancient religion, not modern science. *Glatt* kosher is the strictest standard.

The Union of Orthodox Synagogues puts a seal of approval on many kosher products, but the only universal standards come from Jewish law, where explicit instructions for "clean and unclean" food preparation can be found.

Some foods, mostly pork and shellfish, never can be kosher. Because the mixing of dairy and meat is strictly forbidden, some households have separate eating and cooking utensils for meat and dairy.

Marks such as this one (Vaad Harabonim of Greater Detroit and Merkaz) found on food products indicate the kosher supervision. Other marks are: **D** (dairy), **DE** (dairy equipment but no actual dairy in ingredients, hence it can be eaten even after a meat meal), **P** (Passover kosher), **Pareve** (nondairy), **Cholov Yisroel** (kosher supervised milk used in ingredients), **Pas Yisroel** (Jewish baked foods), **Yoshen** (not from current grain crop).

NATHAN'S DELI
581 E. Jefferson, Detroit; (313) 962-3354
Mon-Fri 8am-6pm, closed Sat and Sun.
Popular, downtown "Big City" deli offers
breakfast favorites, fresh salads, well-stacked
sandwiches, including lavash.

THE WOODWARD BAGEL BAKERY
COFFEEHOUSE
4200 Woodward, Detroit; (313) 832-3000
*Mon-Fri 6:30am-midnight, Sat 8am-midnight,
Sun 10am-4pm.* Fresh New York style bagels
and sandwiches, salads, sumptuous
desserts and gourmet coffees. Hosts art
openings, poetry readings and musical performances; 10- by 45-foot mural on ceiling
painted by Jorge Galvez.

ANN ARBOR

ZINGERMAN'S DELICATESSEN
422 Detroit St., Ann Arbor
(734) 663-3354
and
ZINGERMAN'S NEXT DOOR
(734) 663-5282
*Daily 7am-9pm, open until 10pm during day-
light-saving time.* Huge corned beef sandwiches and long list of combos on variety of
homemade breads. Considered the best deli
in the Midwest. Whitefish sandwiches and
mushroom-barley soup are renowned. Large
assortment of cheeses; knowledgeable staff.
Monthly themes and specials.

WINDSOR

PERETZ HOUSE
**1653 Ouellette, Windsor; (519) 973-1772
Ext. 32**
Mon-Fri 5:30pm. Restaurant, at the Windsor
Jewish Cultural Center/Senior Complex, is
open by appointment only for luncheons,
meetings and parties. Only Glatt kosher
restaurant in the Windsor area, all the food
and baked goods are homemade; catering. **K**

KOSHER FOOD MARKETS
& BUTCHERS

DEXTER-DAVISON KOSHER MEAT &
POULTRY MARKET
**13181 W. 10 Mile, Oak Park
(next to Farmer Jack)
(248) 548-6800**
Mon-Thu 9am-6pm, Sun 8am-3pm.

FARMER JACK
**10 Mile and Coolidge, Oak Park
(248) 542-1920**
and
**Orchard Lake and Maple, W. Bloomfield
(248) 851-3850**
*Mon-Sat 7am-11pm, Sun 8am-9pm.
(Butcher closed Sat.)* Extensive selection of
kosher foods.

HARVARD ROW KOSHER MEATS
**6221 Orchard Lake Rd., W. Bloomfield
(in Sugar Tree Plaza)
(248) 539-8806**
*Sun 7:30am-2pm, Mon-Thu 8:30am-6pm, Fri
8:30am-2pm.* Retail kosher meats, rotisserie
chickens cooked on location. Also Kosher
frozen foods and spices. Delivery available
on Tuesday and Thursday.

LAKEWOOD SPECIALTY FOOD CENTER
**25250 Greenfield, Oak Park
(between 10 Mile Rd. and I-696)
(248) 967-2021**
*Mon-Thu 9am-7pm, Fri 9am-4pm, Sun 9am-
5pm.* Kosher products; Israeli, vegetarian,
Jewish foods; full deli and kosher ethnic food,
full line of baked goods (from New York) and
candy. Glatt kosher. Catering.

ONE STOP KOSHER
25040 Southfield Rd., Southfield
(248) 569-5000
Mon-Wed 7:30am-7pm, Thu 7:30am-9pm, Fri 7:30am to 2 hours before sundown, Sun 8am-5pm. Thousands of kosher items, including fresh meats and poultry; frozen foods. Great service and delivery available.

STRICTLY KOSHER MEATS, INC.
26020 Greenfield, Oak Park
(248) 967-4222
Mon-Thu 8am-5:45pm, Sun 8am-2pm. Glatt kosher, homemade kishka, retail kosher meats, limited spices and other foods.

SUPERIOR KOSHER MEATS
23059 Coolidge, Oak Park; (248) 547-3900
Mon-Tue 7:30am-7pm, Wed-Thu 7:30am-8pm, Fri 7:30am-2pm, Sun 7:30am-6pm. Kosher meats, deli products, prepared foods, and a full line of unusual and hard to find ingredients (many from New York).

BAGELS ARE BIG BUSINESS

Less than a generation ago, bagels were considered rather exotic fare by anyone outside the Detroit area's Jewish community. And even there, they weren't so easy to come by. Times have certainly changed! Virtually every grocery in every town offers many bagel varieties in the same aisle with Wonder bread—and the freezer offers even more, along with Bagel Dogs (kosher hot dogs wrapped in bagel dough), and Bagel Bites (little pizzas made on mini-bagels).

Bagel shops have replaced yesterday's donut shops, with one seemingly on every corner. Their zoom in popularity over the last decade is probably due to the fact that bagels are low- or no-fat (except egg bagels); boiled and then baked (never fried); versatile—happily holding everything from lox, tomato and raw onion to strawberry-flavored cream cheese; and portable—fitting in well with today's packable fast-track living.

There are many stories concerning the origin of the bagel. One version centers on the saving of Vienna from Turkish attack in 1683 by Jan Sobieski, the King of Poland ("Vanquisher of the Turks"). The grateful townspeople made sweet bread in the shape of "beugels" or stirrups, to commemorate the event. Another story refers to Abigail's flight across the Negev. Before leaving, her servants loaded the camels with many lumps of dough on sticks. When they arrived at their destination, they found the sun had baked the dough. They were named *Abigails*, then *bigails*, and finally *bagels*.

But regardless of origin, until recently, bagels seemed to be confined to American Jewish culture, particularly New York.

There are many great places for bagels in the metro area—and everyone has a personal favorite; **Brothers Bagel, Detroit Bagel Factory** and **New York Bagel** have been local institutions for over a generation.

BAKERIES

Look for New York-style cheese cake, honey cake, challah bread, rugelach (rich cookies usually containing nuts and fruit or chocolate chips), sour cream cakes, hamentashen (three-cornered, filled pastries), mandel bread and kichel (an airy sugar-covered cookie).

JEWEL BAKERY
21784 W. 11 Mile, Southfield
(Harvard Row)
(248) 353-5688
European-style breads and cakes.

STAR BAKERY
26031 Coolidge, Oak Park
(at Lincoln, main location)
(248) 541-9450
and
15600 W. 10 Mile Rd., Southfield
(New Orleans Mall)
(248) 559-4808
and
29151 Northwestern Hwy., Southfield
(248) 352-8548
Daily 7am-7pm. Jewish style, not kosher. Sour cream cakes, breads and cookies.

SUNSHINE TREATS
29960 W. 12 Mile Rd., Farmington Hills
(248) 851-2920
Large selection of kosher treats and goodies, and of course, service with a smile. Delivers to all the local Jewish nursery schools.

ZEMAN'S NEW YORK KOSHER BAKERY
25258 Greenfield, Oak Park
(248) 967-3905
Sun-Thu. 6am-7pm, Fri. 6am-5pm. The Greenfield site is the oldest kosher bakery in the area. Join the hustle and bustle Fridays and savor the scents of a variety of breads.

ZINGERMAN'S BAKEHOUSE
3711 Plaza Drive, Ann Arbor
(734) 761-2095
Daily 7am-6pm. Specialty breads of all types from challah rolls to European tsitsel. Zingerman's breads also can be purchased at many stores in the Detroit area.

SHOPS

BORENSTEIN'S BOOKS & GIFTS
25242 Greenfield, Oak Park
(at Royal Plaza, S of I-696)
(248) 967-3920
Sun 9:30am-5pm., Mon-Thu 9:30am-7pm, Fri 9:30am-4pm, Sat closed. Originally in Detroit, specializes in ritual Judaica, religious jewelry and Israeli giftware. Offers a large selection of religious books and tapes.

ESTHER'S JUDAICA
4301 Orchard Lake Rd., W. Bloomfield
(Sugar Tree, N of Maple)
(248) 932-3377
Sun 10:30am-5:30pm, Mon-Tue 10am-6pm, Wed 10am-7pm, Thu 10am-8pm, Fri 10am-4pm, Sat closed. One of the newest stores carrying a large selection of Judaica ritual objects, books, tapes of modern and traditional music, skin care products from the Dead Sea, kosher gift baskets, cards and candles.

SPITZER'S BOOKS AND GIFTS
21790 W. 11 Mile Rd., Southfield
(Harvard Row at Lahser)
(248) 356-6080
Sun 9:30am-5:30pm, Mon-Tue 9:30am-6 pm, Wed-Thu 9:30am-7 pm, Fri 9:30am-4pm, Sat. closed. Religious books and objects, toys and games at one of the oldest Jewish bookstores in the area.

TRADITION! TRADITION!
Southfield
(248) 557-0109 or 1-800-579-6340
By appointment only. A gallery and resource of unique Jewish ritual objects to celebrate the Sabbath or holidays. Specializing in special orders; everything from limited edition Kitubot to hand made tallit. Contact: Alicia Nelson.

ZYZYX!
6885 Orchard Lake Rd., W. Bloomfield
(Boardwalk Shopping Center)
(248) 539-3309
Mon, Tues, Wed, Fri, Sat 10am-6pm, Thu 10am-8pm, Sun noon-4pm. Pronounced *Zi-zicks*, this eclectic shop offers extensive collection of Judaica, from whimsical to elegant.

KLEZMER

KLEZMER is the Yiddish word for musician—not a specific type of music or instrument. Klezmer musicians played folk music, as opposed to classical music, all over Central and Eastern Europe. Klezmer was once considered a derogatory term suggesting that these musicians were only good enough to play for Bar Mitzvahs, not classical concerts. However, things have definitely changed; now Klezmer is hip!

This music is a combination of Central and Eastern European folk music, songs that came from specific geographic regions, some Yiddish, some Hebrew, some show tunes from the Yiddish theater. This was a type of music without a country. When many of the Klezmer musicians immigrated to the United States, they brought with them the folk music from their homeland and then incorporated touches of popular music (ragtime and jazz). After World War II, the Klezmer sound had almost vanished. In the '70s a second-generation revival took place, and this is where the term "Klezmer" was actually coined. Today there are many Klezmer bands throughout the United States—they even have a variety of sites on the Internet: **(www.well.com/user/ari/klez/)** will link you to them.

PERFORMING ARTS

HORA AVIV FOLKDANCE TROUPE
(248) 626-0126.
Contact: Shelley Komer Jackier
The spirit of Israel and its multicultural nature is presented in energetic dance. Call for information about performances and instruction.

STORYTELLING
(248) 356-8721
Corrine Stavish rekindles the ancient art of storytelling with programs for all ages in Jewish folklore, from ancient to modern, and across cultures. Performs for celebratory events of all types and monthly at Borders Book Store on Orchard Lake Road.

JEWISH ENSEMBLE THEATRE (JET)
(248) 788-2900
One of only 12 professional Jewish theatres in the nation, JET performs throughout the year at the Jewish Community Center in West Bloomfield with 4 main stage shows, 3 educational outreach tours (off-site), and Festival of New Plays (4 weeks in the spring). Bookings for educational outreach programs are available. Contact the JET office for information on shows or bookings.

THE ETHNIC CONNECTION
(734) 662-5253
Contact: David Owens
Ann Arbor-based foursome—vocal and instrumental—perform Yiddish folk songs, Hebrew and Eastern European music for dancing or concerts.

THE KLEZMER FUSION BAND
Ann Arbor; (734) 662-7465
Contact: Neil Alexander.

ZEMIR CHORALE OF METROPOLITAN DETROIT
(313) 861-8990
Contact: Larry Katkowsky.
Music reflects the entire Jewish experience, secular and religious songs in Hebrew, English, Yiddish and Ladino (Judeo-Spanish language which evolved in Portugal and Spain).

The Jewish calendar is lunar (about 354 days in a year), differing from the secular "solar" calendar (about 365 days). Each month begins with the new moon. The Jewish "day" actually begins in the evening because the Bible says, "God created darkness first, and then there was light." So the Sabbath *(Shabbat)* and all holy days begin at sundown.

Jewish calendars begin with the biblical tradition of the date of the Creation of the World. The Christian calendar year 2000 AD corresponds to the Jewish year 5760.

Rosh Hashanah is the Jewish New Year. It is a time of self-appraisal—a spiritual cleansing of sorts. It falls in the seventh month *(Tishrei)* of the Hebrew Calendar (in the early autumn) because that is believed to be the month in which God created the world. Indulging in a "new" fruit is a common practice.

Yom Kippur (the "Day of Atonement" or forgiveness) is the holiest day of the year. It follows Rosh Hashanah, and marks the end of the **High Holy Days.** While apples and honey are traditionally eaten on Rosh Hashana to symbolize God's blessings for a "sweet" new year, Yom Kippur is observed with prayer and a day-long fast. It is ended by "breaking the fast" and engaging in a meal together with friends and family. It is a time to be spent in **Shul** (Synagogue) praying, not a day of work.

Sukkot is the eight-day festival of the harvest—"the feast of tabernacles or booths" which begins four days after Yom Kippur. A *sukkah* ("booth") is a temporary and "hastily built" hut, reminding celebrants of the time of wandering in the wilderness after the Exodus. Often erected in the back yard, or connected to the patio, the sukkah is made of wood and branches, sometimes cornstalks, and adorned with greenery, fruits and gourds. Meals and snacks are eaten in the hut.

Simchat Torah ("the celebration of the Torah") reflects the completion of the year's cycle of Torah readings (the Five Books of Moses).

Hanukkah (Chanukah) is the "Festival of Lights," lasting eight days usually in December. It commemorates the recapture of the Temple in Jerusalem by Judah Maccabee, when one day's supply of lamp oil miraculously lasted eight days.

One new candle is lit on the **menorah** (a candelabra-like stand with eight holders for candles and one more, the "shamash" for lighting the others), each night, along with the one(s) lit the night before (as the prayers are said), until all are aglow. Generally a gift or **gelt** (money) is given to the children in the home each night of Hanukkah as part of the celebration. Chocolate gold-foiled coins in a small mesh bag are often seen as part of the holiday sweet treats. While this holiday does not require certain foods to be prepared, traditional holiday cuisine would most definitely include *latkes* (fried potato pancakes) and jelly donuts. In part, the reasoning stems from the use of oil, as it was accountable for the eight days of continual light from the menorah.

Purim (meaning "lots") is the Feast of Esther, celebrated in **February or March,** to commemorate the deliverance of the Jews by Esther from the dreaded Hamen in 473 BC. The scroll of Esther is read and *Hamentashen* (three-cornered, cake-like cookies filled with fruit or poppy seeds) are eaten in remembrance of Hamen's three cornered hat, while noise makers **(groggers)** are sounded to drown out Hamen's name. A festive occasion, gifts of food are exchanged as well as given to the needy.

Passover ("the passing over"), also called **Pesach,** is an eight-day spring festival which commemorates the exodus of the Israelites from Egypt and the Angel of Death "passing over" the Jewish houses, sparing the first born sons. Before the first **Seder,** great preparation is made in the home—a cleansing,

the changing of the dishes, and removal of the *Hametz* (bread and all other leavened food products, along with anything fermented or that can be ground into flour). **Kosher for Passover** food products replace the foods in the pantry and are used in preparation of the two Seders and the week-long holiday. **The Seder** is a traditional liturgy of the story of the Exodus retold from the Haggadah. Questions are asked and answered in remembrance of the Exodus. A Seder Plate is prominent on the table—representational of symbols from the story, and a large meal with specific foods is prepared and eaten.

Shavuot is celebrated 49 days after the beginning of Passover and commemorates the giving of the Torah to Moses on Mt. Sinai. Traditional foods are dairy, including blintzes and kugels.

VISUAL ARTS

JANICE CHARACH EPSTEIN GALLERY
Jewish Community Center
West Bloomfield; (248) 661-1000
Works by Jewish artists, contemporary art addressing Jewish issues and themes, and special shows of local or historical interest.

LYNNE AVADENKA
(248) 541-0109
Original, beautifully hand-painted *ketubot* (Jewish marriage contracts) in English and Hebrew calligraphy—accurate according to Jewish law. All art work is specifically created to capture the personal taste and personality of the couple. Avadenka's work is recognized in the United States and internationally, and hangs in museums and major corporations.

DANIELLE PELEG GALLERY
4301 Orchard Lake Rd., W. Bloomfield
(Crosswinds Mall)
(248) 626-5810
A fine selection of art by noted Israeli and Jewish-American artists.

RENEE WASSERMAN GRUSKIN
(248) 661-1681
Original, handpainted Chupahs (ritual wedding canopy) for rental or purchase are hand-painted. Can later be transformed into a painting, a bed covering or sewn into a piece of sentimental clothing.

RICHARD KOZLOW
(248) 642-5512
Internationally renowned Jewish American artist exhibits frequently at local galleries as well as his Royal Oak studio. His prolific works include both paintings and sculpture with subjects ranging from landscapes to female figures to the Holocaust.

EXHIBITS

MICHIGAN JEWISH SPORTS HALL OF FAME
(248) 476-3803
Michigan Jewish Sports Hall of Fame honors athletes of Jewish descent. Exhibit is at Jewish Community Center in West Bloomfield.

TEMPLE BETH EL EXHIBITS
6400 Telegraph Rd. (at 14 Mile)
Bloomfield Hills
(248) 851-1100
Display of miniature historic synagogues from around the world, handcrafted by the late Aid Kushner, can be viewed in the library Mon-Fri 9am-5pm. Call for other dates and times. Also a large Judaic art and artifact collection.

DETROIT JEWISH HISTORICAL SOCIETY
(248) 647-5613
Contact: Judy Cantor.
Conducts number of Jewish tours of old Detroit, as well as other programs throughout the year. The group is a rich resource of information about Jewish Detroit.

HOLOCAUST MEMORIAL CENTER
6602 W. Maple Rd.(at Drake)
West Bloomfield
(248) 661-0840
Photographs, artifacts, film clips and video displays enhance awareness and understanding of World War II's greatest tragedy, in order that history not repeat itself. Closed Friday afternoons and Saturdays.

JEWISH HERITAGE WEEK
(248) 353-8828
During the second full week of May, the Michigan Region office of the American Zionist Movement (21550 W. 12 Mile, Southfield) provides display-case and bulletin-board exhibits for local public libraries.

INSTRUCTION

COHN-HADDOW CENTER FOR JUDAIC STUDIES
Wayne State University Campus
(313) 577-2679
Coordinates activities with the needs of the Jewish community and institutions of higher learning, as well as sponsoring programs and activities for the community at large.

JEWISH COMMUNITY CENTER
(248) 661-1000 (West Bloomfield)
(248) 967-4030 (Oak Park)
Offers a number of instructional programs throughout the year. Call for class schedule.

ISRAELI FOLK DANCING
Jewish Community Center
Offered Tue 7-9:45pm at the 10 Mile Jewish

Community Center, (248)-967-4030. Each evening starts out with instruction and beginning dances. Also offered at the Maple Campus Tuesday evenings 7pm-8pm (teaching), 8pm-10pm (dancing). Attendance can be at one or both sessions.

JCC EVENTS

The Jewish Community Center (JCC) hosts special events in conjunction with several other local Jewish organizations. Call (248) 661-1000 for more information about the following:

WALK FOR ISRAEL
Usually during May, this all-day affair starts with a 3.5 mile walk through local neighborhoods and past the Temple Israel complex. There are activities for the entire family and a concert.

YOM HAZIKARON
Held in April, this emotional event pays tribute to those fallen in battle for Israel.

YOM HASHOAH
Held during April, this moving event pays tribute to those who perished in the Holocaust.

JEWISH BOOK FAIR
This annual book fair was founded in 1951, and is the oldest and largest Jewish book fair in the United States. Held yearly in November, at both campus sites of the Jewish Community Center—West Bloomfield and Oak Park. All of the books sold at the book fair are either penned by Jewish authors or contain Jewish content. This 10-day event features speakers, demonstrations, workshops, authors and children's programs.

THE MACCABIAH GAMES
(734) 761-1693
Contact: Sharon Newman. Annual celebration of Jewish unity, culture and education through a world athletic competition, sanctioned by the International Olympic Committee. In 1998 Detroit played host to this huge event.

BAR OR BAT MITZVAH

Bar *Mitzvah* means "Son of the Commandment," a *Bat Mitzvah* means "Daughter of the Commandment." At the age of 13 (12 for girls), Jewish law deems a young person to be an adult, with adult responsibilities—the most important being the observance of the *Mitzvot* (the commandments handed down by God).

In a Bar or Bat Mitzvah ceremony, the child accepts and affirms his or her responsibility and commitment. In doing so, recitation of blessings, reading a portion from the *Torah* (the Five Books of Moses) and *Haftarah* (a passage from the Book of Prophets), and speaking to the congregation (in some synagogues and temples) is part of this acceptance.

The child's parents often host a large party after the service, either at lunch time or for dinner.

If invited to a Bar/Bat Mitzvah, it is more important to attend the service than the reception.

It is not appropriate to give the Bar/Bat Mitzvah gift at the service, rather at the party. If the gift is money, it should be placed in an envelope with the Bar/Bat Mitzvah person's name on the front, and handed to the parent. There is usually a table set up for boxed or larger-sized gifts.

YOU'RE INVITED

Weddings and Bar/Bat Mtizvahs are joyous occasions to which Gentile friends are often invited. Here is a brief guide for those unfamiliar with the customs.

SYNAGOGUE ETIQUETTE

Synagogue etiquette varies depending on whether you are attending an Orthodox, Conservative or Reform synagogue or temple; but in general:

Men should wear slacks and shirts (suits and sport coats with a tie are preferred). Women should wear appropriate skirts or dresses, shoulders should not be bare. There are synagogues that frown upon women wearing slacks.

Some synagogues prefer women to wear hats or have their heads covered. Men should wear a *yarmulke* (skull cap) in an Orthodox or Conservative synagogue; in Reform temples, this is an option. Some Jewish men and women will wear a *tallis* (prayer shawl) draped over their shoulders (it is more common for men to wear them). If a man does not have a yarmulke, one will be provided. (If it is a synagogue that considers a yarmulke the norm, the man should put one on in respect for the tradition.) Prayer shawls also are provided, but are less mandatory.

Visitors may sit anywhere in the sanctuary, unless it is an Orthodox synagogue, where the men and women are seated separately. Regardless of your religious affiliation, you should stand when the congregation is asked to rise from their seats. The service can be followed along in the prayer book provided, and it is considered polite to at least open the book and follow along, regardless of your participation.

SYNAGOGUES *(A partial list)*

CONSERVATIVE

ADAT SHALOM SYNAGOGUE
29901 Middlebelt, Farmington Hills
(248) 851-5100

BEIT KODESH
31840 W. Seven Mile Rd., Livonia
(248) 477-8974

BETH ABRAHAM HILLEL MOSES
5075 W. Maple Rd., W. Bloomfield
(248) 851-6880

BETH ACHIM
21100 W. 12 Mile Rd., Southfield
(248) 352-8670

BETH SHALOM
14601 W. Lincoln Rd., Oak Park
(248) 547-7970

BETH TEPHILATH MOSES
146 South Ave., Mt. Clemens
(810) 465-0641

B'NAI MOSHE
6800 Drake Rd., W. Bloomfield
(248) 788-0600

**ISAAC AGREE
DOWNTOWN SYNAGOGUE**
1457 Griswold, Detroit
(313) 961-9328

SHAAREY ZEDEK
27375 Bell Rd., Southfield
(248) 357-5544

SHAAREY ZEDEK B'NAI ISRAEL CENTER
4200 Walnut Lake Rd., W. Bloomfield
(248) 681-5353

HUMANISTIC
THE BIRMINGHAM TEMPLE
28611 W. 12 Mile Rd., Farmington Hills
(248) 477-1410

JEWISH CULTURAL SOCIETY
JCC of Washtenaw County
2935 Birch Hollow Dr., Ann Arbor
(734) 665-5761

MESSIANIC
CONGREGATION BETH MESSIAH
25835 Southfield Rd., Southfield
(248) 559-1535

CONGREGATION SHEMA YISRAEL
28600 Lahser, Southfield
(248) 358-3850

RECONSTRUCTIONIST
CONGREGATION T'CHIYAH
404 S. Pleasant, Royal Oak
(248) 542-0900
Meets at Royal Oak Women's Club.
4605 Cass, Detroit
(313) 822-0009
Meets at Wayne County Medical Society

ORTHODOX
AGUDAS YISROEL-MOGEN ABRAHAM
15751 W. Lincoln, Southfield
(248) 552-1971

BAIS CHABAD OF FARMINGTON HILLS
32000 Middlebelt Rd., Farmington Hills
(248) 855-2910

SHOMREY EMUNAH
25451 Southfield Rd., Southfield
(248) 559-1533

YOUNG ISRAEL OF OAK PARK
15140 W. 10 Mile Rd., Oak Park
(248) 967-3655

YOUNG ISRAEL OF SOUTHFIELD
27705 Lahser, Southfield
(248) 358-0514

REFORM
TEMPLE BETH EL
7400 Telegraph Rd., Bloomfield Hills
(248) 851-1100

BETH ISAAC
2730 Edsel Dr., Trenton
(734) 675-0355

TEMPLE EMANU-EL
14450 W. 10 Mile Rd., Oak Park
(248) 967-4020

TEMPLE ISRAEL
5725 Walnut Lake Rd., W. Bloomfield
(248) 661-5700

TEMPLE KOL AMI
5085 Walnut Lake Rd., W. Bloomfield
(248) 661-0040

TEMPLE SHIR SHALOM
3999 Walnut Lake Rd., W. Bloomfield
(248) 737-8700

CONGREGATION SHIR TIKVAH
3633 W. Big Beaver Rd., Troy
(248) 619-9669

SEPHARDIC
SEPHARDIC COMMUNITY OF GREATER DETROIT
21100 W. 12 Mile Rd., Southfield
(248) 788-1006

TRADITIONAL
CONGREGRATION B'NAI DAVID
5642 W. Maple Rd., W. Bloomfield
(248) 855-5007

JEWISH WEDDING GLOSSARY

Aufruf: Calling up of a couple to the Torah on the Shabbat before their wedding.

B'deken: The ritual veiling of the bride by the groom.

Breaking of the Glass: Done by the Chatan (groom) at the conclusion of the ceremony. Guests usually respond with "Mazel Tov!"

Chupah: The wedding canopy. Usually fabric with four corners attached to four poles and stretched over the couple. Many couples use a tallis (prayer shawl). It is a sign of God's presence and symbolizes the couple's new home.

Groom's Tish: The groom's table, where the Chatan, his groomsmen, and male family members gather for song and dance before the wedding ceremony.

Kallah: The bride.

Ketubah: Marriage contract.

Mizinke: A joyous dance towards the end of the simcha (reception), which honors parents who have brought their last daughter or son to the wedding canopy.

Yichud: A short time of seclusion immediately following the marriage for the Chatan & Kallah. Because of this, receiving lines are not a traditional part of Jewish weddings.

ORGANIZATIONS

JEWISH COMMUNITY CENTER (JCC)
Main Campus
6600 W. Maple Rd., W. Bloomfield
(248) 661-1000
JCC—Oak Park Campus
15110 W. 10 Mile, Oak Park
(248) 967-4030
The JCC main campus in W. Bloomfield is a huge facility housing organizations, educational programs, entertainment and art programs, clubs, a health and fitness center and swimming pool. Recreational classes for all ages, day camps, art and music classes, religious festivities and other activities are held there.
The **Oak Park campus** is smaller, but offers a similar mix of programs and athletic facilities.

WINDSOR JEWISH COMMUNITY CENTRE
1641 Oullette Ave., Windsor
(519) 973-1772

JEWISH COMMUNITY COUNCIL
6735 Telegraph Rd., Bloomfield Twp.
(248) 642-5393
Provides services to promote Jewish interests and values; also advocates on behalf of Jews locally and around the world. The Council serves as an umbrella body for more than 200 organizations.

JEWISH FEDERATION OF METROPOLITAN DETROIT
6735 Telegraph Rd., Suite 30
Bloomfield Hills; (248) 642-4260
In partnership with its agencies, it serves as

an umbrella for a large number of agency related services: Agency for Jewish Education, B'nai Brith Youth Organization, Jewish Day Schools, Fresh Air Society, Hebrew Free Loan Association, Hillel Foundations, Jewish Community Center, Jewish Community Council, Jewish Family Service, Jewish Federation Apartments, and Jewish Home for the Aged. Other programs sponsored by the Federation include; Jewish Community Archives, Jewish Information and Referral Service, Michigan/Israel Connection, Michigan Jewish Conference and the Neighborhood Project. FEDERATION RESOURCE LINE: (248) 559-4411 Helpful volunteers answer questions related to the Jewish community.

JEWISH GENEALOGY SOCIETY OF MICHIGAN
(249) 855-3970
Contact Bomi Silverman. Hosts workshops and special events.

NATIONAL COUNCIL OF JEWISH WOMEN (NCJW), Greater Detroit Section
26400 Lahser Road, Ste. 100, Southfield
(248) 355-3300
Established in 1893, it is the oldest women's volunteer organization in America. It is inspired by Jewish values and works through a program of research, education, advocacy and community service to improve the quality of life for women, children and families and strives to ensure individual rights and freedoms for all. NCJW also is the local organizer of the "Race for the Cure."

SOCIETY FOR HUMANISTIC JUDAISM
28611 W. 12 Mile Rd., Farmington Hills
(248) 477-1410
Organized in 1969, the Society's mission is to mobilize people to celebrate Jewish identity and culture consistent with a humanistic philosophy of life. Gathers and creates educational and programmatic materials, including holiday and life cycle celebrations; publishes a tri-quarterly journal available by subscription.

AMERICAN ARABIC AND JEWISH FRIENDS OF METROPOLITAN DETROIT
6985 Woodward Ave., Bloomfield Hills
(248) 489-3858
Contact: Shelly Komer Jackier
A program of Greater Detroit Interfaith Roundtable established in 1981 to promote greater understanding between two communities in southeastern Michigan. Welcomes as members all American citizens of Arabic and Jewish descent who support this objective. Sponsors annual dinner to fund scholarship.

MEDIA

PRINT
THE JEWISH NEWS
27676 Franklin Rd., Southfield
(248) 354-6060
Weekly newspaper (every Thursday) for the greater Detroit Jewish community. Includes world events and local interest stories that affect or involve the Jewish community. Also covers entertainment, charity events, single social network, obituaries, real estate and food, plus special annual supplements such as school and summer camp guides.

WASHTENAW JEWISH NEWS
2935 Birch Hollow Dr., Ann Arbor
(313) 971-1800
A free publication for the Ann Arbor area loaded with local information, articles of Jewish interest and events.

JEWISH BUSINESS EXCHANGE
33290 W. 14 Mile Rd., Ste. 423, W. Bloomfield
(248) 932-5797
Comprehensive Jewish business and professional networking directory.

RADIO
WPON AM 1460
(248) 332-8883.
"Jewish Hour" with Rabbi Herschel Finman Friday 3-4pm.

WEB SITES

These sites have many links:

www.thinkjewish.com

www.koshernet.com

rashi.tiac.net/yihud

www.uscj.org/uscjo1

www.JewishAmerica.com

www.jewishdetroit100.org

OY DU JOUR (Jewish Post of New York's website of the month)

www.melizo.com/jewishpost/jpoye

SHAAREYZEDEK

Local site has many links of Jewish interest plus listings for Detroit area activities.
www.shaareyzedek.org

The Torah is a scroll of parchment containing the first five books of Hebrew Scriptures. It is used in a synagogue during services.

YIDDISH EXPRESSIONS

Yiddish is a High German language written in Hebrew characters that is spoken by Jews and descendants of Jews of central and eastern European origin. Short for *yidish daytsh*, literally, "Jewish German," from Middle High German *judisch diutsch*. Just a few examples of expressions that have become part of American English:

• I've never seen such *chutzpah!* (nervy, unmitigated gall)

• Don't be such a *kvetch!* (complainer —usually a constant complainer.)

• *Mazel tov!* (Congratulations!)

• *Oy Vey!* (Oh No! Literally, "Woe is me!")

• Now there's a real *mensch.* (a real human being—in reference to a good and decent person)

• Have a little *nosh.* (snack)

• I've been *schlepping* these shopping bags all day long. (hauling, dragging)

• Isn't that just like Howard Stern, he's always doing the same *schtick.* (particular routine)

• He loves to *kibbitz!* (kid or joke around)

• When it comes to wine, she is quite the *mavin.* (expert, connoisseur)

• Before setting up a business meeting, *shmooze* a little bit. (chit chat, idle talk)

• And finally, the difference between a *schlemiel* and a *schlemazel:* A schlemiel steals a car from a schlemazel (who left his keys in it)...and gets caught (before he leaves the parking lot).

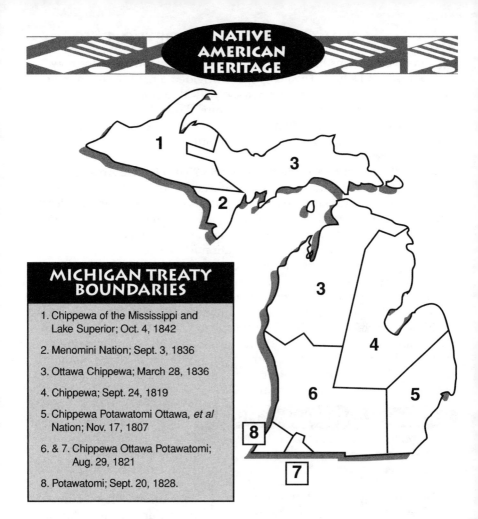

MICHIGAN TREATY BOUNDARIES

1. Chippewa of the Mississippi and Lake Superior; Oct. 4, 1842

2. Menomini Nation; Sept. 3, 1836

3. Ottawa Chippewa; March 28, 1836

4. Chippewa; Sept. 24, 1819

5. Chippewa Potawatomi Ottawa, *et al* Nation; Nov. 17, 1807

6. & 7. Chippewa Ottawa Potawatomi; Aug. 29, 1821

8. Potawatomi; Sept. 20, 1828.

The Great Lakes region is the traditional home to more than 33 different American Indian tribes, bands and nations. Most speak a dialect known as Ojibwa. Others come from the Iroquois Confederacy or have more recently migrated to this area from throughout the American continent, also known as "Turtle Island."

The original lifestyle of American Indians was tied closely to the land and what it offered. Game animals, fishing, food gathering and some small family supportive gardening were more than sufficient to meet the needs. Villages were often relocated based on the cycles of the year, weather, the need for trade and sometimes in the interest of avoiding or preventing conflict.

By necessity, all housing, clothing and transportation items were made from what was provided by nature. Possession of material wealth was not the goal of any individual; instead the benefit of all—the family, clan, village, band or tribe—was the primary concern.

NATIVE AMERICANS IN DETROIT

American Indians have always gathered to trade in the place now known as Detroit. The geography provided a natural site to travel by either land or water. The area was so critical to commerce between tribes that only the traders themselves were allowed into the territory. War parties and the other members of the tribes were required to wait in outlying areas (such as Walpole Island, Point Pelee, Wyandotte, Tecumseh and Pontiac).

Today, the Detroit area is home to nearly 25,000 Native Americans from as many as 90 different tribes, bands and nations from across the United States and Canada. To serve the needs of this population at least 12 different agencies offer a range of services—from social activities to tending to critical health needs, including medical, dental, substance-abuse counseling and prevention education for teens.

In the past, much effort was expended in dealing with the "Indian problem." Aggressive actions such as wars, chemical warfare and forcible removal to lands in the west took place in order to force the Indians off the land to make room for lumber and agriculture industries. Children were removed from their homes to "educate the Indian out of them," and were punished for speaking their language and clinging to traditional ways. These actions almost caused the fabric of the Native American lifestyle—clan identification, language, songs, ceremonies and prayers—to wither and disappear.

In the past 30 to 35 years however, there has been a resurgence of tradition and culture through the spiritual and language reconnection to previous generations. More Native Americans are attending ceremonies, going to activities, going to universities, becoming substance-free, learning ancestral songs and dances, and returning to their language. Native American communities around the state sponsor pow wows almost every weekend.

INDIAN NAMES IN MICHIGAN

The Ojibwa language is the probable source of many place names in Michigan. Here's a partial list:

Cheboygan	Munising
Chesaning	Muskegon
Dowagiac	Naubinway
Genesee	Newaygo
Ishpeming	Okemos
Kalamazoo	Onaway
Kawkawlin	Ontonagon
Keweenaw	Otsego
Mackinac	Owosso
Island	Petoskey
Manistee	Pinconning
Manistique	Port Sanilac
Manitou Beach	Saginaw
Mecosta	Saugatuck
Menominee	Sebewaing
Michiana	Tecumseh
Michigamme	Wyandotte

MICHIGAN CHIPPEWAS

Seven distinct tribes comprise the 20th century Michigan Chippewas. Each modern tribe is the descendant of historic 19th century bands which have continued to occupy a site in or near their historic village. The name has two consistent spellings, with some groups favoring Chippewa and others Ojibwa. The most consistent translation connects the word with an Ojibwa root word meaning "puckered up" and refers to the gathered stitching of the Chippewa-styled moccasin.

—*James M. McClurken, Ph.D.*

Chippewa moccasins with one-piece front seam, late 18th century.

TOUR — FRIDAY FARE

[D-F/2-4] A Detroit-area itinerary for exploring Native American culture focuses on exhibits at **Cranbrook Institute of Science** in Bloomfield Hills and a visit to the **Southeastern Michigan Indian (SEMI) Center** in Center Line for lunch (Friday only) and shopping. *To get to the SEMI Center, take I-696 to the Van Dyke exit. Go south to the first light, and turn right on Bernice. At the stop sign, turn right on Lawrence and proceed to 26641.* Arrive about noon when the cafeteria opens, and choose from the various entrées on the American Indian menu. Then visit **Crafts of Many Tribes,** where genuine Native American-made jewelry, pottery, dream catchers and paintings are for sale.

To get to Cranbrook, return to I-696 and take it west to I-75 north. Exit I-75 at Big Beaver (16 Mile) and go west to Woodward. Proceed north on Woodward; watch for the Cranbrook entrance on the west side between Lone Pine (17 Mile) and Long Lake (18 Mile) Roads. Follow the signs to the **Science Institute.** The Hall of Anthropology on the main floor features dioramas depicting the lifestyle of Woodland Indians and a collection of clothing and artifacts. (The exhibit is not on view when major traveling shows are in town.) Display cases on the lower level are devoted to crafts such as basketry, quilling and beadwork. At the **planetarium show,** gaze at constellations named after Indian legends. When you're done with the exhibits, visit the **Wigwam Village** set up most of the year on the grounds of the Nature Place behind the museum.

[A-B/2-3] One of the best places in Michigan to learn about American Indians is East Lansing, 1-1/2 *hours west of Detroit via I-96.* This tour explores the **Nokomis Learning Center** in neighboring Okemos, a craft shop in East Lansing and a museum on the campus of Michigan State University.

To get to the Nokomis Learning Center, take the Okemos Road exit north from I-96. When you reach the town, turn right on Hamilton. Turn left at the first light, which is Marsh Road. Take Marsh past Grand River and Central Park Drive, behind Meridian Mall. The center is part of the Meridian Township complex, which includes municipal buildings and an historic village. The center's American Indian exhibits and programs focus on the **Woodland Indians of the Great Lakes**—the Ojibwa, Ottawa and Potawatomi tribes, also known as the People of Three Fires. *(For hours and program information, see "Museums" listing.)*

To find **Beads 4 U,** a small craft shop just east of the MSU campus, *go west on East Grand River to 1017.* Many of the traders at pow wows shop here for materials and supplies to make crafts. Beads 4 U stocks everything from raw materials, patterns and tools to beads, quills, raw hide, garment leather and hackle (chicken feathers). It's also a good place to find finished Native American art, books, calendars, records, tapes and CDs.

To learn more about Native American history and culture, venture onto the MSU campus *(Abbott entrance on Grand River)* to visit the **MSU Museum**. *It's on West Circle Drive next to Beaumont Tower.* Exhibits change frequently, but generally a gallery is devoted to Great Lakes Indians.

OPTION FOR AN EXTENDED TRIP

From the Lansing area, it's only an hour *(on U.S. 27 north)* to **Mount Pleasant,** home of the Saginaw Chippewa Indian Tribe of Michigan. The tribe runs a gambling casino, campground and hotel. **Soaring Eagle Casino** *(2395 S. Leaton Rd. at Broadway)* offers blackjack, a money wheel, high-stakes bingo, and 1,700 slot and video poker machines. *Call 1-888-7-EAGLE-7 or (517) 775-7777.*

LACROSSE

Lacrosse is the oldest organized sport in North America. French and English colonists found the Indians playing a fast, rough game called *baggataway.* Around 1840, Canadians revised the rules and called it *lacrosse* because the curved end of the playing stick resembled a bishop's staff, or *crosier.* For information about local lacrosse teams, contact:

● The Michigan Scholastic Lacrosse Association, Bingham Farms; (810) 644-7400

WHAT DID WE CALL OURSELVES BEFORE COLUMBUS CAME?

When the first Europeans arrived—Columbus and his crew—they called us Indians, because of the obvious reason: Columbus thought he was lost in India. But what did *we* call ourselves? … In every single tribe, even today, when you translate the word that we had for ourselves … it was always something that translated to basically the same thing. In our language it's *Ninuog,* or "the people," "the human beings."… So when the Pilgrims arrived here, we knew who we were, but we didn't know what they were. So we called them *Awaunageesuck,* or "the strangers," because they were the ones who were alone, they were the ones that we didn't know, but we knew each other. And we were the human beings.

—Tall Oak of the Narragansett Tribe

A great deal of what we know as Michigan has been influenced over the years by the presence of the original people. We didn't journey here for the jobs, the better life and all the things recent emigres look for here. We were always here; so when the Archie Bunkers and John Waynes out there tell us to "go back where you came from," we just stand there and smile, for we are back where we came from.

—Thurman Bear

INDIAN TRAILS

The impact that American Indians made on the Detroit area is visible in the many trails that branch out from the city today. Michigan Avenue, or U.S. 12, was the **Sauk Fox Trail.** Grand River, Fort Street, Jefferson, Woodward, Gratiot and Van Dyke all followed the original trails that led into the interior of the state.

Interestingly, several streets follow trails the Native Americans used so they could come and go without being detected by the occupants and residents of early Detroit. East and West Grand Boulevard was built on a trail that gave the tribes a route to come downstream south, portage around the fort or town, and then reenter the river out of view. The same is probably true of East and West Outer Drive.

The faint remains of the **Saginaw Trail,** which led to Pontiac and beyond, can still be seen in Royal Oak behind the Starr House on Crooks Road, just south of 13 Mile. Rochester Road is the former **Paint Creek Trail.**

For more information about Native American Indian trails, contact the Michigan Historical Center at 1-800-827-7007.

CULINARY CONTRIBUTIONS

The Indians of the Great Lakes region planted corn, beans and squash. They tapped trees for maple syrup and gathered wild rice. They hunted deer and other wild game, including the indigenous wild turkey. (When the British introduced the bird to Europe, they named it after what they called guinea fowl, which were birds apparently imported from Turkey.) Buffalo hunting was limited primarily to the Great Plains, where other food sources (that were far less dangerous to hunt) were not so abundant.

Corn bread was a winter staple and was often sweetened with maple sugar and dried berries. The Northeast Indians were the first to barbecue; later the Southwest Indians added spices to create the sauces we know today.

Women—who did the farming—raised sunflowers, the seeds of which they pounded into flour. They also gathered many greens, onions, garlic, mushrooms, tubers, roots, nuts and more than 30 varieties of fruits, which they dried for winter use.

● *March is maple-sugaring time. Demonstrations are offered at Cranbrook Institute of Science, Bloomfield Hills (248-645-3200); University of Michigan– Dearborn (313-593-5338); Lloyd A. Stage Outdoor Education Center, Troy (248-524-3567); Indian Springs, Hudson Mills and Kensington Metroparks (1-800-477-3191); and Independence Oaks, Clarkston (248-625-6473).*

FOOD

Although there are no bonafide Native American restaurants in the Detroit area, the Southeastern Michigan Indian Center in Center Line serves authentic foods on Fridays at lunchtime (see "Friday Fare" tour). Also, food booths at pow wows offer "Indian dogs" (fry-bread, or fried bread, wrapped around a hot dog), corn soup, wild rice, buffalo meat and sometimes even bear.

**SOUTHEASTERN MICHIGAN
INDIAN CENTER
26641 Lawrence, Center Line
(810) 756-1350**
Fri noon: Luncheon based on a Native American Indian menu includes fry-bread, buffalo, whitefish, turkey and Indian tacos.

**BUTCHER BOY FOOD PRODUCTION
13869 Herbert St., Warren
(810) 779-0600**

Mon-Fri 9am-5pm, Sat 9am-3pm. Specializes in wild game, including buffalo and venison.

SHOPS

In the past, genuine "Native American-made" goods were available only at pow wows or local Indian centers. But the popularity of American Indian design has given rise to the growth of commercial shops and art galleries. Be sure to ask whether the artwork, crafts and other items for sale are made by Native American Indians.

**CRAFTS OF MANY TRIBES
Southeastern Michigan Indian Center
26641 Lawrence, Center Line
(810) 756-1350**
Mon-Fri 9am-5pm. Shop contains jewelry, books and pottery. Most items are made by local craftspeople. All profits support the SEMI Center.

THE AMERICAN BISON, more commonly called buffalo, is the largest North American land mammal. Huge herds once ranged from Mexico to Canada and from Pennsylvania and the Carolinas to west of the Rockies.

When Europeans arrived in America, there were an estimated 30 million to 60 million bison in this area. By 1870, the bison numbered 5.5 million. The westward-moving pioneers and railroad workers were killing bison by the thousands, taking only the choicest pieces—the hump and tongues—to eat. By the 1880s, fewer than 1,000 were left on the continent—two-thirds of them in Canada. Today, the herds have increased to more than 100,000; they're kept mostly on privately owned ranches and government preserves.

For the Plains Indians, the bison was the most important game animal. Its hide furnished material for tepees and robes; its meat was eaten fresh or preserved as *pemmican* by drying and pounding.

Bison meat is becoming increasingly popular with health-conscious people for its purity and extremely low fat content.

For a list of sources that sell buffalo meat or to see a herd grazing on Michigan grass, contact the Michigan Bison Association, 4721 Taber Rd., South Branch, MI 48761; (517) 257-4821.

● **The Buffalo Cookbook: The Low Fat Solution to Eating Red Meat** *is filled with bison facts and is beautifully illustrated with photos of Native American artifacts provided by local collectors. The book's author is Franklin-based food writer Ruth Mossok Johnston; the cover illustration of a Native*

American buffalo hunter was painted by local artist David McCall Johnston. The cookbook is available at local bookstores.

BEADS 4 U
1017 E. Grand River, East Lansing
(just E of MSU campus)
(517) 351-8168
Mon-Fri 10am-7pm, Sat 10am-5pm. Raw materials, supplies and patterns for making Native American arts and crafts *(see "Mid-Michigan" tour),* including beads, shells, quills, hides, horse hair and feathers. Also finished art, books, records, tapes, CDs and calendars. For a catalog, send $2 to P.O. Box 868, East Lansing, MI 48826.

FOUR DIRECTIONS
329 S. Main St., Ann Arbor
(734) 996-9250
Mon-Tue 10am-7pm, Wed-Thu 10am-9pm, Fri-Sat 10am-10pm, Sun 1-5pm. American Indian jewelry, books, fossils and more.

GREAT CANADIAN
TRADING POST COMPANY
3025 Huron Church Rd., Windsor
(Lambton Plaza)
(519) 966-4716
Sat-Thu 9am-7pm, Fri 9am-9pm. Features Six Nations Indian art and sculpture, wild rice and maple syrup, Native American-made moccasins and mukluks, and a wide selection of Eskimo and Inuit soapstone carvings.

BRUSHER'S ANN ARBOR ANTIQUES MARKET
5055 Ann Arbor-Saline Rd., Ann Arbor (Washtenaw Farm Council grounds; Exit 175 south off I-94) (313) 662-9453
First and third weekends of the month, early spring through late fall. Among the 300 vendors are some specialists in American Indian crafts and artifacts.

ART GALLERIES
Although not owned by American Indians, these galleries specialize in Native American art of the Southwest.

COWBOY TRADER
251 Merrill, Birmingham (248) 647-8833
Tues-Fri 10:30am-5pm, Sat 10am-4pm. Authentic Indian artwork. Hosts annual all-American Indian art show featuring dealers from three states in January.

MESA ARTS
32800 Franklin Rd. (at 14 Mile), Franklin (248) 851-9949
Tue-Sat 11am-5pm. No longer exclusively devoted to Southwest design, this eclectic gallery features Native American wall art, jewelry, textiles, ceramics and kachinas.

NATIVE WEST
863 W. Ann Arbor Trail, Plymouth (734) 455-8838
Mon-Wed, Sat 10am-6pm; Thu-Fri 10am-8pm; Sun noon-5pm. Southwest art, including jewelry, handmade Navaho rugs, sand paintings and kachinas. Member of the Indian Arts & Crafts Association.

THE PARK GALLERY
22 S. Main, Clawson; (248) 288-9383
Tue-Fri 11am-7pm; Sat 10am-5pm. Authentic American Indian antiquities, including arrowheads, headdresses and blankets.

MAIL ORDER
NOC BAY TRADING COMPANY
P.O. Box 295, 1133 Washington Ave. Escanaba, MI 49829; (906) 789-0505
Beadwork supplies, jewelry findings, trade silver, bells, porcupine quills, books, blankets, recordings, custom-made bustles, finger weaving and much more. The $3 catalog comes with a coupon for $3 toward your first order.

MUSEUMS
CRANBROOK INSTITUTE OF SCIENCE
1221 N. Woodward, Bloomfield Hills (248) 645-3200
Mon-Thu 10am-5pm, Fri-Sat 10am-10pm, Sun noon-5pm. Display of American Indian history in Hall of Anthropology contains artifacts of local significance; crafts on lower level. Outdoor Wigwam Village on Nature Place grounds. (Call ahead: Sometimes major traveling shows replace Native American exhibit in Hall of Anthropology.)

DETROIT INSTITUTE OF ARTS
5200 Woodward, Detroit (313) 833-7900
Wed-Fri 11am-4pm, Sat-Sun 11am-5pm. American Indian collection in Gallery N101 displays artifacts from the Plains, Northeast and Southeast Woodlands, Great Lakes, Southwest and West, Northwest Coast, Alaskan and Arctic cultures.

DREAM CATCHERS
are thought to have originated in the northeastern United States. American Indians believed that the power of the dream catcher was enhanced with prayer, and that when the catchers were hung over a baby's crib, only sweet dreams would come to the child.

DETROIT HISTORICAL MUSEUM
5401 Woodward, Detroit; (313) 833-1805
Wed-Fri 9:30am-5pm, Sat-Sun 10am-5pm.
Exhibits include American Indian involvement in the history of the city from the time the first French fur traders arrived.

RUTHVEN EXHIBIT MUSEUM
University of Michigan
1109 Geddes, Ann Arbor
(734) 764-0478
Tue-Sat 9am-5pm, Sun 1-5pm. Campus museum contains artifacts from Native American and Inuit cultures and dioramas of daily life.

MICHIGAN STATE UNIVERSITY MUSEUM
W. Circle Dr., East Lansing
(517) 355-2370
Mon, Wed, Fri 9am-5pm, Thu 9am-9pm, Sat 10am-5pm, Sun 1-5pm. Hall of Great Lakes depicts the culture and history of American Indians of Michigan. Rotating collection and traveling shows. Call for current showings.

NOKOMIS LEARNING CENTER
5153 Marsh Rd., Okemos
(517) 349-5777
Tue-Fri 10am-5pm; Sat noon-5pm; first Sun of month noon-5pm, with special program at 2pm. Programs and exhibits concern the history of the tribes living in the Great Lakes region before the arrival of settlers. Traditional and contemporary Native American art is featured. Plans call for a Woodland Indian Village on the grounds. Arts festivals, with dance and musical performances, are scheduled. Gift store stocks arts and crafts.

WYANDOTTE MUSEUM
Ford-McNichols Home
2610 Biddle Ave., Wyandotte
(734) 246-4520
Mon-Fri 9am-5pm, guided tours noon-4pm; first Sun of month 2-5pm. Displays chronicle the development of the town from an Indian village through the 19th century.

The downriver city of Wyandotte owes its name to the term Wendat, *which the Huron Indians used to refer to themselves. The Hurons were an Iroquoian tribe whose original homeland was in southwestern Ontario. After 1650, they joined the Ottawas in controlling the fur trade in the Upper Lakes region. By the 1800s, most lived near Detroit.*

The Thunderbird motif is one of many used in quill- and beadwork.

PORCUPINE QUILLWORK is the best known decorative technique of the Woodland Indians—a tradition that has been unique to North America since a few hundred years before Columbus landed. The quills are dyed and then sewn, wrapped, spliced, plaited, chained or netted to decorate buckskin clothes, knife sheaths, pipe stems, birchbark boxes and medicine bags. Because of the amount of time and patience it takes to make one piece, only a few Native Americans produce elaborately quilled items today. On a bark box that's just a few inches wide, there can be more than 1,000 individual quills! These handicrafts can command high prices, but often you can find simple quilled pieces for sale at pow wows. Examples of fine quillwork art are on display at Cranbrook Institute of Science.

MICHIGAN TRIBES

*There are 11 federally recognized tribes
and four historic tribes in Michigan.*

LOWER PENINSULA
**SAGINAW CHIPPEWA
INDIAN TRIBE**
7070 E. Broadway, Mt. Pleasant
(517) 772-5700
Pow wows, campground, hotel, casino, bingo
and other games.
**Soaring Eagle Casino & Hotel; 1-888-7-
EAGLE-7 or (517) 775-7777**

**GRAND TRAVERSE BAND
OF OTTAWA AND CHIPPEWA INDIANS**
2605 N.W. Bayshore Dr., Suttons Bay
(616) 271-3538
Pow wows, casino, super bingo palace.
Leelanau Sands Casino; 1-800-922-2946

POKAGON BAND OF POTAWATOMI
53237 Town Hall Rd., Dowagiac
(616) 782-6323
Labor Day Weekend pow wow in South
Bend, Indiana.

**LITTLE TRAVERSE BAY
BAND OF ODAWA INDIANS**
1345 U.S. 31 N., Petoskey; (616) 348-3410
Homecoming Pow Wow in August at Ottawa
Stadium on M-119.

**LITTLE RIVER BAND
OF OTTAWA INDIANS**
409 Water St., Manistee; (616) 723-8288
Pow wow in July at Manistee County
Fairgrounds on M-22.

HURON POTAWATOMI
2221 1-1/2 Mile Rd., Fulton
(616) 729-5151

WIGWAMS AND OTHER DWELLINGS

In the Great Lakes region, perhaps the most widely used housing was the bark-covered wigwam. This dwelling could be either dome- or cone-shaped. Construction started with a frame of small, flexible trees, or saplings. These were stuck firmly into the ground in a circle, then bent overhead in an arch and tied together with tough bark fibers or with rawhide. Next, more slender branches were wrapped in circles around the bent poles and fastened to them. Slabs of bark were tied to this frame to form the roof and walls. Openings were left for a door and a smoke hole. Platforms inside served as beds, chairs and shelves.

The Iroquois and other New York tribes built the larger longhouse. Five to a dozen families might live together in such a structure.

The tepee, or tipi—used by nomadic Plains tribes—usually consisted of buffalo hides stretched over a cone formed of tent poles; it was strong and easy to move. Tribes in the South and West used the wickiup, made of brush or mats stretched over arched poles.

Also in the South, certain tribes built winter houses using clay plastered to a framework of poles and woven twigs, with a domed or cone-shaped roof. The Seminoles in Florida used palmetto-thatched shelters without sidewalls; many still live in this type of house. The early Pueblos in the Southwest built multistory "apartment houses" high in the cliffs.

● *Six Michigan State Parks rent authentic tepee
replicas to campers. For details, see "Camping" listing.*

Modern "pop tents" are patterned after wigwams>

INDIAN GAMING IN MICHIGAN

Seven federally recognized American Indian tribes run nine gaming casinos in Michigan *(see "Michigan Tribes")*. Two are in the Lower Peninsula (Soaring Eagle Casino in Mount Pleasant and Leelanau Sands Casino in Suttons Bay); the others are in St. Ignace, Sault Ste. Marie and other Upper Peninsula locations. The casinos offer a variety of games, including bingo, poker, blackjack, dice, slot machines and video poker machines.

Indian gaming is big business with most profits going to the tribes. Gaming is credited with creating jobs, boosting local economies and Michigan tourism, and raising capital for tribal community development.

UPPER PENINSULA
**SAULT STE. MARIE TRIBE
OF CHIPPEWA INDIANS**
523 Ashnum St., Sault Ste. Marie
(906) 635-6050
Pow wows, hotel, restaurant, museum,
casinos, bingo, shopping.
Vegas Kewaden Casino, Sault Ste. Marie
(906) 632-0530 or 1-800-539-2346
Kewaden Shores Casino, St. Ignace
(906) 643-7071 or 1-800-626-9878

**BAY MILLS CHIPPEWA
INDIAN COMMUNITY AT BRIMLEY**
(906) 248-3241
Campground, pow wows, casino, bingo.
King's Club Casino; (906) 248-3227
Bay Mills Hotel & Casino; (906) 248-3715

**KEWEENAW BAY
INDIAN COMMUNITY AT BARAGA**
(906) 353-6623
Pow wow, campground, motel, casino, bingo.
Ojibwa Casino; (906) 353-6333

**LAC VIEUX DESERT BAND
OF LAKE SUPERIOR CHIPPEWA
INDIANS AT WATERSMEET**
(906) 358-4577
Pow wows, gift shop, casino, bingo hall.
Lac Vieux Desert Casino
(906) 358-4226 or 358-4227

**HANNAHVILLE POTAWATOMI
INDIAN COMMUNITY AT WILSON**
N. 14911 Hannahville B-1 Rd.
(906) 466-2932
Chip-In Casino
(906) 466-2686 or 1-800-682-6040

HISTORIC TRIBES
**BURT LAKE BAND OF OTTAWA
AND CHIPPEWA INDIANS**
6461 E. Brutus Rd., Brutus
(616) 529-6113

**SWAN CREEK BLACK RIVER CONFED-
ERATED OJIBWA TRIBES OF MICHIGAN**
1220 Court St., Saginaw
(517) 799-0006

**GUN LAKE BAND OF GRAND RIVER
OTTAWA INDIANS**
5721 Grand River Dr., Grand Ledge
(517) 627-0244

**GRAND RIVER BAND
OF OTTAWA INDIANS**
307 Michigan N.E., Grand Rapids
(616) 458-8759

POW WOWS

Pow wows take place nearly every weekend in Michigan starting in the spring. They include dance competitions, pageants and telling of tribal legends, as well as food booths and traders selling souvenirs, arts and crafts. A complete calendar of events is available from the Michigan Commission on Indian Affairs in Lansing (517-373-0654).

Originally, pow wows, or "celebrations," took place in the spring to celebrate the new beginning of life. It was a time for people to get together to sing, dance, renew old friendships and make new ones. Pow wows are still an important part of the lives of Native Americans. Many families pack up and go "on the circuit," camping and enjoying the traditional activities. The celebrations incorporate the entire lifestyle and heritage of American Indians, including trading, music, dance, family and spirituality.

CIRCLES AND CEREMONIES

The circle is an important symbol to American Indians. At pow wows, the dancers are in the center of a circle, the drums and the audience form a circle around them, and the concessions form yet another circle around the gathering. The circle brings people closer together—closer to family, friends and their culture.

The dance arena is in the shape of a circle, representing the cycles of life, the moon, the sun and the earth. The arbor, in the center of the circle, is constructed to shade the drum and drummers. The veteran dancer carries the flag and leads the dancers—first the oldest males, then the youngest males, followed by the oldest and youngest females—into the arena from an eastern entrance. Traditional dancers wear natural items and colors for their motif. Fancy dancers use bright, more eye-catching colors in their dance outfits.

—excerpted from OYAKA, *Native American Indian newsletter*

CEREMONY PROCEDURE AND RULES OF CONDUCT

- **GRAND ENTRY:** Stand for the beginning of the Pow Wow.

- **FLAG SONG:** Remain standing silently for the Indian Anthem.

- **BENEDICTION:** Remain standing quietly for the Indian Prayer.

- **VARIABLE SONGS:** Veteran's Song, Honor and Social Dances follow.

- **GIVE AWAY:** On Sunday only, there is a gift of appreciation.

- **CLOSING SONG:** Stand.

POW WOWS

MARCH
ANN ARBOR POW WOW
University of Michigan
(734) 763-9044 or 763-1207
Celebrates Native American culture
and heritage.

APRIL
MT. PLEASANT POW WOW
Finch Fieldhouse
Central Michigan University
(517) 774-3945

WESTERN MICHIGAN UNIVERSITY
POW WOW
Kalamazoo; (616) 387-2279

JUNE
ANNUAL DAY OF THE EAGLE
POW WOW
Mill Street, East Jordan
(616) 536-7351

SARNIA POW WOW
Sarnia, Ontario; (519) 336-8410
Last weekend in June.

JULY
HONORING OUR HERITAGE POW WOW
Fireman's Park, Clio; (810) 239-6621
Sponsored by the Genesee Valley Indians
Association of Flint.

SAULT STE. MARIE POW WOW
(906) 635-6050
July 4th weekend.

AUGUST
MICHIGAN STATE UNIVERSITY
AMERICAN HERITAGE POW WOW
East Lansing
(517) 351-6620 or 1-800-935 FEST
Part of the 10-day Michigan Festival.

LITTLE ELK'S RETREAT
Isabella Indian Reservation, Mt. Pleasant
(517) 775-4000
Traditional pow wow.

PESHAWBESTOWN POW WOW
Suttons Bay (Grand Traverse area)
(616) 271-3538

FALL FESTIVALS

INDIAN FALL FESTIVAL
Gibraltar Trade Center North
I-94 and North River Rd., Mt. Clemens
(810) 465-6440
On weekends in early October, traders from
the United States and Canada offer craft-
work, books, jewelry, pottery, leatherwork,
basketry and other art. Foods, music and traditions also shared. Proceeds benefit
Southeastern Michigan Indians Inc.
(810-756-1350).

NATIVE AMERICAN DAYS
Cranbrook Institute of Science
1221 N. Woodward, Bloomfield Hills
(248) 645-3200
Museum's fall lineup of special events
includes a weekend in October and
November devoted to Native American
culture.

NATIVE AMERICAN FESTIVAL
Novi Expo Center, Novi
(I-96 Exit 162)
(248) 352-0990
November event features Native American
Indian drumming, dancing and singing,
demonstrations by artisans, storytelling, food,
arts and crafts, and hands-on learning activi-
ties for children. Opportunities for Scout troops
to earn badges. Presented by *Metro Parent
Magazine* in cooperation with Southeastern
Michigan Indians Inc. and the North American
Indian Association of Detroit

CAMPING

Campgrounds are available at or near some of the pow wow sites. For information, call the contact number listed for that particular pow wow.

MICHIGAN STATE PARK RESERVATIONS
P.O. Box 3393, Livonia, MI 48151
1-800-44 PARKS

Campers can rent authentic replicas of the traditional American Indian tepee at six Michigan State Parks. The 20-foot-tall canvas version is pitched on a wooden platform and comes equipped with cots and pads to sleep four. The closest site is Holly State Park, 30 miles northwest of Detroit. Tepees are limited, so make reservations in advance by calling (248) 634-8811.

CANOES

Though many believe that the first canoe was developed in the 1600s by the Woodland Indians of North America, this is not entirely accurate. The first canoes were adaptations of the seagoing dugouts used by the Carib Indians of the Caribbean islands. The Carib word kenu, which served as the basis for the word canoe, is defined as "a boat that is dug out of a tree."

In the early 1600s, North American Indians started fabricating the more well-known version of the canoe from hollowed-out trees and also by attaching the strong, lightweight birch bark (sometimes elm) to wooden frames. These boats, which have remained virtually unchanged in design for the past 400 years, proved to be ideal for traveling streams, rivers and lakes, which were often quite shallow. The joints of the canoes were held together by the root of the white pine and then made waterproof by applying hot pine or spruce resin.

● *Paddle a replica of a fur-trader's canoe through backwoods channels on the Huron River. Special tours are guided by an Oakwoods metropark naturalist. Call to make "Great Canoe" reservations. Other Metroparks also offer canoe rentals. For information call 1-800-477-3191.*

● *Modern canoes aren't made of birch bark, but they're available for rent at liveries. Paddling down some of the smaller rivers, like the Clinton, from spring through fall, is a great way to take in sights unseen by land travel. Check the Yellow Pages under "Canoe Rentals."*

EXPEDITIONS

APPLE ISLAND TOUR
West Bloomfield Parks
and Recreation Department
(248) 738-7800

Orchard Lake fall color tours in September and October provide the opportunity to explore Apple Island, the legendary burial site of Chief Pontiac. Participants take a pontoon boat to the island and are led on trails by a naturalist or historian guide.

SANILAC PETROGLYPHS
Germania Rd., Port Austin
(517) 373-1979

Weather-dependent; call ahead. See fascinating images left by ancient Native American Indians in Michigan's Thumb area. From the Detroit area, take M-53 (Van Dyke) north past Cass City Corners to Bay City/ Forestville Road. Turn right and go east for five miles, then south on Germania Road for 3/4 mile to the entrance.

ORGANIZATIONS

AMERICAN INDIAN SERVICES
1110 Southfield Rd., Lincoln Park
(313) 388-4100

Provides social services, programs for youth, and Native American cultural activities.

AMERICAN INDIAN HEALTH AND FAMILY SERVICES OF SOUTHEASTERN MICHIGAN
4480 Lawndale, Detroit; (313) 846-3718

Provides health and dental services to the American Indian population in Wayne, Oakland and Macomb Counties. Cultural programs for American Indians are also offered.

DETROIT INDIAN EDUCATIONAL AND CULTURE CENTER
2750 Selden, Detroit; (313) 596-3773

Center supplements existing school activities for students enrolled in the Detroit Public Schools. Seminars, workshops and in-service training for teachers is available.

MICHIGAN COMMISSION ON INDIAN AFFAIRS
611 W. Ottawa, Lansing; (517) 373-0654
Bill LeBlanc, director

Publishes pow wow and events schedule.

NORTH AMERICAN INDIAN ASSOCIATION
22720 Plymouth, Detroit
(between Outer Dr. and Telegraph)
(313) 535-2966

NAIA serves as a meeting center to preserve and promote Native American Indian culture. Participates in Native American Festival each fall and sponsors cultural potlucks on Wednesday nights, featuring drumming, dancing and arts and crafts.

SOUTHEASTERN MICHIGAN INDIANS INC.
26641 Lawrence, Center Line
(810) 756-1350

SEMI provides liaison and social services, including job placement, employment training referrals, and emergency food and clothing. It aims to preserve Native American Indian culture through social and cultural programs throughout the year.

A great number of petrograms (if they're drawn or painted) and petroglyphs (if they're carved) can be found in the western United States and Canada. Although these prehistoric forms of written communication are rare in Michigan, some can be seen at a site in the state's Thumb area. (See Sanilac petroglyphs.)

SCHOOLS

MEDICINE BEAR AMERICAN INDIAN ACADEMY
6325 W. Jefferson, Detroit
(313) 849-6244

Charter school for Native American children located at Historic Fort Wayne.

CHIEF PONTIAC'S REBELLION

The most famous of the conflicts between the French, the British and the Native American Indians was the Rebellion of Chief Pontiac. Inspired by the spiritual leader known as the Delaware Prophet, Pontiac besieged Fort Detroit and captured many forts from as far west as Green Bay, Wisc., and as far east as Pennsylvania. The Rebellion of Pontiac ended with the Treaty of Paris in 1763, which guaranteed that there would be no further non-Indian expansion. The promise was obviously ignored, and Chief Pontiac was assassinated in 1769. A local legend says that Pontiac is buried on Apple Island in the middle of Orchard Lake, north of Detroit.

MEDIA

PRINT

NATIVE PEOPLES MAGAZINE
5333 N. Seventh St., Ste. C224
Phoenix, AZ 85014
(602) 252-2236
Four issues yearly, $13.95. Full-color national publication with emphasis on the arts, issues, people and entertainment.

NATIVE AMERICAS
1-800-9-NATIVE
An award-winning publication filled with information on Native American community life. Call for additional information.

WEB SITES

AMERICAN INDIAN HERITAGE FOUNDATION
Designed to preserve and share Indian culture and heritage and promote understanding among non-Indians. Many links.
www. indians.org/aihf/

NATIVE TECH
Information and resources on historic and contemporary arts and crafts.
www.lib.uconn.edu/NativeTech/

NATIVE AMERICAN HOME PAGE SITES
www.pitt.edu/~lmitten/indians

NATIVE AMERICAN INFORMATION CENTER
www.nnic.com

RESEARCH SOURCES

BURTON HISTORICAL COLLECTION
Detroit Public Library
5201 Woodward, Detroit
(313) 833-1000
Tue, Thu-Sat 9:30am-5:30pm; Wed 1-9pm.
Genealogical material on Cherokee Nation, Ottawa, Chippewa, Dakota and other tribes.

NATIVE AMERICAN music is becoming more popular and available around the world. In addition to traditional drumming, chanting and pow wow music, there is *watla* (also called chicken-scratch)—the party music of the Tohono O'odham tribe of Arizona—and **Andean** music—based on the Quechua Indians' pan pipes, flute and guitar.

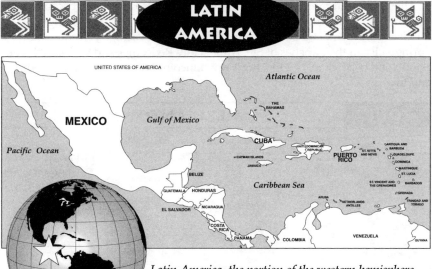

Latin America, the portion of the western hemisphere south of the United States, consists of Mexico, Central America, South America and the West Indies. The term **Latin** *refers to the derivation of the languages spoken by the Spanish, Portuguese and French explorers who colonized much of the area.*

Mexico, *south of the U.S. border, is bounded by the Gulf of Mexico on the east, Belize, Guatemala and the Caribbean Sea on the south, and the Pacific Ocean on the west.*

Cuba, *south of Florida and east of the Yucatan Peninsula of Mexico, is the largest island in the West Indies.*

Puerto Rico, *a commonwealth of the United States since 1952, is about 1,000 miles southeast of Florida, bordered by the Atlantic on the north and Caribbean Sea on the south. The Virgin Islands are to the east and the Dominican Republic is to the west.*

LATINOS IN DETROIT

An estimated 90,000 to 100,000 Latinos live in metro Detroit. Latinos of Mexican descent make up the largest group, followed by those of Puerto Rican and Cuban descents.

In the late 1800s, many Latinos came to Detroit primarily as workers for the railroads, as well as the sugar beet and meat packing industries. By 1920, 15,000 Latinos lived in Detroit—mainly in Corktown, the old Irish neighborhood along Michigan Avenue.

In the 1930s, Mexican muralist **Diego Rivera,** who painted the *Detroit Industry* frescoes at the Detroit Institute of Arts, was involved in forming the *Liga de Obreros y Campesinos Mexicanos de Michigan* (Mexican Laborers League of Michigan). Rivera ultimately contributed much of his artist's commission to the repatriation cause. (During the Depression, a Detroit "Mexican Bureau" had been formed to encourage Mexican Americans to return to Mexico.) Latino communities in Detroit lost significant numbers and endured considerable hostility as they were portrayed and perceived as alien competitors.

The Latino community grew again during the 1940s and '50s, becoming *"La Colonia."* At present, many Latinos live in Detroit's southwest neighborhoods—Corktown, Hubbard-Richard, West Vernor, Michigan Avenue and Springwells, in the parishes of Ste. Anne, Holy Redeemer and St. Gabriel. The population has fanned out to Allen Park, Lincoln Park, Southgate, Dearborn and Livonia.

TOUR	MEXICANTOWN

[E-F/4-5]
Southwest Detroit, near the Ambassador Bridge, is the center of Latino activity. From southbound I-75, take the "Bridge to Canada" Exit and turn right on Porter Street. Turn right on 24th Street and go north to Bagley. From northbound I-75, take the Clark Street Exit to W. Grand Blvd. Turn left on Grand Blvd. and right on Bagley and go two blocks to 24th Street.

Mexicantown, an area made up of ethnic restaurants and shops, is centered *on Bagley, two blocks north of the Ambassador Bridge.* The district runs *between 17th and 25th Streets, divided by I-75,* and there is plenty to see and do on both sides of the freeway. The majority of the restaurants are on Bagley between 18th and 24th Streets. The east side of Bagley is most active on Sunday afternoons from June through September when the **Mexicantown Mercado,** an outdoor market, is in operation.

Start the day with a quick stop at the **Jalisciense Tortilla Factory** for some fresh-made tortillas, then head over to **La Gloria Bakery** *(3345 Bagley)* for Mexican pastries and coffee. Morning people can get an early start: The factory opens at 5 a.m. and the bakery at 6 a.m. Next, stop by **Xochi's Gift Shop** *(3437 Bagley)*. Owners German and Gloria Rosas offer a variety of Mexican products such as *sarapes*, Mexican flowers, clay pots, kitchenware, sombreros, cowboy boots and traditional apparel. **Taqueria Lupita,** next to Xochi's *(3443 Bagley)*, features cuisine from Jalisco, Mexico, and is ideal for a snack, meal or take-home treat. Taqueria Lupita is known for its *tacos al pastor, aguas frescas* (fresh fruit drinks) and special salsas, which are sold by the quart or gallon.

Along the strip are many restaurant choices, including **Xochimilco** (3409 Bagley), **El Zocalo** (3400 Bagley), **Mexicantown Restaurant** (3457 Bagley) and **El Comal** (3456 W.Vernor at 24th). If you crave tamales, try **Evie's** *(3454 Bagley)* or the lunch buffet at **Los Galanes** *(3362 Bagley).* Don't miss the mural representing Detroit's rich cultural heritage on the outside back wall of Los Galanes.

Across the freeway is **Algo Especial,** meaning "something special" *(2668 Bagley),* a video rental and music store with a variety of other Mexican products. One block north on Vernor are more Mexican establishments. **Armandós** *(4242 Vernor),* noted for its Cuban dishes and buffets, is another good choice for lunch. Next, visit the **Museo Indigenista** at *4000 W. Vernor (on the corner of Hubbard).* Open by appointment only, the museum tracks Latino history in Detroit and environs. Then stop at **Casa De Unidad** *(1920 Scotten)* for a tour of the galleria.

Proceed six more blocks west on Vernor to the corner of Junction to visit **Holy Redeemer Church** and observe its rich architectural style. Back outside, take a whiff. That delicious aroma is coming from **Luna's Bakery** *(5620 W. Vernor)* right across the street. Some favorite baked goods include *molletes* (rolls), *empanadas* (turnovers filled with yams or pineapple), cookies, *cortadillos* (pink cake), *mantecadas* (cupcakes) and *pan bolillo* (similar to French bread). Don't forget *la abuelita* (Mexican hot chocolate) to go along with your sweet-bread. After Luna's, head down to **E&L Supermercado** *(6000 W. Vernor),* where you can purchase some *chorizo* (Mexican sausage), tortilla chips, co-jack cheese and *jarritos* (Mexican soft drinks). Ready for dinner? Try **El Rancho** *(5900 W. Vernor)* or **Las Brisas** (8445 W. Vernor) for an authentic Mexican meal.

TOUR	FRIDAY NIGHT FIESTA

[E-F/2-3] Begin in **Royal Oak** with an early dinner (to beat the *crush*-hour crowd, arrive before 6:30pm) at **Monterrey Cantina** *(314 S. Main).* Then *go south on Main two blocks* to **The Hot Zone** *(501 S. Main)* and take in the selection of more than 500 hot sauces, snacks, oils and cookbooks.

Back in the car, *proceed north on Main Street to Maple (15 Mile) and turn left.* The restaurant **Trini & Carmen's** will be about three quarters of a mile on the left. Here you can listen and dance to nationally known recording artists in a Latin nightclub atmosphere.

RESTAURANTS

DETROIT–BAGLEY STREET

TAQUERIA LUPITA
3443 Bagley, Detroit
(313) 843-1105
Sun-Thu 9am-10pm, Fri-Sat 9am-11pm.
Featured in *Hispanic Magazine* as one of the best. Tacos al pastor (meat-filled rolled tortillas) served with tray of garnishes. With chips come samples of various salsas. Carryouts and bottled salsas.

LOS GALANES RESTAURANT
3362 Bagley, Detroit
(313) 554-4444
Mon-Thu 10am-11pm, Fri-Sat 10am-3am, Sun 10-2am. Fiesta buffet daily. Street-side patio and carryouts. Specialty: Camaron al mojo de ajo (shrimp in garlic sauce) and fresh tortillas. Live music and dancing weekends.

MEXICAN VILLAGE
2600 Bagley, Detroit
(at 18th St.)
(313) 237-0333
and
47350 Van Dyke, Utica
(at 21 Mile)
(810) 254-2290
Sun-Thu 11am-midnight, Fri-Sat 11am-2am.
Mexicantown location is the original. Private banquet facilities available.

EL ZOCALO
3400 Bagley, Detroit
(313) 841-3700
Sun-Thu 11am-2am, Fri-Sat 11am-2:30am.
Favorites include seafood and fish selections, as well as regional soups such as caldo jardinero (red snapper stock with fresh vegetables).

EVIES TAMALES & FAMILY RESTAURANT
3454 Bagley, Detroit
(313) 843-5056
Mon-Sat 8am-6pm, Sun 8am-3pm. Known for the best tamales in Detroit, including miniature ones.

MEXICAN TOWN
3457 Bagley, Detroit
(313) 841-5811
Sun-Thu 11am-2:30am, Fri-Sat 11am-4am.
Famous for fajitas and margaritas.

XOCHIMILCO
3409 Bagley, Detroit
(corner of 23rd St.)
(313) 843-0179
Daily 11am-4am. Popular tourist stop for Mexican fare and margaritas.

DETROIT–VERNOR AVENUE

ARMANDO'S
4242 W. Vernor, Detroit
(313) 554-0666
Sun-Thu 7am-3:30am, Fri-Sat 7am-4am. All-you-can-eat daily fiesta buffet. **Caribbean** and **Central American** buffet on Thursday. Also grocery items such as spices, breads, cheeses, coffees and teas. Live Latin entertainment.

EL COMAL
3456 W. Vernor, Detroit
(at 24th St.)
(313) 841-7753
Tue-Thu 11am-10pm, Fri-Sat 11am-midnight, Sun 11am-10pm. Specializes in food from **Guatemala, El Salvador** and **Mexico.** Named for clay pan used to cook tortillas. Interesting shawls decorate walls.

EL RANCHO RESTAURANT
5900 W. Vernor, Detroit
(313) 843-2151
Sun-Thu 8am-11pm, Fri-Sat 8am-4am.
Casual, family-owned restaurant with authentic Mexican food including stews (menudo and caldo de res). Carryout available.

LAS BRISAS
8445 W. Vernor, Detroit
(313) 842-8252
Mon-Thu 11am-10:30pm, Fri-Sat 10:30am-1:30am, Sun 10am-10:30pm. Mariachi band on Friday and Saturday. Banquet hall and catering available.

DON PEDRO'S
24366 Grand River, Detroit
(3 blocks W of Telegraph)
(313) 537-1450
*Mon-Wed 11am-10pm, Thu-Fri 11am-11pm,
Sat 3-11pm, Sun 2-9pm.* Traditional Mexican
cuisine. Specialty: fajitas.

CASA DE ESPANA
6138 Michigan (E of Livernois), Detroit
(313) 895-4040
Tue-Sat 11am-11pm. Only true **Spanish
restaurant** in Detroit area is in 100-year-old
firehouse transformed with Spanish patio and
balcony, stained glass and mosaic map of
Spain. Serves paella (seafood, rice, green
beans, chicken, pork, oysters). Flamenco
dancers Friday and Saturday nights.

MEXICAN DINING

Most Detroiters have eaten a taco, burrito or enchilada, even if they've never been to Mexico. But "breakfast burritos" at McDonald's and lunch at Taco Bell are only tiny bites of Mexico's traditional culinary delights.

Of all cuisines in this hemisphere, Mexican is the most original. Even though it has integrated a share from the Spanish conquistadors, it's fair to say that it differs from Spanish cuisine more than American cooking does from Continental European cuisine, or French-Canadian from French cuisine.

The originality of Mexican cooking partially results from the contributions of the indigenous nations—Aztec, Toltec and Maya—and partially from its own developments based on the major cultivated crops of grain, corn and kidney beans.

Corn and *frijoles* (beans) are staple foods in Latin America. Cornmeal is used to make *tortillas,* and beans appear in the best internationally known Mexican dish, *chili con carne.*

Chili peppers are used in many ways, in many dishes, but Mexican food in most U.S. restaurants is relatively mild and guests often are expected to request extra "heat" or add their own at the table with *salsas,* pickled peppers or bottled hot sauce.

Mexico has a diverse cuisine. All regions serve their own specialties, such as *mole poblano* (a sauce made up of chocolate, chiles and spices served over chicken) in Puebla and *heuvos rancheros* (eggs sunny-side up, served on a tortilla and covered with red chili sauce) in Sonora. Other signature dishes are *frijoles refritos* (refried beans), *arroz* (rice with peas and carrots), *pescado a la veracruzana* (red snapper with tomato sauce, olives and chiles), *barbacoa* (seasoned shredded beef), *menudo* (stew made with tripe, hominy and spices), and *caldo de res* (vegetable stew made with cabbage, carrots, potatoes and beef chunks).

Desserts include *flan* (smooth, firm custard with a topping of caramel syrup), *arroz con leche* (rice pudding, with raisins and ground cinnamon) and *pastelitos* (pies).

DEARBORN

MEXICAN FIESTA
24310 Ford Rd., Dearborn Hts.
(313) 274-3066
Mon-Thu 11am-12:30am, Fri-Sat 11am-1:30am, Sun 11am-11pm. Variety of Mexican and American food.

SENOR SALSA
13277 Michigan, Dearborn
(313) 581-6661
Daily 11am-11pm. Variety of Mexican and vegetarian dishes served in casual atmosphere. Specialty: fresh fruit drinks.

TIJUANAS MEXICAN KITCHEN
18950 Ford Rd., Dearborn; (313) 441-6210
Mon-Wed 11am-9pm, Thu-Fri 11am-10pm, Sat noon-9pm. Authentic Mexican dining in casual atmosphere. Dine-in or carryout.

NORTH

CHEVY'S FRESH MEX
2085 W. Big Beaver, Troy; (248) 643-7720
Mon-Thu 11am-10pm, Fri-Sat 11am-11pm. Large, festive restaurant (formerly Casa Lupita) offers made-to-order Mexican fare, express lunch and famous Sunday brunch.

LA MERIENDA CAFE
3377 Elizabeth Lake Rd., Waterford Twp.
(248) 683-9760
Mon-Fri 11am-9pm, Sat 4-10pm. Traditional Mexican fare, including fajitas, burritos, tamales and nachos.

MARGARITA'S CAFETAL
27861 Woodward., Berkley; (248) 547-5050
Mon-Tue 11:30am-10pm, Wed-Thu 11:30am-11pm, Fri-Sat 11:30am-11:30pm, Sun 11:30am-9pm. Traditional Mexican and vegetarian dishes, including entomatadas, corn tortillas, potato-stuffed flautas and machacado (shredded beef with scrambled eggs). Lots of coffee drinks.

MONTERREY CANTINA
314 S. Main, Royal Oak; (248) 545-1940
Mon-Thu 11am-midnight, Fri-Sat 11am-1am, Sun noon-11pm. Very casual atmosphere, funky decor, arroz con pollo, quesadillas, enchiladas and chicken ranchero.

OLD MEXICO
5566 Drake Rd., W. Bloomfield
(at Walnut Lake Rd.)
(248) 661-8088
Mon-Thu 5-10pm, Fri noon-11pm, Sat 5-11pm. Offers innovative, fresh foods, lively entertainment in a festive atmosphere.

TRINI & CARMEN'S
1019 W. Maple, Clawson; (248) 280-2626
Mon-Thu 11am-11pm, Fri 11am-midnight, Sat noon-midnight, Sun 1-9pm. Gourmet Mexican cuisine, live Latin music Friday and Saturday nights.

JALAPENO PETE'S
212 W. Nine Mile, Ferndale; (248) 545-5650
Lunch weekdays 11:30am-2:30pm, dinner Tues-Sat 5-10pm, Sun-Mon 5-9pm. Southwest cuisine is spicy, colorful and served in large portions in candle-lit setting decorated with Ansel Adams prints.

EAST

DON CARLOS
33025 Gratiot, Clinton Twp.
(810) 791-9120
Mon-Thu 11am-9pm, Fri 11am-11pm, Sat 2-11pm, Sun 2-8pm. Offers burritos, fajitas, 46-ounce margaritas and festive music in authentic Mexican atmosphere.

EL SOMBRERO
8601 Old 13 Mile Rd., Warren
(810) 268-5060
Mon-Thu 11am-9pm, Fri 11am-11pm, Sat 2-11pm, Sun 4-9pm. Authentic Mexican cuisine.

JUAN'S HACIENDA
31313 Dequindre, Madison Hts.
(248) 583-9792
Mon-Thu 11am-10pm, Fri 11am-11pm, Sat 2-11pm, Sun 4-9pm. Operated by Juan and Gloria Abundis since 1984; offers authentic dining in casual atmosphere. All tortillas come from Juan's brother's factory in Mexicantown. Flaming fajitas are a favorite.

WEST

DON PABLO'S
39895 Ford Rd., Canton Twp.
(734) 844-7836
Sun-Thu 11am-10pm, Fri-Sat 11am-11pm. Traditional Mexican cuisine in a casual atmosphere.

DOS PESOS
11800 Belleville Rd., Belleville
(S of I-94)
(734) 697-5777
Mon-Thu 11am-9:30pm, Fri 11am-10:30pm., Sat 3-10:30pm, Sun noon-9pm. Small, family-run storefront offers full range of fresh Mexican dishes, attractively served.

THE BASICS:

Burrito: A flour tortilla folded and rolled to enclose any of several fillings, including shredded or chopped meat, refried beans, grated cheese, sour cream and lettuce.

Carnes: (meats), *pescado* (fish), *mariscos* (shellfish), *legumbres* (vegetables), *arroz* (rice), *frutas* (fruits), *nueces* (nuts), *bebidas* (drinks), *especies* (spices), *condimentos* (condiments), *postres* (desserts), *dulces* (sweets).

Chorizo: *(chor-EE-zoh)* A highly seasoned, coarsely ground pork sausage flavored with garlic, chili powder and other spices. It's widely used in Mexican and Spanish cooking, making a tasty addition to many dishes including casseroles, soups, stews and enchiladas.

Enchilada: A softened corn tortilla rolled around a meat or cheese filling. Served hot, usually topped with salsa and sprinkled with cheese.

Guacamole: A popular Mexican specialty of mashed avocado mixed with lemon or lime juice and various seasonings (usually chili powder and red pepper). Sometimes finely chopped tomato, green onion and cilantro are added. Used as a dip, sauce, topping or side dish.

Mole: *(MOH-lay)* From *Nahuatl molli,* meaning "concoction," mole is a rich, dark, reddish-brown sauce usually served with poultry. There are many variations, but generally mole is a smooth, cooked blend of onion, garlic, several varieties of chilies, ground seeds (such as sesame or pumpkin seeds—*pepitas)* and a small amount of Mexican chocolate, its best-known ingredient.

Salsa: "Sauce," cooked or fresh. *Salsa cruda* is "uncooked salsa;" *salsa verde* is "green salsa," which typically is based on tomatilloes, green chiles and cilantro. A broad selection of salsas—fresh, canned or in jars—are available in supermarkets.

Taco: *(TAH ko)* "Sandwich," eaten as an entrée or snack, consisting of a folded corn tortilla filled with ingredients such as beef, pork, chicken, sausage, tomatoes, lettuce, cheese, onion, guacamolé, refried beans and salsa. Most tacos are made with crisp (fried) tortilla shells, but there are also "soft" (pliable) versions made with flour tortillas.

Tortilla: *(tohr-TEE-yuh)* Mexico's everyday bread, the unleavened tortilla is round and flat, shaped by hand, resembling a thin pancake. Tortillas can be made from corn flour *(masa)* or wheat flour, but always are baked on a griddle *(comal).* They can be eaten plain or wrapped around various fillings. Both types of tortillas are sold prepackaged in the refrigerator section of most supermarkets.

EL NIBBLE NOOK
27725 Eight Mile, Livonia
(248) 474-0755
*Mon-Thu 11am-10pm, Fri-Sat 11am-11pm,
Sun noon-10pm.* Traditional Mexican cuisine.
Many choices in burritos, including spinach,
broccoli and mushroom, and seafood.
Strolling mariachi band Friday and Saturday.

OLD MEXICO
28407 Five Mile, Livonia
(734) 421-3310
*Mon-Thu 10:30am-9pm, Fri-Sat 10:30am-
10pm, closed Sun.* Innovative fresh foods in
a festive atmosphere. Live entertainment.

RIO BRAVO CANTINA
19265 Victor Pkwy (at 7 Mile), Livonia
(734) 542-0700
and
Fairlane Town Center, Dearborn
(313) 271-2900
*Mon-Fri 11am-11pm, Sat 11am-midnight,
Sun 11am-10pm.* Tortillas made in view of
diners. Growing chain owned by Applebee's.

ANN ARBOR/YPSILANTI
THE BURRO
619 E. William St., Ann Arbor
(at S State St.)
(734) 994-1888
*Mon-Thu 11am-9:30pm, Fri-Sat 11am-11pm,
Sun noon-9:30pm.* Voted Ann Arbor's "Best
Mexican Restaurant."

LA FIESTA MEXICANA
529 W. Cross St., Ypsilanti
(734) 483-1666
Hours vary by season. Regional specialties
from all over Mexico. Catering available.

TIOS
333 E. Huron, Ann Arbor
(734) 761-6650
Daily 11am-11pm. Huge menu features more
than 250 hot sauces and salsas. Free tastings first Sunday of every month.

BEVERAGES

SPIRITS: *Margaritas* are basically
lemon juice and tequila with salt around
the rim of the glass. Tequila is to Mexico
what champagne is to France. (The Mexican
government has declared that only tequila
from Jalisco, Nayarit and Tamaulipas are "legiti-
mate"—as France has done with its "official" champagne regions.)

Mezcal, the cousin of tequila (also distilled from the cactus-like
plant called *maguey* or *agave),* has the infamous worm in the bottle.
Corona is the most well-known Mexican beer. *Kahlua* is Mexico's
world-famous coffee-flavored liqueur. *Sangria,* an iced red-wine
punch with fruit and fruit juices, gets its name from the Spanish word
for "blood" but is now also available in a white-wine version.

SOFT DRINKS: *Aguas frescas* (fresh fruit drinks) come in pineapple, *tamarindo* and *orchata* flavors. *Jarritos,* a brand name of
Mexican carbonated soft drinks, comes in tropical fruit flavors.
Licuados are shakes made of fruit and milk with cinnamon, vanilla or
other flavors.

TAKING THE HEAT

There are more than 200 varieties of chilies grown throughout the world, about 100 of which are indigenous to Mexico. They vary in length from 12 inches to a quarter-inch. Some are long, narrow and no thicker than a pencil, while others are plump and globular. Their heat quotient varies from mildly warm to mouth-blistering, tooth-rattling hot!

Why do we endure the pain? Some say because we get an adrenaline rush (similar to a "runner's high") which then whets our appetites. Also, the first taste stuns the tongue, anesthetizing the mouth to further pain.

A chili's color can be anywhere from yellow to green to red to black. Dried chilies are available year-round. The availability of fresh chilies varies according to the type and season. **As a general rule, the larger the chile, the milder it is.** Small chilies are much hotter because, proportionally, they contain more seeds and veins—which can contain up to 80 percent of a chili's *capsaicin,* the stuff that gives chilies their fiery disposition. Since neither cooking nor freezing diminishes capsaicin's intensity, removing a chili's seeds and veins is the only way to reduce its heat. After working with chilies, it's important to wash your hands thoroughly to avoid painful burning of the eyes or skin (wearing rubber gloves can remedy this problem).

Chilies are cholesterol-free and low in calories and sodium. They're a good source of vitamins A, C and E, folic acid and potassium. Folklore has them curing everything from colds to arthritis.

BAKERIES AND MARKETS

E&L SUPERMERCADO
6000 W. Vernor, Detroit
(313) 554-2140
Mon-Thu and Sat 8:30am-5:45pm, Fri 8:30am-6:15pm, Sun 9:30am-3pm. Offers full line of Latin American products, fruits and vegetables. Fresh tortillas sold daily.

HACIENDA FOODS
6016 W. Vernor, Detroit; (313) 842-8823
Mon-Fri 8:30am-5pm, Sat 8:30am-3pm. Wholesale distributor and manufacturer of tortilla products. Specializes in hard-to-find Mexican products, chilies and dried chili peppers.

LA COLMENA
Honey Bee Market
2443 Bagley (at 17th St.), Detroit
(313) 237-0295
Mon-Sat 8am-8pm, Sun 8am-6pm. Imports from Mexico and Latin America. Specialties: Mexican chorizo (sausage), carnitas (seasoned pork) and barbacoa (shredded beef); flour and corn tortillas; fresh Mexican produce such as tomatillo, Jamaica (hibiscus) flowers and tamarindo fruit; and Mexican beverages including jarritos, sangria, aguas frescas and licuados. Piñatas, pots and pans, and other imports.

LA GLORIA BAKERY
3345 Bagley, Detroit; (313) 842-5722
Daily 6am-8:30pm. Sweetbreads, cookies, pastries and other Mexican specialties.

MEXICANTOWN BAKERY
4300 W. Vernor, Detroit; (313) 554-0001
Mon-Thu 7am-8pm, Fri-Sat 7am-9pm. Latin American baked goods such as Puerto Rican bread and fruit pastelitos (pies), Cuban pastelitos (with meat, cream cheese or coconut), Caribbean pastries, Mexican fruit-filled empanadas and a complete spice selection. Carnitas (seasoned pork by the pound) available on weekends.

LA JALISCIENSE
2650 Bagley (at 18th St.), Detroit
(313) 237-0008
Daily 5am-1:30pm. Manufacturer and distributor of corn and flour tortillas.

LA MICHOACANA
3428 Bagley Ave., Detroit; (313) 554-4450
Mon-Sat 7am-2pm. Fresh corn and flour tortillas available from a neighborhood factory famous for the flour variety.

LA PLAZA MARKET
1139 Clark St., Detroit
(across from Clark Park)
(313) 843-1211
Mon-Sat 9am-8pm, Sun 9am-6pm.
Everything from pots and pans to imported soft drinks. Recorded music from Brazil, Mexico and the Caribbean.

LUNA'S BAKERY
5620 W. Vernor, Detroit; (313) 554-1690
Mon-Sat 6:30am-9pm, Sun 6:30am-7pm.
Molletes (rolls), pan boliloio (bread), empanadas (fruit turnovers), Spanish cookies, cakes and other treats.

MEXICANTOWN MERCADO
Bagley and 21st St., Detroit
(313) 842-0450
Marketplace set up from mid-June to September 1 with fresh produce, specialty food booths, imports and gift items.

THE HOT ZONE
501 S. Main (at Fifth St.), Royal Oak
(248) 547-6610
Mon-Tue and Thu 10am-8pm, Wed and Fri-Sat 10am-10pm, Sun noon-5pm.
Chili sauces, salsa, peppers, spices, chips and pottery. Also features tortilla chips in holiday colors and shapes (hearts, stars, shamrocks), manufactured by Erevia, a local company.

CALIDO CHILE TRADERS
Lakeside Mall, Sterling Hts.
(M-59 E of Schonenherr)
(810) 247-0691
Mon-Sat 10am-9pm, Sun 11am-6pm. Salsa, chili products and other specialty foods from south of the border.

MOLAS are the needlework creations of the Cuna Indians of the San Blas Islands, on the Caribbean side of the Republic of Panama. Molas are almost exclusively made by Cuna Indian women. This form of embroidery has been handed down from generation to generation. The designs have evolved from simple, yet intricate, geometric and symmetrical designs and shapes to later include animals, plants, and flowers. In making the mola, the Cunas are inspired by their surroundings in tropical Panama. One of the most unique features of the mola is a sewing technique known as reverse appliqué.

(See Pa Ndau, the embroidery of the Hmong people, in the Southeast Asia chapter.)

FOOD OF THE GODS

CHOCOLATE, which is derived from the Theobroma cacao tree, goes back at least 4,000 years. The plant was regarded by the Aztecs as being of divine origin (*Theobroma* means "food of the gods"). They also used the tree's beans as currency.

The Aztecs created what we now know as chocolate by fermenting, drying and roasting the beans, then grinding the kernels to produce *cocoa mass* (chocolate liquor). When the Spanish conquistadores led by Cortes were in Mexico in 1520, they observed the emperor Montezuma drinking *chocolatl*, a beverage consisting of powdered cocoa beans and ground corn, flavored with *tlilxochitl* (ground black vanilla pods) and honey.

Mayan altar tablet. Palenque, Mexico.

Today, **Mexican chocolate** is flavored with cinnamon, almonds and vanilla. This sweet chocolate has a much grainier texture than other chocolates and is used for the hot chocolate drink, *la abuelita,* and *mole* sauce.

VANILLA, which the Aztecs also gave us, is from the plant *vanilla planifolia,* a tropical orchid that grows as a vine. The flowers develop slowly over several months into long, narrow pods. Vanilla needs a process of curing similar to cocoa to develop its characteristic aroma. Vanilla extract is made by cutting the beans into small pieces and soaking them in successive quantities of hot alcohol.

SHOPS

ALGO ESPECIAL
2668 Bagley, Detroit
(313) 963-9013
Mon-Sat 9am-8pm, Sun 10am-6pm. Latino (Spanish and English) video rental, magazines, cassettes and compact discs.

ANDES INTERNATIONAL
508 Monroe, Detroit
(313) 961-4341
Mon-Thu 11am-9pm, Fri-Sat 11am-11pm, Sun noon-7pm. Greektown boutique at Trapper's Alley features Latin American jewelry, artifacts, art and apparel.

DISENOS ORNAMENTAL IRON
2701 Bagley, Detroit
(313) 961-6966
Mon-Fri 9am-5pm. Spanish-style columns, fences, gates, porch rails and step rails.

DOS MANOS
Hand Crafts of Latin America
A long-time fixture in Royal Oak, specializing in folk art and gifts made "of the hands," the shop has recently closed but will operate from their web site at *www.dosmanos.com.*

MEXICAN GIFT SHOP
5631 Michigan Ave. (at Junction), Detroit
(313) 897-4830
Mon-Sat 10am-5pm. Wide selection of Mexican art, cultural items and imports.

XOCHI'S GIFT SHOP
3437 Bagley (at 24th St.), Detroit
(313) 841-6410
Daily 11am-10pm. Many authentic artifacts, flowers, clothes, sarapes, Mexican hats and ponchos. Custom-made piñatas for parties.

DANCING TO THE LATIN BEAT

Many dance movements have emerged from Latin America over the past few years, with new ones appearing regularly. *The* bossa nova, *the* lambada *and* macarena, *for instance, have become extremely popular at ballrooms and dance clubs all over the world. Below is just a sampling of what to look for as a spectator or participant.*

BALLET FOLKLORICO is a style of music and dance derived from the diverse regional cultures of Mexico. Each region has its distinctive costumes, dance steps and music. For example, *la bamba* is a traditional dance from Veracruz and *el jarabe tapatio* is one from Jalisco.

CHA CHA, one of the most popular dances ever in the United States, is derived from the mambo.

CUMBIA began as dance music with an Andean Indian-Latin-Afro beat, played on flutes and drums. It is characterized by dancers' feet remaining one directly in front of the other, probably because it originally was danced while holding a lit candle.

FLAMENCO, the traditional song and dance of Andalucia in southern Spain, retains its gypsy and Moorish origins. *Zapateado,* the intricate toe- and heel-clicking steps, characterize the men's dance; the traditional women's dance is based more on grace of body and hand movement.

MAMBO combines American Jazz with Afro-Cuban beat. In the 1940s, it became one of the first Latin dances to capture the fascination of North Americans.

RANCHERA is Mexican country-western, usually played by acoustic guitar, bass and the accordion.

RUMBA, inspired by African rhythms and Spanish melodies, began the Cuban and Latin American dance crazes.

SAMBA, rhythmic dance music from Brazil, was made famous by the energetic, swaying dancers during *Carnival* in Rio de Janeiro.

TANGO is a type of music as well as a dance, native to Argentina. Despite modern variations, it is dramatic, emotional and even poetic.

TEJANO MUSIC or **WAILA** is a blend of Mexican cumbias, polkas and rancheras with flavorings of country, rock and pop.

(See also "Caribbean" chapter)

PERFORMING ARTS

CARMEN GRUPO ESPANA
Spanish Dance Theater; (734) 525-4313
Senora Maria Del Carmen, director
Classic, regional and flamenco dancers
available for full-length concert performances,
mini-concerts, lecture demonstrations,
performances with community orchestras,
workshops and private parties. Also offers
dancing classes.

BEAN GALLERY
**90 Macomb St., Mt. Clemens
(1 block N of Cass)
(810) 783-1100**
Coffeehouse with classical flamenco and
Spanish music Fridays at 8pm. Serves
coffees, teas, sandwiches and sweets.

CLUB INTERNATIONAL
6060 W. Fort, Detroit; (313) 841-0020
Dance and banquet hall hosts musical
groups from Puerto Rico, South America and
Mexico. Annual music awards to performing
groups, artists and DJs from Michigan, Ohio
and Indiana usually given in December.
Call (248) 443-1986 for award program.

SALERO DE ESPANA
**Maria Durante/Gene Agopian
(313) 562-6726**
Spanish flamenco dancers and accompaniment for festivals, social functions, school
assemblies and restaurant entertainment.

LATIN DANCE LESSONS AND CLUBS

*Find ballroom studios, such as Arthur
Murray, in the Yellow Pages under
"Dancing Instruction."*

ARGENTINE TANGO CLUB
**25340 Van Born Rd., Dearborn Hts.
(313) 292-1897**
One of the newest and fastest-growing tango groups in North America
offers tango workshops for the more
advanced and Latin and tango classes
for beginners.

ARRIVA NIGHTCLUB
**6880 E. 12 Mile (W of VanDyke), Warren
(810) 528-2430**
8:30pm-1am. Salsa music and Latin dancing
on Thursday nights.

BOMBAY BICYCLE CLUB
**3150 Boardwalk, Ann Arbor
(734) 668-1545**
Night club with salsa, merengue and conga
line dances.

EISENHOWER DANCE ENSEMBLE & CENTER FOR DANCE
**1541 W. Hamlin, Rochester Hills
(248) 852-5850**
Ballroom classes on Tuesday, Friday and
Sunday evenings provide instruction in Latin
dances.

KICK'S ENTERTAINMENT LOUNGE
**Troy Marriott, 200 W. Big Beaver, Troy
(248) 680-9797**
Summer Salsa Nights with Latin Buffet on
Thursdays from 5:30-7pm and music 7:30 to
midnight. Call for dates.

PARABOX
**1927 Michigan Ave., Detroit
(at Rosa Parks Blvd.)
(313) 843-2579**
Latin nights every Saturday feature salsa,
merengue and Latin house. Register for
lessons.

SERENGETI BALLROOM
2957 Woodward, Detroit; (313) 842-3010
Regularly scheduled Latin music and dance
nights. Call for details.

MARIACHI BANDS *are ensembles
composed of five to eight
members (guitars, guitar-
ron, violin, trumpets and
maracas). No salsa or
merengue here—only*
rancheras. *Many of the
mariachis play at local
restaurants and grand opening events, as well as weddings and private parties.*

• **MARIACHI 90**
Salvador Torres, (313) 961-8442

• **MARIACHI ALMA DE MEXICO**
Raul Hernandez, (313) 963-9013

• **MARIACHI NUEVO ZAPOPAN**
Melchor Huerta, (313) 849-2494

STARDUST BALLROOM
28651 Northwestern Hwy., Southfield
(just E of 12 Mile Rd.)
(248) 356-5678
Latin dance parties Fri 9pm-midnight; Argentine Tango Club Mon 7-9pm; Monday morning Latin dance classes; group lessons by appointment.

PAPA CHINO'S
24587 W. Eight Mile, Detroit
(just W of Telegraph)
(313) 255-7989
Latin nights Friday and Saturday.

CAFE VIOLETA
5671 Vernor, Detroit
(Holy Redeemer Arts and Cultural Center)
(313) 842-3450
Friday night series of coffee house parties. Presentations by local and national musical performers followed by open salsa dancing.

THE VELVET LOUNGE
29 S. Saginaw, Pontiac
(248) 334-7411
Free mambo lessons every Monday 8-10pm. Latin rhythms and swing on Saturday nights.

PIÑATAS

The Star of Bethlehem, not Santa, brings candy and goodies to children in Mexico. Originally, piñatas, the decorated vessels filled with treats, were shaped like stars. Now they are made in shapes to match every occasion, from burros to soccer balls to Batman, and can be found at most large party supply stores and shops in Mexicantown.

Piñatas may be used as table centerpieces or hung from the ceiling or wall. Today, many parties include a piñata either as the traditional party game or as a festive accent.

In Latin America, piñatas are used to entertain children at most festive occasions. In Mexico, the word *piñata* literally means "party." Piñatas traditionally are filled with candies, small toys, coins and confetti. To play the game, blindfolded children take turns using a colorful stick to hit the piñata. An adult pulls a rope causing the piñata to go up and down, making it more difficult to hit. When all the treats fall to the floor, a mad scramble to get a share of the goodies ensues.

To fill the piñata, first locate the best place to cut the piñata flap. This is usually on the back. Next, carefully cut a flap 3 inches down, 3 inches across, and 3 inches up. If there is newspaper filling inside, carefully pull it out through the flap. Then fill the piñata with small toys and candies.

TIPS AND SAFETY SUGGESTIONS

- The birthday boy or girl should have the first turn. The smallest child should go next so that everybody gets a turn before the piñata is completely broken.
- Blindfolding makes the game more interesting, but may not be necessary with very small children.
- Spin the blindfolded child around a few times, then guide him or her to the piñata. Make sure all the party guests keep away from the piñata hitter and that the swinging has stopped before kids scramble for the spilled candy.

VISUAL ARTS

DETROIT INSTITUTE OF ARTS
5200 Woodward, Detroit
(313) 833-7900
Wed-Fri 11am-4pm, Sat-Sun 11am-5pm.
Diego Rivera's "Detroit Industry" frescoes in
Rivera Court, on the main level of the DIA in
Gallery C200, are the finest examples of the
Mexican muralist's work in the United States.

GALLERIA BIEGAS
35 E. Grand River (at Woodward), Detroit
(313) 961-0634
Hours vary according to exhibition schedule.
Gallery features paintings, sculpture and
others works by Latino artists.

FIESTA GARDENS
21st Street and Bagley, Detroit
(313) 842-0450
Authentic brick plaza with double-tiered
fountain, antique lamp posts and iron entry-
way modeled after quaint plazas in Mexico.
Park is site of many celebrations.

MEXICANTOWN MURALS
"Diversity Is Our Strength" mural is at 3362
Bagley on the back wall of Los Galenes
Restaurant. The Aztec World, conquistadores
and other scenes are depicted on the
Citizens's District Council Building at the
corner of Bagley and Ste. Anne Street.

CULTURAL EXHIBITS

MUSEO INDIGENISTA
4000 W. Vernor, Detroit
(corner of Hubbard)
(313) 841-5470
Dr. Lucile Cruz Gajec, director
Open by appointment only. Cultural and
historical exhibits, artifacts and costumes are
dedicated to Hispanic history of Detroit.
Museum also sponsors lectures and food
exchanges.

CASA DE UNIDAD
1920 Scotten (at Vernor), Detroit
(313) 843-9598
Mon-Fri 10:30am-4:30pm. Cultural arts and
media center offers concerts, poetry readings
and art exhibits as well as workshops in
photography, writing and graphics.

DETROIT PUBLIC LIBRARY
Bowen Branch
3648 W. Vernor at Grand Blvd., Detroit
(313) 297-9381
Meeting place for Latino Poets Association.
Photographic installation of Diego Rivera's
murals. Mounts Hispanic art exhibit every fall
during Hispanic Heritage Month. Programs
feature Hispanic authors and speakers.

CINCO DE MAYO

Cinco de Mayo commemorates
the victory of the Mexican
people who joined to defeat a
larger and better-equipped
French Army on May 5, 1862.
When the second French invasion
began in 1861, during the admin-
istration of Benito Juarez,
Mexican guerrilla forces decided
to make their stand defending the
strategic town of Puebla.
Outgunned and outnumbered
two to one, these untrained forces
under General Zaragoza successfully defended their positions,
then attacked and scattered the
French troops, achieving
victory over soldiers deemed
among the best trained in the
world. The victory advanced the
cause of the liberation movement
and eventually led to the end of
European domination.

The Cinco de Mayo celebration symbolizes the right of
people to self-determination and
national sovereignty, and the
ability of non-Europeans to
defend those rights against
modern military organizations.

December
A MEXICAN CHRISTMAS

Posadas: During the eight nights before Christmas, groups of friends will re-enact Joseph and Mary's search for shelter *(posadas)* by going from house to house, singing traditional songs and asking to be let in. After first refusing, the owner will invite them to enter. At one house, a posadas party takes place.

In Detroit, the tradition is carried out at **Ste. Anne's Church** on Bagley Avenue near West Lafayette. December 15-23, Latinos gather in the evening to sing and pray as they go to different doors of the church in search of shelter. Posadas take place the Sunday before Christmas, during which celebrants follow a donkey through parts of the Mexican community in southwest Detroit to the church.

January 6
FESTIVAL OF THE THREE KINGS

Epiphany commemorates the visit of the Three Wise Men to the Christ child. In the Latino community, children receive gifts from the Three Kings, just as the baby Jesus received gold, frankincense and myrrh from the visitors. Families also gather for singing, prayers and a special meal that includes *champurrado* (thick hot chocolate drink).

Rosca de reyes (cake of the kings) is bread that is baked with little plastic replicas of the baby Jesus inside. Anyone who gets a slice with a baby in it has the honor of holding a family party later in the year.

Spring
EASTER TRADITION

Cracking Cascarones: A longstanding Easter tradition among Hispanic families is the cracking of *cascarones* (elaborately painted eggshells filled with confetti). Cascarones require many days, even weeks, to prepare. During an Easter egg hunt, children search not only for the Easter basket, but also for the cascaron.

Just before sundown, everyone chases each other around, smashing dozens of eggshells on delicate craniums. Although it may seem irreverent, the activity is a respected tradition. And, unlike hard-boiled Easter eggs, the cascaron eggs don't have to be eaten.

November
DIA DE LOS MUERTOS

Families go to cemeteries on this "Day of the Dead" to clean and decorate graves of ancestors. At home, *ofrendas* (altars) are set up and decorated with gifts favored by the deceased.

Dia de los Muertos officially starts at midnight. It is believed that overnight between November 1 and 2, the souls of the dead return to earth to mingle with the living.

ACTIVITIES

HOLY REDEEMER ARTS AND CULTURAL CENTER
5671 Vernor, Detroit
(313) 842-3450
Affiliated with Holy Redeemer Church, the cultural center offers classes in music, voice and instruments; many forms of dance with an emphasis on Latino ballroom dancing; mural painting and crafts. Instructors are paid professionals. Fall and spring semesters available, drop-ins welcome. Call for class information.

ROBERTO CLEMENTE RECREATION CENTER
2631 Bagley, Detroit
(313) 224-0228
Community center, named after Pittsburgh Pirates baseball player who died on relief mission to Puerto Rico, offers various recreational activities. Hispanic heritage mural in multipurpose room.

EVENTS

CINCO DE MAYO CELEBRATION
Mexican Patriotic Committee
7280 Senator, Detroit
(313) 843-2940 or 843-6214
Street fiesta, featuring mariachis, dancing and ethnic food, is held on Vernor between Springwells and Central Avenue on weekend of Cinco de Mayo. Parade on Saturday usually starts at 1pm at Clark Park.

MEXICAN FESTIVAL
Yack Arena, downtown Wyandotte
(313) 246-4515
Event usually celebrated in late May. Food, crafts, music and dancing, including Ballet Folklorico performances.

SUMMER
MERCADO FIESTAS
Mexicantown Community Development Corporation
(313) 842-0450
Mexicantown Mercado takes place every Sunday noon-6pm at Bagley and 21st Street from June through September; features music, dance, crafts and food following a different theme each week. Performers include local and national musicians, dancers, artists and poets.

CARROUSEL OF NATIONS
Multicultural Council of Windsor
(519) 255-1127
Mexican Village is part of Windsor ethnic festival held two weekends in June.

LATINO WORLD FESTIVAL
Hart Plaza (Downtown Detroit riverfront)
(248) 443-1986 or 224-1184
Latino food, music, entertainment and cultural gallery, usually last weekend in June.

PONTIAC INTERNATIONAL ETHNIC FESTIVAL
Pontiac Growth Group
(248) 857-5603 or 791-6952
Mexican food and entertainment part of festival at Phoenix Plaza over July 4 weekend.

FIESTA MEXICANA
Hart Plaza (Downtown Detroit riverfront)
(313) 843-2940 or 224-1184
A three-day celebration filled with authentic Mexican food, dances, mariachi bands, arts and crafts is usually held the first weekend in August.

FESTIVAL OF MICHIGAN FOLKLIFE
Michigan State University, East Lansing
(517) 355-2281 or 355-2370
Ten-day festival in early August brings together storytellers, musicians, cooks and dancers representing the state's diverse ethnic traditions.

FALL
MEXICAN INDEPENDENCE DAY
Celebrations on September 16 mark the end of abolition. Fiestas are sponsored by various committees in southwest Detroit. Check community newspapers for dates and times.

UNITY IN THE COMMUNITY FESTIVAL
Casa de Unidad
1920 Scotten, Detroit
(313) 843-9598
A three-day festival at Clark Park celebrating the unity of the Latino community in southwest Detroit is in connection with Mexican Independence Day (usually the second weekend in September). Mariachis, various bands (jazz, blues, salsa), folkloric and traditional dances performed. Also featured are ethnic foods, games, workshops, children's area, and information and sales booths.

HISPANIC HERITAGE MONTH
The annual observance begins September 15 to coincide with several Hispanic countries that celebrate their independence day in mid-September. Extending to October 15, it covers Dia de la Raza (Day of Our Race), a celebration of heritage on October 13 for many of Latin America's indigenous Indian peoples. During September and October, schools and universities (University of Michigan, Michigan State University, Wayne State University, Eastern Michigan University and Oakland University, for example) schedule programs featuring Hispanic poets, dancers, artists and guest lecturers. Community organizations also sponsor cultural activities. Check community calendars and school bulletins for events.

CHURCHES
The majority of Latinos are Roman Catholic and the churches historically have been a vital element of the community.

STE. ANNE DE DETROIT
1000 St. Anne St., Detroit
(313) 496-1701
Second oldest Catholic parish in the United States (established in 1701) has vaulted ceilings, ornate woodwork and stained glass. Bilingual Masses and celebrations attract people from all parts of the city to this stately anchor in Mexicantown neighborhood. Tours available.

HOLY REDEEMER
1721 Junction, Detroit
(313) 842-3450
Modeled after the Church of St. Paul in Rome, Holy Redeemer serves as a religious, social and cultural center for the Latino population in southwest Detroit.

Other churches with Masses in Spanish:
ST. GABRIEL CHURCH
8118 W. Vernor (at Springwells), Detroit
(313) 841-0753

MOST HOLY TRINITY
1050 Porter, Detroit
(313) 965-4450

ST. STEPHEN/MARY, MOTHER OF THE CHURCH
4311 Central, Detroit
(313) 841-0783

ST. FRANCIS XAVIER
4250 W. Jefferson, Ecorse
(313) 383-8514

ST. JOSEPH
937 E Third St., Monroe
(734) 241-9590

● ●

The Aztec stone calendar (from ancient Mexico), with a sun motif, shows the year divided into 18 short months. The central position of the sun emphasizes its importance in the agricultural cycle.

Rio Carnival

O f the many colorful festivals that take place in Brazil, the **Carnival of Rio de Janeiro** is the most famous. For four days before the Christian observance of Lent, the celebration features parades with thousands of costumed street dancers and many magnificent floats. Lively musicians and dancers swaying to samba rhythms crowd the streets of Rio. In Detroit, the Brazilian Cultural Club hosts a pre-Lenten masquerade ball modeled after the celebration in Rio.

ORGANIZATIONS

MEXICANTOWN COMMUNITY DEVELOPMENT CORPORATION
7752 W. Vernor, Detroit
(313) 842-0986
Mission is to foster economic development in the Hubbard-Richard community of Southwest Detroit as a means of eliminating blight and providing opportunities for local entrepreneurs. Sponsors Mexicantown Mercado.

BRAZILIAN CULTURAL CLUB
P.O. Box 37360 (Oak Park Branch)
Detroit 48237
(313) 861-2177 or (248) 258-8722
Organization publishes quarterly newsletter about events, which include Carnival, the colorful, pre-Lenten masquerade ball modeled after the February celebration in Rio de Janeiro. The Feijoa dinner dance in the fall features a typical Brazilian meal with black bean soup.

PUERTO RICAN CULTURAL AND EDUCATIONAL CLUB
613 W. Huron, Pontiac
(248) 332-5540
Volunteer organization promotes the values, traditions, achievements and heritage of Latinos through cultural, civic and educational programs. Sponsors Cultural Festival in September in conjunction with Hispanic Heritage Month.

ASSOCIACION ARGENTINA DE DETROIT
(248) 855-4948
Cultural and social club sponsors performances of music and dance groups from Argentina touring the U.S. Hosts annual dinner dance in spring and picnic in July. Participates in Latino Festival at Hart Plaza.

MICHIGAN HISPANIC CHAMBER OF COMMERCE
32450 N. Avis Rd., Madison Heights
(248) 577-0730
Organization of Mexican businesses and companies hosts Fiesta Hispana annual dinner dance at The Ritz-Carlton in May and annual Hank Aguirre Memorial Golf Outing in August.

THE SOCIEDAD MUTUALISTA MEXICAN CLUB
2165 Pontiac Rd., Auburn Hills
(248) 338-6657
This 55-year-old state-certified nonprofit organization aims to empower the Hispanic community through scholarships, financial help and other programs. Fund-raising breakfasts are the second Sunday of each month.

SOUTHWEST DETROIT BUSINESS ASSOCIATION
7752 W. Vernor, Detroit
(313) 842-0986
Coalition of businesses and community interests committed to enhancing the stability and economic health of southwest Detroit.

MEDIA

PRINT

EL CENTRAL
4124 W. Vernor, Detroit
(313) 841-0100
Weekly newspaper serving tri-state Hispanic communities. Covers business news, community news, culture and arts, educational news, employment information, sports, entertainment and international news.

LATINO PRESS
P.O. Box 36970, Grosse Pointe
(313) 884-3125
E-mail: latino.press.detroit@mci2000.com
Web site: www/infolat.com/latino
Published monthly for Latino communities in Michigan, Ohio and Ontario. English and Spanish articles about the economy, education, art, events, children, health and food.

MICHIGAN HISPANIC DIRECTORY
(313) 365-6410
Annual listing of Hispanic professionals, businesses and services in Michigan.

BOWEN BRANCH LIBRARY
W. Vernor and Grand Blvd., Detroit
(313) 297-9381
Huge selection of Spanish books. The name of the library is in both English and Spanish on the front of the building.

RADIO

WDTR FM 90.9
(313) 596-3507
"La Voz de Esperanza" Tuesday 11am and Friday 7:30pm. Contact Frederick Feliciano, (313) 963-7177.
"Caribe Serenade" Tuesday 5pm and Saturday 7:30pm. Contact: Ozvaldo Rivera, (313) 596-3507.

WNZK AM 690 DAYS/680 NIGHTS
(734) 557-3500
Music, news and more. Monday-Friday 6am-7am. Contact: Olivia Galan (313) 284-2424 for current times. Religious programming 11pm-midnight Thursday and Friday.

WPON 1460 AM
(248) 332-8883
"La Hora Cristiana" Saturday 10-11am.
"Latino Expression," Sunday 5-6pm

TELEVISION

To access Spanish TV programs on Univision, GEMS or Telemundo, contact your local cable system.

WEB SITES
CULTURE & SOCIETY OF MEXICO
www.public.iastate.edu/~rjsalvad/scmfaq/scmfaq

LATIN AMERICAN CULTURE LINKS
www.yahoo.com/regional/regions/latin_america/society_and_culture/organizations

Hidden in the dense rain forest of Central America are massive stone pyramid temples built by the Mayans between 300 and 900 A.D.

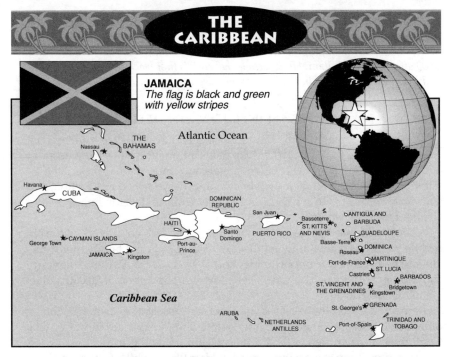

THE CARIBBEAN

JAMAICA
The flag is black and green with yellow stripes

Atlantic Ocean

THE BAHAMAS
Nassau

Havana
CUBA

George Town
CAYMAN ISLANDS

JAMAICA   Kingston

HAITI
Port-au-Prince

DOMINICAN REPUBLIC
Santo Domingo

San Juan
PUERTO RICO

Basseterre
ST. KITTS AND NEVIS

ANTIGUA AND BARBUDA

GUADELOUPE
Basse-Terre

Roseau DOMINICA

Fort-de-France MARTINIQUE

Castries ST. LUCIA

BARBADOS
Bridgetown

ST. VINCENT AND THE GRENADINES   Kingstown

St. George's GRENADA

Caribbean Sea

ARUBA
NETHERLANDS ANTILLES

Port-of-Spain

TRINIDAD AND TOBAGO

North America's Caribbean Islands are in the clear, warm Caribbean Sea, where Christopher Columbus landed in 1492. Named after the indigenous Carib people, the islands also are known as the West Indies. Since World War II, the favored term for the region has been the Caribbean.

The chain of hundreds of islands stretches 2,000 miles from Florida to Central and South America. With legendary beaches and winter temperatures averaging 70° F, tourism is the Caribbean's major industry. Popular destinations include **Aruba, Barbados, Bermuda, the Grand Caymans, Haiti, Jamaica, Puerto Rico** and **Trinidad.**

The largest Caribbean island is **Cuba** (44,218 square miles), with Spanish-speaking people of Spanish, African and mixed descent (see "Latin America"). However, about two-thirds of the Caribbean islands are tiny. Many are grouped by a common political domain. The **U.S. Virgin Islands** comprise 68 islands, including **St. Croix, St. John** and **St. Thomas.** The **Bahamas** consist of 700 islands, though only 22 are inhabited.

To the south of Cuba is **Jamaica,** the third-largest island, which has 500 miles of coastline and a mountainous interior with mineral deposits. The population is primarily of African or African European origin, from British colonization and the slave trade of the 17th to 19th centuries.

The Caribbean also includes mainland countries such as Panama, Belize and Guyana. In all, 30 Caribbean countries have a combined population of 33 million. The broad ethnic diversity, including language and religion, reflects the Caribbean's indigenous **Arawak** and **Carib** population; its British, French and Dutch colonization; plus an influx of Chinese, East Indians, Portuguese and other groups. The majority, however, are descendants of the millions of Africans shipped to the islands to work as slaves on plantations and in sugarcane mills.

*Art is what sets **Haiti** apart from other Caribbean countries. Haitian artists are internationally known as the most prolific in the world. Despite civil strife in recent years, Haitians remain proud that the country won its independence from France in 1803 after a slave rebellion. Haiti became the world's first black republic and the second independent country in the Western Hemisphere, preceded only by the U.S.*

CARIBBEAN INFLUENCE IN DETROIT

C aribbean people from the West Indies, Guyana and Belize have been in Detroit since the early 1900s. Like other immigrants, they came to study and work. Among them were professionals and tradespeople, especially tailors, who established their own businesses. They formed a close-knit, supportive group, with cricket teams, dinner clubs and a club house on Canfield near St. Antoine.

After World War II, a new wave of immigrants arrived to work in the automobile plants. Magnets drawing them to Detroit included family members already here, economic opportunities and Detroit's large African American community with its rich culture. There now is a population of 50,000 in the greater Detroit area.

In the mid-1970s, the West Indian American Association, national clubs and other Caribbean special interest groups united to form a Caribbean Carnival Committee, now known as the Caribbean Cultural and Carnival Organization. They stage a big festival at Hart Plaza, which features a Caribbean *Carival* parade—a Mardi Gras-type activity in August.

TOUR	CARIBBEAN EVENING

[D-F/3-5] Plan for a dusk-to-dawn adventure and wear dancing shoes. Start with a late afternoon trek to the **Detroit Institute of Arts** *(see Cultural Center map)* to view the small but treasured collection of Haitian art.

Then drive northwest for dinner at **The African Caribbean Restaurant** on Grand River in Detroit's Rosedale Park neighborhood where you can experience Detroit's only dine-in restaurant featuring Caribbean and African cuisine—one owner is from Nigeria, the other from Trinidad. From the Cultural Center, *take Woodward north to West Grand Boulevard, going west on the Boulevard to Grand River and continuing north. Parking lot is on the north side of the restaurant.*

Continue on to the **Tropical Hut** for live music. *Left (south) on Grand River; just past Southfield Freeway, turn left. Go one block to Fenkell, then turn right. Continue to Livernois, turn right, continue one block to the club.* After listening to a variety of Caribbean and R&B music in a cozy setting, head out for a festive finalé. *Go north on Livernois to Seven Mile Road. Turn left onto westbound Seven Mile. Continue to* **Splendor International,** a club where patrons Reggae till dawn.

This tour works any time of the year, but it might be best appreciated as a mini-vacation on a bleak or blustery Michigan day.

[E-G/1-5] Begin with breakfast and a cup of Jamaican Blue Mountain coffee at **Irie'n Mellow** *(211 Dougall at Chatham, Windsor. See map on page 394).* Gracious co-owner Irene Hammond's brother, Beres, is an internationally renowned Reggae performer and writer. Next proceed to **Lil Ochie** *(521 Wyandotte St. E.)* for some carry-out Jamaican specialities to have for lunch later. Also check out the **West Indian Variety Food Store** *(722 Wyandotte St. E.).*

Take the Ambassador Bridge back to Detroit to Mexicantown (see map on page 130). The **Mexicantown Bakery** *(4300 W. Vernor)* offers a number of Caribbean pastries and **La Plaza Market** *(1139 Clark)* features island imports and recordings.

Now go north on I-75 to I-696 west to the **Detroit Zoological Park** *(Woodward and I-696, Royal Oak).* Head for the coral reef. The beautiful, brilliant fish can be observed from many angles and it doesn't require much imagination to get the feeling that you're snorkeling off a warm island. Then you have only to walk through a doorway into a tropical paradise where butterflies and hummingbirds fly freely around you as they sip nectar from exotic flowers. Another doorway leads to the aviary where birds of a color too bright to flock anywhere but the Caribbean roost happily in brilliant bougainvillea and lush palms. Listen to their call, breathe in the floral perfume, the moist tropical air. Sit on a park bench and watch them glide right over your head. Ask a zoo keeper for a good place to eat the lunch you've brought.

Go north on Woodward to Fourth St., just north of Lincoln (10 1/2 Mile). Turn right and follow it to Main St. in Royal Oak. Find a place to park, then walk to Keep walking east, across the tracks to Main St. and up one block to **The Hot Zone** *(510 S. Main)* for spices of the Caribbean. *Walk west on Fourth St.* to **Off the Record** *(401 S. Washington)* to check out their extensive Reggae and Ska recordings.

Now it's time to head to the beach. *Go south on Main to I-696 E. 10 miles to I-94 E. exit. Take 94 to Gratiot exit 231. Go north to Cass Ave. and turn left, then right onto Main St., then left onto Macomb Place* to **Kokomo's Seafood & Oyster Bar** *(76 Macomb Place)* in Mount Clemens for casual but fine Caribbean dining (outdoors in summer).

After dinner head to **Waves** *(24223 Jefferson)* for key lime pie, calypso and other island sounds (alternatively choose to have dinner there). *Go back down Gratiot to I-94 W. Take 10 Mile Rd. Exit 228. Turn left on 10 Mile and right onto Jefferson.*

…And if, after all this, you're still in the Reggae mood, you can go to **Splendor International** *(see previous tour).*

- **Barbecue** first was encountered by Europeans in 1492, when Columbus journeyed to the island of Cuba.

- **Pineapples** originated as a symbol of hospitality from the indigenous *Tainos* living in Cuba. (Look for pineapple motifs on colonial furniture and architecture.)

- An important staple among the native population was the starchy root vegetable **yuca,** also known as *manioc* and *cassava,* and from which we derive tapioca and other products.

- The African slaves brought such foodstuffs as **yams, okra** and *akee* to the island, as well as introduced the use of **bananas** and **plantains,** which had been transplanted from Asia.

- Words such as *tobacco, yam, hammock* and *barbecue* are derived from native Caribbean languages.

RESTAURANTS

DETROIT

ARMANDO'S
4242 W. Vernor (at Clark), Detroit
(313) 554-0666
Sun-Thu 10:30am-3:30 am, Fri-Sat 10:30-4am. Caribbean, Central American buffet on Thursdays. Also grocery items. Live Latin entertainment.

CARIBBEAN CITCHEN
10500 W. McNichols, Detroit
(313) 345-3746
Mon-Thu 10:30am-10pm, Fri-Sat 11am-midnight, Sun 10:30am-8pm. Carryout restaurant, some groceries. Traditional Caribbean cuisine including Tropical Treat ice cream and Irish Moss juice.

RONO'S
20211 W. McNichols, Detroit
(313) 531-0660

Tue-Sat noon-midnight. Carryout Caribbean restaurant, noted for courtesy, is the oldest of its peers in Detroit. Traditional menu includes oxtail with broad beans, brown stewed fish and bread pudding.

AFRICAN CARIBBEAN RESTAURANT
18456 Grand River (W of Southfield)
Detroit; (313) 270-3060
Mon 11:30am-9:30pm, Tue-Sat 11:30am-10:30pm.Closed Sun. Caribbean and African cuisine (one owner is from Trinidad, the other from Nigeria). Exotic beef, poultry, fish and vegetarian choices. Caribbean beverages (all nonalcoholic) occasionally include the lemony, homemade Mauby.

SUBURBS

JAMAICA JOE'S ISLAND GRILL
6041 Haggerty Rd., W. Bloomfield
(248) 926-5300
Daily 11am-2am. Extensive menu includes tropical-inspired specialities like jerk chicken, Rasta Pasta and coconut onion rings. Tiki bar offers 30 different rum drinks.

KOKOMO'S SEAFOOD & OYSTER BAR
76 Macomb Place, Mt. Clemens
(810) 469-4774
Mon-Thu 11am-11pm, Fri-Sat 11am-midnight. Candlelight Caribbean dining; carryout and patio.

WAVES
24223 Jefferson Ave., St. Clair Shores
(810) 773-3840
Mon-Wed 11am-10pm, Thu 11am-11pm, Fri-Sat 11am-midnight, Sun noon-10pm. Varied specialities include Rajin Cajin, Margarita Shrimp, Chicken Havana Banana, live entertainment.

WINDSOR

IRIE 'N MELLOW UNDER DE CORNER
211 Dougall Ave., Windsor
(519) 254-3110
Mon-Fri 8am-2pm, Sat-Sun 8am-10pm. A taste of the Caribbean (as well as Canadian) cuisine in the heart of Windsor.

LIL OCHIE
521 Wyandotte St. E., Windsor
(519) 253-4655
Mon-Wed 11am-10pm, Thu 11am-11pm, Fri-Sat 11am-midnight, closed Sun. Strictly carryout features authentic Jamaican specialties (the name comes from the famous resort, Ocho Rios) like curried goat, akee and plaintain. Large variety of Caribbean soft drinks.

WEST INDIAN VARIETY FOOD STORE
722 Wyandotte St. E., Windsor
(519) 977-5683
Mon-Sat 10am-6pm. Specialties such as jerk chicken and oxtail cooked on premises for dine-in or carryout orders on Friday, Saturday and some weekdays.

ANN ARBOR
BEV'S CARIBBEAN KITCHEN
1232 Packard, Ann Arbor; (734) 741-5252
Tue-Sat 11:30 am-9pm. Jerk chicken and pork; curried chicken and goat. Five stools and a counter; mainly carryout.

ZANZIBAR
216 S. State, Ann Arbor; (734) 994-7777
Mon-Sat 11am-11pm, Sun 5-10pm. "Pan-Tropical" gourmet menu includes spiced yellowfin tuna and roast pork loin.

GROCERIES

CARIBBEAN GROCERY STORE
18927 W. Seven Mile, Detroit
(313) 534-5202
Mon-Fri 9am-6:30pm, Sat-Sun 9am-7pm. Stock includes yams, jerk seasoning and other spices, nonalcoholic Caribbean Cola "champagne;" and imported ginger ale.

CARIBBEAN AND AFRICAN TROPICAL FOOD STORE
16926 W. McNichols, Detroit
(313) 838-6637
Mon-Sat 10am-8pm, Sun 10am-6pm. Imported items and spices from Caribbean and Africa.

CARIB BAKERY
17550 W. Seven Mile, Detroit
(313) 534-3226
Tue-Thu 9am-8pm, Fri-Sat 9am-9pm. Hard dough bread, spiced buns and Bulla cakes. Carryout food includes curried shrimp.

THE HOT ZONE
501 S. Main (at Fifth St.), Royal Oak
(248) 547-6610
Mon-Tue and Thu 10am-8pm, Wed and Fri-Sat 10am-10pm, Sun noon-5pm. Chili sauces, jerk sauces, salsa, peppers, spices, chips and pottery.

MEXICANTOWN BAKERY
4300 W. Vernor, Detroit
(across from Clark Park)
(313) 554-0001
Sun-Thu 7am-8 pm, Fri-Sat 7am-9pm. Cuban pastelitos, Puerto Rican bread and other Caribbean pastries.

CARIBBEAN MENU FAVORITES

Ackee: The cooked yellow pulp of this fruit resembles scrambled eggs and is paired with salt fish in a tasty Jamaican dish.

Breadfruit: The flavor, texture and color of cooked breadfruit resemble a somewhat grainy bread.

Conch: (pronounced "konk") A shellfish that is served either pounded, minced and frittered, or marinated and grilled. A specialty in the Bahamas and Key West, Fla. (which is known as the "Conch Republic").

Dirty Rice: Brown and white rice seasoned with cumin and turmeric.

Empanadillas: Crescent-shaped spicy pastries filled with everything from crab to pork.

Goat Water: A ragout of goat meat and vegetables.

Jerk: Blend of seasonings used as a dry or wet rub on meat, fish or poultry.

Kalik: The beer of the Bahamas, light and wheaty.

Key Limes: Smaller, rounder and more tart than "regular" (Persian) limes.

Plantain: Resembles a banana but is classified as a vegetable. Plaintain chips are similar to potato chips.

Oildown Stew: Salt pork and breadfruit stewed in coconut milk.

Roti: Chick-pea flatbread wrapped around curried meat and potatoes.

Souse: Pickled vegetables and pig parts.

Rum: A liquor distilled from fermented cane product. Rum first was made in Barbados in the 1600s in pot stills next to the wind-driven sugar mills found on every plantation.

LA PLAZA MARKET
1139 Clark St., Detroit; (313) 843-1211
Mon-Sat 9:30am-8pm, Sun 9:30am-6pm.
Hot sauces, imported soft drinks, canned
soups and beans. Recorded music from
the Caribbean.

TROPICAL FOOD MART
3020 E. Grand Blvd., Detroit
(313) 972-5656
Mon-Sat 10am-6pm. Features foods from
Caribbean, Africa and Asia.

SHOPS

(See also "Latin America.")

DOS MANOS
For many years in Royal Oak, this shop
recently closed, but will continue to offer
folk art and gifts hand-crafted in the
Caribbean on their web site at
dosmanos.com.

STRICTLY ROOTS
RECORDS, VIDEOS AND BOOKS
15734 W. Seven Mile, Detroit
(313) 836-8686
*Mon-Wed noon-7:30 pm, Thu-Sat 11am-
8pm.* Extensive Caribbean and African
American audio and video selections, including music, poetry, historic speeches, movie
classics, educational documentaries and
some comedy.

SUNKEN TREASURE

The great Spanish treasure galleons traveled
throughout the Caribbean in the 16th and 17th
centuries—subject to pirates and wrecks, becoming very much a part
of island lore and heritage and giving rise to many a swashbuckling
tale.

One of the most famous shipwrecks is the *Atocha*. The bulk of the
treasure comprised nearly 47 tons of silver and more than 150,000 gold
coins and bars. Divers also brought up millions of dollars in precious
gems. In 1986, these precious gems rained down on recovery divers,
led by Mel Fisher.

Silver coins from the *Atocha* were measured in *reales*, often called
"pieces of eight." They were quite valuable at the time—a common
working man might earn just one piece of eight a month. Two silver
pieces of eight equaled one *escudo* gold coin, hence the term *doubloon.*

● *Atocha Treasure Collection: Limited edition reproductions made from
pure Atocha silver and accompanied by a numbered certificate of authenticity
signed by Mel Fisher are available from Rizzo Jewelers of Rochester,
414 Main St. Plaza #108, (248) 651-3334 (Tue-Sat 10am-5pm).
Prices start at $50; catalog available.*

For the smaller budget:

● **RYDER HOBBIES, 30118 N. Woodward, Royal Oak; (248) 549-5262**
Mon-Fri 11am-7pm, Sat 11am-6pm, Sun noon-4pm. Old and new coins and stamps from
around the world, priced from ten cents to hundreds of dollars.

KEY WEST

The Florida Keys are a chain of about 60 small islands that extend from Miami Beach to Key West. (Key is from the Spanish cayo, meaning "rock" or "islet.") The southernmost city in the United States, outside of Hawaii, is Key West. Key West's history has been colorful. Pirate ships hid in the passes and waterways between the keys. The offshore coral reefs still hold the sunken wrecks of ships lost in sea battles of long ago. Closer to Havana than it is to Miami, it has a strong Caribbean influence. Since 1938 the Overseas Highway has linked Key West to the mainland.

VISUAL ARTS

DETROIT INSTITUTE OF ARTS
5200 Woodward, Detroit; (313) 833-7900
Wed-Fri 11am-4pm, Sat-Sun 11am-5pm.
Haitian art exhibit is in North Court area, adjacent to the African Collection. A hallway is lined with more than a dozen pieces by artists of the primitive school, including Philome Obin, Bouta, Sbneque Obin and Edward Callrie-Duval.

INTERNATIONAL INSTITUTE
111 E. Kirby, Detroit; (313) 871-8600
Mon-Fri 8:30am-5pm. Doll exhibit in Hall of Nations.

MUSEUM OF AFRICAN AMERICAN HISTORY
315 E. Warren, Detroit; (313) 494-5800
Tue-Sun 9:30am-5pm. Largest collection of Haitian art in Michigan. Changing exhibits sometimes focus on Caribbean, such as "Sacred Arts of Haitian Voodoo."

ENTERTAINMENT

(Also see Latin America chapter)

THE DECK
2301 Woodward, Detroit
(Second City Bldg., third floor)
(313) 965-9500

Fri 5pm-2am, Sat 7pm-2am Memorial Day to Labor Day. A Reggae band plays in this indoor/outdoor club above the Second City Comedy Club. Full bar service and limited sandwich menu. Cover charge after 9pm.

MAJESTIC THEATRE AND CAFE
4124 Woodward (near Warren), Detroit
(313) 833-0120
Tue-Fri and Sun 11:30-2:30am, Sat 4pm-2:30am. Mediterranean fare, live music, billiards and bowling. Reggae once or twice a month in nightclub.

FIFTH AVENUE
215 W. Fifth, Royal Oak; (248) 542-9922
Sun-Tue 6pm-2am, Wed-Sat 5pm-2am. Live Reggae included in weekly mix of roots music.

PAGE ONE LOUNGE
17740 W. Seven Mile, Detroit
(1 block W of Southfield Rd.)
(313) 532-6060
DJ Michael Julien hosts Reggae *Wed 6pm-2am. Fri-Sat 8pm-2am.* Reggae is mixed with R&B and other sounds, often by a live band. Cover charge after 9pm.

ROYAL KUBO
25234 Greenfield, Oak Park; (248) 968-7550
Filipino nightclub features "Caribbean Vibes" on Tuesdays broadcast live on WNZK 680 AM, 10pm-midnight.

SERENGETI DANCE STUDIO
2957 Woodward, Detroit; (313) 832-3010
Reggae and other West Indian, jazz and African sounds are heard here during live performances. Special cultural events. Most showtimes are 9pm, days vary by event.

SIERRA AFRIQUE
19325 Plymouth Rd., Detroit
(313) 838-3833
In addition to hosting dances and other special events, this banquet hall caters African food.

SPLENDOR INTERNATIONAL
13701 W. Seven Mile, Detroit
(313) 861-8844
Fri-Sat 11pm-4am. Reggae party 'til dawn with some R&B mixed in. Serves juice and Caribbean soda (no alcohol) and baskets of Caribbean cuisine. Dance crowd of mixed ages, but skews young. Hosted by DJ.

TROPICAL HUT
14925 Livernois, Detroit
(3 blocks S of Fenkell)
(313) 861-5340
Wed-Sat 9pm-2am. Intimate club decorated with Caribbean and African art—a favorite of transplanted West Indians. DJ hosts Caribbean music with some R&B; live band about once per month. Cover charge.

PERFORMING ARTS

WRITHM DANCE COMPANY OF DETROIT
2751 E. Jefferson, Ste. 450, Detroit
(313) 396-5666
Among its broad repertoire, troupe performs Haitian dances with authentic drums. Also presents lecture demonstrations for school groups. Associated with the Pemajju School of Dance and Related Arts.

UNIVERSAL XPRESSION
(313) 272-3798
The band plays Soca, salsa, Zouk, Reggae, calypso and R&B.

REGGAE AMBASSADA
(313) 483-4462
The band plays Reggae and other Caribbean sounds.

JO-NAB
(248) 616-8040
Percussion and vocal group features "Reggae to Rock yo' Soul." Appears regularly at some of the clubs listed here.

CLASSES

CARIBBEAN INITIATIVE
Selected Recreation Centers, Detroit
This summer program offers youngsters and adults the opportunity to learn about Caribbean culture, make colorful costumes and help decorate floats for Detroit's "Carival" Parade. Contact the Detroit Recreation Department, (313) 877-8077, or the Caribbean Cultural and Carnival Organization, (313) 538-4452.

DETROIT DANCE CENTER
820 W. Baltimore, Detroit
(313) 873-2623
Carole Morisseau, director
Instruction given in African, Haitian and other Caribbean dances.

PEMAJJU SCHOOL OF DANCE AND RELATED ARTS
2751 E. Jefferson, Ste. 450, Detroit
(313) 396-5666
Among its broad curriculum, Haitian dance and drum classes are offered for children, adult novices and professionals. Penny Godboldo, director, occasionally hosts artists from Haiti as guest teachers.

WENDY'S SCHOOL OF DANCE
17600 James Couzens, Detroit
(313) 863-0458
Haitian and other Caribbean dances are among the studio's class offerings.

CULTURAL INSTITUTIONS

CARIBBEAN CULTURAL AND CARNIVAL ORGANIZATION
18423 W. McNichols, Detroit
(313) 538-4452, 836-3227 or 577-4479
Organizes Hart Plaza festival and parade in August. Countries represented include Jamaica, Bahamas, Haiti, Belize, Panama, Guyana and Trinidad/Tobago.

ESPOIR CENTER
(313) 871-4594 or 342-6174
Contact: Julio Bateau
Detroit-area Haitian cultural group organizes exhibits, conferences, lectures, student exchanges and other activities. New quarters are at 421 E. Ferry near Museum of African American History.

WEST INDIAN AMERICAN ASSOCIATION
2015 E. Seven Mile, Detroit
(313) 893-3311
Social and cultural club for Jamaicans and others from the Caribbean.

SPECIAL EVENTS

JUNE
CARROUSEL OF NATIONS
Multicultural Council of Windsor
(519) 255-1127
A Caribbean Village is always among the dozens of ethnocultural villages offering displays, arts, crafts and entertainment during this event in Windsor.

Music always has been a dominant factor in Caribbean life. The distinctive **steel drum** or **pan** evolved in Trinidad as a result of islanders having their native drums outlawed by the government because they were used to call neighborhood gangs to collect and "mash up." In the 1930s, someone discovered that the dented section of an oil barrel could make a good sound. Now street fights have been replaced by highly competitive band playoffs each year at Carnival.

CALYPSO emerged early in the 20th century and became popular with U.S. folksingers in the 1950s. The words often are improvised and concern satirical themes. Guitar and maraca are the usual accompaniment, as well as steel drums.

MERENGUE is a Dominican folkloric dance, considered by many to be the Dominican Republic national dance, in vogue since the mid-1800s. There are many modern variations, including ballroom style.

REGGAE is a vibrant style of music that originated in Jamaica and is noted for its drums. Popularized in the 20th century by Bob Marley, it became known for its rebellious lyrics about poverty, politics and Rastafarianism. It influenced rock music of the 1980s.

Newer dance-music styles:

SOCA is an upbeat derivative of calypso with electric bass and guitars.

SALSA comes in three types in the Puerto Rican style: straight (high energy), romantica and erotica.

ZOUK is a high-energy French Caribbean style. Its name means "party" in Créole.

(See also "Latin America.")

● *Bands performing Caribbean music appear regularly throughout the area. For current choices, call the West Indian American Association at (313) 893-3311.*

CARIBBEAN FAMILY REUNION
Belle Isle, Detroit; (313) 538-4452
First organized in 1991, this annual gathering is at Shed 8 near the police station on the last Saturday in June. Daylong activities include games for kids and adults such as Caribbean and American music and maypole dancing. All are welcome to bring a picnic lunch to the free event, which celebrates Caribbean unity and international friendship.

JULY
JAMAICAN INDEPENDENCE DANCE
West Indian American Association Hall

2015 E. Seven Mile, Detroit
(313) 893-3311
Jamaican social club plans to annually celebrate Jamaica's colonial independence from British with event on or around July 27.

AUGUST
WINDSOR'S CARIBFESTE
(519) 254-7721
This Canadian celebration of Caribbean culture, usually on the second weekend in August, traditionally features riverboat cruises, live music and a street parade.

"CARIVAL" CARIBBEAN INTERNATIONAL FESTIVAL
Hart Plaza, Detroit
(313) 538-4452 or 224-1184
Colorful festival with food booths, music, arts and crafts. Parade features floats, musicians and celebrants in costume. It starts in the Detroit Medical Center at Mack and "jumps up" Woodward Avenue to Hart Plaza.

FALL
HAITIAN ART EXHIBITION
(313) 871-4594 or 342-6174
Contact: Julio Bateau
Espoir Center for Caribbean Culture usually sponsors a weekend exhibit and sale.

UNIA
(UNIVERSAL NEGRO IMPROVEMENT ASSOCIATION)
4847 St. Aubin, Detroit
(313) 838-3010
Marcus Garvey founded the UNIA in his native Jamaica in 1914. He came to the United States two years later and by 1919, the organization claimed 30 branches and two million members. Detroit's chapter was one of the largest UNIA branches, continuing to function even after Garvey's imprisonment and eventual deportation. Today, the UNIA office houses a collection of books, historical materials, photographs and memorabilia on the UNIA and Pan-Africanism.

MEDIA
PRINT
The weekly *Jamaican Star* and *Jamaican Gleaner* newspapers are sold at Detroit's Carib Bakery. A third newspaper, **Caribbean Week,** is available by mail subscription from Caribbean Communications, Inc., 1320 Route 9, Champlain, NY 12919 (514) 398-9934.

HOT CALALOO
PO Box 429, Riderwood MD 21139
Bi-monthly newsletter focuses on issues the Caribbean as well as sports, entertainment, poetry, music and culture. $8 per year.

RADIO
WCBN 88.3 FM, "Radio-Free Ann Arbor"
(734) 763-3500
"Road to Skaville" featuring Caribbean oldies Tuesday 8pm and "Dance Hall Reggae" Saturday 7-10pm.

WDET 101.9 FM Detroit
(313) 577-4146
George Collinet hosts "Afropop" Sun 6-7pm. Michael Julien hosts "World Music" Sat 10pm-2am. Both feature Caribbean music.

WDTR 90.9 FM Detroit
(313) 596-3507
Regular Reggae programming weekly.

WEMU 89.1 FM Ypsilanti
(734) 487-2229
"Cuban Fantasy," Sat 1-3pm, includes Salsa. "World Dance Party," Saturday 3-5pm, includes Reggae, ska and calypso.

WNKZ 680-AM Detroit
(248) 557-3500
Features "Caribbean Vibes" from the Royal Kubo Tuesday 10pm-midnight.

WEB SITES
CARIBBEAN CONNEXION
www.caribbean-connexion.com/

RAINBOW VOYAGER
www.wow.net/rainbows
Internet magazine about Caribbean arts and life.

GLOBAL JOURNEYS
IN METRO DETROIT

EUROPEAN ROOTS

NOTES

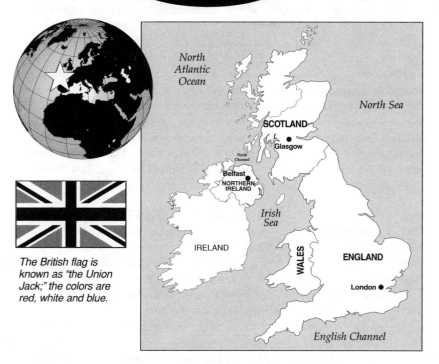

The British flag is known as "the Union Jack;" the colors are red, white and blue.

The British Isles consist of two main islands—Great Britain and Ireland--and make up a total area of 93,602 square miles (slightly smaller than Michigan). Although Great Britain is the island composed of England, Scotland and Wales, it is also the shortened name for the **United Kingdom of Great Britain and Northern Ireland.** The U.K. includes England, Scotland, Wales, and Northern Ireland.

The population of Great Britain is approximately 60 million, with a population density of about 620 per square mile (compared to Michigan's 37 per square mile). The largest cities are London (the capital and largest), Birmingham, Manchester, Liverpool, and Glasgow (Scotland). Most Britons (94%) are either English, Irish, or Scottish. The remainder include Indians, West Indians, Pakistanis, Chinese, Africans, Bangladeshis and Arabs. The country's official language is English.

The Church of England (Anglican) is the largest religious organization (54%). Other major Protestant religions are Presbyterian and Methodist. The second largest religion, statistically, is Roman Catholic (13%). Islam, Judaism, Hinduism and Sikhism also are well-represented.

The British monarch is theoretically chief of state, but executive power is held by a prime minister and a committee of ministers called the cabinet.

Scotland is a mixture of many cultural backgrounds, but it is the Celtic influence on its people that is perhaps the best known. (See Ireland chapter for more on Celtic heritage.)

British Commonwealth

The largest, richest, and most powerful empire in the world's history was the British Empire. At its zenith, Great Britain ruled broad lands on every continent and islands in every ocean (America as well, of course). It was a common saying that the sun never set on Britain's dominions.

As one after another of these lands have become independent states, they have joined together in the Commonwealth of Nations (from 1931 until 1949, called the British Commonwealth of Nations). The territory of its member states covers almost a quarter of the land surface of the Earth and contains nearly a fourth of its people. It comprises peoples of every race and many religions and includes some of the oldest as well as some of the youngest civilizations.

The Commonwealth is a free, voluntary association of sovereign states, together with dependencies for which certain states are responsible. The sovereign member states are free and equal partners with Great Britain in the association. When a dependency achieves full sovereignty, it may decide whether or not to be a member.

BRITISH IN DETROIT

The French settlements founded by Cadillac were taken over in 1763 by the British, who quelled a Native American uprising under Pontiac in the same year. During the American Revolution, Michigan was a base for British-instigated raids by Native Americans against the colonists.

Although the Michigan posts were assigned to the United States by the Treaty of Paris (1783), the British occupied them until 1796.

Today the Detroit area has a relatively small community of people directly from Great Britain. Most of the Brits here have connections to the auto industry. Uncountable numbers of residents, however, are of British, Scottish or Welsh heritage, and just across the river is an actual Commonwealth country.

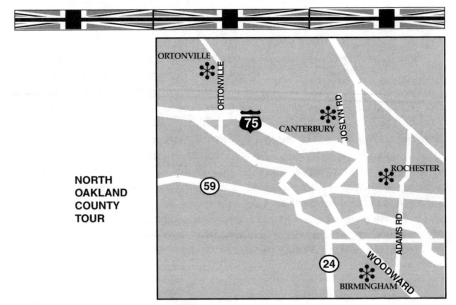

NORTH
OAKLAND
COUNTY
TOUR

ORTONVILLE
ORTONVILLE
75
CANTERBURY
JOSLYN RD
59
ROCHESTER
ADAMS RD
24
WOODWARD
BIRMINGHAM

MOTORING FROM BIRMINGHAM TO CANTERBURY

After preparing a "proper English Breakfast" (see British Cuisine), head for Birmingham, named after the U.K.'s industrial city in the Midlands. Get to **Ackroyd's Scottish Bakehouse** *(300 Hamilton Row, between "old" and "new" Woodward, a block north of Maple)* in time to buy some baked goods for *Elevenses* (see British Cuisine). Take some goodies to eat along the way, because there won't be another refreshment stop until tea-time. You might want to try some "Smarties" (English M&Ms) or "licorice allsorts." Nearby coffee shops will pack you up a *cuppa* (cup of tea) to take as well.

Now proceed *north on Woodward to Lone Pine Road (about a mile and a half).* Turn left and very quickly you will notice a "British" look...rolling green hills, rambling "country homes" with slate roofs, Range Rovers or Jaguars parked in the drives. Soon you will come to a dale with a flowing brook *(Cranbrook Road)*. Immediately to the right is **Brookside School,** marking the beginning of the **Cranbrook** complex, named after the English village of Cranbrook. Just up the hill to the left is **Christ Church Cranbrook,** a masterful adaptation of an English Gothic parish church. Then, on the right, after the entrance to Cranbrook Academy of Art, will be **Cranbrook School,** a beautiful representation of a medieval collegiate complex. (These may all be toured by pre-arrangement. See listings.)

Proceed to Lahser Road, then turn right, go one mile to Long Lake, turn right again. On the left will be bit of Scotland—a golf course at **Bloomfield Hills Country Club.** (St. Andrews in Scotland is where the game originated in the 16th century.) As you cross Woodward Ave., look for the small "castle" to the southeast; it's the **Fox & Hounds** restaurant. Soon on the right is another "English country house," now the **Village Club** (a private women's club). Coming up on the left, at Kensington Rd., is the **Bloomfield Open Hunt Club,** where you might well catch a glimpse of English-style equestrians on cantering, trotting or jumping horses.

Continue to Adams Road (about 2 miles), then turn left (north) and drive about 6 miles to **Meadow Drook Hall** *on the east side of Oakland University's campus.* The one-hour Hall tour begins at 1:30 p.m. (Sundays have a different schedule). There is much to see in this great house, architecturally inspired by the manor houses of Compton Wynyates and Hampton Court.

After the tour, follow the directional signs and take University Drive west to I-75, go north approximately 3 miles to Joslyn Rd. (exit 83). Go north (right) on Joslyn about 3 miles to **Canterbury Village** *(2356 Joslyn Court) to shop at the* **Highland Fling** *and other shops, and have tea in the* **Tea Room.**

It should now be time for dinner, so get back on *I-75 north for about 8 miles to Ortonville Road (M-15) Exit 91. Go right (north) on Ortonville about 6 miles to* **Annie MacPhee's Family Restaurant** (650 Ortonville Rd., Ortonville). Relax and enjoy warm hospitality and an authentic Scottish supper. If it's Saturday, there'll be live Celtic music.

B&B OPTION:

Instead of driving home after dinner, pre-arrange a stay at a nearby Bed and Breakfast. The British custom of converting large houses or "empty nests" into guest rooms, complete with breakfast, has become extremely popular in the U.S. Guests are usually treated to warm and personal hospitality and a large home-cooked breakfast to send them on their way. Just like the private homes they once were, B&B's vary considerably, from small and simple (often sharing a bath with other guests) to opulent master suites in former mansions, with corresponding prices.

Some B&Bs near the Ortonville area are:

HOLLY
Cooper Carl
304 S Saginaw St.
(248) 634-7075

**Holly Crossing Bed &
Breakfast**
304 S Saginaw St.
(248) 634-7075

LAPEER
Hart House
244 W Park St.
(810) 667-9106

AUBURN HILLS
Cobblestone Manor
3151 Five Points Ct.
(248) 370-8000

PONTIAC
Emily's Bed & Breakfast
1684 Baldwin Ave.
(248) 333-7499

or call:
**Bed & Breakfast
Reservations of Michigan**
(248) 682-2665

B&B Association
(313) 438-1990

CANADA

Windsor, London and **Chatham** are all within daytrip distance from Detroit. Tea Rooms, pubs, gardens and shops reflect Canada's British connection. You'll find famous British stores like Marks & Spencer, English china, scones and crumpets, jams and jellies. For overnight get-aways, great Bed and Breakfasts are plentiful throughout southern Ontario.

Stratford (about 3 hours from Detroit) is world-renowned for its Shakespearean productions. The Stratford Festival runs from mid-May to early November at three venues. Several of the 12 plays presented each season are Shakespearean. *Call the Stratford Festival Box Office for information: 1-800-567-1600. Website: www.Stratford-Festival.ON.CA*

The Convention & Visitors Bureau of Windsor, Essex County & Pelee Island has a wealth of free information. Call 1-800-265-3633, or stop by the Ontario Visitors Center, just a block from the tunnel, and the staff will help you plan your journey.

William Shakespeare (1564-1616), English playwright and poet, is recognized in much of the world as the greatest of all dramatists. Shakespeare's plays communicate a profound knowledge of human behavior, revealed through portrayals of a wide variety of characters.

THE HIGHS & LOWS OF AFTERNOON TEA

"**I** shudder when I hear Americans say 'High-Tea' because they think they are referring to something quite 'posh.' But the opposite is true. In England, High-Tea refers to a meal that usually is eaten at 5:30 or 6:00 p.m. (commonly containing a meat dish such as Toad-in-the-Hole or Bubble & Squeak [see next page]). It is consumed by (a) young children or (b) working class families. 'Proper' Englishmen (a snobbish term for the upper classes) eat their evening meal, i. e. dinner, at 7:30 p.m. or later.

One of the reasons a High-Tea (i.e. a light supper) is eaten in the late afternoon or early evening is because many working people eat their heavy meal in the middle of the day.

Just to confuse the issue, 'High' *can* refer to something in England that is 'high' either in elevation or status. Examples are:

 • **High-Church:** where greater importance is attached to the influence of the priesthood than in 'Low-Church.'

 • **High-Table:** a table of honor, usually placed on a dais.

 • **High-Life:** way of life of the upper classes.

What Americans refer to as *High-Tea* is really ***Afternoon Tea***. This meal may consist of tea (Earl Grey, Darjeeling, etc.), sandwiches, biscuits (cookies) and cake. When one has a much fancier tea, there might also be hot buttered toast served from a covered dish, and small sandwiches of thinly sliced cucumber, chopped egg, watercress, or anchovy paste. These sandwiches have all crusts removed and are cut into tiny triangles. Usually, two types of tea are served. The guest is asked if he or she prefers 'Indian' or 'Chinese.' (Meaning tea from either India or from China)."

–Patricia Pilling, Detroit area anthropologist, born and raised in England

---

Although tea is often associated with the English, drinking it has only been an afternoon habit since about 1840. Before that, it was only ordered after dinner when the ladies and gentlemen gathered in the drawing room. By the 1860s, five o'clock became the social ritual for tea, and by 1877, there was even a special costume for it--the tea gown.

While tea dates back almost 5,000 years to ancient China, Great Britain was one of the last of the sea-faring nations to be introduced to it. By 1650, Americans were already drinking tea, yet because of the Cromwellian Civil Wars, the first tea sample did not reach England until around 1652-54.

Tea quickly replaced ale as the national drink of England. In 1699, Englishmen were drinking only 40,000 pounds of tea a year. By 1708, the annual average was 240,000 pounds. The price remained artificially high due to trade monopolies, so tea was often placed in locked chests called *tea caddies.* By the 1800s, tea rivaled beer in popularity, even among the poor. It was a hot item to warm the often cold meals of the indigents, and boiling the water made it a safe drink.

 • *Afternoon tea, in the British tradition, is served at the Ritz Carlton-Dearborn, the Townsend Hotel in Birmingham, the Sweet Afton Tea Room in Plymouth, and Fiona's Tea House in Detroit. (See Restaurant section.)*

BRITISH CUISINE

There is no cuisine in the world about which there are as many jokes as the British. The British bear them with their typically wry sense of humor. Perhaps they can't boast a wide array of internationally renowned dishes, but they've contributed a lot to the world's appreciation of beef steak. The British elite troops were referred to as beefeaters. Worcestershire sauce was invented to go with it. Other good foods by the Brits are Cheddar, Wensleydale, Cheshire and Stilton cheeses. And of course, beer, ranging from pale ale to dark porter and stout.

And where would we be without the **sandwich,** named for its inventor, the Earl of Sandwich (1718-1792). Probably in accordance with their great belief in sports and sportsmanship, the British have always been betting and gambling buffs. But the Earl of Sandwich overdid it. Finding it annoying to have to forsake the gaming table for the dinner table, he assembled his meal between two slices of bread so he could eat and play simultaneously. For better or worse, Americans owe many of their eating habits to the Earl.

It appears to be a character trait of the British not to be overly proud of their cuisine—a state of mind that makes one open to learn. In the case of their foods and drinks, they did learn quite a bit from the colonies conquered by British soldiers all over the world. From East Asia (China), they adopted **tea** (and re-exported the habit to India), and from India they adopted curry-style seasoning and chutney.

FOOD

ACKROYD'S SCOTTISH BAKEHOUSE
300 Hamilton Row, Birmingham
(248) 540-3575
Mon-Fri 9:30am-6pm, Sat. 9am to 5pm.
and
25566 Five Mile Rd., Redford
(313) 532-1181
Mon-Fri 9am-6pm; Sat 8:30am-5pm.
Homemade meat pies, pastries, breads (Scottish white and Irish soda bread) and scones. Also imported condiments, teas, jams, T-shirts and gift items.

ALBIE'S PASTIES
16709 Middlebelt, Livonia
(734) 427-4330
Mon-Fri 10am-8pm, Sat 10am-6pm, closed Sun. Pasties, subs, salads.

BARB'S COPPER COUNTRY KITCHEN
610 S. Main St., Clawson; (248) 435-5250
Mon-Sat 8:30am-9pm, Sun noon-9pm.
Huge homemade pasties.

PRIME CHOICE QUALITY MEATS
580 W. 14 Mile Rd. (btw Crooks & Main), Clawson
(248) 288-4145
English groceries, sausage, prime English beef, carries the *Union Jack* newspaper.

VILLAGE BAKERY
1715 Coolidge, Berkley; (248) 541-2090
Mon-Fri 7am-6pm, Sat 7pm-5pm. Many kinds of meat and/or vegetable (including spinach or rutabaga) pasties. Order in advance.

(Also see "Multicultural Detroit" market listings.)

BRITISH CUISINE

A traditional ("proper") **English breakfast** is meant to be savored, not rushed. Fruit juice, cereal, a *rasher* (portion consisting of several thin slices) of bacon, sausage, eggs, *kippers* (herring, cured and smoked, available in tins similar to sardines) could be accompanied by grilled tomatoes and mushrooms, as well as **fried bread** (slices of bread fried to golden brown in lard). To round it off: coffee or tea served with a rack of toast (toast is held in wire racks to let it cool before serving), butter and marmalade.

Then in late morning is *Elevenses* (a "coffee break") consisting of coffee or tea and a pastry.

Lunch precedes **Tea Time** *(see separate heading this chapter)*, followed by supper—unless Tea is "High," which means it includes supper as well.

Looking at the names of some of the most common British dishes begs the question: Do the British assign these titles because they laugh at their own cooking—or do the names of the dishes inspire the jokes? Perhaps the names were thought up by well-intentioned nannies hoping to inspire their charges to eat their supper. For instance:

- *Toad-in-the-Hole:* a small chunk of rump steak and kidney or sausage fried and then baked in a batter "cave"
- *Cock-a-Leeky:* chicken soup with prunes, herbs and leeks
- *Bubble & Squeak:* made from leftover mashed potatoes and cabbage, beef or lamb, with many variations
- *Bangers & Mash:* sausage and mashed potatoes (goes well with peas)
- *Spotted Dick:* a boiled suet pudding studded with raisins.

Pudding: English puddings are nothing like Jello Instant. They can be sweet, but are more often savory and are essentially a mixture of ingredients (suet and bread crumbs are staples), steamed or boiled for hours, usually in a "pudding basin" or mold. Examples: *Steak & Kidney Pudding*—just as it sounds; *Yorkshire Pudding*—served with roast beef, it's light pastry baked in drippings; *Plum Pudding*—traditional Christmas fare, does not contain plums, but a mixture of dried fruits, bread crumbs, suet and spirits, mixed together, steamed and aged, then steamed for a few more hours and served very warm with chilled brandy butter.

In fairness, British cooking, like American, has improved greatly over recent decades in terms of health consciousness, fresh ingredients and preparation.

TOMATOES, which are indigenous to the Andes, were long thought by the European colonists to be poisonous. When they were brought to England some 200 years ago, they were discovered not to be toxic, but were thought to be a powerful aphrodisiac and dubbed "love apples." They have been extremely popular ever since.

Scotland has a distinct cuisine, arguably based on barley and oats. According to a definition in Samuel Johnson's 1755 *Dictionary of the English Language*, oats were "a grain which in England is generally given to horses, but which in Scotland supports the people." Since oats are by far the most nutritious of the cereal grasses, it would appear that the Scots were ahead of the rest of us. Today, whole oats are still used as animal fodder. Humans don't usually consume them until after the oats have been cleaned, toasted, hulled and cleaned again, after which time they become oat *groats* (which still contain most of the original nutrients). When steamed and flattened with huge rollers, oat groats become regular rolled oats (also called old-fashioned oats). Scotch oats or steel-cut oats or Irish oatmeal are all names for groats that have been cut into two to three pieces and not rolled. They take considerably longer to cook than rolled oats and have a decidedly chewy texture.

● *Porridge:* Made from oats and is often eaten for breakfast, with the addition of milk. Porridge must be cooked with salt to obtain the correct flavor. Those eating porridge outside Scotland have been known to cook it without salt and add sugar or even syrup, a habit which would turn the stomach of any Scotsman (or Scots-woman).

● *Bannock:* (oatcake) A barley and oat-flour biscuit baked on a griddle. In modern times bannocks are often eaten with cheese.

● *Scotch Broth* or *Hotch-Potch:* A thick, rich soup traditionally made by boiling mutton, beef, marrow-bone or chicken then adding vegetables.

● *Scone:* [SKOHN; SKON] A quick bread said to have taken its name from the Stone of Destiny (or Scone), the place where Scottish kings were once crowned. The original triangular-shaped scone was made with oats and griddle-baked. Today's versions are more often flour-based and baked in the oven. They come in various shapes including triangles, rounds, squares and diamonds. Scones can be savory or sweet and are usually eaten for breakfast or tea.

● *Haggis* (a savory pudding): Perhaps the best known Scottish delicacy, its devotees find it wonderful stuff. However, those partaking of it for the first time are often put off when they hear what it is made of…sheep's offal mixed with beef suet and lightly toasted oatmeal. This mixture is placed inside the sheep's stomach, which is sewn closed. The resulting haggis is traditionally cooked by further boiling for up to three hours. *(See Burns Suppers.)*

● *Scotch Whisky* (or simply "Scotch"): Certainly the best known Scottish drink, Scotch Whisky (only the Irish and American varieties are spelled with an "e" before the "y") is distilled from a barley liquor and flavored with peat-tainted water. Known as the *Water of Life* or *Uisge-Beatha* in Gaelic. There are two basic classes of whisky: *Malt Whisky*—more expensive, the product of a single distillery. *Blended Whisky*—cheaper and more popular, this comes from several distilleries and is mixed, often with some proportion of industrial spirit, to give a standard flavor.

RESTAURANTS/PUBS/TEA SHOPS

(Also see "Ireland" chapter.)

ANNIE MACPHEE'S
650 Ortonville Rd., Ortonville
(248) 627-2891
Mon-Fri 11am-10pm, Sat-Sun 6:30am-10pm.
"Michigan's only Scottish Restaurant" offers
bridies (meat and onion wrapped in a pastry),
haggis (ordered 24 hours in advance) and
pork sausage rolls. Members of the Scottish
community rate the food as very authentic.
Live Scottish music on Saturdays, including
"Celtic Pipes and Drums."

ASHLEY'S
338 S. State St., Ann Arbor; (734) 996-9191
Mon-Sat 11:30am-2am, Sun 11:30-midnight.
English ales, domestic microbrews, regular
Porter & Stout tastings; 45 Scotch Single
Malts, 75 bottled beers. Pub food, live music.

BUBBLE AND SQUEAK
363 Commerce Rd., Commerce Twp.
(248) 363-6489
Hours: Tue-Fri 11am-10pm, Sat & Mon 5pm-
10pm. English-style dining featuring
Shepherd's Pie and Yorkshire Pudding.
Famous for its fish & chips.

COMMONWEALTH CLUB
30088 Dequindre, Warren; (810) 751-9560
Wed, Fri, Sat, dinner served at 7pm and for
special events. Menu offers English pies, fish
& chips, as well as traditional American fare.
This is a private club, but the general public is
welcome. Live entertainment.

DEACON BRODIES
75 Macomb Place, Mt. Clemens
(810) 954-3202
Kitchen Hours: Mon-Thurs 11am-10:30pm,
Fri-Sat 11am-11pm, Sun 3pm-9pm. British
and Scottish foods, beers, draft cider. Live
Celtic music on weekends. Authentic **double-
decker bus** (available for hire) is used for
regularly scheduled pub crawls.

FIONA'S TEA HOUSE
945 Beech St. (3 blks N. of Michigan,
between Third & the Lodge Fwy.), Detroit
(313) 967-9314
Mon-Fri 7am-4:30 pm, Sun 11am-4:30pm,
closed Sat. Charm and elegance abound in
tiny restored cottage, on what was originally
part of a ribbon farm *(See "France").*
Available for private dinner parties. Catering
services include breakfast trays for corporate
meetings as well as gift baskets.

NESBITT INN PUB FARE
131 Elliott St. W., Windsor; (519) 256-0465
Tue-Wed 11am-midnight, Thu-Sat 11am-
1am, Sun 4-10pm. Pub at Bed & Breakfast
offers all the authentic foods, including steak
& ale mushroom pie and fish & chips.

THE PUB
Nordstroms at Somerset
2800 W. Big Beaver, Troy; (248) 816-5100
Mon-Sat 10am-9pm, Sun noon-6pm. Several
authentic dishes (shepherd's pie, fish & chips
and English pasties) and many English
beers. A comfortable waiting place for spous-
es of shoppers.

RITZ CARLTON-DEARBORN
Fairlane Plaza 300 Town Center Dr.,
Dearborn; (313) 441-2000
Afternoon tea served daily in elegant sur-
roundings, often with live piano. Special teas
throughout the year, including Mother's Day.

SWEET AFTON TEA ROOM
450 Forest Ave., Plymouth; (734) 454-0777
Mon-Sat 11am-5pm (private parties on Sun).
Tea sandwiches, scones, tarts as well as
more hearty luncheon fare like shepherd's
pie and Beef Wellington. Devon cream,
lemon curd and 25 varieties of tea.

THE TOWNSEND HOTEL
100 Townsend St., Birmingham
(248) 642-7900
Wed-Sat 3-5pm. Tea Time in elegant surroundings. Special teas at various times of
the year, including a "Children's Tea" at
Christmas time. **Rugby Grille** *(Sun-Thurs*
6:30am- midnight, Fri-Sat 6:30am-1am)
serves breakfast, lunch and dinner in a
"pricey pub" atmosphere.

A Pasty or
"Cornish Pasty" is
pronounced PASS-
tee and has been known
in England since the Middle
Ages. These pastries stuffed with
meat and vegetables became a sta-
ple midday meal for the Cornish
miners who settled in Michigan's
Upper Peninsula in the mid-19th
century.
● *May 24 is Michigan Pasty Day.*

SHOPS

For Staffordshire and other English china, see Heslops, Hudsons, Jacobson's, Shanfields-Meyers and Somerset Collection in "Multicultural Detroit" chapter.

ADAMS ENGLISH ANTIQUES
19717 East Nine Mile (btw I-94 & Harper)
St. Clair Shores, (810) 777-1652
Mon-Fri 9am-5pm, Sat 10am-5pm. Huge selection from primitive pine pieces to garden effects. New shipment from England every eight weeks.

CANTERBURY VILLAGE
2356 Joslyn Court, Lake Orion
(248) 391-5700
Mon-Thurs. 10am -8pm, Fri-Sat 10am-9pm, Sun. 11am-7pm. Inside the complex of quaint shops is a stained glass window from 19th century Scotland, a chandelier from the Michigan Theater circa 1924, authentic swords and armor. One of the shops, **Highland Fling** (248-391-5819) features high-quality Scottish jewelry, clan badges, tartans, music, books, kilts, pottery, cassettes and T-shirts. Kilts can be special-ordered, as well as rented (popular for wedding parties).

STEWART FABRICS
1835 Woodward Ave., Birmingham
(248) 646-0065
Mon & Thu 10am-8pm, Sun 12-5pm, Tue, *Wed, Fri, Sat, 10am-6pm.* Carries authentic tartans, buttons and accessories from around the world.

SOMERSET COLLECTION
2800 & 2801 W. Big Beaver, Troy
Mon-Sat 10am-9pm, Sun noon-6pm. Has branches of some of London's most famous stores: **Jaeger** (248-649-9390) offers women's sportswear and other apparel. **Burberry's** (248-643-8555) features their world-famous raincoats with the distinctive plaid lining. **Laura Ashley** (248-649-0890) has original designs for women, children and the home.

STORE OF KNOWLEDGE
Somerset Collection, Troy
(248) 637-7200
and
Lakeside Mall, Sterling Heights
(810) 566-0649
and
Briarwood Mall, Ann Arbor
(734) 669-8350
Regular mall hours. Videos, books, gifts and other offshoots of BBC network shows, including *Masterpiece Theatre,* British sitcoms and documentaries.

TARTANS

The Highlands are a mountainous region in northern Scotland. (Many 18th century immigrants felt right at home in the Appalachians and settled there.) In the early days the rugged land led to the separation of the Highlanders into small groups called *clans.* Each clan was ruled by a chief. All the people of a clan had the same surname, which often began with Mac--such as *MacDonald, MacKinnon, MacLean* or *MacLeod.* The clansmen wore kilts (short, pleated skirts) which are suitable for climbing the rough hills, and blankets for cloaks. Each clan had its own colorful pattern--called a tartan--for weaving cloth. (These tartans are now commonly called plaids, and they are marketed throughout the world.) Today the kilt is a national costume, proudly worn for special occasions.

Half-timbering, steeply pitched eaves, and leaded glass windows lend charm to the "Tudor Revival" style houses built in the late 1920s to early '30s. The metro area's older residential areas offer an abundance of examples, from small cottages to enormous "manor houses."

ART & ARCHITECTURE

DETROIT INSTITUTE OF ARTS
5200 Woodward, Detroit
(313) 833-7900
Wed-Fri 11am-4pm, Sat-Sun 11am-5pm.
British Isles Exhibit *(3rd floor)* displays artwork from the 15th -19th century English painters (1700-1800's), sculpture pieces, silver and pottery, including creamware with colored glazes from Staffordshire. Stained glass display of six heraldic panels includes Arms of England and Arms of Lord Clifford. There also is a replicated paneled room made of oak taken from a house in Exeter, Devonshire. Another room exhibits Neo-Classical style architecture from England, referred to as the "Adam Style."

CRANBROOK EDUCATIONAL COMMUNITY
380 Lone Pine Rd., Bloomfield Hills
(248) 645-3149
Hours and tours change seasonally, call for schedule updates and special events.
Begun in 1907, the Cranbrook complex embodies the belief of its founder George G. Booth, along with its architects Eliel Saarinen and Albert Kahn, that art should permeate every aspect of life. The Booths' former home—Cranbrook House and Gardens— along with Brookside School, Christ Church and the Cranbrook Schools, embodies the best of traditional English architecture, as well as the essential principles of the *Arts and Crafts* style.

EDSEL & ELEANOR FORD HOUSE
1100 Lakeshore Rd.,
Grosse Pointe Shores
(E of I-94, N of Vernier Rd)
(313) 884-4222
Public tours Wed-Sat 1pm-5 pm year-round. Prescheduled tours may be arranged any day. Closed holidays. Elegant Cotswold-style home has been preserved as a reminder of how America's industrial aristocracy lived during the early days of the auto industry. Set on acres of landscaped gardens and grounds, it offers a tea room that is open for lunch and there is also a gallery shop.

MEADOW BROOK HALL
Oakland University, Rochester Hills
(248) 370-3140
Tours daily at 1:30 pm, Sun1-4pm.
On their honeymoon trip to England, the Wilsons (Matilda, widow of John Dodge and her second husband Alfred G. Wilson) took along architect William Capp and visited English country and manor houses for inspiration. The 100-room Tudor-style mansion was completed in 1929. Knole Cottage, a six-room playhouse was built and furnished in the same style as Meadow Brook Hall. Special events include the **Garden Show** in June; a classic car show, **Concours d'Elegance** on the first Sunday in August; and the **Christmas Walk,** the first two weeks in December.

WILLISTEAD MANOR
Willistead Park
1899 Niagara St., Windsor
(519) 255-6545
Built by Edward Chandler Walker, the second son of Hiram Walker, the house, coach house and gate house were all designed by Albert Kahn in Tudor-Jacobean style. The building was begun in 1904 by stone masons from Scotland. Set on 15 acres, it is the scene for annual Yuletide festivities in December, an art fair in June, and a classic car show in August. The facilities are available for private events. Call for tours and additional information.

CHURCHES

These churches hold special events or are of special architectural interest.

CATHEDRAL OF ST. PAUL
4800 Woodward Ave. (at Warren)
Detroit
(313) 831-5000
Christmas season tradition at Episcopal church in Detroit's Cultural Center is to have service with carols and lesson followed by English dinner and church music.

CELTIC CROSS
PRESBYTERIAN CHURCH
11451 E. 10 Mile Rd (West of Hoover)
Warren
(810) 757-7832
Special "Kirking of the Tartans" throughout the year.

CHRIST CHURCH CRANBROOK
470 Church Rd, Bloomfield Hills
(248) 644-5210
English Gothic architecture (see tour).

JEFFERSON AVENUE
PRESBYTERIAN CHURCH
8625 E. Jefferson (at Burns), Detroit
(313) 822-3456
"Scottish Sunday" held annually before Thanksgiving. Service includes Scottish music, "Kirking of the Tartans," followed by a dance performance.

KIRK IN THE HILLS
1340 Long Lake Rd., Bloomfield Hills
(248) 626-2515
Modeled after Melrose Abbey in Scotland. Brief tours given on Sundays after 11am service. In-depth tours scheduled several times a year.

DANCES OF SCOTLAND

Dance contests are usually a part of Highland Games. "Highland" dances, requiring great skill and stamina, were traditionally performed solely by men (in kilts) before and after battle. "National" dances were devised for female interpretation and are less athletic and more grace-ful. There are 15 official traditional dances. Costumes are as varied as the dancing.

● The **Highland Fling** is probably the most wide-ly known of Scottish dances. It is performed on one spot without stepping away—due to the fact that it was originally performed by Highland warriors on their *targes* (shields).

● *Seann Triubhas* (Gaelic for "old trousers") sym-bolizes the Scots' rebellion at the British law of Proscription, enacted in 1746, which forbade the wearing of kilts. The dance suggests the kicking off of trousers and the subsequent freedom of movement of the kilt.

● The *Sword Dance* traditionally was performed by Highland warriors on the eve of battle.

● In the *Scottish Lilt,* the dancers seem to float across the stage, wear-ing traditional 17th *Arisaidh* dress. Prior to its introduction in 1952, female dancers wore the same costumes as their male competitors.

PERFORMING ARTS
(Also see "Ireland" chapter.)

MICHIGAN DANCE HOTLINE
(734) 913-2076
Call for information on English and Scottish
dances and events.

A REASONABLE FACSIMILE
P.O. Box 294, Rochester, MI 48308
Anne and Rob Burns perform English
Renaissance and Elizabethan music for
adults and children at festivals and schools.
CD available.

BAGPIPE MUSIC UNLIMITED
(313) 836-8528
Contact: Donald Varella
Lessons; bag pipe music for special
occasions (mainly weddings and funerals).

CELTIC PIPES AND DRUMS
(248) 684-2822
Contact: George Tate
Group's 33 members mostly perform for
special occasions (weddings, funerals,
parades, events, etc.). They can be found
performing at Annie MacPhee's quite often.

FALCONBANE ANCIENT GUARD
(517) 725-1725
Competition level pipers and drummers in
medieval costume perform for weddings or
other smaller ceremonies.

**MCKELLAR/BENNETT SCHOOL OF
HIGHLAND DANCE**
Sterling Heights
(810) 752-4979
Contact: Elaine McKellar
Adults and children, beginners to advanced.

**ROYAL SCOTTISH COUNTRY
DANCE SOCIETY**
(810) 296-3282
Contact: Cathie Lavery
Scottish country dancing is different from
Highland dancing. It usually consists of three
to four couples in formations. Classes offered
in Ferndale or Roseville.

**RENAISSANCE DANCE COMPANY
OF DETROIT**
15 E. Kirby, Suite 903, Detroit
(313) 875-6352

MORRIS DANCING

Morris Dancing in the British Isles goes back thousands of years. Probably a remnant of pre-Christian fertility rites, the dance's various figures, implements, beasts and other characters depicted by the costumed dancers relate to pagan rituals. Shakespeare refers to morris dancing as an "ancient" tradition.

Often there are "extra characters" accompanying the traditional six dancers and one musician. One character-type is the *fool*, acting as a go-between with the team and the audience. Another is the *hobby-horse*, usually a dancer in the middle of a horizontal cloth-covered hoop designed to resemble a man riding a horse.

There are over 150 morris teams active in the U.S. and Canada. Often several teams will get together for a weekend "ale" in which they'll go to dance in a variety of places, sample the local brew, sing, then dance some more. The teams are usually available for hire to perform at special events.

For information on morris dancing in the metro area, contact Jill Baker, (734) 677-1498.

Contact: Harriet Berg, artistic director
Elizabethan court and country dances with
authentic music and costume.

SCOTTISH HIGHLAND DANCERS
(248) 652-2134 or (248) 616-0710
Contact: Rene Kinwen
Demonstrations for groups; program on
Scottish Heritage; individual performances.

THE STONE CIRCLE BAND
(313) 882-1429 or (810) 832-2248
Allan Cayn, Jim Perkins, Frank Kennedy,
Steve Wahalen, Geno Zwolek play music
from the British Isles.

ST. ANDREW PIPES AND DRUMS
(313) 464-0468
Contact: Dave Martin
Will give beginning instruction to youngsters
between the ages of 10 and 15 who are
willing to commit the time and effort it takes
to be a proficient player.

WHITE HEATHER CLUB
150 Vester, Ferndale
(248) 546-5037
Social club offers Scottish Country dance
lessons.

HIGHLAND GAMES

Highland (or Caledonian) Games are athletic meets which originated in the Scottish Highlands as part of regular clan gatherings. The modern version began in Braemar and Strathdon, in northeast Scotland, in about 1835.

Competition usually includes wrestling and various track events. **Tossing the hammer** (a metal ball with a wood handle), **shot-putting** with a stone, **hill racing** (racing through the brush to the top of a hill), and **tossing the caber** (a long heavy fir-wood pole), are specialties.

Pageantry, highland dancing and Celtic music accompany the games, which also include a pipe band competition. Many also feature sheep-herding dog demonstrations, vendors, craftspeople, and Scottish food and drink.

HIGHLAND GAMES

ALMA HIGHLAND FESTIVAL & GAMES
(517) 463-5525
One of the largest Celtic celebrations in
North America is held over the Memorial
Day Weekend on the Alma College
campus in mid-Michigan. *(See "Let's
Celebrate" Chapter.)*

CELTIC FESTIVAL AND GAMES
Saline
(313) 429-4907
Sponsored by the city of Saline, a parade
opens the event held at Mill Pond Park,
usually the first Saturday in July.

CHAMPIONSHIP SUPREME HIGHLAND GAMES
Chatham, Ont.
(519) 436-3237
Held second Saturday in July.

ST. ANDREW'S SOCIETY OF DETROIT ANNUAL HIGHLAND GAMES
Greenmead Historical Village
Newburgh Rd. at 8 Mile, Livonia
(313) 832-1849
*Held the first Saturday of August, 9am-
5pm.* Held every year since 1850 (some
former locations include Bob-Lo Island,
Historic Fort Wayne and Edsel and
Eleanor Ford House), these are North
America's oldest Highland Games and
attendance is at nearly 10,000.

THE BURNS SUPPER

Scotland's most famous poet, Robert Burns (1759-96), beloved for his songs and poems in the Scottish vernacular, is honored every year on or around his birthday, **January 25.** Traditionally, the food consists of haggis served with *'tatties and neeps*—boiled potatoes and turnips (actually what we call rutabagas), a meal frequently served in poor households in Scotland in Burns' time and still popular today.

The haggis is carried into the dining room, usually led by a piper in full dress. It is then traditionally "addressed"—an appointed person recites Burns' *"Address to a Haggis:"*

> *Fair fa' yer honest, sonsie face,*
> *Great chieftain o' the pudden race!*

After the meal, a series of toasts are normally proposed:
A toast to the Immortal Memory (of Burns)
A toast to the Lassies
A reply by the Lassies

There may be other entertainment, often including singing and recitation of Burns' songs and poems, and pipe music. The Burns Supper traditionally ends with all present standing and singing *Auld Lang Syne.*

● *Burns Suppers are held by local Scottish organizations. See listings.*

FESTIVALS & EVENTS

(Also see "Highland Games.")

SUMMER/FALL

SCOTTISH DAYS
Canterbury Village
2356 Joslyn Court, Lake Orion
(248) 391-5700
Bagpipers and Scottish dancers entertain at Canterbury Village during early July weekend festival. Meat pies and other Scottish foods.

MICHIGAN RENAISSANCE FESTIVAL
Holly Grove, Dixie Highway, Holly
(248) 634-5552
Weekends, mid-August to late September.
Recreates the harvest festival of late medieval Renaissance England, where farmers displayed their crops, inn keepers offered specialty dishes and craftspeople hawked their wares. Artists, musicians, jugglers and actors in period costumes amuse and entertain fair goers.

Many of our current ideas about the way Christmas "ought to be" derive from the English Victorian Christmas, such as that described in Charles Dickens' *A Christmas Carol.*

The caroling, the gifts, the feast, and the wishing of good cheer to all.

The custom of gift-giving on Christmas dates only to Victorian times. Before then it was more common to exchange gifts on New Year's Day or Twelfth Night (Epiphany). Santa Claus is known by British children as *Father Christmas.* The old-fashioned Father Christmas was depicted wearing long robes with sprigs of holly in his long white hair. Children write letters to Father Christmas detailing their requests, but instead of dropping them in the mailbox, the letters are tossed into the fireplace. The draft carries the letters up the chimney, and theoretically, Father Christmas reads the smoke. Gifts are opened Christmas afternoon.

From the English, we get a story to explain the custom of **hanging stockings** from the mantelpiece: Father Christmas once dropped some gold coins while coming down the chimney. The coins would have fallen through the grate and been lost, if they hadn't landed in a stocking that had been hung out to dry.

Singing carols is also of English origin. During the Middle Ages, groups of serenaders called "waits" would travel from house to house singing ancient carols and spreading the holiday spirit. The word *carol* means "song of joy." Most of the popular old carols sung today were written in the 19th century.

The **hanging of greens,** such as holly and ivy, is a British winter tradition with origins far before the Christian era. Greenery was probably used to lift sagging winter spirits, freshen the air, and remind the people that spring was not far away. The custom of kissing under the mistletoe is descended from ancient Druid rites. The decorating of Christmas trees, though primarily a German custom, has been widely popular in England since 1841 when Prince Albert had a Christmas tree set up in Windsor Castle for his wife, Queen Victoria, and their children.

The word *wassail* is derived from the Anglo-Saxon phrase *waes hael,* which means "good health." Originally, wassail was a beverage made of mulled ale, curdled cream, roasted apples, nuts, eggs, and spices. It was served for the purpose of enhancing the general merriment of the season. The custom arose of carrying the bowl into a room with great fanfare, singing a traditional carol about the drink, and finally, serving the steaming hot beverage.

The celebration of **Boxing Day,** which takes place on December 26, the feast of St. Stephen, is a part of the holiday season unique to Great Britain. Traditionally, it is on this day that the alms box at every English church is opened and the contents are distributed to the poor. Also, servants traditionally got the day off to celebrate with their families. It became traditional for working people to break open their tip boxes on this day.

DECEMBER

WASSAIL FEAST
Detroit Institute of Arts
5200 Woodward, Detroit; (313) 833-4005
Mid-December. A tradition for over 25 years at the Detroit Institute of Arts. The main event takes place in the Great Hall, adorned in winter finery with tapestries, candlelight and trumpets heralding the entrance of guests. Features jugglers, mimes, acrobats and strolling musicians who entertain at a sumptuous Elizabethan feast (vegetarian option available). Make reservations well in advance.

A CHRISTMAS CAROL
Meadow Brook Theatre
Oakland University, Rochester
(248) 377-3300
Month-long run of Charles Dickens tale during Christmas season.

VICTORIAN CHRISTMAS
Holly Hotel
110 Battle Alley, Holly; (248) 634-5208
A December tradition for more than 15 years, this historic hotel (now an elegant restaurant) hosts a special Victorian Feast as well as a series of holiday dinners. (Spaces are filled quickly, book well in advance).

JANE AUSTEN'S BIRTHDAY
(734) 522-7638
Local chapter of Jane Austen Society holds an annual celebration (see below).

HOLIDAYS

APRIL

WILLIAM SHAKESPEARE BIRTHDAY AND ST. GEORGE'S DAY
April 23 is the birthday of both the English language's greatest author and the Patron Saint of England.

NOVEMBER

GUY FAWKES DAY
The English have been burning effigies to mark Guy Fawkes Day for almost 400 years. The practice of burning the effigies —which today are called "guys"—on the night of November 5th was started in 1606, the year after the failed Gunpowder Plot. In some parts of England, children continue the tradition by carrying the "guy" as they walk through the streets begging passersby for "a penny for the guy." The collection is used to buy firecrackers for the night. It is equivalent to the American tradition of trick-or-treating. Cranbrook holds an **annual Guy Fawkes Ball.** Call (248) 645-3149 for information.

JANE AUSTEN

Jane Austen was born in 1775 near Basingstoke, in the parish of Steventon, of which her father was rector. The seventh of eight children, she was educated at home and never lived apart from her family. In meticulous detail, she presented the quiet, day-to-day country life of the upper-middle-class English. Because of her sensitivity to universal patterns of human behavior, she has been regarded by many critics as one of the greatest of all novelists.

With the release of several films based on her books, Jane Austen is currently enjoying more popularity than ever. *Sense and Sensibility* is the story of two sisters and their love affairs; *Pride and Prejudice*, the most popular of her novels, deals with the five Bennet sisters and their search for suitable husbands; *Northanger Abbey* is a satire on the highly popular Gothic romances of the late 18th century. *Mansfield Park, Emma* and *Persuasion* all deal with the romantic entanglements of strong heroines.

● *For information on joining the local chapter of the Jane Austen Society, see listing under "organizations."*

RUGBY

Founded at Rugby School, Rugby, England in 1864, the game is similar to American football—except that the play is continuous, without time-outs or substitutions; interference and forward passing are not permitted; and kicking, dribbling, lateral passing, and tackling are featured. No helmets or protective padding are worn—players rely on the principles of good sportsmanship. It's traditional for both teams to gather in the clubhouse after the game to drink beer and sing songs in an expression of camaraderie.

Rugby season is May-June and teams often play on Saturdays behind the Light Guard Armory on Eight Mile Road in Detroit. Windsor hosts a large tournament each year. The Detroit clubs welcome spectators and are always looking for new players. Call either number for details on all local events.

DETROIT RUGBY FOOTBALL CLUB
(248) 542-8641

DETROIT TRADESMEN RUGBY CLUB
(248) 589-5699

SOCCER

The modern game of soccer began in the 19th century in England, where a variety of football games developed, all of which involved both handling and kicking the ball.

At a meeting of the London Football Association (FA) in 1863, the game of football was split into **rugby football** (the parent sport of American football), in which handling and carrying the ball was allowed, and **association football (soccer)**, which banned the use of the hands. The FA established the first set of rules for **soccer**, which was played at that time mostly in private schools and universities. Before long, soccer became widely played by people of the working classes, and in 1885 the FA reluctantly recognized the legitimacy of professional players.

Today, soccer is played by both girls and boys all over the metro area, indoors and out. Detroit boasts two professional soccer teams.

DETROIT SAFARI SOCCER TEAM
(248) 377-0100
Plays June-Oct at the Palace, Auburn Hills.

DETROIT ROCKERS SOCCER TEAM
(313) 396-7070
Plays Nov-April at Joe Louis Arena, Detroit.

CROQUET

Most historians believe that croquet evolved from *paille-maille*, played in France as early as the 13th century. It was later imported into England as "pall-mall." By the 1850s, croquet had become one of England's most popular outdoor sports, and by 1870 it was played throughout the United States. Simply put, players use wooden mallets to drive balls through wickets (hoops) on a lawn.

For information on croquet in the metro area, including indoor tournaments held at River Place Inn, contact:

DETROIT CROQUET CLUB
(313) 278-2396

POLO

The origin of polo is uncertain, but it was played by British officers in India in the 19th century and then spread to England and the U.S. Outdoor polo is played by two teams of four on a grass field with goalposts at either end. Play is directed toward striking a ball with a long, flexible mallet into the goal. Because of the frequent collisions between horses (called polo ponies), each player must change mounts several times during a match.

THE DETROIT POLO CLUB

Holds competitions at Evergreen and Nine Mile Roads in Southfield. For information, contact Southfield Community Relations at (248) 354-4854.

TENNIS

Major Walter Clopton Wingfield was one of the first great sports promoters. In 1873, he pub-

lished the first rule book for "Sphairistike" (Lawn Tennis). He then patented a "new and improved portable court."

Major Wingfield began advertising lawn tennis sets with special balls and bats, shoes with India-rubber soles, and special tape measures for the net. To make it an all-season game, he even suggested it could be played on ice skates.

Lawn tennis was sanctioned when championship matches were held at Wimbledon in 1877 on the grounds of a club that had been renamed the All-England Croquet and Lawn Tennis Club. Familiarly called the Big W, it is still the shrine of lawn tennis and holds the only Grand Slam event still played on a grass surface.

For information on playing or watching tennis matches, contact:
SOUTHEAST MICHIGAN TENNIS ASSOCIATION
1-800-789-8782

GOING CRACKERS

Party crackers are a British Christmas tradition dating back to Victorian times. In 1840 a confectioner started selling sugared almonds, each with a motto, as love tokens. One Christmas day a loud "crack" came from his log fire, inspiring him to make a log-shaped package that would produce a surprise "bang" and inside would be an almond and a motto. It soon became a favorite at parties, with trinkets, paper hats, riddles, fortunes or jokes inside each cracker.

Traditionally, each person at the dinner table is given a cracker at the start of the meal. Hold one end of the cracker in one hand, then with arms crossed, take one end of the cracker of the person seated next to you, forming a "chain" around the table. The crackers are all pulled at once, making a loud snap, and out fall the items inside, the hats are donned and worn throughout the meal and the jokes, riddles or fortunes are read aloud.

● *Crackers are becoming quite popular in the U.S., and are fairly easy to find at department stores and import shops (See "Multicultural Detroit"). They are now available for other special occasions including birthday parties and showers.*

CLUBS

COMMONWEALTH CLUB
30088 Dequindre, Warren; (810) 751-9560
Social club for those of British heritage.
Sponsors special events and entertainment.

DAUGHTERS OF THE BRITISH EMPIRE
(810) 774-6798
Joyce Bratt, state organizer. A service and
social organization for women of British
heritage.

JANE AUSTEN SOCIETY
(313) 522-7638
Detroit area chapter of national organization
meets regularly to discuss and celebrate one
of England's greatest novelists.

WHITE HEATHER SOCIAL CLUB
150 Vester, Ferndale; (248) 541-9757
Sponsors events, classes and promotes
Scottish cultural heritage.

THE RICHARD III SOCIETY
**9842 Hawthorne Glen Dr., Grosse Ile;
email: BATCHDG@aol.com**
Devoted to exploring the historical truth about
Richard III and the times in which he lived.

ST. ANDREW'S SOCIETY OF DETROIT
(313) 832-1849
Membership is open to all persons of Scottish
birth or descent. Social events and activities
that are open to public: Burns Supper in
January; Annual Highland Games in August;
St. Andrew's Day Celebration in November
(Patron Saint of Scotland).

MEDIA
PRINT
U.S. SCOTS MAGAZINE
**Department WWW, P.O. Box 21587,
Columbus, OH, 43221-0587.**
Articles on modern Scottish and Scottish-
American culture, history, and traditions.
Guide to Highland Games and Celtic festivals
around the world. Quarterly. $9.95 year.

UNION JACK

"America's Only British Newspaper" is
available at Prime Choice, Clawson; The
White Heather Club, Ferndale; and
The Commonweath Club, Warren.

RADIO
WDET 101.9 (DETROIT)
(313) 577-4146
Folks Like Us, Sat. 12-3pm. Host Matt
Watroba plays a variety of Gaelic and Celtic,
as well as international folk music. *Thistle &
Shamrock,* 7pm Sunday.

WUOM 91.7 (ANN ARBOR)
(313) 764-9210
Daily broadcasts of the BBC World News,
9-10am. *Thistle & Shamrock,* 7-8pm Sunday.

TELEVISION
WTVS CHANNEL 56 (DETROIT)
(313) 873-7200
Broadcasts of interest to Anglophiles including Brit-Sitcoms (old and new), *Masterpiece
Theatre,* and other gems from the BBC. Call
for info or how to receive *Signals,* the monthly
publication of schedules and news.

CBET CHANNEL 9 (WINDSOR)
(519) 255-3411
Programs, including soaps, from all over the
Commonwealth.

WEB SITES
GATHERING OF THE CLANS
www.tartans.com/

AUTHENTIC KEEWENAW PASTIES made
by retirees and shipped frozen anywhere.
www.pasty.com/home.html

U.S. SCOTS MAGAZINE
Online edition
www.infinet.com/~dlaird/usscots/usscots.html

LONDON SUNDAY TIMES
Online edition www.sunday-times.co.uk

BRITISH ENGLISH		
Sidewalk: *Path or Pavement*	**Living Room:** *Lounge*	
	Speed Bump: *Sleeping Policeman*	**Cookie:** *Biscuit*
Delivery or Semi Truck: *Lorry*	**English Muffin:** *American Muffin*	
Elevator: *Lift*	**Eraser:** *Rubber*	**First Floor:** *Ground Floor,*
Car Trunk: *Boot*	**French Fries:** *Chips*	**Second Floor:** *First Floor, etc.*
Car Hood: *Bonnet*	**Potato Chips:** *Crisps*	

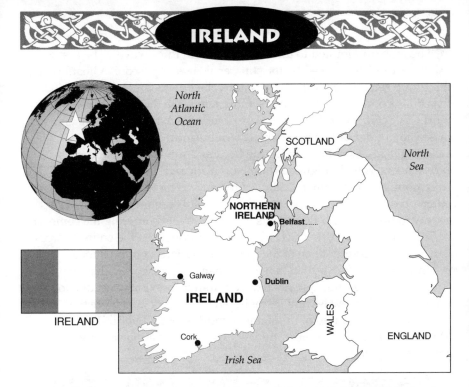

IRELAND

Ireland is the westernmost and second largest of the British Isles. Politically, the island is divided into **Northern Ireland,** a constituent part of Great Britain, and the **Republic of Ireland,** formerly *Éire.* The colors of the flag are orange, white and green.

The island's maximum length is 302 miles and its width is 174 miles. The population is about five million. The eastern coast is fairly regular but the western coast is fringed by submerged valleys, steep cliffs and hundreds of small islands that literally have been torn from the mainland by the forces of the Atlantic. The climate is moist, mild and changeable.

The Irish are descendants primarily of the ancient Celts, but the Vikings, Normans and English contributed to the ethnic nature of the people. Centuries of English rule largely eliminated the use of the ancient **Gaelic,** or Irish, language. Since Ireland became independent in 1922, the government has attempted to revive Gaelic by requiring its use in schools. English is the dominant language in the educational system and is spoken throughout Ireland except in certain areas of the west coast. Government documents are printed in Gaelic and English.

In the sixth century, extensive Roman Catholic monasteries were founded, in which religion and learning were zealously cultivated during the early Middle Ages. About 96 percent of the people are Roman Catholics. Most of the remainder are Anglicans and belong to the Church of Ireland. The Irish have a rich literary and artistic heritage. Irish literature has been largely in English rather than Gaelic. The late 1800s and early 1900s, a period known as the Irish literary renaissance, produced great writers such as William Butler Yeats, James Joyce, George Augustus Moore and Samuel Beckett.

IRISH IN DETROIT

The Irish immigrated to the United States in three waves. The first was prior to 1700, sparked by the stiff penal laws imposed by Great Britain; this group settled primarily in the south. The potato famine of the 1840s forced a second wave of about one million to leave their homeland. The third wave came in the 1890s because of increased unemployment and dissension under British rule in Northern Ireland.

In the 1830s, **Corktown** in Detroit became a miniature Ireland to the early settlers as Irish migrated from New York and Boston. Detroit, with its large population of Roman Catholic French, was more hospitable than other, predominantly Protestant, cities. Each street represented a different county in Ireland, with Protestants living on streets bordering the community. Today, people of Irish descent are spread throughout the entire metropolitan area and represent one of the Detroit area's largest populations.

Since the Irish first settled here more than a century-and-a-half ago, Corktown (though now greatly reduced from its previous size, due to urban renewal, freeways and re-zoning) has been home to more than a dozen successive waves of immigrants, most recently Puerto Rican, Mexican and Maltese families, mingled with preservationists, professionals and "urban pioneers."

SHAMROCKS AND SHILLELAGHS

● **Cork:** The city and seaport of County Cork in the Republic of Ireland and the inspiration for Corktown's name. Henry Ford's first car factory outside the United States was in Cork City, from where Ford's father had emigrated during the famine.

● **Shamrock:** The national symbol of Ireland, it can be any of several clover-like plants (finding a rare four-leafed one is said to bring good luck). As a young bishop, St. Patrick used the three leaves to illustrate the mystery of the Trinity (Father, Son and Holy Spirit) to the ancient High Kings of Ireland. Shamrocks are worn by Irish Americans on St. Patrick's Day in his honor, but also because it's like wearing a little bit of home.

● **Shillelagh:** (shi lā' la) An Irishman's cudgel—a short heavy club made from oak or blackthorn in the village of Shillelagh.

● **Classic Irish Blessing:** *May the road rise up to meet you; may the wind be always at your back; the sun shine warm upon your face; the rain fall soft upon your fields; and until we meet again, may God hold you in the hollow of his hand.*

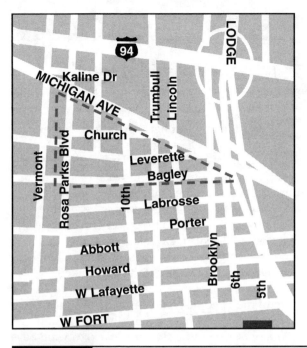

Directions to Corktown

From I-94, I-75, I-96 or I-696: take the Lodge (US 10) south, and exit at Howard Street. Turn right on Howard and right again on Sixth Street.

TOUR	AROUND CORKTOWN

[E-F/4-5] First stop at the **Corktown Citizens' District Council** (corner of Bagley & Trumbull) to pick up a printed guide to the historic points of interest. (The CCDC also sponsors a festive public tour in June. A great place to finish your walk is **O'Leary's Tearoom** *(1411 Brooklyn)* for lunch or tea (weekdays only). You can pre-arrange to have your tea leaves, palm or tarot cards read by calling ahead. If the Detroit Tigers are playing, parking will be virtually impossible until the new stadium is ready in the Theater District; otherwise there's plenty of free parking on the street.

BED-AND-BREAKFAST OPTION:

Make reservations to stay at the **Corktown Inn** *(1705 Sixth Street; 313-963-6688)*. Detroit's oldest brick residence offers artistically renovated rooms and wonderful breakfasts, featuring dishes from all the ethnic cultures of Corktown. Weather permitting, brunch is served in the charming walled garden. **Note:** *Proprietors Chet and Richard will happily prepare breakfasts for non-overnight guests by prior arrangement.*

Dinner and Irish musical entertainment can be found close by at the **Gaelic League** *(2068 Michigan Ave.)*, which also has an Irish gift shop that's open evenings. **Nancy Whiskey** *(2644 Harrison at Spruce)* has entertainment on weekends, and a bit farther away, in Greektown, the **Old Shillelagh** *(349 Monroe)* features Irish fare and entertainment nightly. Another choice is crossing over to Windsor to **Patrick O. Ryan's Irish Public House** *(25 Pitt Street East)*.

Céad m'ile f'ailte!
—*Gaelic for "One hundred thousand welcomes!"*

Perhaps the greatest heritage of Irish cooking is hospitality. Offering guests to share whatever you have—whether it is a great feast from a full larder and kitchen, or a few boiled potatoes with a glass of buttermilk to wash them down—is an Irish tradition. Any stew can be stretched, any loaf of bread cut a little thinner, to make the "stranger in the gate" welcome.

Essentially, the Irish kitchen was the house's fireplace. The interior was where the fire itself burned. Hot coals were raked over a stone or brick hearth to heat it for a cooking surface, then pushed back again. Breads such as *oatcakes* or *farl,* a kind of soda bread, were baked directly on the hearth.

Because there was plenty of fuel, people could easily bake at hearthside or right in the fire, in covered containers—originally pottery and later, iron. One of these containers, called the *Bastable oven,* can still be found in antiques shops. It was what a North American cook might call a dutch oven—a three- or four-legged pot with an unusual concave cover. The covered pot would sit surrounded by the coals of the fire, producing an even heat that baked or roasted from all sides. **Irish stew** (potatoes, mutton and onion), *colcannon* (a cabbage and potato dish, traditionally served on All Hallow's Eve) are examples of this one-pot cooking. Probably 90 percent of Irish cooking, for hundreds of years, was done in pots like these, and Irish cooks became remarkably versatile with them.

Beverages

Dry stout is Ireland's most famous type of beer. It's nearly black in color with a rich, creamy, roasted flavor, drier than those made in England. Guinness is most popular, with Murphy's and Beamish right up there.

Irish coffee, a blend of Irish whiskey, coffee and whipped cream, began as a promotion at Ireland's Shannon Airport in 1947 as an official welcoming beverage.

SIR WALTER RALEIGH introduced the potato to Ireland in the late 16th century. It soon became the main staple, until the great potato famine in the 19th century.

[O/E-2/3]   Begin with an early lunch in **Birmingham** at **Dick O'Dow's** *(160 W. Maple)* where you can enjoy Irish fare surrounded by authentic furnishings imported from Dublin.

Now go east *on Maple to Woodward Ave. South.Turn right on 12 Mile Rd., then left at the first light onto Coolidge.* The first stop is **St. Patrick's Books & Gifts** *(2826 Coolidge).* A recording of Irish music can be obtained here for playing along on your journey. Further down Coolidge, just before 11 Mile, is **Raphael's Magificent Possessions** *(1799).* Authentic reproduction Celtic crosses and Irish tiles are just some of the treasures to be found.

Next, head *west on 11 Mile to Southfield. Turn left on Southfield and continue on Southfield Fwy to I-96.* Go west to Livonia and **Madonna University.** In the **Library's Irish Room** *(signs will tell you where to exit for Madonna),* you'll find artifacts on display and an extensive collection of Irish books. Browse at your leisure, or join the literary guild so you can borrow them. (*Hours vary; call ahead.*)

With a bit of luck you'll still have time to nip up to **The Celtic Shamrock** *(33335 Grand River; take I-96 east to Farmington Road north into downtown Farmington)* for a great selection of imported Irish goods. Then hop across the street to **Cowley's Old Village Inn** *(33338 Grand River)* for a meal and some live Irish music.

DINING

DICK O'DOW'S
160 W. Maple, Birmingham; (248) 642-1135
Daily 11am-midnight. Interior, which was constructed in Dublin and then shipped over in pieces, is beautifully decorated with authentic Irish artifacts from 18th century farmhouse floors to beamed ceiling. The bar is constructed partly of stone from a castle. A huge fireplace dominates the cozy dining room. Innovative Irish fare, exclusive Irish ales and stouts on tap, live entertainment; "Proper Irish Breakfast" served on Sundays.

O'GRADY'S IRISH PUB
585 W. Big Beaver, Troy
(E. of I-75, next to Drury Inn)
(248) 524-4770
Mon-Thu 11am-midnight, Fri-Sat 11am-2am, Sun 11 am-11pm. Extensive menu by award-winning chef includes Guiness-flavored corned beef. Designed for socializing, family-oriented entertainment. Live music.

OLD SHILLELAGH
349 Monroe St., Detroit; (313) 964-0007
Irish traditional music and sing-alongs every night. Irish fare is always on the menu.

O'LEARY'S TEA ROOM
1413 Brooklyn, Detroit (Corktown)
(313) 964-0936
Mon-Fri 9am-4pm, Sun brunch 10:30am-3pm. Open only for breakfast, brunch and tea, but they do serve alcoholic beverages and accommodate private parties at other times by reservation. Menu features such classics as mulligan stew, shepherd's pie and pasties, as well as a variety of sandwiches and salads. A selection of gifts, teas and baked goods are available. Tea-leaf, palm and tarot-card readings by appointment.

O'MARA'S
2555 W. 12 Mile, Berkley; (248) 399-6750
Daily 11am-11pm. Five specials daily; home-cooked fare such as stuffed cabbage and pot roast. Home-baked bread, microbrewery on premises, regular live entertainment.

PATRICK O. RYANS IRISH PUBLIC HOUSE
25 Pitt Street E., Windsor; (519) 977-5722
Authentic Irish Pub offers over 25 beers on tap, genuine Irish fare. Live entertainment nightly and Saturday afternoons.

● IRISH COOKERY (313) 363-9634
Chef John W. Pollard specializes in catering innovative and traditional Irish cooking.

PUBS

The TV show "Cheers" perfectly depicts a classic Irish American pub—a place "where everybody knows your name and they're always glad you came"—serving up warm conviviality, food and drink. A number of pubs are in the area, but the ones following offer live Irish/Celtic music as well. Call for performance times and additional information.

COWLEY'S OLD VILLAGE INN
33338 Grand River, Farmington
(248) 474-5941
Irish entertainment weekends. The Sons of Erin come from Newfoundland to perform several times yearly.

CONOR O'NEILL'S
318 S. Main, Ann Arbor (734) 665-2968
Sunday brunch, Irish music 4 nights per week.

FINNEGAN'S BAR & GRILL
115 Ouellette, Windsor; (519) 971-8127
Sandwiches and full meals, outdoor patio, entertainment weekends.

FOUR GREEN FIELDS
30919 N. Woodward, Royal Oak
(248) 280-2902
Friday and Saturday night entertainment by performers such as Pat McDunn & The Gales; sing-alongs other nights.

GAELIC BEER WORKS
5491 12 Mile (W. of Mound), Warren
(810) 751-1230
Irish/English/American/vegetarian pub fare. Sunday brunch. Live entertainment nightly.

INNESFREE IRISH PUB & GRILL
6327 Middlebelt, Garden City
(734) 425-2434
Proprietors John and Mick offer up Irish music, food and spirits.

KENNEDY'S IRISH PUB
1055 W. Huron, Waterford; (248) 681-1050
Kitchen open daily until 1:30am. Guinness on tap, plus 81 different beers, private dining room and carryout available. Live Irish music.

O'HALLORAN'S TIPPERARY PUB
8287 Southfield, Detroit; (313) 271-5870
Tommy O'Halloran has owned this authentic Irish pub for a quarter-century. On weekends, entertainment is offered by the likes of John McGlinchey.

NANCY WHISKEY
2644 Harrison, Detroit (at Spruce)
(313) 962-4247
Corktown location, true pub atmosphere and food. Irish entertainment on weekends.

O'SHEA'S TAVERN
543 Main St., Rochester; (248) 650-8170
Its riverfront location makes it a favorite spot for the warmer months. Irish entertainment Monday and Saturday.

ROSIE O'GRADY'S
175 W. Troy, Ferndale; (248) 399-8888
Occasional Irish bands; performers include Ron Coden.

GAELIC FOOTBALL
could be called a combination of soccer and rugby. A soccer ball is kicked, but hand-passing is permitted. To see a game first hand, or possibly even join a team (the season runs from June to August), contact the **Padraig Pearse** men's team at (734) 462-2423 or **St. Anne's** women's team and **Wolfetones** men's team at (734) 453-8550.

SPECIALTY MARKETS

R. HIRT JR.
2468 Market St., Detroit (Eastern Market)
(313) 567-1173
Tue-Fri 8am-5pm, Sat 7am-4pm. Irish cheeses such as blarney, Irish teas, imported shortbread; shamrock-shaped cheese and green tortilla chips for St. Patrick's Day.

THE IRISH BAKER
5472 Schaefer Hwy., Dearborn
(313) 584-2444
Wholesale Irish baked goods and sausage. Call for more information.

SHOPS

CELTIC SHAMROCK
33335 Grand River, Farmington
1-800-672-7238
Mon-Fri 10am-6pm, Sat 10am-5pm. Irish imports, Galway crystal, jewelry, books, tapes, christening gowns and Irish linen.

GAELIC LEAGUE IRISH IMPORT SHOP
2068 Michigan, Detroit; (313) 963-8895
Wed-Sun 2pm-10pm.

RAPHAEL'S MAGNIFICENT POSSESSIONS
1799 Coolidge, Berkley; (248) 546-0194
Mon-Sat 10am-6pm, open till 8pm Thurs. Large selection of full-size reproduction Celtic crosses as well as other Celtic items.

ST. PATRICK'S BOOKS & GIFTS
2826 Coolidge, Berkley; (248) 544-2955
Mon-Fri 10am-5:30pm, Sat 10am-5pm. Carries statues, pins, T-shirts, teapots, books and tapes. A portion of sales benefits the HAVEN Shelter for Women.

SHANFIELDS-MEYERS
188 Ouellette, Windsor; (313) 961-8435
Mon, Tue, Thu, Sat 9am-6pm, Wed 9am-7pm, Fri 9am-8pm, Sun 10am-6pm. Remarkable selection of fine china and glassware at discount prices.

THE IRISH ROSE
207 Huron Ave., Port Huron; (810) 982-5487
Mon-Thu 9:30am-6pm, Fri 9:30am-9pm, Sat 9:30am-5pm, Sun noon-4pm. Michigan's largest selection of Irish and Scottish gifts, foods and embroidery.

BELLEEK PORCELAIN AND WATERFORD CRYSTAL
Heslop's, Hudson's and Jacobson's offer wide selections of Belleek porcelain and Waterford crystal and regularly feature guest artisans *(See "Multicultural Detroit.")*

The Celtic cross, which brings together the cross and the circle, predates Christianity by many centuries. Its original symbolism was associated with fertility. Within Christianity, it represents the union of heaven and earth.

CULTURAL ARTS

MADONNA UNIVERSITY LIBRARY
36600 Schoolcraft, Livonia
(on I-96 service drive)
(734) 591-5000
An extensive collection of artifacts on display, as well as books that may be borrowed by members ($25 annual fee). Call for hours, as they vary with the school year.

CELTIC JEWELRY
(734) 426-0558
Contemporary and traditional creations in gold and platinum by Katherine Grace and Saint Ryan.

CELTIC TRADITIONS LIMITED
1921 Bellaire, Royal Oak; (248) 544-2662
Cast compound stone Celtic Crosses and genuine Irish peat briquettes. Primarily mail order; call for brochure.

SEAN SHAMROCKS; (313) 882-5661
Hand-sculpted Irish tiles. Artist accepts commissions.

HISTORIC BUILDINGS

HENRY FORD ESTATE—FAIR LANE
University of Michigan—Dearborn
4901 Evergreen Rd.; (313) 593-5590
Mon-Sat 10am-3pm, Sun 1-4:30pm. April-Dec. Call for Jan-March schedule. Henry Ford is probably Detroit's most famous "son of Eire" and this was his residential estate, built in 1915 on 1300 acres bordering the Rouge River. The 56-room residence and estate were named "Fair Lane" in honor of Ford's maternal stepfather who was born on a road in County Cork, Ireland which led to the county fair grounds. Now open for tours and used as a conference center, it is available for rental. St. Patrick's Day festivities, sponsored by the Dearborn Arts Council, are held there.

MOST HOLY TRINITY CHURCH
1050 Porter, Detroit (Corktown)
(313) 965-4450
The oldest Irish Catholic church in Detroit; holds the "sharing of the green" Mass each St. Patrick's Day. Begun by Father Kern, this sentimental service is attended by leading politicians and celebrities.

CLASSES

COMHALTAS
Ceolto'iri' E'ireann
Meets Thursday evenings at the White Heather Club in Ferndale. *(See Scottish listings for more information on the White Heather.)* Comhaltas is a national organization devoted to promoting and preserving Irish culture and traditions through language, music, song and dance. About 100 members are in the Detroit chapter. New members are welcome—you don't have to be Irish, just interested. Classes in Sean Nos singing, bodhran, concertina, fiddle, tin whistle, ceili and set dancing. Contact Sean Fallon, (734) 420-0962, for details.

IRISH CANADIAN CULTURAL CLUB
Windsor club offers classes in drama, harp, guitar, fiddles, concertina, tin whistle, bodhran, Gaelic language, Celtic lettering, choral singing and Ceili. Also sponsors Scoil Samhraidh, a week-long event in midsummer offering classes, lectures, concerts and ceilis. Call Justin Manning at (519) 252-5013 or Lynn Reid at (519) 973-1263.

GAELIC LANGUAGE CLASSES
(248) 288-3575
Taught by Breege Kelly from September-May at Lockman School in Royal Oak.

IRISH LANGUAGE CLASSES
(248) 646-6193
Virginia Blankenhorn

IRISH COOKING CLASSES
Coach House, Botsford Inn
Grand River at Eight Mile, Livonia
(248) 540-6687
Annually in early February, includes buffet lunch and book of recipes.

THE O'HARE SCHOOL OF IRISH DANCE
(248) 593-8100
Mike and Tim O'Hare teach all ages and levels at various locations.

CEILI DANCING
(734) 522-5787
Contact Kitty Heinzman

THE MUSICIAN OF IRELAND
(248) 547-1461
Music and dance lessons, often scheduled at the White Heather Club in Ferndale.

(Also see GAELIC LEAGUE under "Social Groups.")

The harp symbolizes Ireland's rich musical heritage. According to tradition, one of Ireland's earliest kings was named David and he took the harp of the psalmist as his badge. It was first used as an official symbol during the reign of Henry VIII.

BASIC COMPONENTS OF IRISH DANCE:
● *Ceili, or group dance which is performed with eight people.*
● *Set, which is considered to be the earliest type of Irish dance where counties were identified by their own style.*
● *Step dance, which resembles tap dance, made extremely popular by the musical* Riverdance.

PERFORMERS

BRIAN BONNER; (313) 565-4833
Irish music for all occasions.

CORKTOWN; (313) 365-5585
Offspring of the defunct band Geezers, performs at area social clubs and events.

ROLLANDE KRANDALL ; (248) 543-4756
Sings ancient ballads and plays traditional Celtic music on mandolin and ocarina; also gives instruction.

PAMELA MIESEL; (734) 665-9984
Ann Arbor-based Irish fiddler.

ODD ENOUGH; (248) 548-0459
Serious, hard-edged Irish band performs regularly at the Friendly Sons of St. Patrick and the Gaelic League.

JIM PERKINS; (248) 474-8316
Long-time local folk entertainer.

LEPRECHAUN RECORDS
(810) 294-0643
Features the renowned Charlie Taylor.

PIPERS AND PIPE BAND SOCIETY OF ONTARIO; (248) 477-7542.
Contact: Kathy McMahon
Windsor/Detroit branch performs and gives workshops on pipes and drums.

SHILLELAGH SADDLE TRAMPS
(313) 386-3643
Contact: Icie Frady-Alley

Traditional music for Ceilis, weddings, funerals and wakes.

STRATHMORE; (519) 948-9149
Contact: Frank Edgley, who plays the uilleann and long pipes. Windsor-based group plays traditional music for social functions.

MURPHY'S MEN; (313) 383-0511
Plays a variety of music at local pubs.

AL PURCELL; (734) 420-0962
A world-renowned uilleann piper and tin whistle player, also gives private lessons

Note: Referrals to a number of other performers can be obtained by contacting Comhaltas or the social clubs..Also see The Irish Connection *newspaper and web sites for appearance updates.)*

SOCIAL CLUBS

ANCIENT ORDER OF HIBERNIANS
24242 Grand River, Detroit; (313) 535-4110
Traditional music first and third Friday each month, featuring bands such as Inis-Ceol or Shillelagh Saddle Tramps.

DOWNRIVER IRISH-AMERICAN CLUB
1926 West Rd., Trenton; (734) 671-0990
Meets monthly in the lower banquet hall of Mr. Nick's (owner Nick McGrath is "a born-in-Ireland Limerick man").

FRIENDLY SONS OF ST. PATRICK
8269 Eight Mile, Warren; (810) 758-7602
Entertainment every Friday; performers such as Odd Enough, John Sullivan.

GAELIC LEAGUE
2068 Michigan, Detroit
(313) 963-8895 or 964-8700
Corktown League sponsors many "outreach" activities and cultural programs, including live music weekends, an Irish fair in the summer, and Gaelic language and dance classes.

INCORPORATED SOCIETY OF IRISH-AMERICAN LAWYERS; (313) 224-5736
Contact: George Ward
Sponsors St. Patrick's Day celebration, dances, speakers and scholarships. Meets at Gaelic League and various Detroit locations.

IRISH-AMERICAN CULTURAL INSTITUTE
Metro Detroit Chapter; (248) 540-6687
Sponsors discussion groups on Irish music, dance, literature and politics. Hosts annual Bloomsday Celebration. National organization publishes quarterly journal, "*Eire-Ireland.*"

IRISH FOLKLORE

● **Leprechauns:** Antisocial fairy shoemakers, about two-feet tall who look like small old men dressed in cocked hats and leather aprons. If you hear the sound of their hammers, you may be able to track one of them down and force him to tell you where his pot of gold is hidden. But if he tricks you into taking your eyes off him for even a second, he vanishes—and so do your hopes for the gold.

● **Blarney:** The Blarney Stone is set in the wall of Blarney Castle tower in the Irish village of Blarney. Kissing the stone is supposed to give one the gift of gab or persuasive eloquence—hence the expression "full of blarney." The original stone is almost impossible to reach, so a substitute has been provided for would-be kissers. It's still not easy—you have to lie on your back and bend over and down while holding on to iron bars (and trying not to think of who might have kissed it before you). The substitute is said to work as well as the original.

ANNUAL EVENTS

MARCH 17
ST. PATRICK'S DAY PARADE
St. Patrick is the Patron Saint of Ireland and March 17 is his day, celebrated with far greater fanfare in the United States than in Ireland, where it is a more solemn occasion. Most of the organizations listed in this chapter will offer special activities then, but the biggest is the parade on the Sunday preceding St. Patrick's Day, sponsored by the United Irish Societies. Call (313) 963-5745.

MAY
COMHALTAS CEILI MOR (BIG DANCE)
(734) 420-0962

JUNE
HISTORIC CORKTOWN HOME TOUR
(313) 962-5660
Sponsored by the Corktown Citizens' District Council. Detroit's oldest neighborhood opens its doors to welcome guests.

ANNUAL BLOOMSDAY CELEBRATION
(248) 540-6687
Members of the Detroit chapter of the Irish American Cultural Institute present readings and music of various Irish writers and poets as they join other James Joyce fans worldwide in celebrating the day when Leopold Bloom set out on his day-long journey through Dublin.

OCTOBER
COMHALTAS CONCERT TOUR
Brings music, song and dance from Ireland. Call (313) 386-3643.

MEDIA
PRINT
COMHALTAS NEWSLETTER
(313) 386-3643
Covers Irish cultural events in the Detroit-Windsor-Toledo area.

GAELIC LEAGUE NEWSLETTER
(313) 964-8700 or 963-8895
Calendar of events and local happenings.

MUSIC PROLIFERATION DEVICE
(248) 543-4756
Includes a new traditional Celtic tune every issue, as well as announcements of local events and performances.

THE IRISH CONNECTION
P.O. Box 36775
Grosse Pointe Farms, MI 48236
(248) 363-9634
Monthly available at select book stores, clubs and pubs as well as by subscription. Extensive coverage of news and events of interest to local Irish community.

RADIO
WNZK AM 690 DAYS/680 NIGHTS
"Irish Radio Hour" with Kathleen O'Neill
Sunday 1:30-3pm.

CJAM 91.5 FM Canada
Free Passage to Canada, Celtic program 9-11am Tues.

WOUM FM 91.7 Ann Arbor
Sunday 7-8pm.
and
WDET FM101.9
Sunday 1-2pm
"The Thistle & Shamrock," nationally syndicated program features music and commentary by host Fiona Ritchie, Sunday 7-8pm.

WEB SITES
IRISH IN MOTOWN
www.tln.org/~irish/index.htm

VIRTUAL IRISH PUB
www.visunet.ie/vip

(Also see "British Isles" chapter for Celtic-related information.).

ST. PATRICK

The enduring legends of St. Patrick are that he used a shamrock to explain the Trinity and that he banished all snakes from Ireland. The true story of Patrick, however, survives not in his myths but in his work. Patrick was responsible for converting the people of Ireland to Christianity.

Patrick was born to a Romanized family in Britain, probably in the first half of the sixth century. At age 16 he was taken to Ireland by pirates and sold into slavery, where he worked as a herdsman. Patrick escaped, and after studying in continental monasteries, he returned to Ireland, where he succeeded in converting almost the entire population of the island. Patrick's writings have come to be appreciated for their simplicity and humility. The patron saint of Ireland, his feast day is celebrated on March 17.

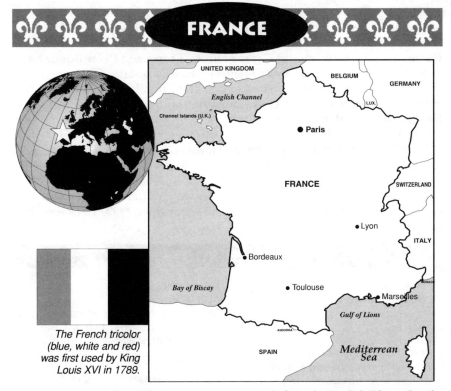

FRANCE

The French tricolor (blue, white and red) was first used by King Louis XVI in 1789.

France, western Europe's largest country, extends from the English Channel and Straits of Dover on the north to the beaches of the Mediterranean Sea on the southeast. The Alps and Jura Mountains form the border with Italy and Switzerland on the east. Germany, Luxembourg and Belgium lie to the northeast. The Pyrenees in the south form a mountain boundary with Spain. The Bay of Biscay, an arm of the Atlantic Ocean, is on the west.

Paris, the capital and largest city, is in northern France and has long been a center of art, learning and commerce. The south of France includes the French Riviera, the seaport of Marseilles and the countryside of Provence. Between are the vineyards of the Bordeaux and Alsace regions, the chateaux of the Loire Valley and industrial centers around Lyon and Toulouse.

DETROIT'S FRENCH HISTORY

D etroit was founded in 1701 by Antoine Laumet de la Mothe Cadillac, who named the site *d'étroit*, meaning "of the strait." Cadillac led a group of French fur trappers, explorers, soldiers and missionaries, who built a fort where the Ford-UAW National Training Center (formerly Veterans Memorial Building) and Pontchartrain Hotel now stand at the riverfront downtown.

By the time Cadillac's wife, Marie-Thérèse Guyon Cadillac, and the families of the settlers arrived in 1702, French colonial land patterns were established. The property was divided into *arpents*, or "ribbon farms," that consisted of long narrow strips that ran from the river inland for several miles. *(See "French Ribbon Farms.")*

Although the French surrendered Detroit to the British in 1760, the early settlers left a lasting heritage. The names of many streets—**Livernois, Gratiot, Cadieux, St. Antoine, Orleans, Rivard, Riopelle, Beaubien, Campau**—and places such as **Grosse Pointe, Ecorse** and **River Rouge** are remaining evidence of the area's French roots. Of the states that have French place names, Michigan ranks sixth in the number of cities, third in counties and ninth in rivers. Only Louisiana and Minnesota have more French names in all three categories.

The French remained prominent in Detroit into the early part of the 20th century, when the city's bicentennial was celebrated in 1901. A brief resurgence of French activity occurred in the 1970s and '80s when the French automaker, Renault, had a presence here. Now, in preparation for the tricentennial of Detroit, plans are under way for tourism and cultural exchanges with France and local events to commemorate Detroit's French founding.

FRENCH ROOTS

The following spots in Detroit have historical markers, monuments or art commemorating the city's French history:

HART PLAZA
Woodward and Jefferson Avenues
"Landing of Antoine Laumet de la Mothe Cadillac" marker has explanation in French and English.

HOTEL PONTCHARTRAIN
2 Washington Blvd.
(at E. Jefferson across from Cobo Hall)
"Fort Pontchartrain" marker indicates the site that extended from the Detroit River to Congress between Third and Woodward Avenues.

JEFFERSON AND GRISWOLD
Southwest Corner
"First Home of Cadillac" bronze tablets.

RIVER PLACE
Jos Campau at Detroit River
"Le Côte du Nord-Est" marker contains information about the founding of Detroit.

DETROIT PUBLIC LIBRARY
5201 Woodward Ave.
The Arrival of Mme. Cadillac and Mme. Tonti, a mural painted in 1921 by Gari Melchers, is in Adam Strohm Hall (third floor, Woodward side).

CADILLAC SQUARE STATION
Detroit People Mover
"Landing of Mme. Cadillac," a bronze plaque by Carlos Romanelli, was commissioned in 1901 by the Women's Committee of Detroit's Bicentennial.

MARYGROVE COLLEGE
Mme. Cadillac Hall
8425 W. McNichols
Site of Mme. Cadillac marble statue, erected in 1922.

INDIAN VILLAGE
Iroquois and E. Vernor
Northeast Corner
"Land Purchase" marker denotes sale of land by two French farmers, François Rivard and Gabriel St. Aubin, to Abraham Cook in early 1800s.

Louis VII of France adopted the iris as his emblem during the Crusades. It then evolved from the *fleur-de-Louis* to the *fleur-de-lis,* the three petals symbolizing faith, wisdom and valor.

SCHOOLS WITH FRENCH NAMES

GABRIEL RICHARD
Catholic high schools in the Downriver suburb of Riverview and in Ann Arbor are named after Gabriel Richard, a frontier ambassador who arrived in Detroit in 1789. The Catholic priest helped establish schools, published Michigan's first newspaper and books, was a co-founder of what became the University of Michigan, and was elected Michigan's territorial delegate to the U.S. House of Representatives. He was pastor at Ste. Anne's Church (see "Historic Churches").

DE LA SALLE
De La Salle Collegiate school in Warren is named after St. John Baptist de la Salle, who founded the Institute of the Brothers of the Christian Schools in France in 1680. Incidentally, French explorer Robert Cavalier la Salle christened Lake St. Claire (now Lake St. Clair) on August 12, 1679.

L'ANSE CREUSE
A bay of Lake St. Clair and a school district in northeastern Macomb County share this name, which loosely translated means "little bay" or "shallow bay." L'Anse Creuse Road, which still exists in part, once ran from the water's edge into Pontiac; it was the route farmers took to transport their produce to the bay for sale along the water.

HISTORIC CHURCHES & TOURS

Ste. Anne de Detroit Church *(1000 Ste. Anne St.; bounded by Howard, 18th and West Lafayette Streets)* was founded by Antoine Laumet de la Mothe Cadillac in 1701. One hundred years later, Father Gabriel Richard became its pastor. Visitors can view his coffin in the chapel. He died assisting victims of Detroit's cholera epidemic of 1832.

Ste. Anne's Church is the second-oldest continuously operating Catholic church in the United States. The current structure was completed in 1887. The names of many of Detroit's prominent French-speaking families are memorialized by stained-glass windows.

FRENCH HERITAGE TOUR
Detroit Upbeat
(313) 341-6810
Explores Detroit's French roots. Available to groups of 25 or more.

HISTORIC CHURCH TOURS
Detroit Historical Society
(313) 833-7934 or 833-1805
Historical and architectural tours highlight churches and their contributions to Detroit's religious and cultural life.

CHURCH ARCHITECTURE/
EARLY FRENCH HISTORY TOURS
Stewart McMillin
(313) 922-1990
Church Architecture Tour features Ste. Anne's and other historic churches. Early French History Tour explores the Detroit riverfront from the time of Cadillac's arrival in 1701, including the site of Fort Pontchartrain and ribbon farms. Call for dates or to arrange a customized tour.

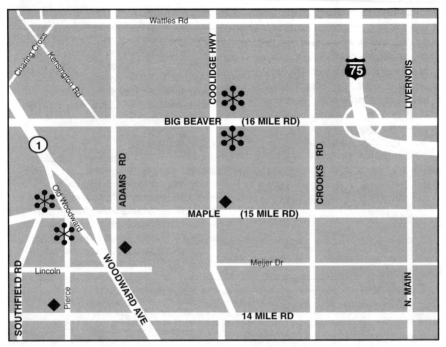

BIRMINGHAM AND SOMERSET SHOPPING

[E-F/2-3] Say "France" to most people, and the images of master chefs, fine wines and haute couture come to mind. Though there's no French Quarter in metro Detroit, you can experience a bit of France by visiting the Birmingham area. By the end of the day, you'll exclaim, "Vive les achats (long live shopping)!" *Take Woodward north through the city of Birmingham to* **Gallery Row** *(Old Woodward at Harmon Street). Park at one of the metered spaces and begin at* **A Touch of Lace** *(722 N. Old Woodward).* Displayed on a table in the back are the luxurious towels and travel accessories of French linen manufacturer D. Porthault, a company that has been supplying linens to Europe's royalty for nearly a century. How exclusive are they? A palm-size, velvet-lined jewel case costs nearly $50; a bath towel, $110.

Walk about a block south to **Lori Karbal,** a cosmetics and skin-care shop at *554 N. Old Woodward.* Ask the knowledgeable staff about the wall of French perfumes and soaps. L'Artisan Parfumeurs are made with natural ingredients (one contains bourbon). Pré de Provence's hefty hand-milled soaps come in scents such as honey and citrus. L'Occitane body and hair-care products are also on display. Point à la Ligne makes candles shaped like fruit.

You can drive to the next stop, which is in the heart of Birmingham. *Go south on Old Woodward to Merrill, turn right (west) on Merrill and park in the Pierce Street garage, just south of the corner of Pierce and Merrill Streets.* From the garage, walk north on Pierce to **Barbara's Paper Bag,** a stationery store, *at*

147 Pierce (248-642-3860). Here you'll find G'Lalo paper, with its deckle-edge finishes, and Récife pens. *Head north to West Maple, turn left and walk about a block west to* **La Belle Provence** *(185 W. Maple),* a store packed with French country accessories. Gien dishes and Limoges figurines share space with colorful furniture, throw pillows and pottery. It's like taking a trip to the sun-drenched Mediterranean coast and visiting rural homes in the south of France. At **Caruso Caruso,** a clothing store *at 195 W. Maple (248-645-5151),* you'll find Aviatic denim jeans, a French product known for its fit on both men and women. Then stop at **L'Esprit** *(243 W. Maple, 248-646-8822)* where you'll find rustic country antiques, cheerful prints and accessories for Country-French decorating. The owners scour France for whatever catches their eye—from mantelpieces to pottery.

Cross Maple and wander around **Merchant of Vino's Cellar Collection** *(254 W. Maple; 248-433-3000). (Another Merchant of Vino is near Somerset at Maple and Coolidge.)* Consider a Rhône wine or one of the 15 French champagnes on hand, such as La Grande Dame, or a red table wine such as Châteauneuf-du-Pape. For a memorable side trip, ask to see the vintage Bordeaux kept in the cellars downstairs. On the way out, don't forget a rich bar of Valrhona chocolate, considered one of the world's finest.

Walk two-and-a-half blocks east to find more shops featuring country furnishings from Provence. **Watch Hill Antiques** *(330 E. Maple)* sells European antique and reproduction pine furniture and home accessories.

Head back west to Old Woodward and walk about two blocks south to **Harp's Lingerie** *(265 S. Old Woodward)* to see sexy lace bras and shapers from France. The shop, renowned for its helpful staff, offers Lou, Gemma, Vabien and Chantelle products. "They know how to style their bras," say staffers. *Head north on Old Woodward, then west on Merrill and south on Pierce, and you're back at the garage.*

To find an authentic French bakery, *take Pierce south to 14 Mile and turn right into a parking place in front of* **Le Petit Prince** *(124 W. 14 Mile).* You'll feel as though you're right in Paris—clerks speak French to each other while they ring up fresh baguettes, buttery croissants and handmade candies. Ask about their *croquembouche,* a puff-pastry delight made for special occasions.

For a shopping excursion at **The Somerset Collection** via a new store, **Savoir Faire,** *drive east on 14 Mile to Woodward, go north a few blocks to Adams and head north; within a couple of blocks on your right is* **Savoir Faire** *(1157 S. Adams),* an elegant home store that specializes in French antiques and reproductions. *From here, proceed north on Adams to Big Beaver (16 Mile eastbound). Take Big Beaver right (east) about one mile to Coolidge. Park on the south side,* where anchor stores **Saks Fifth Avenue** and **Neiman Marcus** carry merchandise from French designers and manufacturers.

Head to the second floor of the mall for **Rodier of Paris**. In this shop dedicated to women's fashions, customers will find a selection of Kasha knits, a line of day and sport clothing that's always produced in black, navy, ivory and charcoal so that items purchased one year can be mixed and matched with future buys. Take a look inside **Louis Vuitton**, *on the first level on the Neiman Marcus side,* to see the selection of luxury luggage and handbags. A new arrival from Paris is the home linens boutique called **Carré Blanc** located *near Saks on the first level.* Here you'll find fine French-designed linens, from beach towels to bedding.

Before venturing into the northern half of the mall via the skywalk over Big Beaver, take a break at **Café Jardin** in the center court to refuel. Quiche du jour, soups, sandwiches, salads and pastries are on the menu.

Take the skywalk to **Somerset North** and visit **Nordstrom's** *(248-816-5100) at the west end. In the couture department on the second floor,* see the work of French designers such as Jean-Louis Scherrer and Christian LaCroix. Isabelle Allard designs elegant dinner suits and evening gowns exclusively for the store. *On the first floor of the store,* take in the House of Caron's fragrances, including Bellodgia; it's made with pansies.

For refreshment, **Le Petit Bistro** *in the Peacock Café food court on the third level* offers croissant sandwiches, quiche and salads.

FRENCH RIBBON FARMS

The main French settlement in the early 1700s lined the Detroit River from the mouth of the Rouge River on the southwest to the great swamp *(grand marais)* just east of Belle Isle. Because waterways were the only transportation route, each parcel of land had water access. This "ribbon farm" system provided landowners with long, thin strips of land— 400 to 900 feet of river frontage that extended inland as far as three miles.

The Allard, Ellair, Renaud, Rivard, Socia and Trombley families were among the first French settlers to travel up the river from Detroit to trap for the fur trade and establish ribbon farms in the Grosse Pointes.

As more French came, farms lined the shores of Lake St. Clair and the Detroit River to Lake Erie. From 1776 to 1783, settlements spread to the banks of the Rouge River to the west, the River Raisin to the south (Monroe) and the Clinton River to the north.

Harper Avenue, which parallels the Detroit River and Lake St. Clair, served as the outer boundary for the ribbon farms. As the population increased, the old French farms were subdivided as each owner saw fit.

● *Fiona's Tea House (see "British Isles" chapter), 945 Beech St., Detroit, stands on land that was once part of a ribbon farm owned by the Forsyth family, who probably purchased it from one of the original French families.*

THE ART OF CUISINE

Many people consider French cooking to be the standard against which all other cuisines are measured. This standard was introduced into the French courts by **Catherine de Medici** in the 1500s and later perfected by **Auguste Escoffier** (1846-1935), who is considered to be the father of French cooking.

The French word *cuisine* literally means "kitchen," but it also pertains to a specific style of cooking (as in "Chinese cuisine") or to a country's food in general. Many regional Western cuisines have adopted a number of French methods of preparing food and the terminology to go with it.

Haute cuisine is the richest and most elaborate style, using classic recipes with numerous ingredients and intricate techniques. *Cuisine bourgeoisie,* which originated in homes and farms, usually consists of hearty dishes that require long cooking times and often feature ingredients from a particular region. *Nouvelle cuisine* is a movement that started in the 1970s in rebellion against heavy flour-based sauces, which often are high in fat. Nouvelle cuisine focuses on lighter fare, fresh ingredients, presentation and the chef's creativity.

Regional cooking reflects the character of the land and its surroundings. The fertile land in Burgundy, for instance, contributes to this region's robust cooking style. Provence is bordered by the Mediterranean Sea, and its specialties naturally involve fresh seafood. Adjacent to Switzerland and Germany, the Alsace region shows influences of its neighbors in its cooking style, as in the dish *choucroute* (sauerkraut, pork and potatoes). Parisian cooking has many influences, and restaurants there reflect the French belief in experimentation and education.

TERMS

Alsacienne: typically with white wine, sauerkraut and pork

Basquaise: normally with ham and tomatoes

Bourguignonne: typically with red wine, bacon and onions

Normande: often cream, butter, apples, brandy, white wine

Provençal: usually with olive oil, garlic, herbs and tomatoes

SAUCES

Most French sauces are wine-based. Wine is used in combination with cream or spices and stock. The most common:

Béarnaise: egg and butter with white wine

Béchamel: flour, milk and butter with onion

Bordelaise: red wine with shallots

Hollandaise: butter and egg yoke with lemon juice

Rouille: pepper, tomato, olive oil and garlic

ABOUT FRENCH RESTAURANTS

There's a type of French restaurant to satisfy every dining mood The most formal of these is the *grand restaurant,* which features elegant ambience, food and service—with prices to match. Here, diners might find a *prix-fixe* (fixed price) menu, consisting of a series of courses from a set menu at a set price. *(For other types, see box.)*

A standard fine dinner starts with *hors d'oeuvres* (appetizers), perhaps a *pâté* (a spread of finely mashed and seasoned meat) or *escargots* (snails).

Next is a *potage* (soup), most likely a *consommé* (broth). The famous thick French onion soup is seldom served as part of a menu; it's usually a small meal in itself. *Poissons et fruits de mer* (fish and shellfish) or a *soufflé* (a light, savory custard) may be served next.

Sorbet, a fruit sherbet, comes next in order to refresh the palette for the *entrée* (the main course, usually meat or poultry). A side dish of vegetables *(légumes)* is served at the same time as the entrée, but not on the same plate. Unlike the American custom, the salad *(salade)* is served after the main dish. *Fromage* (cheese) is next, followed by *entremets* (sweets or dessert). The most typical French desserts are *mousse* and *crêpes.* After dessert come coffee and *cognac* (French brandy).

There are various wines *(vins)* to accompany different courses, from an *apéritif* (herbal-flavored or sweetened) to whet the appetite at the beginning to a *digestif* of brandy to help settle the stomach at the end.

Not all restaurants will offer all these courses. Often *à la carte* dining is an option, meaning one can order items individually from the menu *(carte).*

Other types of French restaurants:

Bistro: a less formal, often less expensive restaurant offering classic as well as creative fare

Brasserie: "beer hall;" similar to a bistro but serves from a limited menu and is more casual

Auberge: "inn;" offers dining in a country atmosphere, formal or informal

Café: casual, usually fairly inexpensive restaurant, often limited to breakfast, lunch or snacks

RESTAURANTS

DETROIT

COURTHOUSE BRASSERIE
1436 Brush, Detroit; (313) 963-8887
Call for hours. Only 10 tables; creative French cuisine served with care.

HARLEQUIN CAFE
8047 Agnes, Detroit; (313) 331-0922
(2 blocks N of Jefferson)
Tue-Thu 11:30am-10pm, Fri 11:30am-11pm, Sat 4:30-11pm, Sun brunch 11am-3pm. French-inspired cuisine in urban café setting. Live entertainment.

OPUS ONE
565 E. Larned, Detroit; (313) 961-7766
Call for hours. Closed Sun. French cuisine served in a luxurious atmosphere. Menu changes seasonally and typically features seafood en croute and rack of lamb.

TWINGO'S CAFÉ
4710 Cass, Detroit; (313) 832-3832
Mon-Thu 11am-10pm, Fri-Sat 10am-midnight, Sun noon-11pm. Café just south of Wayne State University serves baguettes with salads, soups, quiches. Banana bread with tangerine cream cheese and French custard are teatime and dessert favorites. Live music at night.

EAST

VINTAGE BISTRO
18450 Mack Ave., Grosse Pointe Farms
(between Cadieux and Moross)
(313) 886-9950
Tue-Fri 11am-9:45pm, Sat 5-9:45pm. Jon-Louis Seat's Paris-style bistro has changing à la carte menu with light and substantial dishes. Soups include bisques and consommé.

NORTH

CAFÉ JARDIN
Somerset Collection
2815 W. Big Beaver, Troy
(248) 649-1348
Mon-Fri 10am-8:30pm, Sat 10am-7pm, Sun 11am-6pm. Garden courtyard café in Somerset South offers salads, quiche, soups, sandwiches and pastries.

CHEZ PIERRE ORLEANS
543 N. Main, Rochester
(248) 650-1390
Mon-Sat 5:30-9:30pm. Classic French and Creole cuisine in elegant setting overlooking Paint Creek.

THE FRENCH GOURMET
23421 Woodward, Ferndale
(248) 541-1200
Tue-Sat 11am-9pm, Sun brunch 10am-2pm. Restaurant and bakery features classic French dishes, including bouillabaisse and escargot, as well as tarts, breads and pastries.

LA FONDUE
111 S. Main, Royal Oak; (248) 399-1440
Mon-Thu 5-9pm, Fri-Sat 5-11pm. Named for the French word *fondre* (to melt), this Swiss method of cooking features a communal pot of bubbling oil or melted cheese. Diners spear chunks of meat and seafood to cook in oil or chunks of bread with melted cheese. Dessert is cake or fruit dipped in melted chocolate.

LE METRO
29855 Northwestern Hwy., Southfield
(in Applegate Square)
(248) 353-2757
Call for hours. French and American food served in a bistro setting with paper-covered tables and dishes like French onion soup and ratatouille.

MORELS: A MICHIGAN BISTRO
30100 Telegraph Rd., Bingham Farms
(248) 642-1094
Mon-Thu 11am-11pm, Fri 11am-midnight, Sat 5pm-midnight. Extensive French wine list at restaurant specializing in contemporary American cuisine.

WEST

CAFÉ BON HOMME
844 Penniman, Plymouth; (248) 453-6260
Mon-Thu 11:30am-10pm, Fri 11:30am-11pm, Sat noon-11pm. Café next door to antique shop in downtown Plymouth features contemporary French cooking and Country-French decor. Specialties include rack of lamb, swordfish and salmon.

CAFÉ GIVERNY
307 S. Main St., Plymouth; (248) 453-6998
Tue-Thu 9:30am-9pm, Fri-Sat 9:30-9:30pm. Crêpes served from breakfast through dessert, along with soups, salads, coffee in arty "Left Bank" atmosphere.

COUNTRY EPICURE
42050 Grand River, Novi;
(248) 349-7770
Mon-Fri 11-10pm, Sat 5-11pm. Menu is French-inspired eclectic, but decor is Country-French.

THE LARK
6430 Farmington Rd., West Bloomfield
(248) 661-4466
Tue-Sat 6-11:30pm. French cuisine served in a sophisticated European-style country inn whose dining room overlooks a brick-walled garden. Has been voted top restaurant in Michigan and U.S.

TOO CHEZ
27155 Sheraton Dr. (at I-96 and Novi Rd.)
Novi; (248) 348-5555
Mon-Thu 11:30am-10pm, Fri-Sat 11:30am-11pm. French influence is present on changing eclectic menu that also includes Italian, Polish, Russian and vegetarian/vegan dishes.

TRIBUTE
31425 W. 12 Mile, Farmington Hills
(248) 848-9393
Tue-Sat 5:30-9:30pm. French restaurant with Asian accents offers fine dining and wines. Specialties include steak, duck, salmon and other fish, as well as appetizers such as foie gras.

WINDSOR
LA CUISINE
417 Pelissier St.; Windsor
(519) 253-6432
Tue-Fri 11:30am-9:30pm, Sat 11:30am-10pm. François and Janet Sully prepare French specialties in their second-floor bistro. Mostly French is spoken. Closed September and October while owners travel around France.

ANN ARBOR
ESCOFFIER
300 S. Thayer, Ann Arbor; (734) 995-3800
Mon-Sat 5:30-9:30pm. Nationally recognized wine list and menu that includes mushroom soup, a specialty. Salads and about a half dozen main courses.

KERRYTOWN BISTRO
415 N. Fourth, Ann Arbor; (734) 994-6424
Tue-Thu 11:30am-9pm, Fri 11:30am-10pm, Sat 10:30am-10pm. French country inn at Farmer's Market serves stews, mixed grills, cassoulets and other provincial classics.

MENU EN FRANÇAIS

TERMS

Aioli: made with garlic, olive oil and eggs

Brûlé: burned

Florentine: with spinach

Fumé: smoked

Fricassée: cut-up pieces of meat stewed in gravy

Gratiné: with toasted cheese or crumb topping

ITEMS

Boissons: beverages

Bouillabaisse : fish chowder

Cassoulet: baked beans and meat combination

Coq au vin: chicken stewed in wine sauce

Coquille Saint-Jacques: sea scallops

Cuisses de grenouille: frog's legs

Fromage: cheese

Jambon: ham; also refers to thigh or shoulder of meat, usually pork

Mousse: a molded chilled dish made with whipped cream or egg whites, usually dessert

Poulet: chicken

Quiche: a pastry shell filled with an egg and cream custard

Ratatouille: Provençal eggplant and zucchini casserole

Salade Niçoise: named after the city of Nice on the Mediterranean coast; lettuce, eggs, tomatoes, olives, tuna and anchovies, dressed with vinegar and olive oil (classic French dressing)

Tartare: chopped raw meat with egg, onion, parsley and capers

Tornedos: beef filet (boneless center cut)

Viande: meat

Vin: wine

DESSERTS

Crêpes: very thin pancakes filled with fruit or chocolate.

Glacé: ice cream

Crème brûlée: custard with carmelized sugar topping

AT THE BOULANGERIE

French bread is light, crusty, yeast-raised bread made with water instead of milk. The brown, crisp crust is created by brushing or spraying the loaf with water during the baking process. French bread comes in many shapes, including rounds, fat ovals and the classic long, thin *baguette*.

Croissant is the French word for "crescent." Originally, the croissant was made from a rich bread dough. It wasn't until the early 1900s that a creative French baker made it with a dough similar to puff pastry. Croissants can be made with buttered layers of yeast dough or puff pastry. They're sometimes stuffed (often with chocolate or cheese) before being rolled into a crescent shape and baked. Croissants were originally thought of as breakfast pastries but now are used for sandwiches and meal accompaniments.

BAKERIES AND MARKETS

In French, *boulangerie* is "bakery," *pâtisserie* is either "pastry" or "pastry shop," and *marché* is "market."

DETROIT
R. HIRT JR. COMPANY
2468 Market St. (Eastern Market), Detroit
(313) 567-1173
*Tue-Fri 8am-5pm, Sat 7am-4pm.*Huge selection of French cheeses and other imports.

NORTH
LE PETIT PRINCE
124 W. 14 Mile (at Pierce), Birmingham
(248) 644-7114
Tue-Sat 7am-7pm, Sun 7am-2pm. Bread, baguettes, croissants, miniature French pastries and wedding cakes in shop where French is spoken.

THE BAKERS LOAF
29480 Northwestern Hwy., Southfield
(248) 354-5623
Mon-Fri 8am-6:30pm, Sat 8am-6pm. Breads, quiche, all-chocolate specialty cake (cake, mousse, chips, shavings).

BONNIE'S PÂTISSERIE
29229 Northwestern Hwy., Southfield
(248) 357-4540
Mon-Fri 8am-6pm, Sat 8am-5pm. Bakery specializing in pastries.

MACHUS PASTRY SHOP
633 S. Adams (Adams Square)
Birmingham; (248) 644-1031
and
71 W. Long Lake (W of Woodward)
Bloomfield Hills; (248) 594-7675
Mon-Wed 8:30am-7pm, Thu-Sat 8:30am-8pm. Tortes, pastries, eclairs, petits fours.

PARIS PASTRY
22171 Coolidge, Oak Park; (248) 541-6550
Mon-Sat 10am-9pm, Sun 10am-7pm. French pastries and croissants are among selections at European/Middle Eastern bakery.

EUROPEAN ACCENT BAKERY
76 N. Adams, Rochester Hills
(248) 375-5599
Mon-Sat 8am-9pm, Sun 9am-6pm. Chef Alain Fournier prepares breads and cakes.

EAST
FRANÇOIS-RICHARD PASTRY SHOP
2751 14 Mile, Sterling Hts.
(810) 264-4370
Tue-Fri 7:30am-6:30pm, Sat 8am-4pm. European pastries, butter-cream and coffee tortes, mousse, croissants.

LA PETITE PASTRY SHOPPE
37156 Dequindre, Sterling Hts.
(810) 795-2929
and
41714 Hayes, Clinton Twp.; (810) 228-7986
Mon-Fri 8am-6:30pm, Sat 8am-4pm. French pastries, European tortes, sweets table, wedding cakes.

JOSEF'S FRENCH PASTRY SHOP
21150 Mack Ave., Grosse Pointe Woods
(313) 881-5710
Tue-Sat 8am-6pm, Sun 8am-1:30pm.
European pastries, cheesecake, specialty
cakes and fresh floral decorations.

WEST
VIE DE FRANCE
Twelve Oaks Mall, Novi; (248) 348-3944
Mon-Sat 9am-9pm, Sun 10am-6pm.

Bakery/café with French breads, quiche,
croissants, coffee cake, sandwiches, soups
and salads.

PARIS BAKERY
28418 Joy Rd. Livonia; (734) 425-2060
(between Inkster and Middlebelt)
Mon-Fri 9am-7pm, Sat 9am-6pm. French
pastries, sourdough bread, coffee cakes,
specialty cake creations.

BLEUS & BRIES

"No one can simply bring together a
country that has 265 varieties of cheese."
—*Former French President
Charles de Gaulle*

Whether it's Brie or bleu, the French love their *fromage*. In fact, the
average French person consumes about 40 pounds of cheese each year—
twice the amount of the average North American.

● *In Detroit, the Traffic Jam
restaurant makes its own award-winning
cheeses (as well as many different
breads), available for carryout.*

TRAFFIC JAM
511 W. Canfield Detroit (at Second)
(313) 831-9470
*Mon 11am-3pm, Tues, Wed 11am-9pm,
Thu 11am-10:30pm, Fri 11am-
midnight, Sat 5pm-midnight.*

⚜ ⚜ ⚜ ⚜ ⚜ ⚜ ⚜ ⚜ ⚜ ⚜ ⚜ ⚜ ⚜ ⚜ ⚜ ⚜ ⚜ ⚜ ⚜

TOUR   ARTFUL AFTERNOON

[E-F/4-5] Lunch at **Twingo's Cafe** *(4710 Cass, just south of the Wayne
State campus)* in Detroit's Cultural Center can be a prelude to a French art
tour at the **Detroit Institute of Arts** *(5200 Woodward)*. The recently
renovated galleries devoted to French decorative arts on the second floor
of the museum resemble rooms that would be found in 18th-century Paris.
An elaborate period drawing room and eight other small
rooms showcase the collection of 18th-century
French paintings, sculpture, tapestries, furniture,
ceramics and rare silver. Nineteenth century French
painters—Impressisonists and Post-Impressionists—
are featured on the first floor and 20th-century
French artists are on the second floor.

Stop by the **Traffic Jam** *(see above)* for some
cheese and bread to take home.

The vine-clad slopes along the Côte d'Or, the valleys and chateaux of the Loire, and the quaint farms of Alsace have given us the great prototypes of the world's fine wines: **Bordeaux, Burgundy, Chablis, Champagne** and **Sauternes.** The popular names **Chardonnay, Cabernet Sauvignon, Merlot, Sauvignon Blanc** and **Syrah** are all French grapes.

An excellent bottle of wine can be quite an investment, and the terms and types of wines available can be overwhelming. Beginners to seasoned connoisseurs, however, can find plenty of help in metro Detroit.

WINE MERCHANTS

ELIE WINE COMPANY
405 S. Main St., Royal Oak
(248) 398-0030
Mon-Thu 11am-9pm, Fri-Sat 11am 10pm, Sun noon-7pm. Exclusively French wines. Owner S. Elie Boudt, who hails from North Africa, has been a wine merchant for 12 years and congenially shares his knowledge with customers.

MERCHANT OF VINO
(See Multicultural Detroit chapter for locations and hours.)

MERCHANT'S WAREHOUSE
126 N. Main St., Royal Oak
(248) 546-5969
and
22250 Michigan Ave., Dearborn
(313) 563-8700
Mon 11am-7pm, Tue-Fri 10am-9pm, Sat

9am-9pm, Sun noon-5pm. Great selection of imported wines, with helpful, knowledgeable staff. Sponsors wine tastings in conjunction with restaurants throughout the year.

WINE TASTING/CLASSES

FRENCH WINE CLASSES
Instructor: Betty Delsener
(313) 823-3495
Classes take place at Grosse Pointe War Memorial in Grosse Pointe Farms and at Macomb Community College in Clinton Township.

WINE APPRECIATION
The Community House
380 S. Bates, Birmingham
(248) 644-5832
Offers wine appreciation classes, including two on French wines.

WINE COURSE
Schoolcraft College
18600 Haggerty Rd., Livonia
(734) 462-4448
Continuing Education division usually offers one or two wine classes each semester.

● *The following restaurants offer special wine-tasting dinners at various times of the year:*

MORELS: A MICHIGAN BISTRO
30100 Telegraph Rd., Bingham Farms
(248) 642-1094

GOLDEN MUSHROOM
18100 W. 10 Mile, Southfield
(248) 559-4230

RISTORANTE DI MODESTA
29410 Northwestern Hwy., Southfield
(248) 358-0344

TRIBUTE
31425 W. 12 Mile, Farmington Hills
(248) 848-9393

TOO CHEZ
27155 Sheraton Dr., Novi
(at I-96 and Novi Rd.)
(248) 348-5555

SHOPS

A TOUCH OF LACE
722 N. Old Woodward, Birmingham
(248) 647-LACE or 647-5223
*Mon-Fri 10am-5:30pm, Sat 10am-4pm
(Closed Sun and also Sat during August).*
Towels and travel accessories of D. Porthault,
a company that has been supplying linens to
Europe's royalty for nearly a century.

LA BELLE PROVENCE
185 W. Maple, Birmingham
(248) 540-3876
*Mon-Sat 10am-5:30pm, Thu 10am-8pm,
Sun noon-5pm.* French-Country decor,
design and gifts. Carries Pierre Dieux,
Quimper Faience pottery, Limoges, Majolica,
MacKenzie Childs, Stonehouse Farm Goods,
Vera Bradley and Christopher Radko
designs.

CARRÉ BLANC
Somerset Collection
2801 W. Big Beaver, Troy; (248) 637-7077
Mon-Sat 10am-9pm, Sun noon-6pm.
Paris-based linens boutique features French
designs on duvet covers, pillow shams and
sheeting. Also carries table linens, bath and
beach towels.

L'ESPRIT
243 W. Maple, Birmingham; (248) 646-8822
Mon-Sat 10am-5:30pm, Thu 10am-8pm.
French-Country antiques, home accessories
and interior decor.

HARP'S LINGERIE
265 S. Old Woodward; Birmingham
(248) 642-2555
Renowned for its helpful staff, offers Lou,
Gemma, Vabien and Chantelle products.

LORI KARBAL
554 N. Old Woodward, Birmingham
(248) 258-1959
Mon 11 am-5:30 pm, Tue-Sat 10am-5:30pm.
Fine French perfumes, cosmetics, soaps and
skin care products.

LOUIS VUITTON
Somerset Collection
2869 W. Big Beaver, Troy; (248) 643-8930
Mon-Sat 10am-9pm, Sun noon-6pm. Luxury
luggage and handbags.

RODIER OF PARIS
Somerset Collection
2801 W. Big Beaver, Troy; (248) 643-9300
Mon-Sat 10am-9pm, Sun noon-6pm.
Women's fashions in classic colors.

SAVOIR FAIRE
1157 S. Adams, Birmingham
(248) 644-0560
Tue-Sat 10am-6pm; closed Sun and Mon.
An elegant store for the home featuring fine
antique French furniture and accessories.

WATCH HILL ANTIQUES
330 E. Maple, Birmingham
(248) 644-7445
*Mon, Wed, Fri, Sat 10am-6pm, Thu 10am-
8pm, Sun noon-5pm.* Painted armoires and
European country furniture, antique and
reproduction pine furniture.

MUSEUMS AND EXHIBITS

DETROIT INSTITUTE OF ARTS
5200 Woodward Ave., Detroit
(313) 833-7900
Wed-Fri 11am-4pm, Sat-Sun 11am-5pm.
Nineteenth century European art features
French painters in S130, S131 and S132
(Impressionists and Post-Impressionists).
Works by 20th century French artists are in
N286. Galleries housing the extensive
collection of 17th and 18th century French
decorative arts on the south side of the
second floor have reopened after renovation.

DETROIT HISTORICAL MUSEUM
5401 Woodward Ave., Detroit
(313) 833-1805
Wed-Fri 9:30am-5pm, Sat-Sun 10am-5pm.
Exhibits tracing Detroit's 300-year history
begin with French explorer Antoine de la
Mothe Cadillac landing on the banks of the
Detroit River in 1701.

FRANÇOIS BABY HOUSE
Windsor's Community Museum
254 Pitt St. W., Windsor; (519) 253-1812
*Tue-Sat 10am-5pm year-round. Sun 2-5pm
May-Sept.* One of the older surviving brick
buildings along the Detroit River, it served as
Gen. William Hull's headquarters during the
War of 1812. Displays feature artifacts,
firearms, tools, agricultural implements and
furnishings of French settlers and Indians.

PÈRE MARQUETTE

Père (Father) Jacques Marquette was a French voyageur and Roman Catholic missionary who explored the Great Lakes and the Mississippi River. In 1668, he established a mission among Ottawa Indians in Sault Ste. Marie. He moved to St. Ignace in 1671.

During his travels through Michigan's Upper Peninsula, Père Marquette entrusted a silver chalice to the Indians. He told them that if he did not return for it, they were to wait for another black-robed priest to request it. The chalice remained in sacred trust for more than 200 years, buried under a great tree until 1912.

That year, two elderly Native American Indians asked Father Patrick Dunigan, a chaplain for the Michigan National Guard in the Upper Peninsula, if he would like to see the "treasure" they wished to give him. Father Dunigan willed the chalice to the **Manresa Retreat Home** *(1390 Quarton Rd., Bloomfield Hills; 248-644-4933),* where it is now used at the concluding mass of each retreat.

MONROE COUNTY HISTORICAL SOCIETY
126 S. Monroe St., Monroe
(734) 243-7137
Summer daily 10am-5pm. Winter closed Mon-Tue. The city of Monroe, 38 miles south of Detroit, was founded by French families who moved from Detroit in the second half of the 18th century. The **Historical Museum** at 126 Monroe St. contains archeological and art exhibits related to the early French settlement at the mouth of the River Raisin.

The Historical Society also maintains the **Navarre-Anderson Trading Post**, located two miles west of town at 3775 N. Custer. It was established by the French in 1789 and contains two early French buildings. The oldest log cabin house remaining in Michigan was built in the *pièce sur pièce* style of French Canadian architecture.

The **Battlefield Visitors Center** (1403 E. Elm St.; Exit 14 off I-75) is the site of the Battle of River Raisin. Open daily 10am-6pm Memorial Day to Labor Day. Open remainder of year on weekends and by appointment. Call (734) 243-7137.

GROSSE POINTE HISTORICAL SOCIETY
381 Kercheval, Grosse Pointe Woods
(313) 884-7010
Tue-Wed 10am-12:30pm, 1:30-4pm.
Resource Center in the historic Provencal-Weir House contains artifacts, archives, photographs and land records. Group hosts series of programs and events and produces booklets and videos. *Pointe to Pointe* guidebook outlines tour along East Jefferson-Lakeshore Road from Windmill Pointe to Gaukler Pointe. Two documentary videos — *Recollections of the Past (1650-1900)* and *The Past As Prologue (1900-Present)*— are available.

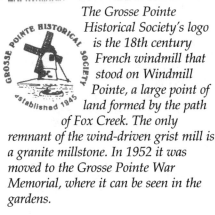

The Grosse Pointe Historical Society's logo is the 18th century French windmill that stood on Windmill Pointe, a large point of land formed by the path of Fox Creek. The only remnant of the wind-driven grist mill is a granite millstone. In 1952 it was moved to the Grosse Pointe War Memorial, where it can be seen in the gardens.

EVENTS

APRIL
FRANCOPHONE FESTIVAL
Place Concorde, Windsor
(519) 948-5545
"Francophone" refers to a population, such as Canada's, that uses French as its first or second language. This 10-day event for Windsor's French-Canadian community features traditional meals, entertainment, theater, a floor-hockey tournament and other activities.

JUNE
ST. JEAN BAPTISTE CELEBRATION
Place Concorde, Windsor
(519) 948-5545
Around June 24. Festivities honor the patron saint of French Canadians.

JULY
FRENCH HERITAGE FESTIVAL
St. Ignace; (906) 643-9394
Mid-July. Living history encampment and candlelight tour at Father Marquette National Memorial and Museum in the Upper Peninsula.

BASTILLE DAY
July 14. The French Revolution began in 1789 when crowds of Parisians assaulted the Bastille prison, freed the prisoners and dismantled the building stone by stone. In France, the holiday calls for fireworks, parades, festive dinners and balls. Though the French community in Detroit does not celebrate on that scale, the French American Chamber of Commerce and other local organizations sometimes host receptions or special events.

AUGUST
OLD FRENCH TOWN DAYS
Monroe County Historical Society
Hellenberg Park, Monroe
(734) 243-7137
Fourth weekend in August. Festival recalls early pioneers who settled at the mouth of the River Raisin and named their village French Town. Battles re-enacted from the Revolutionary, 1812, and French & Indian Wars. Canoeists depict life of the voyageurs, men who carried the cargoes of the fur trade on the River Raisin in the 18th century.

NOVEMBER
NOUVEAU BEAUJOLAIS TASTINGS
The new wine from Beaujolais in southern Burgundy is released a month after the harvest, usually the third Thursday in November. When the new wine arrives in Detroit, French organizations and wine merchants often have wine-tasting parties.

FRENCH FILMS

ANN ARBOR FILM FESTIVAL
(734) 995-5356
Held in early-spring, it's the oldest 16mm festival in the country for independent and experimental filmmakers. French filmmakers featured.

DETROIT FILM THEATRE
5200 Woodward Ave., Detroit
(at the Detroit Institute of Arts)
(313) 833-7900
Fri-Sat 7 and 9:30pm; Sun 4 and 7pm; Mon 7pm. Alternative and foreign films presented in original language with English subtitles. Crystal Gallery Café upstairs offers soups, sandwiches, pastries and beverages one hour before each day's first performance until start of last performance. Free calendars available at book and music stores and DIA shops.

LANDMARK-MAIN ART THEATRE
118 N. Main St., Royal Oak
(NE corner of 11 Mile)
(248) 542-0180
Often shows French films with English subtitles.

STAR SOUTHFIELD
25333 W. 12 Mile Rd, Southfield
(between Northwestern and Telegraph)
(248) 372-2222
Occasionally shows French films with English subtitles.

THOMAS VIDEO
122 S. Main St., Clawson
(248) 280-2833
Daily 10am -midnight. Largest selection of foreign films on tape in Michigan, including many in French. Sales and rentals.

FRENCH COURT & COUNTRY DANCES

Dance was the principal form of recreation and entertainment in 17th and 18th century France. Aristocratic children started taking lessons at an early age to learn the *minuet, allemande, gavotte, quadrille, passepied* and other court dances.

The intricate steps of French court and country dances of that period influenced the development of square and country dancing and inspired contemporary ballet.

To celebrate the 17th and 18th century history of Detroit, Michigan and the Great Lakes, the **Mme. Cadillac Dance Theatre** *(see "Performing Arts")* performs and demonstrates folk-style French and English country dances, as well as the more formal court dances. The group's repertoire includes:

- *Branles:* country dances from various regions of France

- *Court dances:* allemande, gavotte, minuet and passepied

- *Danse de l'épée:* sword dance requiring fencing skills

- *Danse carré:* a lively Québecois quadrille

PERFORMING ARTS

MME. CADILLAC DANCE THEATRE
15 E. Kirby, Ste. 803, Detroit
(313) 875-6354
Founded by artistic director Harriet Berg, this touring group performs authentic 17th and 18th century music and dance in costume to depict life in the French Colonial period of the Great Lakes. Dance dramas include *First Lady of Detroit—The Adventures of Marie-Thérèse Guyon Cadillac; Jean-Baptiste Pointe-du-Sable—Black Man in the Wilderness;* and *Chevalier St. George— Black Baroque Composer.* Workshops in French court and country dances available. For booking information, call Cally Kypros (313-881-8024 or 882-2100).

ORGANIZATIONS

ALLIANCE FRANÇAISE
Founded in 1902 to promote French culture and language, the organization hosts lectures by persons eminent in French literature, art, travel, history and science. Members attend films, plays, receptions, wine tastings and other programs of interest to Francophiles. There are several affiliated groups in the Detroit area:

Grosse Pointe Chapter
c/o Grosse Pointe War Memorial
32 Lake Shore Dr.
Grosse Pointe Farms
(313) 886-0269 or 881-8844
Chapter hosts conversation groups and monthly events.

Greater Detroit Chapter
(313) 584-7296 or (248) 645-5176
Contact: Didet McPhail, president
Monthly programs.

SOIRÉE LITTÉRAIRE
(248) 644-2692
Contact: Ed Chalom
This subgroup of Alliance Française hosts French Great Books discussions.

FRENCH INSTITUTE OF MICHIGAN
400 W. Maple Rd., Bimringham
(248) 644-4110
Contact: Ludmila von Taube, director
Wed 1-5pm. Affiliated with Alliance Française, the institute offers French language classes and cultural programs.

ÉCOLE FRANÇAISE
6275 Inkster, Bloomfield Hills
(248) 203-5181
Contact: Pascale Corduries, director
Preschool, elementary and secondary school serves children of French Nationals in metro Detroit.

FRENCH-AMERICAN CHAMBER OF COMMERCE
27777 Franklin, Ste. 1200; Southfield
(248) 358-1861
Promotes international commerce between United States and France. Sponsors business seminars and cultural events.

FRENCH TRADE COMMISSION
100 Renaissance Center, Ste. 1670
Detroit
(313) 567-0510
French government agency regulates and facilitates trade between United States and France. Hosts cultural activities.

PLACE CONCORDE
7515 Forest Glade Dr., Windsor
(Lauzon Pkwy. exit off E.C. Row Expy.)
(519) 948-5545
Banquet and convention facility serves as information and resource center for French Canadian community. Classes, activities and special events scheduled throughout the year.

The Eiffel Tower is one of the world's most famous landmarks. Built in 1899 to commemorate the 100th anniversary of the French Revolution, today it still dominates the Paris skyline. A 1/3-scale replica can be toured at Kings Island in Cincinnati (about a 4-hour drive from Detroit).

RESOURCES

BURTON HISTORICAL COLLECTION
Detroit Public Library
5201 Woodward Ave., Detroit
(313) 833-1480
Sources for French Canadian genealogy.

INTERNATIONAL BOOK CENTRE
2391 Auburn Rd., Shelby Twp.
(810) 254-7230
Mon-Sat 11am-5pm. French language instruction, literature and cultural books. Cassettes, videos and computer software. Posters, T-shirts, games, dolls and gifts.

RESOURCEFUL CHILD
Park Street West, Windsor
(second floor of Park Place)
(519) 977-7464
Bookstore with French books and tapes for children.

MEDIA

PRINT
LE RENPART
7515 Forest Glade Dr., Windsor
(Place Concorde)
(519) 948-4139
Weekly French language newspaper.

BROADCAST
CBC RADIO AND TELEVISION
825 Riverside Dr. W., Windsor
(519) 255-3411
540 AM radio with French variety programming.

Channel 54 (UHF) airs CBC network programs from Montreal and Ottawa.

The **International Channel** on cable T.V. offers French programming and movies. Check your local cable guide.

WEB SITES
FRENCH CULTURE
www.francenet.fr/franceweb/fwcarnet

CONNOISSEURS GUIDE
www.connaisseurs.com/indexa

WINE TERMS GLOSSARY
www.bpe.com/drinks/wine/winegloss

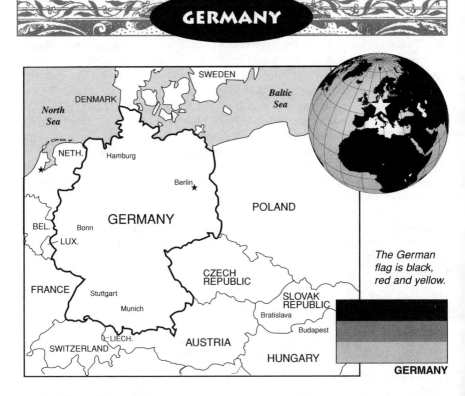

The German flag is black, red and yellow.

GERMANY

Germany, in central Europe, stretches from the Alps to the Baltic and North seas. It is bordered by nine countries: Denmark on the north; Poland and the Czech Republic on the east; Austria and Switzerland on the south; and France, Luxembourg, Belgium and the Netherlands on the west. The German people are descended from Alpine (south and central regions) and Teutonic (northern region) tribes. Most of Germany's major rivers lie in the west. The most important is the Rhine, flowing by fairy-tale castles and forming part of the borders with Switzerland and France before flowing into the Netherlands. There are three major geographical regions: lowland plains in the north, uplands in the center and mountains in the south.

For much of its history, Germany was a geographical term for the area occupied by German states. National unification in 1871 lasted 74 years. In 1945, after World War II, the country was divided into the Federal Republic of Germany (West Germany) and the German Democratic Republic (East Germany). On October 3, 1990, Germany once again became a unified nation when East Germany became part of the Federal Republic of Germany, the capital of which is Berlin.

About 45 percent of Germans are Protestants, the great majority of whom are Lutherans. Most the Protestants live in the north. About 40 percent of the people are Roman Catholics, concentrated in the Rhineland and Bavaria.

GERMANS IN AMERICA

People of German descent make up the largest ethnic group in the United States, constituting 23.3 percent of the population. Although some skilled German workers were in Capt. John Smith's Jamestown settlement in 1607, the first all-German settlement in America was founded in 1683 when 13 German families on the ship *Concord* landed at what is now Germantown, Pennsylvania. Commenting on the rich culture, social- and work-ethics of German colonists, Benjamin Franklin said, "America cultivates best what Germany brought forth."

Later, Germans came to the United States in several waves in search of work opportunities and land for farming. Mass immigration of 6 million Germans between 1820 and 1920 created "Little Germanies" in New York, Milwaukee, St. Louis, Cincinnati and Detroit, as well as rural communities in Michigan and most other states.

Fleeing political unrest in their homeland, Germans came *en masse* to Detroit in the early 1830s. Most of the immigrants were educated and had capital to establish small businesses. They settled mostly on the east side of the city and set up tanneries along Gratiot, the trade route of the trappers. The area north of Jefferson Avenue and along Gratiot Avenue was known as Germantown by the mid-1800s.

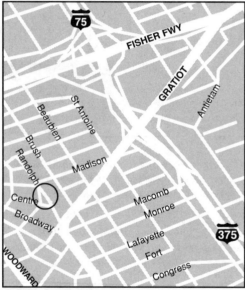

SITE OF GERMANTOWN IN OLD DETROIT

In 1849, four German immigrants formed the *Gesang-Verein Harmonie* to meet and sing *Lieder* (German art songs). Eventually they built a clubhouse, designed by German American architect Richard E. Raseman, at Beaubien and Lafayette. The **Harmonie Club** faces **Harmonie Park** *(circled on map)* and is a massive beaux arts classical design. **Trapper's Alley,** the festival marketplace in downtown Detroit's Greektown *(see "Greece")*, is the former fur processing company of immigrant Traugott Schmidt.

Another wave of immigration, between 1850 and 1880, saw thousands of ambitious arrivals becoming merchants, chemists, engineers, manufacturers, physicians, clergy and professors, the last founding the University of Detroit. By the 1880 U.S. census, the German population outnumbered the combined totals of two dozen other nationality groups represented in Detroit. Twentieth century migrations occurred in response to the World Wars and, more recently, with German firms in auto-related and other businesses establishing operations here. As a result of immigration in Detroit, Ann Arbor, Alpena, Saginaw and surrounding areas, 28 percent of Michigan's population is of German descent.

To experience "Bavarian" heritage and hospitality, plan a day trip to Frankenmuth, *about 80 miles north of Detroit, off I-75, Exit 136.* The town features more than 100 shops and attractions, including the world's largest Christmas store and restaurants famous for chicken dinners. *(See "Michigan Towns" for a suggested tour.)*

Another way to "journey to Germany" is to attend an **Oktoberfest**. Germans can't wait for a good party, so the Oktoberfest season begins in September. *(See "Events.")* *Wochen-Post*, the German-American weekly available in metro Detroit, runs a complete calendar listing in the fall.

PROSIT! (CHEERS!)

Although the Stroh brewing facilities are no longer in Detroit, the company still has its international corporate headquarters here and the Stroh family legacy remains through its many financial gifts to organizations. One might say beer helped build the city.

Virtually every country in the world produces its own beer, but "Germany" and "beer" are synonymous to many people. Germany has more than 1,000 breweries and produces 5,000 varieties of beer. Today, more types of beer are available than ever, with the boom in microbreweries, brew pubs that make their own brands on premises, and home brewing. **Lager** is by far the most popular style, accounting for about 90 percent of beer consumed, with **ale**—being produced in increasingly creative forms—becoming prized by connoisseurs. (Whether the beer is an ale or a lager depends on the yeast used in the brew and the temperature of the fermentation.)

BREWING SUPPLIES

BREW & GROW
33523 W. Eight Mile, Livonia
(800) 734-4195 and (248) 442-7939
Mon-Fri 10am-7pm, Sat 10am-5pm.

DETROIT BREW FACTORY
18065 E. Eight Mile, Eastpointe
(810) 776-8848
Tue-Fri 11am-9pm, Sat 10am-6pm, Sun 12-5pm. Closed Mon. This brew-on-premises microbrewery offers both beer and wine-making for the do-it-yourselfer.

MERCHANT'S WAREHOUSE
126 N. Main St., Royal Oak
(248) 546-7770
and
22250 Michigan Ave., Dearborn
(313) 563-8700
Mon 11am-7pm, Tue-Fri 10am-9pm, Sat 9am-9pm, Sun noon-5pm. Great selection of imported beers (and wines), as well as everything necessary to brew your own. Sponsors festive beer tastings throughout the year.

SHELBY BEER & WINEMAKERS SUPPLY
3665 Christi Lane, Shelby Twp.
(810) 739-0247
Mon-Fri 8am-8pm, Sat 8am-4:30pm. More than 270 types of beer products to make; free classes for new brewers.

See page 223 for information on homebrewing.

Among the many varieties of German sausage (wurst) are:

BAUERWURST
Coarse-textured, smoked and highly seasoned; usually steamed or sautéed.

BIERWURST OR BEERWURST
Cooked sausage flavored with garlic; dark red color; usually sold as sandwich meat.

BRAUNSCHWEIGER
Most popular of the liverwursts; enriched with eggs and milk; spreadable and usually served at room temperature.

BOCKWURST
Ground veal flavored with parsley and chive; generally sold raw and must be cooked well before serving. Traditionally served with bock beer, particularly during springtime.

BRATWURST
Pork and veal seasoned with a variety of spices, including ginger, nutmeg, coriander and/or caraway. Generally fresh; must be well-roasted or sautéed before eating.

KNACKWURST OR KNOCKWURST
Short, thick links of pre-cooked and smoked-ground beef, pork or both, flavored with garlic. Usually boiled or grilled, often with sauerkraut. The name comes from the German *knack* ("crack") because of the crackling sound the sausage makes when bitten into.

LIVERWURST (LEBERWURST) OR LEBERKASE
"Liver sausage" or "liver cheese." Well-seasoned, ready-to-eat sausage made from at least 30 percent pork liver mixed with pork or other meat. It ranges from firm enough to slice to smooth and spreadable. It is smoked or plain and comes in large links, loaves and slices. Generally used for snacks and sandwiches, it goes well with rye bread and crackers.

METTWURST
Also called *schmierwurst* because it's soft enough to "smear" or spread. Bright-red pork sausage, seasoned with coriander and white pepper. Cured, smoked and ready to "schmier" on bread or crackers.

SCHWEINEWURST
Small pork sausages.

THURINGER
Any of several fresh and smoked sausages named for the former German region of Thuringia. Coriander is an important seasoning.

WEISSWURST
German for "white sausage," made with veal, cream and eggs. It's traditionally served at Oktoberfests with mustard, rye bread and beer.

WÜRSTCHEN
Frankfurter made of lightly smoked pork and beef; the forerunner of the American hot dog.

ZUNGENWURST
Dried sausage that can be eaten raw, although it's more often sliced and browned in butter or bacon fat.

RESTAURANTS

BAVARIAN CHATEAU
5251 E. Outer Dr., Detroit
(313) 371-0720
Wed 11:30am-2:30pm for lunch. Bar open until 6pm. Banquet hall with stage and seating for up to 700 is available for rent Monday-Tuesday and Thursday-Sunday at former site of German American Cultural Center. Restaurant specializes in Jäger Schnitzel, Wiener Schnitzel, Bratwurst, Knockwurst, meatballs, ribs and fish.

DAKOTA INN RATHSKELLAR
17324 John R, Detroit
(I-75 McNichols-Six Mile Exit)
(313) 867-9722
Lunch: Tue-Wed 11am-2pm. Dinner: Thu-Fri
11am-1am, Sat 5pm-1am. Beer haus run by the Kurz family since 1933 features German fare, *oompah* music, evening sing-alongs and a month-long Oktoberfest celebration. Among the regulars who gather here are German teachers who have a *Stammtisch* (designated table) on the first Friday of the month.

GERMAN RESTAURANT
114 N. Center St., Stockbridge
(517) 851-7785
Tues-Sat 11am-8pm, Sun 11am-7pm. Rudi and Wilma Kaczmarek serve traditional home-cooked German meals at a small-town restaurant north of I-94 between Ann Arbor and Jackson. The Sausage House adjacent offers hams, bacon, German luncheon meats and fresh baked goods daily, except Monday.

ROBUST AND SUBSTANTIAL

German cooking is simple, robust and substantial. The cuisine is known for *Wurst* **(sausage)** and **cheese,** as well as **pickles, sauerkraut, potatoes, dark breads** and **beer.**

Flavors in German cooking come from herbs and spices such as dill, sorrel, thyme, juniper, caraway seeds and mustard seeds. Combining vinegar and sugar gives the sweet-and-sour taste present in many German dishes.

Germans rely heavily on pork *(Schweinefleisch)* for a main dish. It often is prepared as *Koteletten* (chops) or *Schweinebraten* (roasted in the oven). Meat, vegetables and potatoes are served together on one big plate.

Specialties such as sauerkraut and pickles are prepared in vinegar and brine. To make sauerkraut, cabbage is fermented with salt in its own juice and seasoned with spices.

German wines, usually white, are popular because they are light, fruity and fresh tasting. The most well-known types are *Mosel, Reisling, Rhine* and *Liebfraumilch.*

MENU FAVORITES

Wurstplatte: Sausages and cold cuts

Sauerbraten: Pot roast

Hasenpfeffer: Roasted rabbit

Wiener Schnitzel: Breaded veal cutlets

Rouladen: Rolled beef with pickle and onion

Spätzle: Tiny dumplings or thin noodles

Kartoffelpuffer: Potato pancakes

Schwarzwälder Kirschtorte: Black Forest cake

Bayerische Erdbeercreme: Strawberry Bavarian

HEIDELBERG
215 N. Main, Ann Arbor; (734) 663-7758
Tue-Thu 11am-10pm, Fri 11am-midnight,
Sat 1:30pm-midnight, Sun 11am-10pm.
German favorites such as Bratwurst,
Knockwurst, Hasenpfeffer, apple strudel and
other desserts. German beers and wines.
Bavarian-style Alpine room.

HEINZMAN'S HEIDELBERG
43785 Gratiot (S of Hall Rd.),
Clinton Twp.;(810) 469-0440
*Tue-Thu 11am-9pm, Fri 11am-10:30pm, Sat
3-10:30pm, Sun 11am-8:30pm.* German
specialties and contemporary dishes in castle-like setting. Favorites are Wiener
Schnitzel, Sauerbraten, Rouladen and
Hasenpfeffer.

JACOBY'S SINCE 1904
624 Brush, Detroit
(2 1/2 blocks N of the RenCen)
(313) 962-3334
Mon-Sat 11am-11pm, Sun 11am-10pm.
Downtown bar and restaurant since 1904
serves German dishes such as Rindfleisch,
Rouladen and Kassler Rippchen (smoked
pork chops), as well as barbecued ribs,
prime rib and catfish.

METZGER'S
203 E. Washington at 4th, Ann Arbor
(734) 668-8987
Tue-Thu 11am-9pm, Fri-Sat 11am-10pm,
Sun 11:30am-8pm. German entrées such as
Wiener Schnitzel, Sauerbraten, Rouladen,
Wurst and meat patties, accompanied by red
cabbage and potato dumplings.

BRETZEL BITS

The pretzel was not invented by the
Germans, rather it is believed to have
been invented by an Italian monk in the 6th
century as a reward for youngsters who behaved well in church.

The pretzel probably traveled to America with the **Palantine
Germans** who later were known as the Pennsylvania Dutch. The
German word for pretzel is "bretzel."

Pretzel probably derives from the Latin *pretzola*, or "little
reward," and evolved into the Italian word *brachiola* which
means "little arms." Legend has it the pretzel represents arms
crossed in prayer, and that the three holes represent the Trinity.

In the early days, pretzels were made from bread dough and
therefore were soft. One night while tending the pretzel ovens, a
baker fell asleep. When he awoke, he fired up the oven again,
thinking the pretzels had not been baked enough. The result? A
hard, brittle product that paved the way for the crunchy pretzel
we know today.

Many types of pretzels are on the market, ranging from huge
soft ones to small hard nuggets; spicy flavored to chocolate
dipped. The most popular remains the hard, salted pretzel.

German children often wear pretzels (*Neujahrspretzel*) around
their necks for good luck in the New Year. Pretzels top some
Christmas trees in Austria.

RICHTER'S CHALET
23920 Michigan Ave., Dearborn
(313) 565-0484
*Tue-Thu 11am-9pm, Fri 11am-10pm,
Sat 3-10pm, Sun 12:30-7pm.* Specialties
are Wiener Schnitzel, Sauerbraten,
Rouladen, Knockwurst and potato pancakes.

BAKERIES

BURGHARDT'S BAKERY
33009 W. Seven Mile, Livonia
(SE corner of Farmington Rd.)
(248) 477-7153
Tue-Fri 9am-5pm, Sat 9am-4pm.
Famous for German sourdough rye.

GRAF'S PASTRY KITCHEN
30010 W. 12 Mile, Farmington Hills
(248) 851-8181
Tue-Fri 10am-6pm, Sat 9am-5pm. Tortes,
strudels and coffee cakes.

HERMANN'S BAKERY
317 S. Main (at Fourth St.), Royal Oak
(248) 541-3218
Tue-Fri 9am-6pm, Sat 8am-5pm. Known for
apple strudel and German breads.

OLD VILLAGE BAKERY
4917 Rochester, Troy; (248) 689-5080
and
31821 Mound, Warren (810) 268-0320
Tue-Fri 8am-8pm, Sat 4am-8pm. Specialties
include German nut cookies, strudel and
cakes. Coffee cakes available on Sat.

MARKETS

BYRD'S MEATS
33066 W. Seven Mile, Livonia
(1 block E of Farmington Rd.)
(248) 478-8680
Mon-Sat 9am-7pm, Sun 10am-5pm. Meats,
fish, sausage and Westphalian ham (prized
delicacy made from pork raised on acorns in
the Westphalian forest, then smoked over
beechwood and juniper branches).

FREDRO MARKET
4540 Fredro St. (at Fenelon), Detroit
(313) 366-6275
Tues-Sat 9am-5pm. Polish German market
sells fresh and smoked homemade sausage,
plus a full line of gourmet and lunch meats.

Breads from
Germany range
from light rye bread
(Roggenbrot) to poppy
seed rolls and soft pret-
zels. Another staple is
pumpernickel, a coarse dark bread
flavored with molasses. Caraway
seeds often are used for flavoring.

Stollen is a sweet yeast bread
served at Christmas. The rich loaves
are studded with dried fruit.
Kugelhupf is a light yeast cake made
with dried and candied fruit and
baked in a fluted ring mold.
Traditional Christmas cookies are
Gewurzplatzchen (spice cookies),
Pfeffernusse (pepper balls),
Spritzgeback (hard, flavored with
anise), *Springerle* (cookies shaped
with special molds), *Nusskipferl*
(nut crescents), *Mandel-Halbmonde*
(almond crescents), *Lebkuchen*
(spice bars), and *Tropfkrapfen*
(drop doughnuts).

HANS DELICATESSEN & IMPORT
1049 E. Long Lake Rd., Troy
(NE corner of Rochester Rd.)
(248) 689-3598
Mon-Fri 9am-6pm, Sat 9am-5pm. Market
and café with German meats, breads (fresh
rolls on Thursday and Saturday), pickles, herring, imported chocolate and other grocery
items.

NITSCHE'S MEAT & DELI
52175 Van Dyke, Utica
(between 23 and 24 Mile Rds.)
(810) 739-5500
and
29616 Gratiot, Roseville
(between 12 and 13 Mile Rds.)
(810) 773-5270
*Mon-Thu 9am-6pm, Fri 9am-7pm, Sat 8am-
5pm.* Homemade German sausage, baked
hams. Imported coffee and breads.

THE SMOKE HOUSE
24935 Gratiot, Eastpointe
(810) 773-0150
Mon-Sat 9am-5pm. Homemade German
sausage and meats, full deli.

WINTER'S SAUSAGE
22001 Gratiot, Eastpointe
(3 blocks S of Nine Mile)
(810) 778-7120
Mon-Fri 9am-5pm, Sat 9am-3pm.
Homemade and imported sausage,
lunch meat and hams.

GOING CUCKOO

Peter Henlein, a
locksmith in
Nüremberg, Germany,
began producing portable time-
pieces known popularly as
Nuremberg eggs around 1500.
We now, of course, call them
watches.

Cuckoo clocks, intricately
carved into birdhouses, contain
carved-wood birds that emerge
and "sing" to tell the time.
Made in the Black Forest of
Germany as early as 1730, they
still are popular. For Detroit
area dealers, check the Yellow
Pages under "Clocks."

● Frankenmuth Clock Shops

BOENING'S BAVARIAN CLOCK HAUS
250 S. Main St., 1-800-232-5155

FRANKENMUTH CLOCK COMPANY
966 S. Main St., (517) 652-2933

THE VILLAGE STORE
646 S. Main St., (517) 652-6100

SHOPS

ALWAYS CHRISTMAS
Olde World Canterbury Village
2336 Josyln Ct., Lake Orion
(3 miles off I-75, Exit 83)
(248) 391-5700
Tree ornaments and other German
Christmas decorations.

BUCHHOLZ IMPORTS
8397 Old 13 Mile Rd., Warren
(between Van Dyke and Hoover)
(810) 268-0410
German newspapers and magazines, tapes
and videos, gifts, chocolates, sausage,
smoked fish and other specialties.

OLD COUNTRY TRADITIONS
Harley's Antique Mall
I-94, Exit 127 on Concord Rd., 10 miles W
of Jackson; (517) 531-5300
Alpentraum-classical women's clothing from
Germany.

ROSEVILLE CLOCK SHOP
28085 Gratiot, Roseville
(between 11 and 12 Mile Rds.)
(810) 772-5180
Authentic German Cuckoo clocks.

TRAURIG'S QUILT & PILLOW SHOP
22050 Woodward Ave., Ferndale
(248) 547-2660
White goose-down quilts, quilt covers and
featherbed pillows; cleaning and remaking.

WATCH HILL ANTIQUES
330 E. Maple, Birmingham
(248) 644-7445
Austrian-German furniture, painted armoires,
country antiques and reproductions.

HERITAGE EXHIBITS

DETROIT HISTORICAL MUSEUM
5401 Woodward, Detroit, (313) 833-1805
Wed-Fri 9:30am-4pm, Sat-Sun 10am-5pm.
"Frontiers to Factories: Detroit at Work"
describes how the area's natural resources
and industrial development drew German
and other immigrants to jobs in Detroit.

DEXTER AREA MUSEUM
3443 Inverness St., Dexter, (734) 426-2519
Thu-Sat 1-4pm. Local history items, farm display and changing exhibits at church built in
1883 by German settlers.

BANDS & MUSIC

Among the German bands appearing at festivals and events are:

- **The Vagabonds** (810) 979-5029
- **Enzian** (810) 468-3951
- **Sorgenbrecher** (810) 775-5601
- **Festivals** (810) 786-9058
- **Rhinelanders** (313) 886-8399
- **Tradewinds** (810) 573-3753
- **The Eric Neubauer Orchestra** (810) 771-6964
- **Marv Herzog** Popular band at Frankenmuth events. Call 1-800-Fun Town.

Other performers:

- **Lisa, accordion player** (313) 277-8082
- **Langegger Herbert, yodeler** (810) 286-6964

GERMAN CHOIRS
German American Cultural Center
3800 Utica Rd., Sterling Hts.
(810) 978-0070
Office hours Wed 9am-2pm. Groups that rehearse at the center include Rheingold Male Chorus and Schwabischer Mannerchor.

ACH! THOSE AMAZING BACHS

FIRST FAMILY OF MUSIC

Germany has given the world many of its greatest composers. The first family among them has to be the incredible Bachs, who produced 53 prominent musicians over seven generations. The most famous was **Johann Sebastian** (1685-1750), the organist and composer of the baroque era, who is considered to be one of the most productive geniuses of Western music. He learned to play the keyboard from his older brother **Johann Christoph.** Though J.S. sired a total of 20 children, only 10 survived to adulthood. Organ compositions by his eldest son, **Wilhelm Friedemann,** are played frequently today. **Johann Christoph Friedrich,** a son by J.S.'s second wife, was a prodigious composer of a variety of music. **Carl Philipp Emanuel,** second son of J.S., was a renowned composer who developed the sonata form. **Johann (John) Christian,** 11th and youngest son of J.S., is known as "the English Bach" because he moved to England (to escape some sibling rivalry, perhaps?). There he became a tutor to Queen Charlotte, wrote 13 operas and had a major influence on the young Mozart.

CELEBRATE THE BACH LEGACY

BRUNCH WITH BACH
Detroit Institute of Arts
5200 Woodward Ave., Detroit
(313) 833-2323 for reservations
Series of Sunday concerts in Kresge Court.

MICHIGAN BACH FESTIVAL
(248) 539-3256 or (313) 271-1939
Curtis Posuniak, general director
From March to June, a series of orchestral, chamber, choral and solo instrument concerts are performed at St. Paul on the Lake, Grosse Pointe Farms; Henry Ford Estate, Dearborn; and Kirk in the Hills, Bloomfield Hills.

HISTORIC CHURCHES

ST. MARY (CATHOLIC)
646 St. Antoine (at Monroe)
Detroit; (313) 961-8711
Construction began in 1841, making the parish the third-oldest in Detroit. Features likenesses of King Wenceslas of Bohemia and Queen Elizabeth of Hungary. On the walls are stone plaques engraved with the names of many of the prominent German families that made contributions. Latin Mass every Sunday at 9:30am.

ST. JOSEPH (CATHOLIC)
1828 Jay St., Detroit
(Orleans and Gratiot)
(313) 393-8212
This Gothic Revival church was built in response to the overflow of St. Mary's in the mid- to late 1800s. Designed by Francis G. Himpler, a German-born architect who studied at the Royal Academy in Berlin, the interior is richly decorated with wood carvings and stained glass imported from Germany, as well as by local artisans. German Masses on the fourth Sunday of month at 9am.

HISTORIC TRINITY EVANGELICAL LUTHERAN CHURCH
1345 Gratiot Ave., Detroit
(313) 567-3100
One of the oldest German Lutheran congregations (dating from 1850) in Detroit, this Late Gothic Revival structure was completed in 1931. Its steeple perhaps was designed to soar higher than the Stroh Brewery, then just south of the church. German services on Christmas and Easter.

ST. PETERS LUTHERAN CHURCH
11423 Chicago Rd., Warren
(810) 979-3850
German language services and cultural activities.

VISUAL ARTS

DETROIT INSTITUTE OF ARTS
5200 Woodward, Detroit
(313) 833-7900
Wed-Fri 11am-4pm, Sat-Sun 11am-5pm.
See the bold color of German expressionist painters such as Nolde, Kirchner, Beckmann and Mueller in Gallery N280; German porce-

lain from Meissen (1710-1740) in S230; 20th century prints and drawings created by artists of Die Brücke ("The Bridge") in the graphic arts gallery. Most of the armor from the Middle Ages in the Great Hall (W200) is of German origin.

DETROIT FILM THEATRE
Detroit Institute of Arts
(313) 833-2323
Often features German films presented in original language with English subtitles. *(See "Multicultural Detroit")*

OBSERVANCES

OCTOBER 3
DAY OF GERMANY'S UNIFICATION
In 1989, East Germany's regime suspended border controls, effectively opening the Berlin Wall. By October 1990, East Germany dissolved and its people became citizens of the Federal Republic of Germany.

OCTOBER 6
GERMAN AMERICAN DAY
In 1683, a group of 13 German families on the ship *Concord* arrived in America and founded the first German settlement, in Germantown, Pennsylvania. Commemoration of October 6 was proclaimed by President Reagan in 1987.

EVENTS

JUNE
BAVARIAN FESTIVAL
Heritage Park, Frankenmuth
1-800 FUN FEST
Parade, polka bands, beer and German food tents. (See "Let's Celebrate" chapter.)

GERMAN FESTIVAL
Yack Arena (3131 Third St.), Wyandotte
(734) 246-4515
Usually first weekend in June, features food, shows, souvenirs, music and dancing.

CARROUSEL OF NATIONS
Multicultural Council of Windsor
(519) 255-1127
German Village is set up as part of annual celebration two weekends in June.

JULY

INTERNATIONAL ETHNIC FESTIVAL
Phoenix Plaza, downtown Pontiac
(248) 857-5603
German is one of many nationalities represented at festival over Independence Day weekend.

GERMAN AMERICAN VOLKSFEST
Freedom Hill County Park
15000 Metropolitan Pkwy., Sterling Hts.
(810) 979-7010
Food, song, dance, rides at festival usually the third weekend in July. Sponsored by Carpathia Club, (810) 978-0457.

AUGUST

MULTI-ETHNIC CULTURAL FESTIVAL
Halmich Park, Warren
(810) 574-4950
German dance bands and foods featured.

GERMAN DAYS
Freedom Hill County Park
15000 Metro Pkwy, Sterling Hts.
(810) 979-7010
Bands, singers, folk dancers and entertainers at festival usually held the second weekend in August. Parade of flags, food, rides. Sponsored by German-American Cultural Center, (810) 978-0070.

SUMMER MUSIC FEST
Heritage Park, Frankenmuth
1-800-FUNFEST
On the second weekend in August, summer visitors will find polka bands, big-band shows, dancing and variety of food in Frankenmuth, 80 miles north of Detroit (see "Michigan Towns").

OKTOBERFEST

Munich, Germany, plays host each year to the world's largest public festival, the Oktoberfest. The Lord Mayor opens the first barrel of beer and leads the parade of floats, bands and decorated beer wagons pulled by brewery horses. The celebration continues for 16 days with beer and food, music and dance.

It all began in 1810 with the wedding of Crown Prince Ludwig (who later became King Ludwig I) to Princess Therese. For the occasion, the King proclaimed that a festival would be celebrated in four locations with food and drink for all. This event led to an annual fall festival, celebrating the beer brewed in southern Bavaria.

The traditional German polka often is showcased during Oktoberfest celebrations all over the world. Polka began as a folk dance in Central Europe. The highly energetic music, with the oompa-pa of the tuba demanded a one-two-three, one-two-three beat.

The **Frankenmuth Oktoberfest** is the first in the United States to officially operate under the auspices of the city of Munich.

OKTOBERFESTS

APPLE ORCHARD INN OKTOBERFEST
62840 Van Dyke, Washington Twp.
(at 29 Mile Rd.)
(810) 752-2188
Country inn serves hearty German meals, beer and wines Monday-Thursday evenings during October.

EDELWEISS CLUB OKTOBERFEST
German-American Cultural Center
38000 Utica Rd., Sterling Hts.
(810) 978-0070
Austrian group has celebration on last Saturday in September at Carpathia Hall.

FRANKENMUTH OKTOBERFEST
(off I-75 between Flint and Saginaw)
1-800-FUNFEST
Michigan's Little Bavaria hosted its first Oktoberfest in 1989 to celebrate the reunification of East and West Germany. Pretzels, Bratwurst, Weisswurst, roasted almonds and rosettes (fried sweet dough) are served with locally brewed beer. German bands play polkas, waltzes and other music on Oktoberfest weekend in mid-September. (Tents just off Main St. in downtown Frankenmuth.)

GERMANIA CLUB OKTOBERFEST
23155 King Rd., Brownstown
(734) 479-4278
Clubs hosts event Saturday in late October.

OKTOBERFEST WEEKENDS
Olde World Canterbury Village
2369 Josyln Ct., Lake Orion
(3 miles off I-75, Exit 83)
(248) 391-5700
German bands, yodeling contest, food, children's activities on weekends from mid-September to early October.

ST. MARY'S OKTOBERFEST
Orchard Lake Campus, W. Bloomfield
(Orchard Lake and Commerce Rds.)
(248) 683-0402
Fri 6pm-midnight, Sat noon-11:30pm, Sun noon-8pm. Largest Oktoberfest in Detroit area attracts 55,000 on last weekend in September. Chicken and pork chop dinners, Spaten Beer from Munich, hot pretzels made on the spot, German bands, Bavarian dance and folk groups, midway rides and games.

TEUTONIA CLUB OKTOBERFEST
55 Edinborough St., Windsor, Ont.
(519) 969-3815 or 969-3817
Annual event, usually on last weekend in September and first weekend in October.

U.S.S. OKTOBERFEST
Cruise on Detroit River and
Lake St. Clair
(313) 886-5065
German-American Radio Magazine, with Dr. Eugene Carl Strobel, hosts America's largest floating Oktoberfest the last Sunday in September. Ticket includes Bavarian dinner plate, complimentary beer, entertainment and dancing on cruise from 5-9pm.

ORGANIZATIONS

CARPATHIA CLUB
38000 Utica Rd., Sterling Hts.
(810) 978-2292 or 978-0070
Members from German-speaking regions of Hungary, Yugoslavia, Romania, Austria and Switzerland maintain customs and language through activities such as folk dance, song, soccer, holiday observances and social events. Banquet hall is used by many groups. Heritage display in lobby.

GERMAN-AMERICAN CULTURAL CENTER (GACC)
38000 Utica Rd., Sterling Hts.
(810) 978-0070
Office hours Wed 9am-2pm. Based at the Carpathia Club Hall, the center is an umbrella organization for various German American cultural and social groups in the Detroit area. Affiliates sponsor German classes for adults and children, dance and singing groups, concerts, sports teams, recreational and social events. Collection of steins and Black Forest clock on display in library.

O TANNENBAUM

The Christmas Tree is believed to have originated in the Black Forest of Germany as an outgrowth of pagan and Christian traditions. Pagan Germans worshiped the evergreen tree as a sign of life and promise that spring and fruitfulness would return.

Displaying a Christmas pyramid, or *lichtstock* (light pole), was a widespread custom in the Middle Ages. A wooden frame with several tiers of shelves was decorated with candles, green branches and ornaments.

The idea of decorating a fir tree (*Tannenbaum*) probably came from the paradise trees adorned with apples, nuts and wafers for miracle plays about Adam and Eve. The wafers evolved to the Christmas cookies for which Germans are famous. Children looked forward to dismantling the "sugar tree's" edible ornaments on Jan. 6.

In the early 1800s, the Christmas tree tradition was firmly established in Germany and spread elsewhere in Europe. German immigrants in the mid-1800s brought the custom to the United States. Commercially made ornaments from Germany began to appear in the United States in the 1870s. Among the earliest were the silver and gold embossed cardboard ornaments from Dresden, icicle tinsel from Nuremberg, blown-glass ornaments from a tiny village in the Thuringian mountains and *Engelshaar* (angel's hair), also from Germany. A wide selection of ornaments imported from Germany is available at *Always Christmas* in Lake Orion and *Bronner's* in Frankenmuth.

ST. NICHOLAS DAY

In Germany and some other countries in Europe, children don't have to wait until Dec. 25 for presents. On the eve of Dec. 6, St. Nicholas, the patron saint of children, students, sailors and merchants, comes down from heaven on a white horse and leaves treats and gifts for good children. The legend is based on the generosity and compassion of the bishop of Myra in Asia Minor, who mysteriously provided food, clothing and bags of gold for the needy around 325 A.D.

DIE KINDER

KINDERGARTEN: A preschool education that serves as a transition from the home to formal school began in Blankenburg, Germany, in 1837 when Friedrick Fröbel started the first kindergarten. In German, the name means "garden of children." His concept was based on the idea that play is the work through which children learn, and that teaching should involve creative play and social interaction. He employed games, songs and stories in the learning process and used special teaching aids suited to small children. The concept soon spread to other European countries, as well as Japan, Canada and the United States. Kindergartens began in major U.S. cities in the 1870s and '80s. By the 1920s, kindergarten programs were an established part of most public schools nationwide.

ORFF SCHULWERK: Carl Orff (1895-1982) was a German composer known for his educational and theatrical music. In Munich, he conducted in various German theaters and, in 1924, with the dancer Dorothea Günther, founded the Günther School to train children in music, dance and gymnastics. His *Schulwerk* (*Music for Children*, 1930-33, revised 1950-54) begins with simple rhythmic patterns and progresses to sonorous ensemble pieces for xylophones, glockenspiels and other percussion instruments. His methods are employed in select schools in metro Detroit.

WALDORF EDUCATION: Founded in 1919 in Germany by Rudolf Steiner, Waldorf education offers an interdisciplinary approach to academic excellence. Steiner's philosophy and methodology cultivates skills, artistic abilities, moral strength, courage and global understanding. The curriculum balances intellectual progress with character building by encouraging students to develop their "heads, hearts and hands." The three Waldorf schools in the Detroit area are part of a worldwide network that comprises the largest international independent school movement in the world.

OAKLAND STEINER SCHOOL	RUDOLF STEINER SCHOOL	WALDORF SCHOOL OF DETROIT
1050 E. Square Lake Rd., Bloomfield Hills	2775 Newport Rd., Ann Arbor	2555 Burns, Detroit (in Indian Village)
(248) 646-2540	(734) 995-4141	(313) 822-0300

GERMANIA CLUB
Downriver Germania Heritage & Cultural Foundation of Michigan
23156 King Rd., Trenton
(734) 479-4278 or 287-4829 or 282-6852
Social club sponsors German Fest at Yack Arena in Wyandotte. Hosts Oktoberfest, German American Day and other events. Site of John Peter Zenger Memorial Library with books in English and German.

SCHWABENVEREIN
Schwaben-Halle
215 S. Ashley, Ann Arbor
(734) 663-5774 or 662-4964
German American Ann Arbor social club.

RESOURCES

BURTON HISTORICAL COLLECTION
Detroit Public Library
5201 Woodward, Detroit
(313) 833-1480
German genealogy can be traced through passenger and immigration lists and other archival sources.

GOETHE INSTITUTE
220 E. Huron, Ste. 210, Ann Arbor
(313) 996-8600
Sponsors cultural activities in the arts and humanities: conferences, lectures and discussions, concerts, music workshops, art exhibitions. Also experimental, documentary and feature films.

GERMAN AMERICAN BOOK FAIR & CONFERENCE
(313) 886-5065
Sponsored by German American Heritage Foundation first week in November at Eastern Michigan University. Contact Dr. Eugene Carl Strobel, president.

MEDIA
RADIO
WPON AM 1460
(313) 534-9766; fax 534-4542
www.wpon.com
"Deutsche Sprachbrücke/German Communication Bridge" (Melodien der Heimat since 1972) with Roswitha Koch, Saturday 9-10am, and Sunday 9-10am and 2-4pm. German, Austrian and Swiss music; chantey, western, children's and hit music. Features Deutsche Welle programs (originating from Germany); Stadtbummel (with

chances to win trips to Germany); German language lessons, and cultural programs.

GERMAN-AMERICAN RADIO MAGAZINE
(313) 886-5065
English talk, German music and German conversation lessons with Dr. Eugene Carl Strobel.

PRINT
BREWING GUIDES
(from page 211)
GREAT LAKES BREWING NEWS
214 Muegel Rd., East Amherst, NY
(716) 689-5841
and
MICHIGAN BEER GUIDE
P.O. Box 648, Leonard, MI 48367
(248) 628-6584
Home-brewing advice, events, resources. Available free at home-brew supply stores or by subscription.

NORDAMERIKANISCHE WOCHEN-POST
1301 W. Long Lake, Troy; (248) 641-9944
Weekly German language newspaper available at 50 newsstands in Southeast Michigan. Formerly called *Detroit Abend-Post*, it was founded in 1854 as the *Michigan Journal.*

WEB SITES
GERMAN AMERICAN CORNER
www.german-usa.com

AUSTRIAN CULTURE
www.austriaculture.net/AboutAustria5

GERMAN ONLINE DICTIONARY
dictionaries.travlang.com/GermanEnglish

Special thanks to Johann Gutenberg (1390-1468), German printer and pioneer in the use of movable type. Sometimes identified as the first European to print with handset type cast in molds, Gutenberg made the printing of this book possible.

MORE JOURNEYS

Although the most German-speaking people in metro Detroit are of German origin, Austrians, Swiss and Carpathians are represented as well.

AUSTRIA

VEREIN DER OSTERREICHER
(Austrian Society)
38000 Utica Rd., Sterling Hts.
(810) 879-2241
One of the affiliate clubs of the German-American Cultural Center, the Austrian Society sponsors social and cultural activities. The organization's major event is the annual Viennese Strauss Ball in January.

AMADEUS
122 E. Washington St., Ann Arbor
(between Fourth and Main)
(313) 665-8767
Tue-Thu 11:30am-10pm, Fri-Sat 11am-11pm, Sun 10am-3pm. Viennese coffeehouse with Mozart's music and Eastern European cuisines, including tortes and strudels.

VIENNA COFFEE SHOP
15414 Mack, Grosse Pointe Park
(313) 417-0089
Daily 11am-11pm. Sandwiches and salads follow a Viennese theme—Mozart roll, Franz Joseph roll and Strauss Carousel pita. Full line of fancy coffees.

CARPATHIA

Carpathians are Germans who settled in Yugoslavia, Hungary and other areas in the Carpathia Mountain region. A group immigrated to Detroit at the turn of the century in search of greater opportunity. After World War II, Carpathians were displaced from their homeland and fled to Germany, the United States and Australia. From 4,000 to as many as 7,000 came to Detroit where they had sponsors from the first wave of immigration.

The Carpathia Club in Sterling Heights is a social and cultural center serving this population and other German-speaking groups in the Detroit area *(see listings).*

SWITZERLAND

Swiss immigrants from the German-speaking region of Switzerland founded the Detroit Swiss Society in 1868. (Contact the Society through the German-American Cultural Center.)

Edelweiss, immortalized in a song in "The Sound of Music," is the common name for a dense, woolly perennial herb found at high altitudes in Asia and Europe. The inconspicuous blossoms are borne in heads surrounded by woolly, petal-shaped leaves. The edelweiss is cultivated readily in Michigan gardens and grows best in coarse, sandy loam. It is the floral emblem of Switzerland.

● *Edelweiss can be purchased in the spring from a few vendors at Detroit's Eastern Market on Saturdays.*

The Greek flag is blue and white.

GREECE

Greece, in southeastern Europe, occupies the southernmost part of the Balkan Peninsula and numerous islands. The land is mountainous and rugged and has a long, irregular coastline on the Aegean, Mediterranean and Ionian Seas. Mainland Greece and the Peloponnesian peninsula are connected by the Isthmus of Corinth. Islands constitute one-fifth of the country's 50,000 square miles.

Ancient Greece is considered the cradle of Western civilization. About 2,500 years ago, Greece controlled much of the land bordering the Mediterranean and Black Seas. In Athens and elsewhere in Greece, magnificent ruins stand as monuments to the nation's glorious past.

The Greeks came under control of invaders for more than 2,000 years. They lost their independence to the Macedonians in 338 B.C. and did not regain it until 1829, from the Ottoman Turks. Since then, Greece has had many serious political problems.

Nevertheless, Greek art, philosophy and science have become foundations of Western thought and culture.

GREEKS IN DETROIT

Greeks began arriving en masse in the United States during the 1820s while the Greek War for Independence raged. Between 1880 and 1902, 95 percent of Greek immigrants coming to this country were men. Often the money they sent home was used to finance passage for relatives.

While many Greek immigrants had agricultural backgrounds, few became farmers in this country. Those who settled in Detroit sought jobs as railroad and auto factory workers, or opened shops.

By 1880, Greeks had established a small business community on a section of Monroe Street in downtown Detroit. Today, Greektown is bustling with restaurants, bars, bakeries and markets reminiscent of the streets of Athens. Anchored by Annunciation Greek Orthodox Cathedral, St. Mary's Roman Catholic Church (built in 1865) and Second Baptist Church (built in 1836), Greektown is the most walked-about area in downtown Detroit.

Although second- and third-generation Greek Americans—many of whom are professionals, politicians and entertainers—live in suburbs such as Ecorse, Lincoln Park, Farmington and St. Clair Shores, Greektown remains their spiritual home.

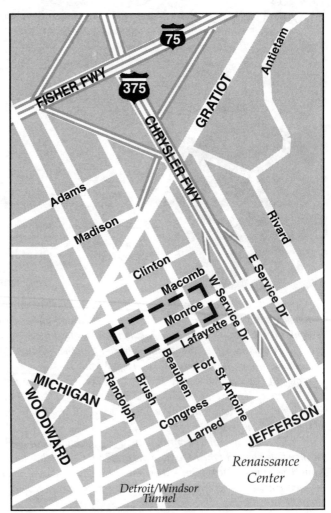

GREEKTOWN

[4-5/E-F] On busy nights, a visitor unfamiliar with **Greektown** might want to flag down a fire truck because so many waiters are lighting up "Opa" cheese appetizers—the baked *kassari* cheese topped with brandy and then set aflame. The process gives the cheese a light crust and a delicate oily flavor.

Greektown is a two-block area in downtown Detroit, on Monroe between Brush and St. Antoine, settled by Greeks in the 1880s who came to America looking for jobs and political asylum. The new immigrants, most of whom were fruit and confectionery vendors, opened their own businesses and prospered. There is still an Old World feel to Greektown —the streets are narrow and merchants step outside to sweep the sidewalk or talk to each other on warm days. Sports fans gravitate here because restaurant service is good and eateries tend to keep late hours, especially on weekends (some stay open until 4 a.m.). The neighborhood offers more than just Greek food. There's Ethiopian, Creole/Cajun, Tex-Mex, Chicago pizza and Cypriot cuisines.

To find Greektown, take I-75 to I-375 south to the Jefferson Street West Exit in downtown Detroit. Take Congress Street west three blocks to Brush Street. Turn right on Brush and go two blocks to Lafayette. Park inside the garage on the corner, which is directly across from **Atheneum Suite Hotel and Conference Center** *(1000 Brush).* This four-diamond, 175-suite hotel is a perfect spot for an overnight getaway.

Start the tour by walking into the lobby of the Atheneum (Greek for "gathering place"). You can't miss the massive murals of Trojan War soldiers and mythological figures. The hotel is known for its luxury suites and oversize marble bathrooms.

When you leave the hotel by walking north through a connector hallway, notice the **world's largest indoor waterfall** at the other end. More than 6,000 gallons of water tumble down the 114-foot marble structure each minute. Visitors sometimes toss coins onto the falls' ledges and make a wish.

Off to the left of the falls is **Fishbone's Rhythm Kitchen Café** (where you may want to grab a Cajun po'boy sandwich some other time). *Proceed north through the building onto Monroe Street,* Greektown's main artery.

Stop by **Trapper's Alley** where a couple of authentic reminders of Greece remain. One is the smoke-filled **Epiros House** *(512 Monroe),* where Greek men slap down playing cards, play backgammon *(tavli)* and sip Greek coffee. The owner will serve visitors a cup at the unadorned counter.

Next door is the **Athens Bookstore** (*520 Monroe*), where visitors will find an array of Greek periodicals and gifts, including *Ta Nea,* a newspaper from Athens, and a *Cosmopolitan*-like magazine called *Einai.* Music, videos, soap, worry beads, sailor hats and books also can be found here.

Shopping inside the rest of Trapper's Alley is spotty, but visitors will appreciate the former fur tannery's rough brick interior. An interesting resident, the **Alley Theatre,** offers musicals and plays throughout the year on the building's third floor. Call (313) 963-9339.

Across the street, the **Monroe Grocery and Bakery** (*573 Monroe*) carries imported and domestic Greek products including Kouros red and white wines, and trays of shiny black olives. Large wheels of cheese are kept cool in the deli cases. Greek customers speaking the native tongue will make you forget you're in the Midwest.

At the east end of Greektown near I-75 is the **Annunciation Greek Orthodox Cathedral** (*707 E. Lafayette*). The church can be opened to visitors who call ahead on weekdays, (313) 864-5433. This church, built in phases between 1968-77, replaced an older one on Macomb Street. Worth seeing: The richly painted icons standing at the front of the stark white sanctuary.

To end the tour, have lunch or dinner at the **Laikon Café** (*569 Monroe*). The difference in the food here, people say, is that the owners do the cooking—and it shows. Recommended: chicken gyros, lamb chops, steaming hot Greek coffee and cool, creamy rice pudding. For a memorable weekend evening, stop by the **Bouzouki Lounge,** a neighborhood nightclub named for the Greek stringed instrument (similar to a mandolin). Open nearly 30 years, this hot spot has a live band, undulating belly dancers and Greek cuisine.

GREEK DINING

A bout 20 percent of Greece is islands and no part of Greece is more than 85 miles from the sea. Geography as well as Greeks' zest for life and love of simple, well-seasoned foods, is reflected at the table. It is an unpretentious cuisine that makes the most of the surroundings and is influenced by the cultures of its neighbors for centuries: Turkey, the Middle East and the Balkans.

Olive trees provide a flavor-packed oil with which to bathe foods. Vineyards produce excellent wines, some resin-flavored. Lemon trees produce the fruit whose tang pervades Greek gastronomy.

The seas offer a variety of fish and shellfish. Lamb is the principal meat, often served braised and stewed in casseroles with assorted vegetables, or skewered and broiled. Pork, beef and game are marinated, grilled or baked. Chicken is broiled or braised. Meat and vegetable combinations are endless, often embellished with the classic lemon sauce, *avgolemono,* or a cinnamon-spiced tomato sauce.

Gyro (pronounced "yeero"or "jeero") is a relatively new addition to Greek restaurants and usually is found at more informal places. The thinly sliced beef, chicken or lamb served on pita bread with a yogurt sauce can be eaten like a sandwich but often is easier to handle with a knife and fork.

Meals are often preceded by glasses of *ouzo,* accompanied by appetizers and salad, olives, nuts, cheese and pickles. Other appetizers are marinated or deep-fried squid or octopus. And, of course, *saganaki,* the flaming cheese dish, which is ignited with a shout of *"Opa!"*

The Greek word for salad, *salata,* encompasses both sliced vegetable mixtures and puréed mixtures (as in *melintzanosalata,* eggplant spread). *Horitaki salata* is what Americans have come to know as "Greek salad." It is usually served in a large bowl to be shared around the table throughout the meal. Key ingredients are **feta** cheese, olives, oregano and beets, with an oil and vinegar dressing, but additional ingredients often are added based on availability and the chef's preference.

Avgolemono (egg, lemon, rice) soup is a signature dish. Rice is used in everything from stuffed grape leaves to rice pudding; rice dishes often are laced with spices and nuts.

Phyllopitas, composed of the wafer-thin pastry and layered with chicken and mushrooms, spinach and feta, or lamb and leeks, is another signature dish. Fresh vegetables, particularly okra and eggplant, are used imaginatively in both cooked and marinated dishes and salads, often strewn with mountain-grown herbs: garlic, oregano, mint, basil and dill.

Honey is often used instead of sugar and is essential to **baklava,** the famous pastry. A visit to a Greek pastry shop reveals the versatility of **phyllo dough** in dozens of different pastries, many of Turkish derivation. The honeyed pastries and buttery nut cookies go well with thick **Greek coffee.** Fresh fruit—generally figs, oranges, apples and melon—usually conclude the late evening dinner.

GREEK ISLANDS (CONEY, THAT IS)

The hot dog aristocracy: Custom-made hot dogs heaped with chili, smothered with sweet Spanish onions and accented with mustard. Look for chili fries, loose hamburgers, chili, gyros, Greek salad and spinach pie at corner and mall Coney Islands.

Detroit was introduced to the Coney Island hot dog in 1924 by Greek entrepreneur Bill Keros, followed a decade later by his brother, Gus, in downtown Detroit. The Keros family still operates the **American Coney Island** in downtown Detroit on West Lafayette and **Lafayette Coney Islands** at Oakland, Westland and Southland Malls. The Keros' cousins own 16 **Kerby's Koney Island** restaurants in the suburbs.

Long-time Greek-owned businesses include **Senate Coney Island,** with locations in Livonia, Dearborn and Taylor. Another Greek, James Giftos, started **National Coney Island** in 1965 and now has 12 restaurants in the area. He makes his own chili sauce which he supplies to other restaurants.

Newcomer Leo Stassinopoulos, with eight **Leo's Coney Island** restaurants in Oakland County, bottles and sells his own Greek salad dressing.

RESTAURANTS

GREEKTOWN

BOUZOUKI LOUNGE
432 E. Lafayette, Detroit; (313) 964-5744
Thu-Sun 5:30pm-2:30am. Authentic Greek entertainment in a taverna setting features dancers, singers, bouzouki players and continuous music. Audience is invited to join in. Menu includes lamb with green beans, rice pilaf and other Greek fare.

CYPRUS TAVERNA
579 Monroe, Detroit; (313) 961-1550
Sun-Thu 11am-2am, Fri-Sat 11am-3:30pm. The island of Cyprus is most famous as the birthplace of Aphrodite, goddess of love and beauty. Specialties include septalies, haloumi, the popular Aphrodite platter, shrimp and spinach pie.

LAIKON CAFE
569 Monroe, Detroit; (313) 963-7058
Mon, Wed-Thu and Sun 11am-1am, Fri-Sat 11am-3:30am. Extensive menu features avgolemono soup, squid, saganaki and Greek sausage.

NEW HELLAS CAFE
583 Monroe, Detroit; (313) 961-5544
Mon-Thu 11am-11pm, Fri-Sat 11-3am, Sun 11am-midnight. "The Grandfather of Greektown," famous for lamb chops, sea bass and vegetarian dishes.

NEW PARTHENON
547 Monroe, Detroit; (313) 963-8888
Daily 11-3am. Greek statuary and murals give this restaurant a striking decor. Famous Greek salad and a variety of lamb and fish dishes.

OLYMPIA SHISH-KEBAB INC.
532 Monroe, Detroit
(313) 964-4774
Mon-Thu 11am-midnight, Fri-Sat noon-3am, Sun noon-midnight. Specializing in shish kabob, a variety of Greek salads, lamb chops, pastitsio and gyro platter.

PEGASUS TAVERNA
558 Monroe, Detroit
(313) 964-6800
Mon-Thu 11-1am, Fri-Sat 11-2am, Sun 10:30am-midnight. Largest restaurant in Greektown is on the ground floor of Trapper's Alley. American dishes served, along with Greek lamb specialties and gyros.

EPIROS (CORFU) COFFEE HOUSE
512 Monroe, Detroit
(313) 964-0149
Daily 7-5am. Until the 1970s, Greektown was home of many coffee houses named after various areas in Greece. Men would meet, play cards, enjoy Greek coffee and discuss politics. The only original coffee house remaining in Greektown.

EAST
ANDREA'S GARDENS
14300 E. 12 Mile, Warren; (810) 775-4300
Daily 7am-11pm. Popular Greek menu featuring the trio combo: dolmathes, moussaka and spinach pie. Lamb chops a specialty.

MYKONOS
22310 Moross (Pointe Plaza, at Mack) Detroit; (313) 343-0500
Mon-Thu 11am-10pm, Fri-Sat 11am-11pm, Sun noon-10pm. Popular Greek restaurant and bar on east side. Full menu features baked fish with vegetables, lamb chops and other traditional Greek cuisine.

NORTHWEST
BIG DADDY'S PARTHENON
6199 Orchard Lake Rd., W. Bloomfield (N of Maple)
(248) 737-8600
Sun-Thu 11am-10pm, Fri 11am-midnight, Sat noon-midnight, Sun noon-9pm. A bright, Greek country house setting and menu (including many vegetarian specialties) makes this a busy gathering place for all ages. Entertainment Thursday and Friday.

GINOPOLIS ON THE GRILL
27815 Middlebelt, Farmington Hills (at 12 Mile Rd.)
(248) 851-8222
Mon-Thu 11am-11pm, Fri-Sat 11am-midnight, Sun 2-9pm. Popular restaurant and sports bar brings Greek classics to the suburbs. Famous for Montgomery Inn ribs.

WINDSOR
PARTHENON
3347 Tecumseh E., Windsor
(519) 948-3331
Tue-Thu 11am-10pm, Fri 11am-11pm, Sat 8am-11pm, Sun 8am-9pm. Menu features lago stefatho, lamb—barbecued, roasted or stewed—and village salad.

THANASIS OLYMPUS
1204 Tecumseh E., Windsor
(519) 977-6650
Mon-Thu 11am-10pm, Fri-Sat 11am-midnight, Sun 4-10pm. Bifteki, barbecued quail, salted cod served with skordalia, house-made pickled beets and lamb chops. Casual atmosphere despite statuary, columns and fountains.

ANN ARBOR
MEDITERRANO
2900 S. State, Ann Arbor
(734) 332-9700
Mon-Thu 11am-10pm, Fri 11am-11pm, Sat noon-11pm, Sun noon-10pm. Varied menu of Mediterranean foods with emphasis on lamb souvlaki, moussaka, octopus and spanakopita.

PARTHENON
226 S. Main, Ann Arbor
(734) 994-1012
Mon-Thu 11am-10pm, Fri-Sat 11am-11pm, Sun noon-10pm. Popular for good, hearty Greek dishes—lamb, chicken, soups and salads.

In markets, Greek olives often are found in barrels or bins to serve yourself. The most popular are:

● **Amfissa:** Black and round with a nutty-sweet taste.

● **Green:** Large and crunchy with a mild flavor.

● **Cracked green:** Made by cracking unripe green olives, placing them in water for several weeks to remove their bitterness, then storing them in brine.

● **Black:** Small, wrinkled, dry-cured olives with a strong flavor.

Arni: Lamb.

Avgolemono: An egg and lemon mixture used as a sauce or a soup base.

Bifteki: Spiced ground beef patties.

Dolmades or dolmathes: Stuffed grape leaves.

Feta: The classic white goat cheese of Greece.

Filo or **Phyllo:** The paper-thin pastry dough essential for appetizers, entrées and desserts.

Glyksmata: Dessert.

Haloumi: Fried Cypriot cheese.

Horitaki salata: "Greek" salad.

Kafes: Coffee.

Kalamaria: Squid.

Kasseri: Creamy farm cheese with a bite.

Kota: Chicken.

Lago stefatho: Rabbit stew.

Loukoumades: Deep-fried honey balls topped with honey, served warm topped with a light honey/sugar syrup.

Moussaka: A layered casserole usually made with eggplant and chopped meat, topped with a custard sauce.

Melintzano: Eggplant.

Melintzanosalata: Puréed eggplant dip.

Oktopodi: Octopus.

Orzo: Tiny melon-seed-shaped pasta.

Ouzo: A colorless alcoholic drink flavored with anise.

Patitsio: A layered casserole of macaroni and chopped meat topped with a custard sauce.

Pilaf: Rice boiled in broth and flavored with onion and spices.

Psari: Fish.

Retsina: White or rosé wine flavored with pine resin.

Rigani: Oregano, used in countless dishes.

Rizolgao: Creamy rice pudding with a sprinkling of cinnamon.

Saganaki: Melted cheese sprinkled with lemon juice and brandy and ignited with a shout of "Opa!"

Salata: Salad.

Septalies: Broiled ground meat with onion, garlic, parsley and spices.

Skordalia: Mashed potatoes and garlic.

Souvlakia: Skewered food.

Spanakopita: Spinach filo pastries.

Tahini: Crushed sesame seed paste.

Tarama: Fish roe from gray mullet.

Taramosalata: Fish roe spread.

Tiropita: Filo stuffed with Greek cheese.

Tsatziki: Cucumber yogurt dip.

COOK IT YOURSELF

These cookbooks are published by local organizations.

The Joy of Greek Cooking with an American Accent
222 pages, $12.50

To order, call Annunciation Cathedral in Greektown, (313) 965-2988.

Yasso: An Adventure in Greek Cooking
180 pages, $15

To order, call St. George Church in Bloomfield Hills, (248) 335-8869.

GROCERIES AND BAKERIES

*These Greek groceries, or **pantopoleon**, feature an array of imported foods, cheese, olives, delicacies, breads and pastries.*

GREEKTOWN

ASTORIA PASTRY
541 Monroe, Detroit
(313) 963-9603
Sun-Thu 8am-11pm daily, Fri-Sat 8-1am.

ATHENS GROCERY
527 Monroe, Detroit
(313) 961-1149
Mon-Thu 10am-10pm, Fri-Sat 10am-midnight, Sun noon-10pm.

MONROE GROCERY AND MARKET
573 Monroe, Detroit
(313) 964-9642
Mon-Tue 10am-9pm, Wed-Sun 10am-8pm. The only bakery in Greektown that bakes the popular whole wheat bread koulouria with sesame and tsoureki (twisted sweetbread) daily. Supplies Greek restaurants with baked goods. Also noted for lamb and baked lamb, feta, kasseri, kefaloteri (grated for macaroni), kolamata and green olives. Greek wines from various regions.

SIMEON BAKERY
501 Monroe, Detroit
(313) 963-2860
Mon-Thu 7am-11pm, Fri, Sat 7-1am.

STEMMA CONFECTIONERY
514 Monroe, Detroit
(313) 962-1898
Mon-Wed 9am-8pm, Thu 9am-10pm, Fri-Sat 9am-11pm, Sun noon-6pm. Oldest pastry shop in Michigan, in business since 1904, is in Trapper's Alley.

SUBURBS

HELLENIC MARKET
33308 Seven Mile, Livonia
(248) 476-2080
Mon-Sat 9am-5pm, Sun 9am-2pm. Features imported Greek food: halva, loukoumi, olives and cheese. Breads and pastries baked on premises.

PASTRI DELITE
912 Dix, Lincoln Park; (313) 381-7766
Mon-Fri 7:30am-4pm, Sat-Sun 10am-5pm.

SIMEON BAKERY
3159 Telegraph, Dearborn
(313) 274-6312
Mon-Sat 8am-4pm.

STOUKAS IMPORTING
20705 E. Nine Mile, St. Clair Shores
(810) 771-1369
Mon-Sat 10am-6pm. Popular with Eastsiders; an array of cheese, olives and peppers. All pastries are homemade.

AT THE BAKERY

Follow the scent of walnuts and honey and there you will find Greek sweets. Among the most popular are:

Baklava: Aristocrat of Greek pastry is made of layers of pastry and ground walnuts topped with honey.

Galatoboureko: Delicately flavored custard baked with layered phyllo pastry with honey syrup.

Kourabiedes: (good luck cookies) Butter cookies shaped by hand and covered with powdered sugar.

Koulourakia: Traditional crisp cookie served with Greek coffee.

Karithopita: Moist walnut cake with honey syrup.

Melomakarna: Honey-dipped cookie with cinnamon and walnuts.

Loukouma: Feather-like deep-fried honey puffs.

Diples: (honey ripples) Dough that is deep-fried and twisted then sprinkled with honey, cinnamon and ground walnuts.

SHOPS

ATHENS BOOK STORE
520 Monroe, Detroit; (313) 963-4490
Mon-Thu 11am-8pm, Fri-Sat 11am-9pm, Sun noon-7pm. In Greektown since 1930, it is the only place in town you can purchase Greek newspapers from New York and Athens. Stocks Greek books, Divry dictionaries, Stefana wedding crowns, Greek baptismal crosses, icons and music.

BOUTIQUE OF FAVORS
(by appointment only)
(810) 978-8433
Wedding, christening and religious supplies for Greek Orthodox faith; wedding invitations and favors; artifacts; jewelry; and laces.

DETROIT INSTITUTE OF ARTS SATELLITE GIFT SHOPS
Somerset Collection, Troy; (248) 649-2222
Mon-Fri 10am-9pm, Sat 10am-7pm, Sun noon-6pm.
and
Twelve Oaks Mall, Novi; (248) 380-8050
Mon-Sat 10am-9pm, Sun 11am-6pm.
Jewelry and gift items related to the museum collection. A variety of ancient Greek art reproductions, books, calendars and stationery.

CLASSIC ART & ARCHITECTURE

Inspired by the monumental stone sculpture of Egypt and Mesopotamia, classic Greek art and architecture flourished from about 1100 B.C. to the first century. Its unique qualities have made it one of the strongest influences on subsequent Western art. During Roman times, most sculptors were Greeks who continued the Hellenistic tradition in Greece, Asia Minor, Africa and Italy. Stone and clay sculptures were painted brightly (those elegant white statues we see today in museums were only the "base" of what once were colorful pieces).

Athenian vase decoration was in the black-figure style, which had been brought from Corinth to Athens about 625 B.C. and blended with the more linear and larger-scale Athenian style. The decoration was painted in black slip on the red ground of the clay. Details were incised and sometimes emphasized and given three-dimensionality by the use of red and white highlights.

The term *classical* has become not only the name of a period in Greek art but also a term for Greek and Roman art in general, and beyond that a term meaning the best of its kind.

● High-quality reproduction Greek statuary for indoors and out is available from:

DECOR STATUETTE INC., 43756 Mound Rd., Sterling Hts., (810) 739-5838

LA ROCHE ARTIFACTS INTERNATIONAL, 509 S. Washington, Royal Oak, (248) 543-2770

PACHINI STATUE MANUFACTURING INC., 20199 Van Dyke, Detroit, (313) 891-6606

CLASSIC COLUMNS

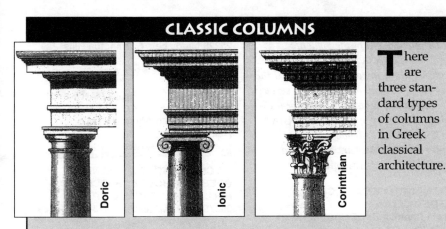

There are three standard types of columns in Greek classical architecture.

● The oldest, **Doric,** is topped by a simple abacus (slab).

● The **Ionic column** has a base and a capital made of scroll-shaped volutes directly beneath the abacus.

● The most elaborate column is the **Corinthian.** It has the most complex base and the capital is made of layers of carved acanthus leaves ending in volutes. All three columns have fluted shafts.

Examples can be found throughout the area in Greek-revival-style public buildings and private homes. They are used widely in the neoclassic style that started becoming popular in restaurants and office buildings in the 1980s.

VISUAL ARTS

DETROIT INSTITUTE OF ARTS
5200 Woodward, Detroit; (313) 833-7900
Wed-Fri 11am-4pm, Sat-Sun 11am-5pm.
Classical Greek art collection (galleries C205 and C266) features statuary, vessels and artifacts tracing developments of the classical world of ancient Greece.

DONNA JACOBS GALLERY
574 N. Woodward, Birmingham
(248) 540-1600
Thu-Fri 11am-5:30pm, Sat 1-5pm and by appointment. Specializes in Persian, Egyptian, Greek, Etruscan and Roman antiquities.

KARRES GALLERY
206 W. Sixth St., Royal Oak; (248) 542-1720
Call for hours. Greek American painter Sam Karres has achieved national recognition for his colorful depictions of cityscapes from Detroit and other metro areas.

ASSUMPTION GREEK ORTHODOX CHURCH AND CULTURAL CENTER
21800 Marter Rd., St. Clair Shores
(810) 779-6111
Church tour available for groups. Guide points out Byzantine works of art (sacred iconography) and explains their role in the Orthodox faith. *(See Byzantine Churches in "Ukraine" chapter.)*

GREEK HERITAGE ROOM
Manoogian Hall, Room 171
Wayne State University, Detroit
(313) 577-2246
Call for hours. The beauty of the Greek Isles and the significance of Greek contributions to modern culture are represented. Doric columns are framed at the ceiling level with a frieze using typical Greek patterns. The stucco textured walls are complemented by a floor of magnificent Greek Thassos marble.

CHURCHES

Nearly 98 percent of the Hellenic Republic is Greek Orthodox. Congregations are active throughout the metropolitan area. Most conduct services in Greek and English and sponsor festivals and other events promoting Greek heritage. Many also have a cultural center where classes are offered and banquet facilities are available.

GREEK ORTHODOX DIOCESE OF DETROIT
19405 Renfrew Rd.; Detroit, MI 48221
(313) 869-5433

ANNUNCIATION GREEK ORTHODOX CATHEDRAL
707 E. Lafayette Blvd., Detroit
(313) 965-2988
Greek and English language liturgy Sun 10:30am.

ASSUMPTION GREEK ORTHODOX CHURCH AND CULTURAL CENTER
21800 Marter Rd., St. Clair Shores
(810) 779-6111
Greek language Mass Sun 10am.

HOLY CROSS GREEK ORTHODOX CHURCH
25225 Middlebelt, Farmington Hills
(248) 477-1677
Greek language service Sun 10:15am.

NATIVITY OF THE VIRGIN MARY GREEK ORTHODOX CHURCH
39851 Five Mile, Plymouth Twp.
(734) 420-0131
Greek language service Sun 10:30am.

ST. CONSTANTINE & HELEN GREEK ORTHODOX CHURCH & HELLENIC CULTURAL CENTER
36375 Joy Rd., Westland; (734) 525-6789

ST. GEORGE GREEK ORTHODOX CHURCH
1515 S. Woodward Ave., Bloomfield Hills
(248) 335-8869
Greek liturgy Sun 10am.

ST. JOHN GREEK ORTHODOX CHURCH & HELLENIC CULTURAL CENTER
11455 Metropolitan Parkway, Sterling Hts.
(810) 977-6080
Greek language service Sun 10am.

ST. NICHOLAS GREEK ORTHODOX CHURCH
760 W. Wattles Rd., Troy; (248) 362-9575
Greek language service Sun 10am.

IDEAL PROPORTIONS

Ever wonder why a legal-size sheet of paper measures $8\,1/_2$ by 14 inches? It's just another gift from the Greeks. The **Golden Section** (also called the **Golden Mean** or **Divine Proportion**) is the visually satisfying ratio first constructed by Greek mathematician Euclid in about 300 B.C. and used ever since in art and architecture. Simply put: The ratio of the whole to the larger part is equal to the ratio of the larger part to the smaller.

The Golden Section

Visitors to the Detroit Institute of Arts will notice how often this ideal has been used in paintings (one of the reasons subjects often are not in the center, but about one -third of the way across the canvas), sculpture and even the building itself. All because the eye seems to find this proportion most pleasing.

In ancient Greece the owl was sacred to Athena, goddess of wisdom and night, and came to symbolize the city named after her, as well as wisdom.

The Greek language dates back three-and-a-half millennia. Modern Greek derives from the same dialect used by Homer. Greek is also the language of the Gospels. The Greek alphabet and the Greek language have contributed much to all western languages.

OLYMPIC GAMES

The Olympic Games, the most famous of the four great national festivals of the ancient Greeks, were celebrated in the summer every four years in the sanctuary of Zeus at Olympia from 776 B.C. to 393 A.D.

The competitions were open only to honorable men of Greek descent. The order of the events is not precisely known, but the first day of the festival was devoted to sacrifices. The second day began, in all probability, with **footraces,** for which the spectators gathered in the *stadion,* an oblong area enclosed by sloping banks of earth. On other days, **wrestling, boxing** and the *pancratium,* a combination of the two, took place.

Horse racing, in which each entrant owned his horse, was confined to the wealthy but was nevertheless a popular attraction. After that came the **pentathlon,** a series of five events: **sprinting, long jumping, javelin hurling, discus throwing** and **wrestling.** The victors were awarded crowns of wild olive. Celebrated by poets, winners often lived the rest of their lives at public expense.

The Olympic Games, which rose to their height in the fifth and fourth centuries B.C., were suppressed in about 393 A.D. by the Roman emperor Theodosius I.

They were revived in Athens, Greece, in 1896, by French educator and thinker Pierre de Coubertin, who proposed them in order to promote a more peaceful world. The program for the 1896 games, comprising only summer events (the Winter Olympics were not established until 1924), included about 300 athletes from fewer than 15 countries competing in 43 events in nine sports. In contrast, 100 years later, the 1996 Summer Olympics in Atlanta included more than 10,000 athletes from more than 190 countries competing in 271 events in 29 different sports.

GREEK FOLK DANCES

YASSOO!
The glories of ancient Greece are depicted in dance. Greek folk dancing can be divided into two categories: **village folk dances** and **city folk dances.** A fundamental aspect is that food, drink, conviviality, music and song accompany dance. Greek dancing is performed at public celebrations—religious festivals, national or provincial holidays—as well as family celebrations such as engagements, weddings, births, baptisms and anniversaries.

Among the popular dances are:

● *Syrto* ("dragging dance"), the oldest of all Greek dances, is depicted on many ancient vases and Byzantine frescoes. In addition to the simple enjoyment of the steps and music is the human continuity of experiencing a dance performed by Greeks 2,000 years ago.

● *Hassapiko* ("the butcher's dance"), is a fast, spirited Panhellenic dance led by the men.

● *Kalamatiano* refers to Kalamata, a town in southern Peloponnese that was one of the centers of silk manufacturing during the Byzantine Empire. Kerchiefs from Kalamata were highly prized, and men presented them as a symbol of love—much as red roses are given today. Because holding hands was either a public scandal or a declaration of intent to marry, men gallantly (or perhaps prudently) offered their kerchiefs instead of their hands for partners to hold while dancing. Though its traditional significance is largely forgotten, the kerchief still plays a prominent role in many Greek dances.

● *Syrtaki,* the Greek sailor dance made popular in the movie "Zorba the Greek," is performed in a straight line, shoulder to shoulder, accented with smooth steps and bent knees.

● *Pentozala,* from the Island of Crete, comes from *pento,* meaning "five" and *zali,* meaning "dizzy"…thus a dizzy five-step dance. As the music gets livelier, the dancers leap higher and improvise variations in an attempt to outdo the others' movement.

FESTIVALS & SPECIAL EVENTS

Feasts and festivals are integral to Hellenic life. Name days, saints' days, weddings and holidays are the occasion for merriment, a bounteous table and spirited folk dancing.

MARCH
GREEK INDEPENDENCE DAY
Celebrated March 25 with religious and secular events in the Greek American community. In 1821, the Greek War of Independence from the Ottoman Turks began. This struggle defined the modern Greek nation and demonstrated the continuity of Greek culture.

MAY
GREEKTOWN ART FAIR
Features artisans and merchants displaying wares from the United States and abroad on the third weekend in May. Sponsored by the Greektown Merchants Association, (313) 963-3357.

JUNE
CARROUSEL OF NATIONS
Annual festival held two weekends in June includes a Greek Village. Contact the Multicultural Council of Windsor at (519) 255-1127.

JULY
OPA FEST
Usually celebrated the second weekend of July on the grounds of St. Nicholas Church (760 W. Wattles, Troy). The three-day event features entertainment, authentic folk dancing and live music, dozens of food specialties and cooking demonstrations. There are special activities for children and a gift boutique. Call (248) 362-9575.

AUGUST
GREEK CULTURE FESTIVAL
At Assumption Greek Orthodox Church (21800 Marter, St. Clair Shores). Call (810) 779-6111

PERFORMING ARTS GROUPS

ATHENIAN PERFORMING ARTS
(248) 348-6236
Contact: John Avdoulos

GREEK THEATER

A classic Greek theater is available for community groups to use for performances during August. The first public building (constructed in 1915) on the George Booth estate, now the Cranbrook Educational Community, this "theater-in-the-round" includes a semi-circle amphitheater for seating, a grassy area for orchestras and a raised stage with a column backing.

It is home to St. Dunstan's Theatre Guild, which performs there in season. For ticket information, call (248) 644-0527.

GLENDI DANCERS
(810) 776-7535
Contact: Sandy Koukoulas
Greek folk-dance ensemble for people 15 and older performs at many functions. Group's instructors teach folk dance at Assuption Greek Cultural Center in St. Clair Shores, (810) 779-6111.

HELLENIC SOCIETY FOR THE PERFORMING ARTS
(313) 881-0101
Contact: Penny Voudoukis

ORGANIZATIONS

Metro Detroiters from various areas of Greece have their own clubs that meet regularly for social and philanthropic activities, such as Association of Stereoelladites, Brotherhood of Mani, Eperotic Society, Pan-Thessalians, Pan-Cretan Federation, National League of Cypriots, Pan-Macedonians, Pan-Messianians, Ikaria Society and Chios Society.

AMERICAN HELLENIC CONGRESS
Ann Arbor; (734) 761-9210
Contact Dr. Demetrios Politis.
Aims to promote action on local, national, international issues pertaining to Hellenic American interests.

AMERICAN HELLENIC EDUCATIONAL PROGRESSIVE ASSOCIATION
(248) 879-2786
Contact John Athans
Has many chapters throughout the United States and Canada.

RESOURCES

MODERN GREEK STUDIES
431 Manoogian Hall
Wayne State University, Detroit
(313) 577-3032
The main goal of the Modern Greek Studies Program is to promote the learning of the modern Greek language and culture at WSU and in the Detroit area at large. Several courses are offered per year in modern Greek language, literature and culture. Program sponsors free public lectures by prominent scholars, scholarships to study in Greece, multimedia library and annual newsletter. Works closely with students of Greek origin on campus, supporting their organization—the Dionysians—and activities.

MEDIA
PRINT
NATIONAL GREEK TRIBUNE
32618 Bunert Dr., Warren, MI 48093
(810) 294-7335
Greek and English biweekly

HELLENIC CHRONICLE
5 Franklin Commons
Framingham, MA 01702
(508) 820-9700
English weekly.

LAOGRAFIA
6 Golden Star
Irvine, CA 92714
(714) 559-8575
Monthly publication of the International Greek Folklore Society covers dance, costumes, food, music, folk customs, book reviews and cultural conferences.

THE GREEK AMERICAN
25-50 Crescent St.; Astoria, NY 11102
(718) 626-7676
English weekly.

NEWS FROM GREECE
Press Office/Embassy of Greece
2211 Massachusetts Ave., N.W.
Washington, D.C. 20008
(202) 332-2727
English biweekly.

RADIO
WNZK AM 690 DAYS/680 NIGHTS
(248) 557-3500
"Detroit Greek Hour" since 1945.
Sat-Sun 3-4pm, with Alexandra & Kostas Karacostas
Sun 4-5pm. "The Next Generation" (English) with Jimmy Karacostas.

WEB SITES
DIA ANCIENT GREEK ART COLLECTION
www.dia.org/galleries/ancient/greece/greece

WAYNE STATE UNIVERSITY MODERN GREEK STUDIES
www.langlab.wayne.edu/cgl/modgrk

GLAVX
glavx.org/index.html
Glavx in Greek means owl. Glavx serves as the Greek world's global connection and a diaspora network.

ANCIENT CULTURES
www.eawc.evansville.edu/index
Extensive coverage of Greek and Roman.

ATRIUM
www.atrium.com
Ancient Greece, with daily updates, tv program schedules, calendar.

GREEK THEATER
www.istos.net.gr/theater/02

The following sites offer much information and many links to both modern and ancient Greek culture:

GREEK CULTURE
www.gogreece.com/aande

HELLAS
www.greece.org/hellas/root

GOGREECE
www.gogreece.com

ITALY

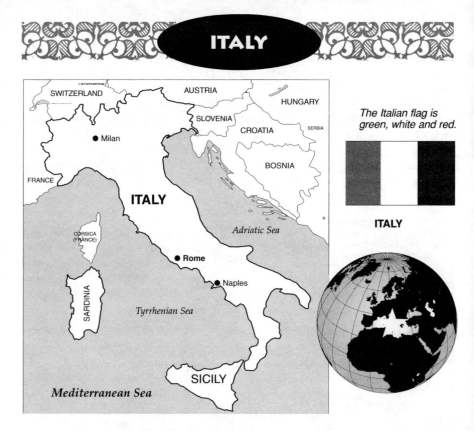

The Italian flag is green, white and red.

ITALY

Italy is the boot-shaped peninsula extending into the Mediterranean Sea from southern Europe. The toe points toward the offshore island of Sicily. The top half of the country, from Rome on the west coast and the port of Ancona on the east coast to the northern border, is more urban and prosperous than the rural south. Italy shares an Alpine border on the north with France, Switzerland, Austria and Slovenia.

Regional differences are marked because of natural geographical boundaries and the diverse cultural heritage that has come down from the Greeks, Etruscans, Arabs, Normans and Lombards. The differences are evident in local dialects, holidays, festivals, songs and cuisine. But central to all Italian life is the tradition of the family as a guiding force and focus of loyalty.

ITALIANS IN DETROIT

While barely a dozen Italians were in Detroit prior to 1855, today about 350,000 Italians are represented in professions throughout the area.

One of the first groups to settle in Detroit was from the town of **Cuggiono,** near Milan. When the townspeople stopped in Detroit en route to work in the mines near Calumet in the Upper Peninsula, they met an Italian businessman who convinced them to stay here. Many who did became successful in the business and industrial communities.

Later, like most other immigrants, Italians usually came seeking better employment, finding work in the auto industry. But some were skilled artisans, particularly in tile work and decorative plaster, whose work graces many early mansions and office buildings. They also brought their appreciation of fine art, music and food.

Today, the Italian population is scattered throughout the area, but is represented most heavily on the east side—in St. Clair Shores and Eastpointe, as well as in the Macomb county suburbs of Harrison and Shelby Townships, Warren, Sterling Heights, Clinton Township, Mt. Clemens and Fraser.

WINDSOR'S LITTLE ITALY

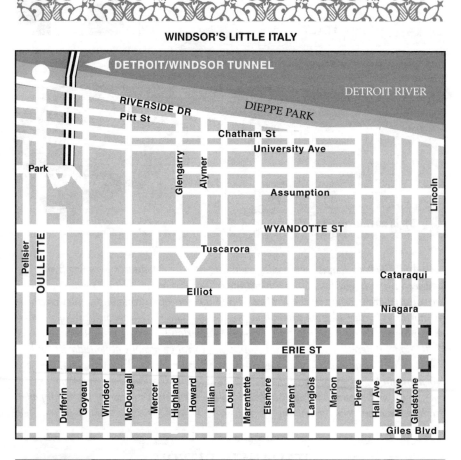

TOUR   BIG DAY IN WINDSOR'S LITTLE ITALY

[E-F/4-5] *Allow a half-day and be sure to center the tour around lunch or dinner.*

The best place to experience the sights, sounds and scents of Italy is a few minutes northwest of the Detroit/Windsor Tunnel. With a population of about 11,300, **"Little Italy"** boasts one of the greatest concentrations of Italians this side of the Atlantic.

The nine-block area, known as **Via Italia,** is packed with fine restaurants, bakeries and markets. Grocers here carry imported spices for neighboring restaurants and residents to purchase. Bakers attract customers from Canada and the United States who come to buy bread and pastries.

Little Italy is *on Erie Street East between Ouellette and Gladstone Avenues. From the Tunnel, turn left and take Ouellette south to Erie Street East and turn left again.*

Shops are closed on Sunday and Monday, but many bakeries and restaurants stay open. It's best to call ahead. Metered parking is available, but occasionally you can find free parking on the side streets. Bring a shopping tote because it'll be hard to resist buying some souvenirs, from soccer balls to salami to beautiful espresso sets. The hardware store is a must-stop for serious cooks, as it offers an amazing selection of pots and pans.

The Via Italia district contains outdoor cafés, restaurants, speciality shops, bakeries, delis and boutiques. At its center is **St. Angela's Catholic Church,** which is a magnet for Italians who have moved to the suburbs. (The homemade lunches served at the church every Wednesday are a true taste of Italy.)

Espresso is ubiquitous: Coffee shops can be found anywhere, from accountants' offices to beauty salons to billiard halls. Check out the many restaurant choices for lunch or dinner *(see listings).* You'll also find freshly made gelato at several places—be sure to have some. One dinner possibility is **Brigantino's** *(on Erie between Parent and Marion Streets),* where hosts Sam and Emilia Ambrosio make you feel like family, and impromptu opera singing or Italian folk music are likely.

Park at the metered space on Erie Street East near Highland and begin meandering across the street to the following shops.

Alderina *(465 Erie St. E.)* carries high-end Italian clothing for women, including the exquisitely tailored Gispa. Reputed to be perfectionists, the owners insist customers leave with clothes that fit.

SUNDAY STROLL

The "Sunday stroll" and gathering in the piazzas of Italian villages and cities are examples of the close feeling of unity Italians have.

The Sunday strolls, which may involve strolling up the same street 100 times, are known to the Italians as *fare le righe* or "to make ruts in the road." The idea is to socialize and gather, but physical appearance is an important part of this ritual. In fact, fashion plays a huge role in the Italian culture. Look at today's top designers and the list is full of Italians such as Moschino, Armani, Valentino, and Dolce & Gabbana.

Borrelli & Sons *(485A Erie Street E., south side)* sells wine grapes and juices. The interior smells a little like fermenting juice. Floors are covered with drums of juice concentrate. The store will help neophytes bottle their own wine.

Europa Imports *(558 Erie St. E., north side)* offers *bomboniere,* the little gifts or favors that traditionally are handed to wedding guests. Shelves are packed with elaborate frames, figurines, teacups, lace doilies and crystal. Don't miss the section devoted to blinding-white first-communion clothing for children.

Italia Bakery *(571 Erie St. E., south side)* sells its own pizza dough and specializes in Italian breads such as white *calabrese* and the hard-to-find *nonna integrale,* or "grandmother's bread," a robust, fragrant loaf made with natural wheat. Another best-seller: the lunch-size potato pizza, traditional pizza topped with thinly sliced potatoes.

The Pasta House *(635 Erie St. E., south side)* offers seven flavors of fresh egg noodles, including tomato and squid. Everything here is carryout, and rumor has it the chef often is asked to bake his lasagna in customers' own baking pans for a little dinner sleight of hand.

La Bottega *(731 Erie St. E., south side)* manages to offer everything from deli meats to taped Italian music. This is the one store with a wide selection of Italian magazines and newspapers such as *Corriere della Sera* from Rome. For a refresher, try a can of *Brio Chinotto,* the national soft drink of Italy. But be warned: It's not nearly as sweet as Coke or Pepsi.

Jammin' Joe's *(743 Erie St. E., south side)* carries Italian CDs, tapes and a wall of videos, including *Il Padrino, Parte II* (*The Godfather, Part II*). Music rules here: The owner doubles as a disk jockey for weddings and parties.

Watch European soccer on television with passionate Italian soccer fans at **Gennaro's Café and Lottery Shop** *(781 Erie St. E., south side)* on Sunday mornings at about 9:30 and afternoons at 2:30. Year-round, the café serves delicious cappuccino, espresso and homemade gelato. Great outdoor seating in warm weather.

Stop by **La Stella Supermarket** *(984 Erie St. E., north side)* for Italian imports such as Pastene's aged balsamic vinegar or *pan ducale Atri,* biscuits that complement a steaming cup of *latte.*

Customers can watch artisans work on stained glass at **A.M. Stained Glass Creations** *(1125 Erie St. E., south side)*. The workshop sells, repairs and makes windows, lamps and custom-designed gifts.

Palumbo Coffee *(1299 Erie St. E.)* sells Gaggia espresso machines and supplies most of the coffee to the area's cafés. Customers can buy espresso by the pound or cup.

One street worth a look in nice weather is **Lillian,** say residents. Here you'll find well-tended gardens and picture-perfect homes. For a real horticultural find, check out the perfect fig trees near *840 Marion.* They're loaded with fruit in late summer.

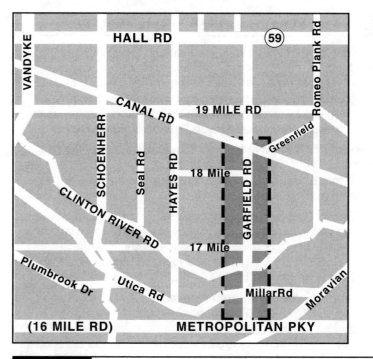

CLINTON
TOWNSHIP

| TOUR | NEW ITALIA |

[F-G/2-3] Clinton Township and other growth areas of Macomb County have become home to many Italian enterprises. Within a three-mile stretch of Garfield Road from Metropolitan Parkway (16 Mile) to Canal Road, you'll find **Vito's Bakery** *(36795 Garfield)*, **Luciano's Fine Italian Cuisine** *(39071)*, **Ciao Coffee House** *(39880)*, **Bonaldi's Italian Imports** *(41740)*, **Vince & Joe's Fruit Market, Deli & Meats** *(41790)*, **Stafano & Asaro Pastry Shop** *(41820)* and **Pizzo's Bakery & Party Store** *(42171)*.

For an authentic Italian experience, visit **Ciao Coffee House** *at Garfield Plaza, north of 17 Mile (810-228-0821).* The rich flavors of espresso, and live soccer games from Italy (September-April) on a big-screen television, beckon everyone to join in on the fun 7 a.m.-7 p.m. Also stop in at one of the bakeries along Garfield—**Vito's** *(south of 16 Mile),* **Stafano & Asaro** *(north of 18 Mile)* or **Pizzo's** *(at Fairway Plaza near Canal Road),* and pick out some cannoli or other pastry, along with homemade Italian bread, to take home. At **Bonaldi's Italian Imports** *(north of 18 Mile),* you'll be able to find magazines, greeting cards and music in Italian, as well as gift items.

For lunch, enjoy fresh pizza or pasta at **Giuseppi's Italian Café,** *at 41830 Hayes Rd. in the Oakwood Plaza (810-228-8022).* Or, for an elegant night out, dine at **Luciano's,** *at Garfield and 17 Mile in the Garfield Pointe Plaza (810-263-6540).*

E-G/4-6] Italy is one of the biggest wine producers in the world, and the south coast of Ontario is one of the biggest wine producers in Canada. From May through October, you can get a Mediterranean feel by taking the coast road along Lake Erie, tasting as you go (unless you're the driver). A complete "Wine Route" tour guide is available from Windsor/Essex County Convention & Visitors Bureau (1-800-265-3633). Some highlights:

Colio Estate Wines, *1 Colio Dr. in Harrow, 20 minutes south of Windsor.* Daily tours conducted year-round at 1, 2 and 3 p.m. At the end of each tour, visitors are taken to the hospitality room where they sample table wines, sparkling spumante and varietals.

Pelee Island Winery offers tours and a barbecued lunch. Guests can sit inside a large wine barrel or picnic in the nearby vineyards. The island is served by a ferry. Land transportation to the wine pavilion is a shuttle provided by the Pelee Island Winery. The winery, open May to September, is at 455 Hwy. 18 East in Kingsville (1-800-59-PELEE).

Twenty minutes from Windsor, **D'Angelo Vineyards,** *5141 Concession 5, RR4, Amherstburg,* (519-736-7959) is open year-round. From May to September, hours are 11 a.m.-6 p.m. daily. Winter hours are Tue-Sat 10 a.m.- 6 p.m., Sun noon-5 p.m. Tours are by appointment. Retail outlet offers 11 varieties of wine displayed among antique radios. Admission is free.

For lunch on the way there or dinner on the way back, try **Rosa's,** *287 Dalhousie St. in Amherstburg* (519-736-2177) for a traditional Italian family-style meal. Open Tue-Sat 4-10 p.m.; Sun 12:30-10 p.m.

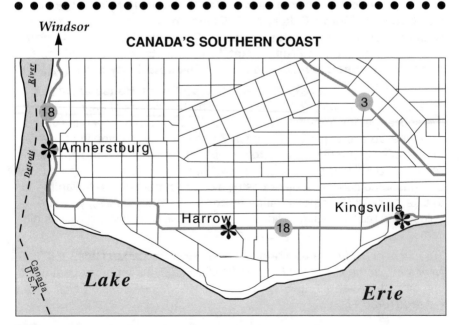

CANADA'S SOUTHERN COAST

RESTAURANTS

"L'appetito vien mangiando"

(Appetite comes with eating)
Italian restaurants are so abundant in metro Detroit that not enough space is here to mention them all. The ones listed represent a sampling in each region.

WINDSOR (LITTLE ITALY)
BRIGANTINO'S
1063 Erie St. E., Windsor; (519) 254-3493
Mon-Thu 11am-11pm, Fri-Sat 11am-midnight, Sun 4-11pm. Northern and southern cuisine in a quaint, romantic setting. Seafood specialties.

CALABRISELLA RISTORANTE
614 Erie St. E., Windsor; (at Lillian St.)
(519) 977-7306
Mon-Sat 11am-11pm. Fresh Italian dishes with southern sauces, including clam, primavera, carbonara. Veal specialties.

COOK'S SHOP/PASTA SHOP
683 Ouellette, Windsor; (519) 254-3377
Sun, Tue-Thu 5-10pm, Fri-Sat 5pm-midnight. Wide selection of fresh pastas and grilled dishes. Intimate, romantic setting downstairs; upstairs Pasta Shop is more casual, with food prepared in front of you.

IL GABBIANO
875 Erie St. E., Windsor; (519) 256-9757
Tue-Fri 11:30am-2pm, Tue-Sat 5-11pm, Sun 4-9pm. Emphasizes seafood such as seafood grill with shrimp, calamari; tuna and red snapper when available.

LA CONTESSA
780 Erie St. E., Windsor
(near Marentette St.); (519) 252-2617
Mon-Thu 11am-10pm, Fri 11am-11pm, Sat 5-11pm. Roman style trattoria with seafood entrees, 21 pasta dishes, appetizers, salads, soups and house-made desserts. New owner Madeline Zavaglia is noted for sauces.

RISTORANTE NICO
851 Erie St. E., Windsor (near Elsmere)
(519) 255-7548
Mon-Fri 11:30am-10pm, Sat 5-10pm. Small, stylish trattoria features adventurous menu, different grilled fish daily, classical guitar weekends.

SANREMO MEDITERRANEAN
900 Erie St. E., Windsor; (519) 252-1292
Daily 11am-2am, Sun buffet 1-9pm. Family restaurant serves fresh fish and seafood from its fish market around the corner, accompanied by the house pasta.

GELATO

Made by combining a low-fat milk (about 8 percent butterfat compared with ice cream's 15 percent), sugar and natural flavorings, gelato is a hot-selling cool, creamy treat that melts on your tongue. Gelato makers take the milk, sugar and flavorings, heat them high enough to kill bacteria, refrigerate the mixture, then batch freeze the treat. Favorite flavors include hazelnut, almond, chocolate, banana and tiramisu. Lemon ice, made with water, sugar and flavoring, is another Erie Street confection in Windsor. *Semifreddo,* which means "half cold," is gelato with whipped cream folded into it.

SPAGO RISTORANTE
690 Erie St. E., Windsor
(E of Howard); (519) 252-1626
Dining room: Mon 5:30-9:30pm, Tue-Sat 5:30-10:30pm, Sun 4:30-9:30pm.
Café: Mon-Tue 4pm-midnight, Wed-Fri 4pm-1am, Sat 11am-1am, Sun 11am-midnight. Casual European-style café on ground floor serves pastas, pizzas, sandwiches and cappuccino. Fine dining upstairs in romantic setting. Top-rated bruschetta.

SPAGO TRATTORIA & PIZZARIA
614 Erie St. E., Windsor
(next to European Café); (519) 252-9099
Lunch: Mon-Sat 11:30am-3pm. Dinner: Mon-Thu 5-10pm, Fri-Sat 5pm-12:30am, Sun 4-9:30pm. Casual atmosphere featuring woodburning pizza oven, homemade pasta and sauces, and a selection of Italian veal and chicken entrées.

TUTTO RISTORANTE
866 Erie St. E., Windsor; (519) 252-7140
Mon-Fri 11:30am-10pm, Sat-Sun 5:30pm-2am. Homemade cheese, complementary fresh fruit plate, imported desserts show the care taken to provide an authentic Italian dining experience.

DETROIT
AMERICA'S PIZZA CAFÉ
2239 Woodward Ave., Detroit
(next to The Fox Theatre)
(313) 964-3122

Pasta!

ITALIAN DINING

Italy has been the crossroads of civilization for thousands of years, and therefore has adopted ingredients from all over the world. In addition, there are a great many regional differences between the cuisines of northern and southern Italy—one being the use of butter and cream in the north instead of olive oil.

Say "Italian food" and the first thoughts almost everyone has are **pasta** and **pizza.** Although many claim that pasta was brought to Italy by the Venetian Marco Polo from China, it is more likely that this food existed in both places, independently, long before Polo's expeditions. Nearly every country has a form of pasta.

As for pizza, this dish is much less important to Italian cuisine in Italy than it is in the United States. Pizza has developed into a full meal only in the United States and northern Europe; for the Italians, it's more like an evening snack. There is evidence that pizza came to Italy via the Greeks who settled in the Naples area. The original Italian pizza primarily consisted of a bread crust and had few toppings.

Mon-Thu 11am-10pm, Fri-Sat 11am-midnight, Sun noon-10pm. More than 27 varieties of pizza, cooked over wood fire. A before- and after-theater favorite.

BUDDY'S RESTAURANT & PIZZERIA
17125 Conant, Detroit; (313) 892-9001
Mon-Thu 11am-10pm, Fri-Sat 11am-11pm, Sun noon-10pm. There are satellites throughout the area, but this is the original Buddy's that's been winning best-pizza awards for more than 50 years. Homemade pastas and huge salads, family-style dining.

IL CENTRO
670 Lothrop, Detroit; (313) 872-5110
Mon 11am-3pm, Tue-Thu 11am-9pm, Fri 11am-10pm, Sat 4-9pm. Open late on Fri-Sat and Sun 4-8pm when there's a show at Fisher Theater. Intimate atmosphere in a charming old house, just across from the Fisher Building. Specializes in southern Italian cuisine.

LA DOLCE VITA
17546 Woodward Ave., Detroit
(313) 865-0331
Wed-Thu and Sun 4pm-midnight, Fri-Sat 4pm-1am. Known for cappuccino, espresso and delicious desserts. Favorite before- and after-theater spot for sophisticated dining.

LELLI'S INN
7618 Woodward Ave., Detroit
(313) 871-1590
Mon 11am-2pm, Tue-Thu 11am-10pm, Fri 11am-11pm, Sat 3-11pm, Sun 3-9pm. In operation for more than 50 years. Noted for thick minestrone soup, fine veal, "steak Lelli" and house-made ice cream.

MARIO'S
4222 Second Ave., Detroit
(between Willis and Canfield)
(313) 832-1616
Mon-Thu 11am-11pm, Fri-Sat 11am-midnight, Sun 3-10pm. Vintage Italian restaurant with wood paneling and checkered tablecloths. A favorite with theatergoers since 1948. Dinners come with antipasto tray, salad, minestrone and pasta.

RISATA
2305 Woodward , Detroit
(313) 965-9500
Sun and Wed-Thu 5-8:30pm, Fri-Sat 5-11:30pm. Creative, contemporary Italian fare in upbeat, urban atmosphere.

ROMA CAFE
3401 Riopelle St., Detroit
(at Eastern Market between
Gratiot and Mack)
(313) 831-5940
Mon-Sat 11am-10pm. Detroit tradition since

1890. Popular lunch spot in Eastern Market area has checkered tablecloths and classic Italian dishes.

VINCE'S ITALIAN RESTAURANT
1341 Springwells; (313) 842-4857
Call for hours, closed Mon. Started by Vincenzo and Maria Perfili nearly 40 years ago and still family-run, Vince's is famous for its manicotti, cannoli and ravioli made with homemade pastas and sauces.

EAST
ANDIAMO ITALIA
7096 E. 14 Mile, Warren
(810) 268-3200
Mon-Thu 11am-11pm, Fri 11am-midnight, Sat 4pm-midnight, Sun 4-9pm.
Northern Italian dining with pastas, breads and sauces made from scratch. Chicken, veal, fish and beef entrées.

ANDIAMO LAKEFRONT BISTRO
24026 Jefferson Ave., St. Clair Shores
(810) 773-7770
Mon-Thu 11am-11pm, Fri-Sat 11am-mid-night, Sun noon-10pm. Seafood, pastas, pizza and steak in casual marine setting.

ARRIVA ITALIA RISTORANTE
6880 E. 12 Mile, Warren; (810) 573-8100
Mon-Thu 11am-10pm, Fri 11am-midnight, Sat 5pm-midnight, Sun banquet only.
Supper club with dinner shows. All-you-can-eat pasta buffet at lunch time.

ANTONIO'S
20311 Mack, Grosse Pointe Wds.; (313) 884-0253
Tue-Thu 6-9:30pm, Fri-Sat 6-10pm, Sun 5-8pm. An intimate restaurant with traditional, sophisticated Italian fare, including seafood, chicken and pasta.

BENEDETTO'S RISTORANTE ITALIANO
15505 15 Mile Rd., Clinton Twp.
(810) 790-1010
Tue-Thu 11:30am-10pm, Fri 11:30am-11pm, Sat 4pm-11pm, Sun 1-8pm. Closed Mon.
Italian dining in an Italian café atmosphere.

ITALIAN DINING

America has adopted the Italian term *pasta* for noodle dishes of Italian origin. In Italian, *pasta* merely means "dough," whereas the Italian term for noodle dishes is *minestre*. Fresh pasta is common in the northern regions, while dried pasta is used almost exclusively in the south. *Semolina,* yellow flour ground from high protein durum wheat, is used in many brands of dried pasta because of its ability to stand up to kneading and molding.

There are many kinds of noodles in Italian cuisine, and they vary greatly in color and shape. Color can come from eggs or vegetables such as spinach, carrots or beets *(rossi).* The available combinations of colors, flavors and shapes of dried pasta seem to increase daily.

Aside from spaghetti and macaroni there are *tagliatelle* (flat and wider than fettuccine), *rigatoni* (short tubular), *vermicelli* (thin and short), *capellini* (thin, long spaghetti), *anelli* (rings), *spirali* (corkscrew shaped noodles), *fusilli* (a wavy, round spaghetti) and *cannelloni* (tubular noodles with a filling of meat and spinach), for example.

The most common Italian noodles, of course, are *spaghetti*. As a dish, they are prepared in many ways. The most well-known is as *bolognese* (with a sauce of minced meat and tomatoes). Another popular way is as *carbonara* (with beaten egg, cream and small slices of bacon). They also may come *al frutti di mare* (with seafood in a tomato sauce), *alla vongole* (with clams) or *al formaggi* (with a light cheese sauce, made of milk and commonly as many as four different cheeses).

COLUMBO'S ITALIAN RESTAURANT
86 Macomb Place
Mount Clemens; (810) 465-7704
Mon-Thu 11am-9pm, Fri 11am-10pm, Sat 4-10pm. Fettuccine Alfredo and other pastas, fish and steaks.

COSTANZO'S VICTORIAN ROOM
3601 E. Twelve Mile, Warren;
(810) 751-6880
Mon 11am-2pm, Tue-Thu 11am-9pm, Fri 11am-10pm, Sat 4-10pm. Homey service, a lush decor and fine dining that includes fresh pasta and homemade minestrone.

DA EDOARDO RISTORANTE
19767 Mack, Grosse Pointe Wds.
(313) 881-8540
Mon-Thu 11:30am-10pm, Fri-Sat 11:30am-11pm, Sun 5-9pm. Divided into romantic formal dining room and casual side. Innovative and classic Italian fare, including veal Bolognese, lasagna, cannelloni and risotto.

GIUSEPPI'S ITALIAN CAFE
41830 Hayes Rd., Clinton Twp.
(810) 228-8022
Mon-Thu 11am-9pm, Fri 11am-10pm, Sat 2-10pm, Sun 2-9pm. Pasta, veal and chicken dishes. Picante lemon-butter wine sauce and marinara sauce notable.

JOE BOLOGNA'S TRATTORIA
2135 17 Mile, Sterling Hts.
(810) 939-5700

Mon-Thu 11am-9pm, Fri-Sat 11am-11pm, Sun 11am-9pm. Casual neighborhood restaurant with sandwiches and deep-dish pizza, traditional Italian fare and some elaborate dishes.

LUCIANO'S
39071 Garfield, Clinton Twp.
(810) 263-6540
Mon-Thu 11am-10pm, Fri 11am-11pm, Sat 4-11pm, Sun noon-10pm. More than 20 pasta dishes, authentic Italian atmosphere, bread smothered with spices and olive oil.

LUIGI'S
104 Macomb St.
Mount Clemens; (810) 468-7200
Call for hours. Traditional fare with pasta, fish, chicken, veal, lamb beef and pizza.

TIRAMI SU
43080 Garfield, Clinton Twp.
(810) 263-5353
Daily 11am-11pm. Former car wash has been transformed into a grape arbor atmosphere with café umbrellas. Home-cooked Italian fare; signature dessert is tiramisu.

TRATTORIA ANDIAMO
20930 Mack Ave., Grosse Pt. Wds.
(at Hampton St.); (313) 886-9933
Mon-Thu 11am-11pm, Fri 11am-midnight, Sat 3pm-midnight, Sun 1pm-9pm. Authentic Italian cuisine with extensive menu from Sicily; brick-oven-baked pizza, calzones.

ITALIAN DINING

In Italian cuisine, noodles are normally not a meal by themselves. In the order of a fine dinner, they are served in between the hors d'oeuvre and the main course. The Italian name for *hors d'oeuvre* is *antipasto*, literally meaning "before the pasta."

There is a wide variety of antipasto; two types of standard mixed plates are the one that includes cold cuts, salami and lightly marinated vegetables in olive oil and vinegar, and the *antipasto di mare,* which mainly consists of cold seafood with a few vegetables added.

Italian cuisine is rich in signature hors d'oeuvres. Among them are many kinds of thinly sliced meats, often served in a marinade containing olive oil. The most famous of these thinly sliced meat dishes is *parma ham* (prosciutto). Air-dried and originating in the region of the northern Italian city Parma, it's much milder in taste than most hams, and therefore suited to be eaten without bread. It is most commonly served with fruit—mostly melon. **Carpaccio** are thin slices of rare beef tenderloin marinated in olive oil, salt, pepper and parmesan cheese.

Soup and salad are served after the antipasto but before the main course. The most typical Italian soup is **minestrone,** a non-thickened soup with plenty of vegetables and noodles, mostly macaroni. Salads are served with an Italian dressing, consisting of oil, vinegar and herbs. *Insalata cabrese* is a tomato salad topped with mozzarella cheese.

Italian main courses are generally meats. Veal *(vitello)* is the most popular, followed by beef *(bue),* pork *(maiale),* chicken *(pollo)* and lamb *(agnello).* Meats often are spiced with two strong-flavored herbs, rosemary and basil. A number of meat dishes use wine.

Italians believe that good wine goes with good food, and, among many other wines, have given us **Chianti** and **Asti Spumante** and **Marsala.** Cheeses too, are important: *mozzarella, parmesan, provolone, romano* and *asiago* are indispensable.

There are hundreds of varieties of Italian bread, which is always on the table. Instead of being spread with butter, it is often dipped in olive oil or used to wipe up the last bit of sauce from the plate.

For *dolci* (dessert), Italian ices, fresh fruits, *biscotti, gelato, spumoni, tiramisu* or *zabaglione* are just a few choices. *(See "On the Menu" and "From the Bakery" glossaries.)*

WEST

ANTONIO'S
26356 Ford Rd., Dearborn Hts.
(313) 278-6000
Mon-Thu 11am-10pm, Fri 11am-11pm, Sat 4-11pm, Sun 1-9pm. Family-owned for more than 30 years, known for fresh authentic sauces, homemade pastas and bread.

CAFE CORTINA
30715 W. 10 Mile, Farmington Hills (at Orchard Lake Rd.); (248) 474-3033
Mon-Thu 11:30am-10pm, Fri 11:30am-11pm, Sat 5-10pm, Sun private parties. Fresh-baked bread, homemade pastas and sauces, and veal selection. In romantic setting, plus outside patio dining.

COLANGELOS
15800 Middlebelt, Livonia
(734) 522-5600
Mon-Fri 11am-10pm, Sat 4-11pm, Sun 2-8pm. Extensive made-to-order Italian dishes and homemade pastas.

DAVINCI'S
Novi Hilton at 21111 Haggerty Rd., Novi
(248) 349-4000
Mon-Sat 6:30am-11pm, Sun 6:30am-10pm.

Breakfast through dinner in marketplace setting. Italian and Mediterranean dishes, award-winning wine list, daily buffets.

DEPALMA'S
31753 Plymouth, Livonia; (734) 261-2430
Mon-Wed 11am-10pm, Thu 11am-11pm, Fri 11am-midnight, Sat 5pm-midnight, Sun 4-8pm (closed Sun June-August). Southern Italian cuisine, including seafood dishes, pasta and veal. Entertainment nightly.

DELUCA
27424 W. Warren, Westland
(734) 422-8900
Mon-Thu 4-10pm, Fri-Sat 4-11pm, Sun 2-10pm. Famous for pizza, pasta and seafood.

FONTE D' AMORE
32030 Plymouth Rd., Livonia
(734) 422-0770
Mon-Fri 11am-11pm, Sat 4-11pm. Northern Italian dining at "Fountain of Love" features 10 specials daily and all-Italian wine list with more than 200 varieties.

GENITTI'S HOLE IN THE WALL
108 E. Main St., Northville; (248) 349-0522

ON THE MENU

Al dente: "To the bite," describes the correct degree of doneness for pasta and vegetables.

Alfredo: Pasta sauce originally consisting of butter, cream and the finest Parmesan cheese available.

Amaretto: Almond liqueur.

Appertivo: Beverage designed to awaken the palate and perk up the appetite.

Balsamic vinegar: Wonderfully fragrant vinegar, sweet and tart, made from the juice of Trebbiano grapes. Well-aged balsamic vinegars can cost $200 an ounce.

Calamari: Squid.

Focaccio: Flat bread baked plain or topped with onions, zucchini, eggplant or cheese.

Formaggi: Cheese.

Fritto Misto: Mixture of vegetables, meat and fish are dipped in a light batter and quickly deep-fried.

Frittata: Fluffy, large omelet usually made with vegetables, meats and cheese but not folded.

Frutte: Fruit.

Gnocchi: Dumplings of potato and spinach in delicate cheese sauce.

Grappa: Strong, clear brandy made from the distilled remains of pressed grapes.

Osso Buco: Slices of veal braised with vegetables, aromatics and stock. Milanese style is served with saffron risotto.

Pane: Bread.

Panino: Sandwich.

Lunch: Mon-Sat 11am-3pm. Dinner theater: Fri 7pm, Sat 6:30pm, parties of 30 or more during the week by reservation. Italian family-style feast. Seven-course dinners followed by interactive theater production.

LA BISTECCA ITALIAN GRILLE
39405 Plymouth Rd., Plymouth Twp.
(734) 254-0400
Mon-Thu 11:30am-11pm, Fri 11:30am-midnight, Sat 5pm-midnight. Closed Sun.
Hearty entrees include steaks and chops plus fish and some pasta dishes. Piano player in the bar Wed-Sat.

MARCO'S DINING & COCKTAILS
32758 Grand River, Farmington
(at Village Commons between Farmington and Orchard Lake Rds.)
(248) 477-7777
Mon-Thu 11:30am-9:30pm, Fri 11:30am-10:30pm, Sat 4:30-10:30pm. Traditional Italian American fare, including specialty pizzas, lasagna, calamari and fritto misto in contemporary neighborhood restaurant.

LITTLE ITALY
227 Hutton St., Northville
(248) 348-0575
Lunch: Mon-Fri 11:30am-2pm. Dinner: Mon-Thu 5-10pm, Fri-Sat 5-11pm. Sun 3-9pm.
Cozy restaurant in Victorian farmhouse with authentic light-and-fresh Italian fare. Proprietor Al Valente also has Ristorante di Maria and Villa Maria in West Bloomfield.

WEST SIDE GRILL
6393 Farmington Rd., West Bloomfield
(248) 626-3722
Daily 6am-9pm. Real home-style Italian food, cooked to order in casual atmosphere.

Tortellini

NORTH
ANDIAMO ITALIA WEST
6676 Telegraph Rd., Bloomfield Hills
(248) 865-9300
Mon-Thu 11am-11pm, Fri-Sat 11am-1am, Sun 4-10pm. Pricey restaurant at site of former Machus Red Fox has been transformed with bright sunflower decor. Menu features classic Italian fare, including pasta, veal, chicken, seafood and steaks. Bolognese sauce, by master chef Aldo Ottaviani, sold by the quart.

BACI ABRACCI
40 W. Pike St., Pontiac
(248) 253-1300
Tue-Thu 11am-10pm, Fri 11am-11:30pm, Sat 5-11:30pm, Sun 2-8pm. Name of Italian restaurant, bar and banquet facility means "kisses and hugs."

CAPRARO'S ITALIAN DEN
1477 John R, Troy (S of Maple)
(248) 588-6000
Mon-Thu 11am-10pm, Fri-Sat 11am-11pm, Sun 11am-9pm. Creative Italian American cuisine. "Grand brunch" a Sunday favorite.

CHIANTI TUSCAN GRILL
28565 Northwestern Hwy., Southfield
(248) 350-0055
Mon-Thu 11:30am-10pm, Fri 11:30am-11pm, Sat 5-11pm, Sun 4-8:30pm. Jimmy Schmidt's festive, family-style spaghetti palace in Tuscan-style villa. Antipasto and pasta in serving sizes to share.

COLANGELO'S
2 N. Saginaw, Pontiac
(248) 334-2275
Mon 11am-2pm, Tue-Thu 11am-10pm, Fri-Sat 11am-11pm. Award-winning restaurant cooks authentic Italian dishes to order.

COMO'S
22812 Woodward, Ferndale
(248) 548-5005
Mon-Thu 11am-2pm, Fri 11-4am, Sat noon-4am, Sun noon-2pm. Outdoor patio, award-winning pizza, Italian specialities.

D'AMATO'S
222 S. Sherman, Royal Oak
(248) 584-7400
Mon-Thu 11am-11pm, Fri 11am-midnight, Sat 5pm-midnight, Sun 4-9pm.. Neighborhood restaurant in the neoclassically restored Washington Square Plaza offers simple, rustic Italian food in large portions.

ON THE MENU

Pasta e fagioli: Rich bean soup with pasta, in which a large sausage has been cooked.

Pesce: Fish.

Pesto: Paste of fresh basil, pine nuts, Parmesan, garlic and olive oil served over pasta or in soup.

Polenta: "Mush" made from coarsely ground cornmeal.

Porcini: Wild mushrooms, fleshy, velvety and earthy in flavor.

Primavera: Sauce with vegetables.

Pumate: Sun-dried tomatoes.

Risotto: Rice dish made by gradually stirring simmering broth into arborio rice.

Sumbuca: Anise-flavored, not-too-sweet liqueur that is usually served with a few roasted coffee beans floating on top.

Scampi: Type of shrimp native to the Adriatic Sea; used in the United States to mean any shrimp broiled with butter, lemon and garlic.

Spumoni: Frozen molded dessert. Two layers of ice cream and sweetened whipped cream flavored with rum, toasted nuts and candied fruit.

Tiramisu: Sponge cake soaked with an espresso syrup and layered with a sweetened *mascarpone* cheese and chocolate sauce.

Verdura or Legumi: Vegetables.

Vitello: Milk-fed veal.

Zabaglione: Custard whipped with wine (usually Marsala) or juices to form a rich, creamy dessert.

Zuppa Inglese: "English soup," refrigerated dessert similar to the British favorite, trifle.

A century ago, the Detroit area was home to enterprising auto barons. Today, two national pizza companies based here thrive. While neither founder is Italian—one is Macedonian, the other Irish—their pizza "dough" has contributed greatly to the city.

Mike and Marian Ilitch opened their first **LITTLE CAESARS PIZZA** in 1959 in Garden City. By 1992, they had built a chain of 4,000 restaurants. Although they have concentrated on developing the carryout concept, they added delivery in 1995. For many years, their pizza has been named the "Best Pizza Value in America" in the annual "America's Choice in Chains" national survey conducted by *Restaurants & Institutions* magazine.

The Ilitch family has more than Little Caesars pizza on its corporate plate. It also owns America's Pizza Café and Tres Vite restaurant. In addition, Little Caesars runs the concessions at the Detroit Zoological Park.

Mike Ilitch owns the Detroit Tigers baseball team. The family owns the Detroit Red Wings hockey team and the Detroit Rockers soccer team. The Ilitches run Olympia Entertainment Inc., which manages Detroit's Joe Louis Arena, Cobo Arena and the Glens Falls (N.Y.) Civic Center. In 1987, the Ilitches bought the Fox Theatre and, after a year of extensive renovation, opened the 5,000-seat building to the public. In 1993, the family opened The Second City-Detroit Comedy Theatre and Risata, an Italian restaurant, next to the Fox.

The Ilitches' total investment in Detroit's Theatre District is $200 million. Construction is under way for a new Tiger ballpark east of the Theatre District, thanks in large part to major contributions by Mike Ilitch.

DOMINO'S PIZZA was founded in 1960 by Thomas Monaghan and credits its success to its limited menu—a hand-tossed pizza and Coca-Cola—offered only through carryout or delivery. Later, the company added new products such as deep-dish and thin-crust pizza and Buffalo wings. Today there are more than 6,000 stores in 60 international markets.

Tom Monaghan built Domino's Farms, the 300-acre world headquarters of Domino's Pizza Inc., in Ann Arbor. Its Prairie House headquarters building serves as a tribute to famed architect Frank Lloyd Wright. The Farms is used by individuals and groups for receptions, picnics and meetings. Call for admission prices and package deals: (734) 930-5032.

IL POSTO RISTORANTE
29110 Franklin Rd. at Northwestern Hwy.
Southfield
248) 827-8070
Mon-Sat 11am-10pm. Northern Italian cuisine served in classic European style.

LARCO'S ITALIAN CHOPHOUSE
645 E. Big Beaver, Troy; (248) 680-0066
Mon-Thu 11am-10pm, Fri 11am-11pm, Sat 5-11pm, Sun 4-9pm. Fine dining, authentic Italian specialties, good steaks and an extensive wine list make it a favorite.

LELLI'S
885 N. Opdyke Rd., Auburn Hills
(248) 373-4440
Mon-Thu 11am-10pm, Fri 11am-11pm, Sat 3-11pm, Sun 3-9pm. Longtime favorite in midtown Detroit now has second restaurant in suburbs.

LEPANTO
316 S. Main, Royal Oak; (248) 541-2228
Mon 5:30-9pm, Tue-Thu 5:30-10pm, Fri-Sat 5:30-11pm. One of the first restaurants to open in "Restaurant City." Award-winning Italian fare in elegant, intimate atmosphere.

LINO'S
50 W. Tienken Rd., Rochester
(248) 652-9002
Mon-Thu 5-10pm, Fri-Sat 5-11pm, Sun 4-9pm. Intimate atmosphere and traditional Italian menu, including chicken cacciatore, linguine with clam sauce, steak Florentine and veal Tosca.

MACARONI GRILL
32729 Northwestern Hwy.
Farmington Hills; (248) 851-3900
Mon-Thu 11am-10pm, Fri-Sat 11am-11pm, Sun noon-10pm.
and
39300 W. Seven Mile Rd., Livonia
(at Haggerty); (734) 462-6676
Mon-Thu 11am-10pm, Fri-Sat 11am-11pm, Sun 11am-10pm. Creative Italian fare prepared in open kitchen, pour your own wine from gallon jugs, waiters likely to break out into arias at any time, fun spot for all ages.

MARIA'S FRONT ROOM
215 W. Nine Mile Rd., Ferndale
(at Woodward); (248) 542-7379
Mon 4-9pm, Tue-Thu 5-10pm, Fri-Sat 5-10:30pm, Sun 4-9pm. Pizza, hot garlic bread, as well as pasta, veal and chicken dishes served in cozy atmosphere.

PICANO'S
3775 Rochester Rd., Troy; (248) 689-8050
Mon-Thu 11am-10:30pm, Fri 11am-11pm, Sat noon-11pm, Sun noon-9:30pm. Classic Italian fare, including eggplant parmigiana appetizer and pastas as you wish. Make your own pasta dish. Strolling musicians at night. Named one of top 25 Italian restaurants in United States.

RUSTICA EUROPA
877 E. Auburn Rd., Rochester Hills
(at John R in Auburn Square)
(248) 852-0011
Tue-Thu 11:30-2am, Fri-Sat 4:30pm-10pm. Closed Sun-Mon. Imaginative Italian fare such as Bistecca con salsa balsamica reflects the chef's classic training; intimate and friendly.

220
220 E. Merrill, Birmingham
(248) 645-2150
Mon-Wed 11am-11pm, Thu-Fri 11am-midnight, Sat 11-1am.. Former Edison building beautifully restored; innovative Italian cuisine. Edison's piano bar downstairs, open Thu-Sat 6pm-2am.

SOUTH
FRATELLOS
4501 Fort St., Trenton; (734) 692-1730
Mon-Thu 11am-10pm, Fri-Sat 11am-11pm, Sun noon-8pm. Two levels, grand piano, pasta and veal Tosca make for an elegant Italian evening.

GIOVANNI'S RISTORANTE
330 S. Oakwood Blvd. (W of Fort St.)
Detroit; (313) 841-0122
Tue-Fri 11am-10pm, Sat 4pm-11pm. Homemade gnocchi, pasta and marinara, plus elaborate veal, chicken and seafood dishes served in lively but cozy, upscale atmosphere.

MORO'S DINING
6535 Allen Rd., Allen Park; (313) 382-7152
Mon-Fri 11am-10pm, Sat 4-10pm, Sun 2-8pm. Noted for scampi cooked tableside, veal, flambéed desserts and large portions.

PEPPINA'S RISTORANTE
1128 Dix Rd., Lincoln Park
(between Outer Dr. and Southfield Rd.)
(313) 928-5523
Tue-Thu 11am-10pm, Fri 11am-11pm, Sat 4-11pm, Sun noon-9pm. Specializes in homemade pastas, pizza, northern Italian cuisine. Banquet facilities and catering.

FROM THE BAKERY

Amaretti: Crisp almond macaroons sprinkled with coarse sugar.

Baba: Sponge cake with rum.

Biscotti: Italian word for all cookies, as well as name for twice-baked dry biscuits that are dipped in vin santo (sweet dessert wine) or coffee.

Cannoli: Fried pastry tube filled with sweetened ricotta cheese, chocolate cream, nuts or pieces of chocolate.

Cassata: Sicilian cake in which a layer of pound cake, iced with almond paste and sometimes decorated with marzipan fruits, surrounds ricotta cheese flavored with chocolate.

Crostata: Tarts filled with jam, marzipan, ricotta or other filling.

Pannetone: Cake made with a dough rich in egg yolks, traditionally served at Christmastime. The dough is studded with raisins, candied fruits and occasionally pistachios.

Torta: Cake.

BAKERIES
WINDSOR
AURORA PASTRIES
839 Erie St., Windsor; (519) 256-8801
Daily 10am-6pm. Assortment of cakes, including rum cake, cassata and baba. In addition, a beautiful assortment of housewares and gifts.

ITALIA BAKERY
571 Erie St. (past Howard St.), Windsor
(519) 252-7066
Daily 8am-6pm. Bakes much of the Italian bread that is imported to Detroit markets; many varieties of bread, rolls, pastries, cannolis and tiramisu, sandwiches and groceries.

LA STELLA MARKET
948 Erie St. E. (at Parent), Windsor
(519) 255-1112
9am-6pm Mon-Fri. Closed Sat-Sun. Food imports and homemade breads and pastas.

DETROIT AND DEARBORN
CAPRI ITALIAN BAKERY
4832 Greenfield, Dearborn
(313) 584-4449
Mon-Fri 7am-5:30pm, Sat 6:30am-4pm. Pizza, pepperoni rolls and breads.

DEARBORN ITALIAN BAKERY
24545 Ford Rd., Dearborn
(313) 274-2350
Mon-Fri 7am-8pm, Sat 7am-7pm. Italian cakes and pastries, pizza.

DIMAGGIO ITALIAN BAKERY & PIZZA
25861 W. Six Mile, Redford Twp.
(313) 538-9665
Tue-Sat 7am-6pm, Sun 7am-2pm. Pizza, cannoli and dinner bread.

ITALIA BAKERY
5717 Schaefer, Dearborn
(313) 846-4600
Tue-Sat 7am-6pm. Cannoli, cookies, cakes and coffee cakes.

PASQUALE'S ITALIAN BAKERY
16056 E. Eight Mile Rd., Detroit
(313) 371-0090
Tue-Sat 8am-4pm, Sun 8am-3pm. Specializes in breads.

REDFORD ITALIAN BAKERY
26417 Plymouth, Redford Twp.
(313) 937-2288
Mon-Fri 9am-6:30pm, Sat 9am-4:30pm. Homemade breads, pizza, cannoli and Italian goods.

ROMA BAKERY
6412 Schaefer Hwy., Rd., Dearborn
(313) 581-5000
Mon-Fri 8am-6pm, Sat 8am-8:30pm.
Pepperoni rolls and other Italian specialties.

SOUTH
CAPRARA BAKERY
13498 Northline Rd., Southgate
(734) 284-2820
Mon-Fri 8am-5:30pm, Sat 8am-3:30pm
Italian bread, buns, pepperoni rolls, pizza, and pastry.

JACK'S ITALIAN BAKERY
18841 Allen Rd., Melvindale
(313) 928-9500
Mon-Fri 6am-6pm, Sat 7am-5pm. Pizza, pepperoni rolls, breads.

EAST
ASARO BAKERY
13689 23 Mile Rd., Mt. Clemens
(810) 566-8900
Mon-Sat 6am-8pm, Sun 7am-6pm. Specialty cakes, pastries, cookies, breads and pizza.

BOMMARITO BAKERY DOLCERIA
21830 Greater Mack, St. Clair Shores
(810) 772-6731
Tue-Thu 9am-8pm, Fri-Sun 8am-8pm.
Submarine sandwiches, cannoli and cakes.

CHIRCO'S ITALIAN DELI AND BAKERY
50262 Van Dyke, Utica; (810) 254-5080
Mon-Sat 9am-6pm. Famous for bread and rolls.

GIOVANNI BAKERY
31014 Harper, St. Clair Shores
(810) 293-0423
Mon-Sat 8am-7pm, Sun 8am-5pm. Baked goods and cakes for all occasions.

AT THE COFFEE BAR

Espresso: A dark, strong coffee made by forcing steam (or hot water) through finely ground, Italian-roast coffee specially blended for making espresso. Served in a tiny espresso (or demitasse) cup.

Espresso breve: Espresso with half-and-half.

Espresso doppio: A double espresso.

Espresso lungo: A shot that is pulled long for a bit of extra espresso.

Espresso macchiato: With a minimal amount (or "mark") of steamed milk on top.

Cappuccino: Made by topping espresso with the creamy foam from steamed milk. Some of the steamed milk is also added to the mix. The foam's surface may be dusted with sweetened cocoa powder or cinnamon.

Caffe amaretto: A caffe latte with almond syrup. (Most espresso bars offer an array of flavored syrups that can be added to coffee or used to make Italian sodas.)

Caffe americano: Espresso that is cut with very hot water to fill an American-size cup.

Caffe latte: Espresso with steamed milk, often topped with foamed milk. In Italian latte means "milk."

Caffe mocha: Can be prepared a variety of ways, basically a chocolate caffe latte.

Granita: Like a caffe latte "Slurpee."

MANNINO'S BAKERY
4061 E. 17 Mile, Sterling Hts.
(810) 978-8166
Mon-Fri 7am-7pm, Sat 8am-4pm. Italian cassata cakes, wedding cakes, cannoli, cream puffs, bread and rolls.

MILITELLO'S BAKERY & DELI
52950 Van Dyke, Shelby Twp.
(810) 254-9700
Mon-Sat 6am-6pm. Sells Sicilian bread, which is heavier than most Italian bread.

PIZZO'S BAKERY
42171 Garfield, Clinton Twp.
(at Fairway Plaza near Canal Rd.)
(810) 286-4650
Mon-Fri 6am-7pm, Sat 6am-5pm. Bread and rolls, cakes for all occasions, pastries.

STAFANO & ASARO PASTRY SHOP
41820 Garfield, Clinton Twp.
(810) 263-5121
Mon-Sat 8am-7pm, Sun 8am-5pm. Mini pastries and cannoli.

TANINO'S ITALIAN BAKERY
233401 Ryan, Warren; (810) 752-2420
Mon-Fri 7am-7pm, Sat 7am-5pm. Donuts, cannoli, eclairs and pizza.

TRINGALI'S BAKERY
29100 Schoenherr, Warren
(N of 12 Mile); (810) 777-9010
Tue-Sat 7:30am-7pm, Sun 7am-1pm. Specializes in large and small cannoli, cannoli shells, cream puffs, cookies, bread, rolls and pizza.

VITO'S BAKERY
36795 Garfield, Clinton Twp.
(S of 16 Mile); (810) 791-0360
Mon-Sun 8am-10pm. Italian breads, cannoli, tortes, cookies and cassata cakes.

WEST
ALONGI'S ITALIAN BAKERY
1055 S. Inkster Rd., Inkster
(313) 561-1020
Mon-Fri 7am-6pm, Sat 7am-3pm. Cannoli, pizza, breads, cakes and pastries.

JOE'S ITALIAN BAKERY & DELI
1058 W. Ann Arbor Rd., Plymouth
(734) 416-1456
and
31236 Five Mile, Livonia
(734) 261-5666
Mon-Fri 7am-7pm, Sat 7am-5pm. Claims to have the best cannoli in town.

LIVONIA ITALIAN BAKERY
33615 Seven Mile, Livonia
(248) 474-0444
Mon-Sat 9am-7pm, Sun 9am-4pm. Cafe, bakery and market with prepared foods, pasta, wines and cookware. Catering menu features Italian style deli trays, antipasto salad, lasagna and other party favorites.

MARIA'S ITALIAN BAKERY & PIZZERIA
115 N. Haggerty Rd., Canton Twp.
(734) 981-1200
Mon-Thu 7am-10pm, Fri-Sat 7am-11pm, Sun 8am-9pm.
and
11700 Belleville Rd., Belleville
(734) 697-3840
Mon-Thu 7am-10pm, Fri-Sat 7am-11pm, Sun 9am-10pm.
and
41706 10 Mile Rd., Novi
(248) 348-0545
Mon-Fri 7am-7pm, Sat 7am-5pm. Homemade pastas, Sicilian deep-dish pizza, stromboli, pastry, cakes, tortes and cannoli.

NORTH
JULIAN BROTHERS ITALIAN BAKERY
518 S. Rochester, Clawson
(248) 588-0280
Tue-Sat 10am-9:30pm. Fresh bread daily, great pizza, unbaked pizza dough and pizza fixings available to make your own at home.

MARKETS

Italian markets carry imports including seasonings, sauces, pastas, wines, olives, oils, vinegars and candies. Many have a deli counter with cheeses, meats and homemade sausage. Italian names are found on many buildings in Detroit's Eastern Market district, at Gratiot Avenue and Russell Street.
(See Multicultural Detroit.)

WINDSOR

ITALIAN DELICATESSEN & SALUMERIA
643 Erie St. E., Windsor
(519) 253-2514
Mon-Sat 8:30am-6:30pm, Sun 8:30am-4:30pm. Many types of salami, cheeses and imported foods; gift baskets.

DEARBORN/DETROIT

ALCAMO'S MARKET
4423 Schaefer, Dearborn
(313) 584-3010
Mon-Thu and Sat 9am-6pm, Fri 9am-7pm. Prepared Italian foods, wines, pastas and 100 varieties of olive oil.

GONELLA'S
259 S. Oakwood, Detroit, (313) 841-3500
Mon-Sat 8:30am-5:30pm. Market and deli near Rouge Bridge sells hundreds of Italian sandwiches daily.

LA CANTINA
1324 N. Telegraph, Dearborn
(S of Ford Rd.)
(313) 565-7573
Mon-Sat 9am-6pm, Sun 9am-3pm. Full line of Italian food specialties and wines.

EAST

ANTONIO'S ITALIAN MEATS AND FOOD
38900 Ryan (at 17 Mile), Sterling Hts.
(810) 939-4440
Mon-Sat 9am-6pm. Deli with Italian groceries, sausage, wines.

GIGLIO'S MARKET
27919 Harper, St. Clair Shores
(810) 774-3767
Mon-Fri 8:30am-7pm, Sat 8:30am-6pm, Sun 8.30am-4pm. Homemade sausage, largest pasta selection in Michigan—120 different cuts. Pastry, cakes, tortes and cannoli.

LOMBARDO FINE FOODS
31065 Ryan Rd., Warren
(810) 939-0580
Tue-Sat 9am-7pm, Sun 10am-4pm. Specializes in meats and sausage. Also cheeses, pastas and oils.

VENTIMIGLIA ITALIAN FOODS
35197 Dodge Park, Sterling Hts.
(810) 979-0828
Mon-Fri 9am-7pm, Sat 9am-6pm, Sun 9am-2pm. Deli selection, baked goods, pastas, olive oils, wine, other Italian food specialties and gifts.

WEST

CHIMENTO'S ITALIAN MARKET
33610 Plymouth Rd., Livonia
(734) 421-3800
Mon-Sat 9am-7pm, Sun 10am-3pm. Specializes in imported and domestic merchandise, over-the-counter butchering, homemade sausage, 50 different olive oils, 100 kinds of pasta.

CANTORO'S ITALIAN MARKET
19710 Middlebelt, Livonia; (248) 478-2345
Mon-Fri 9am-6pm, Sat 8am-6pm. Homemade bread, salami, cheeses, olive oil, pasta and wines surrounded by murals of Dennis Orlowski.

GREEN GROCERS

Italian Americans are renowned for their produce markets in the Detroit area. In the past few years many of these have expanded far beyond the simple corner "green grocer." Here are a few:

Manzella's Fruit Market
St. Clair Shores, (810) 294-8130

Nino Salvaggio
Farmington Hills, (248) 855-5570
St. Clair Shores, (810) 778-3650

Papa Joe's
Rochester Hills, (248) 853-6263

Randazzo Fruit Markets
Dearborn, (313) 563-6800

Tony Serra & Sons
Roseville, (810) 758-0792

Vic's Quality Fruit/World Class Market
Beverly Hills, (248) 647-4646,
Novi, (248) 305-7333
Bloomfield Hills, (248) 454-0700

Vince & Joe's Fruit Market & Deli
Clinton Twp., (810)-263-7870

Westborn Fruit Markets
Dearborn, (313) 274-6100
Berkley, (248) 547-1000
Livonia, (734) 422-8100

SHOPS

NORTH

BELLA LUNA
Summit Place, Waterford; (248) 681-4753
*Mon-Sat 10am-9pm, Sun noon-6pm.
Boutique specializes in handmade glass
beads from Venice. Also carries vases, fig-
urines, paperweights.*

**DETROIT INSTITUTE OF ARTS
SATELLITE GIFT SHOP**
Somerset Collection, Troy; (248) 649-2222
*Mon-Fri 10am-9pm, Sat 10am-7pm,
Sun noon-6pm.* A variety of ancient Roman
through contemporary Italian art reproduc-
tions, books, calendars and stationery.

DONNA JACOBS GALLERY
574 N. Woodward Ave., Birmingham
(248) 540-1600
*Thu-Fri 11am-5:30pm, Sat 1-5pm and by
appointment.* Persian, Egyptian, Greek,
Etruscan and Roman antiquities.

ROMA SPOSA
722 N. Old Woodward, Birmingham
(248) 723-4300
*Mon & Thu 10am-8pm, Tue, Wed, Fri 10am-
6pm, Sat 9am-4pm.* Bridal boutique features
custom-made gowns by Italian designers.

TUTTO BENE
217 N. Old Woodward (N of Maple)
Birmingham; (248) 723-8310
*Mon, Wed, Fri, Sat 10am-6pm, Thu 10am-
8pm. Closed Sun.* "Everything Good" is
name of boutique featuring Italian crafts—
handmade ceramics, jewelry and glassware,
including lamps, vases, dinnerware, wine
pitchers, planters and decorative tiles.

EAST

BONALDI'S ITALIAN IMPORTS
41740 Garfield, Clinton Twp.
(N of 18 Mile); (810) 263-1233
*Mon-Tue and Thu-Fri 10am-8pm, Wed and
Sat 10am-6pm.* Collectibles, artifacts, figurines, religious items, jewelry. Italian language cards, magazines and music.

WEST

DETROIT INSTITUTE OF ARTS SHOP
Twelve Oaks Mall, Novi;
(248) 380-8050.
Mon-Sat 10am-9pm, Sun 11am-6pm.
Roman to contemporary Italian art, including
reproductions, books, calendars and stationery.

WINDSOR

CAPRICCIO GIFTS
839 Erie St., Windsor
(519) 256-8801
Mon-Fri 10am-6pm, Sat 9am-6pm. Coffee
bar and pastries, wedding favors, unique
gifts for baptisms and other occasions.

DECORIA
997 Parent, Windsor
(519) 253-3030
Tue-Fri 10am-5:30pm, Sat 10am-4pm.
Elegant gifts for home and garden,
Renaissance reproductions, stationery.

THERESA'S LINENS & GIFTS
1100 Erie St. E., Windsor
(519) 252-8507
Mon-Sat 9am-6pm. Crystal, linens,
Communion dresses, christening gowns,
bridal gowns and gifts.

VISUAL ARTS

DETROIT INSTITUTE OF ARTS
5200 Woodward Ave., Detroit
(313) 833-7900
Wed-Fri 11am-4pm, Sat-Sun 11am-5pm.
European art includes extensive collection
of Italian works from the Gothic and
Renaissance periods, particularly Venice
and Florence. Artists from the Italian branch
of the Neo-Expressionist movement are represented in the contemporary collection.
Ancient Roman art is particularly well-
represented with sculpture, mosaics and
frescoes, pottery and household objects.

ITALIAN HERITAGE ROOM
General Lectures Hall, Room
Wayne State University, Detroit
(313) 577-2246
Call for hours. The newest addition to the
WSU Heritage Rooms (and the first in
America), features a colonnade based on
the Ufizi Art Gallery in Florence.

TOLEDO MUSEUM OF ART
2445 Monroe St., Toledo, Ohio
(at Scottwood Ave.)
(419) 255-8000 or 1-800-644-6862
The relatively small, but beautiful, museum
has treasures from ancient Rome; a
medieval cloister; paintings, sculpture,
furniture, silver, tapestries and graphic arts.
More than 6,000 examples of art in glass
from antiquity to the present. Well-stocked
gift shop.

HOME OF THE OPERA

Opera began in Italy in the late 16th and early 17th centuries. The word *opera* means "work" in Italian and is short for *opera in musica*. It is a dramatic play in which all or part of the dialogue is sung, and which contains instrumental overtures, interludes and accompaniments. Types of musical theater closely related to opera include musical comedy and operetta.

Opera was developed by a group of musicians and scholars who called themselves the *camerata* (Italian for "salon"). Their goal was to revive the musical style used in ancient Greek drama and to develop an alternative to the highly contrapuntal music of the late Renaissance.

Michigan Opera Theatre (MOT) began in 1963 when Italian American David DiChiera, MOT founder and general director, toured schools across the state, building an audience with his "Overture to Opera" series. "Overture" staged its first full-length opera, "The Barber of Seville," at the Detroit Institute of Arts in 1970 and moved to Music Hall one year later. Although 1971 is MOT's official founding date, the name didn't change from "Overture to Opera" until 1973.

Now housed in a beautifully restored 1922-vintage downtown theater, renamed the Detroit Opera House, MOT continues to be a wonderful resource to the community, carrying its educational programs throughout the state and staging spectacular performances that attract world-class performers.

The works of famous Italian composers such as **Antonio Vivaldi, Gaetano Donizetti, Giacomo Puccini, Gioacchino Rossini** and **Giuseppe Verdi** are presented regularly by MOT. You can also listen to opera on 89.9 FM with Howard Dyck whose show "Saturday Afternoon at the Opera" airs 1:30-6pm.

Call (313) 874-SING for additional information.

PERFORMING ARTS

MICHIGAN OPERA THEATRE
Detroit Opera House
1526 Broadway, Detroit; (313) 874-SING
Box office open Mon-Fri 10am-5pm.
Fall season runs from Sept-Nov; spring from April-June. Line-up usually includes operas in Italian or operas by Italian composers. Call for directions, parking and ticket information.

ANNUAL ITALIAN FILM FESTIVAL/ GREAT LAKES
Michigan Theater
603 E. Liberty, Ann Arbor; (734) 668-8463
Call for information and film schedule.

ITALIAN STUDY GROUP OF TROY PERFORMING ARTS
(248) 585-5246
Contact: Denise Silverio
Special group within Italian Study Group meets at Troy Community Center.

ISGT CHOIR
(810) 677-0104
Contact: Lucia Lester
Based at Troy Community Center.

CORO ITALIANO
(810) 751-2855 or 773-4124
Contact: Luigi LaMarra, choir director
Based at Italian Cultural Center in Warren.

EDUCATIONAL INFLUENCE

The Italian effect on European education dates back to the ancient Roman educators and scholars, including Cicero, Quintilian and Seneca. Later, during the Middle Ages, Italian universities became the model for those of other countries. During the Renaissance, Italy was the teacher of the liberal arts to virtually all of Europe, especially for Greek language and literature. The educational influence of Italy continued through the 17th century when its universities and academies were major centers of teaching and research in the sciences. Latin formed the basis of all modern "Romance languages." Not only was Latin the official language of scholars and the Roman Catholic Church throughout most of the Western World, but its terms are still used in the sciences.

Italian education once again attained international notice in the 20th century, partly as a result of **Maria Montessori's** method for teaching young children.

Quite a few local elementary schools employ Montessori methods; there are also specialized Montessori centers and schools. See the Yellow Pages.

ANNUAL EVENTS

SPRING

FESTA ITALIANA
Banquet, sponsored by the Italian Study Group of Troy, is held every spring to honor the Italian American of the Year. Call Mary Cairo, (248) 588-4425.

ITALIAN FESTIVAL
Food and entertainment highlight **April festival** at Yack Arena in Wyandotte. Call (734) 246-4515.

ST. JOSEPH'S DAY
On **March 19** in Italy, restaurants and entire towns put out the St. Joseph's Table to feed the needy. Several Italian restaurants in the area observe this custom.

SUMMER

CARROUSEL OF NATIONS
Sponsored by the Multicultural Council of Windsor, celebration includes an Italian Village with food, entertainment and crafts on Erie Street East in Windsor's Little Italy. Event is held **two weekends in June.** Call (519) 255-1127.

VIA ITALIA
On Erie Street East in Windsor's Little Italy, this summer celebration has music and dancing, parade, food, outdoor Mass at St. Angela's and other festivities. Sponsored by the Erie Street Business Improvement Association, (519) 977-8024.

PONTIAC INTERNATIONAL ETHNIC FESTIVAL
Event held at Phoenix Plaza over the **Fourth of July weekend** has Italian food booths and entertainers. For information, call Pontiac Growth Corp at (248) 857-5603.

ITALIAN DAYS
Festival, held **first weekend in August** at Freedom Hill County Park in Sterling Hts., features food, music, dancing and booths. Call (810) 979-7010.

MULTI-ETHNIC FESTIVAL
In **late August** at Warren's Hamlich Park on 13 Mile between Dequindre and Ryan, event includes soccer tournament, Italian food and entertainment. Sponsored by Warren City Council, (810) 574-4950.

OCTOBER
COLUMBUS DAY PARADE AND CELEBRATION

Parade down 12 Mile Road from south campus of Macomb Community College to the Italian Cultural Center, is at 11am the Saturday on or preceding Columbus Day (October 12). Other events include a Saturday evening banquet, 11am Sunday Mass at Holy Family Church in downtown Detroit (Lafayette and the I-75 Service Drive), followed by brunch and a commemoration service at the Columbus statue on East Jefferson. Call Columbus Day Celebration Committee, (248) 623-1783.

DECEMBER
CHRISTMAS SINGALONG

Traditional event takes place the first Sunday in December at the Italian Cultural Center in Warren. Call (810) 751-2855.

ORGANIZATIONS

DANTE ALIGHIERI SOCIETY
(248) 559-3455
Contact: Frank DeSantis
Founded in 1889 in Rome, the society promotes Italian culture and language. Sponsors lectures on history, artists, writers, and Italian influence on math, science and art.

ITALIAN AMERICAN FRATERNAL CLUB
5101 Oakman, Dearborn; (313) 582-7433
Contact: Nancy Block
Recently celebrated its 50th anniversary, over 500 members sponsor events and activities for the many people of Italian heritage in the Dearborn area.

ITALIAN CULTURAL CENTER
**28111 Imperial Drive, Warren
(off 12 Mile between Schoenherr
and Hoover)
(810) 751-2855**
Services and activities for people of Italian

heritage. Sponsors festivals, Columbus Day parade, arts and crafts show in November and various social events throughout the year. Offers Italian language classes.

ITALIAN STUDY GROUP OF TROY
**P.O. Box 104, Troy, MI 48098
(248) 588-4425 or 939-5946**
Educational and cultural organization that promotes Italian language and culture. Maintains display of Italian crafts at Troy Community Center, where its classes and activities take place. Oggi is a support group of the Italian Study Group of Troy. Oggi means "today," and its members are young adults with interests in soccer, festivals, Italian sports cars and being exchange students.

ITALIAN AMERICAN CLUB OF LIVONIA
**39200, Five Mile Rd., Livonia
(734) 953-9724**
Sponsors social events, cultural programs and language classes.

WORLD CULTURE

The Romans inherited much from the Etruscans and borrowed many ideas from the Greeks, but from ancient to modern times, Italy has had a major influence on world culture. Italians have contributed some of the world's most admired sculpture, architecture, painting, literature and music. Politically unified less than 150 years ago, most Italians do not consider themselves to be a "new" people, but instead descendants of the ancient Romans.

Many works of the great Italian painters, such as **Giotto, Fra Angelico, Michelangelo, Leonardo da Vinci, Raphael** and **Titian** can be viewed at the Detroit Institute of Arts and the Toledo Art Museum.

MEDIA

PRINT

INTERNATIONAL BOOK CENTRE
2391 Auburn Rd., Shelby Twp.
(810) 254-7230
Mon-Sat 11am-5pm. Books and publications in Italian and other languages.

IL GIORNALE ITALIANO
P.O. Box 26575
Fraser 48026; (810) 292-4856
Monthly tabloid in Italian and English.

THE ITALIAN TRIBUNE
P.O. Box 380407
Clinton Twp. 48038; (810) 783-3260
Biweekly tabloid in Italian and English. Available by subscription or free at restaurants and shops in Italian neighborhoods.

LA GAZETTA
909 Howard Ave.
Windsor, Ontario, Canada N9A 1S3
(519) 253-8883
Weekly newspaper in Italian.

TELEVISION

TV "RAI"
Sat 7-8pm and Sun 8am-2pm. Programming direct from Italy via satellite aired in Macomb County by Comcast Cable.
Also on cable TV, local performer Pino Marelli, (248) 524-9281.

RADIO

MUSICA ITALIA
CHYR FM 96.7
Leamington, Ontario; (519) 326-6171
Vince Mancina, Sun 8am-11am. Ralph DeBenedictis, 12-3pm.

RADIO ITALIANA
(248) 939-5946
Lisa Bica Grodsky features popular Italian hit music (Laura Pausini, Eros Ramazzotti, Umberto Tozzi). For information, contact P.O. Box 1013, Royal Oak 48067-1003.

NOSTALGIA DE ITALIA
(313) 561-7627
c/o Dino Valle
Traditional, classical and operatic music by Italian composers.

WEB SITES

LITTLE ITALY
www.viaitalia.com
E-mail address: erie@igs.windsor.net

DALL'ITALIA VIDEO MAGAZINE
www.dallitalia.it

ITALIAN CULTURAL RESOURCES
www.tcom.ohiou.edu/ou_Language/lang-italian.html

ITALIAN SCULPTURE AROUND TOWN

- *Rasso de Danza* by Giacomo Manzu, one of Italy's most acclaimed sculptors, is in front of the American Natural Resources Building at Jefferson and Woodward in Detroit.

- *The Nymph and the Faun,* another Manzu sculpture, graces Wayne State University's McGregor Conference Center in Detroit.

- *Christopher Columbus* statue, by Augusto Rivalta, is at Jefferson and Randolph in Detroit.

- *Dante Allighieri* statue by Raffaello Romanelli, at Central and Vista avenues on Belle Isle in Detroit, honors Italy's most celebrated poet.

- *Works by Corrado Parducci* are on the Guardian Building, the Buhl Building, the Main Branch of the Detroit Public Library, the U.S. Courthouse in Detroit and the Horace H. Rackham Memorial Fountain at the Detroit Zoological Park.

- Sculptor *Sergio DeGiusti,* a Wayne State University alumnus, has created a commemorative relief for the offices of the U.S. Drug Enforcement Agency at the Rick Finley Building in Detroit, as well as 20 bas-relief panels in the State of Michigan Library in Lansing.

The Polish flag is red and white.

POLAND

Poland is in central Europe, bordered by Lithuania on the northeast, Belarus and Ukraine on the east, Germany on the west, the Czech Republic and Slovakia on the south, and the Baltic Sea on the north. Although the Carpathian Mountains form Poland's southern region and lakes dot the north, most of the country is covered with flat plains and gently rolling hills. In fact, Polanie is the Slavic word for plain or field dwellers. The name was given to one of the westernmost tribes of Slavic people more than a thousand years ago.

POLES IN DETROIT

With a population estimated at 500,000 to 800,000, Polish Americans constitute one of the largest ethnic groups in metropolitan Detroit. Hamtramck had the largest concentration of Poles until the 1970s, when many moved to Warren and Sterling Heights in Macomb County and also to Oakland County. While 18 percent still live in Detroit and Hamtramck, Macomb County has become Michigan's "Polonia." About 25 percent of the county's residents claim Polish ancestry. Many Polish Americans also live in Dearborn, Dearborn Heights, Wyandotte and other parts of Michigan, especially Grand Rapids, Bay City and Alpena.

The first Polish settlers in Detroit arrived in 1762, followed by others in the early and mid-1800s. The establishment of St. Albertus Catholic Parish on Detroit's east side in 1871 marked the formation of a strong Polish American community. A Polish seminary founded nearby in 1885 was the predecessor of the theological and educational center now at Orchard Lake.

The first wave of Polish immigrants in the 1860s came for economic reasons and to escape conscription into foreign armies. By 1880 Poles had settled in Detroit, Cleveland, Chicago, Pittsburgh and Buffalo, N.Y.

The next wave, 1880-1910, saw Poles coming to work in the lumber, coal and auto industries. The opening of Dodge Main in Hamtramck in 1914 attracted more Poles. By the 1920s and '30s, Polish Americans had become a vital part of Detroit's labor movement.

The influx of immigrants continued after World War I, and especially after World War II. More recently, political refugees have immigrated and entered a variety of professions. Polish American organizations continue to be active in preserving the strength and vitality of the community and maintaining cultural ties.

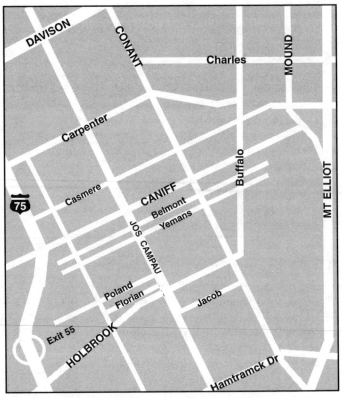

HAMTRAMCK

[E-F/3-4] Hamtramck is on the east side of I-75 between Carpenter (south of the Davison Expressway) and East Grand Boulevard. Exit 55 (Holbrook/Caniff) will take you to the main shopping district on Joseph Campau. Coming from the north, take Caniff east. If you're approaching from the south, immediately turn right on Holbrook and you'll soon pass the neon sausage sign at Kowalski Headquarters on your way to Jos. Campau.

An eagle has been the symbol on the Polish coat of arms since the 1200s.

Best bet for parking is a metered space behind stores, especially the large lot behind Shopper's World on Yemans. Because the lot is sandwiched between the **Polonia Restaurant** and the **Polish Village Cafe,** you can either begin or end your tour with an authentic meal from the homeland.

Start your trek *on Jos. Campau by going a block up* to **Pope Park** at Belmont. Not only is there a towering sculpture of Pope John Paul II (Karol Wojtyla), but also a colorful mural of a Krakow town square. Then wander into **Martha Washington Bakery** *(10335 Jos. Campau, north of Belmont)* or *head south on Jos. Campau* to **New Palace Bakery** *(9833)* or **Kowalski/ Oaza Bakery** *(9405)* for *babki* (coffee cakes), angel wings and Polish breads. Pick up some kielbasa at **Ciemniak's Meat Market** *(9629)*, **Campau Quality Sausage** *(9601)* or **Stan's Grocery** *(11325)*. For a traditional deli, try **Polish Deli & Bakery** *(12015)*, where you can dine in or get a carryout. Plan to spend most of your time browsing for folk art, imports, books, videos and compact discs at the **Polish Art Center** *(9539)*. Owner Joan Bittner serves as a guide to Polish culture and can direct you to any Polish American establishment in metro Detroit.

At Jos. Campau and Holbrook, you'll find the new Town Center development and parking. A **commemorative marker** by the Farmer Jack grocery parking lot designates the site of the Pope's 1987 visit. *Across the street on the corner of Jacob* is the renowned **Under the Eagle** restaurant *(9000)* in an old, red brick, canopied building. *Two blocks farther south* is **Kopytko Meat Co.** *(8609)*, specializing in European homemade sausages.

Before leaving Hamtramck, visit **St. Florian Catholic Church** *(2626 Poland, west of Jos. Campau)* to see an example of the magnificent cathedrals that attest to the strong faith and loyalty of the Polish people. This church, where the movie "Polish Wedding" was filmed, is open every day from 7:30 a.m. to 7 p.m. *(Use the Poland Street entrance.)*

[E-F/2-3] Follow the Polish American migration to Warren and Sterling Heights by traveling Dequindre and other northeast arteries. To get a taste of Polish cuisine and culture in the suburbs, visit the **American Polish Cultural Center** *on the northwest corner of Maple (15 Mile) and Dequindre on the Troy-Sterling Heights border.*

The castle-like banquet facility is open to the public for lunch Tuesday through Friday and dinner on Wednesday and Friday (live entertainment). Note the carved oak columns and pediment surrounding the doorway and the crystal chandeliers and elaborate Polish regional displays in the **Heritage Gallery** restaurant. Select from the hearty homemade fare on the menu and order some pierogi to take home. Plans call for the Cultural Center's 12-acre site to be developed into a Polish Village with stores, delis, bakeries, expanded banquet facilities, an auditorium, office space and a day-care center.

Until then, complete the tour by shopping across the street at the **Polish Market** *(2938 Maple)* and **Old Country Deli** *(38952 Dequindre, on the southeast corner of 17 Mile).*

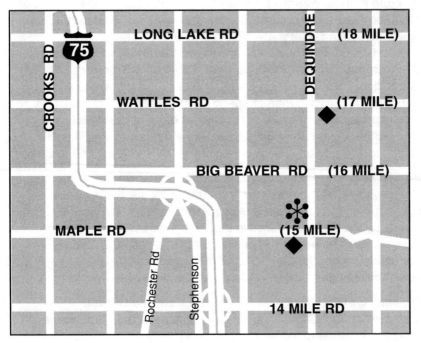

WARREN/STERLING HEIGHTS/TROY

[C-D/2-3] On the first Sunday of any month, head out to the **Orchard Lake Schools and Center,** home of S.S. Cyril & Methodius Seminary, St. Mary's College and Preparatory School, Center for Polish Studies and Culture, Polish American Liturgical Center and Pope John Paul II Center.

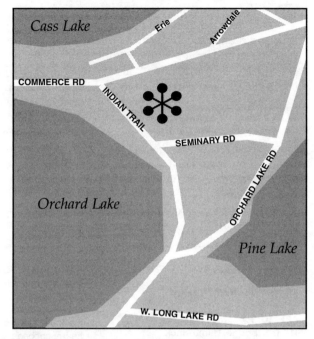

The 120-acre campus on the eastern shore of Orchard Lake is *17 miles northwest of Detroit and five miles south-* west of Pontiac in West Bloomfield Township. From Orchard Lake Road, take either Indian Trail or Commerce Road. If you enter Seminary Road from Indian Trail, you will see the Marian Grotto on the corner. This garden site is used as a prayer area and a setting for graduation and wedding pictures. *Park at the guest lot near the church.*

Mass in the Polish language begins at 1 p.m. in the **Shrine Chapel of Our Lady of Orchard Lake.** Afterward, Polish dinners are served in the dining hall next door. Then tour the campus, starting with the **National Polish American Sports Hall of Fame** at Dombrowcki Fieldhouse on the western edge of campus.

Clustered at the other end of campus are several buildings with exhibits. A former dormitory, called the Ark, now houses the **Pope John Paul II Center, Polish War Veteran Museums, Polish Singers Alliance Museum, Friends of Polish Art Archives** and other collections. Adjacent is the **The Galeria,** a one-story, red brick military structure, which exhibits Polish and Polish American art and hosts lectures and concerts. The nearby Activities Building contains the **campus bookstore** and **Polish Panorama** display.

Be sure to arrive by 4 p.m. to see the presentation with a taped narration in Polish or English. More than 100 handcrafted figures synchronized on a moving track depict the 1,000-year history of the Polish nation. Call Orchard Lake Center at (248) 682-1885 for the schedule of religious services, meals, lectures and tours.

POLISH CUISINE

Polish fare is made primarily of beef, pork and chicken, along with crops that can be grown in cold and damp climates, such as potatoes, beans, cabbage, beets and grains. Dairy products, especially sour cream, also are prevalent in Polish cooking. Dill, marjoram, caraway seed and parsley are the seasonings most often used.

Pierogi, a Polish specialty, are half-moon-shaped noodle dumplings filled with a minced mixture, most commonly pork, onions, cottage cheese and seasonings. Mushrooms, cabbage, potatoes and rice also are used as filling. After the pierogi are cooked in boiling water, they're sometimes sautéed briefly in butter and topped with toasted bread crumbs and/or sour cream. They can be served as a first course or side dish. Pierogi are available fresh or frozen at many local markets.

Polish restaurants serve *kielbasa* (sausage), **kapusta** (sauerkraut), **bigos** (meat stew), **nalesniki** (crepes), **golabki** (stuffed cabbage) and hearty soups.

RESTAURANTS

HAMTRAMCK

CAFE ZUPPA
2917 Trowbridge, Hamtramck
(313) 871-9929
Mon-Tue 10am-7pm,Wed-Sat 10am-midnight. Hearty soups from Polish and other cuisines served in 16-ounce bowls. Also coffees and desserts.

HOLBROOK CAFE
3201 Holbrook, Hamtramck
(313) 875-1115
Daily 11am-9pm. Restaurant, lounge and banquet facility serves traditional Polish fare at site of former Polish American Century Club. Friday night fish fry.

KRAKUS RESTAURANT & BAR
12900 Jos. Campau, Hamtramck
(313) 368-4848
Mon-Thu 11am-7pm, Fri-Sat 11am-8pm. Homemade Polish food; dancing Saturday 9pm-1:30am. Complete carryout, banquets.

POLISH DELI & BAKERY
12015 Jos. Campau, Hamtramck
(313) 365-3731
Daily 9am-8pm. Dine-in or carryout at self-serve Polish deli. Soups, entrées, salads, vegetables and baked goods.

POLONIA-JAWOROWKA
2934 Yemans, Hamtramck
(313) 873-8432
Mon-Thu 11am-7pm, Fri-Sat 11am-8pm. Restaurant and banquet hall known for hearty cabbage soup, cheese and potato pierogi, sausage and other Polish dishes.

POLISH VILLAGE CAFE
2990 Yemans, Hamtramck
(313) 874-5726
Tue-Sat 11am-8pm, Sun 1-7pm. In lower level of red brick building with white shutters and balcony. Specialties include soup, especially dill pickle soup; potato pancakes, pierogi, nalesniki and golabki. President Clinton ate here while on his 1996 campaign tour.

ROSIE O'GRADY'S PUB
11816 Jos. Campau, Hamtramck
(313) 891-2236
Mon-Tue 11am-midnight, Wed-Fri 11am-2am, Sat 4pm-2am, Sun noon-9pm. Polish food, drink specials, entertainment.

UNDER THE EAGLE
9000 Jos. Campau, Hamtramck
(between Jacob and Roosevelt)
(313) 875-5905
Mon-Tue 11am-7pm, Wed closed, Thu-Sun 11am-9pm. Famous Polish eatery noted for roast pork loin, mashed potatoes, tangy sauerkraut, fresh pierogi, dill pickle soup.

See also *"Markets"* for **Srodek's Quality Sausage** and **Stan's Grocery,** which have delis with carryout and dine-in service.

WINDSOR/DETROIT/DEARBORN

JIM'S PLACE
13245 Michigan Ave., Dearborn
(W of Miller Rd.)
(313) 584-5437
Mon-Sat 6am-8pm, Sun 7am-6pm.
Homemade pierogi, stuffed cabbage and other Polish specialties.

POLISH RESTAURANT PIAST
1194 Wyandotte St. E, Windsor
(519) 255-1622
Mon-Tue, Thurs 11am-8pm, Wed, Fri-Sat 11am-9pm. More than 70 old-fashioned homemade Polish dishes using fresh, natural ingredients.

STARLITE RESTAURANT
7511 Michigan Ave., Detroit
(313) 841-3169
Daily 8am-7:30pm. Pierogi, beef soup, potato pancakes, salmon patties and city chicken are specialties.

(STEVE'S) THREE BROTHERS' RESTAURANT
17620 W. Warren, Detroit
(1 block E of Southfield)
(313) 271-1227

Daily 9am-8pm. Dine-in or carryout pierogi, kielbasa and stuffed cabbage. Known for czarnina soup and cabbage soup. Daily lunch specials.

EAST

AMERICAN POLISH CULTURAL CENTER
2975 E. Maple Rd., Troy
(on NW corner of Dequindre)
(248) 689-3636
Open to the public Tue-Fri for lunch, Wed and Fri for dinner. Heritage Room menu offers homemade kielbasa, kapusta, kopytka (long potato noodle), stuffed cabbage and pyzy.

DIANA RESTAURANT
19528 Kelly, Harper Woods
(between Seven and Eight Mile Rds.)
(313) 526-9436
Wed-Sat noon-8pm, Sun and Tue noon-7pm. Soup, pierogi, stuffed cabbage, potato pancakes, crêpes, stuffed beef rolls, city chicken, pork chops and roast pork with dumplings at low prices.

ENZO'S WARREN CAFE
32747 Mound, Warren; (810) 939-7800
Mon-Thu 10:30am-8pm, Fri 10:30am-9pm, Sat 2-9pm. Polish entrees include cabbage rolls and pierogi.

WHAT'S FOR ZUPA?

Polish soups are some of the best in the world. *Chlodnik,* a cold soup made of sour milk and a fermented red-beet extract, also contains chopped vegetables and occasionally meat. Other cold soups, nice starters to a light lunch in the summer, are usually made of sour milk and fresh berries.

Zupa ogorkowa (pickle soup) is made of fermented (not preserved) pickles in a broth. *Zupa grzybowa,* or wild mushroom soup, is a Polish specialty made from the *boletus edulis* mushroom (also called *porcino*). In Polish restaurants, the one soup you will find most often is *barszcz,* a clear beet soup made from a fermented beet extract. It often is served with tiny meat-stuffed dumplings called either *kolduny* or *uszki* (little ears). Sometimes a *pasztecik* (stuffed meat pasty) is served on the side.

Zurek is a sourish soup made from fermented wheat and usually served with a hard-boiled egg or sausage. *Bigos* is a meat and sauerkraut stew. Other soups to try are *szczawiowa* (sorrel), *kapusniak* (cabbage) and *krupnik* (meat and barley). The adventurous diner might try *czarnina,* made from ducks' blood.

WEST
THREE BROTHERS
8825 General Dr., Plymouth
(734) 416-3393
Mon-Sat 8am-8:30pm, Sun 8am-8pm.
Specializing in Polish-American cuisine.

SOUTH
POLONUS RESTAURANT
1744 Biddle, Wyandotte; (313) 283-3530
Tue-Thu 11am-8pm, Fri-Sat 11am-9pm, Sun 11am-6pm. Serves potato pancakes, pierogi, stuffed cabbage, city chicken, marinated duck, crêpes, sausage and pork chops.

THREE BROTHERS II
3840 Oakwood Blvd., Melvindale
(313) 383-3620

Daily 9am-8pm. Pierogi, kielbasa, soups and other Polish fare. Dine-in or carryout.

NORTH
LINZI'S CAFE
1043 Cass Lake Rd., Waterford
(248) 682-6000
Mon-Sat 11am-8:30pm. Polish items on menu include pierogi, kielbasa, stuffed cabbage and sauerkraut.

LUCKICH'S FAMILY RESTAURANT
3900 Rochester Rd., Troy (N of 16 Mile)
(248) 528-9955
Mon 7am-3pm, Tue-Sun 7am-9pm. European fare includes Polish "super combo" with stuffed cabbage, Polish sausage, sauerkraut, pierogi and potato pancake.

ON THE MENU

Appetizers can include smoked salmon and herring in a variety of sauces. *Karp po zydowsku* (carp Jewish style) is an aspic with raisins. Some salads are *surówka*, a raw, grated salad of cabbage, sauerkraut, beets, apples, carrots or leeks; *mizeria*, thinly sliced cucumbers in sour cream; and *salata*, usually a combination of vegetables, fruits and hard-boiled eggs in mayonnaise. Pickles *(ogorki kiszone)* are prepared in various ways.

Potatoes—mashed, fried or boiled—are standard. *Kluski* (dumplings) with various combinations of grated raw and cooked potatoes *(pyzy)* are typical accompaniments to meat dishes. Mushrooms are served in a number of ways. *Golabki* (stuffed cabbage dishes) also are popular.

Golonka (pork) is the main domestic meat in Poland. It is served in various ways—from simple broiled pork chops to *schnitzel* (sausage) and *szynka* (Polish ham). *Kaczka z jablkami* (roast duck with apples) is a classic Polish dish. *Flaczki* (tripe), *kielbasa* (pork sausage seasoned with garlic), *kiszka* (barley and buckwheat sausage) and *parowki* (frankfurters) also are found on most menus.

Szarlotka (apple cake), *sernik* (cheesecake) and *makowiec* (poppy seed roll) are typical Polish dessert cakes. **Polish strawberries** are wonderful and have even inspired festivals in the area *(see "St. Florian Strawberry Festival")*.

Vodka is the Polish national drink, made from either grain or potatoes—the grain version being slightly sweeter, the potato version drier. The only indigenous Polish wine is *miód pitny*, a honey wine, which comes in a variety of strengths and sweetnesses. There are also a number of interesting Polish beers.

BAKERIES/DELIS

HAMTRAMCK/ EAST-SIDE DETROIT

OAZA BAKERY
11829 Jos. Campau, Hamtramck
(between Commor & Caniff)
(313) 365-7010
Mon-Sat 6am-8pm, Sun 9am-5pm.
European-style breads, pastries, angel wings, cookies and a deli counter. Main store has lunch counter and outdoor café. (Satellite shop is near Holbrook in the **Kowalski Market** at 9405 Jos. Campau.)

MARTHA WASHINGTON BAKERY
10335 Jos. Campau, Hamtramck
(313) 872-1988
Mon-Thu & Sat 6am-6pm. Fri 6am-7pm.
Since 1925 has specialized in breads, rolls, and wedding and birthday cakes.

NEW PALACE BAKERY
9833 Jos. Campau, Hamtramck
(313) 875-1334
Mon-Thu & Sat 5am-7pm, Fri 5am-8pm.
Polish specialties.

POLISH DELI & BAKERY
12015 Jos. Campau, Hamtramck
(313) 365-3731
Mon-Thu 10am-10pm, Fri-Sat 9am-11pm, Sun 10 am-8pm. Baked goods, sausages and Polish imports.

NEW DELUXE POLISH BAKERY
11920 Conant (at Eldridge), Detroit
(313) 892-8165
Mon-Sat 5am-7pm. European baked goods, including babki. Deli counter.

NORTOWN BAKERY
7531 E. Seven Mile, Detroit
(313) 892-0880
Mon-Sat 9am-9pm. Polish baked goods, breads and Kowalski lunch meat.

WEST-SIDE DETROIT

TARNOW BAKERY
5804 Tarnow, Detroit
(one block N of McGraw between Livernois and Central)
(313) 894-1680
Tue-Sat 6am-6pm, Sun 6am-4pm. Polish baked goods and custom cakes.

FROM THE BAKERY

Babki: Yeast coffee cake in shape of woman's turban hat or skirt. Varieties include rum, honey, pound cake or regular.

Mazurki: Traditional Easter cake has cookie-dough base topped with apple, fruit preserves, nuts or chocolate.

Chrusciki: (Angel wings) Powdered sugar-covered flaky pastry shaped like a bowtie or wings.

Makowiek: Poppy seed rolls.

Orzechowiek: Nut rolls.

Seven sisters loaf cake: Chocolate-filled torte.

SUNFLOWER BAKERY
18900 W. Warren, Detroit
(313) 271-2551
Tue-Sat 5am-8pm, Sun 6am-4pm. Polish baked goods, decorated cakes.

WEST WARREN BAKERY
15708 W. Warren, Detroit
(2 blocks W of Greenfield)
(313) 584-2610
Mon-Sat 5am-7pm. Polish bakery specializing in wedding and birthday cakes.

WESTWOOD BAKERY
19436 W. Warren, Detroit
(313) 271-6400
Mon-Fri 6am-6pm, Sat 6am-5pm. Polish goods baked daily. Babki a specialty.

CHENE MODERN BAKERY
17041 W. Warren, Detroit
(2 blocks E of Southfield)
(313) 582-0700
Mon-Fri 5am-8pm, Sat 5am-7pm. Polish rye and egg twist breads, chrusciki, tea cookies and babki.

EAST

EAST DETROIT BAKERY & DELI
17530 Nine Mile, Eastpointe
(810) 776-6450
Mon-Fri 5am-6pm, Sat 5am-5:30pm. Polish
specialties, cakes and Kowalski meats.

OLD COUNTRY DELI
38952 Dequindre, Sterling Hts.
(SE corner of 17 Mile)
(810) 977-1740
Tue-Fri 9am-6pm, Mon and Sat 9am-5pm.
Lunch meats and pastries.

OAZA BAKERY & DELI
4140 Nine Mile (at Ryan), Warren
(810) 758-6776
Mon-Fri 8am-8pm, Sat 8am-7pm. Polish
breads, pastries, Kowalski meats.

WEST
NEW PARIS BAKERY
28418 Joy Rd., Livonia
(between Inkster and Middlebelt)
(313) 425-2060
Mon-Sat 7am-6pm, Sun 7am-4pm. Polish
favorites are among the selection of
European baked goods.

MARKETS

BOZEK'S MEATS & GROCERIES
3011 Holbrook, Hamtramck
(313) 873-3665
Daily 9am-7pm. Polish specialties, European
groceries and natural smoked meats.

SRODEK'S CAMPAU QUALITY SAUSAGE
9601 Jos. Campau, Hamtramck
(313) 871-8080
*Mon-Thu 8am-6pm, Fri 8am-7pm, Sat 8am-
4pm.* European deli featuring pierogi and five
kinds of Polish sausage.

CIEMNIAK'S MEAT MARKET
9629 Jos. Campau, Hamtramck
(313) 871-0773
Daily 9am-6pm. Noted for smoked kielbasa
and hams made on premises.

STAN'S GROCERY
11325 Jos. Campau (N of Caniff)
Hamtramck; (313) 365-1165
*Mon-Thu 9am-7pm, Fri 9am-8pm, Sat 9am-
6pm.* Grocery features a number of Polish
specialties and meats. Deli offers carryout
and dine-in service.

DUDEK FOODS

3303 Caniff St., Hamtramck
(313) 891-5226
Mon-Fri 7am-3:30pm, Sat 9am-noon.
Homemade products such as pierogi, potato
pancakes and condiments.

FREDRO'S MARKET
4540 Fredro, Detroit
(corner of Fenelon)
(313) 366-6276
Tue-Sat 9am-5pm. Known for kielbasa.

POLISH MARKET
2938 Maple (at Dequindre)
Troy; (248) 577-5334
*Tue-Wed 10am-6pm, Thu 10am-7pm, Fri
9am-7pm, Sat 9am-6pm, Sun 10am-3pm.*
Large assortment of baked goods, sausages
and other Polish specialties. Also Hamtramck
location.

WARRENDALE MEATS
19340 W. Warren, Detroit
(between Southfield and Evergreen)
(313) 271-6299
Mon-Sat 9am-6pm, Sun 9am-4pm. Fresh
and smoked Polish sausage; deli wiith pierogi, meatballs, stuffed cabbage and lunch
meats. Full line of Polish imports includes
jams, jellies and soups.

MAIL ORDER

POLISH AMERICAN CALENDAR
6261 Artesian St., Detroit, MI 48228
(313) 336-6081
Contact: Donald F. Samull
Calendar with information and recipes
available at Border's Book Shop, Polish Art
Center or from author. Also, mail order Polish
goods and books.

KLASSICS BY KURTIS
6790 Telegraph, Suite 29
Bloomfield Hills, MI 48301
(248) 539-0670
Kurtis Posuniak imports handblown glass
ornaments from Poland of classical composers Chopin, Beethoven and Bach.

SHOPS

POLISH ART CENTER
9539 Jos. Campau, Hamtramck
(313) 874-2242
Mon-Wed 9:30am-5pm, Thu 9:30am-7pm, Fri-Sat 9:30am-6pm, Sun 11am-3pm (closed Sunday late May-August). Owners Joan and Raymond Bittner have been importing items from Poland since 1970 for charming shop with folk art on the walls. Wycinanki paper-cuts, Pajaki mobiles, Pisanki Easter eggs and supplies, handwoven rugs, carved wooden boxes, plates and wall hangings are featured. Shop carries exclusive line of Christopher Radko ornaments, Boleslawiec historic European stoneware, traditional star-burst design crystal and posters by muralist Dennis Orlowski, as well as costumed dolls, military memorabilia and food imports. Book section features best-seller paperbacks translated into Polish, books on old-world tradition, cooking, history and literature, in addition to newspapers and magazines, compact discs and videos. Catalog available.

ST. MARY'S COLLEGE BOOKSTORE
Activities Bldg., Orchard Lake Campus
(248) 682-1885
Open weekdays and first Sunday of the month before Christmas and Easter. Merchandise includes books, cassettes and greeting cards in Polish.

AL'S NYLON JACKETS
11348 Jos. Campau, Hamtramck
(313) 893-4560
Mon-Fri 9am-4:30pm. Custom T-shirts, sweatshirts, jackets and caps with lettering in Polish or other language.

CARVED IN STONE

Statues, busts and other historic markers commemorate famous Polish people and their contributions.

Gen. Thaddeus Kosciuszko: Statue of American Revolutionary War general and "architect of West Point" is at Third Street and Michigan Avenue in downtown Detroit.

Casimir Pulaski: Statue of Revolutionary War hero and Father of the American Cavalry is on Michigan Avenue at Washington Boulevard. (Michigan Avenue has been designated Pulaski Memorial Highway.)

Kosciuszko

Copernicus (Mikolaj Kopernik): Bust of astronomer who discovered that planets revolve around the sun is outside the Main Branch of Detroit Public Library on Woodward Avenue.

Joseph Conrad (Teodor Josef Konrad Korzeniowski): Bust of master English novelist is at Hamtramck Public Library on Caniff.

Pope John Paul II (Karol Wojtyla): A statue, at Jos. Campau and Belmont (Pope Park), and a marker, at Jos. Campau and Holbrook, commemorate the Pope's 1987 visit to Hamtramck.

Copernicus

FOLK ART

WYCINANKI: Polish papercut designs, featuring stylized birds, flowers and trees, as well as farm and village wedding scenes, have been used to decorate rural cottages since the early 19th century (when multicolored paper became readily available).

Designs and colors vary among regions, the two most famous being the Lowicz and Kurpie regions.

PAJAKI: Mobiles, named after the Polish word for spider (the spider web brings good luck), are made out of straw and decorated with beads, paper designs, yarn, feathers or blown-out decorated egg shells. Villagers fashioned these large mobiles, reminiscent of cathedral chandeliers, to hang in their homes. They are called pajaki because when seen from below, the hanging decorations resemble jiggling spider legs.

*Also see **szopki** (creches) under "Christmas Season" and **pisanki** (egg decorating) under "Easter Season."*

FOLK ARTISTS

*Various examples of Polish folk art are on display or for sale at the **Polish Art Center** (9539 Jos. Campau) in Hamtramck, **American Polish Cultural Center** in Troy and **St. Mary's College** at Orchard Lake. Local folk artists demonstrate and display their crafts at festivals and events such as the International Institute's original **All World Market** in October and the **Warren Multi-Ethnic Cultural Festival** in August.*

Marcia Lewandowski, a master folk artist specializing in *pisanki, pajaki,* Polish folk Christmas ornaments, costumes, embroidery and beading, is represented at many festivals. To arrange for an exhibit, workshop, seminar or lecture demonstration, write to her at 5128 Casmere, Detroit, MI 48212 or call (313) 891-0696.

Wycinanki designs by Hamtramck artist **Adele Tarnowski** are displayed at the Polish American Congress (1133 Jos. Campau) and ethnic festivals. For demonstrations at schools and festivals, write to her at 2949 Jacob, Hamtramck, MI 48212.

Artist **Barbara Gronet** gives workshops and lecture/demonstrations on *wycinanki, pisanki,* Christmas ornaments, embroidery and painting on glass. Call (313) 365-8949 for information.

Sandra Wasiak McAlpine creates Christmas ornaments, *pisanki* and *wycinanki* designs.
Call (810) 949-3817.

VISUAL ARTS

DETROIT INSTITUTE OF ARTS
5200 Woodward, Detroit
(313) 833-7900
Wed-Fri 11am-4pm, Sat-Sun 11am-5pm.
Polish art in the museum's collection ranges from the oil painting "Carrousel" (1906) by Witold Wojtkiewicz to "Abakan 27," a contemporary fiber sculpture by Magdalena Abakanowicz. Although these works are featured in "A Visitor's Guide to the Detroit Institute of Arts," they are not always on view. The "Trapped Bird," a stainless steel sculpture by George Zambrzycki, when displayed, is in Gallery N280 (20th Century Art).

HAMTRAMCK MURAL ART
A mural by **Dennis Orlowski** at Hamtramck's **Pope Park** (Jos. Campau at Belmont) depicts a town square in Krakow, Poland. The artist used citizens of Hamtramck as models. Another building (Hamtramck Coney Island) at Jos. Campau and Evaline has a mountain folk dancing scene. Orlowski murals at the **Holbrook Cafe** (formerly the Polish American Century Club at 3201 Holbrook), inside and outside, illustrate the history of Poland. Other murals by Orlowski adorn the **Hamtramck Library.** To contact the artist, call (313) 871-0921.
"Polka Dancers" painted by **Denise Forest** brighten the parking lot side of **St. Florian's Education Center** at Latham and Poland in Hamtramck.

CULTURAL EXHIBITS

AMERICAN POLISH CULTURAL CENTER
2975 E. Maple, Troy
(248) 689-3636
Heritage Gallery contains maps, artifacts and costumes from six regions in Poland; an impressive painting of military leader Thaddeus Kosciuszko and portraits of Polish composers and Nobel laureates. Traditional folk art also is on display.

ST. MARY'S COLLEGE CAMPUS
3535 Indian Trail, Orchard Lake
(248) 682-1885
Many exhibits and collections are housed on the 120-acre campus, where six Polish-Catholic institutions are based. **The Galeria**

features an art exhibit of Polish and Polish American artists. The curator, world-renowned Marian Owczarski, continues to create sculptures for art centers, universities and theaters. **The Ark** (Central Archives of Polonia) contains the historical records of dozens of Polish organizations in Michigan, as well as museum collections of the Polish Veterans and Polish Singers Alliance. The **National Polish-American Sports Hall of Fame** is in Dombrowski Fieldhouse and the **Polish Historical Panorama** is in the Activities Building. Call for times and special event information.

ETHNIC HERITAGE ROOM
Manoogian Hall, Wayne State University,
906 W. Warren, Detroit
(313) 577-2246
Room 105, used as a study lounge and meeting room, features stained-glass windows depicting Generals Pulaski and Kosciuszko, as well as Maria Sklodowska Curie. Artifacts include tapestries and a design of the Copernican solar system, honoring Mikolaj Kopernik.

POLISH AMERICAN HISTORIC ASSOCIATION
St. Albertus Church
4231 St. Aubin, Detroit
(at Canfield)
(313) 832-6886 or 527-9321
Sat 10am-2pm or by appointment. Historic site of first Polish American parish now houses heritage display of folk costumes and historic photos. The first Katyn monument in the United States was erected outside the church at the corner of St. Albertus and Canfield.

DANCE GROUPS

WAWEL POLISH DANCERS

Group performs at many local and statewide functions wearing colorful costumes and head dresses of Poland. For information about performances and instruction, contact Thomas J. Skurski (9910 Yorkshire, Detroit, MI 48224) at (313) 885-7209.

RZESZOW YOUTH ENSEMBLE

Kids 3-19 perform national and regional dances of Poland. Saturday classes are at St. Clements Church Social Hall on Van Dyke, north of 10 Mile in Center Line. Contact Marcia Lewandowski for information about the group at (313) 225-2119 or 891-0696.

ST. MARY'S FOLK SONG AND DANCE ENSEMBLE *(GJALICJA)*

Features young people and adults performing folk songs and dances from Eastern European countries. Rehearsals are Thurdays at 6:30pm during the school year in the old gym on campus, 3535 Indian Trail, Orchard Lake. Call Michael Krolewski at (248) 683-0518 for information.

POLISH ROMAN CATHOLIC UNION ASSOCIATION (PRCUA)

Sponsors a teacher's dance ensemble and many children's groups. Dance schools are in Hamtramck, Detroit, Sterling Hts., Warren, Garden City, Redford Twp., Dearborn and Wyandotte. Write to Shirley Galanty, 5661 Norborne Ave., Dearborn Hts., MI 48128, or call (313) 563-4600.

RODOMIANIE POLISH FOLK DANCE ENSEMBLE

For information, write Cynthia Scheitzer, 1738 N. Lafayette, Dearborn, MI 48128.

NATIONAL DANCES OF POLAND

Polonaise: The oldest national dance, according to tradition, evolved from a procession of noblemen at the coronation of Henry III to the Polish throne in 1573. Stately and dignified, it opened every grand ball, and by the 18th century was performed throughout Europe in slow, three-quarter time.

Krakowiak: Quick, lively dance in two-quarter time with characteristic syncopation, is next in age to the Polonaise. Its basic step is a sliding gallop representing warriors' horses. It is a dance of the Polish peasant with roots in the nobility.

Mazurka: Danced in triple meter, the Mazur originated in central Poland, became accepted in the Polish court in the 17th century, and spread throughout Europe as a social and stage dance. The basic steps are ballet movements and are known by their French names.

Oberek: A quick, circling dance in three-eighths time. The word *oberek* means "to turn or spin." Its intricate steps feature acrobatic whirls, leaps and somersaults by the man who is supported by his sure-footed partner.

Kujawiak: This dance in three-quarter time of moderate tempo draws inspiration from the romantic Polish peasants of north-central Poland. Its movement is graceful and rhythmic, reminiscent of grain swaying in the wind. It is often paired with the Oberek for contrast.

POLAND'S GREAT COMPOSERS

From the Renaissance through the Baroque, Classical and Romantic periods to contemporary times, Poland has produced 86 classical composers. Among the most famous are:

Frederic Chopin (1810-1849): Regarded as the greatest of all composers for the piano, Polish folk music and patriotism influenced his mazurkas and polonaises.

Chopin

Ignace Jan Paderewski (1860-1941): Pianist, composer and statesman especially known for his interpretations of the music of Chopin. He made concert tours in the United States to raise funds to assist the victims of World War I in Poland.

Karol Szymanowski (1882-1937): Father of Modern Polish Music, paved the way for contemporary composers. His early symphonic music used elements from Polish folk music. Virtuoso Polish pianist composer Paderewski made his mazurkas famous.

Henryk Wieniawski (1835-1880): Violinist and composer.

Stanislaw Moniuszko (1819-1872): Father of the Polish National Opera.

Krzysztof Penderecki (born 1933): Contemporary composer and conductor noted for chamber music, opera, orchestral works and religious choral music.

CLASSICAL CONCERTS

MACOMB SYMPHONY
Macomb Center for the Performing Arts
Garfield at M-59, Clinton Twp.
(810) 286-2222
Ethnic night, the season opening for symphony concert series in October, usually features Polish composers to coincide with Polish Heritage Month.

CHOPINIANA
American Polish Cultural Center
2975 E. Maple, Troy
(248) 689-3636
Concert and champagne dinner the last Sunday in October honors Poland's great composer, Frederic Chopin. Classical pianists, 45-piece symphony, dance troupe, soloists and Polonaise Chorale perform.

CHOIRS

POLONAISE CHORALE
Mixed choir and women's ensemble, directed by Daniel Misteravich, practices Tuesday evenings at the American Polish Cultural Center in Troy. For information, call Angie Crongeyer at (313) 863-6209.

LUTNIA SINGING SOCIETY
Michigan's oldest Polish cultural organization sponsors a women's chorus. Group rehearses Thursday evenings at the American Polish Cultural Center in Troy. Call Joann Nawrocki at (810) 783-7847.

CLUB FILARETS
Mixed choir, directed by Wladyslaw Budweil, rehearses Friday nights at the American Polish Cultural Center in Troy. Call (313) 891-3559.

SPECIAL EVENTS

FEBRUARY
MARDI GRAS FESTIVAL
Celebrated at St. Ladislaus, 2730 Caniff, Hamtramck, the weekend before Ash Wednesday. Call (313) 872-0709.

PACZKI DAY
More commonly called Fat Tuesday, the day before Ash Wednesday is the last opportunity to gorge on sweets before Lent. Parade in Hamtramck is preceding day. On Tuesday, bakeries are jammed with customers picking up paczki orders. Call Hamtramck Chamber of Commerce at (313) 875-7877 for parade details.

MARCH/APRIL
HOLY THURSDAY PILGRIMAGE
Bus tour, sponsored by the American Polish Assistance Association, visits seven churches. Call (810) 772-2378.

APRIL
SPRING FESTIVAL
Usually first weekend in April at Our Lady Queen of Apostles, 3851 Prescott, Hamtramck. Call (313) 872-0709.

SPRING FESTIVAL
Hosted by St. Hedwig's (3245 Junction Ave., Detroit). Call (313) 894-5409.

MAY
MAY 1 CELEBRATION
At Holy Cross Parish, 2311 Pulaski, Hamtramck. Call (313) 365-5191.

PATRIOTIC CELEBRATION
Commemorative event takes place May 3, usually on campus of St. Mary's College at Orchard Lake Center. Co-sponsored by Polish American Congress. Call (313) 365-9400.

STRAWBERRY FESTIVAL
The first weekend in May at St. Florian Church, 2626 Poland, Hamtramck. Call (313) 871-2778.

POLISH COUNTRY FAIR
Annual event on St. Mary's College campus in Orchard Lake. Call (248) 682-1885.

JUNE
POLKA FESTIVAL
At Sts. Peter & Paul Church, (76685 Grandville, Detroit.) Call (313) 846-2222.

JULY
POLISH FESTIVAL
At Freedom Hill County Park (15000 Metropolitan Parkway, Sterling Hts.). Polish entertainment, ethnic food, music, dancers and rides. Traditional Mass on Saturday at 4pm with Filarets Choir. Call (810) 979-7010.

PARISH FESTIVAL
At St. Stephens Church (18858 Huron River Dr., New Boston). Call (734) 753-6268.

ANGEL DAYS
A summer festival at Our Lady Queen of Angels (4200 Martin St., Detroit). Call (313) 897-8160.

AUGUST
SUMMER FESTIVAL
At Our Lady of Mt. Carmel (976 Superior Blvd., Wyandotte) in late August. Call (734) 284-9135.

POLKA FESTIVAL
An annual event at St. Aloysius (37200 Neville, Romulus). Call (734) 941-3730.

APPLE FESTIVAL
At Our Lady Help of Christians (12634 McDougall, Detroit) in late August.

WARREN MULTI-ETHNIC FESTIVAL
Polish groups showcase their crafts, music and food at three-day event held at Halmich Park on 13 Mile. Call Warren City Council (810) 754-4950.

SEPTEMBER
HAMTRAMCK FESTIVAL
Labor Day weekend festivities include Polish Day Parade. Call (313) 875-7877 or 365-9400.

PIEROGI FESTIVAL
At Sweetest Heart of Mary Church (4440 Russell St., Detroit) the Sunday after Labor Day. Call (313) 831-6659.

OCTOBER
POLISH HERITAGE MONTH
Events in October include ceremonies at the Kosciuszko and Pulaski statues. Call the Polish American Congress at (313) 365-9400.

BANANA FESTIVAL
St. Hyacinth Church (3151 Farnsworth, Detroit) celebrates Polish ethnicity the first weekend in October. Banana desserts are sold, but banana name was chosen tongue-in-cheek. (Other harvest-time festivals already were dedicated to the traditional crops.) St. Hyacinth also has a Polish Heritage Mass in October.
Call (313) 922-1507.

FALL FESTIVAL
At St. Hedwig's (33245 Junction Ave., Detroit) in October. Call (313) 894-5409.

CHRISTMAS FAIR
At Our Savior Polish National Church (610 N. Beech Daily, Dearborn Hts.). Ethnic dinners Saturday and Sunday; arts and crafts, breads and gifts for sale. Call (313) 561-7281 or 561-5233 for dates.

BIESIADA HOLIDAY FEAST
The Biesiada takes place the last weekend in November at the American Polish Cultural Center in Troy. Features dinner and cultural program of Renaissance period music and literature. Call (248) 689-3636.

WIGLIA DINNER
Takes place on Dec. 24 at the American Polish Cultural Center (Maple and Dequindre) in Troy. Call (248) 689-3636. (See Polish Christmas section.)

PISANKI EASTER EGGS

Polish designs on decorated Easter eggs have changed little over the past thousand years. Colors and motifs vary with the region and range from simplified plant and animal designs to floral lace-like patterns and geometric embroidery-style motifs. *Pisanki* may be single- or multicolored, scratch carved *(drapanki)*, painted *(malowanki)* or decorated by the wax batik method *(batykowane)*. There also are wooden and carved eggs, which are wood-burned, painted or both.

Unique to Poland are blown-out eggshells of various sizes *(wydmuszki)*, decorated with miniature Polish paper cutouts. These are called *nalepianki* and are used as Easter decorations and Christmas tree ornaments.

● Pisanki artists demonstrate the fine art of egg decorating at ethnic festivals and craft shows. The annual **Michigan Egg Guild Show,** featuring Polish and other ethnic egg decorating styles, is held at the Dearborn Civic Center the first weekend in May.

● Local *pisanki* artists include **Joseph Dudzinski** (313-928-7631), **Marcia Lewandowski** (313-891-0696), **Barbara Gronet** (313-365-8949) and **Sandra Wasiak McAlpine** (810-949-3817). The **Rev. Czeslaw Krysa,** an ethnographer, pisanki artist and lecturer on folk art and traditions, has a collection of 1,500 pisanki Easter eggs. They are on display in the **Galeria** at **St. Mary's College** at Easter time. Call (248) 682-1885 ext. 330.

● Complete Pisanki supplies and kits are available from the **Polish Art Center,** (313) 874-2242.

OTHER HOLIDAYS

MARCH 19
FEAST OF ST. JOSEPH
The Polish version of St. Patrick's Day. Parties this day offer a reprieve from strict Lenten regulations.

MAY 1
MAY DAY
Procession and evening prayer in honor of Our Lady at churches.

MAY 3
POLISH CONSTITUTION DAY
Polish American Congress sponsors commemorative event.

LATE MAY/EARLY JUNE
CORPUS CHRISTI SUNDAY
In honor of the Blessed Sacrament, a procession is made to four sites (or altars).

JUNE 23
ST. JOHN'S EVE (Sobotka)
Polish midsummer celebration often includes big outdoor picnics and "wreaths on the Vistula" custom.

AUGUST 15
ASSUMPTION DAY
Commemorates the day when Mary, mother of Jesus, died and was "assumed," body and soul, into heaven.

DOZYNKI
Beginning in mid-August, harvest-time feasts are held to show gratitude for fair weather, good crops and nature's bounty.

NOVEMBER 1
ALL SAINTS' DAY
The dead are remembered by placing candles and flowers on their graves.

EASTER SEASON

LENT
The new year's carnival season of parties and festivities comes to an end when Lent begins on Ash Wednesday. Traditionally, Poles observe the fasting period during the six weeks preceding Easter to recall Jesus' 40 days in the wilderness.

EASTER WEEK
The week preceding Easter, in late March or early April, is filled with religious observances and festive preparation for the holiday.

Palm Sunday: Worshipers receive palm leaves (evergreen or pussy willow branches in northern climates) to commemorate Jesus' entry into Jerusalem, where he was greeted by people waving palm branches.

Holy Thursday: Pilgrimage and visit to seven churches. The day is in honor of the Last Supper of Jesus. Churches elaborately decorate altars that reserve the Eucharist.

Good Friday: Churches create a grave with the figure of Jesus in a tomb, which is displayed from Good Friday until Easter Sunday.

Holy Saturday: Blessing of food baskets for the Easter Sunday breakfast (*Swieconka*).

Easter Sunday: (*Wielkanoc*) Early morning Mass with procession around the church three times in honor of the three days Christ was in the tomb. After, festive meals feature cakes decorated with a lamb and Easter eggs. A small lamb molded out of butter is also traditional for the table.

Dyngus: A humorous custom of frivolity on Easter Monday involves pranks, merrymaking and more eating.

The Paschal Lamb was sacrificed and eaten at the Jewish Passover. For Christians, Jesus Christ was called the Lamb of God, thereby a symbol at Easter time.

PACZKI DAY

Fat or **Shrove Tuesday** is known as *Paczki Day* in the Detroit area. Bakeries sell jelly-filled doughnuts by the thousands for a pre-Lenten gorge. Pronounced *POONCH-key*, *PUNCH-key* or *POOCH-key*, they are made on a bun press from a richer dough than regular doughnuts. Top-selling fillings are raspberry, lemon and custard. Apple, apple-raspberry, blueberry, cherry and prune fillings also are available. Paczki are sold at the bakeries listed in this chapter and at major grocery chains. Farmer Jack's Hearth Oven Bakery has a paczki hot line for orders and store locations (313-270-1084).

RELIGIOUS CENTERS

Roman Catholic churches with services in Polish:

ST. BARBARA
13524 Colson, Dearborn; (313) 582-8383

OUR LADY HELP OF CHRISTIANS
12634 McDougall, Detroit; (313) 892-6116

ST. ANDREW
7060 McGraw, Detroit; (313) 361-1717

ST. BARTHOLOMEW
2291 E. Outer Drive, Detroit
(313) 892-1446

ST. FLORIAN
2626 Poland, Hamtramck; (313) 871-2778

OUR LADY QUEEN OF APOSTLES
3851 Prescott, Hamtramck
(313) 891-1520

OUR LADY OF CZESTOCHOWA
3100 18 Mile, Sterling Hts.
(810) 977-7267

SHRINE CHAPEL OF OUR LADY OF ORCHARD LAKE
St. Mary's Campus, Orchard Lake
(248) 682-1885

OUR LADY OF MT. CARMEL
976 Superior Blvd., Wyandotte
(734) 284-9135

ST. CUNEGUNDA CHURCH
5900 St. Lawrence, Detroit
(313) 841-4000

ST. HEDWIG
3245 Junction, Detroit; (313) 894-5409

ST. HYACINTH CHURCH
3151 Farnsworth, Detroit; (313) 922-1507
Annual Polish Heritage Mass in October.

ST. LADISLAUS
2730 Caniff, Hamtramck; (313) 872-0709

ST. LOUIS THE KING
18891 St. Louis, Detroit; (313) 891-1766

SWEETEST HEART OF MARY
4440 Russell, Detroit; (313) 831-6659

ST. STEPHEN/MARY MOTHER OF THE CHURCH
4311 Central, Detroit; (313) 841-0783

TRANSFIGURATION
5830 Simon K, Detroit; (313) 892-1310

Polish National Churches with services in Polish:

HOLY CROSS POLISH NATIONAL CATHOLIC CHURCH
2311 Pulaski, Hamtramck
(313) 365-5191

ALL SAINTS NATIONAL POLISH CATHOLIC CHURCH
5555 17 Mile, Sterling Hts.
(810) 978-8923

OUR SAVIOR POLISH NATIONAL CATHOLIC PARISH
610 N. Beech Daily, Dearborn Hts.
(313) 561-7281 or 561-5233

SACRED HEART OF JESUS POLISH NATIONAL CATHOLIC CHURCH
18720 Sawyer, Detroit
(313) 336-6127 or 336-5083

CHRISTMAS CUSTOMS

SZOPKI: Ornate paper and foil Christmas crêches, styled after the Renaissance architecture of Krakow, Poland, range in height from several inches to several feet. They often have small figures representing events surrounding the nativity. The large *szopki* are carried about during the Christmas season and are used as puppet theaters to present nativity plays called *Jaselka*.

● *Szopki are on display at the American Polish Cultural Center in Troy.*

OPLATKI: Wafers, like those used for Catholic communion, are stamped with a Christmas scene. When people wish each other a Merry Christmas, they break off and eat pieces of each other's *oplatek*. Sometimes a piece of oplatek is sent in a Christmas card as a symbol of unity with loved ones.

ST. NICHOLAS: People in Poland give special gifts from St. Nicholas to children on Dec. 6. Cookies, candies, fruit, nuts and holy pictures are placed under the pillow or by the Christmas tree. Rather than Santa Claus coming from the North Pole, St. Nicholas comes from heaven dressed in the robes of a bishop and holding a cross. He walks from house to house or travels on a sleigh that does not fly. His helpers, an angel and a devil, help determine if the children have been good, know their prayers and go to church. Children who have not been good get a lump of coal instead of goodies. But St. Nicholas is so forgiving and kind that once the children promise to be better, they are rewarded.

● *St. Mary's College at Orchard Lake Center conducts the **National St. Nicholas Project,** in which volunteers answer letters addressed to St. Nicholas using a specialized handwritten style. The emphasis is on the holiness of the season and the message of St. Nicholas. For information, call (248) 683-0518.*

The Christmas season officially starts on the first day of Advent, four Sundays before Christmas. Polish observance of Christmas lasts at least until January 6, which is Twelfth Night or Epiphany. Some consider Candlemas on February 2 to be the season's close.

Highlights include:

DECEMBER 6
St. Nicholas Day
Polish holiday gift giver makes his visit to children.

DECEMBER 24
Christmas Eve
Polish families gather for a special meatless meal *(see "Wigilia")* and attend Shepherds Mass *(Pasterka)* at midnight.

DECEMBER 25-26
Christmas
Celebration of the birth of Jesus, the long-awaited Christ or Messiah, lasts two days. The extra holiday on December 26 *(St. Stephen's Day)* allows for more visiting.

DECEMBER 27
St. John's Day
Blessing of the wine takes place at church.

DECEMBER 31
New Year's Eve
St. Sylvester's Day celebrations usher in the New Year.

JANUARY 6
Feast of Three Kings *(Trzech Kroli)*. For Twelfth Night or Epiphany, special church services take place to bless water and chalk. Poles use this chalk to write K.M.B. *(Kaspar, Melchoir and Balthazar)* over their doors for good luck.

FEBRUARY 2
Candelmas
Candles are blessed at church for home use. Remaining Christmas decorations are put away.

WIGILIA

A strict 24-hour fast ends with a huge meatless feast on Christmas Eve. The meal, in honor of the star of Bethlehem, cannot begin until the first star appears. Though Christmas in Poland officially is known as *Boze Narodzenie,* it is most often referred to as *Gwiazdka,* which means "little star." Once the star appears, a special rice wafer blessed by the parish priest, called *oplatek,* is broken into pieces and shared by all.

The feast consists of 12 courses, one for each apostle (though some families serve 13 to include Christ). Some people place straw under the tablecloth to symbolize the manger in which Christ was born. Most families set an extra place, for the stranger who might be passing by.

Christmas Eve dishes vary from region to region, but usually include fish soup, almond soup, pickled beets, herring in oil, fish in gelatin, carp in sour cream, cooked sauerkraut with peas or mushrooms, bread and butter, dried fruit compote, poppy seeds and raisins mixed with noodles, poppy seed cake and marzipan. Coffee, tea, cold drinks or dry white wine are served. At the end of the Wigilia meal, the family goes off to Midnight Mass.

CLASSES

AMERICAN POLISH CULTURAL CENTER
Offers Polish language and folk dancing classes in Troy. Call (248) 689-3636.

WARREN COMMUNITY CENTER
Teaches language classes on Monday nights: Polish I 6-8pm and Polish II 8:30-10pm. Call Antoni Walenwender at (248) 581-3181.

JOSEPH DABROWSKI SCHOOL
On the St. Mary's Campus at Orchard Lake Center; offers Polish language classes. Call Alina Paszek at (248) 682-1885.

HENRYK SIEKIEWICZ SCHOOL
Classes taught at St. Ladislaus School (2740 Caniff, Hamtramck) on Tues 6-8pm for children and Wed 5:30-8pm for adults. Call Helen Zmurkiewicz at (810) 772-1267.

ADAM MICKIEWICZ SCHOOL
Meets at Our Lady of Czestochowa (3100 18 Mile Rd., Sterling Hts.) on Fri 5:30-8:30pm for children's Polish language classes. Call Anna M. Szewczyk at (810) 573-0664.

CASIMIR PULASKI ELEMENTARY SCHOOL
19725 Strasburg, Detroit; (313) 581-3181
Contact: Krystyna Kryszko
Saturday Polish lessons for children.

MACOMB COMMUNITY COLLEGE
Continuing education program offers conversational Polish at the Fraser campus, taught by Tamara Kirchner. Call (810) 296-3516.

ST. MARY'S COLLEGE
Offers a four-year degree program in Polish. Contact Dr. Janusz Wrobel at (248) 683-0339.

FRIENDS OF POLISH ART
Presents 3- to 7-week courses in different facets of Polish culture for various community and adult education programs. To book the group for lectures, contact David Troiano at (810) 778-2096.

POLISH CULTURE
Slide presentation and lectures about holidays, given annually by Don Samull at Dearborn Schools (313) 730-0468, Troy Schools (248) 879-7532 and Grosse Pointe War Memorial (313) 881-7511.

TRADITIONS OF POLAND
Presentations by ethnographer Michael Krolewski cover folk art, dress, customs and folk tales from different regions. Programs available for community education, organizations and school districts. Call (248) 683-0518.

ORGANIZATIONS

Polish Americans have more organizations than any other ethnic group in the Detroit area. Dozens of groups have been formed to serve social, political, religious, cultural, educational, business, civic and fraternal interests. The **Polish National Alliance** is the largest Polish fraternal organization and is composed of councils and lodges. Other fraternal organizations include **Polish Falcons of America** (emphasis on athletic activities), the **Polish Womens Alliance**, **Polish League of American Veterans**, **Alliance of Poles** and **Polish Roman Catholic Union of America**.

POLISH AMERICAN CONGRESS
11333 Jos. Campau, Hamtramck
(313) 365-9400
Office open Mon-Fri 9am-4pm. Information on all Polish American community activities is available from this central coordinating organization. PAC represents the interests of Polish Americans and the needs and concerns of Polonia. Sponsors activities, speakers bureau and newsletter to promote the proud heritage of the Polish people and their worldwide contributions. Sponsors annual Polish Day Parade.

FRIENDS OF POLISH ART
21132 Bon Heur, St. Clair Shores
(810) 778-2096
Contact: David Troiano
For more than 60 years, this group has been promoting Polish culture, traditions and holiday customs. Purpose is to better acquaint American public with Polish contributions to the humanities. Group sponsors art exhibition at Orchard Lake Center, concerts, poetry readings and other programs.

POLISH SCOUTS OF MICHIGAN
(248) 476-5598
Zenona Raczkowski, executive director
Troops for boys and girls 3-18 in Hamtramck (St. Florian Thu 6:30pm) and Sterling Hts. (Our Lady of Czestochowa on Thursday

nights, young children Saturday mornings). Groups learn Polish history, cultural, song and dance to earn badges. For girls program, call Teresa Wiacek at (810) 772-9227. Alfred Lis (810-977-8311) is the boys director.

RESOURCES

POLISH HERITAGE HOTLINE
St. Mary's College, Orchard Lake
1-900-370-POLE (English)
1-900-370-KRAJ (Polish)
Three-minute recording about Polish American customs, people, history and literature changes every two weeks. Cost is $4 with proceeds going to St. Mary's Polish Studies Program.

POLISH GENEALOGICAL SOCIETY OF MICHIGAN
Burton Historical Collection
Detroit Public Library
5201 Woodward, Detroit; (313) 833-1000

Hosts regularly scheduled meetings and annual genealogical seminar. Society provides access to surname index to ancestor charts and maintains Polonian Registry database.

LIBRARY AT AMERICAN POLISH CULTURAL CENTER
2975 E. Maple, Troy; (248) 689-3636
Open Wed 10am-2pm or by appointment.
Historical and cultural information. Books and magazines in Polish.

HAMTRAMCK PUBLIC LIBRARY
2360 Caniff, Hamtramck
(313) 365-7050
Polish books and vertical file.

DOWNTOWN BRANCH
Detroit Public Library
121 Gratiot, Detroit; (313) 224-0580
Polish language books are part of International Language Collection (ILC).

BIESIADA

Colorful and convivial feasts called *Biesiada* took place in the courts of kings and manors of the lords of Poland in the 15th and 16th centuries. Such feasts were planned to celebrate a special occasion, such as a wedding, birthday, anniversary, holiday, the visit of distinguished guests or the completion of the harvest. *Biesiada* is defined as food, drink, entertainment and talk.

● In keeping with this festive atmosphere of the Renaissance, the American Polish Cultural Society hosts an annual Biesiada, a holiday feast the last weekend in November at the American Polish Cultural Center in Troy. It begins in the afternoon with a reception and entertainment, followed by appetizers and the Parade of Foods. After the multi-course dinner, a cultural program is staged. Themes have included "Poetry and Music of the Polish Renaissance," "The Legends and Music of Old Poland" and "A Renaissance Sampler of Music and Dance."

POLISH-AMERICAN EDUCATIONAL SEMINARS
St. Mary's College,
3535 Indian Trail, Orchard Lake
(248) 683-0504
Michael Krolewski, director
Educational programs for teachers and community leaders.

MEDIA

RADIO
POLISH VARIETIES RADIO
c/o Jurek Rozalski
P.O. Box 10360, Detroit 48210
(313) 945-0660
News and information. (See WNZK.)

RMF/POLISH STUDIO PLUS
c/o Krystyne Zieleniec
P.O. Box 599, Birmingham 48012
(248) 594-7375
Programming from Poland.

WNZK AM 690 DAYS/680 NIGHTS
(248) 557-3500
"Radio Maria," Daily 8-9pm.
"Polish Varieties Radio," Mon-Fri 7-8am and 7-8pm
"Polka Time America," Mon/ Wed/Fri 5-6am.
"Polkas with Dan Capens," Sat 6-8am and Sun noon-1pm
"Jurek Rozalski," Sat 8:30-11am
"Religious Services from Orchard Lake Center and American Polish National Shrine," Sun 9-10am

WPON 1460 AM
(248) 332-8883
"Radio Pomost," Sat 1-2pm.

PRINT
POLISH WORLD
(Tygodnik Swiat Polski)
11903 Jos. Campau, Hamtramck
(313) 365-1990
Weekly bilingual publication for Polish Americans.

POPE JOHN PAUL NEWSLETTER
St. Mary's College
3535 Indian Trail, Orchard Lake
(248) 683-0504
Published by Pope John Paul II Center.

THE POLISH PHONE BOOK
Index Publications
4250 N. Milwaukee, Chicago
(312) 545-4930
Chicago-Detroit-Windsor edition.

Warsaw Daily News and other newspapers and magazines from Poland, as well as Polish language editions of American publications, are available at the Polish Art Center, 9539 Jos. Campau, Hamtramck; (313) 874-2242. The shop also has Polish travel and history videos in English .

WEB SITES
POLISH WORLD AND CULTURE
www.music.uiowa.edu/~mevans

UM POLISH ASSOCIATION
www-personal.umich.edu/~yep/polish/mpa

POLISH AMERICAN ASSOCIATION
www.polish.org/index

POLISH NAMES

Polish surnames often end in *cki* and *ski*. These suffixes are generally topographical and indicate noble origin. The ending *wicz* (or *visius*) denotes Lithuanian origin, whereas *iak* is from the Poznan area. *Czyk* is a variant of the Galicia area and *czuk* and *czuyk* are of the Ukrainian region. *Ko*, as in Kosciuszko, shows Belarussian influence. Other Polish names that don't have a suffix added often are names of professions. For example *Stolarz* means carpenter and *Krawiec* is a tailor.

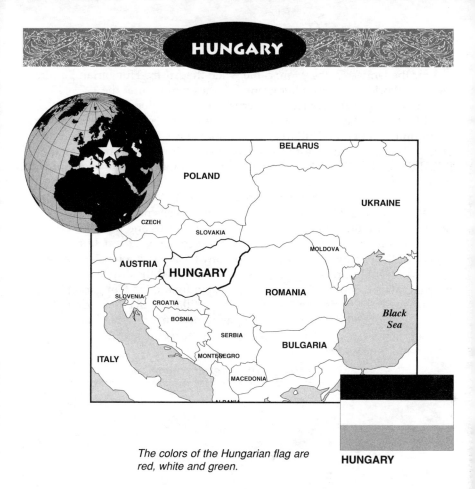

The colors of the Hungarian flag are red, white and green.

HUNGARY

Hungary is a landlocked central European country bordered by Slovakia on the north; Ukraine on the northeast; Romania on the east; Serbia, Croatia and Slovenia on the south; and Austria on the west. Although usually categorized as an Eastern European country, it is actually near the geographical center of Europe. The Danube River cuts through the country, providing a major navigational route from Budapest south through Serbia, Romania and Bulgaria to its mouth in the Black Sea.

The people of Hungary are originally from the steppes or plains of central Russia, near the Volga. Called Magyars, they are related to the Finno-Ugric and Turkish tribes, rather than the Slavic peoples of Eastern Europe. The word Hungarian comes from "Onogur," a Turkish word meaning "10 arrows," as in the 10 Magyar tribes (later seven) that united and moved west to Hungary in the ninth century. The Magyars were fabled archers and excellent horsemen who conquered the Danube Basin area.

HUNGARIANS IN DETROIT

Between 1890 and 1910 about 1.5 million Hungarians left their homeland for the United States. More came when the Austro-Hungarian Empire fell after World War I. Another group left the country after the 1956 Revolution, when the Soviet Army crushed the rebellion.

Although the Hungarian population now is concentrated in Downriver communities and other suburbs, the original "Little Hungary" was in the Delray district of southwest Detroit. In 1905 a Catholic parish was established there. By 1925 Holy Cross Hungarian Catholic Church was built with the help of immigrant craftsmen.

Many second-generation Hungarians moved to the suburbs starting in the 1950s and '60s. However, the Delray-Springwells neighborhoods retained their Hungarian character through the 1970s and into the early '80s. Although much of the area is now blighted, Holy Cross Church, the anchor of the community, continues to draw local parishioners and suburbanites. Recent refurbishing projects have preserved the ornate features of the magnificent church. Another longtime landmark, the Hungarian Village restaurant, at the Springwells exit of I-75, is still a popular gathering place.

Today, about 60,000 people of Hungarian descent are spread throughout the Detroit area, particulary in Downriver suburbs, such as Allen Park, Taylor and Southgate.

ALLEN PARK/SOUTHGATE/TAYLOR/DELRAY

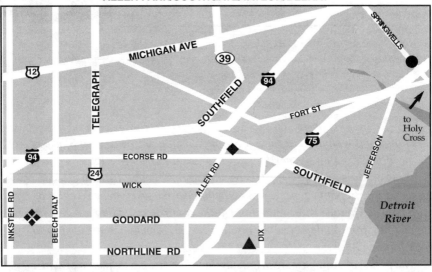

TOUR	DANUBE DOWNRIVER

[D-E/5-6] Downriver is the center of Hungarian activity, with restaurants, bakeries, a cultural center and churches.

Start your tour in Allen Park by sampling Hungarian pastries at **Fancy Pastry Shop** (6543 Park Ave.) and the **Strudel Shop** (6816 Park Ave.) near

Southfield and Allen Roads. Here you'll find a selection of traditional fruit-filled strudels, nut rolls and *kifli (*butter pastry with apricot or walnuts). ◆

For dinner, head to **Hungarian Rhapsody** (734-283-9622) in Southgate. *(Take Southfield to Dix, turn right and go eight traffic lights to Northline, turn right and go two blocks west.)* Steve and Darlene Szatmari have decorated their restaurant with bright garlands of red peppers, colorful *Herend* and *Kalocsa* porcelain plates, and heavily embroidered tablecloths. An alcove in the lobby showcases Hungarian handicrafts, including an embroidered *szur,* the coat worn by shepherds, and other reminders of peasant culture. Noodle dishes reign, such as *turos teszta* and *kaposztas teszta*—but save room for *dobos torte!* ▲

Or, on a Wednesday, Friday or Sunday, enjoy family-style fare at the **Hungarian Cultural Center** (734-946-6261) *on Goddard Road between Beech Daly and Inkster* in Taylor. Learn about the history and culture through exhibits and friendly conversation with members who flock to the center for dinners and a monthly Saturday dinner dance. The dining room is decorated in the traditional style of an old-world Hungarian pub, complete with embroidered curtains and tablecoths, Hungarian waitresses, and the bar and service kitchen recessed in decorative archways. ❖

For weekend entertainment, try the **Hungarian Village** (313-843-5611) restaurant in the original "Little Hungary" in southwest Detroit. *At 1001 Springwells, the restaurant is just a block north of I-75 Exit 45.* A gypsy orchestra and fortune teller add to the ambience on Friday and Saturday nights. ●

IN THE HUNGARIAN KITCHEN

H ungarian cooks depend heavily on **paprika** and will advise that it's well worth the extra effort and expense to get good paprika from Szeged if you're going to prepare specialties such as *goulash* (a classic beef stew), chicken paprikas, *szekely kaposza* (pork sautéed with sauerkraut, paprika and onion served over rice), *töltött paprikas* (stuffed bell beppers) and *burek* (stuffed phyllo).

Noodles also are a mainstay and are an essential part of such traditional specialties as *turos teszta* (with cottage cheese and bacon) and *kaposztas teszta* (with sautéed cabbage).

Pork **"cracklings"** (those crispy bits left after the fat has been rendered) are a favorite flavoring.

Palacsinta (pancakes or crêpes) are prepared in many ways, from appetizers to desserts. But the real dessert is *dobos torte.* The seven- or eight-layer sponge cake is filled with chocolate (and sometimes rum) and finished with a caramel glaze.

RESTAURANTS

BLUE DANUBE
1235 Ottawa St., Windsor
(519) 252-0246 or 800-963-1903
Tue-Sun 11am-10pm, Fri-Sat till midnight.
Hungarian specialties; strolling gypsy
musicians.

DANUBE INN
24 W. Main St., Milan; (734) 439-2626
*Mon-Thu 11am-9pm, Fri 11am-10pm,
Sat 3:30-10pm, Sun noon-8pm.* Traditional
European dishes as well as Hungarian.

ELDORADO
3807 Fort St., Wyandotte; (734) 284-6084
*Tue-Fri 11:30-10pm, Sat 4-10 pm, Sun 4-
8pm.* Hungarian and American dishes,
including chicken paprikash and ghoulash.

EUROPEAN DINER
125 Elm, Wyandotte; (734) 285-8949
Tue-Sat 11am-8pm. Hungarian cook
prepares Hungarian specialties as well as
Serbian, Polish and German fare.

HUNGARIAN KITCHEN
2923 Fort St., Wyandotte; (734) 281-9586
Wed-Sun 11:30am-7:30pm. Home-style dishes: breaded pork chops, stuffed cabbage.

HUNGARIAN RHAPSODY
14315 Northline Rd., Southgate
(734) 283-9622
Tue-Sat 11am-10pm, Sun 11:30am-8pm.
Specialties include turos teszta and dobos
torte. Music in main dining room. Hungarian
dance group performs for banquets.

HUNGARIAN VILLAGE
1001 Springwells (I-75, Exit 45) Detroit
(313) 843-5611
*Mon-Tue 11am-3pm, Wed-Thu 11am-9pm,
Fri 11am-11pm, Sat 3-11pm.* Traditional spe-
cialities. Pianist and vocalist Thursday night,
Gypsy orchestra and fortune teller Friday-
Saturday night.

RIVERSIDE RESTAURANT
740 Dix (E of Schaefer), Detroit
(313) 842-3353
Mon-Fri 6am-5pm. Hungarian specialties
include palacsinta, goulash and soups.

BAKERIES AND MARKETS

DEARBORN SAUSAGE CO.
2471 Wyoming, Dearborn; (313) 842-2375
Mon-Fri 8am-4:30pm, Sat 8am-2pm.
Hungarian and other traditional European

smoked sausages and ham made locally.

ETHNIC BAKERY
24057 Van Dyke, Center Line
(810) 756-2505
Mon-Sat 8am-5pm, Sun 8am-1pm.
Hungarian baked specialties, including pork
and cheese burek. Also Hungarian smoked
meats and "cracklings."

FANCY PASTRY SHOP
6543 Park, Allen Park; (313) 928-7246
Daily 9am-6pm. Hungarian pastries, nut rolls,
strudels, wedding and birthday cakes.

STRUDEL SHOP
6816 Park Ave., Allen Park; (313) 383-3440
Mon 8am-3pm, Tue-Sat 8am-5pm.
Hungarian kifli (butter pastry filled with apricot or walnut), traditional fruit strudel and nut
rolls are among the ethnic selections.

SPECIAL EVENTS

JUNE
HUNGARIAN FESTIVAL
Yack Arena (3131 Third St.), Wyandotte
(734) 246-4515 or (313) 842-1133
Annual festival sponsored by Detroit's Holy
Cross Hungarian Church at Yack Arena.
Features food, music, dancing and crafts.

CARROUSEL OF NATIONS
Multicultural Council of Windsor
(519) 255-1127
Festival takes place two weekends in June,
features dance groups, music, crafts, displays and food. Hungarian villages usually
are set up at two sites in Windsor.

SUMMER FESTIVAL PICNIC
Hungarian Cultural Center
26257 Goddard Rd., Taylor; (734) 946-6261
Tents and booths on the grounds of the cul-
tural center offer foods, crafts and imports.
Entertainment by folk dance groups and
Gypsy musicians highlight event.

HARVEST FESTIVALS

*Dinner dances or other
festive celebrations are held
at the Hungarian Cultural
Center and the Rhapsody
and Hungarian Village restaurants
during the traditional Sureti grape
harvest. Churches also conduct special
events at this time of year. (See individual listings for phone numbers.)*

SEPTEMBER
FALL FESTIVAL PIG ROAST
26257 Goddard Rd., Taylor; (734) 946-6261
September barbecue at the Hungarian Cultural Center features entertainment by Dancers Hungaria and gypsy musicians. Ethnic foods and cultural items sold.

OCTOBER
HUNGARIAN NATIONAL OBSERVANCES
Holy Cross Church, Detroit; (313) 842-1133
Observances commemorate the 1956 uprising in Budapest on October 24 that spread throughout the country. The revolution was crushed by the Soviet Army November 4.

ENTERTAINMENT

GYPSY MUSICIANS
Billy Rose, (313) 584-1647
Joe Vidak, (313) 846-0828
Strolling violinists and Gypsy orchestras, made up of fiddles, guitar, bass and cimbalon, play for restaurants and social events. Repertoire includes folk music as well as semiclassical pieces, show tunes, love songs and other popular music. Hungarian Cultural Center and Hungarian Village restaurant regularly feature Gypsy musicians.

DANCE AND FOLK GROUPS

DANCERS HUNGARIA
Hungarian Cultural Center
(734) 946-6261 or (248) 352-0927
Linda Enyedy, director
Group performs at Hungarian ethnic festivals throughout metro Detroit. Welcomes new members of any nationality from six-year-olds to adults. Rehearses Wednesday evenings at Hungarian Cultural Center.

HUNGARIAN FOLK DANCERS
9901 Allen Rd., Allen Park
(313) 382-1001 or 382-3845
Velma Sabo, instructor
Children to adult groups perform at festivals in traditional costume. They rehearse at Allen Park Hungarian Reformed Church on Wednesday evenings.

HERITAGE DANCERS
14315 Northline, Southgate
(734) 283-9622 or 287-2752
Darlene and Jennifer Szatmari teach children and adult dance groups at Hungarian Rhapsody on Saturday mornings. Groups perform in costume for banquets and special events.

ZITHER ENSEMBLE
Hungarian Cultural Center, Taylor
(734) 946-6261
Group plays Hungarian folk music on zither (mountain dulcimer). Classes and performances held at Cultural Center.

FOLK ART

Embroidered flowers, leaves, birds and spiral designs adorn tablecloths, pillows, curtains, sheets and other linens, as well as clothing.

While the women are noted for their needlework, the men of the *puszta* (the flatland to the east of the Danube) are famous for their intricate carving on wood and bone. They produce canes, pen knives, flutes and pipes decorated with everyday scenes and patriotic symbols. Other characteristic art forms include painted dishes and pottery.

CULTURAL ARTS

CULTURAL PRESENTATIONS
(248) 352-0927
Linda Enyedy, consultant
Presentations to schools and community groups about Hungarian arts and culture.

DETROIT INSTITUTE OF ARTS
5200 Woodward Ave., Detroit
(313) 833-7900
Wed-Fri 11am-4pm, Sat-Sun 11am-5pm.
Collection of 20th century sculpture includes work by Hungarian-born Laszlo Maholy-Nagy, contributor to the international style in Europe and founder of an American version of the Bauhaus school.

WSU ETHNIC HERITAGE ROOM
Alex Manoogian Hall
906 W. Warren, Detroit
(313) 577-3500 or 577-2400
Classroom on second floor (280) features Hungarian decor with hand-painted flower trim, carved woodwork and other folk art, as well as maps and historic murals.

CHURCHES

HOLY CROSS
HUNGARIAN CATHOLIC CHURCH
8423 South St. at Yale, Detroit
(313) 842-1133
Ornate church with stained glass, statues and murals is recognized from freeway by its two green steeples. Various events scheduled throughout the year, including October observance to commemorate 1956 Hungarian uprising against the government. Summer festival is now held at Yack Arena in Wyandotte. Mass in Hungarian Sunday at 10:30am. *From northbound I-75, take Dearborn St. Exit right. At Harbaugh turn left, then right on South St. From southbound I-75, take Springwells Exit left, cross Fort Street and go right on South Street.*

HUNGARIAN REFORMED CHURCH
9901 Allen Rd., Allen Park; (313) 382-1001
Heritage collection at church contains costumes, folk art and artifacts from Hungary. Harvest festival takes place annually on the first Saturday in November. Schedule includes English and Hungarian church services and Bible study.

ORGANIZATIONS

HUNGARIAN CULTURAL CENTER
26257 Goddard Rd., Taylor
(734) 946-6261
A popular banquet facility for Downriver events, the cultural center has a Hungarian style dining room open to public for dinner Wednesday, Friday and Sunday. Major events are summer and fall festivals and monthly dinner dances. Activities held at the center include Hungarian language classes (Tuesday evenings), dance group rehearsals and zither lessons.

HUNGARIAN ARTS CLUB
20447 Carlysle, Dearborn
(313) 278-2629
Organization dedicated to preserving Hungarian heritage and supporting the arts. Sponsors concerts for touring folk music groups from Hungary. Awards scholarships to students of Hungarian descent pursuing the fine arts, and hosts annual debutante ball.

RESOURCES

MAGYAR MARKETING
1-800-786-7851
Catalog of Hungarian cultural items and imports is available from Youngstown, Ohio-based business. Owner Elizabeth Szabo travels to major Hungarian festivals to sell merchandise from a booth.

ORGANIZATION OF HUNGARIAN
CHURCHES & SOCIETIES
20524 Canal Dr., Grosse Ile
(734) 675-5242
Sandor Zoltan, chairman
Umbrella organization for all Hungarian clubs, churches and associations in Michigan. Brochure on Hungarian 1,000th Year Celebration available for $5.

MEDIA

RADIO

WNZK AM 690/680
(248) 557-3500
"Hungarian Hour," with host Zoltan Veres, Friday 9pm.

WEB SITES

HUNGARIAN CULTURE
pacbell.yahoo.com/regional/countries/hungary
ROMANY HOME PAGE
www.troutdream.com/balkanarama/rom

GYPSIES

O riginally nomadic people from India, Gypsies (or *Roma*) migrated to Europe during the Middle Ages. Many speak a dialect called Romany (related to Hindi) and have their own customs. In Hungary, they constitute 5 percent of the population and are the largest minority group.

Gypsy strolling musicians and orchestras are associated with the ambience of Hungarian and other quaint European restaurants. The romantic tunes they play, such as "Red Roses Are Talking," have their origins in 19th-century European café music. A Gypsy orchestra usually consists of fiddles, a bass and cimbalon (similar to a dulcimer but played with a smaller hammer).

Note: This section covers Eastern European countries in the Baltic Region and Balkan Peninsula, plus the Czech Republic and Slovakia. Separate chapters are devoted to Greece, Hungary, Poland and Ukraine.

The **Baltic Region** in northeastern Europe comprises Russia, Lithuania, Latvia and Estonia. The **Balkan Peninsula** in southeastern Europe is surrounded by the Black, Aegean, Mediterranean, Adriatic and Ionian Seas. Countries include Slovenia, Croatia, Bosnia, Montenegro, Albania, Serbia, Macedonia, Greece, Eastern Turkey, Bulgaria, Romania and Moldova. (The historic region of Macedonia is now part of Greece, Bulgaria and Serbia.) The **Czech Republic** and **Slovakia** are north of Hungary and Austria and south of Poland.

EASTERN EUROPEANS IN DETROIT

By 1930, thousands from Eastern Europe were counted among Detroit's immigrant population of 400,000. **Russians, Yugoslavs, Romanians, Czechs, Lithuanians** and **Turks** were among the nationalities represented in Detroit, along with groups recognized today as **Croatians, Serbians, Slovenians, Macedonians, Albanians** and **Bulgarians.**

Many ethnic churches in metro Detroit and Windsor, representing Moslem, Eastern Orthodox, Catholic and other Christian denominations, serve Eastern Europeans and help to preserve their heritage and traditions.

As Detroit grew, some of the groups migrated outward. Although some are in concentrated areas, others scattered throughout the five-county area.

TOUR	DETROIT'S CULTURAL CENTER

[E-F/4-5] Discover some of the little-known gems in Detroit's University Cultural Center by exploring the Hall of Nations at the **International Institute** *(111 E. Kirby, one block east of Woodward).* The exhibit of Old World costumes and handicrafts is the gift of a world traveler who collected 2,000 dolls during half a century. Costumed dolls from many nations, including Bulgaria, Yugoslavia, Macedonia, Croatia, Estonia, Latvia, Belarus, Romania, Serbia, Lithuania, Albania, Hungary and the Czech and Slovak Republics, show off the fine needlework, embroidery and textile design. For lunch, sample an ethnic cuisine in the **Small World Cafe** downstairs (see page 461). *(Call ahead to the Institute, 313-871-8600, to make sure the Hall of Nations is not scheduled for a private function at the time of your visit. Hours are Monday-Friday 8:30am-5pm.)*

Anyone wanting to research Eastern European countries can *go one block west* to the **main branch** of the **Detroit Public Library** at *5201 Woodward (open Tuesday and Thursday-Saturday 9:30am-5:30pm, Wednesday 1-9pm; 313-833-1000)* to find books, videos, maps and research files. Michigan residents may obtain a library card to check out materials. A block west of the Detroit library is Wayne State University's **Purdy Library,** where the **Folklore Archives** document traditions of Detroit's ethnic populations. *Call (313) 577-4053.*

(See "Multicultural Detroit" for map and information about the many museums to visit in the Cultural Center.)

[F-G/3-4] A great way to top off the tour would be a visit to the **Vienna Coffee Shop** *(15414 Mack Ave., Grosse Pointe Park, 313-417-0089)* to enjoy an old-world style meal prepared by the Dulbics, who recently arrived from Sarajevo. *Exit I-94 at East Chalmers and take service drive to Alter Rd. Turn right on Alter, then left on Mack.*

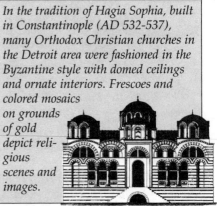

In the tradition of Hagia Sophia, built in Constantinople (AD 532-537), many Orthodox Christian churches in the Detroit area were fashioned in the Byzantine style with domed ceilings and ornate interiors. Frescoes and colored mosaics on grounds of gold depict religious scenes and images.

[D-E/4-5] One of the many examples of Byzantine church design in the Detroit area is **St. Clement Ohridski Orthodox Church.** *Located in Dearborn at 19600 Ford Road, just west of the Southfield Expressway on Altar Road near the Evergreen exit,* the church serves parishioners of **Albanian, Bulgarian, Macedonian, Yugoslavian** and **Greek** descent.

Inside, intricate wood carvings adorn the royal doors, pulpit, Psaltis stand and frames of the icons. Brilliantly colored frescoes in the dome depict Christ, angels, prophets and the four evangelists. Set against a royal blue background flecked with gold stars, a picture of Christ is surrounded by angels in red and gold robes. Rimming the base of the dome are 20 stained glass windows and 20 prophets in vibrant colors. Below them is a circular gold band etched with images of angels, with the evangelists at work writing the four Gospels.

The Rev. Panayot Pamukov, who has been at St. Clement's since 1979, welcomes visitors and is happy to share his knowledge of the religion and the community the church serves. To arrange an appointment, call (313) 271-3110 or 271-2698 Monday-Friday 9 a.m. - 5 p.m.

CHURCHES

As with many immigrants, Eastern Europeans and their descendants have a strong dedication to their churches. Here is just a sampling of area churches that sponsor activities featuring Eastern European traditions and culture.

ALBANIAN
ST. PAUL
ALBANIAN CATHOLIC CHURCH
3411 12 Mile Rd., Warren; (810) 573-8110
Summer festival usually over July fourth weekend.

ST. THOMAS ORTHODOX CHURCH
29150 10 Mile, Farmington Hills
(248) 471-1059
Congregation, composed of Albanians, Russians, Bulgarians, Italians and Greeks, hosts bazaar in October and International Night in spring with music, foods and crafts.

BULGARIAN
ST. CLEMENT OHRIDSKI
ORTHODOX CHURCH
19600 Ford Rd., Dearborn; (313) 271-3110
See tour for church description.

CROATIAN
ST. LUCY CATHOLIC CHURCH
200 E. Wattles, Troy; (248) 619-9910
Croatian congregation, formerly at St. Nicholas Byzantine Catholic Church in Detroit, hosts festival in August on church grounds. Permanent cultural exhibit planned for church hall.

LITHUANIAN
ST. ANTHONY'S
LITHUANIAN CATHOLIC CHURCH
1750 25th St. at Vernor, Detroit
(313) 554-1284
Fall festival picnic on church grounds on last Sunday in October.

DIVINE PROVIDENCE LITHUANIAN ROMAN CATHOLIC CHURCH
25335 W. Nine Mile Rd., Southfield
(248) 356-9721

Food booths and ethnic program are part of Lithuanian Independence Day celebration in mid-February. Lithuanian Scouts participate in St. Casimir Festival in March at church.

MACEDONIAN

ST. NATIVITY OF THE VIRGIN MARY
27740 Ryan, Warren; (810) 757-3490

Sponsors soccer teams and youth dance group. Hosts June festival at Freedom Hill County Park in Sterling Heights.

ST. NIKOLAS MACEDONIAN ORTHODOX CHURCH
5225 Howard, Windsor; (519) 966-6257

Special events at cultural center and hall.

ROMANIAN

ST. GEORGE CATHEDRAL
Romanian Orthodox
18405 W. Nine Mile Rd., Southfield
(248) 569-4833

Romanian dance the week after Easter and a summer picnic on church grounds in July, as well as other events featuring Romanian food, bands, and performers during the year.

ST. JOHN THE BAPTIST
20521 Woodward Ave., Detroit
(at Eight Mile Rd.)
(313) 368-1046

Ethnic food served regularly at church dinners. Romanian choir based here.

RUSSIAN

ALL SAINTS RUSSIAN ORTHODOX CATHEDRAL
22312 Kelly Rd., Eastpointe
(810) 777-6435 or (313) 881-5630

Russian Tea in October features orchestra and folk singers, foods and arts. Church serves as home parish in U.S. for the Moscow Circus. Hosts charity concerts for Russian performing groups on tour.

ASSUMPTION OF THE VIRGIN MARY RUSSIAN ORTHODOX CATHEDRAL
2101 Livernois, Ferndale; (248) 547-5240

SLAVIC

ST. MICHAEL EASTERN ORTHODOX CHURCH
26355 W. Chicago, Redford Twp.
(313) 937-2120

Slovenic services on Orthodox holidays.

STS. ANDREW AND BENEDICT CATHOLIC CHURCH
2400 S. Beatrice, Detroit; (313) 381-1184

Ethnic festival of Slovak and African America cultures is weekend before May 1.

ST. NICHOLAS BYZANTINE CATHOLIC CHURCH
19130 Beaconsfield Rd., Detroit
(313) 521-6827

Slavic foods festival in June or July.

Sunni Muslim families from Detroit's suburbs and Windsor attend the **Albanian Islamic Mosque** in Harper Woods (20426 Harper Ave.; 313-884-6676). The beige brick building with its golden dome, minaret and portico can be seen from I-94 near the Allard Street Exit.

About 400 Albanian families belong to the Bektashi Order of Dervishes and worship at the **Albanian Bektashi Tekke** monastery in Taylor (21749 Northline Rd., 313-287-3646). Some immigrated to the Detroit area before World War I, while others arrived just before the Italian occupation of Albania in 1939 and 1949.

TAMBURITZAS belong to a family of fretted stringed instruments used for playing the folk music of several Balkan countries in southeastern Europe. Because of its popularity among the Croatian people, the tamburitza often is called the national instrument of Croatia. However, its origin was in Persia with the Assyrians more than 5,000 years ago. Its first appearance in the Balkans was in Bosnia about 500 years ago. A little more than 100 years ago, tamburitza orchestras were formed in the Slovenia and Backa regions of Croatia. With the massive emigration from Eastern Europe in the early 1900s, the tamburitza was brought to America. *Tamburitza* is the Americanized version of the Croatian word *tambura*.

SLOVENE-STYLE POLKA BAND

The saxophone and accordion are the dominant instruments in Slovene-style polka, whereas the amplified accordion and trumpets or clarinets are the distinctive sound in Polish polka. The tuba is what puts the oompah in German polkas. *(See Slovene Polka Fest under Festivals.)*

RESTAURANTS

LUKICH FAMILY RESTAURANT
3900 Rochester Rd. (N of 16 Mile), Troy
(248) 528-9955
Mon 7 am-3pm, Tue-Sun 7am-9pm. Eastern European food features Polish and Serbian dishes. Owners are from Yugoslavia.

MASON-GIRARDOT ALAN MANOR
3203 Peter St., Windsor; (519) 253-9212
Tue-Fri 11:30am-2pm, 5-9pm, Sat 5-10pm. Roots in Turkish cuisine with flavors of Africa, Southeast Asia and Europe.

SWEETWATER'S BISTRO
1978 Cass Lake Rd., Keego Harbor
(248) 683-0170
(Call for seasonal hours) Summer: Fri 5-11pm, Sat 5pm-1am, Sun by appointment only. Traditional Russian cuisine plus American entrees.

VIENNA COFFEE SHOP
15414 Mack, Grosse Pointe Park
(313) 417-0089
Tue-Thu 11:30am-10pm, Fri-Sat 11:30am-11pm, Sun 10am-3pm.. Tortes, strudels and other Eastern European fare. Owners are from Sarajevo.

SHOPS

EURO FOOD INTERNATIONAL
15600 W. Ten Mile #12, Southfield
(248) 483-3830
Mon-Sat 9am-9pm, Sun 9am-6pm. Russian market with European imported food products, deli and bakery.

P.L. VIDEO CLUB
15600 W. Ten Mile, Southfield
(248) 557-8641
Weekdays noon-9pm, weekends noon-10pm. Best place in town to get Russian movies, audio tapes and CDs.

PERFORMING ARTS

DETROIT TAMBURITZA ORCHESTRA
(810) 979-2612
Ken Kosovac, director
Nearly 40 years old, this 25-member group is recognized for its authenticity and excellence. Performs classical tamburitza and Croatian folk music at annual Christmas and spring concerts.

NOVA NADA CROATIAN DANCERS
(248) 548-0854
Contact: Steve Talan
Adult group meets Sunday evenings at St. Lucy Catholic Church.

SARISAN SLOVAK FOLK ENSEMBLE
(248) 478-3818
Contact: Milan Straka
Adult group appears at local events (Slovak festivals and International Institute's All-World Market in October and Dance Festival in April) and tours Europe. Welcomes new members at Wednesday evening rehearsals at International Institute. Also sponsors visiting performing groups from Slovakia.

TANEC MACEDONIAN DANCERS
27740 Ryan, Warren; (810) 757-3490
Young people's touring group rehearses at
St. Nativity on Friday nights.

FESTIVALS

JUNE
MACEDONIAN FESTIVAL
Freedom Hill County Park, Sterling Hts.

(810) 979-7010
Food, music, dance, arts, games at annual
ethnic celebration.

CARROUSEL OF NATIONS
Multicultural Council of Windsor
(519) 255-1127
Ethnic festival features Slovakian, Slovenian,
Macedonian, Serbian and other nationalities.

JULY
INTERNATIONAL ETHNIC FESTIVAL
(248) 857-5603
Albanians participate in Fourth of July weekend festival at Phoenix Plaza in Pontiac.

SLOVENE POLKA FEST
Freedom Hill County Park, Sterling Hts.
(810) 979-7010
Polka bands entertain during marathon
weekend of music and dance.

CZECH-SLOVAK FESTIVAL
Yack Arena, Wyandotte; (734) 246-4515
Ethnic foods, music, dance, arts and crafts at
weekend event.

SEPTEMBER
ROMANIAN COUNTRY FESTIVAL
Grass Lake; (517) 522-4800
Romanian Orthodox Episcopate of America
hosts summer fest with food, entertainment,
music and dancing in pavilion.

DECEMBER
CZECH-SLOVAK CELEBRATION
Sokol Cultural Center, Dearborn Hts.
(313) 278-9493
Traditional dinner and ethnic program first
Sunday in December.

ORGANIZATIONS

LITHUANIAN CULTURAL CENTER
25335 W. Nine Mile Rd., Southfield
(248) 356-9721
Divine Providence Church serves as
community center for cultural programs.

CROATIAN LODGE
32851 Ryan Rd., Warren
(810) 979-8154 or 778-8213
Soccer team plays other ethnic groups; lodge
hosts special events for Croatian community.
Call Snjezana Franetovic, president of
Croatian Women (248) 879-0747, for details.

SERBIAN CENTRE & HERITAGE MUSEUM
6770 Tecumseh Rd. East, Windsor
(519) 944-4884
Serbian artifacts and archival material on
exhibit. Groups welcome by appointment.
Viewing of frescoes at the Serbian Church is
also included in the tour. Admission free.

SOKOL HALL
23600 W. Warren, Dearborn Hts.
(313) 278-9493
Home of Sokol Ladies' Auxiliary, and Czech
and Slovak community events.

MEDIA

RADIO
WNZK AM 690 DAYS/680 NIGHTS
(248) 557-3500
"Albanian Hour," Sun 6-7pm and 7-8pm
"Lithuanian Voice," Sun 8-9am.
"Macedonian Hour," Sat 2-3pm, Sun 1-2am.
"Romanian Hour," Sat 11am-noon.
"Yugoslav," Sat 6-9pm, Sun 2-3am
"Serbian," Sat 4-6pm and Sun 7-8am.

WPON AM 1460
(248) 332-8883
"Radio Albania," Sat 1:30-3pm
"Lithuanian Melodies," Sat 8-9am
"Sounds of Croatia," Sat 1pm"

WEB SITES
BALKANARAMA
Many links to Eastern Europe.
www.troutdream.com/balkanarama

ALBANIAN CULTURE
www.albanian.com

CROATIAN CULTURE
www.hr/lookup/wwwhr/abouthr/tradit

MACEDONIAN CULTURE
utwbbwu2.wb.utwente.nl/~vdbelt/macedo1

SERBIAN CULTURE
utwbbwu2.wb.utwente.nl/~vdbelt/serbia1

CAFE BALKAN (MUSIC)
users.computerhaus.at/maricic/b/cafe/music

SCANDINAVIA

DENMARK

FINLAND

ICELAND

NORWAY

SWEDEN

Although the colors vary, the flag design of the Nordic countries is essentially the same.

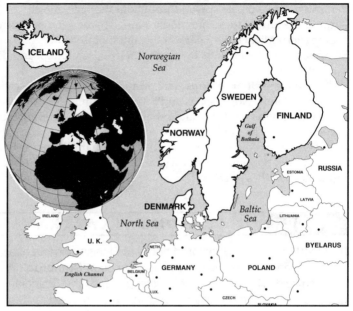

Scandinavia, the "land of the midnight sun," is composed of the two countries on the Scandinavian peninsula, **Sweden** and **Norway**, plus **Denmark**. However, **Finland** and **Iceland** are linked to these three Scandinavian countries by custom, economics and history; together they make up the **Nordic countries.**

Finland, which borders Russia to the east, shares its north-western border with Sweden and northern border with Norway. Sweden's neighbor to the west is Norway and to the south, Denmark. Iceland, 620 miles west of Norway in the Atlantic, has retained much of the same language and customs since the Viking explorers landed there in the ninth century.

The **Lapland** region comprises the northern one-third of Finland, Sweden and Norway; it's within the Arctic Circle. Natives of this region are known as **Sami** *(Lapps)*, whose principal occupation is herding reindeer, from which food and clothing are derived.

Despite their shared borders and history, the holidays and customs of each country are distinctive.

SCANDINAVIANS IN DETROIT

It was around 1849 when immigrants from the Nordic Countries began migrating to Michigan. Many of the Finns and some Swedes settled in the Upper Peninsula, while others spread throughout the state, mostly for farming. Around the turn of the century, Scandinavian immigrants began flocking to southeastern Michigan to work in the automobile industry. Many of the Swedes, skilled toolmakers in their homeland, set up tool and die businesses throughout Detroit.

Unlike some ethnic groups who primarily settled in one section of the city, the Danes, Finns, Norwegians and Swedes assimilated rather quickly. Since some were on the west side and others on the east, the immigrants established numerous clubs and organizations so they could continue to meet with their friends from the "old country," as well as share traditions and holidays with their children born in America. These Scandinavians established many of the Lutheran churches in Detroit.

TOUR　　SCANDINAVIA AT CRANBROOK

[D-E/2-3] The recently restored home of Finnish-born architect **Eliel Saarinen** and his wife, **Loja,** on the grounds of **Cranbrook Academy of Art** in Bloomfield Hills allows visitors to experience the Scandinavian style of a designer who invented rather than copied. Completed in 1930, the Saarinen House was home to this architect responsible for the distinctive "Cranbrook look" we see today. He was also the first president of the Cranbrook Academy of Art. The house and much of its furniture and rugs were designed by Eliel, Loja and their children, son **Eero** and daughter **Pipsan.** Eero became a famous architect in his own right, designing the **General Motors Technical Center** in Warren.

Not far from the Saarinen House is the ***Orpheus Fountain and Triton Pool,*** the most famous image identified with the Cranbrook Community, designed by Swedish-born artisan **Carl Milles.** Throughout the grounds, you will find a number of his sculptures, such as the ***Fountain of Jonah and the Whale, Siren With Fishes*** and ***Europa and the Bull.*** Cranbrook owns the largest collection of Milles' work outside Sweden.

Marshall Fredericks, an American of Danish and Norwegian ancestry, was one of Milles' students in Sweden. When Milles was invited by Cranbrook's founder, George Booth, to come to America, he asked Fredericks to be his studio assistant. One of Fredericks' many works at Cranbrook is ***The Thinker***, which sits outside the Cranbrook Art Museum.

To find out more about the many tours and cultural programs at Cranbrook, call (248) 645-3312. Cranbrook Educational Community is located along Lone Pine Road, east of Lahser. The visitor entrance, at 1221 Woodward Avenue, is between Lone Pine (17 Mile) and Long Lake (18 Mile) Roads, on the west side.

[D-G/3-6] One of the best ways to see the work of the late Marshall Fredericks, a world renowned sculputor from the Detroit area, is to take an afternoon drive. Begin your tour downtown in front of the City-County Building to view *The Spirit of Detroit.* Across Jefferson at the Ford Auditorium is *The Ford Empire and Harlequin Reliefs.* And at the Veterans Memorial Building (UAW-Ford Training Center), the *Victory Eagle* poignantly commemorates World War II. You might also want to head east on Jefferson to go over to Belle Isle. The elegant *Leaping Gazelle* graces the Levi L. Barbour Memorial Fountain there.

Head west to Dearborn, where you can view Fredericks' *Henry Ford Memorial* at the Henry Ford Centennial Library. *(From Detroit, take I-94 west to Michigan Avenue west; the library is just east of the Southfield Freeway.)*

A shopping trip to Northland Mall in Southfield *(Greenfield-Eight Mile exit off the Lodge Freeway)* is an opportunity to view a family pleaser, a sculpture called the *Boy and the Bear,* near Montgomery Ward.

You'll find many of Fredericks' works in the northern suburbs of Rochester and Bloomfield Hills. *Take I-75 north to University Drive exit* to visit the Oakland University campus in Rochester, where you'll find the *Saints and Sinners Fountain* in front of the Kresge Library. Head back south toward Bloomfield Hills and take in the beauty of *Wings of the Morning* in the back garden at Kirk in the Hills Church *(on Long Lake Road, west of Telegraph).* The Cranbrook Educational Community entrance *(on Woodward between Long Lake and Lone Pine Roads)* will lead you to the art museum grounds, where *The Thinker* and other pieces are located.

The final stop on this tour is Fredericks' hometown of Birmingham, where *Freedom of the Human Spirit* graces downtown's Shain Park *(one block south of Maple and two blocks west of Woodward).*

If you'd like to see more of Fredericks' work, visit the **Marshall M. Fredericks Sculpture Gallery** on the campus of Saginaw Valley State University (517-790-5667) *approximately 100 miles north of Detroit, between Saginaw and Bay City.* Here, you can view more than 200 original plaster models and other work. If northern Michigan happens to be in your travel plans, don't miss *Christ on the Cross,* a seven-ton bronze image on the Cross in the Woods in Indian River *(one mile west of I-75, Exit 310).*

● Two other notable works are the beloved *Lion and Mouse* at **Eastland Mall** in Harper Woods and his most recent installation, *Star Dream,* at the **Royal Oak Public Library** *(Eleven Mile Road, one block southeast of Main).*

RESTAURANTS

NANKIN MILL TAVERN
33700 Ann Arbor Trail, Westland
(734) 427-0622
Mon-Thu 10am-midnight, Fri 10am-1am, Sat noon-1am, Sun noon-10pm. Danish-American food all made from scratch.

BAKERIES

GRAF'S PASTRY KITCHEN
30010 W. 12 Mile Rd., Farmington Hills
(248) 851-8181
Tue-Fri 10am-6pm, Sat 9am-5pm. European tortes and coffee cakes.

IVERSEN DANISH BAKERY
22041 W. Outer Drive, Dearborn
(313) 563-5161
Tue-Sat 7am-5pm.
and
31562 Grand River, Farmington
(248) 477-5902
Tue-Fri 7am-6pm, Sat 7am-5pm.

KNUDSEN'S DANISH BAKERY
18601 W. McNichols Rd., Detroit
(4 blocks W of Southfield Rd.)
(313) 535-0323
Mon-Sat 6am-6pm.

LIVONIA DANISH BAKERY
27556 Schoolcraft, Livonia
(734) 425-4930
Mon-Fri 4:30am-5pm, Sat 5am-5pm.

FOODS

BIRMINGHAM COMMUNITY MARKET
130 W. 14 Mile Rd., Birmingham
(248) 644-6060
Mon-Sat 9am-8pm, Sun 10am-6pm. Home-made potatiskorv (Swedish potato sausage).

GOLDEN GATE MEATS INC.
2915 E. Big Beaver, Troy; (248) 689-1550
Mon-Fri 9am-5:30pm, Sat 8am-5pm. Home-made potatiskorv.

HANS DELICATESSEN AND IMPORTS
1049 E. Long Lake Rd., Troy
(248) 689-3598
Mon-Fri 9am-6pm, Sat 9am-5pm. Liver paté, small Swedish sausages.

NORTHERN LIGHTS
407 N. Fifth Ave. (at Kerrytown)
Ann Arbor
(734) 913-4888
Tue-Thu 11am-6pm, Fri 11am-7pm, Sat 9am-6pm. Deli with more than 30 types of Smorrebrod (Danish-style open-faced sandwiches). Eight tables for eating-in.

SHOPPING CENTER MARKET
425 N. Center St., Northville
(248) 344-1030
Mon-Sat 8am-10pm, Sun 9am-5pm. Herring and Norwegian lefse.

T.J. TORPEY MEAT MARKET
3336 Rochester Rd., Troy
(248) 689-2535
Tue-Sat 8am-6pm. Swedish Christmas ham (cured, not smoked) by special order.

(See "Multicultural Detroit" for large markets which carry imported cheeses, herring and potato lefse.)

A DANISH, PLEASE!

Traditional Scandinavian pastries fall somewhere between light coffee cakes and rich pastries. Scandinavians are also known for their appreciation of good coffee (remember Mrs. Olson?)—after all, what goes better with a "danish?"

Some baked goods to look for: *bulla* (Swedish), *pulla* (Finnish) and *kaffee kranz* (Norwegian)—all are braided cardamom coffee bread. *Joulutortut* (prune-filled tarts) and *joululimppu* (rye bread) are Finnish Christmas specialties. *Knäckebröd* (Swedish) or *rieska* (Finnish) is flat bread from wheat or barley, sometimes called hardtack. *Lefse* (Norwegian) is a special thin bread, and *limpa* is Swedish rye bread. *Pepparkakor* is a thin Swedish ginger cookie, and *spritsar* is a Swedish butter cookie.

CHEESE IS BIG

The Danes have made a national name for their excellent copies of French cheeses. *Danablu* is a sharp bleu cheese. *Danbo* belongs to the Samsoe family; it's similar in taste, is mild and firm, and has caraway seed. Danish *camembert* is similar to the French version, but usually stays runny longer. Danish *Brie*, however, bears little resemblance to its French counterpart. *Havarti* is creamy, mild and full-flavored, and sometimes has dill or caraway seeds.

● *Gjetost* has been the national cheese of Norway for more than 100 years. Different from any other cheese, it has the color of caramel, consistency of fudge and tastes like toffee.

Surrounded as they are by seas, Scandinavians are great seafarers and fishermen, and fish is an important staple in their diet. Some specialties: **Gravlax** *is a quickly cured salmon, similar to lox;* **inglad sill** *is marinated herring;* **torsk** *is cod (when poached, it tastes like lobster); and* **lutfisk** *(Swedish) or* **lutefisk** *(Norwegian) is dried cod that's poached and served with cream sauce at Christmas.*

FISH MARKETS

POMEROY'S SEAFOOD CO.
6535 Orchard Lake Rd., West Bloomfield
(248) 626-7595
Mon-Thu 9am-6pm, Fri 9am-7pm, Sat 9am-6:30pm, Sun 11am-4pm. Gravlax, herring.

SUPERIOR FISH
309 E. 11 Mile Rd., Royal Oak
(248) 541-4632
Mon-Fri 8am-6pm, Sat 8am-1pm. Gravlax, herring.

SHOPPING

BANG & OLUFSEN
Somerset North
2801 W. Big Beaver, Troy
(248) 816-9690
Mon-Sat 10am-9pm, Sun noon-6pm. Originated in Denmark in 1925. High quality audio and electronic equipment.

DEL GUIDICE FINE ARTS & ANTIQUES
515 S. Lafayette (at Sixth St.), Royal Oak
(248) 399-2608
Mon-Sat 11am-6pm.
Large collection of Georg Jensen pieces.

HOUSE OF DENMARK
893 S. Rochester Rd., Rochester
(248) 651-9430
and
3325 Orchard Lake Rd., Keego Harbor
(248) 682-7600
and
35555 Plymouth Rd., Livonia
(734) 425-4040
Tue, Wed, Sat 10am-5:30pm; Thu-Fri 10am-9pm; Sun noon-5pm; closed Mon. Danish modern furniture.

SMORGASBORD

A Swedish smorgasbord is traditionally a sandwich buffet; in fact, *smörgås* means "open sandwich" and *bord* is "table." A *kalas* is a more formal buffet, with traditional hot and cold dishes, breads, cheeses and desserts. After partaking of the "cultural smorgasbord" in metro Detroit, your appetite should be whetted for the real thing. The ingredients can be purchased in advance at international markets and the shops listed in this chapter.

**FINNISH CULTURAL CENTER
GIFT SHOP**
35200 W. Eight Mile, Farmington Hills
(248) 478-6939
Hours vary; call ahead. All types of
imported Finnish items.

SWEDE ANNE'S BUTIK
948 Baldwin Rd., Clarkston
(Exit 84 off I-75;
N on Baldwin 4.2 miles)
(248) 814-9000
Mon-Sat 10am-5:30pm, Sun 12:30-5pm.
Scandinavian imports, crystal, clothing,
foods, rugs, linens, art glass, books, tapes.

SWEDISH CLUB'S GIFT CENTER
22398 Ruth Rd., Farmington
(248) 478-2563
Hours vary; call ahead. Variety of imported
Swedish items.

● *For Royal Copenhagen, Bing &
Grondahl porcelain; Orrefors and Boda
crystal; Dansk china and housewares,
see Heslops, Jacobson's and Hudson's in
"Multicultural Detroit" chapter.*

VISUAL ARTS

**CRANBROOK EDUCATIONAL
COMMUNITY**
1221 N. Woodward, Bloomfield Hills
(248) 645-3180
Works by Eliel Saarinen, Carl Milles and
Marshall Fredericks. *(See tour.)*
● *Note: A Carl Milles sculpture, "The Hand of
God" can be viewed outside Detroit's Frank
Murphy Hall of Justice (on Gratiot at St.
Antoine). A copy of this sculpture also stands
at the artist's former estate outside
Stockholm, Sweden.*

DETROIT INSTITUTE OF ARTS
5200 Woodward, Detroit
(313) 833-7900
Wed-Fri 11am-4pm, Sat-Sun 11am-5pm.
Late 19th-century painters Harold Slott-
Moller of Denmark and Eugene Jansson of
Sweden featured in European Gallery.

**MARSHALL M. FREDERICKS
SCULPTURE GALLERY**
Saginaw Valley State University
2250 Pierce Rd., University Center
(517) 790-5667
Sculpture garden, fountain and gallery of 200
original plaster models showcase work of
noted sculptor. *(See tour.)*

BUNADS

A Norwegian *bunad* is a festive costume, varying in design according
to area of origination. They are worn at
christenings, confirmations, weddings
and other ceremonies, but especially on
May 17 (Constitution Day).

Some have intricate embroidery
over the entire dress; others may have
beadwork or needlepoint. Each has its
own style of silver jewelry to complement the costume. They were originally
made from hand-woven wool, plant-dyed, and are cherished heirlooms
today.

● *Bunads may be seen at celebrations held by Norwegian social clubs and
dance groups.*

PERFORMING ARTS

Scandinavian music, dance and choral groups are always looking for new members. Knowing a foreign language isn't a prerequisite.

ARPI MALE CHORUS
(734) 326-6850
Contact: Arthur Elander, director
Swedish choral group.

FINNISH MUSICAL GROUPS
(248) 932-3594
Contacts: Herbert and Dorothy Piilo
The Finnish American Singers and
Soittoniekkojen Klubi folk instrumental group
rehearse at the Finnish Cultural Center in
Farmington Hills.

HOIJAKAT FOLKDANCERS
(248) 478-6939
Contact: Ruth Mannisto, director
Finnish folk dance and drama groups meet at
the Finnish Cultural Center.

MANNISTO PELIMMANIT
(248) 349-3225
Contact: Ralph Mannisto
Finnish music combo.

NORDIC HERITAGE FOLKDANCERS
Scandinavian dance groups meet at the
Finnish Cultural Center. Childrens' group is
directed by Hilkka Ketola (517-548-4461)
and the adult group is headed by Glendine
Heino (519-548-4461).

SCANDIA WOMEN'S CHORUS
(248) 656-8462
Contact: Lillian Lagerkvist
Swedish women's ensemble.

SCANDINAVIAN FOLK DANCING
3337 Ann Arbor-Saline Rd., Ann Arbor
(734) 327-3636
Learn traditional "turning" dances at
Multicultural Folk Arts Center.

SPELMANSLAG ENSEMBLE
(313) 226-2311
Contact: Karin Arneson, director
Scandinavian American instrumental group is
based at the Finnish Cultural Center.

STITCH AN HEIRLOOM

Hardanger is the traditional elegant Norwegian embroidery. Classes and supplies can be found at **Needle Arts Inc.** *(2211 Monroe, Dearborn; 313-278-6266)* and **The Needlework** *(725 S. Adams, Birmingham; 248-645-1180)*. More than 20 different Hardanger instruction books and supplies are available at **The Fancyworks** *(2003 15 Mile Rd., Sterling Heights; 810-978-2660)*.

CHURCHES

In each of the five Scandinavian countries, Evangelical Lutheran is the state religion, supported by government funds. Although Scandinavians are free to choose whatever religion they like, more than 90 percent are Lutheran. The following churches conduct services in a Scandinavian language or observe traditional holidays.

BEAUTIFUL SAVIOR
5631 N. Adams, Birmingham
(248) 646-5041

BETHLEHEM LUTHERAN
35300 W. Eight Mile Rd., Farmington Hills
(248) 478-6520
Orginally a Finnsh congregation.

FAITH COVENANT
35415 W. 14 Mile Rd., Farmington Hills
(248) 661-9191

ST. ANDREW'S
6255 Telegraph Rd., Bloomfield Hills
(248) 646-5207

FIRST APOSTOLIC
26325 Halstead Rd., Farmington Hills
(248) 478-3707
Conducts some services in Finnish.

IMMANUEL LUTHERAN
13031 Chandler Park, Detroit
(313) 821-2380

ST. JOHN'S LUTHERAN CHURCH
13542 Mercedes, Redford
(313) 538-2660
Conducts services in Finnish.

MUSIC THROUGH THE AGES

S candinavia has produced a variety of musically gift-
ed people over the years. **Jenny Lind** (1820-87) was
a Swedish soprano singer, popularly known as the
Swedish Nightingale. She was born Johanna Maria Lind
in Stockholm and attended the school of singing at the
Court Theater, where she made her debut in 1838 as Agathe
in *Der Freischütz*. Her success was instantaneous.

The following selections are just a sampling of the diverse musical
talent from the region:

- *Finlandia,* Jan Sibelius. A classical standard by renowned Finnish
  composer.

- *Gift of Love,* Sissel Kyrkjebò. Norway's most popular singer,
  Kyrkjebò sang at the '94 Winter Olympics in Lillehammer.

- *Du Gamala Du Fria,* Swedish Radio Orchestra. Features well-known
  songs by Swedish composers.

- *Jussi Björling: De Vackraste Sångerna* ("The Beautiful Songs"),
  Royal Orchestra of Stockholm.

- *Peer Gynt,* composed by Edvard Grieg for the play by Henrik Ibsen.

- *Seglarsångar* ("Sailor Songs"), Sven-Bertil Taube. One of Sweden's
  beloved troubadours.

- *Klinga Mina Klocker* ("Rings, My Clock") Benny Andersson.
  Famous Swedish accordion player.

- *Svenska Ballader och Sånger,* Håkan Hagegård. Swedish operatic
  tenor.

- *Chess,* original cast from the musical by Bjorn Ulvaeus of ABBA.

In addition to traditional musicians, **ABBA, Roxette** and **Ace of Base**
are a few of the contemporary Swedish recording artists who have become
popular in America.

ORGANIZATIONS

**DANISH BROTHERHOOD OF AMERICA
LODGE; (734) 464-1110**
and
**DANISH SISTERHOOD OF AMERICA
LODGE; (313) 561-7364**
These local chapters conduct monthly events
perpetuating Danish culture.

**FINNISH CAMP AT LOON LAKE
Near Wixom; (248) 624-2550**
This Finnish summer cottage community
conducts two annual weekend events open
to the public. *(See "Annual Events.")*

**FINNISH CULTURAL CENTER
35200 W. Eight Mile Rd.,
Farmington Hills; (248) 478-6939**
Betty Holmbo, manager
Finnish language classes, the Finn Weavers,
Finnish American Historical Society, Hoijakat
folk dancers, and Finnish Women's Club
meet here. Hosts festivals and bazaars.
(See "Annual Events.")

**KALEVA LODGE
(meets at Finnish Cultural Center)
(248) 549-3669**
An organization for people of Finnish
ancestry.

JENNY LIND CLUB OF DETROIT (SWEDISH)
(248) 656-8462
Founded in 1937 for women of Swedish birth or ancestry who are interested in Swedish art and culture. *(See "Annual Events.")*

SWEDISH CLUB
22398 Ruth St., Farmington Hills
(248) 478-2563
Swedish language classes, Swedish Women's Organization, Ja Da Children's Club (Scandinavian), ARPI Male Chorus and performing groups meet regularly. Monthly Swedish brunch, annual Midsummer Fest. *(See "Annual Events.")*

DETROIT SWEDISH COUNCIL
(248) 641-2999
A member of the American Swedish Council, its purpose is to stimulate interest in Swedish culture for individuals of Swedish ancestry while expanding the public's knowledge.

SWEDISH AMERICAN CHAMBER OF COMMERCE
Michigan Chapter; (248) 644-8170
For companies and individuals interested in creating business opportunities between the two countries.

HOLIDAYS

DANISH

June 5
NATIONAL DAY
Celebrates Denmark's independence in 1849.

June 15
VALDEMAR'S DAY
Flag Day.

FINNISH

March 16
ST. URHØ DAY
This "fun" day was invented by Finnish Americans who wanted to have a patron saint. Green and purple are the colors of the day in remembrance of the legendary Urhø who saved the grape crop by driving out all the grasshoppers from Finland. (St. Henry is the "official" patron saint of Finland; his day is **July 13.**)

First Sunday in December
FINNISH INDEPENDENCE DAY

June 21
ST. JOHN'S DAY
Honors John the Baptist; also **FINNISH FLAG DAY** and Mid-Summer fest.

ICELANDIC

June 17
ICELANDIC NATIONAL DAY

NORWEGIAN

October 9
LEIF ERICSSON DAY
Honors the Viking explorer.

May 17
CONSTITUTION DAY

June 24
ST. HANS' DAY
Longest day of the year.

July 29
ST. OLAF'S DAY
Patron saint of Norway.

SWEDISH

June 6
NATIONAL DAY
Flag Day

December 13
SANTA LUCIA DAY
(See "A Swedish Christmas.")

SCANDINAVIAN

June 22
MIDSUMMER FEST
Celebrates the longest day of the year with dancing and singing around a maypole decorated with flowers. Also, decorating homes with birches and flowers; dancing and singing around a bonfire at night.

During the summer months, visitors from all over the world come to the Lapland region to experience the famous "midnight sun," when daylight lingers all night.

SONS OF NORWAY
Nordkap Lodge, Farmington Hills
(313) 535-6983
Contact: Thad Aardal
and
Samhold Lodge, Pontlac; (248) 332-9647
Contact Gene Steensma.
Local chapters preserve Norwegian culture and history. Offers scholarships to study Norwegian language and culture. Hosts festive celebrations of Norwegian holidays.

VASA LODGE—FRAM LODGE
(313) 371-6413
Detroit chapter has been involved since the early '20s in passing on Swedish tradition.

NORWEGIAN CLUB OF DETROIT
Farmington Hills; (248) 477-8565
A social organization, preserving Norwegian culture and customs.

WHAT'S IN A NAME?

In Scandinavia, family surnames were seldom used until the late 19th century. Before that, most people were identified by *patronymics*, a surname formed by adding a word to the father's first name. For example, Lars Andersson has a son called Olaf. Olaf's surname is *Larsson,* meaning he is the son of Lars. Lars' daughter, named Maja, would be called Maja *Larsdotter.*

Patronymics seldom changed when a person married. In Norway and Denmark, *-sen* is the same as *-son,* and *-datter* is the same as *-dotter.* When new laws were introduced, many people took their patronymics as family names, hence all the Jensens, Hansens, Johanssons and Anderssons.

ANNUAL EVENTS

JUNE
SPRING FEST
Takes place the first weekend in June at the Finnish Cultural Center in Farmington Hills. Call (248) 478-6939.

JENNY LIND CONCERT
Features recipients of the Jenny Lind music scholarship in Sweden. Call (248) 656-8462.

MIDSUMMER FEST
Celebrated June 22 at the Swedish Club in Farmington; call (248) 478-2563. The Finns celebrate the summer solstice with weekend festivities at Loon Lake Finnish Camp near Wixom. Call (248) 624-2550.

AUGUST
FINN FEST
Takes place in August at Finnish Camp on Loon Lake in the Wixom area. Call (248) 624-2550.

DANISH FESTIVAL
Takes place in Greenville (northwest of Grand Rapids). Features sporting events, children's acitivities, arts and crafts fair, food, Grand Danske Parade. Call (616) 754-6369.

NOVEMBER
SCANDINAVIAN BAZAAR
Finns, Swedes and Danes take part in this mid-November event at the Finnish Cultural Center in Farmington Hills. Call (248) 478-6939.

DECEMBER
SCANDINAVIAN NIGHT
Takes place the first Saturday in December at the Finnish Cultural Center in Farmington; features food from all the countries. Call (248) 478-6939.

FINNISH INDEPENDENCE DAY
Finnish American Historical Society hosts program on first Sunday in December at Finnish Cultural Center.

A SWEDISH CHRISTMAS

God Jul! At dawn on **December 13,** the season gets under way with the celebration of **Santa Lucia.** The eldest daughter in each home dresses in a long white gown with a red sash; on her head, she wears a wreath made of greens, adorned with five or seven lighted candles. Lucia usually carries a tray with a copper coffee pot, cups and saucers and special saffron buns *(lussekatter)* and heart-shaped ginger cookies *(pepparkakshjärtan)* to serve the family members. She is accompanied by **star boys,** who wear long white robes and tall white hats with stars on them; they carry large gold stars. **Attendant girls,** dressed in white robes with green sashes and tinsel crowns, carry lighted candles.

The tradition is based on the legend of St. Lucia of Sicily, who was martyred for her Christian faith and for helping to bring food to the poor. Because December 13 was considered on the old calendar to be the longest night of the year, Lucia—meaning "light" in Latin—marks the coming of longer days. The celebration of Lucia takes place in schools, churches and businesses throughout Sweden and in many Swedish American homes and organizations.

A few days before Christmas, families begin to make special paper ornaments to hang on the tree. *Julgranskaramel* are tissue-paper rolls with candy on the inside, and *julgranskorg* are woven paper hearts for hanging candy on the tree. In addition, the tree is decorated with straw ornaments, small Swedish flags and candles clipped on branches with an apple wired underneath to hold the candle upright. A large straw Christmas goat *(julbock),* believed long ago to ward off evil spirits from the home, stands next to the tree.

On Christmas Eve, a large bowl of rice porridge *(julgröt)* is set out for the *jultomten* (Christmas elf), who brings gifts for the children. Families usually gather to exchange gifts and enjoy a smorgasbord. Julgröt is always served for dessert, and one dish will have an almond in it. Whoever gets it is said to have his or her wish granted for the coming year. On Christmas morning, many attend the *Julotta* service at church.

The season ends January 13, St. Knut's Day *(Tjugondag Knut).* A party called *julgransplundring* gives children the opportunity to eat all the sweets left on the tree before it is taken outside…then the Christmas season is officially over.

CHRISTMAS EVENTS

SANTA LUCIA AND LUTFISK DINNER
Sponsored by the **Swedish Club** in
Farmington in mid-December.

**CHRISTMAS BAZAAR
AND SANTA LUCIA PAGEANT**
Takes place at **Beautiful Savior Church**
on Adams Road in Bloomfield Hills.
Sponsored by the **Swedish Women's
Educational Association,** a group dedicat-
ed to preserving Swedish holiday traditions
and customs.

**LUCIA PAGEANT
AND SWEDISH BREAKFAST**
Popular event at **Faith Covenant Church** in
Farmington Hills the first Saturday in
December; includes bazaar selling Swedish
foods and imports. Tickets sell out far in
advance.

SWEDISH CHRISTMAS SERVICE
In early December, **St. Andrew's Lutheran
Church** in Bloomfield Hills conducts a special Swedish Christmas service, followed by
a buffet of Swedish foods.

CHRISTMAS MORNING SERVICE
Immanuel Lutheran Church on Detroit's
east side conducts a special service in
Swedish.
(See "Church" listings for phone numbers.)

MEDIA
PRINT

THE DANISH NEWS
(7334) 464-1110
Published bimonthly for Danish
Brotherhood/Sisterhood members.

FCA NEWS (FINNISH)
(313) 881-8859
Published monthly for Finnish Center
members.

THE NORDIC NEWS (SCANDINAVIAN)
(313) 255-9705
Published five times a year by the Norse
Civic Association. Covers Scandinavian
activities in metro Detroit.

NORDKAPPEN—SONS OF NORWAY
(248) 474-4979
Monthly newsletter.

THE SWEDISH CLUB NEWS
(248) 489-5789
Published bimonthly for Swedish
Club members.

WEB SITES

FINNISH GENEALOGY
postlistegenealogia.org
and
www.genealogia.org

VIKING PAGES
regl0.control.chalmers.se/vikings

LINKS TO SCANDINAVIA
www.nq.com/nordic

NORDIC NEWSGROUP
www.nq.com/nordic/nordisk

SCANDINAVIAN GENEALOGY
www.algonet.se/~floyd/scandgen

THE VIKING AGE

From the eighth to the 11th centuries, the Vikings sailed from
Scandinavia in their highly manueverable longships to trade, fight and
settle throughout most of coastal Europe. They established kingdoms in
the British Isles, Normandy and Russia, where their cultural influence is
still recognized today. They are believed to have sailed as far south as the
Byzantine Empire, where Swedish Vikings formed the Imperial Guard.

Viking explorer Leif Ericsson is thought to have set foot on "Vinland,"
as he called what is now North America, in about the year 1000—nearly
500 years before Columbus.

UKRAINE

The Ukrainian flag is blue (top bar) and yellow (bottom bar).

UKRAINE

BELARUS

POLAND

RUSSIA

UKRAINE

MOLDOVA

ROMANIA

Sea of Azov

RUSSIA

Black Sea

THE TRIDENT, the Ukrainian state emblem, dates back to Kievan Rus, when it was the coat of arms of the Riuryk dynasty. Originating from the symbol of Poseidon, the Greek god of the Sea, the trident has been used as a heraldic symbol and decorative design throughout Ukrainian history.

Ukraine is the second largest country in Europe. Located on the northern shore of the Black Sea and south of Belarus and Russia, Ukraine is often called the bread basket of Europe because of its fertile agricultural land—the steppe—and its moderate climate. Iron ore, coal, manganese, natural gas and oil contribute to Ukraine's abundant natural resources. Ukrainian is the official language and Ukrainian Orthodox is the predominant religion, followed by Catholic and Protestant.

Ukraine's history is one of a centuries-long struggle for national independence. Because of its location in the center of European crossroads, it was divided among empires (including Russian, then Soviet), yet isolated from the mainstream of European growth. As part of the breakup of the Soviet Union, Ukraine emerged as an independent country in 1991. Today, Ukraine enjoys diplomatic relations with 140 countries and takes part in European and worldwide organizations.

UKRAINIANS IN DETROIT

Although some Ukrainians settled in Detroit as early as 1885, sizable numbers began arriving at the turn of the century. Looking for political freedom and economic opportunity, they laid the foundation for the Ukrainian American community by building churches as centers.

The second large influx followed World War II. These Ukrainians were among the thousands caught homeless in displaced-persons camps throughout Europe. They were political refugees who looked to America as a safe harbor. Once settled in Detroit, they contributed their strong work ethic, family values and education to enrich an already active Ukrainian community here.

Today, more than 200,000 Ukrainian Americans populate greater Detroit. Most live in Warren, Troy, Hamtramck, Dearborn, Birmingham, Detroit, Livonia, Sterling Heights and St. Clair Shores. The hubs of Ukrainian-related activities, however, are in Hamtramck and Warren. Windsor has a large and active Ukrainian community as well.

TOUR — HAMTRAMCK

[E-F/3-4] Discover the Ukrainian presence in Hamtramck by *exiting I-75 at Holbrook/ Caniff and following it east to Jos. Campau.* You will find your first stop, **Kopytko Meat Market,** *two miles south at 8609 Jos. Campau on the northwest corner of Andrus.* Kopytko is well-known for its superb *kryana* sausage, made daily, as well as the thin, dried hunter-style sausage, *kabanosy.* Ukrainian-speaking ladies behind the counter will gladly give you a sample. Also available are smoked bacon and ham, rye bread and various kinds of *varenyki* (pierogi).

The second stop is the **White House** *(11672 McDougall),* where on Wednesdays and Fridays you can pick up a special order of potato-, cheese- or cabbage-filled varenyki—as well as special *babka* breads during Easter season—authentically homemade. Be sure to call ahead to place your order and check hours of operation. *(To get to the White House, go north on Jos. Campau past Caniff and turn east onto Casmere. Go two blocks and turn north on McDougall. Look for a white, wooden building just south of the Hamtramck Head Start School on the east side before Commor. Follow the walkway to the back of the house.)*

Immaculate Conception Ukrainian Catholic Church *(11700 McDougall)* is on the north side of the Head Start School. Go to the church office on the McDougall side and ask to view the church, or call ahead for an appointment.

The massive structure is decorated with icons depicting the life of the Virgin Mary, as well as frescoes and paintings above the sanctuary and on the ceiling. An elaborate iconostasis, gilded and meticulously carved, stands as a screen before the altar.

To get to the **Ukrainian Gift Shop** *(11758 Mitchell), turn west onto Commor and then south onto Mitchell.* You may want to pick up a local Ukrainian newspaper here, as well as videos, cassettes, books, greeting cards or wooden carved gift items. *(See list for store hours.)*

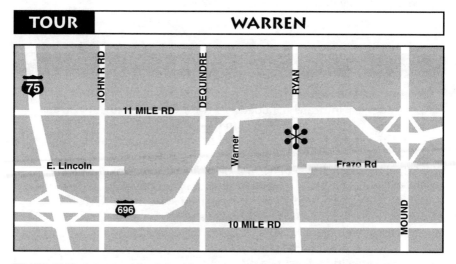

TOUR	WARREN

[E-F/2-3] It's best to schedule this tour around an appointment to visit the Ukrainian Cultural Center. Call (810) 757-8130 for information.

Several points of interest are on Ryan in Warren in or near the **Ukrainian Cultural Center.** *From I-696, take the second exit east of I-75 (Exit 30, marked Dequindre/Ryan). Follow the service road east to Ryan and turn south (right). Within the next block you will see **Eko Art Gallery** (26795 Ryan)* in the **Ukrainian Village Plaza.** Park here to visit Eko, but drive south and park behind the Cultural Center for the rest of the tour. The gallery features works of art by Ukrainian artists from all over the world. In addition, it sells books in Ukrainian and English, embroidered clothing, greeting cards and gifts. Fliers advertising upcoming events are posted on the door.

Just south of the Eko Gallery is the **Ukrainian Cultural Center** *(26601 Ryan, open by appointment)*, where many special events take place throughout the year. It also houses a museum on the second floor. Memorabilia from Ukrainian settlement in Detroit during the 1940s and '50s crowd the walls and tables. The displays of rare and beautiful embroidery, currency and military uniforms are worth the visit. Next to the museum is a well-stocked library filled with Ukrainian books available for loan.

Walk out of the Cultural Center to the **Ukrainian Gift Shop** *(just south, at 26499 Ryan).* A wide assortment of Ukrainian books, cassettes, cards and gift items are available for purchase.

Directly across the street is **St. Josaphat Ukrainian Catholic Church.** The church was refurbished in the 1980s and features Byzantine-style icons and an intricately carved wooden iconostasis. Call (810) 755-1740 for an appointment.

An interesting way to complete your tour might be a stop at the **Ukrainian Social Club, Odesa,** to mingle with Ukrainians from the area. The lounge, located in the Cultural Center, is open Sunday through Wednesday 5pm to midnight, Thursday through Saturday 5pm-2am.

BABKA & BORSHCH

Centuries-old traditions have invested Ukrainian breads with ritual significance. Intricately braided, richly decorated, distinctive breads and pastries play an important role in the customs and traditions of Ukrainian culture. They are symbols of remembrance, happiness, health and prosperity.

Ritual breads include *kolach, paska, babka, korovai* and *holuby* (doves). Traditional baking includes *makivnyk* (poppy seed roll), *medivnyk* (honey cake), *rohalyky* (crescent-shaped sweet rolls), *khrustyky* (deep-fried pastries), *torte* (layered cake) and *pampushky* (with filling).

Ukrainian specialties include *borshch* (beet soup), *varenyki* (dough containing cheese, meat, potato or fruit) and *holubtsi* (cabbage rolls).

The Ukrainian beer *Obolon, Perlova* vodka and *Artyomov* champagne (bottled in eastern Ukraine), plus fortified wines from Massandra, particularly one named "Black Doctor," are highly rated by connoisseurs.

FOOD

KOPYTKO MEAT MARKET
8609 Jos. Campau
Hamtramck
(313) 873-4210
Mon-Sat 7am-6pm. Ukrainian homemade sausages, smoked hams, imported groceries and fresh breads.

EUROPEAN HOMESTYLE SAUSAGE CO.
8616 Michigan Ave., Detroit
(313) 846-6870
Tue-Fri 9am-5pm, Sat 8am-noon. Full line of Ukrainian meats and groceries.

THE WHITE HOUSE
11672 McDougall, Hamtramck
(313) 366-3594
Wed 8am-2pm, Fri 8am-2pm. Call to order Easter breads, pierogi, varenyki and ethnic Ukrainian favorites.

ST. JOSAPHAT UKRAINIAN CHURCH
26401 Ryan Rd. (just S of I-696), Warren
(810) 755-1740.
Friday evening dinners throughout Lent.

WINDSOR
UKRAINIAN RESTAURANT
1148 Marion Ave., Windsor
(519) 253-3981
Daily noon-9pm. Features cabbage rolls and other homemade Ukrainian specialties.

ST. VLADIMIR UKRAINIAN CULTURAL CENTRE
2000 Tecumseh Rd. E., Windsor
(519) 254-8067
Wed 9am-6pm. Center next door to church sells varenyki and holubtsi by the dozen.

UKRAINIAN HOME
1119 Langlois, Windsor; (519) 254-3114
Mon-Sat noon-5pm. Fresh or frozen varenyki. Order ahead.

STS. VLADIMIR AND OLGA UKRAINIAN CATHOLIC CHURCH
1505 Langlois, Winsdor; (519) 254-7927
Varenyki most Sundays after liturgy.

TRADITIONAL ARTS

Woodcarving and inlay, ceramics, embroidery, weaving and *pysanky* (egg decorating) are well-developed traditional Ukrainian handicrafts. Embroidery is especially noteworthy and decorates national costumes, pillowcases, tablecloths and church altars. The designs are usually geometric and predominantly cross-stitched in brightly colored red or orange thread with black accents. Embroidery and ceramic designs vary from region to region, and even from village to village.

GALLERIES & SHOPS
EKO GALLERY
26795 Ryan, Warren; (810) 755-3535
Tue and Thu-Fri 11am-5pm, Sat-Sun 11am-4pm. A large collection of pieces by Ukrainian and Ukrainian American artists, including oil and watercolor paintings, ceramics, sculpture and engravings. Embroidered clothing and tablecloths, books in English and Ukrainian, greeting cards and music.

MRIA
28648 Ryan Rd., Warren (S of 12 Mile Rd.)
(810) 574-0303
Latest in Ukrainian music and art. Import/export service.

UKRAINIAN GIFT SHOP
11758 Mitchell, Hamtramck
(313) 892-6563
Mon-Tue and Thu-Fri 10am-4pm, Wed and Sat 10am-3pm.
and
26499 Ryan Rd., Warren (810) 759-6563
Mon-Fri 10am-4:30pm, Sat 10am-3pm.
Ukrainian newspapers, videos, cassettes, books, greeting cards and gift items.
The shops also serve as offices for the Trident Trade Group, which ships packages directly to Ukraine.

UKRAINIAN CULTURAL CENTER MUSEUM

26601 Ryan, Warren; (810) 757-8130
By appointment. The museum features several pieces of rare Ukrainian embroidery and a rotating exhibit of Ukrainian arts and crafts, as well as historical displays.

WINDSOR

MEEST WINDSOR
1041 Ottawa St., Windsor
(519) 258-5429
Meest (Ukrainian for "bridge"), the Windsor branch of a company that sends packages or money to Ukraine, also sells audio- and videocassettes, Ukrainian greeting cards, a few books and a small amount of art. Manager Peter Mycak also heads the Windsor Ukrainian Canadian Congress.

UKRAINIAN MUSEUM
2000 Tecumseh Rd. E., Windsor
(in lower level of St. Vladimir's Ukrainian Cultural Centre)
(519) 254-8067
Contact: Mary Hnatiuk

PERFORMING ARTS

UKRAINIAN BANDURA CHORUS
(313) 264-9878
World-renowned all-male chorus playing the bandura, the Ukrainian national instrument.

VATRA MEN'S CHORUS
(810) 757-7910
Volodymir Schesiuk, maestro
Call Cultural Center for rehearsal schedule.

ECHOES OF UKRAINE
11739 McDougall, Detroit
(313) 891-6411
Ukrainian dance ensemble directed by world-renowned choreographer Joanna Von Draginda Kulchesky.

WINDSOR UKRAINIAN BARVINOK DANCE SCHOOL AND BARVINOK DANCE ENSEMBLE
(519) 969-8188
Taras and Debbie Rohatyn, directors
Classes for all ages and skill levels.

FOLK ARTISTS

IRENE ZELENEY
(519) 253-1645
Bakes Ukrainian wedding bread (korovai).

ANN MASNEY
(519) 969-2449
Creates pysanky (Easter egg handcrafts).

ROMAN SENIUK
(313) 891-2588
Specializes in pysanky on goose and ostrich eggs as well as crafting unique jewelry.

MARGIE PRYTULAK
(519) 969-8998
Creates Ukrainian embroidery, cooking and pysanky.

FOLK MUSIC

Music and dance have always been important components of Ukrainian culture. Since the 16th century, songs and epic ballads often have been accompanied by the *bandura,* a 30-string, lute-like instrument. Ukrainian songs often reflect their folk origins and medieval church influences. Ukrainians seem to have a variety of songs for most occasions; most love to sing.

Ukrainian folk dancing dates to pre-Christian times, evolving from ritual dances to highly stylized forms. Today, many professional and amateur dance troupes continue the tradition of fast-paced, complex, athletic and colorful performances.

BYZANTINE CHURCHES

Ukrainian churches are traditional Byzantine style with decor featuring frescoes and mosaics, as well as icons painted on wood panels. The architecture is characterized by a central dome space and several smaller domes or half-domes. A distinct style known as Cossack baroque was popular not only in medieval Kiev, but also throughout the small villages of Ukraine, where meticulously structured wooden churches were constructed by hand with minimal tools.

The beginning of Christianity in Ukraine dates to 988 A.D., when St. Vladimir, the Great Prince of Kiev, officially adopted Christianity from the Greeks, creating the Ukrainian Orthodox Church. In 1596, some Ukrainian bishops joined in a union with Rome to create the Ukrainian Catholic Church, while retaining many traditional Byzantine rituals of the Orthodox religion. Most Ukrainians in Ukraine and throughout the world are either Orthodox or Ukrainian Catholic.

Today, the Ukrainian community in metropolitan Detroit and Windsor supports four Orthodox and six Ukrainian Catholic churches, all of which continue traditional services in Ukrainian.

Cathedral of St. Sophia. In Kiev, Ukraine; completed in 1037 and reconstructed in 17th century; now a museum; frescoes and mosaics.

CHURCHES

ST. MARY'S
UKRAINIAN ORTHODOX CATHEDRAL
2010 Mada, Southfield; (248) 356-1636

ST. ANDREW
UKRAINIAN ORTHODOX CHURCH
5130 Prescott, Detroit; (313) 893-1569

HOLY TRINITY
UKRAINIAN ORTHODOX CHURCH
7103 Normile, Dearborn; (313) 581-8781

IMMACULATE CONCEPTION
UKRAINIAN CATHOLIC CHURCH
11700 McDougall, Hamtramck
(313) 893-1710

ST. JOSAPHAT
UKRAINIAN CATHOLIC CHURCH
26401 St. Josaphat (Ryan), Warren
(810) 755-1740

OUR LADY OF PERPETUAL HELP
UKRAINIAN CATHOLIC CHURCH
26606 Ann Arbor Trail, Dearborn Hts.
(313) 278-0470

ST. JOHN
UKRAINIAN CATHOLIC CHURCH
9915 Clippert, Detroit; (313) 897-7300

ST. MICHAEL
UKRAINIAN CATHOLIC CHURCH
6320 Chase Rd., Dearborn
(313) 581-2580

WINDSOR

ST. VLADIMIR
UKRAINIAN ORTHODOX CATHEDRAL
2000 Tecumseh Rd. E., Windsor
(519) 254-8067

STS. VLADIMIR AND OLGA
UKRAINIAN CATHOLIC CHURCH
1505 Langlois, Windsor
(519) 254-7927

EDUCATION

The Ukrainian community supports a grade school and a high school, which is one of only two Ukrainian high schools in the United States. The Immaculate Conception (IC) Ukrainian Catholic High School (810-574-0510) and the IC Grade School (810-574-2480) are in Warren N of 12 Mile between Ryan and Dequindre.

LESIA UKRAINKA SCHOOL
St. Mary Ukrainian Orthodox Church
2010 Mada, Southfield
Ukrainian Saturday School for history, religion and music. Contact the director at (248) 356-1636.

RIDNA SHKOLA
Immaculate Conception Church
11680 McDougall, Hamtramck
Ukrainian Saturday School conducts classes for young people to learn the Ukrainian language. Contact Ola Movchan-Iwanycka, 11222 Olive, Warren, MI 48091.

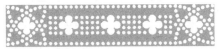

YOUTH ACTIVITIES

SCOUTING ORGANIZATIONS
Ukrainian Cultural Center, Warren
(810) 757-7910
Contact: Borys Potapenko
Youth group meetings at Cultural Center.

CHERNYK SPORTS CLUB
Ukrainian Cultural Center, Warren
(810) 757-8130
Club coordinates an assortment of sports teams for boys and girls.

UKRAINIAN FOLK DANCING
St. Josaphat Parish, Warren
(313) 891-6411
Contact: Joanna Von Draginda Kulchesky
Call for class schedule.

BANDURA SCHOOL
Ukrainian Cultural Center, Warren
(248) 689-7979
Dr. Marko Farion, director
Children learn to play the traditional lute-like instrument.

ADULT ACTIVITIES

UKRAINIAN WOMEN'S LEAGUE OF AMERICA IN DETROIT
27040 Ryan Rd., Warren
(N of 11 Mile Rd.)
(810) 751-8488
Adult activities vary from arts and crafts to cooking. Call for details and schedules.

FESTIVALS AND EVENTS

JANUARY/FEBRUARY
UKRAINIAN NEW YEAR'S DANCE
Called "The Malanka," it takes place two weeks after Orthodox Christmas. Call the Cultural Center for information: (810) 757-8130.

SUMMER
Sunday picnics, sponsored by churches and Ukrainian American organizations, take place at Kiev Resort in Whitmore Lake and the Dibrova Resort in Brighton most summer weekends. Ukrainian Self Reliance Federal Credit Union prints schedules, which are available at local churches. Call the credit union at (810) 756-3300.

CARROUSEL OF THE NATIONS
Multicultural Council of Windsor
(519) 255-1127
A Ukrainian Village is one of 30 groups in Windsor's annual multicultural festival celebrated during two weekends in June.

UKRAINIAN SUNFLOWER FESTIVAL
26401 Ryan Rd., Warren; (810) 755-1740
Takes place first weekend in August at the St. Josaphat Church grounds. Features ethnic food, cultural displays, entertainment, folk dance performances, carnival rides, bingo and Las Vegas-style games at the Cultural Center.

MULTI-ETHNIC FESTIVAL
Helmich Park, Warren
(810) 751-8168 or 574-4950
Annual August festival sponsored by Warren's City Council features food, music, dance and crafts of various countries, including Ukraine.

EASTER SEASON

Easter is the holiest time of the year for Ukrainians. The season focuses on church services, traditional foods such as *paska* (braided Easter bread) and seasonal crafts such as *pysanky*, the elaborately decorated Easter eggs. This spring celebration dates back to pre-Christian Kievan Rus, when tribes conducted fertility rituals to welcome the new growing season.

The Easter Eve church service includes singing, celebration of divine liturgy and the blessing of the food, during which food baskets are placed in a circle with lighted candles in each. The baskets represent a humble offering brought to the resurrected Christ. They then are taken home for the family's morning meal, which ends the Lenten fast.

PYSANKY

Intricately decorated Easter eggs, or *pysanky* (from the Ukrainian word *pysaty*, "to write") intertwine pre-Christian era pagan mysticism and Christian traditions into a world-renowned art form. The eggs are exchanged as gifts and used as decorations throughout the year.

Using a thin metal *kystka* dipped in melted wax, intricate designs are "written" onto the raw eggshell, which is dipped into various dyes and then written on again. Once the wax is melted at the end, the colors beneath are exposed, revealing the complex patterns.

Pysanky are decorated with Christian symbols, such as the cross, fish and triangles denoting the Trinity. Pagan symbols celebrating spring and life include deer and horses to represent prosperity, pine needles and wheat to symbolize youth and health, and birds to represent fertility. Lines encircling the egg without beginning or end represent eternal life.

● *Pysanky supplies are available at the Polish Art Center in Hamtramck (see "Poland") and the Ukrainian Gift Shops in Hamtramck and Warren. Art of Pysanky workshops are given at the Ukrainian Cultural Center. Call (810) 757-8130 for class schedule bulletin. Pysanky classes are also offered at St. Vladimir's Cultural Centre in Windsor, (519) 254-8067.*

ORGANIZATIONS

UKRAINIAN CULTURAL CENTER
26601 Ryan Rd., Warren
(810) 757-8130
Daily 8am-6pm, later for special events. The center is home to more than 40 arts, civic, educational, social, sports and youth organizations. This hub of the local Ukrainian community is a good source for gaining insight into all aspects of Ukrainian activity in the Detroit area. Information is available about professional, political and veterans organizations, as well as senior housing at Ukrainian Village in Warren.

ASSOCIATION FOR THE ADVANCEMENT OF UKRAINIAN CULTURE
2582 Otter, Warren, MI 48092
Contact: Zvenyslava Hayda

UKRAINIAN AMERICAN CULTURAL FOUNDATION
2299 Suite Dr., Troy, MI 48098
Contact: Roma Dyhdalo

THE UKRAINIAN WOMEN'S LEAGUE OF AMERICA IN DETROIT
27040 Ryan Rd., Warren; (810) 751-8488
Originated in Ukraine in 1920s. Nonpolitical but fosters Ukrainian culture and welfare. Sponsors educational, cultural and social activities. Spreads information about the community.

UKRAINIAN WOMEN'S ORGANIZATION
Windsor; (519) 735-4437
Luba Kosak, cultural representative
Women from Ukraine teach cultural heritage and sponsor social activities, including bazaars and exhibits. Also contact Nina Nedin, (519) 969-6338.

MEDIA

RADIO
WNZK 690 AM
(248) 557-3500
"Echo of Ukraine," Tue 9-10pm
"Pohlad," Thu 9-10pm
"Slovo,": Fri 10-11pm
"Ukrainian Religious Hour," Sat noon-1pm. "

CJAM 91.5 FM
"Sounds of Ukraine" by Irene Momotiuk, Saturday 11am-noon. "Ukrainian Catholic Hour" Sunday 7-8pm.

PRINT
UKRAINIAN WEEKLY
(201) 434-0237
20-page English paper distributed throughout North America. Annual subscription is $60 for 52 issues.

Check with individual churches for bulletins that contain current events and activities.

WEB SITES
UKRAINIAN INFORMATION PAGE
www.soma.crl.mcmaster.ca/ukes/ua-links

UKES VILLAGE
www.soma.crl.mcmaster.ca/ukes

WALLPAPER FOR WEB SITES IN UKRAINIAN EMBROIDERY PATTERNS
www.web.beer.by.net/Athens/5734/wall

WINDSOR UKRAINIAN WEB
www.2.uwindsor.ca/~hlynka/ukwin

BYZANTINE ART

Many of the Ukrainian churches in metropolitan Detroit carry on the Byzantine tradition of art and architecture. The most characteristic features of a Byzantine Rite church are the **icons**. The term *icon* is derived from the Greek *eikenai*, "to resemble," and refers to an image, believed to be sacred and able to aid in contacting the represented figure.

The **iconostasis** (from Greek *stasis*, "stand, support") is a colorful picture screen that separates the sanctuary from the nave, surrounding the sanctuary with a feeling of mystery and protection. Usually it is an elaborate work of art in which the skills of architecture, woodcarving or metalwork, and painting are combined harmoniously. To avoid the taint of idolatry, they emphasized otherworldliness rather than human feeling or sentimentality. Gold-leaf backgrounds were common, and strongly geometric designs—emphasizing either angularity or long, sinuous curves—were favored.

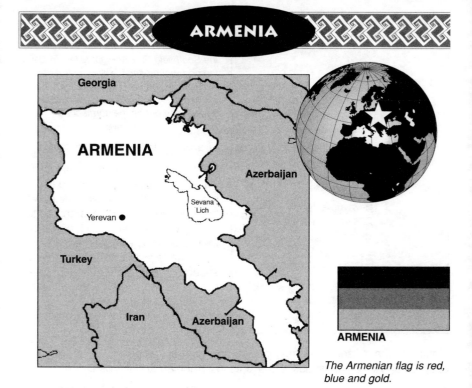

The Armenian flag is red, blue and gold.

Armenia, with 3.3 million inhabitants, is in the southwest corner of what was once the Soviet Union, in the Transcaucasia region of Asia Minor, bordered by Georgia and Azerbaijan. Armenia is north of the border where Iran and Turkey meet. Its capital, Yerevan, is the center of the arts, education and industry. A rugged, mountainous land, Armenia has a dry climate with cold winters and hot summers.

ARMENIANS IN DETROIT

Of the 1 million Armenians in the United States, more than 30,000 live in the Detroit area. Other large Armenian populations reside in New York; New Jersey; Boston; Philadelphia; Washington, D.C.; Chicago; Los Angeles; and Fresno, Calif.

The Armenians originally came to the Detroit area after World War I, while fleeing the Turkish massacres (1915-1918) of 1.5 million Armenians during the Ottoman Empire. Many found employment in the automobile industry and settled in Dearborn, Highland Park and the Delray district of southwest Detroit.

Further immigration took place after World War II, then again during the civil war in Lebanon in the 1970s, followed by the abdication of the Shah of Iran, and after the disintegration and collapse of the USSR.

Over time, many local Armenians moved to Dearborn and Southfield. Many of them now live throughout the Detroit area, mainly in Birmingham, Bloomfield Hills, West Bloomfield, Troy, Southfield, Farmington Hills and Dearborn.

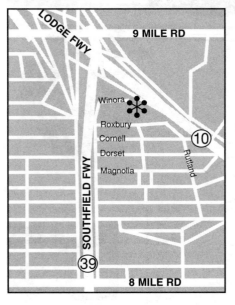

To get to St. John's Armenian Church, exit the Southfield Fwy. at Eight Mile and follow the northbound service drive until it dead-ends at the church. From the Lodge, take the Northwestern service route north to 9 Mile, then get on the northbound Southfield Service Drive.

"Paree looyse" —Good morning!

Treat yourself to an Armenian-style breakfast on a Sunday morning by preparing an omelet with feta cheese, a few onions and butter. Put some marinated black olives on the plate along with *choreg,* a homemade sweet bread laced with sesame seeds. Spread apricot preserves on the choreg and you've started your day off well.

Tune into the **"Armenian Radio Hour"** on WNZK AM 690 days/680 nights at 10 a.m. and you'll hear patriotic songs and sacred music, as well as updates on Armenian issues and events in Armenian and English.

Next, attend services at **St. Sarkis Armenian Church** *(19300 Ford Road in Dearborn)* or **St. John's Armenian Church** *(off the Lodge Freeway at 22001 Northwestern Highway in Southfield)* to experience an Apostolic/Orthodox service, including incense, liturgical music and sermons in Armenian and English. Another choice is the **Armenian Congregational Church** *(26210 W. 12 Mile in Southfield),* where most of the service is in English.

Gather for lunch with friends at a Middle Eastern or Greek restaurant where you can order Armenian favorites such as pilaf with shish kabob or roasted chicken. Or if you've bought Armenian ingredients and foods at a Middle Eastern market or deli, invite friends over for a feast. *(See "Armenian Picnic.")*

After lunch, visit the **Alex and Marie Manoogian Museum of Armenian Artifacts** *(open 1-4pm)* in Southfield, next to St. John's Armenian Church. There, you will find exquisite artworks from ancient to contemporary times. Then browse through the library and view manuscripts, books, maps and other cultural materials.

As a splendid finish to your day, stop by any specialty coffee shop in the area and order some rich Oriental coffee. If you have a backgammon board, bring that with you. Play some *tavlou* (backgammon) while you sip your *soorj* (coffee). Then place the cup upside down on the saucer when you're through. After the grounds fall, take turns in the tradition of reading each other's fortune.

Before you part from your friends, be sure to say *"keesher paree"* (good night). And a good-bye kiss on the cheek is a must with Armenians.

Picnics are a favorite get-together among Armenians. Most of the Armenian churches regularly sponsor picnics and welcome visitors. Call them for a schedule so you can attend, as they are a great way to experience the culture. You also can have your own—invite family and friends for a picnic to enjoy the warmth, closeness and camaraderie of an Armenian gathering. For the feast, buy some string cheese, **basturma** (cured, spicy beef), feta cheese and **lavash** (flat Syrian bread) at a Middle Eastern market. Also buy eggplant and tomatoes to make an Armenian appetizer seasoned with garlic and olive oil.

At **Uptown Deli,** an Armenian-owned catering service in Farmington Hills *(on the east side of Orchard Lake Road between 12 and 13 Mile Roads),* you can buy freshly made **boreg** (Armenian cheese pies), **lehmejun** (Armenian pizza), **mante** (tiny dumplings in broth with yogurt on top) and other delicacies.

For dessert, stop by a Middle Eastern bakery to get phyllo dough pastries such as **paklava** (Armenian spelling for baklava) and **bourma.**

NOAH'S ARK

According to the Bible *(Genesis 6-8),* Noah's Ark landed after the great flood on Mt. Ararat, in the Ararat region near Lake Van in ancient Armenia. Although the area is now part of Turkey, Mt. Ararat remains a symbol of the Armenian nation.

ARMENIAN FACTS

- In 301 A.D., Armenia became the first nation to accept Christianity.
- Armenians have their own alphabet and language thanks to St. Mesrop Mashtots, who invented the alphabet in 404 A.D. It consists of 31 consonants and seven vowels.
- Conversational phrases include "parev" (hello), "Eench bes es?" (How are you?) and "Lav em" (I am fine).
- Most Armenian last names end in *ian,* which means "son of." (However, in Eastern Armenia, it might be spelled *yan.*)
- About half of the approximately seven million Armenians in the world live in Armenia.

RESTAURANTS

UPTOWN DELI
28948 Orchard Lake Rd., Farmington Hills
(between 12 and 13 Mile Rds.)
(248) 626-3715
Tue-Fri 8am-3pm (Sat-Mon catering only).
Busy deli and catering company, owned by
Armenian Gary Reizian, provides traditional
cheese boreg appetizers, mante dumplings,
keofte meat patties, lamb and chicken
kabobs, spinach pie, paklava and many other
delicious foods. A few tables are available for
eat-in orders of lavash or lehmejun.

(See also "Arab World" and "Greece.")

MARKETS
*The following are examples of Middle
Eastern markets that carry Armenian
ingredients and foods. For a more
complete listing, see "Arab World."*

CEDAR MARKET
413 S. Main, Royal Oak; (248) 547.7856
Mon-Sat 9:30am-9pm, Sun noon-4pm.
Middle Eastern, Armenian, Greek and Italian
imported goods, specialty foods and
convenience foods.

GAZALI IMPORTS
10620 W. Nine Mile, Oak Park
(248) 546-6833
Mon-Sat 10am-10pm, Sun 11am-6pm.
Armenian and Middle Eastern foods,
including spices, pastries, bread, rice,
coffees and olive oil.

INTERNATIONAL MARKET
15383 Inkster Rd., Livonia
(734) 522-2220
Mon-Sat 9am-6pm, Sun 10am-2pm. Offers
variety of Middle Eastern foods.

MAJESTIC MARKET
25877 Lahser, Southfield
(248) 352-8556
Mon-Sat 9am-10pm, Sun 10am-8pm. Middle
Eastern food and wine of all kinds.

OASIS MART IMPORTING
4130 Rochester Rd., Royal Oak
(248) 588-2210
Mon-Sat 9am-7pm, Sun 10am-2pm. Middle
Eastern and European foods and groceries.

ARMENIAN FOOD

Lavash: (Armenian
thin bread) A cracker-
like bread basic to the
Armenian diet. It is
served dry or can be
moistened to roll up
with a filling inside.

Choreg: Sesame-
topped sweet rolls
shaped out of twisted
dough, also are called
Armenian knot rolls.

Lamb dishes: Many
kinds are served,
including stew, kebobs,
shanks, chops,
meatballs and hand-
rolled sausages.

Keofte: (Kufta)
Meatballs or patties
made of lamb or other
ground meats.

Lehmejun:
(Lahmajoon) A meat
pie similar to a meat-
covered pizza; has
been served for cen-
turies. *Boreg* is a
cheese pie.

Stuffed vegetables: A
rice and ground-meat
filling used to stuff
large tomatoes, bell
peppers or eggplant.

Pilaf: The Armenian
version is made with
vermicelli and long-
grain rice in chicken
broth.

OF KOMITAS AND KHAZ

Armenian music is rooted in ancient origins, but with a mixture of influences from east and west. Popular music includes vocal and instrumental melodies, which were preserved through the centuries by the efforts of the *ashoughs*—musician-poets who traveled across the country exchanging popular songs and melodies. Shortly before the Armenian genocide and the consequent destruction of a great part of the popular musical heritage, the composer *Komitas (or Gomidas)* collected thousands of pieces of music. Many of the instruments used then are still played today, either with modifications or in their original form. Armenian religious music began when the nation became Christian in 301 A.D. Initially, it was written in its own musical notation called *Khaz.*

Beginning in the 19th century, European influence resulted in Armenian classical music being written in European form. The music, however, continued to receive its inspiration from national sources, as it does today. There have been many famous Armenian composers, in the homeland and in the diaspora, including Raffi Armenian, Aram Khachaturian, Michelle Ekizian and Alan Hovhaness.

CHURCHES

Churches serve as cultural centers for Armenians. See related listings for events, education, arts, bookstores, classes and media.

ST. JOHN'S ARMENIAN CHURCH
22001 Northwestern Hwy., Southfield
(248) 569-3405
Church services Sun 10am-noon.

ST. SARKIS ARMENIAN CHURCH
19300 Ford Rd., Dearborn
(313) 336-6200
Church services Sun 11am-12:30pm.

ARMENIAN CONGREGATIONAL CHURCH
26210 W. 12 Mile Rd., Southfield
(off 12 Mile Rd. and Northwestern Hwy.)
(248) 352-0680
Church services Sun 11am-noon.

MUSIC

HACHIG KAZARIAN ENSEMBLE
(734) 459-1141
Four-piece ensemble includes vocalists plus clarinet, oud (Middle Eastern guitar), dumbeg (Middle Eastern drum) and keyboard.

THE JOHNITES
(248) 478-7827
Four-piece ensemble includes vocalists plus clarinet, oud, dumbeg and guitar.

MUSIC BY MARGARET
(313) 531-7475
An elegant touch—vocalist, pianist and organist who performs in English and Armenian for all occasions—easy listening, vintage standards, show tunes. Portable keyboard available.

THE NIGOSIAN BAND
(313) 278-7646
Four-piece ensemble includes vocalists plus clarinet, oud, dumbeg and guitar.

ARA TOPOUZIAN ENSEMBLE & PRODUCTIONS
American Recording Productions
(248) 851-4149 or 851-9225
http://arp.ic.net
Five-piece ensemble with clarinet, oud, kanun (Middle Eastern zither), dumbeg and guitar, plus vocalists. Also producer and distributor of Armenian and Middle Eastern music recordings and free music catalogs.

EVENTS

OCTOBER
ST. JOHN'S ARMENIAN BAZAAR
Takes place in Southfield the second weekend in October. Taste Armenian delicacies, purchase foods and products to take home, and learn Armenian line dances.
Call (248) 569-3405.

NOVEMBER
ST. SARKIS ARMENIAN BAZAAR
Takes place in Dearborn the first weekend in November. Music, dance and booths featuring foods, crafts and other products.
Call (313) 336-6200.

EVENT SCHEDULE

The Armenian community stays active with dances, dinners, musical concerts and public lectures throughout the year.
Call any one of the churches listed to learn of upcoming events.

ART & ARCHITECTURE

BELIAN ART CENTER
5980 Rochester Rd., Troy
(SE corner at Square Lake Rd.)
(248) 828-1001
Mon-Sat noon-6pm. Armenian-owned gallery features paintings, sculpture, drawings, pottery and glass by local, national and international artists (Armenian and non-Armenian). Also sponsors concert series of chamber music and watercolor classes.

GOMIDAS STATUE
On Jefferson Avenue (adjacent to Hart Plaza) in Detroit, this statue of Gomidas (or *Komitas*, born *Sogomon Soghomonian,* 1869-1935), the Father of Armenian Music, is dedicated to the remembrance of the 1915-1918 genocide of 1.5 million Armenians by the Turks.

ZUBEL KACHADOURIAN, ARTIST
Works by this renowned painter and former educator include the Madonna and Child adorning the altar at St. John's Armenian Church in Southfield. Other works are on display at the Detroit Institute of Arts. Call (313) 961-9821 for a personal appointment.

KEGHAM TAZIAN, ARTIST
Works by this sculptor, painter and multimedia artist include bronze doors of St. Sarkis Armenian Church in Dearborn, 125th anniversary commemorative sculpture in front of Farmington City Hall, sculpture in front of the TRW headquarters in Sterling Heights, and the Forest Lake Country Club lobby sculpture. Tazian's works range from traditional to abstract and include raku, carvings and bronze pieces, as well as paintings in acrylic, oil and watercolor. He teaches art at Oakland Community College. Call (248) 471-7796 to arrange a studio visit.

CHURCH ARCHITECTURE
St. John's in Southfield and St. Sarkis in Dearborn are representative of the unique style of traditional Armenian church architecture. St. John's Church, a replica of the main church in Etchmiadzin (Armenia), has domes covered with genuine gold leaf. A variety of Armenian artwork and ornamentation also can be viewed at the churches.

SUREN PILAFIAN ARCHITECTURE
Works of the Armenian architect can be found at Wayne State University in Detroit. He designed the Kresge Library, which is distinguished by its horizontal lines and cantilevered upper stories. In 1942, he won a competition for his campus design plan. He is also the architect of St. John's Armenian Church in Southfield.

EXHIBITS

ALEX AND MARIE MANOOGIAN MUSEUM OF ARMENIAN ARTIFACTS
22001 Northwestern Hwy., Southfield
(248) 569-3405
Tue-Fri 1-5pm, Sat-Sun 1-4pm. Armenian historical museum next to St. John's Armenian Church offers artifacts from 7th century B.C. to the early 20th century.

ARMENIAN HERITAGE ROOM
Alex Manoogian Hall, Room 226
Wayne State University
(at Lodge Service Dr. N)
906 W. Warren, Detroit
(313) 577-2246
Auditorium, decorated to reflect Armenian culture, includes Armenian woodcarvings, murals and portraits. The building is named after Alex Manoogian, the late benefactor of Wayne State University and other educational and cultural institutions worldwide.

EDUCATION

ARMENIAN CULTURE CLASSES
Language instruction, cooking classes and lectures about Armenian topics take place regularly at St. John's and St. Sarkis. Contact the churches for information.

AGBU ALEX AND MARIE MANOOGIAN SCHOOL
22001 Northwestern Hwy., Southfield
(248) 569-2988
The Armenian General Benevolent Union (AGBU) school is a unique chartered school serving preschool through high school. Armenian language and culture programs are offered on top of the basic core curriculum.

ARMENIAN RESEARCH CENTER
University of Michigan - Dearborn
4901 Evergreen Rd., Dearborn
(313) 593-5198 or 593-5000
Director: Dennis Patazian
Research activities cover Armenian history, literature, art and architecture, as well as history, politics and economics of the surrounding geographical area.

ARMENIAN STUDIES AT UNIVERSITY OF MICHIGAN IN ANN ARBOR
(734) 764-5375
Director: Kevork Bardakjian
Two chairs established by Alex Manoogian are in Armenian history and Armenian language and literature.

ARMENIAN STUDIES WAYNE STATE UNIVERSITY
(313) 577-6237
Director: Dickran Toumajan
Courses in the Department of German and Slavic Studies include Armenian language, 19th/20th Century Armenian Culture, the Changing Face of Europe, and The Immigrant Experience.

Traditional Armenian costume, from 19th century source

BOOKSTORES

ST. JOHN'S BOOKSTORE
22001 Northwestern Hwy., Southfield
(248) 569-3405
Tue-Sun 1-4pm. Sells books, tapes and compact discs. Also extensive library with books, publications, maps and other materials on Armenian culture, history, language, literature, religion and more.

ST. SARKIS BOOKSTORE
19300 Ford Rd., Dearborn
(313) 336-6200
Mon-Fri 9am-4pm, Sun 11am-12:30 pm. Books, tapes, compact discs and other items on all aspects of Armenian culture, history, language, literature, religion and music.

ORGANIZATIONS

ARMENIAN AMERICAN BUSINESS COUNCIL
(248) 646-7847
Organization endeavors to assist Armenians in business through lectures, meetings, networking opportunities, special events, and national and international efforts and communications.

ARMENIAN GENERAL BENEVOLENT UNION (AGBU)
(248) 569-2988
Largest Armenian humanitarian organization in the world; deals with educational and cultural matters.

ARMENIAN RELIEF SOCIETY
(313) 336-6840
Humanitarian organization involved in community education and social welfare programs.

Armenian people are often likened to the Phoenix because they have overcome great tragedy, rebuilding and renewing, while preserving spirit, heritage, intellect and faith.

MEDIA

The following national Armenian American newspapers provide local, national and international news on all aspects of Armenian culture, life, religion and the arts.

PRINT
Local publications include *The Torchbearer*, published by St. John's Armenian Church and *The Illuminator*, published by St. Sarkis Armenian Church.

THE ARMENIAN WEEKLY
80 Bigelow Ave., Watertown, MA 02172
(617) 926-3974

THE ARMENIAN REPORTER
67-07 Utopia Pkwy., Flushing Meadows, NY 11365
(718) 380-1200

THE ARMENIAN MIRROR-SPECTATOR
755 Mt. Auburn St., Watertown, MA 02172
(617) 924-4420

RADIO
WNZK AM 690 DAYS/680 NIGHTS
(248) 557-3500
"Armenian Radio Hour" hosted by Nick Serkaian Sunday 10-11am.

WDTR 90.9 FM
"Heritage of Armenian Culture" Saturday 6-7pm.

WEB SITES
ARMENIA SITES ON THE WEB
www.arminco.com/armenia/web/armweb.html

ARMENIAN ARTS AND CULTURE
www.soros.org/armenia/armearts.html

ARMENIAN RESEARCH CENTER
www.umd.umich.edu/dept/armenian

MUSIC AND DANCES
wotan.wiwi.huberlin.de/~houssik/window/music.html

GENEALOGY FOR ARMENIANS
www.itsnet.com/home/gfa/

GLOBAL JOURNEYS
IN METRO DETROIT

AFRICA AND THE MIDDLE EAST

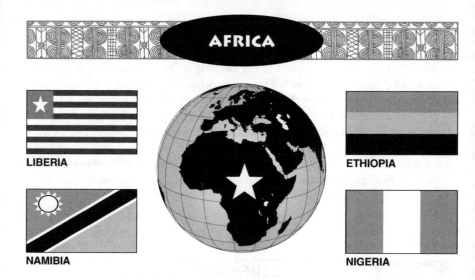

AFRICA

LIBERIA

ETHIOPIA

NAMIBIA

NIGERIA

Africa is the world's second largest continent. With 11.7 million square miles, it covers 20 percent of the Earth. Africa's west coast borders the Atlantic Ocean, its east coast is along the Indian Ocean and its northern edge forms the southern beaches of the Mediterranean Sea. At its northeast corner, it is connected to Asia by a narrow isthmus.

The climate and vegetation vary vastly. At the equator there is year-round rainfall. The open grassland "savanna" areas of Africa's eastern and southern regions contain large numbers of wild animals. Continuing farther from the equator, the Sahara, the Namib and Kalahari deserts are characteristically hot and dry. In Africa's most northern and southern areas, the climate is mild with only winter rainfall.

Africa has about 10 percent of the world's population. Its peoples are divided into more than 50 nations and nearly 3,000 ethnic groups, speaking hundreds of languages. Urban languages include Swahili, Hausa, Wolof and Zulu.

The cultures of Africa also are diverse. North of the Sahara, many of the people have a mixture of Arab and African ancestors and strong cultural ties to the Arabic Middle East.

*South of the Sahara, some countries have populations descended from white settlers who arrived 200 years ago from the Netherlands, Great Britain, Germany and Portugal. The colonial governments they established began to fall in the 1920s, often after bitter wars with the majority black population. The last colony, **Namibia,** gained its independence in 1988.*

*After years of apartheid, especially in South Africa, most African nations now have laws banning racial injustice. Two countries, both sub-Saharan, were never colonies: **Liberia,** founded in the 18th century as a home in West Africa for freed American slaves; and the ancient East African country of **Ethiopia** (formerly Abyssinia).*

AFRICANS IN DETROIT

In the 1990 U.S. Census, 3,837 Detroit residents listed their ancestry as sub-Saharan. They are from the region that is the ancestral home of the majority of African Americans. Many Africans are drawn to Detroit by a sense of adventure and the thrill and challenge of learning a new culture.

The federal immigration count shows **Nigeria** as one of the leading countries of birth, but it is estimated that African immigrants in the Detroit area represent nearly 250 ethnic groups. With freedom of choice highly valued, there is no African cluster in a particular Detroit neighborhood, school or church. Primarily Christian or Muslim, Africans worship in many congregations throughout the area. *(See also "African American Heritage.")*

TOUR — SERENGETI SUNSET

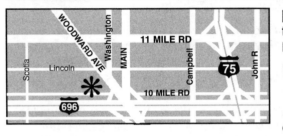

[E-F/3-4] From mid-June through late August the **Detroit Zoological Park** *(Royal Oak, intersection of W. 10 Mile Road and Woodward Avenue; I-696 Exit 16)* is open until 8 p.m. on Wednesdays.

Pack a picnic dinner or snacks and rendezvous at the zoo on a Wednesday at about 5 p.m. You'll be able to view the animals when they are more active, during the sunset hours. (Any day but Wednesday, the hours are 10 a.m.-5 p.m.; 10 a.m.-4 p.m. in winter.)

Enter at the main gate and board the free train for a trip to the **African Station** *(at the opposite end of the park).* Step off the train and take a leisurely stroll back to the main entrance. (Be sure to allow time to browse for interesting African-related objects at the **gift shop** before it closes.)

The paths to exhibits are well-marked, directing you to the African lions, giraffes, hippos, zebras and the **Chimps of Harambee,** a four-acre habitat that's the finest and largest of its kind in the world.

The **art gallery** features multicultural works celebrating and interpreting man's relationship with animals and the natural world. The art ranges from a 4,000-year-old bronze Persian fallow deer to hand-carved African masks and Asian tapestries.

The zoo is open year-round with ongoing special events and programs. Visitors easily can spend an entire day there and still not see everything.

[E-F/3-5] Begin the morning with one of Detroit's little-known treasures: the **African Heritage Cultural Center** *(21511 W. McNichols at Grand River)* in northwest Detroit. *Get there via the Jeffries Freeway (I-96) and exiting at Grand River, then heading north; or via the Southfield Freeway (M-39) or the Lodge (U.S. 10) and exiting at McNichols, then heading west.* Allow about one hour for a guided tour (reservations suggested).

Next, go downtown to enjoy an Ethiopian meal at the **Blue Nile** in Greektown and shop at African specialty shops. *From the African Heritage Center, go east on McNichols to the Lodge. Turn right onto the south-bound Lodge. Continue to Joe Louis Arena Parking Deck Exit. Take the People Mover (fare is 50 cents) to the Greektown station.* The Blue Nile is in the **Trapper's Alley** complex, with an entrance on Monroe.

After experiencing tastes of East Central Africa, visit **Djenne Beads and Art** in Trapper's Alley for *Kente* and mud cloth, baskets and beads. *Then take the People Mover to the Grand Circus Park station. Exit the David Whitney Building to head south on Washington Boulevard* to **Dabl's Perette's Gallery** in the Book Building to see carvings, textiles and beads. End your journey by returning to the People Mover station and completing the circuit back to the Joe Louis Arena Parking Deck.

If time permits, *head up Woodward Avenue to the Cultural Center museums. (See "Multicultural Detroit" chapter for detailed map of Cultural Center area.)* Visit the **African Galleries** at the **Detroit Institute of Arts (DIA)** *at 5200 Woodward Avenue (north wing, main level),* which include masks, carvings, sculptures, jewelry in gold and ivory, beadwork, veccolo and musical instruments. (At the front desk, ask for a map to the collection of African art.) Also take a look in the **DIA Gift Shop**, where you'll find a number of African-related pieces, including jewelry and books.

On a weekday, *exit from the DIA's Woodward door, turn right (north), and right again on Kirby* and then visit the **International Institute's Hall of Nations** and **gift shop** *(111 E. Kirby).*

Or, stop in at the **Charles H. Wright Museum of African American History (MAAH)** *at 315 Warren. Exit the DIA's Farnsworth door and go 1-1/2 blocks east.* African art abounds at the **MAAH Gift Shop**, with many hand-crafted items from Ghana. *(See "Museum Tour" in African American Heritage Chapter.)*

AFRICAN COOKING

I n the Detroit area, African cooking is most readily appreciated through its influence in African American and Caribbean fare (see corresponding chapters). The only strictly African restaurants are those that specialize in Ethiopian cuisine.

Ethiopian food is based on dishes called *we't* (meat, chicken or vegetables cooked in a hot pepper sauce) served with or on *injera* (a flat, spongy bread). Dishes include *shivro* and *misir* (chick-peas and lentils) and *tibs* (crispy fried steak). There is a wide choice of fish, including sole, Red Sea snapper, lake fish, trout and prawn. Traditional restaurants in larger cities serve food in a grand manner around a brightly colored basket-weave table called a *masob*. Before beginning the meal, guests are given soap, water and clean towels. This is done because the right hand is used to break off pieces of *injera*, which is spread out on top of the table in order to scoop up the we't. Cutlery is not used.

Beverages include *Talla*, a lager beer, and *tej*, honey wine. Ethiopian cuisine uses no sugar (traditionally, even coffee is salted, not sweetened). Among African coffees, **Kenya AA** is generally considered the finest. Grown at high altitudes under ideal conditions, it is known for its strong flavor, excellent aroma and all-around balance.

RESTAURANTS

THE AFRICAN CARIBBEAN RESTAURANT
18456 Grand River, Detroit
(W of Southfield)
(313) 270-3060
Tue-Sat 11:30am-10:30pm, Mon 11:30am-9pm. Choices span West Africa and the West Indies, balanced by the two owners (one from Nigeria, the other from Trinidad). African specialties include tomato-based jollof rice and spicy eguisi soup (fish, beef and ground melon seeds) with fu fu (dumplings).

THE BLUE NILE
508 Monroe, Detroit
(at Beaubien in Greektown)
(313) 964-6699
and
221 E. Washington, Ann Arbor
(at Fifth St.)
(734) 998-4746
Metro Detroit's best-known place for African food. Learn the Ethiopian tradition of eating food communally and without cutlery. Diners use flat bread to scoop up meat or vegetarian dishes, which can be ordered bland to spicy. Enhancing the charm is the authentic decor. Guests dine at low, wooden-basket tables while sitting on carved wood chairs.

CLUB ABYSSINIA RESTAURANT AND BAR
6452 E. Jefferson, Detroit
(313) 259-1384
Mon-Fri 11am-11pm, Sat 2-11pm, Sun 4-9pm. Ethiopian food such as beef, lentils and cabbage. Entertainment once a month.

DEARING LOUNGE & BANQUET CENTER
11234 E. McNichols, Detroit
(313) 3712034
Daily 2pm-2am. Upscale restaurant features African, Barbeque and Cajun fare.

MARATHON ETHIOPIAN RESTAURANT
60 University Ave. W
Windsor, Ontario
(519) 253-2215
Tue-Fri 11am-11pm, Sat-Sun 1pm-midnight. Authentic Ethiopian cuisine featuring meat and vegetarian dishes.

THE PANDA DELI & RESTAURANT
7720 W. McNichols, Detroit
(313) 863-8405
Tue-Sat noon-7pm, Sun noon-5pm. All food is prepared only with natural ingredients. Vegetarian entrées span West African, Oriental, Italian and American cuisine. *(Located between Woodingham and Santa Barbara streets.)*

QUEEN OF SHEBA
1295 Wyandotte St. W.
Windsor, Ontario
(519) 254-4851
Tue-Sun 11am-10pm. Closed Mon. Ethiopian cuisine features spongy injera bread, spicy cabbage, red lentils, beef and lamb stew.

GALLERIES AND SHOPS

(See also "African American Heritage" and "Caribbean.")

DOWNTOWN DETROIT
DABL'S PERETTE'S AFRICAN GALLERY
1257 Washington Blvd., Detroit
(Book Bldg.)
(313) 964-4247
Mon-Sat noon-7pm, Sun 1-5pm. Beads, textiles, carvings and clothes. Exhibits and presentations available for schools and groups.

DJENNE BEADS AND ART, AFRICAN IMPORTS
508 Monroe, Detroit
(Trapper's Alley, Greektown)
(313) 965-6620
Mon-Thu 11am-9pm, Fri-Sat 11am-10pm. Art, masks, baskets, trade beads, Yuroba beadwork, and Kuba, Kente and mud cloth.

NEW CENTER AREA
NATIONAL CONFERENCE OF ARTISTS GALLERY
3011 W. Grand Blvd., Detroit
(Fisher Bldg.)
(313) 875-0923
Mon-Fri 11am-5pm, Sat 11am-4pm. Exhibits the work of local, national and international artists of African descent. Gift shop offers collectibles for every taste.

CULTURAL CENTER AREA
DETROIT INSTITUTE OF ARTS GIFT SHOP
5200 Woodward, Detroit; (313) 833-7900
Wed-Fri 11am-4pm, Sat-Sun 11am-5pm. African jewelry, reproductions, gifts, cards and books.

INTERNATIONAL INSTITUTE GIFT SHOP
111 E. Kirby, Detroit; (313) 871-8600
Mon-Fri 8:30am-5pm. Gift shop includes objects imported from Africa.

MUSEUM OF AFRICAN AMERICAN HISTORY GIFT SHOP
315 E. Warren, Detroit; (313) 494-5800

Bariba engraved calabash design.

Tue-Sun 9:30-am-5pm.
Carved boxes, dolls, frames, king's staffs, decorative pins, fabric, baskets, masks, statues, books, embroidered dresses, Kente cloth purses, shoes and jewelry from Africa.

NORTHWEST DETROIT
AFRIKA HOUSE
19445 Livernois, Detroit; (313) 341-7423
Tue-Sat 10am-6pm. African apparel for children and adults, art, jewelry and gifts.

K&K AFRICAN MARKET
19490 Livernois, Detroit; (313) 862-8660
Mon-Sat 10am-7pm, Sun 11am-5pm. Foods, fabrics, cosmetics, hard-to-find items from Africa, the Caribbean and Europe.

SHRINE OF THE BLACK MADONNA CULTURAL CENTER AND BOOKSTORE
13535 Livernois, Detroit; (313) 491-0777
Tue-Thu 11am-6pm, Fri-Sat 11am-7pm. One of Detroit's best resources for African and diaspora art, artifacts, fabrics, leather goods and rare cultural items.

STRICTLY ROOTS RECORDS, VIDEOS AND BOOKS
15734 W. Seven Mile, Detroit
(3 blocks W of Greenfield)
(313) 836-8686
Mon-Wed noon-7:30pm, Thu-Sat 11am-8:30pm. African and Caribbean music, videos and literature.

NORTH SUBURBS
CULTURAL EXPRESSIONS
1032 N. Crooks, Suite C., Clawson
(248) 288-9275
By appointment only. Wholesale/retail African textiles, masks and artifacts.

DONALD MORRIS GALLERY
Huntington Woods, (248) 584-3445
By appointment only. Museum-quality tribal art.

DETROIT INSTITUTE OF ARTS
SATELLITE GIFT SHOPS
Somerset Collection, Troy
(248) 649-2222
Mon-Fri 10am-9pm, Sat 10am-7pm, Sun noon-6pm.
and
Twelve Oaks Mall, Novi
(248) 380-8050
Mon-Sat 10am-9pm, Sun 11am-6pm.
Publications, jewelry and gift items related to the museum collection. A variety of African art, books, calendars and stationery.

ANDERSON GALLERY
7 N. Saginaw, Pontiac
(Oakland Art Bldg., first floor)
(248) 335-4611
Tue-Fri 11am-4pm, Sat 11am-6pm.
Specializes in historic textiles and contemporary fiber arts. Hosts exhibits and presentations on a variety of African arts.

GALLERY SHAANTIA
361 E. Maple, Birmingham
(248) 647-9202
Mon-Wed and Fri 10:30am-5pm, Thu 10:30am-8pm, Sat 10:30am-6pm. Furniture, gifts, accessories and tribal art.

G.R. N'NAMDI GALLERY
161 Townsend, Birmingham
(248) 642-2700

TEXTILES

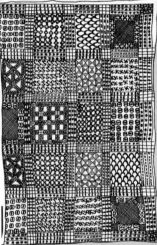

KENTE CLOTH was created by the **Ashanti** people of **Ghana, West Africa,** and is easily identified by its vibrant colors and unique patterns. Kente cloth weaving dates back to the 12th century and was woven, by men only, exclusively for the Ashanti kings and queens.

Modern Kente cloth is made from cotton, silk and rayon fibers, handwoven in four-inch strips and sewn together. The traditional colors are red, gold, blue and occasionally green. Designs are also created in black and white. Each cloth is typically 70 inches long and is worn today as a prized garment.

MUD CLOTH, or *Bogolán Fini,* is an ancient art form of the **Bamana tribe** of western **Mali.** Traditionally worn as wrap-around clothing, each piece of mud cloth is unique and embodies the pride and spirit of the village women. The striking and predominantly black-on-white designs are inspired by everyday objects such as tools, flowers, animals, songs, proverbs and even historical events. One piece, through a laborious and painstaking process, often takes two or more weeks to complete. Locally grown cotton is spun and woven into long, thin strips by the men, then sewn and painted several times by the women using iron-rich mud as the primary pigment.

Genuine handmade Kente and mud cloth is expensive and available at galleries and specialty shops listed in this chapter. Imitation Kente and mud cloth, as well as other African prints, can be purchased at many fabric stores.

Tue-Sat 11am-5:30pm. Specializes in African and African American fine arts.

MOORE AFRICAN GALLERY
304 Hamilton Row, Birmingham
(248) 647-4662
Mon-Sat 10am-6pm, Sun by appointment. Sculptures, paintings and artifacts from Zimbabwe, Malawi, South Africa, Zambia and Mozambique.

NILE GALLERY
3475 Robina, Berkley; (248) 548-8881
Tue-Sat 10am-6pm. Custom-designed clothes in Kente and mud cloth, jewelry, art, beads and antiques from Africa. Classes offered in beadmaking and fabric dying.

ANN ARBOR
KWANZAA HOUSE GALLERY
122 S. Main St., Ann Arbor
(2nd floor); (734) 213-1900
Fri-Sat noon-7pm and by appointment. Original paintings, prints, masks, sculpture, Kente and Kuba weavings, mud paintings and cloth.

DEALERS/CONSULTANTS

EKUA'S FASHIONS
(248) 552-1036
Fabrics imported from West Africa for clothing, scarves and hats designed and manufactured by Evelyn Eames. Designs are mostly African with a western flair.

ELEGANT AFFAIRS BY GRAY
(313) 343-0097
Consultants for African-themed weddings and other events. Services include decorations, gift baskets, hand-crafted accessories.

BE2 DESIGN: AN AFRICAN SHOP
(248) 737-8077
Authentic African imports are sold retail and wholesale, by appointment. Bridal apparel and designs for authentic wedding or naming-ceremony. Owner Beauty Onomake also offers African history lectures for school groups, performing arts, West African cooking classes, catering.

NA NA'S
(313) 881-1155
African artifacts and fashions for men, women and children.

SHADES OF YESTERDAY
(313) 883-2852
By appointment only. African-influenced jewelry, dolls, art and artifacts.

CULTURAL EXHIBITS

AFRICAN HERITAGE CULTURAL CENTER
21511 W. McNichols, Detroit
(at Grand River)
(313) 494-7452
Mon-Fri 10am-4pm. Displays and videos recount African history from $3\frac{1}{2}$ million years ago to 1600, showcasing the accomplishments of Africans before slavery. Allow about an hour for a guided tour; reservations are required for groups and suggested for individuals. Operated by the Detroit Public Schools. Admission is free but donations are welcome.

DETROIT INSTITUTE OF ARTS
5200 Woodward, Detroit
(north wing, main level)
(313) 833-7900
Wed-Fri 11am-4pm, Sat-Sun 11am-5pm. Collection of African art, including masks, carvings, sculpture, jewelry in gold and ivory, beadwork, vessels, and musical instruments. Personalized tours for groups of 10 or more can be arranged through Hospitality DIA at (248) 642-3881. During February, 30-minute guided tours of the African galleries take place each weekend. Authentic African cuisine also rotates through the Black History Month menu in Kresge Court Cafe. Other exhibits and activities are hosted by Friends of African and African American Art.

CHARLES H. WRIGHT MUSEUM OF AFRICAN AMERICAN HISTORY
315 E. Warren, Detroit; (313) 494-5800
Tue-Sun 9:30am-5pm. Tribal masks above entrances define African theme of building's design. Flags of African diaspora and genealogy theme in Rotunda. Core exhibit station devoted to "African Memory." Gift shop with African art. *(See tour in "African American" chapter.)*

DETROIT CHILDREN'S MUSEUM
67 E. Kirby (Cultural Center), Detroit
(313) 494-1210
The Museum routinely focuses on cultural aspects of Africa. Its exhibit on South Africa includes masks, textiles, baskets, carvings and instruments. School groups can enjoy an imaginary journey to Africa or take classes on African heritage and lifestyles.

DETROIT ZOOLOGICAL PARK
(10 Mile and Woodward) Royal Oak
(248) 398-0900
Daily 10am-4pm November-March, 10am-5pm April-October; Sun and holidays 10am-6pm mid-May through Labor Day. Wed 10am-8pm mid-June through August. Many examples of African wildlife and even art in natural settings. Programs for preserving endangered species. *(See "Serengeti Sunset" tour.)*

ENTERTAINMENT

MAJESTIC BALLROOM
4120 Woodward Ave., Detroit
(313) 833-9700
African Funk is part of the regular live performance roster at this popular location.

SERENGETI BALLROOM
2957 Woodward Ave., Detroit
(313) 832-3010
African sounds often are heard here in live performance. Most show times are 9pm, days vary by event.

SIERRA AFRIQUE
19325 Plymouth Rd., Detroit
(313) 838-3833
In addition to hosting dances and special events, banquet hall caters African food.

TROPICAL HUT
14952 Livernois (3 blks S of Fenkell)
Detroit; (313) 861-5340
Mon-Tue 3-9pm, Wed-Sun 5pm-2am. Dance club with schedule of live performances.

PERFORMERS AND CLASSES

THE ART OF MOTION DANCE THEATRE
111 E. Kirby, Detroit; (313) 834-9501
Offers classes in West Africa's Congolese dance for adults and youth at International Institute. Director Karen Prall presents annual June recital at the International Institute. During open house in June, September and December, the organization sells African attire, crafts and foods.

BLACK FOLK ARTS
425 W. Margaret, Detroit
(313) 865-4546
West African dance is the organization's specialty. In addition to performances, Artistic Director Safiya Tsekani offers lectures and classes.

CENTER FOR CREATIVE STUDIES INSTITUTE OF MUSIC AND DANCE
200 E. Kirby, Detroit
(313) 872-3118, ext. 610
Offers World Traditions program for African and East Indian dance. Modern Dance program features Katherine Dunham technique of combining folk styles of Africa, the Australian bush, Cuba, Haiti and Brazil. Classes take place in Detroit's University Cultural Center and Jewish Community Center in West Bloomfield.

INTERNATIONAL AFRICAN CULTURAL ARTS EXCHANGE CENTER
Classes take place at Adams-Butzel Recreation Center (313-935-3119), Joseph Walker Williams Center (313-224-6582) and Wayne County Community College (313-496-2777). Director Ali Abdullah performed internationally with the Senegalese Theatre and became its choreographer. His center offers dance classes at the locations listed above. Lectures, demonstrations are also offered.

The Bayei of Botswana and the Zulu of South Africa weave grass baskets so tightly they can be used for storing liquids such as water and beer.

PEMAJJU SCHOOL OF DANCE
2751 E. Jefferson, Ste. 450, Detroit
(313) 396-5666
Penny Godboldo, director of the Writhm Dance Company of Detroit, offers classes to children, adult novices and professionals in dances of West Africa's Ghana and Benin. Drum classes in West African rhythm also are offered.

NGOMA ZA AMEN-RA
2690 Burlingame, Detroit
(313) 869-2007
New African Cultural Theatre of Detroit performs African drumming and dance.

STORIES AND MUSIC OF AFRICA
(248) 262-6813
Naim Abdul Rauf tailors presentations to the audience, ranging from a storyteller with various African instruments to traditional African dance ensembles. Lecture series highlights African history, social relationships, ethics and values. Hands-on workshops also available.

ANNUAL EVENTS

JUNE
BAL AFRICAIN
Detroit Institute of Arts
5200 Woodward, Detroit
The event is the annual fund-raiser gala of the Friends of African and African American art. Call (313) 833-0247 for details.

AUGUST
AFRICAN WORLD FESTIVAL
Hart Plaza, Detroit
This highlight of the summer Ethnic Festivals celebrates cultures of all people of African descent. Features include traditional dance ensembles, other entertainment, African films, educational lectures, children's activities, art and food. For details, call the event sponsor: Museum of African American History, (313) 494-5800.

AFRICAN WORLD EXPO
Cobo Center, Detroit
(313) 868-4723
More than 150 businesses from Africa are represented at annual event promoting trade between African and American businesses.

AFRICAN MUSIC

Carved wooden panel on Djokwe "bush piano," Congo-Kinshasa.

African rhythms have had major influence on Western popular music styles such as jazz, blues, rock, Caribbean and Latin. On the continent of Africa, one of the most famous types of African popular music also is possibly one of its oldest: **highlife**, a sort of African swing, classically danced in the 1920s (at its peak of popularity) in ball gowns and tuxedos with tails. Its roots are tribal rhythms combined with the brass bands of the Ghanaian soldiers.

Kwela started in the 1940s as street-corner music played by youths with pennywhistles, guitars and voice. *M'bube* is a cappella chorus singing, made popular worldwide by groups such as Ladysmith Black Mambazo. *Rai* is urban music that evolved from regional folk music and bedouin lyric poetry.

(See also "African American Heritage," "Caribbean" and "Latin American.")

OCTOBER
ANCESTORS DAY
Ancestors Day is tied to the African Yam Harvest Festivals, in which ancestor commemorations honor the living, the deceased and those yet to be born. Celebrations include dancing, feasting and the pouring of libations. Call the Museum of African American History, (313) 494-5800, for local event information.

ZOORAMA SAFARI AT BELLE ISLE ZOO
Tours, games, crafts, puppet show, storytelling and treat stations. For dates and more information, call (313) 852-4083.

AFRICAN ART

So many different peoples and cultures have inhabited the vast continent of Africa, that creative endeavors have been numerous and diverse. The art of the sophisticated cities is far different from that of the rural areas. One common thread, as with many other cultures, is that traditional African artwork is linked with religion, and therefore meant for ceremonial or ritual use, paying homage to deities or rulers.

The primitive strength of its motifs has held a fascination for contemporary artists and designers throughout the world and has exercised considerable influence on the development of American and European modern art movements.

MEDIA

Newspapers and magazines published in Africa are occasionally available in campus bookstores at Wayne State University in Detroit, the University of Michigan in Ann Arbor and other colleges.

DETROIT PUBLIC LIBRARY
Downtown Library
121 Gratiot (at Farmer), Detroit
(313) 224-0580
Books in French and English by African authors, and dictionaries in Zulu, Swahili, Somali and Yoruba are available in the International Language Collection. Recent additions to the collection include *Afrique Magazine* in French.

RADIO
WDET 101.9 FM
(313) 577-4146
George Collinet hosts "AfroPop" Sun 6-7pm. Michael Julien hosts "World Music" Sat 10pm-2am. Both feature African music.

TELEVISION
WTVS CHANNEL 56
"The Americas' Family Kitchen," the influence of African Cooking in the New World, with Vertamae Grosvenor, storyteller, poet and culinary anthropologist. Check local TV listings for times.

WEB SITES
AFRICA ONLINE
info@africaonline.com
Home pages for various African countries, interest groups and individuals, on-line reference materials, music, art and cultural exchanges, travel information and a kids' educational section.

AFRICA-AMERICAN MOSAIC
lcweb.loc.gov/exhibits/africa
.american/intro.html
Library of Congress reviews 500 years of black history, culture and contributions.

BLACK/AFRICAN RELATED RESOURCES
wwwafrican/upenn.edu/African.studies/AS

AFRICAN INTERNET RESOURCE PAGE
www.newtown.demon.co.uk:80/africa.html

ARAB WORLD

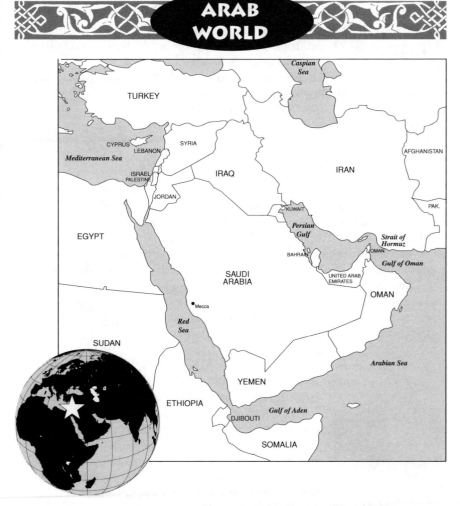

*The Arab World consists of nine countries in North Africa and 12 in West Asia. Historically, **Arab** refers to the Arabic-speaking tribes of the Fertile Crescent and Arabian Peninsula, inhabiting the region defined by the Mediterranean Sea, Red Sea, Arabian Sea and Persian Gulf. However, not all countries in the Middle East are Arab. The term **Arab** is more of a cultural, linguistic and political designation than a geographic reference.*

In North Africa, the following countries belong to the League of Arab States: Morocco*, Algeria, Tunisia, Libya, Egypt*, Sudan, Djibouti, Mauritania and Somalia.

Arab countries in West Asia or the Middle East are Yemen**, Oman, Saudi Arabia, United Arab Emirates, Bahrain, Qatar, Kuwait, Iraq**, Syria*, Lebanon**, Jordan* and Palestine**.

---

* Representation in Detroit Arab community.

** Largest Arab immigrant groups in metro Detroit.

COMING TO AMERICA

For nearly a century now, the Detroit area has been home to diverse people of the 21 countries that make up the Arab World. While immigration from the Arab World began with a small number of people from the area now known as Lebanon and Syria, they soon were followed by Iraqi-Chaldeans, Palestinians, Yemenis, Jordanians and Egyptians. In fact, it was not long before pretty much all the countries and most of the people from Asia Minor, North Africa and the Gulf area were represented.

LEBANON

Initially, the people of this region used New York as a point of entry. The opening of Ford Motor Company's Model T plant in Highland Park played a pivotal role in the establishment of Detroit's Arab community. By the early 1900s, Highland Park had a number of Arab grocery stores, coffeehouses and other businesses within walking distance of the plant. At this time, the community was mainly Christian in faith, but many Muslim immigrants began to arrive. This trend continued and has resulted in an Arab community that is roughly half Muslim and half Christian.

IRAQ

Another important event that affected the geographic makeup of Detroit's Arab community was the opening of the Ford Rouge plant just

PALESTINE

prior to World War I. By the 1940s, the Rouge had become the largest industrial complex in the world, employing more than 90,000 workers. A large number of Muslims from Lebanon and other areas of the Arab World began to settle in Dearborn's South End next to the Rouge plant. This worker reserve was written up by "Ripley's Believe It or Not" as an area in which 52 languages were spoken. Today, southeast Dearborn is 90 percent Arab American.

During the years that followed, chain migration, war and economic disaster in the Middle East resulted in a huge influx of people from the Arab World.

YEMEN

The Lebanese Civil War and the Israeli incursion into Lebanon have been responsible for the arrival of tens of thousands of people from **Lebanon.** An attempt to repress the culture and human rights of the **Chaldean** minority in Iraq, and the most recent Gulf War, caused many to come to the United States from **Iraq.** The Palestinian conflict has become a daily news story, with many coming to the states to seek a better life. Additionally, **Yemeni** workers have come for economic reasons, hoping to find work to support their families here and abroad.

DETROIT'S ARAB COMMUNITY

Since the beginning of the 20th century, metro Detroit has attracted a steady stream of Arab immigrants who, like their European counterparts, sought the refuge and promise of America. Today the Arab-American community numbers more than a quarter of a million people and reflects the religious and ethnic diversity of the Arab World. The major nationalities represented in the Detroit area are Lebanese, Syrian, Jordanian, Palestinian, Iraqi-Chaldean, Egyptian and Yemeni.

Like most immigrant groups, they settled in enclaves reflecting the common bonds of the extended family, nationality, and/or religious persuasion. The ethnic community concept persisted throughout the 20th century, as successive generations migrated out into the expanding metropolitan area.

Lebanese and **Syrian** Christians (Antiochian and/or Greek Orthodox, Melkite, Maronite and/or Roman Catholic) and Muslims (Sunni and Shi'a) represent over 55% of metro Detroit's Arab-American community. Lebanese and Syrian Christians established roots on Detroit's east side and eventually expanded in a northeast path, into Eastpointe, the Grosse Pointes, St. Clair Shores, Harper Woods, Roseville, Sterling Heights, Troy and Rochester Hills. Lebanese and Syrian Muslim residential patterns have concentrated in the Dearborn area, particularly in the city's South End, northeast Dearborn, Dearborn Heights and the western suburbs.

Palestinians and **Jordanians** comprise over 20% of metro Detroit's Arab World community. This group has settled along the ethno-religious, east-west corridors of Detroit and its suburbs, established by the Lebanese and Syrian communities.

The **Iraqi-Chaldeans** are a unique cultural minority with historical ties to ancient Mesopotamia and linguistic links to Aramaic, the language spoken at the time of Jesus Christ. *(See Chaldean Heritage chapter.)* Detroit's Seven Mile Road-Woodward area, with its row of small shops and restaurants, sports bilingual signs and names reminiscent of ancient history, earning its well-deserved designation as Detroit's "Little Baghdad."

Metro Detroit's **Yemeni** community escalated during the latter half of the 20th century, with its members resettling in both Dearborn and Hamtramck. Yemeni-American students represent over 70% of the enrollment in the school district of the City of Hamtramck, a city of two square miles located in the heart of the city of Detroit. In addition to being the homebase of eastern European-Americans, Hamtramck has become an Arab community.

Egyptians, **North** and **West Africans** and immigrants from the **Arab Gulf States** constitute the group of "newer arrivals," enriching the Detroit metro community with their distinctive cultural contributions.

Whatever the country of origin, or the religious affiliation, Arab-American identity is built on the bonds of a shared language and culture and a commitment to fulfill the dream of America.

PAN-ARAB UNITY

Although these groups are different religiously, and to some extent ethnically, they have much in common. The Arab American or Pan-Arab community has a long and unified history and common language (Arabic). In spite of many differences, the family life-styles of most people from the Arab World are much the same. They believe that their heritage, culture and religion are worth preserving, and that they must work together for that purpose. Today's Arab American community increasingly has come together in the form of dozens of organizations that work to assure a place for themselves and their traditions in the mainstream of American life.

Whether on the assembly line or in one of 6,000 businesses, Arab Americans are contributing to the economic and cultural life of Detroit. To truly get to know the Arab American community, take the time to visit their neighborhoods: Dearborn's Warren Avenue and Dix Avenue business strips and the Chaldean community in Detroit's Woodward and Seven Mile area. In these places, as in the homes of Arab Americans, you will enjoy Middle Eastern hospitality at its best.

ARAB HOSPITALITY: COFFEE AND TEA

Arab Americans are forever visiting each other at home and on the job. Togetherness is enjoyed and strongly encouraged. Arab families often can be seen sitting on their front porches, drinking spiced tea, smoking water pipes and sharing meals with friends.

Throughout the Middle East, coffee is a symbol of hospitality. It is considered impolite for a guest to refuse a cup, and an even greater insult for a host to fail to offer some. Coffee is drunk in small, heavily sugared doses throughout the day.

Tea is now as popular as coffee, but tea drinking has been influenced by the traditions that grew up around coffee. Tea and coffee are considered social beverages and reflect the Arab values of hospitality and good company.

Some authorities believe coffee first was grown in Arabia near the Red Sea about 675 A.D. Coffee cultivation was rare until the 15th and 16th centuries, with extensive planting in the Yemen region of Arabia.

CALLIGRAPHY

"AHLAN WA SAHLAN"
"We Welcome You"

Calligraphy is a highly developed form of stylized manuscript writing characteristic of Islamic art. Initially used to reproduce the beauty of the spoken Quran (Koran), the Holy Book of Islam, the fluid, lyrical calligraphy is also incorporated into the architecture, metalwork, carvings and ceramics of the Arab World. Domestic pottery, decoration and jewelry often bear a calligraphic blessing or quotation from the Quran.

Since Islamic tradition restricts figurative representation, Arabic calligraphy, combined with elaborated geometric design, became the creative venue for visual artistic expression. For the Arab artist, the beauty of the written word has become both the inspiration and an end in itself.

Read from right to left, Arabic calligraphy's infinite number of styles are distinguished by the serifs or "hooks" at the tops of vertical strokes, by the shape of letter endings, the compactness or slant of the strokes, vertical or horizontal "stretching" and by the contours of the letters.

DEARBORN NEIGHBORHOODS

Most of Dearborn's Arab citizens live in the neighborhoods that line West Warren Avenue (north of I-94) and Dix Avenue (south of I-94). This heavy concentration of immigrant families supports two thriving business districts, each with a unique character.

A Mediterranean ambiance prevails in the neighborhoods north of Michigan Avenue, along Schaefer and Warren Avenues. Here Lebanese, Palestinian and Yemeni merchants have carved out the fastest-growing business district in Arab America. In addition to its many restaurants, bakeries and groceries, Warren Avenue is home to Arabic music, book and video stores, and specialty and gift shops.

Not far from the Warren area lies the South End (Dix Avenue) Arab community in the shadow of the Ford Rouge complex. Its working-class residents are more than 90 percent Arab, primarily immigrants from Yemen. The restaurants and shops along Dix offer sights and sounds of the Arabian Peninsula. The call to prayer is broadcast five times daily from the local mosque. Men in headdresses (*kafieh*) are commonplace. Some women are in long robes (*abaheh*), and scarves (*hejab*) cover their heads. Autoworkers gather to play cards or talk politics in coffeehouses. The signs and billboards often are in Arabic and English.

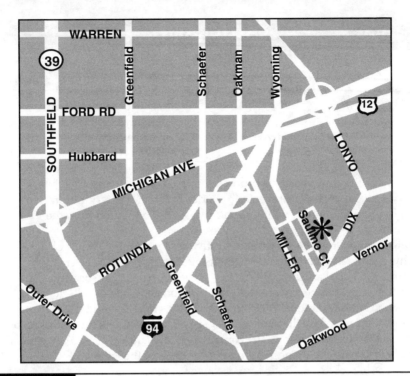

[D-E/4-5] To get a feel for the Arab community, all visitors should start at **ACCESS** (Arab Community Center for Economic and Social Services), *2651 Saulino Court,* in Dearborn's South End. The Center has a small museum and docent-guided or audio tours. For groups, it is wise to call ahead: (313) 842-7010.

Directions:

From I-94 westbound, *exit at Lonyo. Turn left on Lonyo and travel south until Lonyo ends at Dix Avenue. Turn right on Dix and continue about half a mile until you spot a sign for St. Bernadette's Church on the right. Turn onto Saulino Court, where the ACCESS headquarters is at 2651, across from the church. Parking and entrance are behind the last building.*

From I-94 eastbound: *Take the Rotunda Drive East Exit to where it dead-ends at Miller Road. Turn right on Miller and proceed south through the Rouge complex to Dix. Turn left on Dix and travel past Vernor to the small complex of buildings on the left with blue awnings. Turn left on Saulino Court and park behind the last building on the left.*

From Southfield Expressway: *Take Michigan Avenue East Exit about 2 ½ miles east. Turn right on Oakman, which becomes Miller Road, and pass through the Rouge complex. At Dix, turn left and proceed two or three blocks past Vernor to the small complex of buildings with blue awnings. Turn left at Saulino Court and park behind the last building on the left.*

The **ACCESS Museum** chronicles the lives of those of Arab descent—raising a family, wedding traditions, religion, working, politics and education, as well as Islamic contributions to science and medicine.

You might include a visit to **Arabian Village Market** *(10040 Dix Avenue)* and **Arabian Village Bakery** *(10045)*. It is best to get to the bakery in the early morning because much is sold out by afternoon. Usually there are packages of freshly baked puffy pita bread for 50 cents, which makes a nice midmorning snack. As soon as you walk into the market, you will smell the brine-soaking grape leaves and green olives, sold fresh by the pound. Walk around to the back of the store and you will find six kinds of dried beans, cracked yellow peas and lentils. Bulgur comes in four varieties, from coarse- to fine-ground grains, and rice is sold by the 25-pound bag. Or maybe you'd like to try pickled eggplant. After browsing the food sections, take a look at the backgammon sets and water pipes.

When you come out of the market, you can see the **American Muslim Society** mosque across Vernor *(9945)*. The inside consists of a large carpeted room with no chairs or ornamentation. If you want a tour, call ahead or make arrangements through ACCESS (313-842-7010). Women are not permitted to enter the mosque unaccompanied by a believer, except by appointment. Please note that everyone must take off their shoes when entering and women must cover their heads and wear a long skirt or pants. Men also should dress modestly in pants and long-sleeve shirts—no shorts or tank tops.

Some of the best dining and shopping is a few miles north on West Warren Avenue *(From Vernor, take Wyoming north. It weaves around a bit but eventually crosses Michigan Avenue and Ford Road. Go a mile farther north and turn left on West Warren)*. Here you can choose from a variety of shops and restaurants. Some favorites are **Al-Ameer** *(12710 W. Warren)* and **Cedarland** *(13007)*. Many other restaurants are on Michigan Avenue and Schaefer Road *(see list)*.

Optional: If you have time, you might visit the **Islamic Art Gallery,** a permanent collection in the Detroit Institute of Arts (DIA). *Take I 04 back to the Woodward Avenue Exit. Travel south on Woodward. You will see the DIA on the left. You can park in the underground structure.*

DEARBORN RESTAURANTS

SOUTH END
ARABIAN VILLAGE RESTAURANT
10421 Dix Ave., Dearborn; (313) 841-2550
Mon-Fri 7am-midnight, Sat-Sun 8pm-midnight. Yemeni and Middle Eastern cuisine including sandwiches, entrées—especially lamb—and fish specials; carryout and catering. Live entertainment Friday and Saturday.

WEST WARREN AVENUE
AL-AMEER RESTAURANT
12710 W. Warren, Dearborn; (313) 582-8185
Daily 11am-11pm. Sandwiches to full entrées, including shawarma.

AL-BERDOUNI
5821 Chase (at Ford Rd.), Dearborn
(313) 582-6116
Mon-Thu and Sun 10am-midnight, Fri-Sat 10-1am. Sandwiches to full meals such as lamb and grape leaves. Catering available.

AMANI'S RESTAURANT
15411 W. Warren, Dearborn
(313) 584-1888
Sun-Thu 10am-10pm, Fri-Sat 10am-midnight. Sandwiches, complete meals and desserts.

CEDARLAND RESTAURANT
13007 W. Warren, Dearborn
(313) 582-4849
Mon-Thu 9am-midnight, Fri 2pm-midnight, Sat-Sun 3pm-midnight. Casual dining, including lamb and vegetarian dishes, in family setting.

JIMMY'S NILE CAFE
12807 W. Warren, Dearborn
(313) 846-9644
Sun-Thu 10am-midnight, Fri-Sat 10am-1am. Extensive menu includes fish shawarma and fresh juices.

TUHAMAS
10613 W. Warren, Dearborn
(313) 581-0714
Mon-Sat 9am-1am. Sandwiches, kafta, falafel, kabobs, grilled chicken and salads.

EAST MICHIGAN AVENUE
COUNTRY CHICKEN
5131 Schaefer, Dearborn
(S of Ford Rd., N of Michigan)
(313) 582-6677
Daily 11am-11pm. Specialty grilled chicken and Turkish shawarma, special falafel and full Middle Eastern meals.

KABOB VILLAGE
13823 Michigan Ave., Dearborn
(at Maple next to City Hall)
(313) 581-0055
Mon-Thu 10am-midnight, Fri-Sun 10am-1am. Large selection of Lebanese and Mediterranean food, including meat gallaba, mafrouki and arayees. Raw juice bar.

KING OF FALAFEL
5728 Schaefer, Dearborn; (313) 582-3500
Mon-Thu 10am-11pm, Fri-Sun 11am-midnight. Specializes in sandwiches and lamb and chicken shawarma. Carryout service.

LA SHISH EAST
12918 Michigan Ave., Dearborn
(313) 584-4477
Daily 10am-midnight. Casual dining, including specialty salads, sandwiches, lamb shawarma, dinner platters and juice bar.

COFFEEHOUSE CULTURE

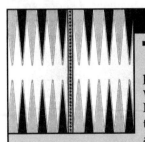

The coffeehouse is a thriving institution in Arab culture. More than a business enterprise, coffeehouses serve as informal men's clubs where a wide range of activities take place. Neighborhood men gather after work to talk politics; read poetry and discuss literature; perform and listen to music; smoke water pipes, play cards, backgammon and other games; or simply watch television.

Backgammon *(tawela)* is a favorite pastime in homes and coffeehouses. A balance of strategy and chance, it is said to be the game that most resembles real life. Like chess, this game first came to the West from the Arab World.

The water pipe *(nargila, sheesha* or "hubbly bubbly") is smoked among friends throughout the Arab World. It contains a stove for the coals, a compartment for the tobacco (or sometimes dried fruit), a glass canister for the bubbling water and a connecting flexible pipe.

WEST MICHIGAN AVENUE
LA PITA
22435 Michigan (at Military), Dearborn
(313) 565-7482
Mon-Sat 10am-11pm, Sun 11am-10pm.
Mediterranean sandwiches; casual dining.

L.A. EXPRESS MEDITERRANEAN BISTRO
22018 W. Michigan (W of Monroe)
Dearborn; (313) 277-5999
Mon-Sat 10am-9pm. Spicy soups, roll-up
sandwiches, fattoush salad, stuffed grapes
leaves, Moroccan-style chicken phyllo dish.

LA SHISH WEST
22039 Michigan, Dearborn; (313) 562-7200
*Sun-Thu 10am-11pm, Fri-Sat 10am-mid-
night.* Casual and intimate dining. Salads,
sandwiches and dinner platters, including
many lamb dishes.

TALAL'S RESTAURANT
22041 Michigan, Dearborn
(between Monroe and Mason)
(313) 565-5500
*Sun-Thu 10am-11pm, Fri-Sat 10am-mid-
night.* Full menu, appetizers to entrées.

ROTUNDA DRIVE
UNCLE SAM'S VILLAGE CAFE
3337 Greenfield, Dearborn; (313) 271-8040
*Mon-Thu 11am-midnight, Fri 11am-2am, Sat
5pm-2am.* Middle Eastern restaurant, bar
and night club.

DEARBORN BAKERIES
*Bakeries specialize in spinach pies, meat
pies and a variety of bread.*

SOUTH END
ARABIAN VILLAGE BAKERY
10040 W. Vernor (at Dix), Dearborn
(313) 843-0800
Mon-Sat 9am-9pm, Sun 9am-6pm. Bakery
and groceries, assortment of Arabic pies,
Yemeni bread and catering of whole lamb.

WEST WARREN
CEDARS BAKERY
10451 W. Warren, Dearborn; (313) 582-2306
Daily 6am-5pm. Lebanese breads and
sweets.

GOLDEN BAKERY
13750 W. Warren, Dearborn; (313) 581-5349
Mon-Sat 5:30am-8pm. Breads, manaecsh
and Arabic pies.

NEW YASMEEN BAKERY
13900 W. Warren, Dearborn
(313) 582-6035
Mon-Sat 5:30am-8pm, Sun 5:30am-7pm.
Breads, sweets and Middle Eastern pies. Deli
with fattousch, tabbouleh, hummus, baba
ghanooj and grape leaves.

SULTAN'S BAKERY
6851 Schaefer Rd., Dearborn
(N of Ford Rd.)
(313) 581-6688
Mon-Sat 9am-5pm. Middle Eastern meat,
cheese and spinach pies, bu-aa bread, sandwiches, cookies and Arabic groceries.

DEARBORN PASTRY SHOPS
*Baked goods and sweets include baklava,
lady fingers, bird's nests, kanafi,
mamoul and European-style cakes and
cookies.*

WEST WARREN AVENUE
NEW AFRAH BAKERY
12741 W. Warren, Dearborn
(313) 582-7878
Daily 5:30am-8pm. Traditional Arabic pastries, baklava, lady fingers, mini roses and
bird's nests.

AL ZAHRAA PASTRY
12741 W. Warren, Dearborn
(313) 582-7878
Mon-Sat 9:30am-10pm. Baklava and variety
of traditional sweets.

YASSINE'S ROYAL BAKERY
10609 W. Warren, Dearborn
(313) 945-1550
Daily 7:30am-5pm. Variety of traditional
Arabic pastries and baked sweets.

SCHAEFER ROAD
MASRI PASTRY
5125 Schaefer (N of Michigan), Dearborn
(313) 584-3500
Daily 8am-10pm. Traditional Arabic and
European pastries.

SHATILA FOOD PRODUCTS
6912 Schaefer Rd., Dearborn
(N of Ford Rd.)
(313) 582-1952
Daily 8am-11pm. Traditional Arabic and
French pastries, including a variety of sweets
and trays with baklava and cookies.

ARAB CUISINE

In the Arab World, people of different regions have unique culinary traditions that reflect local resources, contact with other cultures and the cooks' skills. The nomadic tribes (*Bodovins*) depended heavily on portable staples such as rice and dates, and herdable animals such as sheep.

Lebanon, for example, has been influenced heavily by Turkish cooking. In turn, the entrepreneurial Lebanese have had great influence on modern Middle Eastern cuisine. In **North Africa,** Arabs eat many Berber dishes. Nonetheless, there are aspects of Middle Eastern cuisine that all Arabs, from Morocco to Oman, have in common.

Lamb is the preferred meat and is served to guests in virtually every Arab country. The spices common to Arab cooking—**cinnamon, cloves, garlic, cardamom, coriander** and **saffron**—spread throughout the Middle East on ancient trade routes, as did other foods. Yogurt, dates, *tahini* (a sesame paste), rice, garbanzo beans (chick-peas) and parsley are used in every region, always in locally distinctive ways.

In regions where people sit on the floor, a large basket doubles as a table, with people squatting around it as they eat. Smaller baskets, used as platters, are stacked with steaming meats, seasoned rice, bread, and colorful fruits and vegetables. Today, baskets made with plastic instead of palm leaves take advantage of modern materials while keeping the old tradition of basketweaving alive.

Menus at Middle Eastern restaurants vary from Arabic sandwiches and vegetarian fare to full entrées, using fresh produce and whole grains. Some favorite dishes are *hummus* (a dip made of ground chick-peas, sesame seed oil, lemon and spices), **stuffed grape leaves,** *kibbee* (cracked wheat mixed with fresh tender ground lamb and spices; *kibbeh naye* (raw lamb eaten like steak tartar), *baba ghanooj* (an appetizer or dip made with grilled eggplant), *tabbouleh* (finely chopped parsley, tomatoes, mint and bulgur with an olive oil and lemon dressing), *kabob* (marinated, grilled, skewered chunks of meat or fish). *Falafel* is a small deep-fried patty of delicately spiced ground chick-peas. *Shawarma* is a cone-shaped sandwich of shaved roasted lamb, chicken or beef.

Favorite beverages are **Turkish** or **Arabic coffee** (dark, rich and sweet); teas *(shai)* of many types, including Iranian tea which is served in a glass and meant to be sipped through a sugar cube placed between one's teeth); *Ayran,* a frothy yogurt drink, and *Laban,* a tangy milk drink. Arabs who do not adhere to the Islamic restriction on alcohol consumption often enjoy an alcoholic beverage with their food, including *Arak,* an anise-flavored apértif.

Bread *(khubz arabi, pita, lavash)* is round and flat and can be split to make a sandwich or used as a utensil for scooping food.

Sweets and pastries include *baklava* (layered pastry filled with nuts and steeped in honey-lemon syrup), *halwa* (sesame paste, studded with fruit and nuts), *ma'amul* (molded date or nut cookies), *mutabak* (sweet or savory turnovers) and *um ali* (a pastry pudding with raisins, coconut and milk).

DEARBORN MARKETS

SOUTH END

ARABIAN GULF MARKET
10001 Vernor, Dearborn; (313) 841-7888
Mon-Sat 9am-9pm, Sun 9am-6pm. Middle Eastern foods and nuts. Arabic cultural items and kitchenware.

ARABIAN VILLAGE MARKET
10040 Dix, Dearborn; (313) 841-4650
Mon-Sat 9am-9pm, Sun 9am-6pm. Middle Eastern groceries and Hallal meat. Some cultural items and Arabic audiocassettes.

FAIRWAY VARIETY GROCERIES
10135 Dix, Dearborn; (313) 849-1088
Mon-Thu 9am-8pm, Fri-Sat 9am-9pm, Sun 9am-6pm. Grocery and five-and-dime store.

MADINA STORE
10035 W. Vernor, Dearborn; (313) 843-0130
Mon-Sat 9am-9pm, Sun 9am-6pm. Groceries, spices and Arabic clothing and cultural items.

WEST WARREN AVENUE

AMANA MEAT MARKET
15242 W. Warren, Dearborn; (313) 582-6262
Daily 8am-6pm. Hallal meats and food imports.

ALSALAM MARKET
10394 W. Warren, Dearborn; (313) 846-5120 (in Warren Plaza)
Mon-Sat 9am-10pm, Sun 9am-6pm. Grocery store with cultural items such as water pipes.

CEDARS FRUIT MARKET
13110 W. Warren, Dearborn; (313) 582-8057
Mon-Sat 9:30am-9pm, Sun noon-4pm. Produce and Middle Eastern imports.

DEARBORN VILLAGE FRUIT MARKET
13738 W. Warren, Dearborn; (313) 582-4749
Mon-Sat 8am-9pm. Produce.

ISLAMIC MEAT MARKET
13130 W. Warren, Dearborn; (313) 584-2211
Mon-Sat 9am-9pm, Sun 9am-6pm. Groceries and Hallal meats, variety of imported food. Also cultural items, Arabic clothing, musical instruments and Islamic books.

MEHANNA MARKET
6934 Schaefer, Dearborn; (313) 581-3972 (S of Ford Rd.)

Daily 8am-midnight. Middle Eastern nuts and Arabic grocery with a variety of cultural items and gifts.

MUSDALAH HALAH MEATS
10601 W. Warren, Dearborn; (313) 846-1660
Mon-Sat 8am-4pm.

NUTS AND COFFEE GALLERY
13041 W. Warren, Dearborn; (313) 581-3212
Mon-Sat 10am-10pm, Sun 11am-8pm. Arabic food, nuts, and traditional Arabic items such as coffee pots and inlaid wood backgammon game boards.

SAAD BROTHERS SUPER MARKET
10646 W. Warren, Dearborn; (313) 846-0444
Daily 9am-10pm. Regular groceries and Arabic foods and cultural items.

SULTAN'S
(See "Bakeries, West Warren.")

The arabesque style, based on "leaf scroll" and the Egyptian palmette, has become one of the most popular and enduring motifs in the world.

DEARBORN SHOPS

For cultural items, see also "Markets."

FAIRWAY VARIETY
10135 Dix Ave., Dearborn; (313) 849-1088
Mon-Sat 9am-9pm, Sun 9am-6pm. Variety five-and-dime store that also carries Yemeni jewelry and gold items (ask for viewing).

GENEVA GIFTS
13806 W. Warren, Dearborn; (313) 581-7777
Daily 10am-6pm. Gifts, watches and some cultural items.

HARB'S IMPORTS
13114 W. Warren, Dearborn; (313) 581-0525
Daily 7am-10pm. Imported goods from Arab World and other countries. China, gifts, kitchenware and imported foods.

HOUDA FASHIONS
10503 W. Warren, Dearborn; (313) 581-2949
and
10513 Dix, Dearborn; (313) 843-4144
Daily 9am-10pm. Islamic items including scarves and men's clothing.

JACK'S MEN'S AND LADIES' WEAR
13816 W. Warren, Dearborn; (313) 584-1912
Daily 9am-10pm. Arabic dresses, scarves and men's Arabic clothing.

KITCHENWARE PLUS
15228 W. Warren, Dearborn; (313) 945-6155
Mon-Sat 9am-9pm. Large selection of housewares, kitchenware and gift items. Traditional Arabic items such as coffee cups.

MECAH ISLAMIC SUPERSTORE
13300 Michigan Ave. (at Bingham), Dearborn; (313) 84-MECAH
Mon-Sat 10am-8pm, Sun 11am-5pm. One-stop shopping center for clothing, books, pictures, video tapes, jewelry and other Islamic items.

METRO RESTAURANTS

(See beginning of chapter for Dearborn listings. See also "Chaldean" chapter.)

DETROIT
HARMONIE GARDEN CAFE
87 W. Palmer, Detroit (Cultural Center) (313) 831-4420
Mon-Fri 7am-9pm, Sat 8am-8pm. Middle Eastern specialties available, ranging from falafels to tabbouleh, hummus and shish kabobs.

MAJESTIC CAFE
4124 Woodward, Detroit; (313) 833-0120
Best known for its world music performances.

MEDITERRANEAN CAFE
1212 Beaubien, Detroit; (313) 962-1931
Daily 10-4am. Greektown eatery with Lebanese and Mediterranean food.

EAST
AL-ALMEER
37246 Dequindre (N of 16), Sterling Hts. (810) 795-1700
Sun-Thu 10am-11pm, Fri-Sat 10am-midnight. Lebanese and Chaldean cuisine.

BEIRUT PALACE
2095 15 Mile Rd., Sterling Hts. (810) 795-0424
Mon-Thu and Sun 10:30am-11pm, Fri-Sat 10:30am-midnight. Middle-Eastern cuisine including ethnic plates, vegetarian dishes and raw juice bar.

CEDAR GARDEN RESTAURANT
23417 Greater Mack (at Nine Mile) St. Clair Shores; (810) 778-5999
Mon-Thu 11am-10pm, Fri-Sat 11am-11pm, Sun 4-10pm. Middle Eastern cuisine and raw juice bar.

HAMMURABI RESTAURANT
21570 Dequindre, Warren; (810) 757-6920
Daily noon-2am. Banquet hall, dining and cocktails. Middle Eastern cuisine.

IKE'S FAMILY DINING
39064 Van Dyke, Sterling Hts. (shopping plaza near 17 Mile Rd.) (810) 979-4460
Mon-Fri 7am-10pm, Sat 8am-10pm, Sun 8am-9pm. Lebanese as well as Italian and American food.

JACQUES' MEDITERRANEAN
3720 Rochester Rd., Troy; (248) 680-0480 (Troywood Plaza at 16 1/2 Mile)
Daily 10am-10pm. Lebanese and American cuisine. Live entertainment Thursday-Sunday.

LA SHISH VAN DYKE
32401 Van Dyke, Warren (between 13 and 14 Mile Rds.) (810) 977-2177
Mon-Thu and Sun 11 am-11pm, Fri-Sat 11am-midnight. Lebanese and Middle Eastern dishes served with freshly baked puffy pita bread. Same ownership as the two La Shish restaurants in Dearborn.

STEVE'S BACK ROOM
19872 Kelly Rd., Harper Woods (313) 527-5047
Mon-Sat 11:30am-9pm. Middle Eastern market in front, cozy restaurant with Lebanese cuisine in back. Carryout available.

SAHARA RESTAURANT
22114 Harper, St. Clair Shores
(810) 777-9600
Tue-Sat 11am-8pm. Middle Eastern cuisine.
Noted for eggplant dishes (baba ghanooj).

WEST

ALADDIN'S CUISINE
146 Mary Alexander, Northville
(Downtown)
(248) 380-3807
Mon-Thu 11am-10pm, Fri-Sat 11am-11pm,
Sun 11am-8pm.Vegetarian and non-vegatari-
an entrees, raw juice bar.

PINELAND RESTAURANT
8207 Middlebelt, Westland
(between Joy and Ann Arbor Trail)
(734) 421-4084
Mon-Sat 9am-midnight. Sun 9am-11pm.
Lebanese menu features mixed grill combo
with hummus and salad. Raw juice bar.

NORTHWEST

ANITA'S KITCHEN
31005 Orchard Lake Rd., Farmington Hills
(248) 855-4150
*Mon-Thu 10am-9pm, Fri-Sat 10am-11pm,
Sun 10am-9pm.*Hummus, sandwiches, vegetarian chili and Middle Eastern dinners.

LA SHISH
37610 W. Twelve Mile, Farmington Hills
(248) 553-0700
and
6203 Orchard Lake Rd., West Bloomfield
(248) 538-0800
*Mon-Thu and Sun 11am-11pm, Fri-Sat
11am-midnight.* Location #4 also has extensive menu and raw juice bar.

STEVE'S BACKROOM
7295 Orchard Lake Rd., West Bloomfield
(in plaza at Northwestern Hwy.)
(248) 851-1133
*Mon 11:30-9pm, Tue-Thu 11:30am-10pm, Fri
11:30am-11pm, Sat 4-11pm.* Lebanese
menu with lamb dishes and vegetarian
dishes such as mujadarah stew. Carryout.

THE SHEIK
4189 Orchard Lake Rd., Orchard Lake
(248) 865-0000
*Mon-Thu and Sun 10:30am-11pm, Fri-Sat
10am-midnight.* Lebanese and Middle
Eastern cuisine in upscale setting. Modeled
after the Ghanem family's original Sheik
restaurant in Detroit.

VIRGINIA'S MID-EAST CAFE
2456 Orchard Lake Rd., Sylvan Lake
(248) 681-7170
Mon-Thu 11am-9pm, Fri-Sat noon-10pm.
Ethnic café in suburban strip mall offers
fatoush salads, shawarma and lentil soup.

NORTH

AL-RAUSHEE
411 S. Washington, Royal Oak
(248) 546-8080
Daily 11am-11pm. Mediterranean menu.

ANITA'S KITCHEN
110 W. Maple Rd. (W of Livernois), Troy
(248) 362-0680
*Mon-Thu & Sat 6am-10pm, Fri 6am-11pm,
Sun 7am-9pm.* Full Middle Eastern menu.

BEIRUT PALACE
105 Eleven Mile (at Main), Royal Oak
(248) 399-4600
Daily 10:30 am-1am. Lebanese cuisine with
ethnic plates, appetizers, raw juice bar.

ELIE'S CAFE
263 Pierce St., Birmingham
(248) 647-2420
Mon-Sat 11am-10pm. Middle Eastern food
such as fattoush, kibbee, baba ghanooj and
stuffed grape leaves. Raw juice bar.

FLAMING KABOB CAFE
29702 Southfield Rd. (at 12-1/2 Mile)
Southfield; (248) 423-9777
Mon-Thu 11am-9pm, Fri-Sat 11am-10pm.
Lebanese, Chaldean and Greek cuisine.

LA FENDI RESTAURANT
27060 Evergreen, Lathrup Village
(248) 559-9099
Sun-Thu 11-1am, Fri-Sat 11-2am. Middle
Eastern decor and music. Daily lunch and
dinner specials. Raw juice bar.

PHOENICIA
588 S. Woodward, Birmingham
(248) 644-3122
*Mon-Thu 11am-10pm, Fri 11am-11pm, Sat
5-11pm.* Upscale restaurant serving
Lebanese cuisine. Weekend entertainment.

PITA CAFÉ
25282 Greenfield (near 10 Mile Rd.)
Oak Park; (248) 968-2225
and
237 N. Woodward, Birmingham
(248) 645-6999
Mon-Wed 11am-10pm, Thu-Sat 11am-11pm.
Lebanese food, raw juice bar.

METRO BAKERIES

AL-RAYEES PASTRY
8236 W. Nine Mile, Oak Park (248) 548-4444
Mon-Sat 10am-9pm, Sun 10am-7:30pm.

CEDARS BAKERY
2147 17 Mile (at Dequindre), Sterling Hts.
(810) 795-1670
Mon-Sat 8am-8pm, Sun 8am-6pm.

MID-EAST PASTRY DELIGHT
2097 15 Mile (at Dequindre), Sterling Hts.
(810) 979-3960 or 1-800-MIDEAST
Mon 9am-9pm, Tue-Sat 8am-9pm, Sun 8am-6pm. Meat and spinach pies, Lebanese pizza, pastry trays with lady fingers, bird's nest, half moon crunch and baklava.

PARIS PASTRY
22171 Coolidge., Oak Park; (248) 541-6550
Mon-Sat 10am-9pm, Sun 10am-7pm.
Middle Eastern and European pastries.

METRO MARKETS

GABRIEL IMPORTS
42899 Dequindre (at 19 Mile), Troy
(248) 879-0927 or 879-6330
Mon-Sat 9am-8pm, Sun 10am-4pm.
Nuts, cheeses, olives and other Middle-eastern imports; meat market adjacent.

GAZALI IMPORTED FOODS
10620 W. Nine Mile, Oak Park
(248) 546-6833
Mon-Sat 10am-10pm, Sun 11am-6pm.

ARABIC TOWN
24721 Coolidge, Oak Park (at I-696)
(248) 544-0362
and
2105 15 Mile, Sterling Hts.
(NE corner of Dequindre)
(810) 264-0510
Mon-Sat 10am-9pm, Sun 11am-5pm.
Largest importer of MIddle East foods.

HASSAN & BROS. MEAT MARKET
2904 Long Lake Rd. (at Dequindre), Troy
(248) 619-0909
Mon-Sat 9am-8pm, Sun 10-5. Hallal meats, groceries, imported foods.

JERUSALEM FOOD WHOLESALERS/RETAILERS
13080 Inkster Road (S of Jeffries Fwy)
Redford; (313) 538-1511
Mon-Sat 8am-6pm. Groceries, imported foods.

JOUNI MEAT MARKET
37234 Dequindre (N of 16 Mile)
Sterling Heights; (810) 274-0760
Mon-Sat 9am-7:30pm, Sun 10am-5pm. Hallal beef, lamb, goat and chicken.

MID EAST MARKET
24133 10 Mile Rd.at Telegraph, Southfield
(248) 350-1919
Mon-Sat 10am-9pm, Sun 11am-6pm.

OASIS MARKET
4130 Rochester Rd., Royal Oak
(248) 588-2210
Mon-Sat 9am-7pm, Sun 10am-4pm.

NIGHT CLUBS

PRESTIGE CLUB
22925 W. Eight Mile, Detroit; (313) 537-3860
Fri-Sat-Sun evenings. Middle Eastern food and entertainment.

UNCLE SAM'S VILLAGE CAFE
3337 Greenfield, Dearborn; (313) 271-8040
Entertainment Fri-Sat 9:30pm-2am. Middle Eastern restaurant and bar has belly dancers, band and singers on weekends.

CULTURAL ARTS

MUSEUM OF ARAB CULTURE
2651 Saulino Ct., Dearborn (at ACCESS)
(313) 842-7010
Mon-Fri 9am-5pm. Contains more than 100 photographs showing the diversity and dynamic growth of metro Detroit's Arab American community during the past 100 years. Displays with cultural artifacts, heirlooms and handicrafts provide an introduction to the history, culture, religions and art of the Arab World. Guided tours available by arrangement. Audio tours also available. *(See "Dearborn Tour" for directions.)*

ACC CULTURAL ARTS CENTER
111 W. Seven Mile, Detroit
c/o (248) 559-1990
Arab-American and Chaldean Council maintains extensive collection of educational resource materials, art and artifacts of the Arab World. Arts Center schedules special exhibits and events featuring contemporary visual and performing artists.

CONTRIBUTIONS TO SCIENCE

While Europe was in its Dark Ages, the Arab World was experiencing a spectacular growth in the arts and sciences. When the scientific revolution occurred later in the West, it was built on the groundwork that Islamic civilization had established. The following are examples of Arab contributions to the scientific disciplines:

Medicine: Arabs established the first hospitals, clinics and medical schools (circa 760 A.D.); were the first to treat smallpox and measles successfully, to use alcohol as an antiseptic and mercury as a purgative, and to realize that diseases were spread by contagion. They proposed theories of evolution 900 years before Darwin.

Chemistry: Arab chemists perfected methods for refining metals and producing alloys. They also built the best furnaces of their day. The word *chemistry* is from Arabic *(al-kimiya)*.

Physics: Arab physicists were the first to determine that light rays travel in straight lines, that objects radiate light in all directions, that light weakens as it travels from its source and that vision results from light rays being reflected into the eye. This led to the development of parabolic mirrors, predecessors of the telescope.

Mathematics: Arab mathematicians introduced "Arabic numerals" to the West, invented the "zero" (from the Arabic, *zifr*) and algebra *(al-jabr)*, as well as perfected analytical geometry.

Astronomy: Arabs theorized that the Earth rotated on its own axis at least 600 years before Galileo proposed the idea. Their calendars and astronomical calculations were by far the most accurate of the day. Arab astronomers also developed the altitude and longitude measures used in mapmaking.

> *Geometry plays an important role in Islamic architecture and decorative arts.*

ARABIC HERITAGE ROOM
Alex Manoogian Hall
Wayne State University
906 W. Warren, Detroit; (313) 577-2446
Room 105, in Arabian decor, contains cultural displays and worship area.

A COMMUNITY BETWEEN TWO WORLDS: ARAB AMERICANS IN GREATER DETROIT
(313) 842-7010
Traveling photographic exhibit installed by ACCESS and the Smithsonian Institution showcasing a century of immigration of Arabs to the United States was featured at the National Museum of American History in 1996. Michigan showings are scheduled at the Detroit Historical Museum and Michigan State University Museum in East Lansing. Auxiliary programs such as concerts, lectures, poetry readings and folk artists will take place

in conjunction with the exhibit. A portion of this exhibit is permanently installed at ACCESS in Dearborn.

AMERICAN SYRIAN ARAB CULTURAL ASSOCIATION
20834 Dequindre, Warren; (810) 757-5440
Conducts events throughout the year to promote the arts and presents educational programs about the history and civilization of the Arab World. Sponsors folkloric dance group.

ARAB AMERICAN ARTS COUNCIL
c/o ACCESS
2651 Saulino Ct., Dearborn; (313) 842-7010
Board oversees and helps organize art programs focusing on the classical, contemporary and folk traditions of the Arab World.
Performing Art Series, presented by ACCESS, features a wide range of concerts,

DANCE

Dance is an integral component of all celebrations of rites of passage. Guests at wedding, engagement, baptism, graduation and birthday parties often take part in the *dabkah* line dance and group Arabic (belly) dancing.

Dabkah is a graceful line dance in which participants support each other by grasping hands as they plunge to the ground and spring up again without missing a beat. Usually men lead the dabkah line, followed by women, then children. This vivacious and enthusiastic dance is a way for celebrants, especially those closely related, to communicate their joy and extend good wishes to the bride and groom or guest of honor. There are variations of the dabkah dance among different Arab groups.

Arabic dance is Oriental-style belly dancing in groups or couples. This type of belly dancing involves moving different parts of the body, including head, shoulders, arms, hips, belly and legs, to the rhythm of the music. Although Americans are more aware of solo belly dancing performed at nightclubs, there are variations of belly dancing related to folk traditions that are performed in a group.

exhibits and readings throughout the year at various locations. ACCESS Cultural Arts Department also hosts the **Artistry of Arab American Cuisine,** a series of festive feasts, which include cooking demonstrations by the chef.

ARAB WORLD MOSAIC; (313) 842-7010
Publication on cultural diversity for use by elementary school teachers. Available for loan or purchase from ACCESS. Ask for ACCESS Cultural Arts Department.

TALES FROM ARAB DETROIT
(313) 842-7010
Documentary produced by Olive Branch Productions and ACCESS about Detroit's Arab American community blends voices, poetry, song and dance into everyday stories of cultural conflict and resilience. Video available from ACCESS Cultural Arts Dept.

PERFORMING ARTS

Regional folk dances often performed by touring ensemble groups might include a Saudi woman's dance, a shepherd's cane dance, Egyptian acrobatic sword dance, Turkish Kashlama, and Lebanese, Palestinian and Iraqi line dances.

AJYAL "NEW GENERATION" PLAYERS
Najee Mondalek, director
(810) 296-7022/1-888-442-5925
Dearborn-based Lebanese theatrical troupe performs in Arabic and English, locally and nationwide.

DEARBORN ARABIC ENSEMBLE
(313) 842-7010
Eight professional Arab musicians present traditional, classical and contemporary music performances for weddings and other celebrations. Group travels throughout the United States and performs on traditional Arabic instruments such as the bamboo flute, oud, kanoun, rababa, kamanja, riq and tabla. Also provides private music classes and sells high-quality musical instruments.

MIDDLE EAST DANCE ENSEMBLE
Andrea Hughes and Aida Al Adawi
(248) 332-2042
Lecture demonstration of Middle Eastern music includes explanation of families of instruments used, performance of regional folk dances and showing of artifacts (jewelry and regional clothing).

ST. SHARBEL DANCE TROUPE
Rosine Soyad, director
(810) 773-8454
Maronite Church in Warren has youth and adult Lebanese dance groups that perform at festivals and special events.

TROUPE TA-AMULLAT
Middle Eastern Dancers
Pauline Costianes, director
(734) 427-6592
Performances of regional folk dances with explanation of the dances.

DANCE CLASSES

CITY OF DEARBORN; (313) 730-0468
Middle-Eastern dance classes offered by Continuing Education Department.

MIDDLE EASTERN DANCE
Najwa Al-Qamar, director
(734) 495-3007
Seminars and classes at various locations.

DANCE AND DRUM
Aida Al Adawi, instructor
(248) 332-2042
Classes taught in Varner Hall at Oakland University.

ARAB MUSIC

To the Western ear, Arab music has a strange, exotic sound. Its notes seem closer together, and its melodies have a continuous, gliding quality. Middle Eastern scales have smaller intervals between notes. These intervals, called "quarter tones," fill the gaps between Western notes, producing sensitive tonal distinctions. The Arab musician, if given a range of only four notes on the Western scale, can create a rich, intricate melody.

Arab music emphasizes repetition more than Western music. Each passage is savored, prolonged and played again. Melodies tend to be short, but their notes can be lengthened by the performer. The sound is characterized by lively rhythms, deep emotion and the supple flow of its melodies.

Many Western instruments—the mandolin, dulcimer, zither, psaltery, guitar, violin and tambourine—have their origins in the Middle East. Among the most common are:

Daff: A popular percussion instrument used as rhythmic accompaniment by singers and dancers. Also called the *tambour*, from which comes the English word "tambourine."

Durbakka: A vase-shaped drum, with a skin of fish or lamb stretched over one end, is played under the left arm or between the legs. Group singing, at weddings and other celebrations, often is accompanied by the *durbakka*.

Mizwij: A double-reeded, wooden flute is the ancestor of the oboe, bassoon, clarinet, and other reed instruments.

Nay: An end-blown flute made of dry reed. Due to the limited number of keys, musicians use several nays of varying lengths in order to play different scales.

Oud: Related to the lute and guitar, it produces a mellow, gentle tone, in contrast with the metallic sound of the guitar.

Qanun: An ancestor of the psaltery or zither, it consists of a trapezoid-shaped board over which strings are mounted in groups of three (usually 24 groups).

Rababa: The ancestor of the violin, it is a simple, one-stringed instrument made of wood, skin, hide and hair.

VISUAL ARTS

DETROIT INSTITUTE OF ARTS
5200 Woodward, Detroit
(313) 833-7900
Wed-Fri 11am-4pm, Sat-Sun 11am-5pm.
Gallery of Islamic Art (N150) contains large collection of rugs and textiles, as well as paintings, metalwork, ceramics, and wood and ivory carvings. Islamic art is noted for its geometric shapes, the arabesque (classical vine scroll) motif and calligraphy. Art of Ancient Egypt and the Near East is in galleries C234-236 and N201-202. Egyptian collection features tombs and a mummy.

KELSEY MUSEUM OF ARCHEAOLOGY
University of Michigan campus
434 S. State St., Ann Arbor
(734) 763-3559 or 764-9304
September-April: Mon-Fri 9am-4pm, Sat-Sun 1-4pm. May-August: closed Mon. Collection of nearly 100,000 artifacts from the ancient, early and medieval cultures of Egypt, Middle East, Greece and Rome. Since 1930, the museum has sponsored expeditions to Syria, Libya and Turkey and is exploring sites in Egypt, Tunisia and Israel.

UKADH ART GALLERY
16241 W. Warren, Dearborn; (313) 846-0250
By appointment Mon-Sat 9am-5pm. Owner Nouhad El-Hajj showcases Arab American visual artists and writers. Decorated with unique as well as antique pieces, the gallery features permanent and temporary exhibits.

MIRANDA'S ARABIC GREETINGS
(810) 257-7405
Call for stores that carry greeting card line.

THE SILK WORM
400 Main St., Rochester; (248) 651-1900
Gallery displays include Egyptian art. Famous ancient paintings have been reproduced by hand on genuine papyrus.

ARABIC INSTRUCTION

International Institute, Detroit
(313) 871-8600

City of Dearborn Continuing Education
(313) 730-0468

Henry Ford Community College, Dearborn
(313) 845-9600

University of Michigan-Dearborn
(313) 593-5600

SPECIAL EVENTS
MAY
ARAB CULTURE WEEK
(313) 842-7010
During the first week of May, Arab organizations present cultural events, featuring music, poetry, storytelling, educational workshops, art exhibits and film showings.

JUNE
ARAB INTERNATIONAL FESTIVAL
East Dearborn
(313) 842-7010, 582-3421 or 581-7540
Free shuttle service from Dearborn Civic Center to festival site on Warren between Oakman and Manor. International performances of music and dance by more than 25 groups, children's tent, carnival, artisans' tent, food from various cuisines and traditional Arabic coffee.

JULY
ARAB WORLD FESTIVAL
(313) 877-8077
Detroit riverfront ethnic festival at Hart Plaza, celebrated the third weekend in July, features food and entertainment.

FALL
FANN WA TARAB
(313) 842-7010
Fann Wa Tarab, which translates into "art and sublime music," is a cultural event that fosters understanding of Arabic music, poetry and visual art. Renowned and highly regarded artists are invited each year. Presented annually during late September or early October by ACCESS, the Arab American Arts Council and the Detroit Institute of Arts.

MUSLIM HOLIDAYS

Muslims follow a lunar calendar that is based on the phases of the moon. The Islamic calendar moves ahead of the Gregorian (solar adjusted) calendar at a rate of 10 days a year.

✴ **RAMADAN** The holy month of fasting set aside to celebrate God's revelation of the Koran (the holy book of Islam) to the Prophet Mohammed. During this time, Muslims abstain from all food and drink from dawn until sunset. When a large number of kin and friends are invited, special feast dishes are prepared and enjoyed after breaking the fast. People who are sick, traveling or not in a position to fast are allowed to make up lost fast days later in the year. Children usually do not fast until they reach puberty.

✴ **EID AL-FITR** A feast that marks the end of Ramadan. During this holiday, Muslims give alms to the poor and attend the mosque. Families, neighbors and entire communities take this holiday as an opportunity to make peace. It is a time to celebrate good news such as wedding engagements and job promotions.

Children are given new clothes, small amounts of money and candy.

✴ **EID AL-ADHA** "Feast of the Sacrifice" commemorates Abraham's willingness to sacrifice his son, Ishmael, in obedience to God, and God's mercy in substituting a lamb for Ishmael. Eid Al-Adha falls on the 10th day of the month of pilgrimage and marks the apex of the Hajj, the holy pilgrimage to Mecca. Muslims celebrate this holiday by visiting each other and by slaughtering a sheep or goat. The meat is shared with the poor.

WEDDING CELEBRATIONS

For many Muslim Arabs, the legal marriage ceremony, overseen by a religious authority figure, takes place at the engagement party. This celebration occurs a few days, or even a few years, before the actual wedding day, after which the bride and groom move in together.

The wedding day itself is not a religious event, merely a social one. Gifts of money given to the bride and groom are meant to offset the cost of the wedding party, which usually is as lavish as the families can afford, and help the groom pay for the gold and furnishings he has given to his bride.

The *zaffah* is the initial and obligatory procession of the bride and groom and their attendants in the public space of the party. As the couple enters the hall, a traditional wedding song is played to announce their entry. Two musicians, playing the *mizmer* (a folk oboe) and *tabla* (double-headed drum), and sometimes a singer or dancer accompany the celebrants.

Traditionally, at the front of the hall is an elaborately decorated tiered stage where the bride and groom sit on a raised platform. In a Lebanese wedding, a group of older women then approach the couple and perform *awiha*, stylized humorous poems. Throughout the evening, guests are invited to join in the *dabkah*, a graceful line dance, and group belly dancing.

ISLAM

Islam is based on the teachings of Muhammad, who is called the last Prophet sent by God. The Arabic word *islam* literally means "to submit." In the Koran *(Quran)* it means "to surrender to the will or law of God." One who practices Islam is a Muslim. Muslims regard the Koran as the word of God dictated to Muhammad, mediated by the angel Gabriel.

● **Five Duties**, known as the "Pillars of Islam," are regarded as central to the life of the Islamic community and are professions of faith, prayer, almsgiving, fasting and pilgrimage. Other important laws of Islam include the prohibition of alcohol consumption and of eating pork. As with most other religions, there are variations in degree of practice among Muslims.

● **Mecca**, in western Saudi Arabia, is the birthplace of Muhammad and the most sacred of the Muslim holy cities. According to Islamic tradition, Muslims around the world must face Mecca during their daily prayers. Every year during the last month of the Islamic calendar, more than one million Muslims make a pilgrimage, or *hajj*, to Mecca.

● **Call to Prayer** for Muslim worship occurs five times daily by a lyrical, melodious summons, delivered over the loudspeakers of the mosque or traditionally by a *muezzin*, one who calls to prayer.

● **Hejab**, the head scarf many Muslim women wear in public comes from the Arabic word *hejab* meaning "to cover" or "conceal." The term also is used to describe the Islamic dress code that requires Muslim women and men to dress modestly and not draw attention to their bodies. In Arab Detroit, interpretation of the dress code varies and head covering depends on the individual's religious understanding, country of origin and personal belief, as well as societal pressures. Some Muslim women cover their heads only when entering a mosque. Others wear a scarf covering their hair, ears and neck every time they leave their homes.

ISLAMIC ORGANIZATIONS

MUSLIM STUDENTS ASSOCIATION
4646 Cass Ave., Detroit, MI 48201
(313) 831-9222
Publishes map with locations of Detroit-area mosques. To order the Detroit Masjid Map, send $2.50 payable to MSA.

COUNCIL OF ISLAMIC ORGANIZATIONS
1605 W. Davison Ave., Detroit 48238
(313) 883-3330
Umbrella organization for Michigan.

ISLAMIC MEDIA

THE MUSLIM AMERICAN
1605 W. Davison, Detroit 48238
(313) 730-1677
Monthly newspaper for Muslims in southeast Michigan. Available free at area mosques.
E-mail: muslimamer@aol.com

MOSQUES: Buildings used for Muslim worship range from simple assembly halls for prayer to elaborate structures in the Islamic architectural style. The inner wall *(qibla)* closest to the holy city of Mecca has a niche or arch called a *mihrab,* which indicates the direction to face when praying. Next to the mihrab is the *mimbar,* a pulpit from which the Friday sermon is preached in the prayer hall. A minaret tower is where the *muezzin* (crier) calls the faithful to prayer. Usually there is a courtyard with a fountain or well for ceremonial washing before praying.

Detroit area Muslims worship at mosques located in Dearborn, Detroit, Canton, Farmington Hills, Harper Woods, Rochester and other communities.

AMERICAN MUSLIM BEKKA CENTER
6110 Chase, Dearborn; (313) 581-9349

AMERICAN MUSLIM SOCIETY
9945 W. Vernor, Dearborn; (313) 842-3106
Guided tours of the mosque are offered.

ISLAMIC MOSQUE OF AMERICA
16427 W. Warren, Dearborn
(313) 582-0500

ISLAMIC CENTER OF AMERICA
15571 Joy Rd., Detroit; (313) 582-7442

ISLAMIC INSTITUTE OF KNOWLEDGE
6345 Schaefer, Dearborn; (313) 584-2570

ISLAMIC CENTER OF GREATER TOLEDO
25877 Scheider Rd. (I-75, Exit 193)
Perrysburg, Ohio
(419) 874-3509
Best local example of Islamic architecture is the mosque that dominates the landscape on northbound I-75 near the Ohio-Michigan line. Tours by appointment.

ARAB CHRISTIANS

CATHOLIC CHURCHES

Many Lebanese Christians belong to the Maronite (Antiocian) and Melkite (Greek) groups within the Eastern Rite of the Roman Catholic church. They use ancient liturgies that differ from those recited in European and American Roman Catholic Churches.

ST MARON ADORATION CHAPEL
11466 Kercheval, Detroit; (313) 823-8412

ST. SHARBEL CHURCH
1601 Schoenherr, Warren; (810) 826-9688
Parishioners from all over greater Detroit attend Saturday or Sunday services at this Maronite Catholic Church. As the center of activity for the east-side Lebanese community, it is the site of an annual festival/carnival in late May and a St. Maron's Feast Day celebration in honor of Patron St. Sharbel in February.

OUR LADY OF REDEMPTION MELKITE CHURCH
8525 Cole, Warren; (810) 751-6017

ST. BASIL BYZANTINE CATHOLIC CHURCH
4700 Metro Parkway (between Ryan & Mound) Sterling Heights; (810) 268-1082

(See also Chaldean chapter for Chaldean Catholic Diocese of America churches.)

ORTHODOX CHURCHES

Other Arab Christians are affiliated with orthodox churches, which use similar religious rites but do not accept the authority of the Pope.

ST. GEORGE'S ORTHODOX CHURCH
2160 E. Maple, Troy; (248) 589-0480
Outstanding Byzantine architecture with several bell-shaped domes jutting up to the sky. Built in 1994, the interior is modern with a muted gray tapestry in the lobby. Inside the sanctuary is a high dome with a colorful painting of Christ and the Apostles.

ST. MARY'S ANTIOCHIAN ORTHODOX
18100 Merriman, Livonia; (734) 422-0010

ST. MARK COPTIC ORTHODOX CHURCH
3603 Livernois, Troy; (248) 689-9099
Egyptian congregation uses ancient Coptic language in church services.

ORGANIZATIONS

ACCESS
2651 Saulino Court, Dearborn
(313) 842-7010
Community center provides economic and
social services to Arab Americans and sponsors cultural programs.

AMERICAN ARAB CHAMBER OF COMMERCE
38705 W. Seven Mile, Ste. 435
Livonia 48152
(313) 336-8500
Distributes a biannual directory of Arab
American businesses in metro Detroit.

ARAB AMERICAN AND CHALDEAN COUNCIL
28551 Southfield Rd., Suite 204
Lathrup Village; (248) 559-1990
Tri-county human services agency with outreach centers in Detroit, Warren and Lathrup
Village also serves as a facilitator of cross-
cultural training and education for the public
and private sectors. The W. Seven Mile location houses art and artifact collection.

BINT JE BAIL CULTURAL CENTER
6220 Miller, Dearborn
(313) 584-0011
Lebanese social hall sponsors community
events.

CHALDEAN FEDERATION OF AMERICA
18740 W. 10 Mile, Southfield
(248) 557-2362
(See "Chaldean Heritage" chapter.)

PALESTINIAN AID SOCIETY
3325 Dluett Dr., Ann Arbor; (734) 913-0232
Conducts annual spring concert to raise
funds for Palestinian relief.

AMERICAN & SYRIAN ARAB CULTURAL ASSOCIATION
20834 Dequindre, Warren; (810) 757-5440
Presents education programs and
cultural arts.

YEMENI AMERICAN CULTURAL CENTER
2770 Salina, Dearborn; (313) 841-3395
Organization to preserve Yemeni culture.

MEDIA

RADIO
WNZK AM 690 DAYS/680 NIGHTS
(248) 557-3500
"Arab Network of America" Monday-Friday
8am-5pm, Saturday-Sunday 9am-1pm.

TELEVISION
*Most of these programs are community-
based and broadcast Arabic news, music,
feature films, soap operas, local interviews
and commercials.*

"A NEW VISION FOR DEARBORN"
Cable CUI (DUBAI TV)
Channel 40 (24 hours a day)
(313) 336-4300

AL SALAM TV
6932 Hartwell, Dearborn; (313) 584-8506

ARAB WORLD TV
33014 Shrewsbury Dr., Sterling Hts.
(810) 264-2233 or 431-9095

MIDDLE EAST TV
4031 Gloucester, Sterling Hts.
(810) 826-9685

ARABIC TIME TV (ATV)
7001 Wyoming, Dearborn; (313) 581-3443

SADA EL ARAB
6121 Oakman, Dearborn; (313) 582-2315

TV ORIENT
800 Livernois, Ferndale; (248) 399-0090

UNITED TELEVISION NETWORK INC.
20998 Bridge, Southfield; (248) 357-1700

PRINT
THE ARAB-AMERICAN NEWS
(Sada Al-Watan)
7520 Greenfield, Dearborn; (313) 582-4888
Bilingual newspaper deals with political and
social issues in the Arab community and
covers business, arts and culture. Distributed
every Thursday, free of charge. Available at
many stores in Dearborn.

WEB SITES
*All the following web sites have great links
to Arab culture.*

ISLAMIC INTERLINK: www.ais.org/-islam
Based in Ann Arbor, many local and international rresources and links.

ARAB NET: www.arab.net

ARAB WORLD ON LINE: www.awo.net

CAFE ARABICA:
www.cafearabica.com/index

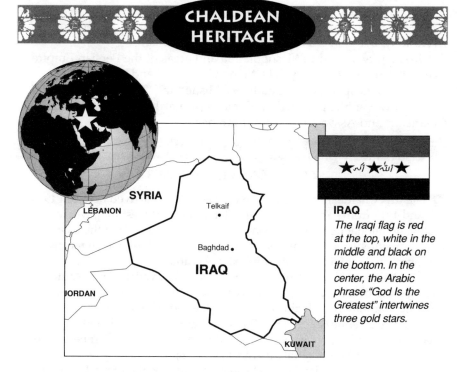

IRAQ

The Iraqi flag is red at the top, white in the middle and black on the bottom. In the center, the Arabic phrase "God Is the Greatest" intertwines three gold stars.

Chaldeans (pronounced kal-DEE-ans) are among the ancient groups that inhabited Mesopotamia—the "land between the two rivers" (the Tigris and the Euphrates) and the "cradle of civilization"—which is present-day Iraq. Since the time of the Sumerians, Akkadians, Assyrians and Chaldeans, Mesopotamia (Iraq) has been a land of many "firsts," making enormous contributions to civilization. Mesopotamia is where the world's first empire was created, where the Towers of Babylon were constructed, where Abraham came from Ur of the Chaldeas, where Hammurabi developed the world's first code of laws and where the discovery of the wheel took place. This civilization was the first to use bronze weapons and horse-drawn chariots. Its irrigation systems and aqueducts were highly developed long before the Egyptian, Greek and Roman Empires acquired them.

Present-day Chaldeans trace their roots to the ancient inhabitants of Mesopotamia: the Babylonians, the Assyrians and the seventh century B.C. Chaldeans, sharing ancestry, culture and leadership. They speak a dialect of Aramaic, the language of Jesus Christ.

During the seventh and sixth centuries B.C., the Chaldeans reached the peak of their glory under the rule of Chaldean King Nebuchadnessar. During his reign (605-562 B.C.), one of the seven wonders of the world, the Palace of Nebuchadnessar with the famous Hanging Gardens of Babylon, was constructed.

As merchants, Chaldeans kept large herds of horses and cattle. They traveled with exotic luxuries—ebony, ivory, elephant hides and gold. Eventually, Babylon fell into the hands of the Persians.

Christianity spread to Mesopotamia and areas of the Persian Empire as early as the first century A.D. Many Chaldeans and Assyrians accepted the gospel and gradually established the "Church of the East." Today, however, the population of Iraq is primarily Islamic. Christian Chaldeans and Assyrians account for 6 percent.

CHALDEANS IN DETROIT

The first Chaldean immigrants to the Detroit area arrived between 1910 and 1912 from various Chaldean villages in northwest Iraq, where multigenerational families lived on small farms. A majority of them came from a quaint village near ancient Nineveh called **Telkaif**, which means "Hill of Stones" in Aramaic. The site originally was an Assyrian fortress.

The Chaldeans chose Detroit because work was available in the auto factories and because an Arabic-speaking community with a Lebanese Catholic Maronite church already was established. The newcomers settled in the Jefferson Avenue/East Grand Boulevard area. A few of them bought small grocery stores. They succeeded in their enterprises, in part because of their strong tradition of family members working together. Other new arrivals followed their lead to establish an occupational pattern. During the 1930s and '40s, many Chaldean families moved to neighborhoods around Chicago Boulevard, Boston Boulevard, Virginia Park and Highland Park.

After the 1967 riots in Detroit, many of the chain grocery stores left the city. It was the Chaldeans, in large part, who provided neighborhood food stores, jobs and services to inner-city residents. The extended family played a key role in the business success of the Chaldean community, providing a reliable and economic labor force to operate their grocery and party stores.

Chaldean immigration grew dramatically in the '60s and '70s when immigration quotas were reformed. But this time, the majority came from urban areas in Iraq, mainly from Baghdad, the capital. The largest number settled in Detroit between Six and Eight Mile Roads, between Woodward and John R. Another concentration was in Southfield.

Many second-generation Chaldeans can recall their parents starting life in Detroit in the Seven Mile/Woodward area; many worked long hours—70-90 a week—in various jobs in gas stations and small grocery and party stores, always putting aside money either to eventually buy the business or to send their children to college. Once established, they often moved to other areas of metro Detroit.

More recently, the Gulf War caused many Chaldeans to leave Iraq and come to the United States. About 100,000 Chaldeans now live in the United States, with the largest concentration in metro Detroit. The rest reside primarily in California, Chicago and Arizona.

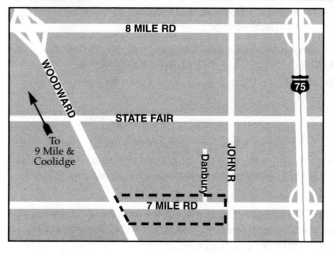

[E-F/3-4]
The one-mile row of Chaldean-owned stores, restaurants, bakeries, meat markets, hair salons and collision shops on *West Seven Mile Road between Woodward and John R* is commonly referred to as

Chaldean Village. The Chaldeans live and work with other ethnic groups in a close-knit community where East meets West.

The neighborhood is reminiscent of Telkaif, the Iraqi village that is the ancestral home of many Detroit Chaldeans. Many store signs are in Arabic and English, and the Aramaic language can be heard at every corner. The enticing aromas of puréed lentil soup, stuffed grape leaves, spiced shish kabob and marinated chicken kabob fill the neighborhood eateries. Shops provide coffees, teas, cheeses and spices of the Middle East, as well as music and videos. Fresh produce, meats, fish and stone-oven-baked breads are sold at many markets here. The area is bustling with people shopping, meeting at the local coffee shops and going to church. **Sacred Heart Chaldean Church** (236 W. Seven Mile at Danbury) provides the religious base for the community.

For a look at "village life," concentrate your exploration in the 400-to-600 blocks of West Seven Mile. Heading east on Seven Mile from Woodward, you'll pass **Sullaf Restaurant** (954), **Modern Meat & Fish Market** (738) and **California Market** (736) on the north side.

Among the buildings with Arabic writing in the 600 block are **Spring Productions** *(635),* which sells Mid-Eastern music and videos, and **Al-Nahrain Restaurant and Coffee Shop** (625) on the south side. Across the street are **Tigris Restaurant** (620) and the **San Diego Club** (600).

In the 500 block, **Bahi Restaurant** *(524),* a diner with Mid-Eastern cuisine, is next door to **Iraqi Bakery & Shorga Imported Foods** *(528).* Here you will find imported cheeses, juices, olives, spices, Iraqi and Lebanese breads, and gift items.

Chaldean specialties at **Al-mosul** (433) include kebobs, gyros, cream chops, stews and rice dishes. The restaurant is in the same cluster as **Beirut Pastry** *(441),* which offers Lebanese baked goods, and **Golden Star Bakery** *(427),* which sells fresh bread and imported foods.

A block down is the **Chaldean Center of America** (310), the church hall for **Sacred Heart** (236). Across the street is **7 Brothers Food Market** (341) and an **Almost 99 Cents** store (309) that, in addition to the usual merchandise, carries ethnic items.

OPTION: OAK PARK

[D-E/3-4] A few miles northwest in Oak Park, businesses at the intersection of Coolidge and Nine Mile serve various ethnic groups. Interspersed with the usual array of shopping strip retailers are several Chaldean establishments with both Arabic and English signage.

At Oak Park Shopping Plaza on the northwest corner, you'll find Middle Eastern specialties at **Kashat Imported Foods** (23111 Coolidge) and fine dining at **New Sahara Restaurant** (23133 Coolidge)**.**

On the southwest corner, another Chaldean market, **Jerry's Imported Foods** (13745 Nine Mile), stocks ethnic novelty items. Even the pink-painted **Paris Pastry** *(22171 Coolidge)* around the corner has a sign in Arabic. The bakery specializes in European and Middle-Eastern pastries.

POPULAR MENU ITEMS

Chicken Cream Chop: Sliced chicken breast, butter-dipped and deep-fried to a golden brown

Dolma: Grape leaves stuffed with meat, rice, onions and tomatoes, seasoned with garlic and spices

Iraqi Salad: Finely cubed cucumbers, tomatoes and onions, beets and chick peas in lemony oil and vinegar

Kubebi (Kibbee): cracked wheat stuffed with fine ground meat, boiled or fried

Lentil Soup: Delicate puréed soup spiced with turmeric

Masgoof: Grilled fish smothered with onions, tomatoes and green peppers

Matabac: Chicken, beef or shrimp sauteed with tomatoes, onions, parsley and spices atop basmati rice.

Maza: Appetizer assortment—hummus, baba ghannooj, tabbouleh, falafel, fried chicken wings, feta cheese, black olives, turnips and curried cabbage with pita bread

Pacha: Beef tripe stuffed with rice, chopped beef and herbs

Potato Chop: Mashed potatoes stuffed with ground beef and fried

Quozi or Kuzy: Whole lamb stuffed with yellow rice, raisins and pine nuts

Shish Kabob (Tika): Chunks of beef tenderloin charbroiled with onions and herbs

Baklava: Phyllo dough pastry with honey and nuts

Coleche: Baked dough stuffed with dates or walnuts

Halawa: Vanilla candy, stuffed with nuts

Zlabia: Bread batter-fried in hot oil, dipped in baklava syrup

Doddly: Cream of wheat and sugar balls, fried and dipped in thick syrup

Fruit Tarts: Puff pastry dough with custard, topped with fruit

(See also "Arab World.")

RESTAURANTS

Lentil soup, chicken cream chop, dolma, kabobs (tika) and Iraqi salad are among the Middle Eastern favorites at Chaldean restaurants.

DETROIT
The Chaldean section of W. Seven Mile between Woodward and John R has the following neighborhood eateries:

AL-MOSUL RESTAURANT
443 W. Seven Mile; (313) 366-4914

AL-NAHRAIN COFFEE SHOP
625 W. Seven Mile; (313) 892-1333

BAHI RESTAURANT
524 W. Seven Mile Rd.; (313) 368-5400

ORIGINAL ASHTAR CLUB
814 W. Seven Mile Rd., (313) 892-0222

SAN DIEGO CLUB & RESTAURANT
600 W. Seven Mile, (313) 892-1311

SULLAF RESTAURANT
954 W. Seven Mile; (313) 893-5656

TIGRIS RESTAURANT
620 W. Seven Mile; (313) 891-6077

SUBURBS
BABYLON RESTAURANT
21411 John R, Hazel Park; (248) 548-6656
Daily 10am-2am. Middle Eastern food, including gyros, kebobs.

FLAMING KABOB CAFE
29702 Southfield at 12 1/2 Mile
Southfield; (248) 423-9777
Mon-Thu 11am-9pm, Fri-Sat 11am-10-pm.
Owner is a native of Baghdad.

HAMMURABI RESTAURANT
21570 Dequindre, Warren; (810) 757-6920
Daily noon-2am. Popular restaurant and banquet hall for Middle Eastern cuisine.

KHAN MERJAN
6431 Miller Rd., Dearborn; (313) 581-8585
Daily 11am-11pm. A new and stylish restaurant offering Iraqi home cooking in a friendly atmosphere where you can dine seated on cushions or western style.

LA FENDI
27060 Evergreen Rd., Lathrup Village
(248) 559-9099
Sun-Thu 11am-1am, Fri-Sat 11am-2am.
Popular Mid-Eastern restaurant with Iraqi specialties: chicken cream chop, matabac and kuzy (roasted lamb shanks with rice). Banquets, catering and carryout.

MIRAGE
12702 W. Nine Mile Rd., Oak Park
(at 9 Scotia Plaza)
(248) 543-9400
Daily 11am-4am. Middle Eastern and Greek cuisine.

NEW SAHARA RESTAURANT
23133 Coolidge, Oak Park
(Oak Park Shopping Plaza)
(248) 399-7744
Daily 11am-4am
Large variety of Middle Eastern fare in fine dining atmosphere.

SENDIAN RESTAURANT
3625 15 Mile Rd., Sterling Hts.
(810) 264-7060
Daily 11am-2am. Chaldean, Greek and American specialties.

BAKERIES

AL-MEENA BAKERY
2685 Coolidge, Berkley
(248) 399-6794
Mon-Sat 9am-6pm. Wedding cakes, baklava, candy and other sweets.

GOLDEN STAR BAKERY
427 W. Seven Mile Rd., Detroit
(313) 366-5700
Mon-Sat 9am-9pm, Sun 9am-6pm. Fresh breads, imported foods.

IRAQI BAKERY
528 W. Seven Mile Rd., Detroit
(313) 891-8932
Mon-Sat 8am-9pm, Sun 8am-8pm. Bakery section of market features various Iraqi and Lebanese breads, sweets.

GROCERS

Specialty and import grocery stores sell bulgur, basmati rice, dried apricot paste, barley, spinach and meat pies, tabbouleh, hummus, international cheeses, candies and breads fresh from stone ovens. (See also "Arab World.")

DETROIT
CALIFORNIA MARKET
736 W. Seven Mile Rd., Detroit
(313) 366-3322 or 366-4429
Mon-Sat 8am-9pm, Sun 8am-8pm. Whole sale and retail grocery has fresh breads, imported coffees, teas, rice, spices. Also novelty items, specialty china and tea sets.

MODERN MEAT & FISH MARKET
738 W. Seven Mile Rd., Detroit
(313) 366-3153
Daily 9am-9pm. Fresh lamb, veal, beef and live fish.

S&J MEAT MARKET
217 W. Seven Mile Rd., Detroit
(313) 368-5155
Daily 9am-6pm. Fresh lamb and beef.

7 BROTHERS FOOD MARKET
341 W. Seven Mile Rd., Detroit
(313) 892-8686
Mon-Sat 10am-10pm, Sun 10am-9pm. Groceries and novelty items.

SHORGA IMPORTED FOODS
528 W. Seven Mile Rd., Detroit
(313) 891-8932
Mon-Sat 8am-9pm, Sun 8am-7pm. Sells bakery items, imported food, novelties and cultural items.

NORTH
KASHAT'S IMPORTED FOODS
2311 Coolidge Hwy., Oak Park
(248) 546-8898
Mon-Sat 10am-9pm, Sun 11am-6pm.

JERRY'S IMPORTED FOODS
13745 W. Nine Mile Rd., Oak Park
(248) 546-1414
Mon-Sat 9am-9pm, Sun 9am-6pm.

NARI'S IMPORTED FOODS
8521 W. Nine Mile Rd., Oak Park
(248) 547-5127
Mon-Sat 9am-10pm, Sun 11am-6pm.

MID-EAST MARKET
24133 W. 10 Mile Rd., Southfield
(248) 350-1919
Mon-Sat 10am-9pm, Sun 10am-6pm.

GALIL'S IMPORTED FOODS
27120 Evergreen, Lathrup Village
(248) 552-9898
Mon-Sat 10am-9pm, Sun 10am-8pm.

WEST
BABYLON ETHNIC FOOD
6609 Orchard Lake Rd. at Maple
West Bloomfield
(248) 851-4343
Mon-Sat 9:30am-9pm, Sun 10:30am-6:30pm.

This lion frieze in color-glazed brick relief symbolizes the power and strength of the Nebuchadnessar Empire of Babylon.

Mother of God Church in Southfield is the largest Chaldean Catholic church in the U.S.

CHURCHES

Many Chaldeans look to their church as the nucleus of their community. These churches are affiliated with the Chaldean Rite of the Roman Catholic Church. Chaldeans were converted to Christianity by St. Thomas the Apostle and his disciples, Mar Addai and Mar Mari. Aramaic, spoken by Jesus Christ and the Apostles, is the language of the Chaldeans. Churches in Detroit (Seven Mile Road), Southfield, Troy and West Bloomfield have ancient Babylonian architectural design.

Along with their many other innovations, the Babylonians are credited with designing the arch—an important element to today's architects and engineers.

MAR ADDAI CHALDEAN CHURCH
24010 Coolidge Hwy., Oak Park
(248) 547-1618

MOTHER OF GOD CHURCH
25585 Berg Rd., Southfield
(248) 356-0565

SACRED HEART CHALDEAN CHURCH
310 W. Seven Mile Rd., Detroit
(313) 368-6214

ST. JOSEPH CHALDEAN CHURCH
2442 E. Big Beaver, Troy
(248) 528-3676

ST. THOMAS CHALDEAN CHURCH
6900 Maple, West Bloomfield
(248) 788-2460

FESTIVALS

EASTER SEASON
PALMS PARADE
Sacred Heart Chaldean Church
310 W. Seven Mile Rd., Detroit
(313) 368-6214
Parade on Seven Mile takes place after Palm Sunday Mass.

MAY
SOUTHFIELD CARNIVAL
Mother of God Church
25585 Berg Rd., Southfield
(248) 356-0565
Chaldean Federation sponsors fair on church grounds.

JULY
INTERNATIONAL FESTIVAL
Phoenix Plaza, downtown Pontiac
(248) 857-5603
Chaldeans participate in this multi-ethnic festival on July 4th weekend.

ARAB WORLD FESTIVAL
Hart Plaza, downtown Detroit
(313) 877-8077 or 877-8078
Chaldeans are part of this major festival on the Detroit riverfront.

AUGUST
AUGUST FESTIVAL
Mother of God Church
25585 Berg Rd., Southfield
(248) 356-0565
Festival on church grounds features amusement rides, games, ethnic food booths and music.

CHALDEAN CULTURE DAY
Mother of God Church
25585 Berg Rd., Southfield
(248) 356-0565
Celebration of Chaldean heritage includes historical displays, costume exhibits and musical programs.

Although not always annual, Chaldean festivals and booths are sometimes part of the summer event schedule in Sterling Heights (810-979-7010), Oak Park (248-691-7555) and other communities.

ORGANIZATIONS

ARAB AMERICAN & CHALDEAN COUNCIL
28551 Southfield Rd., Lathrup Village
(248) 559-1990
Tri-county human services agency with training and educational programs for the public and private sectors. A new office on W. Seven Mile houses art and artifact collection.

CHALDEAN FEDERATION OF AMERICA
18470 W. 10 Mile Rd., Southfield
(248) 557-2362
In addition to providing many services and programs, the federation promotes racial harmony and public awareness and understanding of the Chaldean family, history and culture. Booklets, brochures and videos are available.

CHALDEAN IRAQI ASSOCIATION OF MICHIGAN
25626 Telegraph, Southfield
(248) 352-9020
The CIAM operates the Southfield Manor and Shenandoah Country Club (West Bloomfield). These private clubs each have public banquet and meeting facilities. Shenandoah also has a public 18-hole golf course and grill room.

MEDIA

TELEVISION
ARABIC/CHALDEAN TELEVISION
Aired nightly on local cable in Southfield, Oak Park and West Bloomfield from United Television Network (248-357-1700). South-field-based TV Orient (248-569-2020) broadcasts Arabic/Chaldean programming on seven cable systems in metro Detroit.

RADIO
CHALDEAN VOICE
(248) 353-1083

The huge lion-like Assyrian/Babylonian mastiff, depicted here in a stone carving, is thought by many to be the forefather of the St. Bernard, as well as the other mastiff relatives.

PRINT
CHALDEAN VOICE WEEKLY BULLETIN
c/o Rev. Manuel Boji, 25585 Berg Rd., Southfield; (248) 356-0565
CHALDEAN DETROIT TIMES
17135 W. 10 Mile Rd., Southfield
(248) 552-1989
Biweekly newspaper.

WEB SITES
CHALDEAN CULTURE AND HISTORY
Information for social studies classes at site provided by community liaison for West Bloomfield schools.
http://members.aol.com/chaldeans7

CHALDEAN AMERICAN STUDENT ASSOCIATION
University of Michigan–Dearborn offers historical and contemporary information with graphics and links.
www.umd.umich.edu/%7esdkjr/casa/index.html

ASSYRIAN FOODS
value.net/~stoma/book_assyria.html

CHALDEAN ASSYRIAN HOME PAGE
home.cwnet.com/samir/index.html

Dragon of Babel, from a tile relief at the Ishtar Gate in Babylon, 6th century B.C.

GLOBAL JOURNEYS
IN METRO DETROIT

ASIAN ROUTES

NOTES

Designed as a symbol of freedom, the Indian flag has three horizontal colors of equal proportions. The saffron color on the top stands for courage, sacrifice and the spirit of renunciation; the white band in the middle is for purity and truth; the green at the bottom is for faith and fertility. The Ashoka wheel in the center is the wheel of law.

INDIA

Stretching from the majestic Himalayas in the north to the Indian Ocean on the south, the Arabian Sea on the west and the Bay of Bengal on the east, the Republic of India forms a natural subcontinent of Asia. India is bordered by China, Nepal and Bhutan to the north, Pakistan to the northwest and Myanmar (Burma) to the northeast. On the east, Indian territory surrounds most of Bangladesh.

The country is divided into 25 states and seven centrally administrated union territories. The former British colony became an independent nation 50 years ago on August 15, 1947, after a long struggle for freedom led by Mahatma Gandhi, India's apostle of truth and peace.

The mystique and beauty of India lie in its diversity and rich heritage derived from one of the oldest known civilizations. Each region has its own culture, language and way of life. About 30 percent of the population speaks Hindi, the official language. In addition, there are 16 officially recognized regional languages, and English is widely used.

Indian culture is primarily Hindu-oriented. Many Hindu institutions, including the caste system and dietary proscriptions, have wide-ranging effects on secular Indian society. Sanskrit, the ancient language of Hindu scriptures, was also the medium for a vast body of religious and secular writing that constitutes the core of classical Indian literature.

INDIAN COMMUNITY IN DETROIT

According to U.S. Census data, Indians constitute the largest Asian group in metropolitan Detroit. Asian Indians, who began entering the area roughly 40 years ago, are for the most part a professional group. Many are doctors and engineers, the latter drawn by opportunities with the Big Three automakers.

Though heavier populations of Asian Indians are concentrated on the East Coast of the United States, metro Detroit is now home to about 35,000 Asian Indians. The west-side community, with a shopping district in Garden City, is anchored by the Hindu Temple in Canton. In the northeast suburbs, the Bharatiya Temple in Troy and shops in Sterling Heights serve surrounding communities. In Farmington Hills, Indian restaurants line Orchard Lake Road.

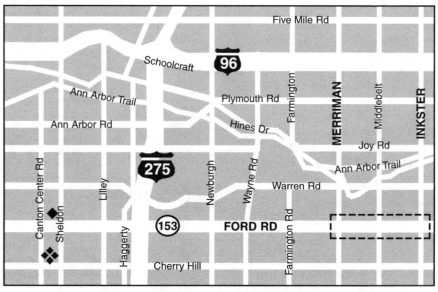

FORD ROAD, GARDEN CITY

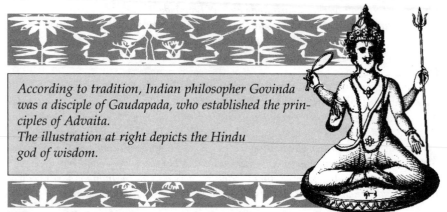

According to tradition, Indian philosopher Govinda was a disciple of Gaudapada, who established the principles of Advaita.
The illustration at right depicts the Hindu god of wisdom.

GARDEN CITY, CANTON, ANN ARBOR

[C-D/4-5] Ford Road between Inkster and Merriman in Garden City offers the largest array of Indian stores and restaurants in the Detroit area. To begin a day of Indian culture, get to this area around 11 a.m., when most of the stores open; this will give you ample time to browse at clothing, jewelry and grocery stores.

The clothing stores, such as **Saheli Boutique** *(28682 Ford Road)* and **India Sari Palace** *(28241)* offer yards and yards of fabric, including cottons, chiffon and beautiful silks. They also carry a range of ready-made Indian outfits for men, women and children.

The jewelry stores, such as **Highglow Jewellers** *(28231)* and **Ruby Jewellers** *(28544),* carry some of India's unique style of jewelry. Jewelry designs in 22-karat gold that are common in India are hard to find in American jewelry stores.

The grocery stores, such as **India Grocers** and **Patel Brothers Inc.,** are chains carrying many Indian and Pakistani food items, including spices, sauces and vegetables. *(See listings for locations.)* They also have Hindi movies on videotape, Indian audiotapes, magazines and other items unique to Indian culture.

Some good choices for lunch or Indian snacks are **Krishna Catering** *(28636),* **Viceroy of India/Neelam's Cafe** *(28233/28235)* and **Bombay Curry House** *(28542)* for meat and vegetarian selections.

Set aside part of the day to watch an Indian movie on the big screen. India is the largest producer of movies outside the United States, and Hindi films are a big part of Indian culture. Some grocery stores, such as **India Grocers** *(in Garden City and Sterling Heights)* and **Foods and Flavors** *(7260 Sheldon Rd., Canton),* rent local theaters to show Hindi movies. They run at various times and days every week. Fliers are posted at the stores. (Check to see if the film has English subtitles.)

The evening ceremony at the **Hindu Temple** *(44955 Cherry Hill)* in Canton provides a glimpse of Hindu rituals, as well as a display of Indian art and sculpture. *(Take Ford Road west to Sheldon Road, then go south one mile to Cherry Hill and go west.)* Call (313) 981-8730 for times of services.

The best way to end your excursion is with a full-course dinner at an Indian restaurant. If you head further west to Ann Arbor, your choices include **Shalimar** *(307 S. Main St.)* and **Raja Rani** *(400 S. Division).* Both offer extensive Indian menus, with specialties ranging from vegetarian meals to fish, chicken, lamb and seafood. The spices used are distinctly Indian and can range from mild to extremely hot. These restaurants also feature a full line of Indian breads, beverages and desserts. *(See restaurant list for choices in Farmington Hills and other cities.)*

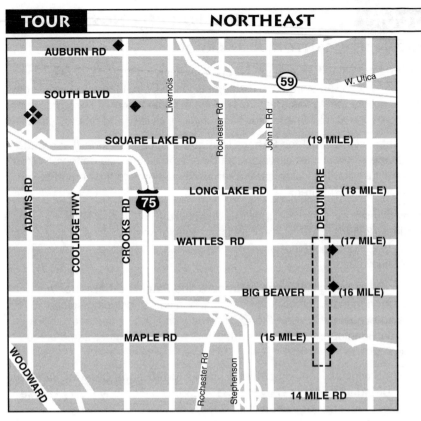

TROY AND STERLING HEIGHTS

[E-F/1-3] On the east side of town, Dequindre between Maple (15 Mile) and Wattles (17 Mile) is the place to find Indian shops and restaurants.

Indian establishments at the plaza on the *southeast corner of Maple and Dequindre* include **India Grocers** and **Rajmahal Restaurant,** which offers the Thali platter (vegetarian and nonvegetarian) as a lunch special. On the northeast corner, **Worldwide Video** rents Hindi movies and Indian and Pakistani dramas.

Continue north on Dequindre to 16 Mile (becomes "Metropolitan Parkway"). At Sunny Plaza *on the northeast corner,* you'll find **Ruby Jewellers** and **Life & Style Fashions.** Next to **Patel Brothers** grocery is **New Delhi Cuisine,** which features a menu of vegetarian and meat entrées, snacks and sweets.

Other specialty groceries in the area include **Laxmi Foods** *at Franklin Square on Dequindre and Wattles* and **Asian Foods** *on the southeast corner of Crooks and South Boulevard in Troy. At Auburn Place on the northwest corner of Crooks and Auburn* is **Moti Mahal** restaurant.

The **Bharatiya Temple** *(6850 Adams between Square Lake Road and South Boulevard in Troy)* serves as a religious, cultural and educational center. Hindu services take place daily. *Call (248) 879-2552 for times.*

In Hinduism, **Krishna** is one of the most widely revered and popular gods, the focus of a large number of devotional cults. In 1965, a Hindu mystic, the swami Prabhupada, arrived in the United States and founded the **International Society for Krishna Consciousness** (more commonly known as Hare Krishna from the chant its members use).

The public became aware of the Hare Krishna movement from seeing its followers dressed in saffron robes and singing, dancing and chanting on street corners and in public buildings. To achieve peace and happiness, believers try to return to an original relationship, called Krishna Consciousness, with the god. This is done through a type of yoga called *bhakti*, which involves recognizing Krishna as a god and doing his work with no thought of reward. All possessions are surrendered to the organization.

Members live in communes in which unmarried men and women live separately in celibacy, while married members have their own quarters. There are prohibitions against gambling, the use of alcohol and eating meat.

TOUR — ON A SUNDAY AFTERNOON

FISHER MANSION

[F-G/4-5] During its Sunday open houses, the **Bhaktivedanta Cultural Center** *(383 Lenox Ave.)* on Detroit's east side offers an in-depth look at the **Hare Krishna** movement. The temple is in the Fisher Mansion, one of several historic auto-baron homes in metro Detroit. *(From downtown, take East Jefferson a few blocks east of Conner to Dickerson, which becomes Lenox after you cross Essex.)* The mansion is on a canal leading to the Detroit River. **Govinda's** vegetarian

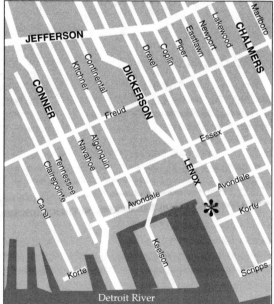

restaurant and gift shop, run by a Krishna Consciousness group, opens at noon. Follow lunch with the 2 p.m. tour of the house.

The Hare Krishna program begins with a religious ceremony at 4:15 p.m. The group conducts classes for religious readings and offers a free full-vegetarian meal for attendees in the evening. The temple also has a large collection of Indian art, including sculptures, handicrafts and paintings on clothing, silk and canvas. *Call (313) 331-6740 for house tours and (313) 824-6000 for temple information.*

INDIAN CUISINE

Most Indian food is prepared with similar spices and many types of vegetables. But that doesn't mean it all tastes the same. The terrain, religion and social systems of the regions of India contribute to local styles of food preparation.

Coastal kitchens make strong use of fish and coconuts. The desert cuisines of Rajasthan and Gujarat use *dals* (lentils) and *achars* (preserves) to make up for the lack of fresh vegetables.

Along the northern plain, from Punjab through Uttar Pradesh and Bihar, a variety of flours are used to make *chapatis* and other breads. In the rainy regions of the northeastern foothills and along the coasts, many kinds of rice are used.

Although most restaurants will automatically provide eating utensils, it's perfectly acceptable to eat in the traditional Indian fashion: with your hands. A dish of fennel seeds will often be placed on the table after the meal; chewing a few seeds will refresh the palate and aid digestion.

At least one fresh or cooked **chutney** (made with vegetables, fruits and herbs) or pickle will accompany the meal, as will rice or bread. Many restaurants also offer a selection of Indian beer, tea, juice and yogurt.

RESTAURANTS

DETROIT

GOVINDA'S
383 Lenox Ave., Detroit
(at the Fisher Mansion)
(313) 331-6740
Irregular hours; usually Fri-Sat noon-9pm, Sun noon-7pm. Total vegetarian menu with dishes such as basmati rice with pine nuts, vegetables and spices; lentil or split-pea soup; and cucumber and yogurt salad. Run by a Krishna Consciousness group.

TAJ MAHAL
2314 Caniff, Hamtramck
(313) 356-4444
Tue-Sun 11am-10pm; buffet lunch 11am-3pm. Bangladeshi and Indian cuisine featuring exotic dishes made in a tandoor.

EAST

MOTI MAHAL
2076 Auburn Rd., Rochester Hills
(248) 852-0077
Tues-Sat 11:30am-10:30pm, Sun-Mon 4:30-10:30pm. Madras curries, Persian dhansak dishes, tandoori and other regional dishes.

NEW DELHI CUISINE
37222 Dequindre, Sterling Hts.
(next to Patel Brothers)
(810) 264-3333
Daily 11am-9pm. Full range of vegetarian and meat entrées, snacks and sweets. Bread basket has naan, methi roti, stuffed paratha, masala paratha, Punjabi fulka.

RAJMAHAL RESTAURANT
344726 Dequindre, Sterling Hts.
(810) 978-8090
Daily lunch buffet 11:30am-2:30pm, dinner 5:30-9pm. Vegetarian dishes, cucumber and yogurt salad, lentil soup, Indian breads. Thali platter lunch special. Carryout and catering.

NORTH

PASSAGE TO INDIA
3354 W. 12 Mile, Berkley; (248) 541-2119
Mon-Fri 11:30am-10pm, Sat 1-10pm, Sun 4:30-9pm. Northern Indian dishes and Bengali selections. Specialties include tandoori dishes, shrimp poori, curries, biryanis, and fresh, hot breads.

PRIYA INDIAN RESTAURANT
72 W. Maple (just W of Livernois), Troy
(248) 269-0100
Mon-Fri 11am-2:30pm, 5-10pm; Sat-Sun 11am-10pm. Features cuisine from tropical southeast coast (hotter and lower in fat than northern cuisine). Vegetarian and nonvegetarian menu includes curries and masalas. Dosas (crepes filled with onions, chilies or curries) are served with sambar, a lentil-vegetable soup.

STAR OF INDIA
3736 Rochester Rd., Troy
(248) 528-2517
Daily 11:30am-2:30pm, 5-10pm. Closed Tue. Fine Indian dining features naan bread, lentil soup, range of rice dishes.

INDO-PAK RESTAURANT
27707 Dequindre, Madison Hts.
(248) 541-3562
Tue-Sat 10am-9pm, Sun 10am-8pm. North Indian cuisine, including variety of breads, curries and rice dishes. Buffet, carryout and catering.

NORTHWEST
SHALIMAR
29200 Orchard Lake Rd., Farmington Hills
(248) 626-2982
Tue-Sun 11:30am-3pm, 5-10pm. Authentic haute cuisine of India, including vegetarian and nonvegetarian dishes and samosas. Full viewing of tandoori cooking. Carryout and catering available.

UDIPI RESTAURANT
29210 Orchard Lake Rd., Farmington Hills
(between 12 and 13 Mile)
(248) 626-6021
Mon, Wed, Thu 11:30am-9pm; Fri-Sat 11:30am-10pm; Sun 5:30-9pm. Closed Tue. Vegetarian Indian cuisine. Daily lunch buffet.

HOUSE OF INDIA
28841 Orchard Lake Rd., Farmington Hills
(248) 553-7391
Daily 11:30am-9pm; buffets Sat-Sun noon-4pm. Authentic Indian cuisine, setting and decor. Tandoori lamb and rice specialties; Hallal meats. Curries, masalas, tandoori breads and dishes, mild-spiced lentil soup.

SITAR
29550 Grand River, Farmington Hills
(just W of Middlebelt)
(248) 477-9000
Mon-Thu 11:30am-10pm, Fri-Sat 5-10pm. Rice specialties, chicken, lamb and seafood entrées, as well as 13 kinds of Indian bread baked in a tandoor. Curries prepared to order—mild, medium or hot. Indian beers and exotic drinks.

VAATIKA
39241 Grand River, Farmington Hills
(SE corner of Haggerty)
(248) 477-7427
Sun-Thu 11:30am-9pm, Fri-Sat 11:30am-10pm. Full selection of dishes from northern and southern India.

WEST
NEELAM'S CAFE/VICEROY OF INDIA
28235/28233 Ford Rd., Garden City
(734) 261-2233
Tue-Sun 11:30am-9pm. Indian cuisine, including curry specialties and chana (chick peas) on bhatura bread. Snack foods and fresh sweets daily. Catering and carryout.

KRISHNA CATERING
28636 Ford Rd., Garden City
(734) 513-FOOD [3663]
Tue-Sat 11am-8pm, Sun noon-5pm. Pure vegetarian foods for dine-in, carryout or catering. Full line of South India specialties.

HIMALAYA RESTAURANT
44282 Warren, Canton; (734) 416-0880
Mon, Wed, Thu 11:30am-9pm; Fri 11:30am-10pm; Sat noon-10pm; Sun noon-9pm. Lunch buffet offers two meat dishes and four vegetarian selections, naan (hot bread), raita (yogurt and cucumber salad), rice and dessert. Indian beers, wines and lassi (yogurt-based drinks).

SOUTHWEST
THE PEACOCK
4045 Maple, Dearborn
(between Schaefer and Rotunda)
(313) 582-2344
Mon-Thu 11am-11pm, Fri-Sat 5-11:30pm, Sun 4:30-9pm. Chicken, lamb and bread cooked in a tandoor. Curry and vegetarian entrées. Homemade mango ice cream. Lunch buffet.

CURRYING FLAVOR

In Indian and Pakistani cuisine, dishes are named according to the type of seasoning in the sauce. The most common of these is **curry**—as in "mutton curry," "chicken curry," "fish curry," or "vegetable curry."

The dominant spice of the 10 or so seeds and roots in all curries is **coriander.** Other generally used ingredients are **turmeric, ginger** and **cumin.** Some curry mixtures contain mustard and poppy seeds.

The degree of hotness depends solely on the amount of **chili** that is added. Coriander and cumin, once crushed, do not maintain their flavor for long, particularly when exposed to light. Therefore, a fresh curry powder mixture tastes different from (and much better than) any bought in a spice jar.

Another common sauce in Indian cuisine is *garam masala.* The preparation of garam masala is similar to the preparation of curries, and it includes many of the same spices. Here, **cardamom** is the predominant spice, which gives the sauce a gray-brown appearance.

Lentils are a common Indian vegetable. They are often puréed and served as a spiced pulp called *dal* (or *dahl*).

ANN ARBOR
RAJA RANI
400 S. Division, Ann Arbor
(734) 995-1545
Mon-Fri 11:30am-10pm, Sat 5:30-10pm. Situated in a Victorian-era house, restaurant offers Indian fare, spiced to order. Lunch buffet features eight main dishes (mostly vegetarian), salad and hot Indian bread.

SHALIMAR
307 S. Main St., Ann Arbor
(734) 663-1500
Tue-Thu 11:30am-2:30pm, 5-10pm; Fri 11:30am-2:30pm, 5-11pm; Sat noon-3pm, 5-11pm; Sun noon-3pm, 5-10pm. Extensive vegetarian and nonvegetarian menu. Tandoori dishes, curries, homemade stuffed breads, Indian beers.

WINDSOR
NEW ASIAN CURRY HOUSE
1139 University W., Windsor
(at Elm)
(519) 977-1234
Mon-Thu 11am-9pm, Fri-Sat 11am-11pm, Sun noon-8pm. Features broad selection of curries, rice dishes, naan, masalas, cucumber and yogurt salad. Dine-in or carryout.

THE TANDOORI TRADITION

The traditional rounded-top *tandoor* is an oven made of brick and clay and used throughout India to bake foods over direct, intense heat produced from a smoky fire. Food prepared in this manner is referred to as *tandoori* cuisine. The dough for Indian bread is placed directly onto the oven's clay walls and left to bake until puffed and lightly brown. Meat cooked in the tall, cylindrical tandoor is usually skewered and placed inside briefly; a chicken half can be cooked in less than five minutes.

Tandoori coloring or paste is available in Indian markets and is used to give foods the traditional red-orange tint of tandoori cooking.

MARKETS

Most markets carry a full line of Indian groceries, including spices, snacks, sweets, breads, prepared frozen food and ice cream. Some also have videos, compact discs, audiocassettes and other ethnic items.

ASIAN FOOD
1961 South Blvd. (at Crooks), Troy
(248) 828-1937
Tue-Sat 11am-8pm, Sun 10am-5pm.

FOODS & FLAVORS
7260 Sheldon Rd. , Canton
(North Canton Plaza)
(734) 455-0160
Tue-Sun 11:30am-8pm. Market and video store.

INDIA BAZAAR
23626 Van Born, Dearborn Hts.
(313) 295-2121
Tue-Sat 11am-8pm, Sun noon-6pm.

LAXMI FOODS INC.
38948 Dequindre, Sterling Hts.
(810) 977-1770
and
29113 W. Eight Mile, Livonia
(248) 476-0400
Mon-Sat 11am-8pm, Sun 11am-5pm. Full line of Indian groceries. Video- and audiocassettes, movies, CDs.

INDIA GROCERS INC.
28251 Ford Rd., Garden City
(734) 422-5121
and
28958 Orchard Lake Rd.
Farmington Hills; (248) 737-9909
and
45480 Ford Rd., Canton
(734) 459-2016
and
34714 Dequindre, Sterling Hts.
(810) 795-0012
Tue-Sat 11am-8pm, Sun 11am-5pm. Fresh Indian vegetables, ready-to-eat snacks, Kulfi, ice cream, frozen foods, naan, roti. Videocassettes of Hindi, Tamil, Telugu and Malayalam dramas.

PATEL BROTHERS INC.
29212 Orchard Lake Rd., Farmington Hills
(248) 851-7470
and
28684 Ford Rd., Garden City
(734) 427-4445
and
37196 Dequindre, Sterling Hts.
(810) 795-5120
Mon, Wed-Sat 11am-8pm; Sun 11am-5pm. Fresh Indian produce, groceries, snacks and sweets; imported food and spices; frozen food and Indian flavors of ice cream.

ON THE MENU

Aloo: potatoes

Biryanis: spiced rice

Dosas: similar to crepes, filled with potatoes, onions and spices

Gobi: cauliflower

Keema: ground meat

Lassi: a yogurt shake; comes in plain or mango flavor

Masala: mixture of spices

Mutter: peas

Mutton: lamb meat

Pakora: small deep-fried balls of graham flour dough, usually flavored with onions, potatoes, chilies or cauliflower

Paneer: cheese, similar to ricotta

Raita: yogurt mixed with tomatoes, cucumbers and other vegetables with light spices

Sambar: spicy lentil, vegetable soup

Samosa: a pastry shell filled with vegetables (such as peas, potatoes and carrots); also comes with meat

TYPES OF BREAD:

Naan: baked in a tandoor

Puri: deep-fried bread

Roti, Chapati, Fulka: types of bread dry-roasted on stove top, made of whole-wheat flour

Paratha: pan bread often stuffed with ground lentils, potato, onion, cauliflower or other vegetables

SARI AND BINDI

The graceful **sari** is a single piece of material that's five to six yards in length. Styles, colors and fabrics vary. Although India has many traditional garments, the sari has become the national dress of Indian women. It can fit a person of any size, and if worn properly, it can accentuate or conceal. How it's worn, its color and its texture indicate the status, age, occupation, region and religion of a woman. The tightly fitted, short blouse worn under a sari is called a *choli*.

Many Indian women still wear traditional dress, but most men have adopted Western clothing. The traditional *kurta,* or Nehru jacket, as well as *lungis, dhotis* and pajamas are still worn outside urban areas.

The reasons behind the *bindi, tilak* or *kumkum*—the "red mark" on the foreheads of Hindu women (and men)—are as varied as the tenets within the Hindu religion. Sometimes it can mean a woman is married (but children wear them as well). Some wear it merely as a beauty mark; for others it has deeper spiritual meaning. Some wear it to bring prosperity and good luck for their families. The colors vary, with the pigments considered by some to be medicinal. The shapes also vary—with various sects applying various marks in various places.

CLOTHING STORES

CHANDANI PALACE
28538 Ford Rd., Garden City
(between Middlebelt and Inkster)
(734) 522-6090
Mon-Sat 11am-8pm, Sun 11am-6pm.
Fabrics and Indian-style clothing for all ages; men's suits.

SAHELI BOUTIQUE
28682 Ford Rd., Garden City
(734) 513-0040
Mon-Sat 11:30am-8pm, Sun 11:30am-5pm.
Indian clothing styles.

SARI PALACE
28241 Ford Rd., Garden City
(734) 525-5470
Tue-Sat 11am-8pm, Sun 11am-5pm. Men's and women's clothing, chiffons, Indian CDs, luggage, jewelry and watches.

LIFE & STYLE FASHION
37188 Dequindre, Sterling Hts.
(810) 264-2036
Mon-Sat 11am-8pm, Sun 11am-8pm.
Women and children's Indian clothing, saris, men's suits, costume jewelry.

JEWELRY STORES

RAM CREATIONS
Novi Town Center
26024 Ingersol Dr., Novi
(248) 305-8686
Tues-Fri 11am-8pm, Sat 11am-6pm. Custom jewelers.

RUBY JEWELLERS
28544 Ford Rd., Garden City
(734) 427-8320
and
Sunny Plaza Store, Sterling Hts.
(Dequindre and Metropolitan Pkwy.)
(810) 939-7728
Indian, Pakistani and Middle Eastern designs; 22-karat gold jewelry, precious and semiprecious stones.

HIGHGLOW JEWELLERS
28231 Ford Rd., Garden City
(734) 422-6810
*Tue-Sat 11am-7:30pm, Sun 11am-5pm.
Selection of 22-karat gold, ruby, emerald,
sapphire and pearl jewelry.*

VISUAL ARTS

DETROIT INSTITUTE OF ARTS
5200 Woodward, Detroit
(313) 833-7900
Wed-Fri 11am-4pm, Sat-Sun 11am-5pm.
Indian and Southeast Asian Gallery (N141)
features Hindu art in bronze, sandstone and
ivory and a relief sculpture from a
temple.

LOCAL HINDU TEMPLES
See "Temples."
Nothing depicts the beauty of Indian art more
than the hand-sculpted statues of religious
deities. Hindu temples provide examples of
Indian statues, paintings, handicrafts and
some architecture.

BHAKTIVEDANTA CULTURAL CENTER
383 Lenox Ave., Detroit
(at the Fisher Mansion)
(313) 824-6000
The temple, in this former home of an auto
baron, features a large collection of Indian
art, paintings, sculpture and handicrafts.
Fisher Mansion tours *take place Fri-Sat
12:30, 2 and 3:30pm; Sun 2 pm. Call (313)
331-6740.*

UNIVERSITY OF MICHIGAN
MUSEUM OF ART
525 S. State St., Ann Arbor
(734) 764-0395
*Tue-Sat 10am-5pm, Thu 10am-9pm, Sun
noon-5pm.* Gandaharan sculpture and other
Hindu temple art.

*Typical
paisley
print>*

FABRIC CLASSICS

*Some of our finest, most enduring
clothing fabric originated in India:*

CASHMERE is the fine wool
spun from the soft undercoat of the
Kashmir goat, from the province of
Kashmir. Cashmere fabrics look
beautiful and luxurious and are
soft to the touch, providing
warmth without weight.

MADRAS, the capital of Tamil
Nadu, was a small village until
1640 when it began to be developed into a port by the East India
Trading Company. The term
madras is used for a specific type of
woven cotton, usually plaid.

KHAKI is a Hindu word
meaning "dusty" or "dust-col-
ored." It was eventually adopted
as the standard uniform color for
soldiers of many countries.

PAISLEY is a particular type of
pear-shaped, often floral design
that originated in India on cashmere shawls. Around 1800, British
soldiers brought it home. The town
of Paisley in western Scotland
copied these fine wool shawls,
adapting the design to their
Jacquard looms. Manufacturing
ended about 1850, and the few
genuine paisley shawls
still in existence are
museum pieces. Paisley
designs, however, con-
tinue to be used on
many fabrics and deco-
rative items such as
wallpaper.

PERFORMING ARTS

BHAKTIVEDANTA CULTURAL CENTER
383 Lenox Ave., Detroit; (313) 331-6740
Religious dramas and classical Indian dance lessons.

CENTER FOR CREATIVE STUDIES INSTITUTE OF MUSIC AND DANCE
(313) 872-3118, ext. 601
Bharat Natyam style of East Indian classical form taught at Jewish Community Center in West Bloomfield.

MALINI'S DANCES OF INDIA
1355 Wynnstone Dr., Ann Arbor
(734) 994-3167
Malini Srirama conducts workshops and directs dance troupe, which performs classical and folk dances at many events.

NADANTA INC.
CHAULADEVI INSTITUTE OF DANCE INC.
30362 Southfield Rd., Southfield
(248) 642-6663
Director Chaula Thacker offers dance instruction in Indian folk, classical and creative styles. Nadanta touring group performs throughout Michigan and gives lectures and demonstrations.

NARTAN
3081 Burlington Ct., Rochester
(248) 377-9122
Classical dance classes taught by Raksha Dave.

VIDYANJALI EAST INDIAN DANCE
24611 Seneca Ave., Oak Park
(248) 399-0259
Classes taught by Sudha Chandrasekhar.

FESTIVALS & EVENTS

Many local Indian groups put on cultural shows throughout the year. Indian shows presented by student groups at universities feature dancing, singing and comedy.

INDIAN AMERICAN STUDENT ASSOCIATION
University of Michigan, Ann Arbor
Contact: Renuka Kher
(734) 668-1788; rkher@umich.edu
IASA's main event is the Diwali cultural show each fall.

INDIAN STUDENT ASSOCIATION
Wayne State University
5221 Gullen Mall, Box 53
Detroit, MI 48202
ISA has an annual cultural show. Garbas, Indian dance parties originating in the state of Gujarat, take place every few months.

BHAKTIVEDANTA CULTURAL CENTER
383 Lenox Ave., Detroit
(at the Fisher Mansion)
(313) 331-6740
Religious dramas staged during Hare Krishna holidays. Call for schedule.

INDIAN DANCE

Nadanta is the cosmic dance of Shiva (the Hindu god of destruction and regeneration, also called Siva) and the name of a Southfield-based dance troupe. Directed by Chaula Thacker, the group presents Indian musical dance dramas as well as folk, classical and creative dance styles. The troupe performs Indian folk dances characterized by whirling color and movement. Dancers also portray India's rich culture and heritage in the 2,500-year-old classical dance form Bharat Natyam, which is known for its beauty, elegance and precision.

The dance company's logo (right) is a *natraja* of the dance of Shiva. It represents the fusion of Hindu mythology and philosophy, showing the universal balance of creation and destruction, and the ultimate ascension of good over evil.

HINDU HOLIDAYS

DIWALI (DEEPAWALI), one of the main Hindu holidays, is the festival of light. Usually in October or November, it signifies the homecoming of **Lord Rama** after he killed the demon **Ravana.** People throughout India decorate their homes with candles and lights and celebrate with firecrackers and sparklers to welcome him home. In some Indian states, Diwali is considered the New Year celebration. In the Detroit area, Diwali is celebrated by many Indian groups, including those at the University of Michigan and Wayne State University, with cultural programs that feature dancing and singing.

HOLI, the festival of colors, is celebrated in the spring. It signifies the destruction of a demoness, Holi. Considered the "most fun" holiday, it includes the splashing of colored powder and water on one's family and friends.

NAVARATRI or **DASHARA,** the festival of nine nights for the Goddess Durga, is celebrated in autumn and signifies the victory of good over evil. Celebrants burn effigies of the demon Ravana and worship Mother Durga. People from the state of Gujarat are famous for conducting all-night *garbas* (dance parties) celebrating Navaratri. The people of northern India (New Delhi) celebrate Dashhara. Locally, many Indians gather at the University of Michigan's Dearborn campus to dance for several weekends surrounding the festival.

Ravana

ANNUAL BAZAAR
Bharatiya Temple
6850 Adams Rd., Troy; (248) 879-2552
August event features stalls selling Indian food, clothing, jewelry.

DEEPAWALI PROGRAM
India Cultural Society
Surinder Sud; (734) 455-7199
Annual dinner and cultural program takes place at Clarenceville High School, Livonia.

TEMPLES

Worshipers and visitors remove their shoes before entering the sanctuary.

BHARATIYA TEMPLE
6850 Adams Rd., Troy; (248) 879-2552
Daily services at 10am, 7pm; Sun program 10:30am-12:30pm. Cultural and educational programs include Hindu heritage, language, Indian classical dance and math classes.

HINDU TEMPLE
44955 Cherry Hill, Canton
(734) 981-8730
Sunday program 10:30am-noon.

SIKH TEMPLE (GURU DWAR)
990 Lincoln, Madison Hts.
(248) 547-0927

SIKH GURDWARA
6780 Orion Rd., Rochester Hills
(248) 651-1139

HARE KRISHNA TEMPLE
Bhaktivedanta Cultural Center
383 Lenox Ave., Detroit
(at the Fisher Mansion)
(313) 824-6000
Daily services and elaborate services on Sundays and all Hindu festival days.

JAIN SOCIETY OF GREATER DETROIT
29250 12 Mile, Farmington Hills
(248) 851-5246
Study masses, lectures by scholars from the United States and India, and social events take place at new temple and cultural hall.

INDIAN RELIGIONS

India's major religious groups are Hindus (83%), Muslims (11%), Christians (2%), Sikhs (2%), Buddhists (0.7%) and Jains (0.5%).

Hinduism is a major world religion (estimated at more than 700 million believers) and has had a profound influence on many other religions during its history, dating from about 1500 B.C.

Although many divinities may be worshiped, modern Hindus are generally divided into followers of *Vishnu, Shiva* or *Shakti.* Each group of followers holds the *Vedas* (the four sacred books of the Brahmins) in high regard, but each also has its own scriptures. In addition to the three primary deities, several others also are worshiped. Many animals and plants are also regarded as sacred, the most notable of which is the cow. All cattle are protected, and even among castes that are not vegetarian, beef is not eaten. Monkeys, tree squirrels and some snakes are also considered holy. All rivers are holy, but the holiest is the **Ganges,** focus of pilgrimage for millions. People are revered according to their station in life—parents are holy to their children, teachers to their students.

The **Jains** exert an influence far out of proportion to their numbers; they are mainly traders, and their wealth and authority have made their comparatively small sect one of the most important. Jainism is similar to **Buddhism**. A core belief is that the path to salvation is through peaceful action, characterized by humility and detachment. They take care to avoid any useless killing, including plants and insects.

Sikhism *(Gurmat)* fuses elements of Hinduism and Islam. It rejects the caste system, priesthood, image worship, and pilgrimage; but retains the Hindu doctrines of transmigration and karma. Sikh males are expected to join the *Khalsa* (Punjabi for "pure"), a religious and military brotherhood. They must observe **the five K's:** no cutting of the beard or hair *(kes)*; wear soldiers' shorts *(kacch)* and an iron bangle *(kara)* against evil; and carry a steel dagger *(khanda)* and a comb *(khanga).*

The **Taj Mahal,** *designed as a tomb for the wife of a 17th century Mughal emperor, was constructed by about 20,000 workers from 1631 to 1648 in Agra.*

YOGA

Yoga (from the Sanskrit *yuga*, meaning "yoke") is one of the six classic systems of Hindu philosophy. It affirms the doctrine that through the practice of certain disciplines, one may achieve liberation from the limitations of the flesh, the delusions of sense and the pitfalls of thought, and thus attain union with the object of knowledge.

In the United States, **hatha** (physical) yoga is most common. It is concerned with developing those bodily controls from which all else follows. Perhaps the most widely practiced system in India is **bhakti** (devotional) yoga. Other popular systems are **mantra** yoga, which devotes itself to uttering the name of Krishna and other incantations; **karma** yoga, the path of work and service; and **jnana** yoga, the way of intellect. The synthesis of bhakti, karma and jnana yogas is called **raya** (royal) yoga.

Yoga has been one of the most influential features of Hinduism worldwide. The strong influence of yoga can be seen in Buddhism, and it has been attracting European and American followers since the 19th century. In recent years, yoga exercises have been recommended by some physical fitness experts as a means of cleansing the body of impurities, reducing weight, toning nerves and muscles, and generally improving health without undue stress to the body.

● *Yoga classes are offered through Ys, community education programs and parks and recreation departments. Yoga studios and schools are listed in the Yellow Pages under "Yoga Instruction."*

INDIAN MUSIC

Traditional Indian music includes the classical *raga,* the unique tune pattern on which most of India's other music is based. *Ghazals,* sometimes found in films, are light, lyrical and poetic. *Qawwali,* Muslim religious music, is especially popular in Pakistan.

Bhangra is Punjabi folk-rock, and there is **Indipop** and **Pakistani** folk music. The sitar and drums are traditional instruments.

To find shops where you can purchase tapes or CDs, see "Multicultural Resources" as well as the stores mentioned in this chapter.

ORGANIZATIONS

INDIA CULTURAL SOCIETY
(734) 455-7199
Contact: Surinder Sud
Dedicated to the enhancement, enrichment and promotion of Indian heritage and culture.

ISLAMIC ASSOCIATION
OF GREATER DETROIT
Rochester Hills; (248) 852-5657

VIDYA NIKETAN
Indo-American Educational Center
2260 Nixon Rd., Ann Arbor
(734) 996-3833
Center provides sociocultural activities including dance, voice and harmonium. Celebrates festivals such as Diwali, Republic Day and Spring Festival. Its Bharat Bhaven Library has more than 700 books on Indian culture, literature and philosophy.

MEDIA

RADIO

GEETANJANLI - MUSIC OF INDIA
(248) 348-0788
"Subhash Kelkar, host.

WNZK AM 690/680
(248) 557-3500
"Swar Bahar," Sun 11am-noon
"Sur Sangit - Punjabi Radio," Sun 5-6pm. and Sat 7-8am.

WPON 1460 AM
(248) 332-8883
"Geet Mala," Narendra Seth, Sat 11am-1pm.

WEB SITES

INDIA CORNER
www.indiacorner.com

INDIA NET
www.cs.uiowa.edu/~rraman/india.html

INDIA WORLD (includes chat room)
www.indiaworld.com/

NET INDIA COMPANY
www.net-india.com/

FILM

India has a thriving film industry that produces nearly 700 movies a year (nearly twice that of Hollywood). More than 13 million tickets are sold daily, filling 13,000 theaters. For information about local Hindi film showings, call:

FOOD & FLAVORS MOVIE HOTLINE:
(734) 455-3900
(store number: (734-455-0160)

INDIA GROCER MOVIE INFORMATION:
(810) 795-0012

INDIA'S WILD WEALTH

The forests, plains, hills and mountains of India are inhabited by a variety of animal life. In the cat family are tigers (India's national animal), panthers, cheetahs and leopards. Elephants are found along the northeastern slopes of the Himalayas and in remote forests. Other large quadrupeds include rhinoceroses, black bears, wolves, jackals, wild buffalo, wild hogs and several species of apes, antelope and deer. Venomous reptiles, including cobras, are especially numerous in India. Pythons usefully consume destructive rodents. Among the abundant tropical birds of India are parrots, peacocks (the national bird), kingfishers and herons.

*You can see many of these animals at the **Detroit Zoological Park** (Woodward and 10 Mile in Royal Oak). The zoo is open daily April-October 10 a.m.-5 p.m., Wed 10 a.m.-8 p.m. (June 15-Aug 31) and 10 a.m.-4 p.m. remainder of year. Call (248) 398-0900; hot line (248) 541-5835.*

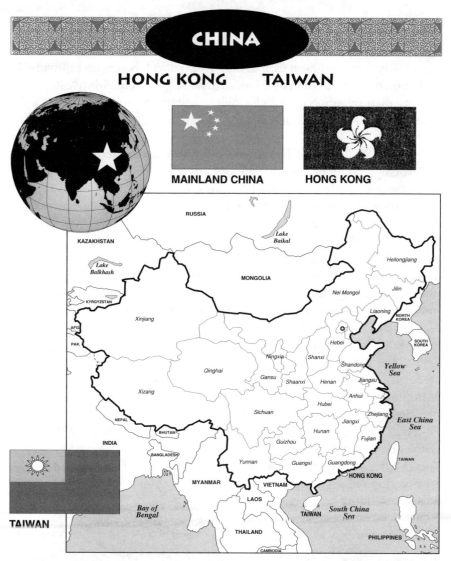

CHINA

HONG KONG   TAIWAN

MAINLAND CHINA   **HONG KONG**

TAIWAN

Mainland China, *for centuries known as the Middle Kingdom, is as large as the United States, but has four times as many people. At last count, its population totaled more than 1.1 billion.* **Taiwan,** *the island to the southeast, has more than 20 million people and is home to the exiled Nationalist government.* **Hong Kong,** *a British-crown colony for 155 years, became a special administrative region of Mainland China on July 1, 1997.*

The flag of the **People's Republic of China** *(Mainland China) is bright red with a constellation of five gold stars—one large star surrounded by four smaller ones. The flag of* **Taiwan** *is red, white and blue; in the left-hand corner of the bright red background is a small rectangle with a 12-point white sun in the center. The new* **Hong Kong** *flag shows a white bauhinia flower on a red field.*

CHINESE IN AMERICA

The first Chinese to come to the United States in the late 1800s were mostly from southern China; they worked as laborers on railroads and in gold mines in the West. Later, many settled in the Midwest, earning their livelihood through Chinese restaurants and laundries. After World War II, their descendants began to mainstream into other professions.

In the 1940s, the first Chinatown in Detroit was situated around Third and Michigan Avenues. By the late '60s, during Detroit's urban renewal, Chinatown moved to Cass and Peterboro. Today, this area houses the **Association of Chinese Americans Drop-In/Outreach Center** *(420 Peterboro),* as well as a small enclave of elderly Chinese and newcomers to Michigan.

The Chinese immigrants who came in the '60s and early '70s were mainly from central and northern China and Taiwan. They were professionals: engineers, scientists and physicians who staffed the big universities, hospitals and automotive companies. Following President Nixon's détente with Communist China, another wave of Chinese came in the late '70s. This time there was an exodus from the big cities of China. The people who came were mostly scholars and graduate students who stayed to work in various industries. Others were entrepreneurs who established small businesses to serve the needs of the growing Chinese American population.

Today, more than 25,000 Chinese Americans live in metro Detroit, with concentrations in Ann Arbor, Detroit, Canton, Troy, Madison Heights, Rochester Hills, Farmington Hills, West Bloomfield and surrounding communities.

COOK IT YOURSELF

Cookbooks by local authors:

- *A Wok a Week: 52 Lite and Easy Meals* by Elizabeth Chiu King is available at bookstores and by mail order (check to Chinese Cultural Publications for $23 to P.O. Box 601, Bloomfield Hills, MI 48303-0601). *The 15-Minute Chinese Gourmet,* also by the author, is available by mail order for $22.

- *Nutritional Chinese Cooking* and *More Nutritional Chinese Cooking by Christine Liu;* available at local bookstores.

[E-F/2-3] John R between 13 and 14 Mile Roads in Madison Heights is the new commercial center for Chinese Americans in the Detroit area. *Take I-75 to East 14 Mile/ Oakland Mall exit; keep in the right-hand lane on 14 Mile to turn south on John R. A half-mile down on the east at Whitcomb is* **John R Square.** At this small shopping center, you'll find everything you need to prepare a Chinese feast, including the decorations.

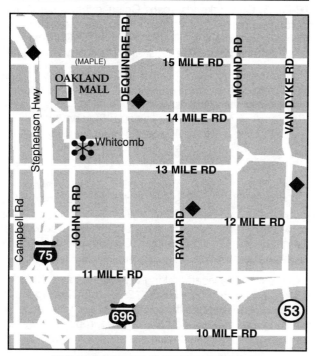

NEW CHINATOWN IN MADISON HEIGHTS

China Merchandise *(31722 John R)* carries groceries, including breads, snacks, rice and noodles, sauces and dim sum items, as well as cooking supplies and giftware. *Next door to the north* is **Mandarin Dining** restaurant. *To the south* is **Tai Pan Bakery,** specializing in Chinese cakes and pastries; **Duck Oriental BBQ,** offering succulent barbequed meat and fowl; and **World Business Corporation** (the sign is in Chinese), selling computer software, books, magazines, newspapers and tapes in Chinese. You'll find other Chinese establishments at **Madison Square** *(13 Mile and John R).*

At **Oakland Mall** *(14 Mile and John R),* a branch of the **Far East Trader** *(middle level, northeast wing)* offers a selection of gifts and furnishings. **Far East Ginseng, Herbs & Tea** *(a mile east on the northeast corner of 14 Mile and Dequindre in Sterling Heights)* has something soothing for just about anything that ails you.

If you're ready for either lunch or dinner, nearby restaurants include **Mon Jin Lau** *(1515 Maple [15 Mile] at Stephenson Highway in Troy)* for Asian fare of various cultures and **Ming Wah** *(4235 E. 12 Mile Rd. at Ryan in Warren)* for Chinese buffet. If you'd like **dim sum** at lunchtime, proceed a few miles further east to Van Dyke to find **Golden Harvest** *(29900 Van Dyke between 12 and 13 Mile in Warren)* or **Ping On** *(42300 Van Dyke between 18 and 19 Mile in Sterling Heights).*

[E-F/4-5] On weekends, many Chinese families from the Detroit area cross the border to shop at Asian groceries and have dinner or a dim sum lunch at a Chinese restaurant in Windsor. Most of the Chinese businesses are along two main streets: *Wyandotte West and University Avenue West.*

Taking the tunnel is the easiest and quickest way to get to Windsor's Chinatown from Detroit. *The tunnel entrance is off East Jefferson, just east of Woodward and west of the Renaissance Center. Upon exiting the tunnel, turn left onto Park and left onto Ouellette Avenue. Stay on the right for about two blocks to the next light, which is Wyandotte West. Turn right onto Wyandotte West and go 1.3 miles until you come to* **Wah Court I** *(2037 Wyandotte W., between Rankin and Partington Streets),* where you can get dim sum every day until 5 p.m.

After lunch, stop by **Sun Hong BBQ** *(2045 Wyandotte W.)* to bring home half a roast duck and several strips of *char siu* (roast pork). For Chinese baked goods, stop by **Majestic Bakery** *(2065)* or **Tong's Bakery** *(2130)*, then proceed to **A-Dong** *(2060)* for selections of Chinese greens, fresh tofu and a Chinese bamboo steamer. If "homestyle" Cantonese cooking is your preference, go a block farther to **Dragon Inn** *(2240)*.

More shops are located along Wyandotte West, including **Sun Chong BBQ** *(309)* and **Ly Hoa Tran BBQ** *(1295)*. The **Cheung Trading Co.** *(2030)* is a Chinese herb and health-food store where you can browse and pick up some ginseng root or packaged ginseng tea, reputed to increase your energy and nurture your *chi* (the intrinsic energy of the universe).

The other enclave of Chinese restaurants and stores is on University Avenue West. If you would like custom-designed invitations or business cards in traditional Chinese calligraphy and motifs, stop by **Canasia Graphics** *(1766 University Ave. W.)*; Tony or Sue Wong will be most happy to oblige. Then enjoy dim sum at **Ho and Wong** *(1457)* or **Wah Court II** *(1689)*. Or, if you enjoy the spicier food from the western region of China, **Shin Shin** *(978)* is a good Szechuan restaurant. Afterward, stop by **Oriental Supermarkets** *(1664)* or **Sun Ying Chong Supermarket** *(1785)* to purchase some Chinese sauces or vegetables for your own kitchen.

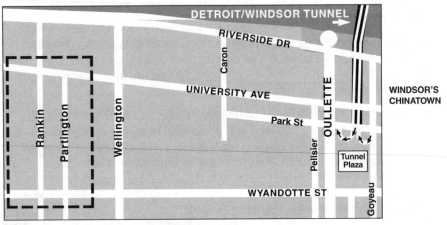

"If there is anything we are serious about, it is neither religion nor learning, but food. We openly acclaim eating as one of the few joys of this human life."
—*Lin Yutang, renowned Chinese lexicographer-author*

Dr. Lin documented more than 9,000 words used in the Chinese language to describe food. No other cuisine in the world has as much variety of foodstuffs, preparation, spices and sauce combinations as Chinese. It's no wonder that eating is the "national pastime."

Chinese restaurants in the Detroit area have common characteristics:

- Most serve Cantonese specialties, including meat, poultry, seafood and vegetarian entrées.

- Prices are comparable, although there are variations in ingredients, flavor and portion.

- Many of the restaurants almost never close. Thanksgiving is the one day in the year that restaurant owners take time off for themselves and their families.

- Reservations are usually not necessary. However, if it's a special occasion and you want to make sure you can dine in the restaurant of your choice, call ahead. Reservations are necessary for a large group or for a party of four or more on weekends.

- Tipping in Chinese restaurants is the same as it is in other dining establishments. Fifteen percent is the custom.

- Many restaurants serve exotic Polynesian drinks or standard cocktails. *WanFu*, a white wine, and *Tsingtao* beer are available in many restaurants. Of higher alcoholic content are *Shaoshing*, a rice wine, and *Kaoliang*, a strong sorghum liquor.

- Tea is preferred as a drink during all meals—more to cleanse the palate of one dish before proceeding to the next than for its own taste.

- Chopsticks have been the standard eating utensil ever since Chinese philosopher Confucius (551-479 B.C.) advocated their use. They were invented because he did not believe in using the same implements for eating as for killing. (At that point in history, knives were the primary eating utensils in all cultures.)

- More restaurants have begun offering **Chinese buffet**—all you can eat for a set price.

- **Banquets** celebrate special events (graduations, weddings, promotions and anniversaries) with more elaborate fare. Although most restaurants can prepare one and seat 10 or 12 at round tables, it is mandatory to book a banquet and place the order in advance.

RESTAURANTS

Metro Detroit and Windsor have more than 250 Chinese restaurants and mom-and-pop carryouts. Many of the restaurants on the partial list that follows were selected by food expert Elizabeth Chiu King for their authentic cuisine.

DETROIT
CHUNG'S
3177 Cass, Detroit; (313) 831-1100
Mon-Thu 10 am -9:30pm, Fri-Sat 10am-11pm, Sun 11am-9:30pm. Cantonese cuisine still going strong in the last of Detroit's original Chinatown restaurants.

EAST
GOLDEN CHOPSTICKS
**24301 Jefferson, St. Clair Shores
(810) 776-7711**
Mon-Thu 11am-10pm, Fri 11am-11pm, Sat noon-11pm, Sun noon-9pm. Hunan, Szechuan, Mandarian, Cantonese and Hawaiian cuisine.

GOLDEN HARVEST
29900 Van Dyke, Warren; (810) 751-5288
Daily 11am-2am. Cantonese, dim sum (daily during lunchtime) and banquets.

MING WAH CHINESE BUFFET
4235 E. 12 Mile, Warren; (810) 573-3845
Daily 11am-3pm, 4:30-10pm, Sun 11am-10pm. Cantonese Chinese buffet with more than 70 varieties.

PING ON
**42300 Van Dyke, Sterling Hts.
(810) 254-3511**
Sun-Thu 11am-11pm, Fri-Sat 11am-midnight. Cantonese, dim sum and banquets.

SOUTHWEST
LIM'S VILLAGE
**24418 Michigan Ave., Dearborn
(313) 565-5788 or 565-5789**
Mon-Thu 11am-10:30pm, Fri-Sat 11:30am-midnight, Sun noon-10:30pm. Cantonese.

WEST
DYNASTY CHINESE FOOD
447 Forest Ave., Plymouth; (734) 459-3332
Mon-Sat 11am-11pm, Sun noon-10pm. Szechuan and Mandarin.

NEW PEKING
**29105 Ford Rd., Garden City
(734) 425-2230**
Mon-Thu 11:30am-9:30pm, Fri 11:30am-

CHOP STICKS

Here's how to use them:
1. Hold the lower chopstick with the base of your thumb and the tip of your ring finger in a fixed position.
2. Hold the upper chopstick with the tips of your thumb, index and middle fingers (just like holding a pencil).
3. Manipulate the upper chopstick to meet the lower chopstick.
4. This manipulation will form a V, which allows you to pick up the food.
   (Don't hold them too low or you'll have no leverage.)

• When you're not using the chopsticks, place them on the chopstick rest or on the lowest dish or saucer on the table.

• It is perfectly acceptable to lift the bowl to your mouth so you don't have to carry the rice too far.

• Soup is meant to be sipped from the bowl and solid bits picked out with chopsticks.

• If you can't master using chopsticks, stay serene; just ask your host for a fork and spoon.

REGIONAL CUISINE

In a country as large and diverse as China—with its varied climate, terrain and resources—it's natural that there are many regional styles of cooking. Long ago, the regional styles of cooking were more distinct than they are today because of poor transportation and communication among regions. When communications improved, regional cuisines borrowed from one another. As a result, it became increasingly difficult to attribute certain dishes exclusively to a particular region.

The adaptability and flexibility of Chinese ways of cooking allowed for much inventiveness and mixing of styles. Today, it's possible to make some generalizations about the distinct characteristics of each major regional cuisine. These four major categories can be divided geographically: **Shanghai** (east), **Szechuan** (west), **Canton** (south), and **Mandarin,** or **Peking,** (north).

10:30pm, Sat noon-10:30pm, Sun noon-9pm. Mandarin and banquets.

NORTH

CHINA BAO
5377 Crooks Rd., Troy; (248) 267-9989
Mon-Thu 11am-10pm, Fri-Sat 11am-11pm, Sun noon-9pm. Lunch buffet with 16 most popular menu items. Dine in and carry out.

CHUNG'S OF WATERFORD
4187 Highland Rd., Waterford
(248) 681-3200
Mon-Thu 11am-9:30pm, Fri-Sat 11am-11pm, Sun noon-10pm. Branch of Detroit's Chung's, offers Szechuan, Hunan and Mongolian fare as well as traditional Cantonese.

EMPIRE DYNASTY
29505 W. 9 Mile Rd., Farmington Hills
(248) 967-6940
Call for hours. Brother chefs, one from New York, the other from San Francisco, specialize in Cantonese and Szechuan dishes.

EMPRESS GARDEN
21734 W. 11 Mile Rd., Southfield
(at Lahser in Harvard Row)
(248) 356-4750
Mon-Fri 11am-10pm, Sat 11am-11pm, Sun noon-10pm. Cantonese.

JADE TIKI
3250 South Blvd., Bloomfield Hills
(248) 852-8181
Daily 11am-9:30pm, except Fri-Sat 11am-10:30pm. Cantonese and dim sum (lunchtime on weekends).

MEI'S KITCHEN
Wattles at John R (in Harlan Plaza)
(248) 528-8490
Tue-Fri, Sun 10:30am-9pm,10:30am-10pm

Sat, closed Mon. "Country style" Chinese. Generous portions and reasonable prices.

MON JIN LAU
1515 Maple Rd., Troy; (248) 689-2332
Mon-Thu 11am-midnight, Fri 11am-1am, Sat 4pm-1am, Sun 3pm-midnight. Pan-Asian fare; recent innovations include wine-tastings and special theme dinners.

OCEANIA INN
3176 Walton Blvd. (at Adams Rd. in the University Shopping Sq.)
Rochester; (248) 375-9200
Daily 11am-10pm. Featuring foods from different regions including Mongolian stir fry.

PEKING HOUSE
215 S. Washington, Royal Oak
(248) 545-2700
Mon-Fri 11am-10pm, Sat-Sun noon-11pm. Cantonese and banquets.

P.F. CHANG'S
Somerset Collection South
2801 W. Big Beaver, Troy; (248) 816-8000
Lunch and dinner daily. Intimate feeling atmosphere with Cantonese, Shanghai, Szechwan, Hunan and Mongolian cuisine.

SHANGRI-LA
6407 Orchard Lake Rd., W. Bloomfield
(248) 626-8585
Daily 11am-2am. Dim sum a specialty, along with Cantonese and Szechuan dishes.

SZECHUAN GARDEN
2855 W. Maple Rd., Birmingham
(248) 280-0362
Mon-Thurs11:30am-9:30pm, Fri 11:30am-10pm, Sat 12:30-10pm, Sun 4:30-9:30pm.

ANN ARBOR
CHINA GATE
1201 S. University, Ann Arbor
(734) 668-2445
Daily 11am-10pm. Szechuan, Hunan and Peking prepared by award-winning chef. Dine in or carryout.

GREAT LAKES CHINESE SEAFOOD RESTAURANT
2910 Carpenter Rd., Ann Arbor
(734) 973-6666
Mon-Sun 11am-2am. Cantonese, dim sum and banquets.

LAI LAI CHINESE RESTAURANT
4023 Carpenter Rd., Ypsilanti
(734) 677-0790
Sun-Thu 11:30am-10pm, Fri-Sat 11:30am-11pm. Cantonese, dim sum.

WINDSOR
DRAGON INN
2240 W. Wyandotte, Windsor
(519) 258-7613
Daily 4pm-5am. Cantonese (good home cooking).

EMPRESS GARDENS III
675 Goyeau, Windsor
(inside Day's Inn)
(519) 253-3332
Daily 11am-11pm. Authentic Hong Kong, Cantonese and Szechuan-style cuisine. Dim sum daily.

HO & WONG RESTAURANT
1457 University Ave. W., Windsor
(519) 256-5548
Mon-Fri 11am-midnight, Sat-Sun 10am-midnight. Cantonese, dim sum.

SHIN SHIN
978 University Ave. W., Windsor
(519) 252-1449
Mon-Thu 11:30am-10pm, Fri-Sat 11:30am-11pm, Sun 11:30am-9pm. Szechuan and Mandarin.

WAH COURT I
2037 Wyandotte W., Windsor
(519) 258-1344
Mon-Fri 11am-11:30pm, Sat-Sun 10am-11:30pm. Cantonese, dim sum (daily until 5pm) and banquets.

WAH COURT II
1689 University Ave. W., Windsor
(519) 256-4755
Mon-Sun 11am-midnight, Sat-Sun 10am-2am. Cantonese, dim sum (daily until 5pm) and banquets.

MONGOLIAN BARBEQUE

This type of cooking is named for the ancient area of east-central Asia that was united by Genghis Khan, who forged a great empire in the 13th century. The food consists of a variety of raw meats, vegetables, sauces and spices that you choose, mix together in a bowl and then take to the grill area to have cooked. Mongolian Barbeques also have a wide selection of beer and wine.

GENGHIS KHAN MONGOLIAN RESTAURANT
37546 Six Mile Rd., Livonia
(in Laurel Park)
(734) 432-9996 or 432-9997
Mon-Thu 11am-9:30pm, Fri 11am-10:30pm, Sat noon-10:30pm, Sun noon-9pm. Elegant atmosphere.

GENGHIS KHAN HOUSE
1600 Rochester Rd., Troy; (248) 689-2123
Mon-Thu 11am-10pm, Fri 11am-11pm, Sat noon-11pm, Sun noon-10pm.

SZECHUAN CUISINE

A lthough the Szechuan climate is warm and humid, the natives of this region have developed a love of peppery, spicy-hot food. *Fagara* pepper, known as Szechuan pepper, and the five basic Chinese spices—**star anise, pepper, fennel, cloves** and **cinnamon**—are used more often here than in the other regions. Garlic, salt and vinegar also are used liberally.

The texture of food is usually dry and chewy. Seafood is not as readily available in Szechuan as it is in the east and south of China, so vegetables are substituted for fish. Dried fungi, such as **cloud ears** and **wood ears,** are found in many dishes. Szechuan food can be prepared with varying degrees of hotness. Specify your preference when ordering—or you may find yourself extinguishing the fire in your throat with many pitchers of ice water!

SHANGHAI CUISINE

S hanghai style is exquisite and refined, with emphasis placed on fine cutting. Many dishes are appreciated for the dainty slivering of the ingredients. The food tends to be less spicy than other regional styles. Soy sauce, wine, sugar and vinegar are the main condiments.

A favorite ingredient—the preserved mustard green, or **red-in-the-snow**—is included in both meat and seafood dishes. The result is food less spicy than Szechuan dishes and sauces less starchy than those of Cantonese cooking.

Classic Shanghai dishes include **boneless fish** (slices of fish, stir-fried); **crab Shanghai** (crabmeat sautéed with eggs and peapods); **drunken chicken** (white-cooked chicken marinated in wine); **happy family** (selected seafood and meat with Chinese greens); **lion head** (meatballs cooked with celery cabbage and cellophane noodles); **west lake duck,** or *sai woo opp* (braised duck with vegetables); and **yangchow fried rice** (fried rice with baby shrimps, roast pork and eggs).

MONGOLIAN BARBEQUE
310 S. Main St., Royal Oak; (248) 398-7755
Mon-Thu 11am-11pm, Fri-Sat 11am-12:30am, Sun noon-10:30pm.

MONGOLIAN BARBEQUE
200 S. Main St., Ann Arbor
(734) 913-0999
Mon-Thu 11am-10:30pm, Fri-Sat 11am-11:30pm, Sun noon-10pm.

THIELK'S MONGOLIAN GRILLE
18480 Mack Ave.
Grosse Point Farms; (313) 884-3686
Mon-Fri 11:30am-10pm, Sat 11:30am-11pm, Sun noon-10pm.

BBQ STORES

A number of stores in metro Detroit and Windsor offer ready-to-eat and utterly mouth-watering roast duck, chicken, char siu (strips of pork), spare ribs and many varieties of Chinese "down-home" food (stomach, intestines, gizzards, etc.). You can buy a whole pig or just half a duck or chicken. Several stores double as eateries, offering simple but hearty fare. Succulent BBQ meat and fowl are delicious in sandwiches or pita bread or with pasta or rice.

DUCK ORIENTAL BBQ
31692 John R, Madison Hts.
(248) 588-7007
Daily 10am-8pm.

EVERGREEN MARKET
20736 Lahser, Southfield; (248) 354-8181
Mon-Sat 9am-7pm, Sun 10am-7pm.

LY HOA TRAN BBQ
1059 Wyandotte W., Windsor
(519) 258-5323
Daily 11am-10pm. Closed Tue.

SUN CHONG BBQ
309 Wyandotte W., Windsor
(519) 258-6881
Daily 10am-6pm.

SUN HONG BBQ
2045 Wyandotte W., Windsor
(519) 255-7808
Daily 11am-8pm. Closed Thu.

BAKERIES

Chinese bakeries offer a variety of cakes and buns. These pastries are light, not too sweet, and delicious.

EASTERN ACCENTS
214 S. Fourth St., Ann Arbor
(734) 332-8782
Mon-Thu 7am-10pm, Fri 7am-midnight, Sat 8am-midnight, Sun 10am-7pm. Features Hong Kong-style baked goods, other Asian pastries and Euro/American items.

MAXIM'S BAKERY
1939 E. Wattles Rd., Troy; (248) 528-8490
Mon-Sat 10am-9pm, Sun 11am-9pm. Variety of Chinese pastries, fruit-filled cream cakes, dim sum appetizers and express Chinese food carryout.

TAI PAN BAKERY
31666 John R, Madison Hts.
(248) 583-3088
Sun-Thu 9:30am-8pm, Fri-Sat 9:30am-9pm. Great selection of Chinese cakes and pastries.

MAJESTIC BAKERY
2017 Wyandotte W., Windsor
(519) 254-6164
Daily 11:30am-7pm.

TONG'S BAKERY
2130 Wyandotte W., Windsor
(519) 256-9773
Daily 11am-7:30pm. Closed Tue. Specializes in Hong Kong-style buns.

GROCERS

Chinese grocery stores are treasure troves. You'll find not only canned and dried goods by the hundreds, but also all kinds of fresh vegetables, tofu and soy products. Wide or thin noodles made from rice, mung beans or wheat—as well as fresh seafood, clawing crabs and shrimp of all sizes—are also available. Many stores offer ready-to-eat foods, gifts, greeting cards, Chinese newspapers and magazines, as well as kung fu videotapes and some Chinese herbs and medicine. It's an adventure to browse and shop. Most items cost less than in regular supermarkets.

CANTONESE COOKING

The adventurous Southerners were the first of the Chinese to leave their homeland for America and Europe in the early 1800s. They were the ambitious entrepreneurs who opened many restaurants and passed this business tradition on to their descendants.

Cantonese cuisine is considered to be the most versatile and diverse of the regional cuisines. While it is simple, it is also subtle and fine. The main flavorings used are fermented soy beans known as black beans, oyster sauce, plum sauce, *hoisin* sauce (made with soy, chili, garlic and spices; sharp but slightly sweet) and ginger root. Many dishes mix seafood with meat, as in **lobster Cantonese.** Other dishes use fresh fruit and nuts.

The barbecued suckling pig and roast pork *(char siu)*, as well as the roast ducks of Canton, are world-renowned, as are the one-meal snacks of noodles and rice, and the **dim sum,** tiny appetizers that touch the heart. The Polynesian style of cooking, which uses a variety of fruit and sweet sauce, is a variation of Cantonese cuisine, adapted to the Western fondness of sweets.

MANDARIN CUISINE

The cuisine of Peking is often referred to as the *Mandarin* style of cooking. A mandarin was a high-court official of Imperial China. Today, the official dialect used by the Chinese people is known as Mandarin.

In this region, the staple food is wheat, not rice as in Canton. You'll find wheat in a variety of forms: flour, noodles, steamed bread, dumplings, pastry, rolls and buns. You'll also find more meat in the Peking diet, especially lamb and beef. The cuisine, therefore, is broad and varied. The chief flavorings used are soy and sesame, wine, scallions, leeks and garlic. The style is simple, yet superb.

This cosmopolitan tradition, which was fostered in the great palace kitchens, still exists in Peking. Famous northern dishes are **Peking duck,** as well as the **Mongolian barbecue** and the **Mongolian fire pot,** which were introduced by the Mongolian invaders, who loved lamb and hot spices.

EAST

**HAN KUK ORIENTAL
FOODS & GIFTS**
33717 Gratiot, Mt. Clemens
(810) 791-8877
Mon-Sat 10am-8pm, Sun noon-6pm.
Chinese and other Asian groceries.

NORTH

ASIA MARKET
30925 Dequindre, Madison Hts.
(248) 588-8383
Sun-Thu 10am-9pm, Fri-Sat 10am-10pm.
Carries a full line of merchandise—from fresh meats, seafood and produce to canned goods. Vietnamese, Chinese, Thai, Korean, Filipino and Laotian foods.

ASIA MART
36949 Dequindre at 13 Mile, Troy; (248) 689-6090
Mon-Sat 10am-9pm, Sun noon-6pm. All types of oriental foods and gifts.

CHINA MERCHANDISE
31722 John R, Madison Hts.
(248) 588-0450
Mon-Sun 10am-9pm.

CHINESE GROCERY CORPORATION
4951 Rochester Rd., Troy
(248) 689-5529
Mon-Thu noon-7pm, Fri noon-9pm, Sat 10am-6pm, Sun 10am-5pm.

EVERGREEN MARKET
20736 Lahser, Southfield; (248) 354-8181
Mon-Sat 9am-7pm, Sun 10am-7pm.
Asian groceries.

FRIENDLY MARKET
28733 Dequindre at 12 Mile
Madison Hts.; (248) 548-6288
Mon-Fri 10am-7pm, Sat-Sun 11 am-7pm.
Exotic foods, medicinal herbs.

KAI SUN MARKET
1059 E. Long Lake Rd., Troy
(248) 524-1250
Mon-Sat 9am-8pm, Sun 9am-7pm.
Oriental discount market.

**ORIENTAL MARKET &
ORIENTAL RESTAURANT**
31806 John R, Madison Hts.
(in Madison Square at 13 Mile)
(248) 583-9533
Daily 9:30am-9pm. Groceries, carryouts, and porcelain and other imports.

ANN ARBOR
CHINA MERCHANDISE
2767 Plymouth Rd., Ann Arbor
(734) 668-7642
Mon-Thu 10am-8pm, Fri 9am-10pm, Sat 10am-9pm, Sun 10am-8pm.

SING TUNG INTERNATIONAL FOOD
3115 Oak Valley Dr., Ann Arbor
(734) 995-0422
Mon-Sat 10am-8pm, Sun 11am-6pm.

ROSEWOOD PRODUCTS AND TOFU INTERNATIONAL
738 Airport Blvd., Suite 8; Ann Arbor
(734) 665-2222
Daily 8am-3pm. Tofu and soy products.

WINDSOR
A-DONG GROCERIES INC.
2060 Wyandotte W., Windsor
(519) 252-7111
Daily 11:30am-8pm. One of the largest and best in the area.

ORIENTAL SUPERMARKETS
1320 Wyandotte W., Windsor
(519) 252-2484
Daily 10am-8pm.

SUN YING CHONG SUPERMARKET
1785 University Ave. W., Windsor
(519) 255-7530
Daily 11am-8pm.

HERB STORES

Chinese herbs and medicines are rapidly gaining popularity, so it's not surprising to see several Chinese "apothecaries" flourishing in metro Detroit and Windsor. Here you will find different kinds of teas (in addition to the oolong tea usually served in restaurants), ginseng (to restore your energy) and cures for all kinds of ills and aches.

THE CHINESE ZODIAC

The legend goes like this: Buddha was old and dying and invited all the animals to which he had been so kind over the years to visit him one last time. Of the thousands that might have come, only 12 did so. So to honor them, he told them that each would be assigned a year, and those born in the year of that animal would embody all that animal's good qualities. The years are named from the beginning of the century, according to who came first to see him, rotating every 12 years.

The Tiger	1902	1914	1926	1938	1950	1962	1974	1986	1998
The Rabbit	1903	1915	1927	1939	1951	1963	1975	1987	1999
The Dragon	1904	1916	1928	1940	1952	1964	1976	1988	2000
The Snake	1905	1917	1929	1941	1953	1965	1977	1989	2001
The Horse	1906	1918	1930	1942	1954	1966	1978	1990	2002
The Goat	1907	1919	1931	1943	1955	1967	1979	1991	2003
The Monkey	1908	1920	1932	1944	1956	1968	1980	1992	2004
The Rooster	1909	1921	1933	1945	1957	1969	1981	1993	2005
The Dog	1910	1922	1934	1946	1958	1970	1982	1994	2006
The Pig	1911	1923	1935	1947	1959	1971	1983	1995	2007
The Rat	1912	1924	1936	1948	1960	1972	1984	1996	2008
The Ox	1913	1925	1937	1949	1961	1973	1985	1997	2000

FAR EAST GINSENG, HERBS & TEA
33162 Dequindre, Sterling Hts.
(810) 977-0202
Mon-Sat 11am-7pm, Sun noon-7pm.

CHEUNG'S TRADING COMPANY
2030 Wyandotte W., Windsor
(519) 252-9228
Daily 11am-7pm. More than 2,000 items. Chinese herbs and health foods, teas and tea sets. Acupuncture and massage.

JOY OF HERBS
620 Wyandotte E., Windsor
(519) 254-4220
Mon-Sat 10am-5:30pm. More than 1,000 bulk herbs. Acupuncture and reflexology.

GIFT SHOPS

FAR EAST TRADER
Tel-Twelve Mall
28620 Telegraph, Southfield
(248) 354-3993
Mon-Sat 10am-9pm, Sun noon-5pm.
and
Oakland Mall
534 W. 14 Mile, Troy; (248) 585-2267
Mon-Sat 10am-9pm, Sun noon-5pm.
and
Lakeside Mall
14000 Lakeside Circle, Sterling Hts.
(810) 247-7600
Mon-Sat 10am-9pm, Sun 11am-6pm.
and
Summit Place
315 N. Telegraph Road, Waterford Twp.
(248) 681-6260
Mon-Sat 10am-9pm, Sun 11am-6pm.
Large selection of gifts and furnishings

HONG KONG GIFT SHOP
271 Ouellette
Windsor, Ontario
(519) 971-8918
Mon-Sat 11am-6pm, Sun 11am-5pm.

ANTIQUES

HAGOPIAN WORLD OF RUGS
850 S. Woodward, Birmingham
(248) 646-7847
and
3410 Washtenaw, Ann Arbor
(734) 973-7847
Sun noon-5pm; Mon, Thu 10am-8pm; Tue, Wed, Fri, Sat 10am-6pm. Exclusive collection of authenticated furniture and accesssories from the Qing Dynasty (1820-1890).

HAIG GALLERIES
311 Main St., Rochester
(248) 656-8333
Mon-Sat noon-6pm. Museum-like art gallery with international antiques, including Chinese porcelain and textiles.

GENE PURDUM ANTIQUES
P.O. Box 212, Williamston, MI 48895
(517) 521-4156
Specializes in fine porcelain and pottery including Chinese export. Call or write for a catalog, or visit the shop via the Web: http://www.tias.com/stores/purdum/ch_exp.htm (Links to fine china discussion group.)

BOOKSTORES

WORLD JOURNAL BOOK STORE
30805 John R, Madison Hts.
(248) 585-6007
Mon-Fri 11:30am-6pm, Sat-Sun 10:30am-6pm. Chinese books, magazines, newspapers, stamps, tapes, gift items, and Chinese writing and painting brushes and inks.

WORLD BUSINESS CORPORATION
31662 John R, Madison Hts.
(248) 589-2380
Mon-Fri 9:30am-7pm, Sat 10am-6pm. Chinese books, magazines, newspapers, computer software, tapes and gift items.

PRINT SHOPS

B K PRINTING
12863 Eureka Rd., Southgate
(313) 283-7774
Mon-Fri 9am-5pm. Kam Leung, general manager, can assist you with custom-designed invitations, business cards and other printed pieces in traditional Chinese calligraphy and motifs.

CANASIA GRAPHICS
1766 University Ave. W., Windsor
(519) 254-4536
Mon-Fri 10am-6:30pm, Sat noon-6pm. Owners Tony and Sue Wong can help custom-design invitations for any occasion with Chinese graphics and motifs. The storefront is unpretentious, with only a large Chinese sign. (The store can be identified by its address number.)

FENG SHUI

Although the *Feng Shui* approach to home and office decoration and design is 3,000 years old, it has only recently come into vogue in the Western world.

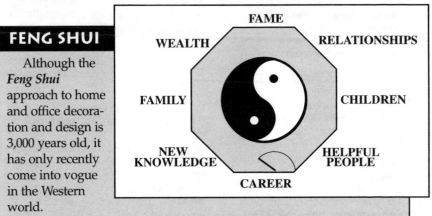

FAME

WEALTH   RELATIONSHIPS

FAMILY   CHILDREN

NEW KNOWLEDGE   HELPFUL PEOPLE

CAREER

Feng Shui means "the way of wind and water, the natural forces of the universe." The ancient Chinese believed in and lived their lives by these natural forces. Europeans call this science *geomancy,* and Hawaiians and Native American Indians practice their own form of it.

Feng Shui uses the *ba-qua* shape and the eight stations of life (see chart above): fame, relationships, children, helpful people, career, new knowledge, family and wealth. Each life station correlates to a location in your home or workplace. These physical locations house the energy (the electromagnetic field) that you have created for that station of your life.

The chart is placed over the floor plan of the building with the career location (the "door swing" side of the chart) directly over the front door. The sides and corners of the ba-qua shape relate to the physical walls and corners of the building.

Of course, there's far more to the science than this. To learn more, enroll in one of the numerous Feng Shui courses available at community education centers.

VISUAL ARTS

DETROIT INSTITUTE OF ARTS
5200 Woodward Ave., Detroit
(313) 833-7900
Wed-Fri 11am-4pm, Sat-Sun 11am-5pm.
The Chinese collection, on the first floor of the north wing (N140), features scrolls, screens, lacquers, porcelain, sculpture, ceremonial objects and other works. Pieces on view change seasonally.

MIDWEST ORIENTAL ART CLUB
(248) 334-8527 or 656-1403
Contact: Yu-Ping Liang Yung
Group dedicated to the preservation and presentation of Asian arts holds regular meetings and exhibitions.

ETHNIC HERITAGE ROOM
Wayne State University
Alex Manoogian Hall
906 W. Warren, Detroit
(313) 577-3500 (University Scheduling)
Room 112 is a classroom decorated in Chinese style.

UNIVERSITY OF MICHIGAN MUSEUM OF ART
525 S. State St., Ann Arbor
(734) 764-0395
Tue, Wed, Fri, Sat 10am-5pm, Thu 10am-9pm, Sun noon-5pm. Chinese ceramics, scrolls, court paintings, jade ritual objects, calligraphy, furnishings and textiles (Imperial robes of Ch'ing Dynasty) in second floor gallery.

CALLIGRAPHY

Pictographs in China date from 1400 B.C. and are similar to Egyptian hieroglyphs. Thousands of characters represent various concepts. Classic Chinese calligraphy employing special brushes and ink, rather than modern pens, is regarded as a fine art.

CHINESE CALLIGRAPHERS
Cheng, Winston (Po-Ling) and Peter
Farmington Hills; (248) 788-9513
Samuel Yung
Bloomfield Hills; (248) 334-8527

CHINESE BRUSH PAINTERS
Winnie Liu
Bloomfield Hills; (248) 646-5768
Yu-Ping Liang Yung
Bloomfield Hills, (248) 334-8527 or 656-1403

PERFORMERS

CATHAY MELODIERS
(248) 641-8264
David Chang, director
This renowned choral group, with a membership of more than 75, has won many accolades for its concerts at home and abroad. Call for performance dates.

DETROIT CHINESE CHOIR
(248) 344-8815
Judy Chen, director
Formed in 1992, this 25-member choral group performs often in the area. Call for concert dates.

DRAGON DANCE GROUP
(248) 879-0984
Performing youth group, affiliated with Wayne County Chinese Language School, meets in Livonia.

MARTIAL ARTS

The martial arts employ various methods of unarmed combat, originally used in warfare in the Far East and shaped by Eastern Asian philosophical concepts, notably Zen Buddhism. In the early sixth century A.D., Bodhidharma—an Indian priest and knight—brought Zen Buddhism to China along with a system of 18 self-defense exercises. The exercises evolved into a form of boxing, which spread, with Zen, throughout China.

The martial arts are popular in many parts of the world as self-defense and law enforcement tactics, competitive sports, and exercises for physical fitness. Among the better known forms are *karate, kung fu, jujitsu, judo, aikido, t'ai chi chu'an, tae kwon do, sumo wrestling* and *kendo.*

Kung fu (Chinese boxing) is, along with karate, the most popularly known of all the martial arts. It employs kicks, strikes, throws, body turns, dodges, holds, crouches, starts, leaps, falls, handsprings and somersaults.

T'ai chi chu'an is a series of 108 complex, slow-motion movements, each named (for example, *the White Crane Spreads its Wings*) and designed to ensure effective circulation of the *chi,* or intrinsic energy of the universe, through the mind and body. It is derived partly from Shaolin Martial Arts of China and partly from Taoism. Over the past few years, t'ai chi has become extremely popular with Americans, for both physical and mental fitness. T'ai chi is designed to prevent the effects of age upon the body and mind. Most community education facilities, as well as Ys, offer classes in t'ai chi. Academies are listed in the Yellow Pages.

The "official" religion of the Chinese Republic is atheism, but Taoism, Confucianism and Buddhism still exert a heavy influence. Muslims, Catholics and Protestants also are strongly represented, all observing their own holy days. The goal of all Chinese festivals is family unity and harmony—to attain the **Five Virtues** or **Happinesses: long life, wealth, peace, kindness** and **honor.**

A few of the major celebrations are described below.

For information about local New Year and Moon Festival events, call the Chinese American Educational and Cultural Center in Ann Arbor at (734) 971-3193.

APRIL 5 OR 6
CHING MING

(Tomb Sweeping Day) Observed since 3700 B.C., Ching Ming marks the beginning of planting, spring and outdoor activities. Similar to Easter traditions, eggs are boiled, colored and eaten to symbolize the renewal of life. It's also known as All Souls Day, because it's a time when families remember their ancestors by visiting cemeteries. When they arrive at the grave sites, family members clear weeds and sweep away dirt. Foods favored by the ancestor are presented as an offering; incense and a pair of long red candles are lit. Spirit paper money in gold and silver and paper drawings and images of necessary items are burned as a way of providing the departed with all their needs. Firecrackers are lit to conclude the ritual. The deceased are given time to extract the essence of the meal, and then, in a happy picnic, the family eats the food. The Chinese also enjoy kite flying during this time—including at night, with lights attached.

SEPTEMBER
MOON FESTIVAL

The Chinese celebrate the Moon Festival on the 15th day of the Eighth Moon, which roughly coincides with the Fall Harvest in September. On this day, Chang O, the Moon Lady, is brighter and more beautiful than at any other time of the year. Celebrations include feasting, enjoying mooncakes *(see "Bakeries" in listings)*, reciting and composing poetry and making much merriment. Each member of a family eats a piece of one mooncake to promote unity and harmony within the family. Children make or receive lanterns in the shape of rabbits, fish, birds and butterflies. Today, many families still gather outdoors to nibble on mooncakes, sip tea and enjoy the full moon.

DRAGON BOAT FESTIVAL

Celebrated around **June 21** (summer solstice), this festival has a patriarchal theme. In Chinese legend, the dragon, which is considered to be benevolent, symbolized *yang*— the active or positive male principle. The Chinese believed that there were innumerable dragons, varying in size, color and power.

CLASSES

CHINESE CULTURAL CENTER SCHOOL
18600 Haggerty Rd., Livonia
(313) 390-8599
Saturday classes in language, dance and martial arts.

WAYNE COUNTY
CHINESE LANGUAGE SCHOOL
18600 Haggerty Rd., Livonia
(248) 879-0984
Saturday classes in Chinese and other activities.

SOUTHERN MICHIGAN
CHINESE SCHOOL
210 W. Square Lake Rd., Troy
(248) 828-2765 or (810) 575-4230
Language classes Friday nights.

ORGANIZATIONS

CHINESE AMERICAN EDUCATIONAL
AND CULTURAL CENTER OF MICHIGAN
296 W. Eisenhower Pkwy., Ann Arbor
(734) 971-3193
Mon-Fri 9am-5pm. Chen-oi Chin-Hsieh, director. In the past 20 years, the CAECC has sponsored and coordinated many symposia, exhibits and activities to foster better understanding and appreciation of Chinese cultural heritage. Its archives include a history of the Chinese Americans in Michigan, Chinese folk art and more. It regularly designs and provides China-bound programs for corporations and industries, in-service training for teachers, field trips for school-children, translation and referral services, and symposia and banquets to celebrate the Lunar New Year and Moon Festival. Call for current exhibits or upcoming functions.

CHINESE NEW YEAR

The New Year begins the first day of the first new moon after the winter solstice. The Chinese calendar is based on the waxing and waning of the moon, so the holiday fluctuates between January 20 and February 20.

The New Year celebration is the most joyous, colorful and elaborate of all the holidays. It begins with a thorough house cleaning, perhaps purchasing new clothes for the entire family and making sure debts are paid up. Up to two weeks of cooking, feasting, rejoicing and visiting follow. Red envelopes containing coins are handed out to friends for good luck.

Two usual New Year greetings are *Kung hay fat choy* ("May you be blessed with prosperity," in Cantonese) and *Hsin nien kuai loh* ("Much happiness in the New Year," in Mandarin).

Virtually every restaurant and organization in this chapter observes the New Year with special events and celebrations, so call to find out what's happening.

● *Stamps commemorating the Chinese New Year are available from the U.S. Postal Service, with new editions issued annually through 2004. The stamps were designed by Chinese American Clarence Lee.*

**DETROIT CHINESE
CULTURAL SERVICE CENTER**
625 E. Big Beaver Rd., Troy
(248) 689-5667
Wed-Mon noon-7pm. Frank Hsing, director.
Activities and functions are mostly conducted
in Chinese. Aerobics, kung fu, t'ai chi and
calligraphy classes are offered regularly, as
well as ping-pong, golf and basketball tournaments. The center provides facilities for
meetings and events of Chinese associations
and schools. Visitors are welcome.

**ASSOCIATION OF CHINESE
AMERICANS**
420 Peterboro, Detroit
(313) 831-1790
Mon-Thu 8am-4:30pm, Sun 10am-4pm.
ACA provides assistance in Cantonese and
Mandarin to non-English-speaking Chinese
and the elderly at the Detroit Chinatown
Drop-In/Outreach Center. Services include
health and social, counseling, education, a
lending library and activities such as hot
lunches, field trips, seminars and workshops.

MEDIA

PRINT
ACA NEWSLETTER
P.O. Box 615, Warren, MI 48090-0615
(313) 831-1790
Published quarterly by the Association of
Chinese Americans. Chronicles events and
news of Chinese Americans in metro Detroit.

WEB SITES
CHINESE CULTURE
www.1stchina.com/1st/artscult_music.html-
curriculum

CHINESE HERITAGE
fllcjm.clements.smu.edu/languages/chinese

CHINESE CULTURE LINKS
www.hk.super.net/~hsuricky/hk/ch_education

LION & DRAGON DANCES

The lion dance is an important tradition in China.
Usually part of festivities like Chinese New
Year, the openings of restaurants and weddings, the
dance is believed to bring good luck and happiness. Combining art, history
and kung fu moves, every move has a specific musical rhythm.

Lions are not native in China—they arrived via the famous Silk Road.
Rulers in what is today Iran and Afghanistan sent lions to Chinese emperors
as gifts. The lion dance dates back to the Han Dynasty (205 B.C. to 220 A.D).

The lion is enacted by two dancers. One handles the head, made out of
strong but light materials like papier-mâché and bamboo, the other plays the
body and the tail under a cloth that is attached to the head. The "animal" is
accompanied by three musicians, playing a large drum, cymbals and a gong.
A Little Buddha teases it with a fan or a giant ball. The head dancer can
move the lion's eyes, mouth and ears for expression of moods.

Quite often spectators think that they are looking at dragons. The main
difference between a lion dance and dragon dance is that the latter is
performed with more people than two. In traditional communities, the
Dragon Dance is used to expel devils and bring people good luck and fortune. Noisy processions, filled with drumming, fireworks and cheering
crowds, accompany each appearance of the Dragons and Lions in China and
in America's Chinese communities. At least 12 dancers, one drummer and
one leader are needed for the traditional Dragon dance.

SOUTHEAST ASIA

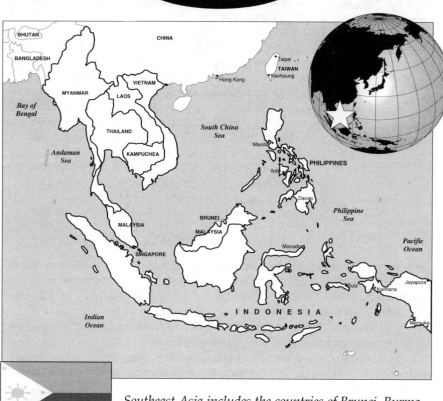

THE PHILLIPINES

The flag has blue and red bars with a sun and stars in red and yellow on white.

Southeast Asia includes the countries of Brunei, Burma (Myanmar), Cambodia (Kampuchea), Indonesia, Laos, Malaysia, the Philippines, Singapore, Thailand and Vietnam. The region is bordered by China on the north, the South Pacific Ocean on the east, the Indian Ocean on the south, and the Indian Ocean, the Bay of Bengal and the Indian subcontinent on the west.

FILIPINOS

The Filipino American population has been settled in the Detroit area since World War II and is not only widely dispersed but also greatly absorbed into mainstream America. In the Philippines, English is required in the school system. The majority of the population is Roman Catholic.

Though the first Filipinos came to Michigan in the early 1900s as auto workers and sent money home, many of the 20,000 Filipino Americans living in the Detroit area today came after 1965 as professionals and brought their families with them. More than a fourth of Detroit-area Filipinos work in health care.

INDOCHINESE

VIETNAM
*The flag is a yellow
star on a red field.*

LAOS
*The flag is a white
circle on a blue field
with red stripes*

The Indochinese—**Vietnamese, Hmong, Laotian** and **Cambodian**—arrived in the Detroit area beginning in 1975, primarily as war refugees. According to the state of Michigan Refugee Office, the number of Southeast Asian refugees resettled here since 1975 is estimated to be more than 10,000. More than half arrived between 1975 and 1981 when the city absorbed about 900 refugees a year.

A large group, the **Hmong,** are ethnic Chinese from the mountains of Laos. However, Hmong and Laotian cultures are unrelated. Although about 100 Vietnamese families are in the Detroit area, a much larger and more organized Vietnamese population is in Windsor.

Few **Thai, Malaysian, Indonesian** and **Singaporean** immigrants are in the area. Although Thai restaurants are popping up all over, most are owned by Chinese, Vietnamese, Laotian or Hmong families.

THE HMONG PEOPLE

Chinese records indicate the Hmong lived on the banks of the Yellow River about 3,000 years ago. It is believed they came to China from the high steps of Tibet, Siberia and Mongolia. Over the centuries, subjugation by the Chinese government led the Hmong to migrate out of China into the mountains of Laos, Thailand and Vietnam. By 1850, the Hmong had established themselves in the mountainous region of Luang Prabang, Laos.

Hmong is classified in the Sino-Tibetan family of languages. Spoken with a slight aspiration through the nostrils as the *m* is enunciated, the word *Hmong* means "freedom."

In the Hmong community, family and clan are the most important social units. There are 18 to 25 clans distinguished by their last names—*Yang, Vang, Kue, Vue* and so on. One must marry outside his or her clan, and relationships among the clans must be maintained. The extended family household constitutes the basic cultural and political unit, with the eldest male as clan leader.

Although many Hmong have become Christians, some retain the spiritual practices of their Chinese ancestors. These include animism, a belief in powerful spirits that can be influenced by shamans (high priests), supernatural beings and reincarnation.

HMONG IMMIGRATION

Hmong tribespeople sided with the United States in the Vietnam War and were foot soldiers in the "Secret War in Laos," defending their homeland and rescuing downed American air crews. When the United States withdrew in 1975, the Communists unleashed a search-and-destroy operation against the Hmong. Although large numbers were killed, thousands of Hmong escaped through the Lao forest to refugee camps in Thailand. They fled to many parts of the globe, including the United States (Michigan, California, North Carolina, Minnesota and Wisconsin).

Detroit's first Hmong family arrived in 1976 as war refugees and settled in the Seven Mile-Hoover area. Today, Hmongtown is between Six and Eight Mile Roads and Gratiot and Hoover on Detroit's east side.

Job opportunities and affordable homes in Michigan have attracted Hmong from other states. In 1995-96, many Hmong immigrants, who had settled in California's Central Valley, left that area because of increasing discrimination. As many as 2,000 resettled in the Detroit area. Of the 130,000 Hmong in the United States, 12,000 now live in Michigan, especially in Detroit, Pontiac, Bay City, Saginaw and Lansing.

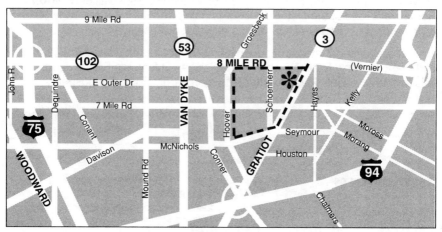

HMONG TOWN

TOUR SOUTHEAST ASIAN SAMPLING

[EF/2-5] The tour begins in Sterling Heights with a late breakfast of fresh Filipino specialties at the **Red Ribbon Bakery** *(26889 Ryan at 15 Mile)*. All the selections are genuine and so is the company. Like most family businesses owned by Southeast Asians, the shop is staffed with fellow immigrants.

Then *head south* to Detroit's Cultural Center area to view the Hall of Nations International Doll Exhibition at the **International Institute** and the Indonesian Room at the **Children's Museum**. They are next door to each other *on Kirby between Woodward and John R. (From I-75, take the Warren Exit west, then go two blocks north to Kirby. From I-94, exit Woodward/John R and go three blocks south to Kirby.)* Call the International Institute (313-871-8600) to be sure that the Hall of Nations is open during the time of your visit. Hmong, Filipino, Thai, Cambodian, Malaysian, Singaporean, Indonesian and other Asian cultures are represented in the 36 showcases of dolls from around the world.

The International Institute also has a gift shop that carries imports and crafts from many Asian countries. Then head for the **Indonesian Room** on the second floor of the **Children's Museum** and get a passport brochure that will guide you to the islands of Java, Sumatra, Borneo and others.

From the Cultural Center, *continue south to downtown and take the tunnel* to Windsor for an authentic change-of-country experience. Turn left out of Customs and left again at Ouellette. Take that to West Wyandotte and you're in a busy Asian community dotted with restaurants and grocery stores. This **Windsor** neighborhood has welcomed its Vietnamese newcomers in the past two decades, and the experience is authentic. Some stores carry traditional cookware to help you prepare Asian fare at home.

Once you've explored the area, choose a restaurant. *Two blocks toward the river* is University Avenue and more Asian establishments. **The Mini** *at 475 W. University* comes highly recommended for Vietnamese specialties. **Saigon Restaurant**, one of the first in Windsor to gain a reputation in the early 1980s, is at *1545 W. University.* Nearly all the businesses accept U.S. dollars.

Back in the United States, try the **Royal Kubo** at *Greenfield and Ten Mile in Oak Park,* the only Filipino nightclub in Michigan. It features Filipino food, cocktails and international karaoke after 9 p.m., in a truly Filipino atmosphere.

RESTAURANTS

DETROIT

SALA THAI
1541-1543 E. Lafayette, Detroit
(313) 567-8424
Mon-Fri 11am-10pm, Sat 5-10pm. Authentic **Thai** salads, appetizers, outstanding soups and noodles.

THAI BANGKOK
9737 Jos. Campeau, Hamtramck
(313) 875-5770
Mon-Thurs 11am-9pm, Fri 11am-10pm, Sat 4-10pm, Sun 4-9pm. **Thai** cuisine.

THAI CHI
630 Woodward, Detroit
(2 blocks N of Jefferson)
(313) 963-8424
Tue-Sun 11am-10pm. Innovative **Thai** and **Chinese** cooking, piano bar at lunch; nightly entertainment.

DOWNRIVER

BANGKOK STAR RESTAURANT
1512 Southfield Rd., Lincoln Park
(313) 388-7288
Mon-Fri 11am-10pm, Sat 4-10pm, Sun 4-9pm.

SOUTHWEST SUBURBS

THAI PALACE #1
22433 Michigan Ave., Dearborn
(313) 278-5252
and
THAI PALACE #2
13919 Michigan Ave., Dearborn
(313) 584-2048
Mon-Sat 11am-10pm, Sun 3-9:30pm.

EAST SUBURBS

JASMINE RESTAURANT
30762 Ryan Rd., Warren; (810) 573-2650
Mon-Sat 11am-9pm. **Filipino** and **Szechuan** cuisine.

PHO HANG
30921 Dequindre at 13 Mile
Madison Heights; (248) 583-9210
Sun-Thu 10am-1pm, Fri-Sat 10am-11pm. **Vietnamese** and **Chinese** fare.

PI'S THAI CUISINE
37180 Dequindre (NE of 16 Mile)
Sterling Heights; (810) 977-8716
and
24940 John R. (at 10 Mile)
Hazel Park; (248) 545-4070
Mon-Fri 11am-9pm, Sat noon-9pm. Home-cooked style **Thai** cuisine.

PA NDAU

Pa ndau (also called *pan dao*) is the centuries-old art created by Hmong women who teach their young daughters how to create reverse appliqué, cross-stitch, embroidery, strip appliqué and antique embroidery.

For generations, the bright designs were the traditional and exclusive expressions of isolated tribes and used on ceremonial clothing, hats, purses, wall hangings and baby carriers. The purpose of pa ndau was to record village life and pass on religious and cultural beliefs, much like a "stitchery bible." Hmong had no written language until the late 1950s, and practiced ancestor worship. Pa ndau is the spiritual companion of individual Hmong people throughout their lives. Bright yellows, pinks and reds on richly embroidered baby backpacks protect children from evil spirits. Pa ndau is given as gifts for important occasions, and the finest work is laid across the chest upon burial. As the pa ndau decays, it delivers its message to the departing soul about the form he or she can expect in the next life.

The reverse appliqué technique, including floral and geometric patterns, shows a contrasting color beneath the folded edges of a top layer, stitched with nearly invisible stitches. The women create the designs without any pattern. They must cut and sew as they go, perhaps following the path of a silk worm, or the cross-section of a cucumber, a squash flower, a crab, a chicken's eye or a Laotian temple.

Bright pink, strong yellow, orange, green and blue on a background of black reflect the Hmong belief that pa ndau must have five or six colors and at least two or three different stitches to be beautiful. In America, however, Hmong refugees have adapted their work to suit the tastes of their customers.

● *Local Hmong artists sometimes have booths at the Greektown Art Fair (May), the Cultural Center Festival of the Arts (September) and the International Institute's All-World Market (October). For an appointment to view Hmong goods, contact Ia Moua Yang at (810) 756-7643.*

THAI CUISINE

Thai has become one of the most interesting cuisines in the world. Contrary to popular belief, **not all Thai food is spicy hot**, and there are plenty of tasty dishes suited to the Western palate. This hybrid cuisine has been influenced by soups and noodle dishes from China, curries from India, and *satays* from Indonesia. Most dishes incorporate four elements: sweet, sour, salty and hot flavors.

Seafood, coconuts, tropical fruits, rice, tapioca, cane sugar, mushrooms, bananas and shrimp are plentiful foods. Thai cuisine varies among regions of the country. Meals in the north are somewhat milder than in the central plains, whereas northeastern food is fiery hot. Seafoods are most common in the south, while the Muslim communities of the deep south are partial to curries.

Many spices and herbs are used in Thai food such as hot peppers, garlic, coriander, ginger, onions and curries. These hot tastes often are offset by steamed rice (eaten at nearly every meal), mild noodle dishes, and sweet Thai teas, coffees, sweet desserts and fruits.

Many types of chili peppers—fresh and dried, whole and ground—are used in Thai cooking. Coconut milk, cardomon, coriander and cilantro are used for curry pastes.

Nam pla, a thin, salty brown extract of small fish such as anchovies, is sold in bottles and used to season many Thai dishes, including *pad Thai*, a noodle dish with spicy peanut sauce and stir-fry of vegetables with choice of chicken or shrimp.

Galanga, a close relative to ginger, has a sharp peppery-lemon taste and is used in large, thin pieces to flavor soups, stews and curries. Lemon grass and lime leaves, fresh or dried, are added to Thai dishes while they are cooking. *Palm sugar*, a dark-brown compressed sugar made from palm trees or coconut palms, is added to sauces, curries and sweets. *Shrimp paste*, sun-dried, salted shrimp with a strong fishy flavor and smell, is used in curries, sauces and soups.

Sticky rice, also called glutinous or sweet rice, is a staple of northern Thailand that cooks to a thick, starchy mass and is used in desserts. *Tamarind* fruit, which has a sweet-sour taste, is sold in small blocks of dark-brown pulp in Asian markets.

Roasted sesame seed and corn kernels are added to *Thai coffee* for an unusual burnt flavor. The beverage is served either ice-cold and sweet with evaporated milk, or hot with sweetened condensed milk.

Cinnamon, vanilla, star anise and food coloring give *Thai black tea* its flavor and terra-cotta coloring. Tea is served at the end of the meal either cold and sweet or hot.

THAILAND RESTAURANT
28742 Van Dyke, Warren; (810) 573-7444
Mon-Fri 11am-10pm, Sat 2-10pm,
Sun 2-9pm.

THAI HOUSE
25223 Gratiot, Roseville; (810) 776-3660
Mon-Thu 11am-9:30pm, Fri 11am-10pm,
Sat 1-10pm. Famous for "7 levels of sauce."

THAI PAN EXPRESS
27872 John R, Madison Heights
(248) 543-1961
Mon-Fri 11am-9:30pm, Sat 4:30-10pm,
Sun 4:30-9pm.

ESSENCE OF THAILAND
37702 Van Dyke, Sterling Hts.
(N of 16 Mile at Sterling Place Plaza)
(810) 978-0110
Mon-Thu 11am-10pm, Fri 11am-10:30pm,
Sat noon-10:30pm, Sun 4-9pm.

BANGKOK CUISINE #1
2149 15 Mile Rd., Madison Hts.
(County Line Plaza on Dequindre)
(810) 977-0130
and
BANGKOK CUISINE #2
2240 16 Mile Rd., Sterling Heights
(810) 977-0130
Mon-Fri 11am-9:30pm, Sat noon-10:30pm,
Sun noon-9pm. **Thai** food.

PHO HANG
30921 Dequindre (at 13 Mile)
Madison Heights; (248) 583-9210
Sun-Thu 10am-10pm, Fri-Sat 10 am-11pm.
Vietnamese specialties, including noodle,
and rice dishes, appetizers and fruit shakes.

NORTH SUBURBS
AL'S BANGKOK EXPRESS
254 W. Nine Mile Rd., Ferndale
(248) 545-3929
Mon-Sat 11am-9pm. Mild, medium or "on
fire" Thai entrees.

BANGKOK CAFE
323 W. Nine Mile, Ferndale; (248) 548-5373
Mon-Sat 11am-9:45 pm. **Thai** food, including curries and spiced noodles.

BANGKOK EXPRESS
29702 Southfield Rd., Southfield
(248) 557-0993
Mon-Thu 11am-9pm, Fri-Sat 11am-10pm.
Thai cuisine.

BANGKOK HUNG
781 E. Big Beaver, Troy, (248) 740-2772
Mon-Thu 11am-9:30pm, Fri-Sat 11am-
10pm. **Chinese** and **Thai** cuisine.

LITTLE TREE SUSHI BAR
107 S. Main, Royal Oak; (248) 586-0994
Mon-Thu 11:30am-10:30pm, Fri-Sat
11:30am-11pm, Sun 4:30-10pm. Three part
menu offers **Japanese, Thai** and **Philippine**
specialities.

MON JIN LAU
1515 E. Maple, Troy
(at Stephenson Hwy.)
(248) 689-2332
Mon-Thu 11am-1am, Fri 11am-2am, Sat
4pm-2am, Sun 3pm-1am. Pan-Asian menu.

RIVER KWAI
297 E. Maple, Birmingham; (248) 594-5758
Mon-Thurs 11am-9pm, Fri 11am-10pm, Sat
noon-10pm, Sun noon-9pm. Fresh and creative Thai food prepared in unique and lively
atmosphere.

ROYAL KUBO
25234 Greenfield, Oak Park
(248) 968-7550
Daily 3pm-2am. Nightclub with **Filipino**
menu. International karaoke (Filipino,
Japanese, Spanish and more) after 9pm.

SIAM SPICY
24838 Woodward, Royal Oak
(248) 545-4305
Mon-Thu 11am-9:30pm, Fri-Sat 11am-
10pm. Voted "Best **Thai** Restaurant" by *The*
Metro Times.

THAI HOUSE EXPRESS
32166 N. Woodward, Royal Oak
(248) 549-4112
Mon-Thu 11am-9:30pm, Fri-Sat 11am-
10pm.

THAI CHILLI
8670 W. Nine Mile, Oak Park
(248) 541-7800
Mon-Fri 11am-9pm, Sat 5-9pm.

THANG LONG RESTAURANT
27641 John R, Madison Hts.
(just N of 11 Mile)
(248) 547-6763
Tue-Thu 11am-10pm, Fri-Sat 11am-11pm,
Sun 11am-10pm. Full-service **Vietnamese**
restaurant; some **Thai** dishes as well.

THAI GARDEN
721 E. Nine Mile, Ferndale; (248) 542-6860
Mon-Thu 11am-9:30pm, Fri 11am-10pm, Sat 4-10pm, Sun 4-9pm. **Thai** dishes.

SY THAI RESTAURANT
315 Hamilton, Birmingham; (248) 258-9830
Mon-Thu 11am-10pm, Fri 11am-11pm, Sat 4-11pm, Sun 4-10pm. **Thai** dishes.

LEMON GRASS
Opdyke at Centerpoint Plaza, Pontiac (248) 335-7435
Mon-Fri 11am-9:30pm, Sat 5-9pm. Authentic **Thai** food.

ORCHID CAFE
3303 Rochester Rd., Troy; (248) 524-1944
and
30 W. Square Lake Rd., Troy (248) 828-4149
Mon-Fri 11am-9pm, Sat noon-9pm. **Thai** restaurant.

BANGKOK HUNG
781 E. Big Beaver, Troy; (248) 740-2772
Mon-Thu 11am-9:30pm, Fri-Sat 11am-10pm. **Thai** restaurant.

BANGKOK CUISINE #2
727 N. Main, Rochester; (248) 652-8841
Mon-Thu 11am-9:30pm, Fri 11am-10:30pm, Sat noon-10:30pm, Sun noon-8:30pm. **Thai** restaurant.

WEST SUBURBS
EURASIAN GRILL
4771 Haggerty at Pontiac Trail W. Bloomfield; (248) 624-6109
Tue-Thu 11 am-10:30pm, Fri 11am-11pm, Sat 4-11pm, Sun 4:30-10pm. Fusion food and Asian specialties such as Vietnamese spring rolls and Indonesian rack of lamb.

VIETNAMESE DINING

Vietnamese cuisine of the past 200 years is a unique combination of Asian and French. Asian influence is seen in the importance of vegetables in the daily diet and in the chopping of food before cooking. Chopsticks are used at the table.

Most Vietnamese soups are consommés (French). Noodles often are added to the soup, making *pho bo.* Also French are many Vietnamese cooking terms. The most common spice, **lemon grass,** is referred to in Vietnam as **citronelle;** and an indigenous paste of mashed shrimp, black pepper and coriander is called *pâté.*

Before the Vietnam War and the Communist takeover, many French restaurants were in Vietnam, particularly in Saigon. Some still offer classic French dishes. Though they do stir-fry, they use very little oil. Most food is simmered, steamed or grilled.

Meats are less important than fish, particularly seafood. There is an abundance of shrimp in Vietnam. Vietnamese prefer beef over pork because pork is often too fatty for their taste.

Vietnamese food is not as spicy hot as other Southeast Asian cuisine because seasoning is left up to the diner. In common with most Southeast Asian cuisines, the Vietnamese have a tasty fish sauce *(nouc mam),* an alternative to soy sauce or salt. It is added to many dishes and is used as a salad dressing. **Table salad** is made up of vegetables, meats, seafood and herbs that are rolled by each diner in lettuce or rice paper.

Spring rolls seem to be adopted from Chinese cuisine. However, the Vietnamese version, named *cha gio,* is prepared largely without fat, unlike deep-fried Chinese rolls. Other signature dishes are *canh chua ca* (hot-and-sour fish soup), *chao tom* (shrimp paste grilled on sugarcane) and *bo nhung dam* (beef fondue).

MAI THAI
6635 Orchard Lake Rd., W. Bloomfield
(248) 626-6313
*Mon-Thu 11am-10pm, Fri-Sat 11am-11pm,
Sun noon-9pm.*

NEW BANGKOK
43436 W. Oaks, Novi
(across from Twelve Oaks Mall)
(248) 347-6098
Mon-Sat 11am-10pm. **Thai** restaurant.

SIAM SPICY
32425 Northwestern Hwy.
Farmington Hills; (248) 626-2092
*Daily 11am-2:30pm, Mon-Thu 5-9:30pm Fri-
Sun 5-10:30pm.* **Thai** cuisine.

THAI BISTRO
45620 Ford Rd., Canton Twp.
(734) 416-2122
*Mon-Fri 11:30am-2:30pm, Mon-Thu 4:30-
9pm, Fri-Sat 4:30-10pm.*

THAI CITY
6534 N. Wayne Rd., Westland
(734) 729-4470
*Mon-Thu 11am-10pm, Fri-Sat 11am-11pm,
Sun 4-9pm.*

THAI PEPPERS
29402 Orchard Lake Rd., Farmington Hills
(248) 932-9119
Mon-Fri 11:30am-9:30pm, Sat 5-10:30pm.

WINDSOR
BASIL COURT
327 Ouellette, Windsor; (519) 252-5609
*Mon-Fri 11am-2pm and 5-10pm, Sat noon-
midnight, Sun 4:30-9:30pm.* **Thai** specialties.

THE MINI
475 University W., Windsor; (519) 254-2221
Tue-Fri 11:30am-10pm, Sat 5-10pm. Highly
rated **Vietnamese** cuisine.

SAIGON RESTAURANT
1545 University W., Windsor; (519) 253-9100
Mon-Thu 11am-midnight, Fri-Sat 11am-2am.
Vietnamese, Saigonese and **Chinese.**

BAKERIES

RED RIBBON BAKERY
26889 Ryan, Sterling Hts.
(corner of Ryan and 16 Mile)
(810) 978-1580
Tue-Sat 10am-8pm, Sun noon-7pm. **Filipino**
sweets and prepared foods. A few café tables.

SAMPAGUITA BAKERY
30905 Dequindre at 13 Mile, Madison Hts.
(248) 616-9824
Limited retail hours; call first. **Filipino** bread
and rolls.

GROCERIES

ASIA MARKET
30925 Dequindre, Madison Hts.
(248) 588-8383

FOOD OF THE PHILIPPINES

Filipino food is not yet well-known in the United States (compared to Thai, for example). Just as Filipinos are part Malay, Chinese and Spanish, so is the cuisine of the 7,000-island nation. Also evident are subtle hints of Indian, Mexican, Arab and American influences. Some classic dishes are: *Adobo*, a rich, dark, well-marinated stew of chicken and pork, with hints of vinegar and soy sauce; *Pancit*, sautéed noodles with bits of fresh vegetables, sausage and tiny shrimp; *Tinolang tahong*, a soup made with mussels steamed in ginger root, spinach and onion; and *Rellenong manok*, chicken, deboned and stuffed with a mixture of ground chicken, pork and ham, plus whole sausages and hard-boiled eggs, so that when it is sliced and served, the dish looks as good as it tastes.

Lumpia can be either fresh *(lumpiang sariwa)* in the form of crêpes filled with vegetables and topped with peanut sauce, or fried *(lumpiang Shanghai)* in the form of small spring rolls filled with ground beef or pork.

For dessert, choose from *halo-halo* (mixed fruits in crushed ice and milk), *leche flan* or *brazos*, which is custard wrapped in meringue.

San Miguel, brewed in Manila, is one of the most popular beers in the world.

Mon-Thu 10am-9pm, Fri-Sat 10am-10pm, Sun 10am-9pm. Fresh meats to produce to canned goods. **Vietnamese, Chinese, Thai, Korean, Filipino** and **Laotian** foods.

ASIAN AMERICAN GROCERY STORE
19612 Schoenherr, Detroit
(between State Fair and Seven Mile)
(313) 526-6137
Daily 9am-7pm. **Thai** groceries.

C&L ORIENTAL FOOD MARKET
37164 Dequindre (at 16 Mile)
Sterling Hts.;(810) 978-8220
Mon-Tue 10:30am-8pm, Wed-Sat 10am-8pm, Sun 11am-7pm. **Filipino** gifts and groceries.

FILIPINAS ORIENTAL FOOD
3866 E. 13 Mile (at Ryan), Warren
(810) 558-8550
Mon 11am-7:30pm, Tue-Sat 10am-7:30pm, Sun noon-5pm. Filipino food, imports, movies.

HAN KUK MARKET
33717 Gratiot, Mt. Clemens; (810) 791-8877
Mon-Sat 10am-8pm, Sun noon-6pm. Filipino, Thai, Chinese, Korean and Japanese foods.

NAM HOA MARKET
30573 John R, Madison Hts.
(248) 589-0831
Daily 11am-10pm. **Vietnamese** groceries.

ORIENTAL MARKET
31086 John R, Madison Hts.
(corner of 13 Mile)
(248) 583-9533
Daily 9:30am-9pm. Oriental groceries.

SOUTHEAST ASIA TRADING
13660 E. Eight Mile, Detroit
(between Schoenherr and Gratiot)
(313) 371-3060
Daily 9am-8pm. Groceries, dry goods, fabric and some gift items.

TASTE OF MANILA
42915 Dequindre (at 19 Mile) ,
Troy; (248) 828-8987
Tue-Sun 10am-7pm.
Filipino grocery.

GO FLY A KITE

Kites are named after the kite bird, a graceful hawk often seen in Asia Minor and Northern Africa. One tradition holds that kites were invented by the Greek scientist Archytas of Tarentum about 400 B.C. But they have been in use among Asian people from prehistoric times. The sport has long been a national pastime of Koreans, Chinese, Japanese, Malaysians and Filipinos.

There are even documents suggesting that kites flying at night over a house were believed to keep evil spirits away. Religious significance remains connected to some ceremonial kite flying. The Japanese once regarded kites as "tangible prayers."

In eastern Asia, special competitions are conducted, through which the kites are elaborately designed and decorated in the forms of birds, fish or dragons, and may be equipped with whistles or pipes that make sounds as the wind blows through them. Kite-fighting contests also are conducted, through which competitors attempt to use their kites to oust those of their opponents.

(See also "Korea.")

THE UNIQUE PLACE, WORLD OF KITES
525 S. Washington, Royal Oak
(248) 398-5900
Pro shop for kite flyers in the Midwest.

KITES & FUN THINGS
1049 S. Main, Plymouth; (734) 454-3760
Offers kites, wind socks and toys.

◆ **GREAT LAKES SPORTS KITE CHAMPIONSHIPS**
Event annually draws crowds of more than 60,000 to Grand Haven in May. Kite ballets, competitions, stunts and exhibitions contribute to the spectacle on the shores of Lake Michigan.
Call (616) 846-7501 for more information.

THE UNIVERSITY OF MICHIGAN LIBRARY has one of the world's best collections of materials on southern Asia. Three professional librarians oversee holdings of more than half a million titles on South and Southeast Asia, including unique research collections in the Thai language (Gedney Collection), Philippines history (Worcester Collection), and the John A. Thierry Southeast Asia Art Collection and Photograph Archive (more than 58,000 images). Also on the Michigan campus is the **Gerald R. Ford Presidential Library** and its archive of records on the Vietnam War. The archaeological and ethnographic collections of the **University Museum of Anthropology** contain bamboo tube and bark manuscripts from Indonesia and the Philippines, and glazed ceramics from Cambodia, Thailand and Vietnam dating from the 10th century. Archaeological field research is ongoing in South and Southeast Asia. For University of Michigan information, call (734) 764-1817.

WINDSOR
SAIGON SERVICES GROCERY
366 Wyandotte, Windsor
(519) 254-6969
Daily 9am-8pm. **Vietnamese** groceries, dry goods and gifts.

CULTURAL EXHIBITS
INTERNATIONAL INSTITUTE
111 E. Kirby, Detroit
(313) 871-8600
International Doll Exhibition includes examples of Southeast Asian costumes, family and festival scenes and artifacts. Gift shop with imports and crafts from many Asian countries. Call for Hall of Nations hours.

CHILDREN'S MUSEUM
67 E. Kirby, Detroit
(313) 873-8100
Mon-Fri 1-4pm, Sat 9am-4pm. Small room on second floor is devoted to the islands of Indonesia. Exhibit includes outrigger canoe, musical instruments, costumes, dolls, tools.

DETROIT INSTITUTE OF ARTS
5200 Woodward Ave., Detroit
(313) 833-7900
Wed-Fri 11am-4pm, Sat-Sun 11am-5pm. South and Southeast Asian collection (N141) includes sculpture from Cambodia and other Indochinese and Island cultures.

PERFORMING ARTS
TAGUMPAY FILIPINO DANCERS
Perform at the International Institute's All-World Market, ethnic festivals and other cul-

tural events. Call Antoine Gosioco at (313) 893-8590.

KYAI TELEGA MADU *(Lake of Honey)*
Performs traditional Gamelan at several concerts annually, often with distinguished guest artists from abroad, featuring 70 instruments and 300 leather puppets. Call Judith Becker, Music Department at University of Michigan, Ann Arbor, (734) 763-3278.

A GAMELAN is a gong-chime orchestra found throughout Southeast Asia. The most well known are those from the islands of Java and Bali. Gamelan music ranges from traditional to contemporary, classical to experimental.

EVENTS
JUNE
CARROUSEL OF NATIONS
Filipino and Vietnamese "villages" are part of Windsor's multicultural festival on two weekends in June. Call (519) 255-1127 for information.

JULY
PONTIAC INTERNATIONAL FESTIVAL
At Phoenix Plaza over the Independence

Day weekend, includes Pacific Rim countries. Call (248) 857-5603.

FILIPINO PICNIC
Sponsored by the Filipino American Association; an annual event in Hamlich Park, Warren. Features cultural show, songs and dances and the spiritual Santacruzan parade, a beautiful and revered tradition. Call (313) 893-8590.

OCTOBER
ALL-WORLD MARKET
Takes place the third weekend in October and includes a Hmong stitchery booth and the Tagumpay Filipino Dancers. Call (313) 871-8600.

NOVEMBER
NOI PEB CAUG CELEBRATION
In preparation for the New Year, Hmong people have many celebrations during the harvest season. It is a time of festive events and family reunions. In following the custom of visiting other villages, the Detroit Hmong community has exchanges with groups in Saginaw and Lansing.

DECEMBER
RIZAL DAY
A celebration and commemoration of Filipino national hero Jose Rizal on the last weekend of December at Cobo Hall in downtown Detroit. Call Antoine Gosioco at

(313) 893-8590 for details.

ORGANIZATIONS

FILIPINO-AMERICAN ASSOCIATION
(313) 893-8590 or 494-2362
Contact: Antoine Goisoco
Sponsors various activities for the community. Hosts a pageant to select a Miss or Mrs. Filipino of Michigan to appear at public events such as the Michigan State Fair parade, consulate programs and festivals.

MEDIA

RADIO
WNZK AM 690 days/680 nights
21700 Northwestern Hwy., Southfield
(248) 557-3500
"Filipino Hour," Wednesday 9pm.
"Karaoke from the Royal Kubo," Friday 10pm.

PRINT
HIMAL AND FILAPINAS
Magazines carried by Paperbacks Unlimited, (248) 546-3282.

WEB SITES
INDONESIAN FORUM
www.cool.mb.ca/indonesia/indoforum

MICHIGAN SOUTHEAST ASIAN STUDIES
www.umich.edu/~iinet/csseas

FILIPINO ARTS AND CULTURE
amsterdam.park.org:8888/
philippines/education/painting

HMONG COMMUNITY
www.hmongnet.org

THAI KITCHEN AND CULTURAL ARTS
www.nectec.or.th/users/joy/sctrecipes

PENCAK SILAT, or *"Seni Silat,"* originated around the seventh century in ancient West Sumatra, spreading throughout Indonesia and on to Malaysia. It is a comprehensive martial art and self-defense system, as well as a spiritual path. For decades, Pencak Silat has been passed on from generation to generation, connecting its mystical and spiritual culture to the time of the Sufis. Hidden in the dance-like movements are self-defense and combat techniques. For more information and/or instruction contact:

PENTJAK SILAT, 3410 Fort St., Lincoln Park; (313) 382-7016

PENCAK SILAT, Satria Muda, Ann Arbor; (734) 930-9963

KOREA

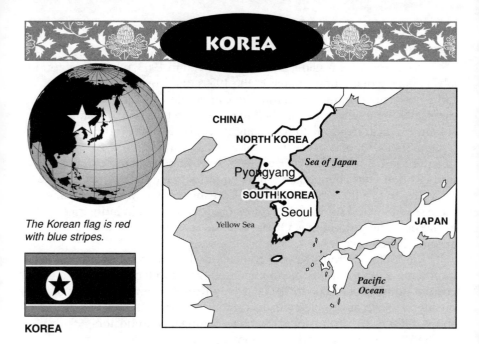

The Korean flag is red with blue stripes.

KOREA

The Korean peninsula is surrounded by the Sea of Japan (also called East Sea) on the east, the Yellow Sea on the west and the Korea Strait on the south. The northern border shares its boundary with China, and 10 miles of the east is shared with Russia. Within 70 miles to the south is **Kyushu,** Japan's major southern island.

The peninsula, which is 600 miles long north to south and ranges from 130 to 200 miles in width east to west, occupies 85,269 square miles, an area nearly the size of Great Britain. The climate of Korea ranges from dry with extremely cold winters in the north to almost tropical conditions in parts of the south.

The Republic of Korea (South Korea) has **Seoul,** the largest city, as its capital. **Pyongyang** is the capital of the Democratic People's Republic of Korea.

Proximity to China and Japan has permitted the flow of peoples and ideas in both directions. Korea has borrowed from and contributed to both cultures, yet the Koreans have remained a homogeneous people, maintaining their own language and traditions.

SOUTH KOREA

The South Korean flag symbolizes the philosophy, thought and mysticism of Asia. In the center of a white background is a circle equally divided into a blue and a red section, each resembling a comma. This symbol (the yin and yang) represents perfect balance and harmony. The bars that appear at each corner of the flag also illustrate the concept of opposites and balances. The yin and yang are red and blue; the bars are are black.

KOREAN IMMIGRATION

The first group of Korean immigrants, seeking freedom from government oppression, arrived in Hawaii in 1903, where they found jobs on sugar plantations. Later, in the 1950s, the Korean War greatly influenced more immigration into the United States. Many Koreans, especially the intellectuals, wished to escape the tensions of war, and sought political freedom. Others sought economic opportunities in the United States. Quotas at this time allowed only a few hundred Koreans to enter the United States yearly. But in 1965, and again in 1968, the immigration laws changed and allowed more to enter.

At the end of the 1960s, about 500 Koreans were in Michigan. Some were students and some were professionals employed in industries such as medical and automotive. Others worked as laborers for the automotive companies.

In the 1980s, Detroit's Korean community began growing quickly. The number of Koreans in Michigan increased from 6,000 or 7,000 to the current number of 25,000 to 30,000. Many Koreans became owners of businesses such as dry cleaners, gas stations, clothing stores and gift shops. Others are professionals, such as engineers and doctors.

The 1980s were a period of economic stability and many Koreans moved to the suburbs, where they sought better living and educational environments. Most of the current Korean population in metro Detroit resides in Oakland County suburbs.

TOUR	ART AND CUISINE

[D-F/3-5] Travel to Detroit's Cultural Center to view the Korean art in Gallery N121 at the **Detroit Institute of Arts** (5200 Woodward Avenue). The Museum is open Wednesday-Sunday. *(See listing for hours.)* Note the love of nature, uninhibited simplicity and boldness of expression that characterize the Korean spirit and are reflected in the art. One of Korea's unique accomplishments is its ceramic art heritage. Look for the celadon pieces, which are characteristic of this heritage.

For a Korean feast, *go north on the Lodge Freeway and exit Telegraph Road north.* To find **New Seoul Garden** *on the Northwestern Highway service drive in Southfield, take the first right (east) and another quick right toward 11 Mile.* If you are with a group, order a variety of dishes and sample them all.

Enjoy your meal, or, as the Koreans say: *"Maan-ee to-say-yo,"* meaning *"Please eat a lot."*

[E-F/1-3] Dequindre and Maple (15 Mile Road) is a special spot to begin an exploration of Korean culture and cuisine. Stop for a Korean lunch at **Shin Sung** *(34744 Dequindre)*, or **Seoul Garden** *(2101 E. Maple)*.

After having your appetite whetted, investigate **Hana Oriental Mart** *(next to Shin Sung Restaurant)* or remain on Dequindre for another Korean treasure, **Asia Mart** *(36949)*, to purchase either some prepared Korean dishes or the ingredients to try your hand at Korean cooking. *(See "Korean Cooking.")* Korean markets *along 18 Mile (Long Lake Road)* include **Jung Won Oriental Mart,** *on the southwest corner of Dequindre,* and **Han Mi,** *at 5060 Rochester Road, north of Long Lake Road.* These Troy markets are near the **Korean United Methodist Church** *(Dequindre between 18 and 19 Mile Roads)* and have delis that sell ready-made Korean dishes. Most of the Korean markets also carry authentic Korean goods such as *han-boks* (traditional garments for men and women) and household items.

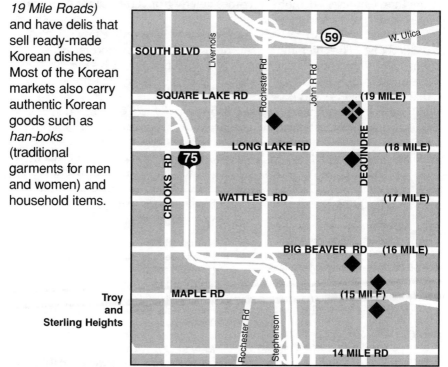

SOUTH BLVD
Livernois
(59)
W. Utica
SQUARE LAKE RD
Rochester Rd
John R Rd
(19 MILE)
LONG LAKE RD
DEQUINDRE
(18 MILE)
CROOKS RD
75
WATTLES RD
(17 MILE)
BIG BEAVER RD
(16 MILE)
MAPLE RD
(15 MILE)
Troy and Sterling Heights
Rochester Rd
Stephenson
14 MILE RD

The Korean language is a genuine native language, part of the Altai group. The vocabulary consists of Korean words, based on Chinese characters and borrowed words. The written language is *Han Geul*. Some Chinese characters also are used.

As a single system, the Korean alphabet is recognized for its originality and logical basis, resulting in Korea having one of the highest literacy rates in the world.

KOREAN COOKING

Like most peoples of the Asian continent, Koreans have made rice the staple of their diet. Rice is always on the dinner table to accompany fish, meat and vegetable dishes. Because of Buddhism's influence over a long period, vegetables have dominated the Korean diet. Some of the most popular are bean sprouts, Korean cabbage, Korean radish, spinach, eggplant, squash, cucumber, and white and sweet potatoes.

In many ways, Korean cooking is different from Japanese and Chinese cuisines. It tends to be spicier than Japanese cuisine and less oily than Chinese. The hotness comes chiefly from chili. Other common spices are sesame and ginger.

Kim-chi, a variety of Korean pickled cabbage, is unlike any other pickled dish. The chief ingredients are Korean cabbage and radishes seasoned with ginger, garlic, red pepper, green onion, fish sauce, chestnuts and pears. Kim-chi is far more important to the Korean diet than anything else and is eaten year-round.

One of the best-known Korean dishes is *bul go ki,* or barbecued beef, which consists of thin-sliced beef roasted over a brazier at the table after being marinated in a mixture of soy sauce, sesame oil, garlic, green onions, sugar and rice wine. A variation is to place a mixture of meat, rice and bean paste on lettuce leaves and roll them into sandwiches.

RESTAURANTS

BELL'S DINER
2167 W. Stadium, Ann Arbor
(734) 995-0226
Daily 6:30am-4pm. Korean items for lunch.

EAST WIND
19160 E. 10 Mile, Eastpointe
(810) 771-7420
Mon-Fri 11am-10pm, Sat noon-11pm, Sun 1-10pm. Chinese restaurant with some Korean items.

HAPPINESS GARDEN
29295 Southfield Rd., Southfield
(248) 569-5720
Mon-Thu 11:30am-9pm, Fri-Sat 11:30am-10pm, Sun 12:30-8:30pm. Korean cuisine.

KANA KOREAN RESTAURANT
114 W. Liberty, Ann Arbor
(734) 662-9303
Mon-Thu 11am-9pm, Fri-Sat 11am-10pm.

Korean cuisine with meat, seafood and vegetarian entrées.

MI-LOC RESTAURANT
23043 Beech (at Nine Mile), Southfield
(248) 356-2155
Mon-Thu 11am-10pm, Fri-Sat 11am-11pm, Sun (sushi bar) noon-9pm. Former Kobe Restaurant offers Korean and Japanese fare.

NEW SEOUL GARDEN
27566 Northwestern Hwy., Southfield
(248) 827-1600
Mon-Sat 11:30am-10:30pm, Sun noon-10pm. Korean and Japanese cuisine. Gal bee (marinated short ribs) and bul go ki.

SEOUL GARDEN
2101 E. 15 Mile, Sterling Hts.
(810) 264-4488
Daily 11:30am-10:30pm. Korean and Japanese fare. Tableside barbeque and hotpot dishes.

SHIN SUNG RESTAURANT
34744 Dequindre (at Maple, NE Corner)
Sterling Hts.; (810) 978-0500
Daily 10:30am-11pm. Korean and Japanese cuisine.

SUSHI KO
30703 Twelve Mile, Farmington Hills
(248) 471-4363
Mon-Sat 11am-10:30pm, Sun noon-10pm.
Japanese restaurant with some Korean dishes.

TAKE SUSHI
1366 Walton Blvd., Rochester Hills
(248) 652-7800
Mon-Fri 11:30am-10pm, Sat-Sun 5-10pm.
Japanese sushi restaurant with some Korean dishes on menu.

MARKETS

Many of the Oriental markets carry cookbooks, household items, gifts and Korean newspapers in addition to groceries.

WEST

URI MARKET
31557 W. 13 Mile at Orchard Lake Rd.
Farmington Hills; (248) 488-0477
Mon-Sat 10am-8pm, Sun 11 am-6pm.
Korean and Japanese groceries.

NORTHEAST

ASIA MARKET
30925 Dequindre, Madison Hts.
(corner of 13 Mile)
(248) 588-8383
Mon-Fri 10am-8pm, Sat-Sun 9am-9pm.
Carries merchandise from fresh meats, seafood and produce to canned goods.

KOREAN COOKING

Other delicious dishes to try are *man doo* (mixed meat and vegetables in a thin wrapper) and *chop chae* (mixed vegetables with transparent noodles). Desserts such as fruit, *duck* (cake), *sikhye* (rice tea) and *whachae* (fruit cocktail) also are part of meals.

If you choose to do your own Korean-style cooking, basic ingredients available for purchase at the markets listed in this chapter include bean curd, bean sprouts, chestnuts, rice wine, dried mushrooms *(pyogo)*, garlic, ginger root, green onions, hot pepper, Korean cabbage *(nappa)*, pickled cabbage *(kim-chi)*, oyster sauce, pine nuts, seaweed, sesame oil, sesame seed, soy sauce, soybean paste and transparent noodles (also known as bean threads or cellophane noodles). Also look for *jujubee*, a dried date-like fruit with puckered skin, sometimes called *dae-choo*, and *naeng-myun*, thin buckwheat-flour noodles.

Koreans pay particular attention to the arrangement of food on plates and the dishes on the table. Foods are placed neatly in concentric circles or parallel columns, never in a disorderly fashion. The colors of the foods alternate in a regular pattern.

Korean Cooking for You, *by local author Moon Ja Yoon, is a colorful gourmet cookbook presenting traditional Korean dishes, customs and celebrations. Instruction includes easy-to-follow recipes, cooking techniques and use of chopsticks. Order direct from the author at special rate of $18 (includes postage and handling) by sending a check to P.O. Box 250160, Franklin, MI 48025.*

ASIA MART
36949 Dequindre, Troy
(SW corner of 16 Mile)
(248) 689-6090
Mon-Sat 10am-9pm, Sun 12:30-6pm.
One of the larger Oriental markets.

HANA ORIENTAL MART
34748 Dequindre, Sterling Hts.
(810) 264-8259
Mon-Sat 10am-9pm,
Sun 10am-6pm.

HAN MI ORIENTAL MART
5060 Rochester Rd.
(N of Long Lake Rd.)
Troy, (248) 528-0022
Tue-Fri 10am-8pm, Sat 10am-8pm, Sun 1-6pm. Large market with Korean and Japanese items.

HAN KUK ORIENTAL MARKET
33717 Gratiot, Mt. Clemens
(810) 791-8877
Mon-Sat 8am-10pm, Sun noon-6pm. Korean, Thai, Filipino, Japanese and other Asian foods.

JUNG WON ORIENTAL MART
2926 E. Long Lake Rd.
(SW corner of Dequindre)
Troy
(248) 528-3911
Daily 10am-9pm.

NORTH
KA GO PA ORIENTAL MART
29037 Southfield Rd., Southfield
(248) 559-7370
Sun-Tue 10am-8pm, Wed-Sat 10am-9pm.

SEOUL ORIENTAL MART
25840 W. Nine Mile, Southfield
(248) 357-2828
Mon-Fri 10am-8pm, Sat 9am-8pm, Sun 10am-7pm.

DETROIT
DONG YANG ORIENTAL GROCERY
18919 W. Seven Mile, Detroit
(313) 534-7773
Mon-Sat 10am-7:30pm, Sun 10am-6pm.

CELADON WARE is stoneware that has been stamped and incised with a delicate floral design, coated with a transparent, iron-pigmented glaze known as celadon. When fired, it results in subtle colors that pool at the edges of the design, creating a shaded effect. Celadon ware was popular in China and Korea.

ENTERTAINMENT

MANNAM NIGHT CLUB
23514 W. Seven Mile, Detroit
(313) 538-4748
Daily 8pm-2am. Offers nightly performances of Korean music.

VISUAL ARTS

DETROIT INSTITUTE OF ARTS
5200 Woodward, Detroit
(313) 833-7900
Wed-Fri 11am-4pm, Sat-Sun 11am-5pm. Closed Mon-Tue. The Korean Gallery (N121) collection includes Korean paintings, sculpture, porcelain and lacquer pieces from the 16th-18th centuries.

KOREAN CERAMICS PROJECT
(313) 577-1823 or (248) 547-5058
Contact: Arthur K.J. Park, Ph.D.
Dr. Park, a potter and art education professor at Wayne State University, coordinates program that offers workshops and educational videos on Korean ceramics.

THE MYSTICAL HERB

Ginseng is an almost mystical herb that has been a part of Chinese culture for about 5,000 years. Many North American Indian nations consumed ginseng for centuries before it was discovered among the Iroquois by a missionary in the early 1700s. Independent of each other, these cultures believed that ginseng gave vitality, relieved stress, increased energy and prolonged life.

Ginseng is an exotic plant that is very difficult to grow properly and harvest. World consumption of this herb has grown to such proportions that 98 percent of all ginseng produced for market is cultivated. Ginseng is costly to grow because it takes as many as six years to harvest, and once a garden has been harvested, the herb cannot be grown in the same soil for at least 20 years.

Although many varieties of the ginseng plant exist, there are only two major ones: *panax ginseng* (commonly called Asian, Korean or Chinese ginseng) and *panax quinquefolius* (commonly called North American, Canadian, Wisconsin or Ontario ginseng).

To distinguish Korean ginseng from those of other countries, it is called *Koryo ginseng,* named after the ancient kingdom of Koryo, from which the nation's current English name "Korea" is derived. Ginseng grown in the wild, deep in the mountains, is known as *sansam* (mountain ginseng). It is, however, found rarely. In the old days, the search for it was almost a spiritual endeavor for those dwelling in the nation's mountainous regions.

Korean ginseng is available in many forms at virtually all health food stores, from bottled sodas to many types of teas to powders and pills.

The family is the most important social unit. In Korea, the surname comes before the given name and adults address each other by their position or surname, but never by their given name. *Kim, Park* and *Lee* are among the most common Korean surnames.

Koreans' ancient beliefs are based on the relationship between humans and their natural surroundings. Confucianism, the philosophy that continues to provide the most widely followed set of beliefs, is concerned with the principles of good conduct, practical wisdom and social relationships. Buddhism, the major organized religion, was brought from China in the 4th century and eventually assumed a Korean character. Christianity was transmitted by missionaries near the end of the Yi Dynasty (1392-1910) and now is a major religion. The Korean community in metro Detroit is primarily Christian.

EVENTS

WINTER
NEW YEAR'S CELEBRATION
Takes place at the Korean United Methodist Church of Ann Arbor and features Korean name writing, flag coloring, learning the deep bow (saebae), music, traditional dress (han-bok), games and a sampling of Korean food. Call the church at (734) 662-0660 or the Families for Children newsletter editor at (313) 389-1846.

SPRING
KOREAN CULTURAL ARTS FESTIVAL
Presented annually by the Korean Student Association of Ann Arbor to promote awareness of Korean and Korean American culture. Contact the student association at (734) 677-1782 or Jeff Galloway at (313) 389-1846.

CULTURAL EXCHANGE
Annual spring event at Korean United Methodist Church in Troy features Korean lunch and children's cultural activities. Call (248) 879-2240 or 828-9451.

SUMMER
MULTICULTURAL FESTIVAL
Bethany Christian Services of Madison Heights hosts event held in Grand Rapids on the last Saturday in July. Features children's activities and booths selling Korean dolls, toys, books and cultural items. Call (248) 588-9400.

INDEPENDENCE DAY CELEBRATION
Sponsored by the Korean Society of Metro Detroit, takes place on the Sunday before August 15 at Island Lake Recreation Area. Call (248) 557-4990 for information.

FALL
KOREAN BAZAAR
Family Adoption Consultants (FAC) in Rochester hosts annual event.
Call (248) 652-2842.

INTERNATONAL BAZAAR
Fair, sponsored by Americans for International Aid and Adoption in November in Birmingham, features Korean artwork, dolls, toys and books. Call (248) 645-2211.

● EVENT INFORMATION
Local Korean churches often sponsor cultural events and special celebrations of Korean holidays. *(See "Religious Centers.")* For information, call the Korean Hotline Service (248-356-4488) at the **Korean Presbyterian Church USA of Metro Detroit.**

Another source of information is a newsletter published by **Families for Children,** an adoptive parent group in the area. Contact Jeff Galloway at (313) 389-1846.

CELEBRATIONS

The dates of many Korean holidays are based on the lunar calendar and vary from year to year. The Korean New Year *(Sol Nal),* for example, is in late January or early February.

Kite flying *(yon-nalligi)* is an important recreational activity during winter for adults and children, and is especially popular during the New Year's holiday, as are other folk games. Bowing to seniors, visiting ancestors' graves and conducting memorial services also are important customs then.

Tano (May or June) began as a spring festival at planting time. Today, this celebration for children includes wrestling matches for boys and swinging competitions for girls. Tall swings are erected in every community so that girls may practice. In some areas, each contestant must ring a bell with her foot when she is high in the air.

The *Chusok* holiday, or Harvest Moon Festival, is considered one of Korea's most important celebrations. It is regarded as their Thanksgiving Day and falls on the night of the full moon of the eighth lunar month. Families make *song poen* (rice cake) and other foods from the newly harvested crops. *Kim-chi* (pickled cabbage), the national food dish of Korea, is prepared to last through the winter months.

Dol Nal, a child's first birthday, is considered an important event in a Korean's life. At this time, a large feast takes place and items such as noodles, money, books, uncooked rice, yarn or a brush are placed before the child. Whatever item the child reachs for is symbolic of the child's future.

EDUCATION

Schools and camps offer cultural programs for children and adults, including language, art, history, customs, dance and cooking.

KOREAN CULTURE DAY CAMP
Korean Presbyterian Church
27075 W. Nine Mile, Southfield
(248) 356-4488 or (734) 416-1446
One-week summer camp *(Tue-Fri 9am-noon)* in July for children 5-12 features activities involving Korean arts and crafts, food, geography, language, tae kwon do and dance.

KOREAN PRESBYTERIAN CHURCH SCHOOL
27075 W. Nine Mile, Southfield
(between Inkster and Beech)
(248) 356-4488
Children's classes *Sun 10-11am.*

KOREAN SCHOOL OF ANN ARBOR
3301 Creek Drive, Ann Arbor
(734) 769-2883
Contact: Ryung-Hwa L. Kim

KOREAN UNITED METHODIST CHURCH SCHOOL
42693 Dequindre, Troy
(between 18 and 19 Mile Rds.)
(248) 879-2240
Children's classes *Sun 9:30-10:30am.*
Korean language school.

SAE JONG SCHOOL
3570 Northfield Pkwy., Troy
(between 16 and 17 Mile Rds.)
(248) 851-5393
Culture and language school *Sat 10am-1:30pm.*

SAE JONG SOCIETY DAY CAMP
Franklin
(248) 851-5393
Weeklong summer camp at which students enjoy outdoor activities and experience Korean history, language and culture.

RELIGIOUS CENTERS

KOREAN CHURCH OF ANN ARBOR
3301 Creek, Ann Arbor; (734) 971-9777

KOREAN PRESBYTERIAN CHURCH OF METRO DETROIT
27075 W. Nine Mile, Southfield
(248) 356-4488

KOREAN UNTED METHODIST CHURCH OF ANN ARBOR
1526 Franklin, Ann Arbor Twp.
(734) 662-0660

KOREAN UNITED METHODIST CHURCH OF METRO DETROIT
42469 Dequindre, Troy; (248) 879-2240

ST. ANDREW KIM KOREAN CATHOLIC CHURCH
21177 Halstead, Farmington Hills
(248) 442-9026

ZEN BUDDHIST TEMPLE
1370 John R, Rochester; (248) 650-2999

ORGANIZATIONS

KOREAN SOCIETY OF METRO DETROIT
17250 W. 12 Mile, Ste. 202, Southfield
(248) 557-4990
Addresses needs of Korean community and provides educational services, including newsletter in Korean.

KOREAN AMERICAN WOMEN'S ASSOCIATION OF MICHIGAN
708 Parkman, Bloomfield Hills
(248) 645-6719

Group provides support for Korean women in interracial marriages, offers scholarships and community services.

KOREAN CULTURAL CENTER OF ANN ARBOR
925 Green Hills, Ann Arbor
(734) 769-2883

KOREAN SOCIETY OF ANN ARBOR
(313) 572-1576

MEDIA

PRINT
KOREAN TIMES
4575 Bantry Dr., W. Bloomfield
(248) 626-9545
Daily paper available at Korean markets.

KOREAN JOURNAL
(313) 531-8772
Biweekly newspaper in Korean. Available at Korean markets.

WEB SITES
WINDOW ON KOREA
http://168.126.70.2/kwin/e2201

KOREAN PAGE
www.koreanpage.com

KOREAN MUSEUM OF AMERICA
www.koma.org/

TAE KWON DO is a martial arts system that originated in Korea. Most famous for its kicks, tae kwon do incorporates jumping and kicking into maneuvers called "flying kicks." Tae kwon do spread worldwide from Korea in the 1960s.

Check the Yellow Pages under "Martial Arts" for local recreation and community centers, studios and Ys that offer tae kwon do instruction.

JAPAN

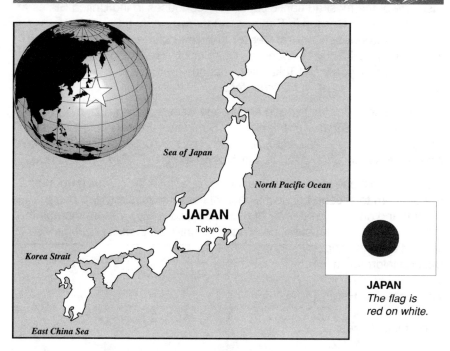

Sea of Japan

North Pacific Ocean

JAPAN
Tokyo

Korea Strait

East China Sea

JAPAN
The flag is
red on white.

Japan is a constitutional democracy in eastern Asia that comprises four large islands as well as the Ryukyu Islands and more than 1,000 small adjacent islands. It is bounded on the north by the Sea of Okhotsk, on the east by the Pacific Ocean, on the south by the Pacific Ocean and the East China Sea, and on the west by the Korea Strait and the Sea of Japan. The Japanese islands extend in an irregular crescent from the island of Sakhalin (Russia) to the island of Taiwan (Republic of China). The total area is 145,841 square miles. Tokyo is the capital and largest city. The Japanese call their country **Nihon** *or* **Nippon** *("the source of the sun")—hence, Land of the Rising Sun. The sun, in red on white, is the emblem on the Japanese flag.*

JAPANESE IN DETROIT

The Japanese American population in metro Detroit numbers about 13,000 and is split between U.S. citizens and temporary residents. Detroit's first Japanese community was established in the 1940s when Japanese American families, who had been kept in internment camps during World War II, moved to the Midwest. There are many second- and third- generation Japanese Americans here, as well as Japanese nationals working for a variety of businesses, who stay for three to five years. Some 350 Japanese-owned facilities in Michigan employ 30,000 Americans. About 70 percent are related to the auto industry, concentrated heavily in Detroit and the tri-county area. In addition, the area supports a number of fine Japanese restaurants and grocery stores.

Visit one of the most authentic Japanese teahouses in the United States at **The Friendship Garden** in Saginaw, *about two hours north of Detroit via I-75.* **The Japanese Cultural Center and Tea House** *(Awa Saginaw An)* was made possible by the Saginaw Chapter of "People to People" and the residents of Saginaw and Tokushima, Japan—sister cities since 1970 *(see "Sister State Program" in this chapter).*

The Friendship Garden is open and free to visitors, giving rest to body, mind and spirit. *Situated in the heart of Saginaw's central parks system along the shore of Lake Linton, you'll find it at the corner of Ezra Rust Drive and South Washington Avenue, north of M-46 off I-75. Parking is nearby.*

An authentic stone lantern sentinel greets guests at the formal garden and invites them to escape the hectic pace of modern life, stroll by a quiet stream and drink in the beauty of nature. A guide leads visitors through the garden and to the teahouse, pointing out significant aspects of Japanese life and customs and offering information about the garden and teahouse. Here, visitors have the opportunity to see the architecture and furnishings of a true Japanese teahouse and acquire an understanding and appreciation of Japanese culture.

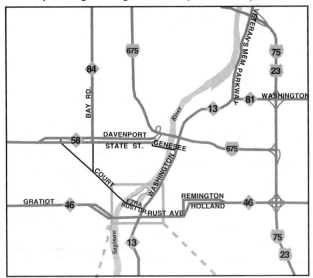

Enjoy an informal tea ceremony or make reservations *(517-759-1648)* to participate in the formal ceremony, or **Cha-no Yu.** Women dressed in Japanese kimonos demonstrate the art of Cha-no Yu, which requires years of study to master.

In the late 15th century, when Japan was enjoying a period of economic and political stability, the tea-drinking ceremony took the form of a religious and aesthetic experience. The formal tea ceremony, *Cha-no Yu*, is the ancient art of preparing and drinking tea, a Zen-based art that is performed in silence. The purpose of Cha-no Yu is to foster gracefulness and harmony, the understanding and appreciation of beauty, and the recognition and appreciation of man's relationship with nature.

During the tea ceremony, the guest leaves the pressures and tensions of the outside world and enjoys an atmosphere of peace and tranquility. The architecture, utensils, art and furnishings of a teahouse are carefully selected to showcase simplicity and the beauty of nature.

The tea used in the ceremony is brewed from finely powdered green tea leaves, or *matcha*, reputed to be rich in vitamins and very healthful. At a formal ceremony, guests usually sit erect on their knees and wear formal dress—the *kimono*.

Awa Saginaw An, Michigan's authentic Japanese teahouse in Saginaw, was designed and furnished by Japanese architect Tsutomu Takenaka in the *sukiya* style. The teahouse rests partially on American soil and partially on land deeded to Tokushima, Japan—Saginaw's sister city. Japanese and American craftsmen worked side by side to build the center.

Awa Saginaw An was dedicated and opened to the public May 21, 1986. *Awa* is the ancient name of Tokushima. *An* is Japanese for "primitive hut," a place in which the first simple tea ceremonies were conducted by Japanese monks. Although teahouses have been built in different locations of the world, this may be the first time two international cities have collaborated to build one in an effort to increase understanding and goodwill between their citizens.

BADGES OF HONOR

Japan developed a system of heraldry in the 12th century, similar to the heraldry that become prominent about the same time in Europe. Japanese heraldic symbols are called *mons*, and are usually circular. The red sun on the Japanese flag is the mon of the Land of the Rising Sun.

TOUR	NIPPON NOTIONS

CLAWSON & ROYAL OAK

[E-F/2-3] Begin in Clawson *(I-75 to West 14 Mile Road exit)* with a sushi/sashimi/tempura lunch at the award-winning **Nippon Kai** *(511 W. 14 Mile, two blocks west of Main Street, south side)*. After lunch, *go back east three blocks to* **Noble Fish** *(45 E. 14 Mile, just east of Main Street),* where you can find everything from carryout sushi to candy, snacks, videos, literature, origami paper, tea and sake sets—not to mention fresh fish.

Now would be the perfect time to visit **Thomas Video** *(see Multicultural Detroit chapter under Films)* to get a Japanese video to watch at home. It's at *122 Main St., two blocks south of 14 Mile.*

Next, *go east on 14 Mile to Rochester Road, turn right (south); go about two miles to* **American Bonsai** *(1602 Rochester Rd., Royal Oak—just south of 12 Mile on the east side).* Even if you resist the temptation to buy one, the miniaturized trees on display are fascinating to see. They evoke the Japanese belief in peace and harmony with nature.

For a large selection of origami supplies and instruction books, plus Japanese calligraphy brushes, inks and rice paper, *go back to 12 Mile and turn left. Head west to Woodward Avenue, then get in the right lane to make the U-turn on Woodward south. Take the first left turn to get back to Woodward north and you'll be at* **Charrette Art Supplies** *(1442 N. Woodward).*

At the **Lotus Import Company** *(419 S. Washington),* you can purchase a miniature Japanese Zen stone garden for $38 or a tin butterfly pin for 35¢, as well as chopsticks and charming ceramic chopstick rests. *To get there from Charrette Art Supplies, take Woodward south to 11 Mile; go east on 11 Mile to Washington and turn right.* Plenty of street parking is available, except evenings.

Now, go buy a kite! Japan's kites are among the most spectacular in the world, treasured as much for their aesthetic worth as for their flying prowess. **The Unique Place, World of Kites** *(525 S. Washington)* is just *one block south* of Lotus Import.

Feeling a bit weary? Amble over to **East-West Futons** *(two blocks east and two blocks north at 306 S. Main St.)* and ask to try out one of the beds for a few minutes *(see next page for more on futons).* Aside from rest, you'll also be able to get Japanese accessories, including rice-paper screens and lamps.

If you're rested and ready for two last stops, *go up Main Street one block to* **Nutri-Foods** *(120 S. Main St.)* to check out the selection of Japanese and Asian herbs, teas and remedies. *Two blocks north,* **The Merchant's Warehouse** *(146 N. Main St., east side, north of the Main Theatre)* is where you'll find a large selection of Japanese beer, sake and tea.

Now, if you're ready for sushi again, or skipped the lunch portion of the tour, head to **Little Tree Sushi Bar** *(107 S. Main St.)* where the offerings include traditional Japanese fare plus a host of Thai dishes.

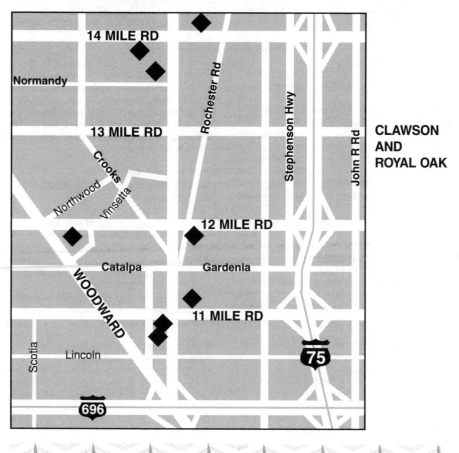

CLAWSON AND ROYAL OAK

RESTAURANT STYLES

A number of restaurants offer a *tatami* room—a traditional room of straw-mat flooring. Guests sit directly on the floor around a low table. You will be asked to remove your shoes to protect the mats. Reservations are usually required.

Yakimono (steak houses) feature *teppanyaki*-style dining—where all the food is cut, prepared and grilled right in front of the diner, with the chef putting on a great show. *Yakitori* (grilled chicken on a skewer) is an extremely popular dish and the main specialty at some restaurants.

In Japan, **sushi bars** play a role similar to that of pubs in England. Patrons sit at tables or booths enjoying their food and beverages (often *sake*, beer or green tea) in a relaxed and informal atmosphere. Others sit on stools at the sushi bar, selecting delicacies from the refrigerated display and watching the master prepare their selections. *Omakase* means "chef's choice"—asking the chef to choose for you. It's not considered impolite to let him know what your budget is.

RESTAURANTS

EAST

BENIHANA
1985 W. Big Beaver, Troy (248) 649-6340
Mon-Thu 11am-2:30pm, 5:30-10pm, Fri 11am-2:30, 5:30-11pm, Sat 5-11pm, Sun 12-9pm. Sushi bar and traditional Japanese menu. Table-side preparation and grilling.

SEOUL GARDEN
2101 15 Mile, Sterling Hts.; (810) 264-4488
Mon-Sat 11:30am-10:30pm, Sun 11:30am-10pm. Japanese and Korean cuisine. Sushi to go, chicken and steak teriyaki.

NORTH

LITTLE TREE SUSHI BAR
107 S. Main, Royal Oak; (248) 586-0994
Mon-Thu 11am-midnight, Fri-Sat 11am-1am, Sun 5pm-midnight. Traditional Japanese fare plus a host of Thai dishes.

MI-LOC RESTAURANT
23043 Beech Rd. (at Nine Mile) Southfield; (248) 356-1955
Mon-Thu 11am-10pm, Fri-Sat 11am-11pm, Sun (sushi bar) noon-9pm. Japanese and Korean food. Carryout, catering.

MUSASHI JAPANESE CUISINE AND SUSHI BAR
2000 Town Center, Suite 98; Southfield (248) 358-1911
Mon-Fri 11:30am-10:15pm, Sat 5:30-11pm,

Sun 5:30-9:30pm. Elegant dining, entirely Japanese atmosphere; tatami room.

NAMI SUSHI
201 W. Nine Mile, Ferndale; (248) 542-6458
Mon-Sat 11:30am-9:30pm. Closed Sun. Traditional and inventive Japanese fare served in an airy atmosphere.

NEW SEOUL GARDEN
27566 Northwestern Hwy., Southfield (248) 827-1600
Mon-Sat 11:30am-10:30pm; Sun noon-10pm. Specializes in Japanese and Korean favorites; sushi bar, tatami room, karaoke.

NIPPON KAI
511 W. 14 Mile, Clawson; (248) 288-3210
Mon-Fri 11:30am-2pm, Mon-Thu 5:30-10:30pm, Fri-Sat 5:30-11pm. Sushi a specialty; also sukiyaki, tempura and chicken teriyaki; romantic setting; tatami room.

SHOGAN JAPANESE STEAKHOUSE
37750 Van Dyke, Sterling Hts. (810) 268-4882
Mon-Thu 11am-10pm, Fri-Sat 11am-11pm, Sun noon-10pm. Sushi bar, tatami room and table-side cooking with knife-wielding chef.

TAKE SUSHI
1364 Walton, Rochester Hills (248) 652-7800
Mon-Fri 11:30am-10pm, Sat-Sun 5-10:30pm. Sophisticated dining with sushi bar and

entrées such as chicken teriyaki, tempura, udon and other hot noodle dishes.

WEST

AJISHIN
42270 Grand River, Novi; (734) 380-9850
Mon & Wed-Fri 11:30am-2:30pm & 5-9:30pm, Sat-Sun 11:30am-9:30pm. Located with other Japanese establishments south of I-96 at Novi Road exit.

AKASAKA
37152 Six Mile, Livonia
(Laurel Park Commons Plaza)
(313) 462-2630
Mon-Sat 11am-2pm, 5:30-10:30pm; Sun 4:30-9:30pm. Kaiseki (fish and beef combo), teriyaki, tempura, sushi bar; karaoke and tatami room.

CHERRY BLOSSOM
43588 West Oaks Dr., Novi; (248) 380-9160
Mon-Sat 11:30am-2pm, Mon-Thu 5:30-10:30pm, Fri-Sat 5:30-11pm, Sun 4-10pm. Yakitori bar (where food is grilled: choices of beef, chicken, seafood); shrimp and vegetable tempura; beef and chicken teriyaki; sushi bar; karaoke; tatami room.

HAKATA JAPANESE RESTAURANT
32433 Northwestern Hwy.
Farmington Hills; (248) 737-7220
Mon-Fri 11:30am-2pm, Mon-Thu 5:30-10:30pm, Fri-Sat 5:30-11pm, Sun 5-9pm. Teriyaki, tempura, sushi bar; tatami room.

BENIHANA
18601 Hubbard Dr., Dearborn
(N side of Fairlane Town Center)
(313) 593-3200
and
21150 Haggerty Rd., Northville
(248) 348-7900
Mon-Thu 11am-2:30pm, 5:30-10pm, Fri 11am-2:30, 5:30-11pm, Sat 5-11pm, Sun 3-9pm. Flamboyant chefs slice, dice and sear right in front of diners.

IZAKAYA SANPEI
43327 Joy Rd., Canton
(at Coventry Commons)
(734) 416-9605
Mon-Fri 11:30am-2pm, Mon-Thu 5:30-10:30pm, Fri-Sat 5-11pm, Sun 5-10pm. Specialty is miso soup; sushi bar, teriyaki, tempura; karaoke, New Year's festivities.

ON THE MENU

Japanese food is very healthy. No cream, cheeses, milk or oily sauces are used. Additional flavor comes from combinations of rice wine (*sake*), soy sauce and sugar.

When most people think of Japanese food, the first thing that comes to mind is *sushi.* Many think sushi is simply raw seafood, but the correct term for that is *sashimi*—slices or slabs of seafood, such as tuna (*akami*) and octopus, served on a platter with thinly sliced ginger, finely shredded radish, soy sauce and *wasabi* (green horseradish mustard).

Sushi types are many, but all are combined with vinegared rice. The *nigiri,* or handmade sushi, is typical and is ordered and served in pairs. Another type includes sushi rolls, or *maki,* which are made with sheets of seaweed (*nori*) and served as six slices. There is also pressed sushi, or *oshi,* which is cut into small squares. And finally, there are stuffed bean-curd rolls, or *inarizushi.*

Shrimp and squid are often dipped in a light batter and quickly deep-fried (*tempura*). Vegetables also are cooked tempura-style. Meat plays a very small role in traditional Japanese cuisine. In fact, at one time it was barely considered fit for human consumption. But as Japan has slowly let in outside influence, meat has become more common.

The most famous Japanese meat is **Kobe beef.** Kobe is a city near Tokyo, but the term *Kobe beef* describes a manner of raising, rather than the origin of, the cattle. Raising beef in Kobe tradition means pampering the cattle with massages and feeding them a special diet, including beer, to keep them relaxed and lazy. It's no surprise that Kobe steaks are too expensive for most people.

Regular beef often is thinly sliced into bite-sized strips, then cooked in a simmering broth and served with glass noodles *(harusame)*, bean curd *(tofu)* and vegetables in a dish called *sukiyaki*. Generally, it's cooked right at the table, and it may contain seafood rather than meat. Pork and chicken are often fried and spiced with ginger and sesame. Another common meat seasoning is *teriyaki*, a sweetened soy sauce.

Japanese cuisine has a number of fish soups, but the most popular is *miso*, made from dissolved soy-bean paste. Noodle soups have become popular in Japan and are available in instant packages in most American supermarkets. Glass noodles, also called cellophane noodles, are translucent, fine "bean threads" made from the starch of green mung beans.

As throughout East Asia, the staple food in Japan is rice *(gohan)*, for which there are varying methods of preparation. Because it's "stickier" than American rice, Japanese rice is easier to eat with chopsticks.

A popular side dish is *chawan mushi*, an egg custard cream. Usually a meal is followed by boiled rice, pickles, fruit and green tea.

Japanese cuisine is not cheap. For fish to be eaten raw, it must be very fresh. Transportation and storage, therefore, are a major expense. Most foods are served in small portions, artfully arranged to showcase their natural beauty.

SANKA TEI
39520 14 Mile, Novi
(248) 960-3363
Mon-Sat 11:30am-2pm, 5-9pm; Sun 4-8pm.
Japanese carryout and sushi to go.

SUSHI-KO
30703 12 Mile, Farmington Hills
(248) 471-4363
Mon-Sat 11am-10:30pm, Sun noon-10pm.
Sushi, sushi teriyaki, udon soup.

THE NOODLE HOUSE
24267 Novi Rd., Novi; (248) 348-5580
Mon-Sat 11am-9:30pm, Sun 11am-8pm.
Sit-down noodle shop featuring miso soup, dumplings and curried rice.

ANN ARBOR

CHAMPION HOUSE
120 E. Liberty, Ann Arbor
(at First Ave.)
(734) 741-8100
Mon-Thu 11am-10pm, Fri 11am-11pm, Sat 5-11pm, Sun 4-9pm. Asian restaurant with Japanese section featuring tatami tables and sushi bar.

HINODAE
215 S. State St., Ann Arbor
(734) 663-7403
Mon-Sat 11am-8pm (except July-Aug: Mon-Sat 11am-7pm). Chicken and steak teriyaki; family-style.

MIKI
106 S. First St. (at W. Huron), Ann Arbor
(734) 665-8226
Mon-Fri 11:30am-2pm, Mon-Thu 5:30-10pm, Fri-Sat 5:30-11pm, Sun 5-10pm. Sushi, sashimi, teriyaki, sukiyaki, yose nab, tempura, udon, vegetarian dishes.

FUJI
327 Braun Ct., Ann Arbor
(at N. Fourth St. across from Kerrytown)
(734) 663-3111
Tue-Thu 11:30am-10pm, Fri 11:30am-10:30pm, Sat 11am-10:30pm, Sun 5-9pm. Authentic Japanese cuisine and complete sushi bar. Karaoke by reservation with dinner parties of 15 or more.

GODAIKO
3115 Oak Valley Dr., Ann Arbor
(at Village Center)
(734) 930-2880
Mon-Sat 11:30am-2:30pm, Mon-Thu 5:30-10pm, Fri-Sat 5:30-11pm, Sun 5-10pm. Tempura, steak teriyaki, three sushi bars; tatami room.

Other Sushi Bars in Ann Arbor:
Take Sushi, 3125 Boardwalk (734) 997-2121
Yamato, in Kerrytown, (734) 998-3484.

CHOPSTICKS *(hashi)* are the basic utensils for eating Japanese food. They are a cultural import from China, where they have been used for thousands of years.

However, hashi are tapered to a sharper tip and are shorter than the Chinese variety (perhaps because Japanese meals involve less reaching around the table than Chinese meals). Japanese chopsticks are often enameled, but most of the less expensive restaurants provide disposable wooden chopsticks. Those are called *waribashi* (pull-apart chopsticks) because they are made from a piece of soft wood that is split in two, except for the top inch or so; before using them you have to pull them apart like a wishbone.

(For more about chopsticks, including instructions, see "China" chapter.)

TOUR · CUISINE SAMPLING

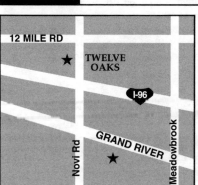

[B-C/2-3] For a taste of Japanese culture and cuisine, *take I-96 west to the Novi exit (#162) and turn right on Novi Road.* Across from Twelve Oaks Mall in the West Oaks complex, you'll find the **Cherry Blossom Restaurant** next to HQ. Make reservations about a week in advance if you want to be served at a low table in one of the tatami rooms.

Cross over the expressway and turn left on Grand River to find new retail strips that house a market, pastry shop and sushi/noodle bar serving metro Detroit's Japanese community. **One World Market**, at *42705 Grand River in the Main Street marketplace* development across from Novi Town Center, offers fresh and frozen Japanese specialties ranging from baked wheat balls with octopus to green tea ice cream. In addition to seafood, imported foods, tea sets, and health and beauty aids, there are magazines, books and Japanese rental videos.

Head farther east on Grand River and make a final stop at **Thomasville Centre** *on the north side.* Take home a carry-out order of sushi from **Ajishin Sushi & Noodles** *(42270)* and a sampling of breads or rolls from the **Pastry House Hippo** *(42130)*.

BAKERIES & MARKETS

*See also the "Nippon Notions" tour in
this chapter, as well as listings in other
Asian chapters and in "Multicultural
Detroit."*

PASTRY HOUSE HIPPO
42130 Grand River, Novi
(248) 347-6408
Tue-Sun 9am-8pm. Owners Linda and
Yusuke Okamoto sell mostly Japanese-style
pastries, including yakisoba, a bun-shaped
bread with pan-fried soba noodles and
ginger. Novelty breads are shaped like pan-
das, turtles and cartoon characters.

KOYAMA SHOTEN
37176 Six Mile, Livonia
(Laurel Park Commons Plaza)
(313) 464-1480
Tue-Sat 10am-8pm, Sun 11am-7pm.
Japanese groceries, video rental.

MERCHANT'S WAREHOUSE
146 N. Main St., Royal Oak
(248) 546-7770
*Mon 10am-7pm, Tue-Fri 10am-9pm,
Sat 9am-9pm, Sun noon-5pm.* Extensive
selection of imported liquors, beers, wines,
spices, seasonings, teas and snacks.

NOBLE FISH
45 E. 14 Mile, Clawson; (248) 585-2314
*Tue-Fri 10am-9:30pm, Sat 10am-7:30pm,
Sun 11am-7pm.* Japanese groceries, fresh
fish, small sushi bar, videos, novelties, tea
services, toys and more.

NUTRI-FOODS
120 S. Main St., Royal Oak
(248) 541-6820
*Mon-Thu, Sat 9am-6pm; Fri 9am-8pm;
Sun 11am-3pm.* Many Japanese and Asian
herbs, remedies, teas, snacks.

ONE WORLD MARKET
42705 Grand River, Novi
(248) 374-0844
Mon-Sun 9am-8pm. Japanese food products.
Sushi Bar open daily except Mon.

SEOUL ORIENTAL MART
25840 W. Nine Mile, Southfield
(248) 357-2828
*Mon-Fri 10am-8pm, Sat 9am-8pm, Sun
10am-7pm.* Asian groceries and gifts.

SING TONG INTERNATIONAL FOODS
3115 Oak Valley Dr., Pittsfield Twp.
(near Ann Arbor)
(734) 995-0422
Mon-Sat 10am-8pm, Sun 11am-6pm.
Asian groceries.

UNAGIYA
32930 Middlebelt Rd., Farmington Hills
(at 14 Mile)
(248) 855-1660
Tue-Sat 10am-8pm, Sun 11am-7pm.
Japanese groceries and gifts.

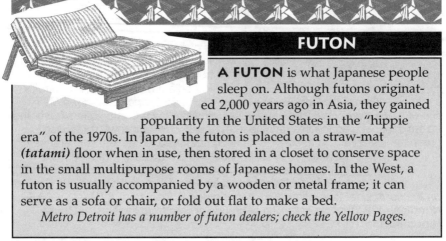

FUTON

A FUTON is what Japanese people
sleep on. Although futons originated 2,000 years ago in Asia, they gained
popularity in the United States in the "hippie
era" of the 1970s. In Japan, the futon is placed on a straw-mat
(tatami) floor when in use, then stored in a closet to conserve space
in the small multipurpose rooms of Japanese homes. In the West, a
futon is usually accompanied by a wooden or metal frame; it can
serve as a sofa or chair, or fold out flat to make a bed.
Metro Detroit has a number of futon dealers; check the Yellow Pages.

SHOPS

JBC–JAPAN BOOK CENTER
37148 Six Mile, Livonia
(Laurel Park Commons Plaza)
(734) 462-1130
Tue-Sun 10am-7pm. Japanese books
and videos.

LOTUS IMPORT COMPANY
419 S. Washington, Royal Oak
(248) 546-8820
Mon-Sat 10am-7pm, Sun noon-5pm.
Clothing and jewelry, primarily from
Asian countries.

CHARRETTE ART SUPPLIES
28878 N. Woodward, Royal Oak
(248) 548-7679
and
4863 Woodward, Detroit
(313) 833-9616
Mon-Fri 10am-7pm, Sat 10am-5pm,
Sun noon-5pm. Art and craft supplies from
many cultures.

EAST-WEST FUTONS
306 S. Main St., Royal Oak
(248) 548-4422
Mon, Tue, Fri, Sat 10am-6pm; Wed-Thu
10am-9pm; Sun 1-5pm. Large selection of
futons, gifts and unique accessories.

THE KIMONO

The kimono is a traditional Japanese wraparound garment with rectangular sleeves. Worn by men and women, it is secured at the waist with a wide sash, or *obi.* The obi is held in place with a narrow silk cord, the ends of which are weighted with jeweled pendants, medicine boxes or beautifully carved toggles *(netsuke).* Kimonos—which can be made from silk, wool, linen or cotton—are usually sewn by hand and are often dyed or embroidered. A complete kimono ensemble requires many accessories, including split-toed socks *(tabi)* and formal sandals *(zori* or *geta)*

Families may pass down especially prized kimonos from generation to generation. Although some older women wear them daily, kimonos are generally reserved for formal occasions, such as weddings, funerals and special holidays.

Kimonos vary according to the wearer and the occasion: Children and young women wear brightly colored kimonos with long sleeves; married women wear kimonos of darker, more subdued hues with shorter sleeves; and men wear solid dark colors. The most formal kimono for married men and women is black and is embroidered with the family crest, or *mon.*

Kimonos were first mass-produced in the early 20th century. Extremely elaborate antique gowns are now museum pieces. *(See "Cultural Arts" list-ings.)* Modern kimonos are available for purchase. *(See "Shops" listings.)*

THE UNIQUE PLACE, WORLD OF KITES
525 S. Washington, Royal Oak
(248) 398-5900
*Tue-Fri 10:30am-6pm, Sat 10:30am-5pm,
Sun noon-4pm.* Kites and supplies from all
over the world.

FAR EAST TRADER
Tel-Twelve Mall
28576 Telegraph, Southfield
(248) 354-3993
and
Oakland Mall
534 W. 14 Mile, Troy; (248) 585-2267
and
Lakeside Mall
14600 Lakeside Circle, Sterling Hts.
(810) 247-7600
Mon-Sat 10am-9pm, Sun noon-5pm.
Kimonos, dolls, sake sets and other
Japanese items.

JAPANESE THEATER

KABUKI is one of Japan's leading forms of classical drama, featuring colorful costumes and makeup, spectacular scenery and a lively, melodramatic acting style. Kabuki became popular throughout Japan in the early 1600s, drawing on the traditions of the older **Noh Theater** and the classical puppet stage, with innovations such as the revolving stage, the *hanamichi* (a processional platform) and trap doors.

Costumes and masks from Japan are sometimes on display at museums listed in this chapter. Kabuki performances are sponsored by various groups in the area. Videotapes of plays are available as well. For more information, contact the cultural organizations in this chapter.

BUNRAKU, Japan's best-known traditional puppet theater, is performed by a team consisting of a narrator, a *shamisen* player and puppets about four feet tall, each one manipulated by three puppeteers.

● *Kids on the Block, a traveling puppet troupe, uses bunraku to educate children on the issues of disability awareness; cultural, medical and educational differences; and social concerns. For information, call 1-800-368 KI0DS (5437).*

CULTURAL ARTS

In ancient Japanese culture, it was believed that all natural objects and phenomena have some degree of divine spirit. Because of this belief, it was necessary to live in harmony with nature to avoid upsetting the natural balance. A reverence for nature and beauty is the foundation of Japanese culture and endures to this day. Nature themes in art (such as the cherry blossom and changes of season) and symbols of strength (mountains, the volcano or the tiger, for instance) are evidence of this reverence.

DETROIT INSTITUTE OF ARTS
5200 Woodward, Detroit
(313) 833-7900
Wed-Fri 11am-4pm, Sat-Sun 11am-5pm.
Japanese Gallery (N120) in the Department of Asian Art has an extensive collection of art and artifacts from as early as the 11th century. Notable examples include screens, scrolls, lacquer, ceramics, weapons, games and textiles.

INTERNATIONAL INSTITUTE
111 E. Kirby, Detroit; (313) 871-8600
Mon-Fri 8:30am-5pm. Silk kimono mounted in the lobby. Doll exhibit in Hall of Nations.

**UNIVERSITY OF MICHIGAN
MUSEUM OF ART
525 S. State St., Ann Arbor
(734) 764-0395**
*Tue-Wed, Fri-Sat 10am-5pm; Thu 10am-
9pm; Sun noon-5pm.* Tea room exhibit; oil
and watercolor paintings on scrolls from the
Edo Period (1615-1868). Margaret Watson
Parker Collection contains more than 600
examples of Japanese woodblock prints,
Asian ceramics and sculpture.

**SCULPTURE BY ISAMU NOGUCHI
Detroit Riverfront at Hart Plaza**
The Pylon, a 120-foot-high spiral stainless-
steel sculpture at Horace E. Dodge & Son
Memorial Fountain, was erected in 1978.

**FROM MANZANAR TO THE MOTOR CITY:
A HISTORY OF MICHIGAN'S JAPANESE
AMERICAN COMMUNITY
(734) 522-7917**
Contact: Mary Kamidoi
This traveling photo exhibit chronicles the
history of Japanese Americans in Detroit.

Available from the Japanese American
Citizens League to tour schools and libraries.

**SAGINAW-TOKUSHIMA
FRIENDSHIP GARDEN
JAPANESE CULTURAL CENTER
AND TEA HOUSE
Parks Division, City of Saginaw
1315 S. Washington Ave., Saginaw
(517) 759-1648**
*Garden hours: June-Sept daily 9am-8pm;
April, May, Oct, Nov Tue-Sat 9 am-4pm.
Center hours: Tue-Sat noon-4pm.* Free tours
of formal Japanese garden. Teahouse open
for informal tea; sweets served throughout
the day. Reservations necessary for formal
tea ceremony. Japanese culture, crafts and
language classes offered periodically; call for
information. *(See Tour.)*

**MINORU YAMASAKI
ARCHITECTURE**
This renowned Japanese American designed
the World Trade Center in New York and the
Shiga Sacred Garden Temple in Shiga,

MUSIC

From the seventh to eighth centuries, cultural
embassies were sent from Japan to China to learn
and acquire China's political and cultural system.
They also borrowed some musical instruments, among which was *cheng* (koto). At first,
the koto was used only at court, and later it was
played mainly by blind musicians. In fact, much of
Japanese pre-modern music was played by blind musicians
and monks. The modern Japanese koto is a 13-string wooden
instrument that's about six feet long and played horizontally either on the
floor or on a short stand.

To sample other styles of Japanese music, try these recordings:

Temple Music: Recorded in Buddhist temples. Sutra chanting in the Jodo
sect, solo chants of Zen priests, and prayers of mountain priests with
Horogai (conch shell) accompaniment.

Gagaku: "Elegant" music, likely the oldest existing form of orchestral
music in the world. Rarely performed in public (and even more rarely in the
West).

Noh Music: Ghosts of warriors, noble ladies, demons, deities, passion
and insanity are the subjects of the famed Noh plays of Japan. With its spectacular costumes and expressive carved wooden masks, Noh Theater has no
counterpart in the West. The music accompanying these plays contributes to

Japan. Yamasaki's Detroit-area-based firm also designed these well-known local structures: De Roy Auditorium, Prentis Hall and McGregor Conference Center on Wayne State University's campus; Temple Beth El (Telegraph and 14 Mile., Bloomfield Twp); and American Natural Resources Bldg. (downtown Detroit, NW corner of Woodward & W. Jefferson).

FUJISAWA ZEN GARDEN
2450 County Rd. #12 (Gesto Road)
Essex, Ontario, (519) 776-4459
Authentic Japanese Zen Garden with Fuji mountain with pond, tea house, cafeteria and gift shop. Japanese Tea Ceremony can be arranged by reservation. Best time to view the garden is Cherry Blossom time, in the Spring. Picnic grounds arranged for large groups. From Windsor, take Walker Rd. south to County Rd. 12, turn left and watch for signs.

PERFORMING ARTS

JAPANESE WOMEN'S CHORUS
3000 Town Center, Ste. 606; Southfield
(248) 355-4899
Contact: Yasuko Sanagi

This chorus, part of the Japanese Business Society of Detroit Women's Club, performs traditional Japanese songs and sings at Christmas Concert of Southfield Symphony Orchestra.

ANNUAL EVENTS
MAY
CHERRY BLOSSOM FESTIVAL
Belle Isle, Detroit
(Jefferson at E. Grand Blvd)
When the cherry blossoms come out in mid-May, Japanese organizations sponsor cultural activities on Belle Isle. Toyota, Japan (Detroit's sister city) and the Japanese Business Society of Detroit donated the 100 cherry trees planted by Scott Fountain. For information, contact the Detroit Recreation Department at (313) 224-1106 or the Japanese Consulate at (313) 567-0120.

JUNE
CARROUSEL OF NATIONS
(519) 255-1127
Windsor's annual multicultural festival, which takes place two weekends in June, includes a Japanese village.

KARAOKE

KARAOKE, which began as an after-work form of relaxation for Japanese businesspeople in the 1970s, has became so popular outside Japan in the past decade that it's now even listed in the *Oxford English Dictionary*. The word is derived from *kara,* meaning "empty," and *oke,* the abbreviation for "orchestra." Karaoke, basically, is singing done by amateurs, accompanied by recorded music, usually in a pub or at a party.

The Japanese like parties. Even in ancient times, someone would usually enliven the party by singing. How *well* the person could sing has never mattered. In fact, an out-of-tune singer sparks laughter and makes the party more lively.

The Japanese are generous and forgiving when they listen to other people sing, which is why they can sing in front of a group without being embarrassed.

● *Karaoke equipment and supplies are available to rent for special events (check the Yellow Pages), and many Japanese restaurants have karaoke nights.*

HOLIDAYS

Japan is a land of many festivals. In every season, in all parts of the country—urban or rural—you can find colorful rites and merrymaking. Some festivals honor historical figures and occasions; others are of religious significance. Shintoism, the ancient national religion of Japan, is a cheerful, optimistic religion that includes a deep reverence for nature.

Many Japanese festivals include souvenir booths, food, singing, dancing and drinking, much like traditional ethnic festivals in America. There are far too many holidays to list them all, but here are a few that Americans might like to borrow:

JANUARY 15
Coming-of-Age Day
Congratulates 20-year-olds with a special ceremony.

FEBRUARY 3 OR 4
Setsubun—Bean-Throwing Festival
Takes place the last day of winter in the lunar calendar. People crowd temple grounds to participate in the traditional ceremony of throwing beans to drive away imaginary devils. Participants shout "Fortune in, devils out!"

THIRD WEEKEND IN FEBRUARY
Kamakura
Popular pastime in snowy areas; children make snow houses in which they enshrine the god of water and hold parties.

MARCH 3
Hina Matsuri
Families with girls display a set of *hina* dolls and miniature household articles on a stepped dais covered with a red cloth; they sometimes have a party for their children. The dolls are dressed in period costume and include an emperor and empress. Kindergartens and schools often set up displays.

APRIL 29
Greenery Day
Celebrated as the birthday of the Emperor Showa up to 1988; now commemorates his love of nature.

MAY 5
Children's Day
Once the celebratory day for boys, it's now to wish that all children grow up well and find happiness.

JULY 7
Tanabata Star Festival
Children set up bamboo branches with colorful strips of paper bearing their wishes.

SEPTEMBER 15
Respect-for-the-Aged Day
To show respect and affection for the elderly who have devoted themselves to the society for many years, and to celebrate their long lives.

SEPTEMBER 22 OR 23
Autumnal Equinox Day
To honor ancestors and remember the deceased. A Buddhist festival day from ancient times.

OCTOBER 10
HEALTH-SPORTS DAY
To foster a sound mind and body; commemorates the 1964 Tokyo Olympiad.

NOVEMBER 15
7-5-3 Day
Children who are 3, 5 or 7 years old dress up in kimonos to go to temples to pray and receive presents.

NOVEMBER 23
Culture Day
Celebrates love, freedom, equality and culture.

BONSAI

Bonsai, meaning "tray planted," is the art of growing miniature trees or other plants in a container. The process involves pruning the roots and branches and repotting the tree. To control the size and shape of the tree, the grower pinches off the new growth and bends and wires the trunk and branches to grow in the desired shape. Although this art form originated in the homes of Japanese and Chinese aristocracy in the 1000s, it did not become widespread in Japanese households until the late 1800s.

AMERICAN BONSAI
1602 Rochester Rd., Royal Oak
(248) 542-2421
Tue-Fri 11am-6pm, Sat-Sun noon-4pm.
Finished plants, stock plants, supplies.
Classes Tuesday evenings.

BONSAI HOUSE
8653 Inkster Rd., Westland
(734) 421-3434
Daily 10:30am-6pm; closed Tue, Sun.
Largest selection of bonsai supplies
in the Midwest.

BONSAI CENTER
101 N. Groesbeck, Mt. Clemens
(810) 465-9555
Tue-Sat 10am-5pm. Plants, supplies
and classes.

FOUR SEASONS BONSAI CLUB OF MICHIGAN
(810) 772-7708
Vance Wood, president
Hosts monthly programs and workshops featuring bonsai masters, as well as a judged annual show. Meets last Sunday of the month at Good Shepherd Lutheran Church, Royal Oak. June exhibition at Washington Square Plaza, Royal Oak.

ANN ARBOR BONSAI SOCIETY
Matthaei Botanical Garden
1800 N. Dixboro Rd., Ann Arbor
(734) 998-7061
Member organization hosts monthly programs, workshops, exhibitions, demonstrations and lectures.

IKEBANA

Ikebana—the art of flower arranging—developed fully in Japan. What distinguishes the Japanese style of flower arranging from the Western style is the use of leaves and stems as major elements in the design, instead of emphasizing only the blossoms. The principles of design and color in ikebana are intended to create a natural effect—to make the arrangement look like it's growing outdoors.

IKEBANA INTERNATIONAL
(248) 356-3089
Contact: Toshi Shimoura
Chapter 85 of the worldwide network based in Tokyo meets the second Wednesday of the month at Southfield Presbyterian Church. Sponsors workshops on Japanese flower arranging and related arts.

KAY MASUDA FLORIST
32502 Northwestern Hwy.
Farmington Hills; (248) 851-0660
Mon-Fri 9am-5pm, Sat usually 9am-2pm (call before coming). Ikebana designs.

TOUCH OF GLASS FLOWERS
3254 West Rd., Trenton; (734) 671-0500
Mon-Fri 9:30am-6pm, Sat 9am-5pm.
Ikebana designs.

WAKABI FLORAL DESIGN
21730 W. 11 Mile, Southfield
(248) 357-6746
Mon-Sat 11am-6pm. Ikebana designs.
Kazuko Bentley offers classes in flower arranging, custom-designed fans, money flowers, calligraphy and artificial bonsai.

KOI

Koi—the large, colorful carp that grace garden ponds at places such as Cranbrook Institute of Science—were developed by the Japanese. Koi were very expensive until the last decade or so; now they are being bred in the United States and are priced within the reach of water gardeners of average means.

GRASS ROOTS NURSERY
24765 Bell Rd., New Boston
(734) 753-9200
Mon-Sat 9am-5pm, Sun noon-5pm.
Enormous selection of aquatic life. Constructs, designs and maintains water gardens.

● *For help designing a formal **Japanese Garden** or **Zen stone garden**, contact the Michigan Cooperative Extension Service. You'll find it in the county government listing in your phone directory, under "MSU" or "Cooperative Extension."*

ORIGAMI

Origami is the Japanese art of decorative paper folding—creating birds, animals, boxes, even balloons. Some are simple enough for children; others are far more complex. Instruction books and the special colorful, square paper are available at art and craft stores. *(See "Nippon Notions" tour and "Markets.")*

HAIKU

Haiku is the shortest poetic form in the world. It usually consists of three lines of five, seven and five syllables each, and it often has nature or the seasons as a theme. Haiku is native to Japan; neither China nor the West influenced its creation. A haiku poet must be concise, while putting deep spiritual understanding into the poem. Although it's difficult to do, haiku is not written only by professionals. Anyone can easily learn to enjoy the form—to love nature, love people and feel things deeply every day. Haiku collections abound in libraries and bookstores. Below are English translations of haiku from two masters:

**The year's first day
thoughts and loneliness;
the autumn dusk is here.**
*Matsuo Basho
(1644-1694)*

**At the over-matured sushi,
The Master
Is full of regret.**
*Yosa Buson
(1716-1784)*

MAIL ORDER

NEKO-CHAN TRADING COMPANY
118 Main Centre, Ste. 321
Northville, MI 48167
1-888-635-6242 for free catalog
Offers books and videos on Zen, martial arts, origami supplies and Japanese incense.

ORGANIZATIONS

The groups below typically cooperate to host events and cultural programs. Call them to find out about the upcoming season.

CONSULATE GENERAL OF JAPAN
400 Renaissance Center, Ste. 1600
Detroit; (313) 567-0120
Organizes and sponsors cultural events. Provides cultural information and offers videos on loan to schools. Coordinates government exchange programs. Sponsors speech contest for high school and college Japanese language students.

GREATER DETROIT AND WINDSOR JAPAN-AMERICA SOCIETY
660 Woodward, Ste. 1541; Detroit
(313) 963-1988
Dedicated to strengthening ties between Japanese and American businesses through better understanding and exchange of culture. Corporate and individual memberships.

JBSD WOMEN'S CLUB
3000 Town Center, Ste. 606; Southfield
(248) 355-4899
Members of the Japanese Business Society of Detroit Women's Club are available to demonstrate origami, flower arranging and other crafts at schools, libraries, senior residences and community group programs. Women's Chorus performs traditional songs.

JAPANESE AMERICAN CITIZENS LEAGUE
7477 Manor Circle, #104; Westland
(734) 522-7917
Contact: Mary Kamidoi
Michigan chapter of JACL was formed in 1946 to protect the rights of Japanese Americans and preserve their unique heritage and culture.

CENTER FOR JAPANESE STUDIES
University of Michigan
204 S. State St., Ann Arbor
(734) 764-6307
Special events include film festivals, art exhibits, concerts. U-M has second-largest Japanese language collection of books and periodicals in the United States.

CLASSES

MUSASHI INTERNATIONAL
2000 Town Center, Ste. 98; Southfield
(248) 358-1072
Japanese language and culture classes, business consulting, travel services and restaurant.

SUZUKI MYERS & ASSOCIATES
P.O. Box 852, Novi, MI 48376
(248) 344-0909
Interpretation and translation, relocation services, language classes, tours for visiting Japanese. Designs cross-cultural classes for businesses and civic organizations.

JAPANESE SCHOOL OF DETROIT
1020 E. Square Lake Rd., Bloomfield Hills
(248) 540-4796
Classes are conducted Saturdays, 8:45am-3:35pm, at Birmingham Seaholm High School (2036 Lincoln) and West Maple Elementary (6275 Inkster). Originally founded to educate children of Japanese businessmen who were here for only a few years, this school currently has an enrollment of more than 800 and also serves children of Japanese Americans who wish to preserve their language and culture.

PALS INTERNATIONAL
900 Wilshire, Troy
(248) 362-2060
Cross-cultural consultation and Japanese language instruction.

JAPANESE MARTIAL ARTS

AIKIDO is a form of Japanese judo—developed from self-defense techniques and sword movements of the samurai—using smooth, balanced, coordinated movements in a noncompetitive setting. Aikido is the way *(do)* of harmony *(ai)* with nature *(ki)*.

To locate classes, check the Yellow Pages under "Martial Arts" or local community education, recreation department and YM/YWCA course listings.

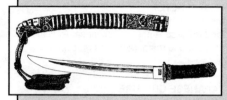

KENDO, the art of Japanese fencing, evolved from a martial heritage that dates back thousands of years to the time of the samurai warriors. Modern kendo is physically and mentally demanding. A kendo bout with a skilled opponent is an intense experience. From the beginning, one must practice hard physically and develop mental control to master simple techniques. Anyone—young or old, even people with some severe physical limitations—can practice kendo. Kendo builds character through the calm manipulation of a sword under great pressure. Physical prowess is less important than doing everything with full spirit, even when there's no hope of winning. The essence of kendo is achieving *ki-ken-tai no itti:* mental, spiritual and physical calm.

● *Detroit Kendo Dojo takes place at West Maple Elementary School, 6275 Inkster, Bloomfield Twp. For details, call Musashi International at (248) 358-1072.*

● ●

←**T**he name "pagoda" refers to a variety of buildings in tower form. Usually part of a temple or monastery, they serve as shrines. Japanese pagodas, usually square and five-stories, are made of wood and showcase fine carpentry and craftsmanship. In India, pagodas are known as *stupa* and are normally pyramidal, elaborately decorated with carvings or sculpture. The Chinese pagoda, of Indian origin, is hexagonal, octagonal, or square, built in as many as 15 superimposed stories. From each story an upward-curving tile roof projects. Brick, faced with tiles, is the most common material.

The Suzuki Method of violin instruction was developed in the 1940s by Dr. Shinichi Suzuki, who theorized that if children naturally learned language at age 3, they could just as naturally learn to play a musical instrument. Parents learn along with the child. For information on instruction, contact:

**CENTER FOR CREATIVE STUDIES
INSTITUTE OF MUSIC AND DANCE**
(313) 872-3118

**SUZUKI MUSIC ASSOCIATION
OF GREATER DETROIT**
(248) 644-1739

**SUZUKI PIANO
TEACHING
COMPANY**
(248) 641-5191

**SOUTH
OAKLAND
YMCA**
(248) 547-0030

MEDIA

PRINT

JAPAN DETROIT PRESS
P.O. Box 252432
W. Bloomfield, 48325-2432
(248) 960-5000
Monthly Japanese language newspaper available at Japanese markets and restaurants.

JAPAN CLUB NEWS
P.O. Box 151
Trenton, 48183-0151
(734) 671-0125
Monthly Japanese language newspaper for Japanese American audience. Available at Japanese restaurants and groceries.

WEB SITES

JAPANESE CULTURE
w.nttam.com/home/index

HAIKU NETWORK
home.sn.no/home/keitoy/haiku

SUSHI PAGES
wwwipd.ira.uka.de/~maraist/sushi/top-misc

SISTER STATE PROGRAM

Michigan's sister state in Japan is the prefecture of **Shiga**. (A prefecture is comparable to an American state.) Sister cities include **Detroit**/Toyota; **Birmingham**/Ritto; **Clinton Township**/Yasu-cho; **Monroe**/Bofu; **Novi**/ Owani-cho; **Pontiac**/Katsasu; **Wyandotte**/Komaki; **Lansing**/Otsu; and **Saginaw**/Tokushima. (*Cho* in a name ending indicates a town.)

The sister state/city program is designed to facilitate goodwill missions, gather and disseminate information, and coordinate activities and home-stay accommodations for visiting delegations. It also sponsors student, teacher and police officer exchanges, as well as government internship programs.

For more information, contact Michigan-Shiga Sister State Program, c/o Michigan State Government, P.O. Box 30008, Lansing, MI 48909; (517) 373-2831 fax (517) 335-4565.

GLOBAL JOURNEYS
IN METRO DETROIT

SIDE TRIPS

NOTES

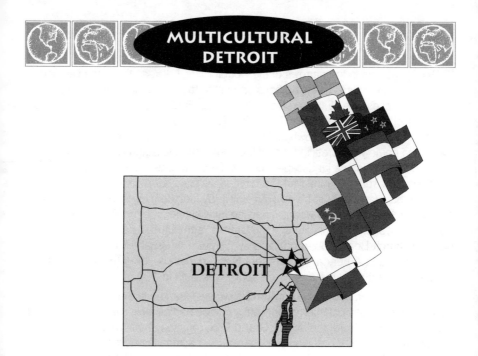

MULTICULTURAL DETROIT

DETROIT

This chapter lists museums and exhibits, tours, boutiques, markets, dining experiences and entertainment offerings that are international in scope. Detroit's multicultural resources also include many educational programs, libraries, community organizations and media that serve the area's diverse population.

Special sections and sidebars highlight:

● CULTURAL CENTER INSTITUTIONS *Right in the heart of the city is a museum district adjacent to the Medical Center and Wayne State University campus. See pages 479-483.*

● SUMMER ETHNIC FESTIVALS *A series of summer festivals are held downtown at Hart Plaza on the riverfront and at suburban venues. See page 484.*

● INTERNATIONAL SHOPPING *Eastern Market, a century-old indoor-outdoor market surrounded by neighborhood meat markets, shops and restaurants, offers foods from around the world. (See page 458.) International merchandise at specialty boutiques and upscale department stores are featured at the Somerset Collection in Troy. See page 462.*

● PARKS & ATTRACTIONS *Belle Isle, a 1,000-acre urban park with zoo, nature center, conservatory and aquarium, and the Detroit Zoo in Royal Oak are favorites for family recreation. See pages 454-457.*

BELLE ISLE

[F-G/4-5] Situated in the narrows of the Detroit River, between the Canadian and American shores, Belle Isle is perhaps one of the most unusual of all urban parks in the U.S. Accessible by the Art Deco **MacArthur Bridge** (or by boat), the park is 2.5 miles long and .5 miles wide. Its original French name, "Isle au Cochons," meant "Isle of Pigs." Also known as Hog Island (due to the wild pigs that lived there), the name was "prettified" about the same time the island was. In 1882, America's most famous landscape architect, Frederick Law Olmstead (he also designed New York's Central Park), submitted his plans for a combined urban/forest parkland that was meant to be enjoyed slowly, by foot, boat or canoe. Standing in contrast to the canals, and woods inhabited by wild deer, are the Renaissance and Spanish-revival-style architecture of the **Detroit Yacht Club, Boat Club** and **Casino.** The Detroit Boat Club, organized by Edmund A. Brush in 1839 was the first of its kind in America. The present Neo-Spanish building (now owned by the Department of Parks and Recreation) was built in 1902.

The **conservatory, zoo** and **aquarium** showcase flora and fauna from around the world. Other glimpses of international color can be had as well: crewing at the **Boat Club,** the **Cricket Field,** the annual **Grand Prix**, regattas at the **Yacht Club**, African-American family-reunion picnics—and just across the water on the south shore, **Canada.** Pack a picnic and take a leisurely drive (and/or bike or walk) through this gem any time of the year.

The Belle Isle Bridge is at E. Jefferson Ave. and E. Grand Blvd. about two miles east of Renaissance Center.

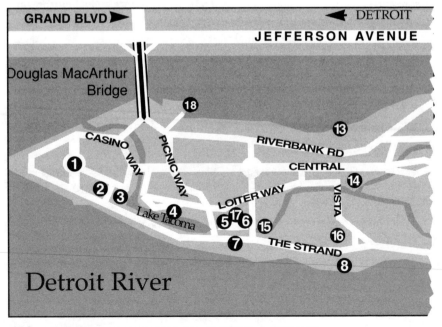

BELLE ISLE NATURE CENTER
(east end at Oakway & Riverbank)
(313) 267-7157

Open year-round Tue noon-4pm, Wed-Sun 10am-4pm. Closed Mon. Museum features natural history exhibits, an animal shelter housing injured wildlife, nature trails and films.

BELLE ISLE ZOOLOGICAL PARK
(313) 267-7160 or 398-0903 ext 65

Daily May-Oct, 10am-5pm. Raised walkway gives visitors a good view of animals from around the world. Zoo entrance and the refreshment area were designed to simulate an African village. Some animals include the maned wolf, an endangered species from South America, described as a "fox on stilts." Spectacled bears are another endangered species native to the Andes Mountains. The Belle Isle Zoo is part of an intensive effort to prevent the extinction of the extremely rare Mexican wolf, the smallest subspecies of timber wolves. A Carnivore Exhibit, featuring African lions and endangered Sumatran tigers, opened in 1994. Other animals include Grant's zebras, South American tapirs, river otters, lion-tailed macaques, ring-tailed lemurs, alpacas, addax (an endangered desert antelope), nilgais (antelopes from India), Bactrian deer, and a variety of birds.

DOSSIN GREAT LAKES MUSEUM
100 Strand Drive (south shore)
(313) 267-6440

Wed-Sun 10am-5pm. Exhibits on Great Lakes shipping, past and present. Real ship's pilot house provides hands-on fun.

WHITCOMB CONSERVATORY and BELLE ISLE AQUARIUM
Belle Isle (313) 267-7133 and 267-7159

Daily 9am-5pm. Both buildings were designed by Albert Kahn around 1900. The Conservatory is a nearly exact replica of the one built for the World's Columbian Exposition in Chicago. A quarter-million plants with origins from all over the globe are displayed throughout the year. Special flower shows are held for every season. Built in 1904, the Belle Isle Aquarium is one of the nation's oldest freshwater public aquariums. It displays more than 100 species of freshwater fish from the Great Lakes, South America, Africa and Asia, including freshwater stingray, electric eels and more than 15 endangered species. It is the only aquarium in North America to propagate the highly endangered Mexican Golden Sawfin. Guided tours offered.

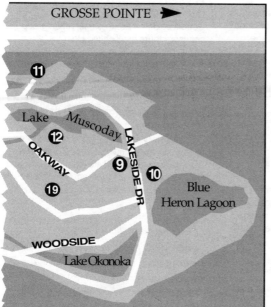

① Scott Fountain
② Cricket Field
③ Casino
④ Skating Pavilion
⑤ Peace Tower
⑥ Whitcomb Conservatory
⑦ Dossin Museum
⑧ Model Yacht Basin
⑨ Nature Center
⑩ Golf Driving Range
⑪ Detroit Yacht Club
⑫ Golf Course
⑬ Beach
⑭ Belle Isle Zoo
⑮ Aquarium
⑯ Athletic Field
⑰ Memorial Gardens
⑱ Detroit Boat Club
⑲ Wooded Area

TOURS

CITY WALKING TOURS
City of Detroit Recreation Department
(313) 224-1100
Guide published by Rec. Dept. and Historic Neighborhood Coalition outlines self-guided tour of Rivertown and a Downtown Art Tour. Also includes schedule of guided tours sponsored by Preservation Wayne, Detroit Historical Society and neighborhood associations.

CONVENTION & VISITORS BUREAU OF WINDSOR, ESSEX COUNTY & PELEE ISLAND
City Centre, Suite 103,
333 Riverside Drive W., Windsor, Ont.
Call 1-800-265-3633
Free information, maps and brochures, from day trips to week-long explorations of Canada's richly diverse international heritage.

DETROIT HISTORICAL SOCIETY TOURS
(313) 833-1405
"Sunday Strolls," highlighting various historical and architectural sites, are scheduled from May through October. Other tours, including self-guided ones, also are available.

DETROIT UPBEAT TOURS
18430 Fairway Dr., Detroit 48221
(313) 341-6810
Detroit Ethnic Series offers custom tours for groups of 25 or more to explore African-American, Arab, French, German, Greek, Hispanic, Irish, Italian, Japanese and Polish heritage in the Detroit area. Contact Jill DeMaris.

DIAMOND JACK'S RIVER TOURS
(313) 843-9376
Board this cruising yacht at docks near the Renaissance Center from spring through fall. Two-hour narrated tours. Snacks available onboard. Group rates available. Call for cruise schedule.

METROPOLITAN DETROIT CONVENTION & VISITORS BUREAU
211 W. Fort St., Suite 1000, Detroit 48226
(313) 202-1800
For information on ethnic attractions and tours, call **1-800-DETROIT**. A visitor's guide, "Legacy of the Northern Star-Guide to Detroit's African-American Community" and other literature are available. Brochures and maps are available at Visitor Information Centers at various metro locations or by mail.

PRESERVATION WAYNE
(313) 222-0321
Detroit's oldest historic preservation group sponsors tours highlighting Detroit's history and architecture. *Mansions, Movie Palaces and Theaters, Auto Industry and the Labor Movement,* and *Eastern Market* are among the themes.

TOURS BY STEWART MCMILLIN
(313) 922-1990
Detroit history expert conducts guided tours in diverse areas, including Ethnic Communities, Art and Architecture, Historical Churches and Cemeteries, Detroit Riverfront, Prohibition, African American History, Cultural Center and Auto History.

(Also check the daily newspapers for announcements of annual tours held in historic neighborhoods, such as Palmer Woods and Indian Village.)

[E-F/2-3] The original tract of approximately 100 acres in Royal Oak was deeded to the City of Detroit by **The Detroit Zoological Society** in 1923. It is the only zoo in America directly designed by Heinrich Hagenbeck, world-famous zoo-designer from Hamburg, Germany. It was the first in America to use dry or water moats (invented by Heinrich's father, Carl) in place of the heavy screen bars and fences found in conventional zoos at that time. The Rackham Memorial Fountain, created in 1939 by sculptor Corrado Parducci and designer Frederick Schnaple, is a favorite with its 10-foot bronze dancing bears.

Animal exhibits from around the world include a Penguinarium, Free-flight Aviary with hundreds of exotic plants and birds, Reptiles & Amphibians, Kangaroo, Bald Eagle, Aardvark, Farmyard, Wolverine, American Alligator (summer only), Giant Tortoise, Hippopotamus, Giraffe and Ostrich, Zebra and Greater Kudu, Saudi Gazelles, Black Rhinoceros, Asian Elephants, African Waterhole, Japanese Macaque, African Lion, Siberian Tiger, California Sea Lion and Harbor Seal Exhibit.

Great Apes of Harambee, a nearly four-acre exhibit, has eight overlooks which provide guests an opportunity to view chimpanzees and gorillas in three environments (forest clearings, meadows, and rock outcropping) resembling their natural habitat. Indoor viewing also is available. **The Bear Dens** are among the most popular exhibits at the Zoo and currently feature polar bears, grizzlies and sloth bears. The **Wildlife Interpretive Gallery** features a coral reef aquarium, touch-screen computers, an art gallery, film theater, changing exhibit hall and butterfly/hummingbird garden.

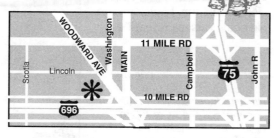

There are several refreshment and souvenir stands, a gift shop, two surface parking lots (with a capacity of 1,330 cars), a four-level parking garage, and two railroad stations for the miniature train. A picnic grove where guests may set up their own grills is available in the summer. Many special events are hosted by the Zoological Society year-round, often after hours. Adult roller chair and "kid kab" rentals are available.

The Detroit Zoological Park is located in Royal Oak at the intersection of West Ten Mile Road and Woodward Avenue (I-696 freeway exit #16). Hours are 10 a.m. to 4 p.m. daily, Nov-March; 10 a.m. to 5 p.m. daily, April-Oct.,10 a.m. to 6 p.m. Sundays and holidays from Mid-May through Labor Day.; 10 a.m. to 8 p. m. on Wednesdays from Mid-June through August. Closed Thanksgiving, Christmas and New Year's Day. For information, call (248) 398-0900.

[E-F/4-5] *"In the market, the rich and the poor met together…stately ministers and noted politicians with baskets on arm, merchants and laborers all alike examined, questioned and bantered side by side…"* —A 19th-century assessment of the market scene:

If Detroit had a corner where all the world meets, it would be Eastern Market. Long the nucleus of the city's fresh meats and produce industry, the market dates back to 1841 (at current site since 1891). Today it's known as the largest bedding-flower market in the world and as a lively gathering place for residents from all over metro Detroit. In recognition of its rich heritage, the market was declared an historic area in 1977 by the State Historical Commission.

Follow your nose and you'll find fragrant spices from the Middle East, rich Italian cappuccino, African kente cloth and other imports. While best known for its open-air Saturday market where thousands gather to buy fruit and flowers, the 11-acre downtown area at the apex of Gratiot Avenue and Russell Street is also surrounded by specialty stores featuring fresh meats, poultry, gourmet foods, spices and fine wines. Goods are imported from as far away as Europe, the Middle East, Asia and South America.

Many of the stores are wholesale only. Those open to the retail trade include **R. Hirt Jr. and Co.**, a family-owned business since 1893, selling imported cheeses and gourmet foods from all over the world; the **Rocky Peanut Company,** for coffees, candies and (of course) fresh nuts; **Ciaramitaro Brothers Wholesale Produce,** originally built between 1885 and 1888 as a saloon; **Salasnek Fisheries,** for fresh seafood; **Rafal Spices,** for a wide variety of spices as well as fresh coffees and gourmet foodstuffs; and dozens of other old-world butchers, importers and produce sellers. **Cost-Plus Wines** offers wines and beers from around the world.

Restaurants include the **Roma Café** (3401 Riopelle) and **Vivio's** (2460 Market), which have added Italian flavor to the market area for more than 50 years. For more informal dining, try the **Butcher's Saloon, Joey's Meatcutters Inn, Louisiana Creole** or the **Russell Street Deli.**

Eastern Market is at the intersection of Gratiot Avenue and Russell Street near downtown Detroit. Hours are Mon-Fri 5 a.m. to noon; Sat 5 a.m. to 5 p.m. From the north take I-75 south to the Mack Ave. exit. From the south take I-75 to I-375 exit.

The Visitors Center is at Adelaide and Market Sts.

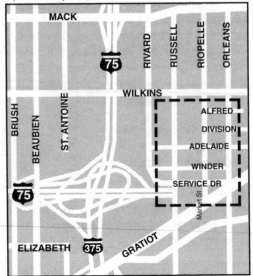

GROCERIES

Southeastern Michigan recently has been blessed with a wonderful assortment of huge international produce markets that feature everything from imported fresh figs to live Dixieland bands.

EASTERN MARKET
2934 Russell, Detroit; (810) 979-6322
Mon-Fri 4am-noon; Sat 4am-6pm; closed Sun; adjacent store hours vary.
Open market vendors sell retail on Saturdays only. (Call for recorded message with events, updates and hours.) Special events include "Flower Day" in May and June. In December, open 24 hours for Christmas tree sales.

GAZALI IMPORTS
10620 W. Nine Mile, Oak Park
(248) 546-6833
Ethnic foods for Middle Eastern, Greek, Armenian, Indian, Italian and Spanish cuisines.

HILLER'S
Commerce Township (Haggerty & 14 Mile)
(248) 960-1990
and
Northville; 425 N. Center St.
(248) 344-4001
and
Plymouth (Haggerty & Five Mile)
(734) 420-5555
and
West Bloomfield (Orchard & Maple)
(248) 851-7100
Produce and imports from around the world, including large selection of British foods and spirits.

HOLIDAY MARKET
1203 S. Main, Royal Oak; (248) 541-1414
and
520 S. Lilley Rd., Canton, (734) 844-2200
Voted "Best of Detroit" by several publications, this grocery features its own breads baked from European recipes; huge selection of cheeses (the only retail outlet for the Traffic Jam's housemade cheeses); espresso and pasta bars, European flower market, wines, waters and liquors from around the world. Large meat and seafood counter.

LOMBARDO FINE FOODS
31065 Ryan Rd., Warren
(N of 13 Mile)
(810) 939-0580
European specialties, especially Italian, Polish and Yugoslavian foods, including homemade sausage, choice meats, cheeses, pasta, noodles, oils, olives, spices, coffee.

MERCHANT OF VINO WHOLE FOODS MARKET
2789 Plymouth Rd., Ann Arbor
(313) 769-0900
and
27640 Middlebelt, Farmington Hills
(248) 473-7600
and
1404 Walton Blvd., Rochester Hills
(248) 652-2100
and
2880 W. Maple (Somerset Plaza), Troy
(248) 649-9600
Food and spirits from around the world; fresh produce, imported cheeses, pastas, candies, teas, coffees and much more. Also **Cellar Collection** on Maple in downtown Birmingham (248-433- 3000) and **Beverage Outlet** on Rochester Road in Troy (248-689-0900).

PAPA JOE'S
GOURMET MARKET PLACE
Hampton Plaza; 2025 Rochester Rd.
Rochester Hills
(248) 853-6263
Carries an assortment of specialty fruits and vegetables such as *carambola, feijoz, lychee and cherimoya,* etc. Extensive fresh meat and seafood counters. Bakeries and deli.

PRODUCE PALACE INTERNATIONAL
29300 Dequindre, Warren
(N of 12 Mile)
(810) 574-3000
Produce, meat, deli and bakery departments with everything from fresh buffalo meat to Norwegian flat bread. Large garden center in season.

R. HIRT JR.
2468 Market St., Detroit (Eastern Market)
(313) 567-1173
Vast array of cheeses from around the world, imported teas, coffees, candies, snacks, gifts.

NINO SALVAGGIO'S INTERNATIONAL MARKETPLACE
6845 Rochester Rd., Troy; (248) 879-9222
and
32906 Middlebelt, Farmington Hills
(248) 855-5570
and
27900 Harper, St. Clair Shores
(810) 778-3650
Produce, bakery and specialty foods, large assortment of fresh produce and meats used in ethnic cuisine.

VIC'S WORLD CLASS MARKETS
31201 Southfield Rd., Beverly Hills
(248) 647-4646
and
42875 Grand River, Novi; (248) 305-7333
and
2055 S. Telegraph, Bloomfield Hills
(248) 454-0700
Produce, fresh pastas, bakery, meats and deli, imported foods and beverages. Culinary consultant available to answer questions.

WESTBORN MARKET
21755 Michigan, Dearborn; (313) 274-6100
and
14925 Middlebelt, Livonia; (734) 524-1000
and
2245 Woodward, Berkley; (248) 547-1000
Produce from around the world, specialty meats and sausages, European flower market; Dixieland band performing regularly on Saturday mornings.

INTERNATIONAL CUISINE

ADVENTURE SERIES
Grosse Pointe War Memorial
3200 Lakeshore Drive
Grosse Pointe Farms; (313) 881-7511
Film and dinner series features different country and cuisine each month.

PIKE STREET THEME DINNERS
18 W. Pike St., Pontiac; (248) 334-7878
Multi-course theme dinners often focusing on international cuisines, such as Russian. Call for current schedule.

DETROIT INTERNATIONAL WINE AUCTION
(313) 872-9463

Annual benefit for Center for Creative Studies held mid-November.

FAMIE'S FINDS; (313) 222-0444
Local chef Keith Famie travels the world to bring back techniques and recipes. He shares on WDIV (Channel 4, Detroit) TV Fridays at noon and Saturdays at 9am.

INTERNATIONAL DINNERS
Culinary Arts Program
Schoolcraft College
18600 Haggerty, Livonia; (734) 462-4488
Student-run American Harvest Restaurant serves International Dinners on Thursdays during the school year. Series features Mediterranean, Pacific Rim, American regional, French and Italian cuisines. Restaurant is in Waterman Center on Haggerty between Six and Seven Mile roads.

GOURMET DINNER SERIES
Hospitality Department
Oakland Community College
Orchard Ridge Campus
Farmington Hills; (248) 471-7786
Gourmet dinners prepared and served by Culinary Arts students, including Mexican Fiesta, Italian Food & Wine Pairing, Wassail Feast, and Culinary Classic in June.

KITCHEN GLAMOR
Novi (248) 380-8600; Redford (313)
537-1300; Rochester (248) 652-0402;
W. Bloomfield (248) 855-4466
Large selection of supplies and equipment for preparing ethnic cuisine plus books and spices. Regular demonstrations, workshops.

MUSICAL FEASTS
400 Buhl Bldg.; 535 Griswold, Detroit
(313) 962-1000 ext. 285
Sponsored by Detroit Symphony Orchestra Volunteer Council, Musical Feasts offer an opportunity to experience a delicious meal—ranging from light luncheons to full-course dinners, accompanied by DSO musicians and hosted in private homes. Costs

range from $25 to $1,000. Some past themes: *Persian Delight, Une Soirée Dans La Cave* and *After the Hunt Brunch.*

MICHIGAN TASTEFEST
New Center Area, Detroit
(313) 872-0188
Held each July 4th weekend, the Tastefest features food from more than 40 metro Detroit restaurants and cuisines of many countries. Also live entertainment at four stages. Proceeds support the charitable activities of the New Center Foundation.

PEACOCK CAFES
Somerset North - Level 3
Big Beaver & Coolidge, Troy
(248) 643-7440
Mon-Sat 10am-9pm, Sun noon-6pm. Cajun, Chinese, French, Greek and Italian food booths, plus a deli, diner and cappuccino

bar are part of the food court. Shoppers looking for a little more ambience, will find a dozen restaurants elsewhere at Somerset, including La Cuisine Jardin, Nordstrom-The Pub and Sebastian's Grill.

SMALL WORLD CAFE
International Institute
111 E. Kirby; (313) 874-2233
Mon-Fri 11am-2pm.
Ethnic lunches are served in cafeteria on the lower level.

SOUTHFIELD INTERNATIONAL SERIES
Southfield Community Relations Dept.
(248) 354-4854
Series of cafe nights held March-June feature dining and entertainment to showcase city's rich ethnic diversity.

BEADS

Beads are made of a variety of materials: seeds, wood, ivory, bone, horn, shell, coral, pearl, jet, amber, gemstones, metals, ceramics, and plastics. They were worn in the Stone Age as amulets or charms (and still are in some communities), probably because magical properties were attributed to the materials from which they were made. Beads also have been worn since early times for decoration. Easily portable, they have, in addition, been objects of currency.

Archaeological finds reveal that a variety of gold bead necklaces were worn in ancient **Mesopotamia** and **India. Egyptian** nobles favored wide collars of colored gemstone, ceramic, or glass beads. **Byzantine** courtiers and Mughal Indian nobility wore ropes of pearls. In **Europe,** glass beads, manufactured since the 13th century, were popular both for jewelry and embroidery. Hundreds of tiny glass beads or seed pearls were embroidered on dresses, church vestments, small pictures, boxes, and baskets or were strung and knitted into ladies' purses or used as fringe on dresses and lampshades.

Native Americans and tribal **Africans** wore strings of small beads and embroidered beads on their clothes and bags as, for example, the skin tunics of the Inuit (Eskimo) and the aprons of the Ndebele. Africans also trimmed headdresses with beads and covered vessels and stools with them. In addition, beads were used for money as, for example, shell wampum on the east coast of North America. Originally the beads were made from natural materials such as shell; subsequently they were replaced by glass beads obtained from European traders (who are thought to have learned the technique from trade in Africa).

● *Bead shops abound in the metro area. (Also look under "shops" listings in various chapters of this book.) For information on where to find beads, contact Lisa Grix, president of Great Lakes Bead Workers Guild, at (810) 977-5935.*

SHOPS

CRISTIONS
215 N. Old Woodward, Birmingham
(248) 723-3337
*Mon-Thurs 10am-7pm, Fri-Sat 10am-5 pm,
Sun 10am-2pm.* Elegant bed and table linens
from Italy, Switzerland, Germany and Ireland.

CULTURAL ACCENTS
3011 W. Grand Blvd., Detroit; (313) 872-5540
Mon-Fri 10 am-6pm, Sat 11am-5 pm. Gallery
in Fisher Building features multicultural dolls,
jewelry and greeting cards.

DIA MUSEUM SHOP
Detroit Institute of Arts
5200 Woodward, Detroit; (313) 833-7944
and Satellite Shops:
Somerset Collection, Troy, (248) 649-2222

Twelve Oaks, Novi, (248) 380-8050. *Open
museum and mall hours.* Publications, art,
jewelry and gift items related to DIA collection
plus those of other renowned museums.

EUROPE DIRECT WAREHOUSE
927 Hilton, Ferndale; (248) 691-9155
Tues-Sat 10am-5pm, Sun noon-4pm. Imported
European furniture, smalls and effects in a
9,000-square-foot showroom.

HESLOPS
(248) 348-7050
Headquartered in Novi with 11 stores in metro
Detroit. Call for locations and hours. Fine crystal, china and housewares designed and craft-
ed in Denmark, Japan, Ireland, England, Germany and many other countries.

SOMERSET COLLECTION

**2800 W. Big Beaver
Troy
(248) 643-7440**
Upscale shopping center,
located 2 miles west of
I-75 Exit 69.

BOUTIQUES

From London, England:
Jaeger (apparel–women)
(248) 649-9390
Burberry's
(apparel–men & women)
(248) 643-8555
Laura Ashley (appar-
el–women & children)
(248) 649-0890

From Paris, France:
Carré Blanc (linens)
(248) 637-7077
Louis Vuitton
(leather goods)
(248) 643-8939

Rodier Paris
(apparel–women)
(248) 643-9300

From Italy:
Gucci (leather goods)
(248) 643-7630
Benetton
(apparel–women
& children)
(248) 816-9995

From Alkmaar, Holland:
Oilily (apparel–children
& women)
(248) 614-9030

From Germany:
Mont Blanc (leather
goods and writing
instruments)
(248) 637-9885

From Denmark:
**Bang &
Olufsen**
(electronics)
(248) 816-9690

From Montreal, Quebec:
April Cornell
(home furnishings and
womens' and girls' cloth-
ing manufactured in
India) (248) 816-9660.
Caché (apparel–women)
(248) 643-9470

ANCHOR STORES
Hudson's
(248) 816-4000
Neiman Marcus
(248) 643-3300
Nordstrom
(248) 816-5100
Saks Fifth Avenue
(248) 643-9000

INTERNATIONAL INSTITUTE GIFT SHOP
111 E. Kirby, Detroit
(313) 871-8600
Mon-Fri 11am-5pm. Crafts, gifts, books, toys and clothing from around the world.

LITTLE FOXES
Fox Theatre Building, Detroit
(313) 983-6202
Tues-Fri 10am-6pm, open two hours prior to special events at FoxTheatre; call ahead. Waterford crystal, French porcelain and many other unique items from around the world fill the shelves of this tiny shop.

LOTUS IMPORT COMPANY
419 S. Washington, Royal Oak
(248) 546-8820
Sun. noon-5pm Mon-Sat 10am-7pm. Clothing, jewelry, unusual gifts from around the world, from tin whistles to zen gardens.

NATURAL WONDERS
Twelve Oaks, Novi
(248) 816-1667
Gifts, books, recordings from around the world, including Celtic and Native American.

THE NATURE COMPANY
The Somerset Collection
2801 W. Big Beaver Road
Troy; (248) 649-3433
Mon-Sat 10am-9pm, Sun noon-6pm. Musical instruments, toys, jewelry, clothing, books, recordings from around the world with emphasis on ecological awareness.

NOMAD IMPORTS
205 W. Nine Mile, Ferndale; (248) 546-7790
Mon-Sat noon-8pm. Imported goods include jewelry, masks, Tibetan clothes, Indonesian wood crafts.

RAND MCNALLY MAP & TRAVEL STORE
Somerset Collection (J226)
2801 West Big Beaver Road, Troy
(248) 643-7470
Mon-Sat 10am-9pm, Sun noon-6pm. Maps, toys, games, videos, globes, books and more.

RAPHAEL'S MAGNIFICENT POSSESSIONS
1799 Coolidge Hwy., Berkley
(248) 546-0194
Mon-Sat 10am-6pm, open till 8pm Thurs. 1920s Tudor-revival style former convent now bursts with antiques, Italian statuary and grottoes, year-round hand-crafted European Christmas ornament display, Lalique crystal, full-size reproduction Celtic crosses, imported china and blown glass.

SHANFIELDS-MEYERS
188 Ouellette Ave., Windsor
(313) 961-8435
Mon, Tue, Thu 9am-6pm, Wed 9am-7pm, Fri 9 am-8pm, Sat-Sun 10am-6pm. Fine china and glassware from all over the world at discount prices.

UNICEF SHOP
111 E. Kirby, Detroit;   (313) 874-1616
Mon-Fri 10am-4pm. Shop in lower level of International Institute sells books, cards, games, puzzles, mugs designed for UNICEF by artists in many countries to benefit the organization.

WTVS STORE OF KNOWLEDGE
Somerset Collection North
(248) 637-7200
and
Briarwood Mall; (313) 669-8350
and
Lakeside Mall; (810) 566-0649
Regular mall hours. Globes, atlases, foreign language tapes, toys and games from around the world, origami supplies. Videos from favorite PBS shows including British sitcoms, *Masterpiece Theatre, National Geographic, Riverdance.* Proceeds benefit WTVS 56.

DEPARTMENT STORES
These well-known stores, firmly rooted in Michigan, carry the high-quality products of international designers.

HUDSON'S
At major malls: Briarwood, Eastland, Fairlane, Lakeside, Northland, Oakland Mall, Somerset Collection, Southland, Summit Place, Twelve Oaks and Westland.
International designs featured in many departments. Frequent fashion shows, demonstrations and special events highlighting artisans, designers and food experts from around the world, as well the U.S.A. Gourmet shops feature delights ranging from truffles (both chocolate and fungus) to chocolate-covered, sprinkle-laden Bavarian pretzels.

JACOBSON'S in Ann Arbor (734-769-7600), Birmingham (248-644-6900), Grosse Pointe (313-882-7000), Laurel Park (734-591-7696), Rochester (248-651-6000). Features clothing and home accesories by renowned European and American designers.

TRIBUTE TO THE WORLDWIDE AUTO INDUSTRY

AUTOMOTIVE HALL OF FAME

Video theater and interactive exhibits at the new Automotive Hall of Fame in Dearborn present an entertaining history of the people and motor vehicles that changed the world. The Hall of Fame is located at 21400 Oakwood Blvd, next door to Henry Ford Museum

The new visitor attraction recognizes and celebrates worldwide motor vehicle industry leaders for the purpose of inspiring others to higher levels of accomplishment in their own work. Exhibits focus on accomplished individuals from every vocational discipline --accountants, designers, engineers, financiers, inventors, marketers and more-- and from countries around the world. Visitors can match wits with Louis Chevrolet, Walter Chrysler, Carl Benz, Eiji Toyoda, Soichiro Honda and other auto industry figures. Interactive displays tell the story of immigrants who came to Detroit in the early 1900s to work in the auto factories and the accomplishments of immigrants such as Fred Dusenberg, Ralph DePalma, Albert Champion and Zora Arkus-Duntov.

The 11x65-foot mural in the Dedication Center depicts nearly 100 scenes associated with the last century of motoring and the impact of the global motor vehicle industry on the lives and lifestyles of humankind. It is believed to be the largest installation of automobile fine art since the Diego Rivera installation at the Detroit Institute of Arts in the 1930s.

A gift shop features educational products, automotive art, books and models and other items from the international motor vehicle industry.

Hours are 10 a.m. to 5 p.m. daily Memorial Day-October; remainder of year closed Monday. Admission is $6 for adults, $5.50 for seniors and $3 for youth 5-12. For further information, call (313) 240-4000.

EXHIBITS

See Detroit Cultural Center for Museum of African American History, Detroit Historical Museum, Detroit Institute of Arts, Children's Museum, Your Heritage House and Detroit Science Center. See Visual Arts section for Cranbrook Academy of Art Museum, Toledo Museum of Art and University of Michigan Museum of Art.

AUTOMOTIVE HALL OF FAME
**21400 Oakwood Blvd., Dearborn
(313) 240-4000**
Daily 10am-5pm Memorial Day-Oct. Remainder of year 10am-5pm daily except Mon. Interactive exhibits focusing on development of motor vehicle industry worldwide. (See sidebar.)

CRANBROOK INSTITUTE OF SCIENCE
**1221 N. Woodward, Bloomfield Hills
(248) 645-3200**
Mon-Thurs 10 am-5 pm, Fri-Sat 10 am-10 pm, Sun noon-5 pm. Natural history exhibits, planetarium, laser shows and special traveling exhibits involving the world around us. Gift shops for adults and children.

HENRY FORD MUSEUM & GREENFIELD VILLAGE
**Village Rd. and Oakwood, Dearborn
(313) 271-1620**
Daily 9am-5pm. Indoor/outdoor museum complex on 93 acres contains historical exhibits from the 1600s to present. *(See tours in Americana chapter.)*

INTERNATIONAL HERITAGE HALL OF FAME
**Cobo Center Atrium, Detroit
(313) 871-8600**
International Institute maintains display at Cobo Center to honor inductees for outstanding service to their ethnic groups and the metro Detroit Community.

VISUAL ARTS

BELIAN ART CENTER
5980 Rochester Rd., Troy; (248) 828-1001
Mon-Sat noon-6pm.
Gallery features African art, Chinese rugs and pottery, Persian and Indian miniatures and other international art. Center also sponsors concert series of chamber music and holds watercolor classes.

BURTON INTERNATIONAL SCHOOL
3420 Cass, Detroit; (313) 494-2394
Multicultural K-8 magnet school in Detroit Public Schools System has mural art by Dennis Orlowski. "Creation of the Universe" panels are in hallway; Media Center mural depicts "Heroes of the World."

CRANBROOK ACADEMY MUSEUM
**1221 Woodward Ave., Bloomfield Hills
(248) 645-3312**
Wed, Fri, Sat 10am-5pm, Thu 10am-9pm, Sun noon-5pm. Displays changing exhibits of contemporary art from throughout the world, as well as work by students, faculty and alumni. Outdoor art by Carl Milles, Academy's first sculptor-in-residence, and contemporary sculptors. (See also Cranbrook tour in Scandinavia chapter.)

GALLERY BIEGAS
35 E. Grand River, Detroit (313) 961-0634
Tue-Fri 9am-5pm, Sat noon-5pm, closed Sun-Mon. Large gallery in "Detroit Art Corridor" in the Harmonie Park area, showcases local artists as well as museum-quality works of artists from Nigeria, Haiti, Spain, Native America and Europe. Nearby galleries include **2-South, Artist's Cooperative, Billiard Gallery, Del Pryor Galleries, Sherry Washington Gallery.**

PHYLLIS-BERG ART INTERIORS
**75 Hillsdale Rd., Bloomfield Hills
(248) 335-0068**
By appointment. Interior designer Phyllis Berg specializes in art imports and designs with ethnic themes.

HAIG GALLERIES
311 Main St., Rochester; (248) 656-8333
Mon-Sat noon-6 pm. Upstairs gallery of Asian, Pre-Columbian, tribal and other ancient art resembles a museum. Indian pottery shares space with Chinese pieces

and Japanese lacquers, ivories and bronzes. Chinese robes on the walls look down on Egyptian ushaptis, Indian saris, African sculptural forms and full-size architectural columns.

HERITAGE INTERNATIONAL GALLERY
275 Iron St. (1 block E of Mt. Elliott)
Detroit; (313) 259-3900
Open to public for special exhibits and shows, call for update. Studio of Korean-born designer (famous for his distinctive neck tie designs) and painter Dominic Pang-born frequently hosts exhibits of other artists as well.

TOLEDO MUSEUM OF ART
2445 Monroe St., Toledo
(419) 255-8000 or (800) 644-6862
Tue-Thu, Sat 10am-4pm, Fri 10am-10pm, Sun 1-5pm. Paintings, sculpture, furniture, silver, tapestries, graphic arts and more than 6,000 examples of art in glass, as well as artifacts from ancient Rome and a Medieval cloister. International traveling shows. Well-stocked gift shop.

UNIVERSITY OF MICHIGAN MUSEUM OF ART
525 S. State St., Ann Arbor; (313) 764-0395
Tue-Wed, Fri-Sat 10 am-5 pm, Thu 10am-9pm, Sun noon-5pm. Western art from sixth century to present, African art and an extensive collection of Asian art. Concerts, family programs and changing exhibits.

VILLA DOMAIN INTERIORS
8469 E. Jefferson, Detroit; (313) 824-4600
Wed-Sat 11am-7pm, Sun noon-5pm. Closed Mon-Tues. Recently restored Italian-Villa-style home originally built for the Book family in 1911 houses an eclectic collection including European antiques, African-American paintings, kimonos, dolls and more. Manager Gloria Robinson knowlegeably points out the mansion's appointments such as intricate parquet floors and mosaic-tiled vaulted ceiling. Also worth a visit is **Harper Galleries** next door (313-821-1952) featuring antiques.

(See "Cultural Center" this chapter for Detroit Institute of Arts.)

THE GLOBAL INSTRUMENT

What do zydeco, celtic, tango, morris, salsa, polka, conjunto, country, klezmer, contradance, not to mention French, Scandinavian, Italian, Dutch and German folk music all have in common? They all employ the sounds of the accordion, or its smaller cousin, the concertina.

What does Detroit have in common with San Francisco, Skokie, Illinois and St. Paul, Minnesota? The accordion has been designated its official instrument.

The accordion, a hand-held instrument, consists of bellows fastened between two wooden sides containing reeds. Stretching and pushing the bellows causes air to pass over reeds producing sound. The notes are produced by pressing buttons and keys.

An accordion-like instrument was invented in **Berlin** in the 1820s. The first actual accordion was patented in **Vienna** in 1829. The piano accordion was patented in **France** in 1852. The hexagonal concertina was invented by **British** physicist and inventor, Sir Charles Wheatstone, who was inspired by the action of the *sheng,* an ancient **Chinese** mouth organ.

In China the accordion is known as *sun-fin-chin;* in Russia, it is *bayan;* in Norway, *trekspill* and in Italy, *fisarmonica.*

PERFORMING ARTS

AMERICAN ARTISTS SERIES
435 Goodhue Road
Bloomfield Hills, MI 48304
(248) 851-5044
Concerts at Kingswood Auditorium, Cranbrook Campus, Bloomfield Hills. Performances have included a "Russian Fete" with Balalaika virtuoso Gennady Zut.

CONCERT OF COLORS
New Detroit Cultural Exchange Network
(313) 664-2000
The main cultural event sponsored by New Detroit, Inc. and its Cultural Exchange Network is the Concert of Colors held in the summer at Chene Park on the Detroit riverfront. Artists from diverse backgrounds collaborate to present traditional, contemporary and crossover music of African, Arab, Latino, Asian and Native American roots.

DETROIT CHAMBER WINDS
Troy; (248) 362-9329
Masterworks by composers such as Mozart, Beethoven, Gabrielli, Stravinsky and Dvorak go largely unheard in today's concert halls due to unusual instrumentation needs. Since its 1982 founding, Detroit Chamber Winds has been the only American ensemble of professional musicians performing these works on an on-going basis. **The Great Lakes Chamber Music Festival** presents performances over a two-week period in **mid-June.** Entirely secular in nature, the event is a joint venture between Catholic, Jewish and Protestant congregations: St. Hugo of the Hills, Temple Beth El and Kirk in the Hills, and Detroit Chamber Winds.

DETROIT SYMPHONY ORCHESTRA
Orchestra Hall
3711 Woodward Ave., Detroit
(313) 576-5100
World-class orchestra presents classical music from around the world and international guests in its concert schedule. Also has outreach programs, summer concerts at Meadow Brook and young people's concerts.

DETROIT YOUTHEATRE
Music Hall Center
Madison and Brush, Detroit
(313) 963-2366
Professional performances especially for young people include luminaries such as Marcel Marceau, Ishangi African dancers. Call for schedule.

CHC PARADE OF NATIONS PEFORMERS
P.O. Box 250452, Franklin 48025
(248) 355-3119
Children Helping Children (CHC) gives local international children a chance to express their artistic abilities and at the same time raise funds for childrens' causes. Children from around the world are available to perform at events sponsored by individuals, organizations or corporations. Contact Nada Dalgamouni, education and enrichment coordinator at the International Institute.

MACOMB CENTER FOR THE PERFORMING ARTS
44575 Garfield Rd., Clinton Twp.
(810) 286-2222
"Discovery Series" offers multicultural sampling of music and dance by touring groups from abroad. Center serves as an eastside venue for Broadway, opera, dance, drama, comedy, rock and pop, country, jazz and children's productions. It also is home to the Macomb Symphony Orchestra and Metropolitan Symphonic Band.

MICHIGAN OPERA THEATRE
104 Lothrop
Detroit, MI 48202
(313) 874-SING
Presents world-class performances in beautifully restored theater. Offers outreach program to schools throughout the metro area.

MOSAIC YOUTH THEATRE OF DETROIT
at Historic Fort Wayne, Detroit
(313) 554-1422
A multicultural arts organization whose mission is to develop young artists through comprehensive theatrical training and to provide high quality performances for audiences of all ages.

MUSICA VIVA INTERNATIONAL CONCERTS
25882 Orchard Lake Road, Farmington Hills
(248) 626-9705
Ginka Gerova-Ortega, artistic director.
Stellar lineup of music and dance from around the world, presented by internationally acclaimed artists.

FOLK MUSIC & ENTERTAINMENT

THE ARK
**316 South Main Street,
Ann Arbor
(734) 761-1451**
Non-profit organization produces nearly 250 concerts throughout the year, and has earned an international reputation for the presentation of music from around the world, including British Isles, Celtic, African, Latin, American, Eastern European, and Caribbean.

BORDERS BOOKS MUSIC CAFE
**34300 Woodward Ave., Birmingham
(248) 203-0005**
and
**5601 Mercury Drive, Dearborn
(313) 271-4441**
and
**30995 Orchard Lake Rd, Farmington Hills
(248) 737-0110**
and
**43075 Crescent Blvd, Novi Town Center
(248) 347-0780**
(Novi Rd. and Grand River)
and
**45290 Utica Park Blvd., Utica
(810) 726-8555**
Stores feature national and local musicians performing live as well as a large selection of world music CDs.

CADIEUX CAFE
**4300 Cadieux, Detroit (btw Mack & Warren)
(313) 882-8560**
Open every evening. Belgian café offers live folk music regularly in addition to feather bowling, over 70 different beers, steamed mussels by the bucket, dart competitions and an annual bicycle race.

FIFTH AVENUE
215 W. Fifth, Royal Oak; (248) 542-9922
Live entertainment nightly. Specializing in "Roots Music" including Zydeco and Blues. Billiards. Private bookings available.

GEMINI
Ann Arbor; (734) 665-0409
National award-winning twin folk singers, Sandor and Lazlo Smolovits, perform world music for youthful audiences all over the metro area.

Their latest recording, *Bright in All of Us*, includes African, Hebrew and Native American folk tunes. Call for information on bookings, performances and recordings.

HARMONY HOUSE
Locations throughout metro area, see yellow pages. Large selection of all types of folk and world music. **Harmony House Classical** store in Royal Oak (248) 398-0422.

MAMA'S COFFEE HOUSE
**Unitarian Church, 651 Woodward Ave. (at Lone Pine), Bloomfield Hills
(248) 546-5153**
Sat. 8-10:30pm. Traditional and modern folk music, American, Celtic, others.

OFF THE RECORD
**401 S. Washington, Royal Oak
(248) 398-4436**
Mon-Tues 10am-8pm, Wed-Thu 10am-9pm, Fri-Sat 10am-10pm, Sun 11am-5pm. Extensive selection of Blues, Soul, Jazz, Reggae/Ska and World Music CDs.

7th House
**7 North Saginaw; Pontiac
(248) 335-3540**
Jazz, Blues, folk and unique entertainment.

FILMS

ANN ARBOR FILM FESTIVAL
(734) 995-5356
Held in early spring, it is the oldest 16mm festival in this country for independent and experimental filmmakers.

BORDERS' FOREIGN LANGUAGE CLUBS
**31150 Southfield Rd., Birmingham
(248) 644-1515**
Borders' French and Spanish foreign language groups host foreign film nights. Call for details or check their website: AtBorders@aol.com.

DETROIT FILM THEATRE
**Detroit Institute of Arts Auditorium
5200 Woodward, Detroit
(313) 833-2323**

Weekends, Aug-May at 7 and 9:30pm, Mon 7 pm. "Cutting edge" foreign films by renowned directors, new and classics, presented in original language with English subtitles. Call for calendar.

MAIN ART THEATRE
118 N. Main St. at 11 Mile, Royal Oak
(248) 542-0180
Sometimes shows foreign films with English subtitles.

STAR SOUTHFIELD
12 Mile Rd. (between Northwestern & Telegraph) Southfield; (248) 372-2222
Sometimes shows foreign films with English subtitles.

THOMAS VIDEO
122 S. Main St., Clawson; (248) 280-2833
Daily 10am -midnight. Largest selection of foreign films on tape in Michigan. Sales and rentals.

TRAVELOGUE SERIES
Birmingham Community House
380 S. Bates, Birmingham
(248) 644-5832
Lineup of colorful, informative and educational travel films scheduled on Wednesday nights.

WORLD TRAVEL & ADVENTURE SERIES
Civic Center, Southfield; (248) 424-9022
Friday night travel film and lecture film series runs Oct-June.

WORLD TRAVEL SERIES
Macomb Center for the Performing Arts
44575 Garfield Rd., Clinton Twp.
(810) 286-2222
Travelogue series scheduled for dates in Sept., Oct., Nov., Feb., March, April and May.

*(Also see travelogue series at **Grosse Pointe War Memorial** under "Dining.")*

LIBRARIES & ARCHIVES

INTERNATIONAL LANGUAGE COLLECTION, DETROIT PUBLIC LIBRARY
121 Gratiot Ave., Detroit; (313) 224-0580

Mon-Fri 9:30am-5:30pm. Books in over 50 languages; 130 newspapers and magazines from around the world. Collection contains fiction, classics, juvenile, popular non-fiction, language acquisition and materials that facilitate intercultural communication.

DETROIT PUBLIC LIBRARY
MAIN BRANCH
5201 Woodward and Kirby, Detroit
(313) 833-1000
Tues, Thurs, Fri, Sat 9:30 am-5:30 pm; Wed 1-9 pm. **Burton Historical Collection** for genealogical research, **Azalia Hackley Collection** of African Americans in the performing arts, **National Automotive History** Collection, and extensive **map collection** are of special interest. Impressive Italian Renaissance building has murals of events from Detroit's early history and beginnings of auto industry.

FOLKLORE ARCHIVES
Wayne State University, Detroit
448 Purdy Library; Gullen Mall
(313) 577-4053
Archives contain the **International Library of African Music,** as well as thousands of manuscripts, recordings, photos, videotapes, slides and other materials on urban traditions of Detroit's diverse population. Collection covers everything from Macedonian wedding customs and Jewish folkways to taped oral histories of Southern whites.

WALTER P. REUTHER LIBRARY
Wayne State University
5401 Cass, Detroit; (313) 577-4024
Archives of Labor and Urban Affairs, WSU Black History Collections, Michigan Dance Archives and more. Exhibits in first floor lobby.

STATE ARCHIVES OF MICHIGAN
717 West Allegan Street; Lansing MI 48918
(517) 373-3559
Group tours contact: (517) 373-2353.
Weekdays 10am to 4pm. With documents dating back to 1797, the State Archives of Michigan houses much of Michigan's record heritage. More than 80 million state and local government records and private papers, 300,000 photographs, 500,000 maps and materials on other media, such as film and audio tapes, are available for public research. The archives' holdings are particularly valuable in tracing genealogy and land surveys.

WHAT'S IN A NAME?

A name identifies a specific person among many persons. Most people have a family or "sur"name (last name) and a "first" or "given" name (first name). Different parts of the world look at names in different ways. In parts of **Africa,** people are named for the day of the week on which they are born, the position in the family, or someone whom the family wishes to honor. In Ghana, a third child born on Wednesday into an Akan family may be called *Kwaku Mensa* ('Kwaku' meaning Wednesday and 'Mensa' meaning third). Even the order of first and last name differs in various parts of the world. In Spain and Mexico, the family name is written first, followed by the first or given name; but in the Western world, the given name is written first and followed by the surname.

In **China,** names are chosen not only because they are part of a family tradition, but because of the meaning of the characters. Given names are especially important in China because there are significantly fewer surnames there than there are in the United States. In 2852 B.C., the Emperor Fuxi decreed the use of surnames. The order of the name is surname (xing, pronounced "shing") followed by the given name (ming, pronounced "ming"). The given name may have one or two characters and usually has an underlying significance. Given names usually have some meaning relating to the place of birth, the name of a relative or friend, or a desirable quality or characteristic.

An example might be Yang Chenbin : "Yang" is the family name and "Chenbin" literally means "(born in the time of) final victory," indicating that the child was born in 1949 when the People's Republic of China was established. Given names are usually used only between very close friends. Nicknames are very popular "Datou" (big head) or "Xiaohu" (little tiger).

For more about names see "Scandinavia," "Korea" and "Poland."

Sung

CLASSES

GENERAL

BIRMINGHAM COMMUNITY HOUSE
380 S. Bates, Birmingham; (248) 644-5832
Wine appreciation and international cooking classes, art history series and foreign policy seminars are among lectures and workshops offered.

CREATIVE ARTS CENTER
47 Williams, Pontiac; (248) 333-7849
Non-profit arts organization offers a number of classes in ethnic visual and performing arts.

DETROIT INSTITUTE OF ARTS
5200 Woodward, Detroit; (313) 833-4249
Department of Education offers drop-in workshops, adult classes, youth art workshops and teacher workshops at all levels of familiarity and interest in art.

GROSSE POINTE WAR MEMORIAL
3200 Lakeshore Dr., Grosse Pointe Farms
(313) 881-7511
Offers many opportunities to experience world culture, including wine-tastings, film series, art and music lectures by experts such as John Guinn and Michael Farrell, and craft workshops. Summer program called "Fun in Foreign Cultures" introduces children to foreign languages, crafts and customs.

DANCE

CCS INSTITUTE FOR MUSIC & DANCE
(313) 872-3118, ext. 610
Judith Sheldon, faculty chair. In addition to formal traditions of Ballet and Modern, the School of Dance at Center for Creative Studies offers *World Traditions* program for African and East Indian dance and *American Heritage* programs for tap and jazz. Modern Dance program features Katherine Dunham technique of combining folk styles of Africa, the Australian bush, Cuba, Haiti and Brazil. Classes held in Detroit's University Cultural Center and Jewish Community Center in West Bloomfield.

DETROIT FOLKDANCE CLUB
(248) 338-0524
International folk dancing on Fridays from 8-11 pm at First Congregational Church in Royal Oak. No partner required. Call for schedule.

DETROIT-WINDSOR DANCE ACADEMY
1529 Broadway, 4th Floor, Detroit
(313) 963-0050
Deborah White-Hunt, director. Instruction in modern, ballet, tap and ethnic dances.

OLD WORLD DANCE CO-OP
(248) 569-5242 or 548-3644
Ethnic dance party held first three Saturday evenings of the month from September-June in Ferndale at St. James Church, on Woodward one light S of Nine Mile. Learn international dances, particularly from the Balkans and Israel. $6 admission. No partner or experience necessary.

SWING CITY DANCE STUDIO
1960 S. Industrial E&F, Ann Arbor
(734) 668-7782
Contact: Susan Filipiak
Offers instruction in traditional dance from around the world. Tap, clogging, ballroom, world dance.

TROY DANCE STUDIO
4963 Rochester Rd, Troy; (248) 689-3393
Classes in various types of dance from ballroom to country & western.

Community Centers and local Parks & Rec departments frequently offer classes and workshops in ethnic dancing, cooking, crafts and other activities.

EDUCATIONAL RESOURCES

A WORLD OF DIFFERENCE INSTITUTE
Anti-Defamation League
4000 Town Center, Suite 420, Southfield
(248) 355-3730
Human relations training that prepares educators to address the needs of racially and culturally diverse students.

CHILDREN'S MUSEUM OUTREACH
67 E. Kirby, Detroit; (313) 494-1210
Office open Mon-Fri 8:15am-4:30pm. (Exhibits open weekdays 1-4pm, Sat Oct-May 9am-4pm.) Operated by the Detroit Public School System, the museum has outreach programs and loans collections to schools in southeast MIchigan.

CULTURAL ENRICHMENT/ GLOBAL LEARNING ASSOCIATES
65 Cadillac Tower Bldg, Suite 2200
Detroit 48226
(313) 965-3379
Brenda Sq. Nuamah, director
Performing artists of various cultures (African, Asian, Caribbean, Hmong, Middle Eastern, Native American, Scottish, Spanish) available for school assemblies, special events, concerts and parties. Multicultural programs include "Harp Beat," American history and the diversity of its cultural roots presented through song and audience participation. Also Black History series, afterschool activities and summer day camp.

GIFTS OF MANY CULTURES
Western International High School
1500 Scotten, Detroit
(313) 849-4758 ext. 2028
Patti Koenig, advisor
Student organization creates activities to foster sharing, belonging and reconciliation among students and school communities in order to erase ignorance, change stereotypes and raise awareness about the many cultures of Detroit. As a model program for schools, it focuses on a different culture each month.

GIRL SCOUTS RAINBOW PROGRAM
Michigan Metro Council
28 W. Adams, Detroit 48226
(313) 964-4475/800-326-0309
Program gives girls opportunity to learn more about themselves and other cultures. Activities celebrating the rich diversity of metro

Detroit cover African American, Native American, Hispanic American, Asian American and Middle Eastern American cultures as well as universal traditions.

MICHIGAN HUMANITIES COUNCIL
119 Pere Marquette Dr., Suite 3B
Lansing, MI 48912-1270
(517) 372-7770
Offers the public a variety of resources on ethnic topics, ranging from video and audio tapes to exhibits and print materials. Renaissance Outreach Alliance for Detroit Area Schools (ROADS) gives tri-county-area teachers resources for classroom exploration of ethnic and world cultural groups.

PASSPORT AMERICA
Interfaith Center for Racial Justice
28640 Campbell, Warren 48093
(810) 751-4292
Weekend program for 7th and 8th graders provides a cooperative living experience to learn about and participate in another culture.

U-M INTERNATIONAL INSTITUTE
340 Lorch Hall
611 Tappan Ave., Ann Arbor
(734) 763-9200
Includes Center for East Asian Studies, Center for Japanese Studies, Center for Chinese Studies, Center for Middle Eastern and North African Studies, Center for Russian and East European Studies, Center for South and Southeast Asian Studies. Currently under development are centers for Turkish, Korean, British and European studies.

COMMUNITY RESOURCES

ACORD (A Community Organization Recognizing Diversity)
343 High St., Northville 48167
(248) 349-8437
Northville group, concerned with fostering harmony and understanding diversity, serves as a resource for the community and schools. Hosts Martin Luther King walk, spring ethnic festival and occasional speakers.

ANTI-DEFAMATION LEAGUE
4000 Town Center, Suite 420
Southfield 48075
(248) 355-3730
Combats anti-Semitism, all forms of bigotry and discrimination and promotes harmonious relations between diverse religious and ethnic groups. Sponsors A World of Difference diversity education program utilized by schools, universities, corporations, community and law enforcement agencies.

BIRMINGHAM-BLOOMFIELD TASK FORCE RACE RELATIONS & ETHNIC DIVERSITY
c/o The Community House
380 S. Bates, Birmingham
(248) 644-5832
Group of area residents concerned about achieving racial equality and ethnic diversity. Speakers and discussion topics are scheduled for the third Monday of the month from 8-9:30am. All interested people are welcome to join in the dialogues and discussions.

CHILDREN HELPING CHILDREN (CHC)
P.O. Box 250452, Franklin 48025
(248) 355-3119
Nada Dalgamouni, director
Multimedia and multicultural enrichment program in which local children from various international backgrounds perform at special events and on radio and TV to raise funds for institutions that help children victimized by various social issues and concerns. Annual telethon is held on United Nations Day in October. CHC promotes harmony, unity, understanding and peace by celebrating cultural diversity and teaching cultural heritage and folklore.

CULTURAL HERITAGE TASK FORCE
City of Detroit Cultural Affairs Dept.
1240 City-County Bldg., Detroit
(313) 224-3470
Representatives from ethnic communities and organizations meet to discuss ways to celebrate the Detroit area's rich and diverse cultural fabric.

DETROIT ORIENTATION INSTITUTE
656 W. Kirby, Detroit; (313) 577-5071
Elaine Driker, director
Activity of Wayne State University College of Urban, Labor and Metropolitan Affairs presents three-day seminar for newcomers and anyone wishing to learn more about the

region. Tour guides and speakers cover history, demographics and population diversity, issues and challenges.

ETHNIC ADVISORY COMMITTEE
City of Sterling Heights
(810) 977-6123 ext. 102
Community Relations Department produced series of brochures called "Getting to Know Your Neighbor," which share information about the culture and history of various nationalities represented in the community.

NATIONAL CONFERENCE FOR COMMUNITY AND JUSTICE
(formerly Interfaith Roundtable)
975 E. Jefferson, Detroit
(313) 567-6225
Non-profit human relations organization specializes in issues relating to diversity -- in schools, the work place and the community. Sponsors breakfast dialogues on the challenges and opportuntiies in a diverse work place; Any Town USA; Rearing Children of Good Will; American Arabic and Jewish Friends youth program, and Different People, Common Ground program.

INTERNATIONAL INSTITUTE OF METROPOLITAN DETROIT
111 E Kirby, Detroit; (313) 871-8600
Mon-Fri 8:30 am-5 pm. Founded in Detroit in 1919 to aid the wave of refugees who came to the area in the aftermath of World War I, the Institute continues to provide immigration and social services to the foreign born. Events and programs build understanding, appreciation and partnerships among diverse peoples that live in southeastern Michigan. (See Cultural Center Institutions.) Activities include International Dance Festival in April, the July 4 Swearing-in Ceremony of New Citizens, Ethnic Sundays, the All World Market in October and Noel Night in the University Cultural Center.

INTERNATIONAL VISITORS COUNCIL OF METROPOLITAN DETROIT
200 Renaissance Center - Suite 627
(313) 259-2680
Julie Oldani, executive director
Sponsors international visitors on short-term visits by arranging for home hospitality, field trips to industrial, scientific and educational facilities, sightseeing and participation in cultural and recreational events.

LAKES AREA COUNCIL FOR DIVERSITY
c/o Walled Lake Consolidated Schools
(248) 788-1062
Samantha Ruetenik, founder
Group made up of representatives from nine communities has a mission to create a community which values multiculturalism. Hosts three to five programs a year, including Martin Luther King breakfast in January and Multicultural Celebration in March.

MICHIGAN ETHNIC HERITAGE STUDIES CENTER
P.O. Box 806368
St. Clair Shores 48080-6368
(313) 886-5065
Multi-ethnic, community-based organization founded by ethnicity expert and professor of Political Science at Wayne State University, Otto Feinstein, to foster inter-ethnic cooperation and the understanding of ethnicity as a primary element in society and education. Produces directory of 2,000 ethnic organizations in Michigan. For information about programs, publications and broadcast activities, contact Germaine Strobel, director.

MELD (MULTICULTURAL EXPERIENCE IN LEADERSHIP DEVELOPMENT)
Center for Urban Studies
Wayne State University, Detroit
(313) 577-2208
Training program to cultivate understanding between leaders from diverse segments of the community. Year-long study involves cross-cultural collaborations emerging from interactive learning, cultural immersion, personal assessments and relationship building.

MULTICULTURAL/MULTIRACIAL COMMUNITY COUNCIL
Farmington Hills City Mgr. (248) 473-9500;
Farmington City Mgr. (248) 474-5500;
Farmington Public Schools (248) 489-3331
Council is dedicated to promoting awareness and acceptance of diversity. Conducts regularly scheduled forums and workshops of interest to entire community, which are broadcast on Community Access Channels 10 and 12.

NEW DETROIT COALITION
645 Griswold, Suite 2900, Detroit 48226
(313) 496-2000
Urban coalition and race relations organization serves as a resource for community-based groups and a catalyst for solving community problems. The Cultural Exchange Network of

its Task Force sponsors a series of cultural events to promote racial, ethnic and cultural inclusion. Also cultural immersion programs.

PALS INTERNATIONAL
900 Wilshire, Troy
(248) 362-2060
Cross-cultural consultation and language instruction.

MEDIA

Local libraries and video stores usually have a good selection of travel documentaries on video tape for rental. The superstores such as Borders and Barnes & Noble (see Yellow Pages for listings) carry vast selections of audio recordings, newspapers and magazines (and of course books) from around the world.

BOOK BEAT
26010 Greenfield, Oak Park
(248) 968-1190
Mon-Sat 10am-9pm, Sun 11am-6pm.
Multicultural books and gifts, exhibitions and special events.

INTERNATONAL BOOK CENTRE
2391 Auburn Rd., Shelby Twp.
(E of Dequindre)
(810) 254-7230
Mon-Sat 11am-5pm. World travelers, foreign-born area residents and foreign language teachers and students come here for books, magazines, cassettes, videos and computer software in dozens of languages. Owner Claudette Mukalla stocks posters, flag T-shirts, games, paper dolls, stickers, and other gift items from various cultures, as well as learning aids for English as a second language. To celebrate diversity, there are multicultural books on holidays and traditions, cooking and folktales.

PAPERBACKS UNLIMITED
22634 Woodward, Ferndale; (810) 546-3282
Mon-Sat 9am- 9pm, Sun 9am-4pm.
Large selection of magazines from around the world.

PRINT
NATIONAL GEOGRAPHIC SOCIETY
1145 17th Street N.W.
Washington, D.C. 20036
1-800-647-5463
Members receive 12 issues of *National Geographic,* at least 5 wall maps, as well as notification of many other programs and opportunities. Other products include *Traveler* magazine, *World* magazine (for kids), books, videos and interactive CDs. Annual dues $27. Website (with online store, forums and news updates): www.nationalgeographic.com.

DETROIT FREE PRESS
600 W. Fort, Detroit 48226
1-800-678-6400
and
DETROIT NEWS
615 W. Lafayette, Detroit 48226
(313) 222-6400
Detroit's two main dailies offer extensive calendars of events weekly with updates on folk performances, festivals, concerts, restaurants, jazz and blues clubs. Frequent articles with ethnic focus.

HOUR DETROIT
117 W. Third St., Royal Oak
(810) 691-1800
Glossy bi-monthly covers arts, events, dining and more.

METRO PARENT
24567 Northwestern Hwy., Ste 150, Southfield
(248) 352-0990
Monthly tabloid Includes Family Fun Guide with events calendar. Available free at 800 locations throughout metro Detroit or by paid subscription.

METRO TIMES
733 St. Antoine, Detroit; (313) 961-4060
Weekly, distributed free at many restaurants and bookstores or available by subscription. Restaurant (categorized by type of cuisine and location) and entertainment guide combined with thought-provoking editorial. Extensive listing of Blues, Jazz and Folk Music performances.

MICHIGAN HISTORY MAGAZINE
Department of State, 717 W. Allegan
Lansing, MI 48918-1805
1-800-366-3703

Published since 1917, colorful 56-page bi-monthly tells the stories of Michigan people and their impact on their communities, the nation and the world.

MICHIGAN DANCE CALENDAR

A listing of virtually all the dance events in Michigan. Send a SASE to the address below. Send three or more SASE's to get each calendar as it comes out.
Dance Calendar; c/o Joan Hellmann
208 Murray, Ann Arbor, MI 48103

The following local news-papers offer features, updates and listings of multicultural interest:

DAILY TRIBUNE
(south Oakland County); (248) 541-3000

MACOMB DAILY
(Macomb County); (810) 469-4510

THE MIRROR
(south Oakland County); (248) 546-4900

NEWS HERALD
(southern Wayne County); (313) 246-0800

OAKLAND PRESS
(north Oakland County); (248) 745-4510

OBSERVER/ECCENTRIC
(Oakland and western Wayne Counties)
(734) 591-2300

SPINAL COLUMN
(western Oakland County); (248) 360-6397

TROY-SOMERSET GAZETTE
(Troy, Rochester Hills, Farmington Hills)
(248) 542-4868

RADIO

CBC-FM (89.9), Windsor
(519) 255-3411
Classical and culturally diverse programming CBC, Canadian Public Radio

CJAM-FM (91.5), Windsor
(519) 971-3630
Alternative music, talk, ethnic.

WDET-FM (101.9)
(313) 577-4146
World music, folk, bluegrass, jazz, eclectic mix. Public radio.

WDTR-FM (90.9), Detroit
(313) 596-3507
Educational, international music

WUOM-FM (91.7), Ann Arbor
(734) 764-9210
World news from the BBC, multicultural programming.

WNZK-AM (680/690), Southfield
(248) 557-3500
"Station of the Nations" airs ethnic and multi-language programming.

WPON-AM (1460), Bloomfield Hills
(248) 332-8883
Some ethnic programs included in lineup.

WYUR-AM (1310), Bloomfield Twp.
(248) 433-9987
Classical music from 7pm-5am.

TELEVISION

Cable TV has a wide range of multicul-tural programming, including foreign-language programs, films and travel documentaries. Check the program guide.

WTVS Channel 56 (Detroit)
(313) 873-7200
Regular broadcasts of global interest, including National Geographic specials and ethnic cooking. Call for information or how to receive *Signal,* the monthly publication of schedules and news. Website: *www.tvs.org*

MICHIGAN MAGAZINE
P.O. Box 503, Rose City MI 48654
(517) 685-2634
Regular broadcasts on PBS channels 56 and 28 (check program guide). Travels throughout Michigan visiting places like The Irish Baker in Dearborn Print magazine available as well. Website: *www.michiganmagazine.com*

ETHNIC HERITAGE ROOMS AT WSU
www.langlab.wayne.edu/ethnicrms/Ethnic-Rooms.html

UNIVERSITY OF MICHIGAN MUSEUM OF ANTHROPOLOGY
www.umma.lsa.umich.edu
Makes images and information about selected collections from the Museum holdings available: Ethnology, Ethnobotany, Asian, Great Lakes, North America, Old World, New World, and Physical.

UM MUSEUMS
www.umma.lsa.umich.edu/Sites/UM_Museums.html

DISTANT CARAVANS
Online catalog of ethnic costumes and accessories E-mail address: barb@distant-car

HOW FAR IS IT?
www.indo.com/distance
Maps and distances between any two places in the world; links to Mapquest which gives detailed driving directions and map.

ONLINE DICTIONARIES
www.facstaff.bucknell.edu/rbeard/diction.html
Interactive dictionaries and translations for over 200 languages, from Ancient Greek to Vulcan.

For local updates of events, restaurants, broadcasts, etc., try these web sites:

CITY NET DETROIT
www.city.net/countries/united_states/michigan/detroit

DETROIT CITY LINKS
usacitylink.com//detroit

DETROIT DOWNLOAD CENTRAL
www.ddc.com

DETROIT EVENTS CALENDAR
www.quando.com

DETROIT FREENET
http://detroit.freenet.org

DETROIT FREE PRESS
www.freep.com

DETROIT METRO GUIDE
www.metroguide.com

DETROIT MUSEUMS ON THE NET
www.detroitnews.com/museums.htm

DETROIT NEWS
detnews.com/TDNHOME/tdnhome.htm

MDCVB
www.visitdetroit.com

METRO TIMES
www.metrotimes.com
Extensive dining and entertainment guide.

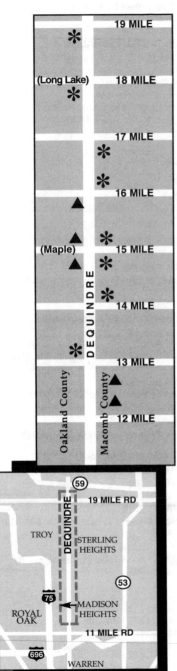

✱ More than one shop

[E-F/1-3] Some of the most culturally diverse communities in metro Detroit are in the northeast suburbs. Dequindre, which starts in Hamtramck and follows the path of I-75 northward, becomes the Oakland/Macomb county line north of Eight Mile. Shopping plazas with ethnic groceries, restaurants and boutiques have cropped up all along Dequindre in Warren, Madison Heights, Sterling Heights and Troy. This tour covering the stretch from 12 Mile to 19 Mile provides a glimpse of European, Asian and Middle Eastern cultures, including Italian, Polish, British, Lebanese, Indian, Chinese, Korean and Filipino.

If you travel north past 12 Mile in Warren, you'll find **Produce Palace International**, an Italian marketplace with produce, wine and food imports, on the east side. A little farther up is the **Commonwealth Club**, where local Brits gather.

In Madison Heights at 13 Mile, Dequindre Plaza on the southwest corner has several Asian enterprises: **Sampaguita Bakery** (Filipino), **Pho Hang Restaurant** (Vietnamese/Chinese), **Asia Market** (Thai, Loatian, Chinese, Korean, Filipino and Vietnamese) and **Asia Video**.

A Chinese cluster at Washington Plaza on the northeast corner of 14 Mile features **Far East Trader Ginseng, Herbs and Tea**, **China Garden** restaurant and **Ocean King Seafood & Oriental Grocery**. Farther north at Melody Plaza is **King's Quality Bakery** (33878) with a selection of European and Mid-Eastern pastries and French bread.

The intersection of Dequindre and 15 Mile (Maple) in Sterling Heights has an even more diverse selection. The plaza on the southeast side includes **India Grocers**, **Rajmahal Restaurant** and **Messina's Meats**, as well as Korean businesses: **Hana Oriental Mart** and **Shin Sung** restaurant. The **Polish Market** is on Maple across from the the **American Polish Cultural Center** on the Troy side of Dequindre. The northeast corner of Dequindre and Maple features the **Mid-East Pastry** shop, **Beirut Palace** restaurant and **Arabic Town** grocery, as well as **Seoul Garden** Korean restaurant and **Weldon's Pasties**.

At 16 Mile, **Asia Market** (26949) is on the southwest corner. Crystal Square on the northeast corner includes **Ho Wah Chinese Restaurant, C&L Oriental Market** and **La Petite Pastry**. Sunny Plaza, also on the northeast side, has a cluster of Indian shops: **New Delhi Cuisine**, **Ruby Jewelers**, **Patel Bros. Grocery**, **Bombay Video** and **L&S Fashions**. **Pi's Thai Cuisine**, **Al-Almeer Restaurant** and **Jouni Halal Meats** add to the corner's ethnic diversity.

Continue to 17 Mile and on the southeast side, you'll find Franklin Square with Indian and Middle Eastern groceries (**Laxmi Foods** and **International Foods**), as well as the **Old Country Deli** (Polish).

Hassan Brothers Meat Market (Middle Eastern) and **Jung Won Oriental Mart** are located on Long Lake (18 Mile) on the southwest corner of Dequindre.

Finally, Gabriel Plaza on the southwest corner of 19 Mile (Square Lake) in Troy has an Asian/Filipino market called **Taste of Manila** and **Gabriel Imports & Meat Market**, with food specialties from Europe and the Middle East.

[E-F/4-5] Bordered by the New Center Area/Fisher Theatre and downtown Detroit, the Cultural Center encompasses the most creative and stimulating environment in the metropolitan Detroit area. A major resource for the city, the state of Michigan and the Midwest region, this district is widely recognized for the premiere arts, education and health care institutions, including the prestigious **Detroit Institute of Arts, Wayne State University, the Center for Creative Studies (CCS)** and the **Detroit Medical Center.**

The **Detroit Historical Museum, International Institute, Detroit Public Library, Children's Museum, Detroit Science Center** and the **Charles H. Wright Museum of African American History** combine with others to create a culturally rich district in the heart of the city.

For a brochure with map and listings of restaurants shops, galleries, organizations and events, contact the University Cultural Center Association, 4735 Cass, Detroit 48202; (313) 577-5088. The website address for the UCAA area guide is www.dia.org/ucca/areaguide.html

For information on specific activities, contact the individual institutions.

Directions: The University Cultural Center Area is bounded by the Lodge Expressway on the west, I-94 on the north and I-75 on the east and south.

From Downtown: take Woodward 2 miles north.

From I-75: Exit Warren, go west 4 blocks to Woodward.

From I-94: Exit Woodward/John R, go south 3 blocks.

From US-10: Exit Warren/Forest, go east 3 blocks to Woodward.

Parking:

● Underground garage at Woodward and Farnsworth for DIA and other museums.

● Parking lot on John R, between CCS Institute for Music & Dance and the Scarab Club.

● Parking lot on Cass between Warren and Forest for proximity to restaurant and WSU campus.

● Lots designated for visitor parking on campus.

● Lot on Frederick Douglass between John R and Brush for sites east of Woodward.

● Metered street-parking.

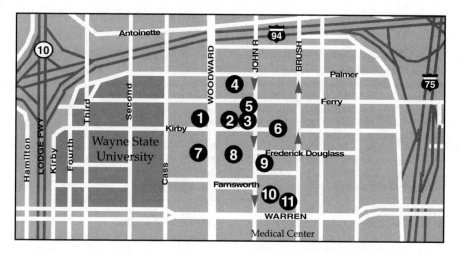

1. Detroit Historical Museum
2. Children's Museum
3. International Institute
4. Merrill Palmer Institute
5. Your Heritage House
6. Center for Creative Studies/ Institute for Music and Dance

7. Detroit Public Library
8. Detroit Institute of Arts
9. Scarab Club
10. Detroit Science Center
11. Charles H. Wright Museum of African American History

CULTURAL CENTER MUSEUMS

CHILDREN'S MUSEUM
67 E. Kirby, Detroit; (313) 873-8100
Exhibits open weekdays 1-4pm, Sat (Oct-May only) 9am-4pm Admission: free. In addition to cultural exhibits featuring Native American, Indonesian and African artifacts, museum offers field trip programs, group tours, Saturday/vacation day activities and outreach and loans. Heritage and geography program covers African, Asian, European, Latin American, Middle Eastern and Native American cultures.

DETROIT HISTORICAL MUSEUM
5401 Woodward at Kirby
(313) 833-1805
Wed-Fri 9:30 am-5 pm. Weekends 10 am-5pm. Admission: suggested $3 adults, $2

seniors, $1 children. Free on Wed. Exhibits on Detroit's growth from Indian days to present include "Frontiers to Factories: Detroit at Work, 1701 to 1901," "Motor City Exhibition" on the auto industry, "Doorway to Freedom" about the Underground Railroad, and "Streets of Old Detroit," plus galleries with vintage automobiles, model railroads, toys and historic costumes.

DETROIT INSTITUTE OF ARTS
5200 Woodward
(313) 833-7900
Wed-Fri 11 am-4 pm, Sat-Sun 11 am-5 pm. Admission: suggested $4 adults, $1 children. World-class art collection with holdings ranging from prehistoric art to sculpture of the late 20th century. Galleries are devoted to American, African, Ancient World, Asian, European, Middle Eastern and Native American art.

DETROIT SCIENCE CENTER
5020 John R (at Warren), Detroit
(313) 577-8400
Mon-Fri 9:30am-2pm, Sat, Sun 12:30pm-5pm.
Admission $6.50 adults, $4 seniors and ages
4-12. Hours subject to change; extended hours
are available during the summer, holidays, and
in conjunction with special events and traveling
exhibits. Exhibit Hall contains special displays,
laser program and hands-on exhibits. Also
IMAX Dome Theater shows, Discovery Theater
science demonstrations and gift shop. For kids
on the net, the DSC has a fun page: Cyber-
space www.sciencedetroit.org/safari.html

INTERNATIONAL INSTITUTE
111 E Kirby, Detroit; (313) 871-8600
Mon-Fri 8:30am-5 pm. Hall of Nations exhibit
features 2,000 dolls from around the world.
Gift shop and café.

CHARLES H. WRIGHT MUSEUM OF
AFRICAN AMERICAN HISTORY
315 E. Warren, Detroit; (313) 494-5800
Tue-Sun 9:30am-5pm. Admission Adults $3,
Children (12 and under) $2. Dedicated to the
preservation and presentation of African and
African American history and culture. New
museum encompasses 120,000 square feet
of expanded exhibition galleries, orientation
theater, classrooms, multi-purpose rooms,
library, and museum shop. *(See Tour in*
African American chapter.)

YOUR HERITAGE HOUSE
110 E. Ferry, Detroit; (313) 871-1667
(Call for appointment.)
Mon-Fri 1-5pm. Historic home serves as
museum and fine arts center for youth. Programs include African American heritage and
international themes.

CULTURAL CENTER
RESTAURANTS

KRESGE COURT CAFE &
AMERICAN GRILLE
Detroit Institute of Arts
5200 Woodward, Detroit; (313) 833-1857
Wed-Fri 11am-3pm, Sat-Sun 11:30am-
4:30pm. Kresge Court is a cafeteria line for
lunch, snacks, desserts and beverages,
including wines and beers, with seating in
Italian Renaissance courtyard. The **American**
Grille is full-service for lunch and Sunday
brunch. Call for reservations.

MAJESTIC CAFE
4140 Woodward Ave., Detroit
(313) 833-0120
Mon & Sat 4:30pm-2am, Tue-Fri 11am-
2am, Sun 11:30am-2am. Features *tapas*
(Spanish appetizers to share), European
and American specialties. Original art on
brick walls and huge windows looking out
on Woodward.

SMALL WORLD CAFE
111 E. Kirby, Detroit; (313) 871-8600
Mon-Fri 11am-2pm. Cafeteria on lower level
of International Institute serves ethnic specialties at lunchtime.

TRAFFIC JAM & SNUG
511 Canfield, Detroit; (313) 831-9470
Mon 11-3pm, Tues-Wed 11am-9pm, Thurs
11am-10:30pm, Fri 11am-midnight,
Sat 5pm-midnight. Creative, international
menu. Freshly baked bread, house-brewed
beer and homemade cheeses and specialty
desserts.

TWINGO'S
4710 Cass Ave., Detroit; (313) 832-3832
Mon-Thu 11am-10pm, Fri-Sat 10am-midnight,
Sun noon-11pm. French café just south of
WSU campus serves baguettes, salads,
soups, quiches and desserts. Live music at
night.

CULTURAL CENTER
INSTITUTIONS

DETROIT PUBLIC LIBRARY
MAIN BRANCH
5201 Woodward and Kirby, Detroit
(313) 833-1000
Tues, Thurs, Fri, Sat 9:30am-5:30pm;
Wed 1-9pm. Burton Historical Collection for
genealogical research, Azalia Hackley
Collection of African Americans in the performing arts, National Automotive History
Collection, and an extensive map collection
of special interest. Impressive Italian Renaissance building has murals of events from
Detroit's early history and beginnings of auto
industry.

CENTER FOR CREATIVE STUDIES
2435 E. Kirby, Detroit; (313) 872-3118
Undergraduate and graduate school for fine arts and liberal arts is noted for its industrial design, graphic communications, multimedia and photography programs. Affiliated Institute of Music and Dance offers community education classes in the performing arts.

WAYNE STATE UNIVERSITY
Detroit 48202; (313) 577-2424
One of the nation's leading urban research universities and the most comprehensive educational institution in the metro area is situated on a 184-acre campus in the Cultural Center. WSU offers 350 major subjects areas, 100 master's programs, 60 doctoral programs and 20 specialist programs.

WSU ETHNIC HERITAGE ROOMS
Alex Manoogian Hall
906 W. Warren; (313) 577-3500
A tangible monument to the world cultures represented by the student body and the community at large are the ethnic rooms that serve as classrooms, auditoriums, student and faculty lounges. They include **African American** (Rm 91), **Arabic** (Rm 105), **Chinese** (Rm 112), **Polish** (Rm 113), **Greek** (Rm 171), **Hungarian** (Rm 280), **Lithuanian** (Rm 288), **Armenian** (Rm 226), **Romanian** (Rm 408), **French** (Rm 480), **Japanese** (Rm 597), **Ukranian** (Rm 297). For more information about viewing the rooms or facility rentals, contact Wayne State University Office for Community Relations at (313) 577-2246.

CULTURAL CENTER EVENTS

MONTHLY
HUDSON'S FIRST FRIDAYS AT THE DIA
The Detroit Institute of Arts presents Friday night programming until 9pm the first Friday of each month. Enjoy art, music, entertainment, film, dining and more. Programs are free with museum admission. Call (313) 833-7900.

FEBRUARY
BLACK HISTORY MIONTH
Special exhibits and programs at museums and Main Branch of Detroit Public Library are scheduled throughout the month of February. Call individual institutions or UCCA at (313) 577-5088.

APRIL
INTERNATIONAL DANCE FESTIVAL
International Institute hosts annual dance festival presenting top folk dance groups from local ethnic communities. (313) 871-8600.

MAY
MUSEUM MONTH programs and events encourage metro Detroiters to discover the treasures of Cultural Center museums. Call individual museums for details.
The University Cultural Center Association museums and their neighbors also host **Family Day** in mid-May. Admission is free at participating museums on that Sunday.
Call UCCA at (313) 577-5088 or museums.

JULY
SWEARING-IN CEREMONY of new citizens is annual tradition conducted by the International Institute on July 4. Call (313) 871-8600.

SEPTEMBER
DETROIT FESTIVAL OF THE ARTS, sponsored by the University Cultural Center Association (UCCA), is held the third weekend in September throughout the 15-block area of the Cultural Center. Festivities include performing, visual and literary arts. A **Children's Fair** is staged on the WSU campus with dance, theatrical and musical performances, as well as a youth arts market, booths and demonstrations. Call (313) 577-5088.

OCTOBER
INTERNATIONAL FAIR
Wayne State University Student Activities Center sponsors a multicultural fair in October. Call (313) 577-2980.

ALL-WORLD MARKET
International Institute holds its annual bazaar in mid-October at the Southfield Civic Center. Shopping booths offer crafts and imports from around the world. Every hour a different international performing group is featured on stage. Call (313) 871-8600.

DECEMBER
NOEL NIGHT
Holiday event in the University Cultural Center features an evening in early December from 4-9pm of joyous singing and cheer. Also, carriage rides, children's activities, arts and crafts, and other Yuletide treats, in addition to holiday music and song. Call (313) 577-2980.

CULTURAL CENTER ART EXHIBITS & SHOWS

CENTER FOR CREATIVE STUDIES GALLERIES at the Park Shelton (115 E. Kirby) is open Tue-Sat 10 am-5 pm. with rotating exhibits of student work. Call (313) 874-1955.

DETROIT INSTITUTE OF ARTS (5200 Woodward) presents special exhibitions at various times of the year and offers related lectures and workshops. Call (313) 833-7900.

MUSEUM OF AFRICAN AMERICAN HISTORY (315 E. Warren) presents special exhibits in changing gallery. Call (313) 494-5800 for schedule.

SCARAB CLUB (217 E. Farnsworth), a local artists' collective with work and exhibition space, has showings certain times of the year. Call (313) 831-1250.

WSU COMMUNITY ARTS GALLERY (150 Art Building) periodically presents special exhibits from around the world. Call (313) 577-2400.

TOUR — WSU CAMPUS

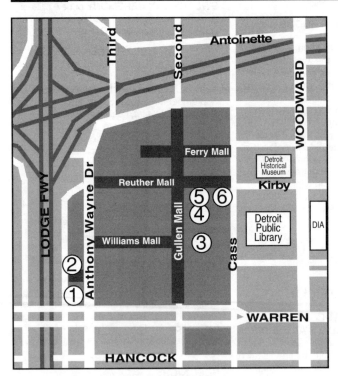

1. Alex Manoogian Hall
2. St. Andrew's
3. De Roy Auditorium and Prentiss Hall
4. Kresge Library
5. Purdy Library
6. Reuther Library

Begin your tour on the west side of the Wayne State University campus at **Alex Manoogian Hall** *at W. Warrren and Anthony Wayne Drive,* where a number of **ethnic heritage** classrooms, lecture halls and study lounges are decorated in the style of a particular country.

An index in the main lobby of **Manoogian Hall** will direct you to the rooms. Don't miss the **Polish Room** *(Rm 113)* with beautiful tile mosaics, carved wood and stained glass. Next door is the **Arab Room** *(Rm 105)* with arches, cultural displays and a worship area. The **Chinese classroom** *(Rm 112)* across the hall is furnished in the Ming tradition and includes a wall mural from a handscroll by Sung Dynasty artist Hsia Kuei titled "Pure and Remote View of Streams and Mountains."

On the lower level, the **African Room** *(Rm 91)* features ceremonial scenes on carved wooden entrance doors, African national flags on a wall mural and showcases for exhibits.

On the second floor, rustic wood flooring adds authenticity to the **Hungarian classroom** *(Rm 280)* with beamed ceiling, carved woodwork, intricate and colorful flower trim and an historical mural. Around the back corridor is the **Ukrainian Room** *(Rm 297)*, containing a wall map with examples from folk art, crafts, folklore, architecture, education and history. The **Armenian Room** *(Rm 226)* is a small auditorium furnished with Armenian wood carvings, murals and portraits.

As you leave Manoogian Hall, look across the courtyard to the large white columns lining the wall of the **Italian Room** in the General Lectures Building. Walk in front of **St. Andrew's**, an English Gothic style church, to take the diagonal sidewalk that veers south to the Anthony Wayne Drive crosswalk. Then go straight into Williams Mall and continue to Gullen Mall. Look across the mall and see **De Roy Auditorium** surrounded by a reflecting pool and beautiful landscaping, and **Prentiss Hall** behind it, both designed by Japanese-American designer Minoru Yamasaki. Another ethnic American, Suren Pilafian, of Armenian descent, won a competition for a campus design plan in 1942. Turn left at Gullen Mall and walk north to see on your right the sweeping horizontal lines and cantilevered upper stories of his design for the **Kresge Science Library** *(5408 Gullen Mall)* and the **G. Flint Purdy Library** *(5244 Gullen Mall)*. The **WSU Folklore Archives,** illustrating the diversity of folk traditions in Detroit, is on the fourth floor. At the **Walter P. Reuther Library of Labor and Urban Affairs**, to the northeast, view special exhibits in the first floor lobby or explore the **Michigan Dance Archives, UAW Labor Archives** or **WSU Black History Collection.**

WSU NEIGHBORS

Cross Cass Avenue to enter the Main Branch of the **Detroit Public Library** (DPL). This Italian Renaissance building features 16th century Italian styling with rich, coffered ceilings on the second floor and wall murals of events from the early history of Detroit, as well as the world's great authors, musicians and artists. *(See DPL listing about special collections.)*

To the north of the library is the **Detroit Historical Museum** and across Woodward is the **Detroit Institute of Arts**. Continue your tour with a visit to a museum or a dining experience. Lunch is served weekdays at the **Small World Café** in the **International Institute** *(111 E. Kirby)* and Wednesday through Sunday in the **Kresge Court Café** and **American Grille** at the DIA. Popular restaurants in the WSU campus area include **Twingo's Café** *(4710 Cass)* and **Traffic Jam & Snug** *(511 W. Canfield)*. On campus is **The Gallery Shop** *(Community Arts Building, Reuther Mall and Cass)* for sandwiches and snacks, weekdays.

SUMMER IN THE CITY

Few cities know how to throw a party like Detroit. Throughout the summer, the Motor City and its suburbs celebrate the area's rich heritage with a series of ethnic festivals.

DOWNTOWN RIVERFRONT FESTIVALS

[E-F/4-5] Downtown Detroit has a long-standing tradition of ethnic festivals on the riverfront. Each year, Hart Plaza attracts thousands of spectators and exhibitors who come together to celebrate diverse backgrounds. Lively events include dancing, special demonstrations of cultural traditions and ethnic imports. The following festivals are included:

> **JULY** Latino World, Ribs 'n' Soul, Afro-American Music, Arab World
>
> **AUGUST** Fiesta Mexicanz, Caribbean International, African World

For more information, call the Detroit Recreation Department's special events line at (313) 877-8077.

Getting there: Take I-75, the Lodge Freeway (U.S. 10) or Woodward downtown to East Jefferson. Hart Plaza is just west of the Renaissance Center on the riverfront.

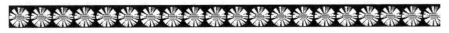

WYANDOTTE

[D-E/5-6] Wyandotte, to the south of Detroit, celebrates the diversity of its community with a series of ethnic festivals at Yack Arena that run April through August. The schedule of events includes:

> **APRIL** Italian Festival
>
> **MAY** Mexican Festival
>
> **JUNE** German Festival, Hungarian Festival
>
> **JULY** Czech and Slovak Festival

For more information, call the Yack Arena events line at (313) 246-4515 or the Wyandotte Recreation Department at (313) 246-4490.

Getting there: Yack Arena is at 246 Sycamore in downtown Wyandotte, one block west of Biddle and one block north of Eureka. From I-75, take Eureka Road (Exit 36) east 4.3 miles to Third Street and turn left. From Detroit, take Fort Street south to Eureka Road, or connect with Fort Street from the Southfield Freeway (M-39).

STERLING HEIGHTS

[E-F/2-3] Sterling Heights is home to a large concentration of residents of Italian and Polish descent. Not surprisingly, those nationalities host summer festivals, as do other ethnic groups that are represented in the community. Freedom Hill Park is the site for the following events:

JUNE Macedonian Festival, *Calabria Festival, *Lebanese Festival

JULY Polish Festival, German Volk Fest, *Slovene Polka Fest

AUGUST Italian Days, German Days

* not annual

For more information, call Freedom Hill Park at (810) 979-7010.

Getting there: Freedom Hill Park is off Metropolitan Parkway (16 Mile) between Schoenherr and Utica Roads. Take I-75 to the Big Beaver (16 Mile) exit and go east about nine miles. Or take I-696 to Van Dyke and go north five miles to Metro Parkway; turn right and go east 2-1/2 miles.

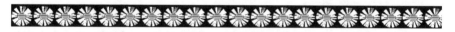

The summer lineup also features international fairs–Carrousel of Nations in June in Windsor, the International Ethnic Festival in July in Pontiac and the Multi-Ethnic Cultural Festival in August in Warren.

CARROUSEL OF NATIONS

[E-F/4-5] During two weekends in June, more than 30 ethnic groups in Ontario gather to celebrate their heritage and set up individual "villages" featuring dance groups, music, crafts, displays and food. Nationalities represented range from Afri-Canadian and British to Filipino, Irish, Scottish, Serbian and Vietnamese. Some of the largest—and most fun, according to a festival spokesperson—include the Greek, Ukrainian and Caribbean villages. Events take place across the city.

For dates and locations, call the Multicultural Council of Windsor at (519) 255-1127.

Getting there: Take the Detroit-Windsor Tunnel or the Ambassador Bridge to Windsor. Get specific directions to the villages of your choice from the festival brochure map available at tourist information centers and Windsor casinos.

INTERNATIONAL ETHNIC FESTIVAL

[D-E/1-2] Recognizing the blend of many ethnic nationalities in the community, Pontiac Growth Group launched an international festival in 1996. Now an annual event, the downtown celebration over the July 4th weekend at Phoenix Plaza features Independence Day fireworks, as well as a Caribbean parade, traditional dances and foods of each culture, and games for young and old. Nationalities represented include African, Albanian, German, Irish, Italian, Mexican, Pacific Rim countries, Puerto Rican and Polish.

For further information, call Pontiac Growth Group at (248) 857-5603.

Getting there: Take Woodward or M-59 to Wide Track Drive in downtown Pontiac.

MULTI-ETHNIC CULTURAL FESTIVAL

[E-F/3-4] The Warren Multi-Ethnic Cultural Festival is a three-day event in mid-to-late August at Halmich Park on 13 Mile Road. Polish, Italian, German, Ukrainian, British, Irish and Native American groups participate, showcasing their music, dance, crafts and food. One of the main events is an adult and youth soccer tournament attracting 100 teams from ethnic clubs and the Michigan Youth Soccer Association.

For further information, contact the Warren City Council at (810) 574-4950 or Walter Ozog at (810) 751-8168.

Getting there: Halmich Park is on 13 Mile Road between Ryan and Dequindre, north of I-696.

✔ *School districts and city parks and recreation departments can be good sources of information about other multicultural fairs. Watch for announcements about fairs held annually in Troy (fall) and West Bloomfield (spring).*

Few people can resist a festival. With lively music and dancing, great food and exciting activities, festivals encourage us to celebrate life and the people and events that have shaped our world.

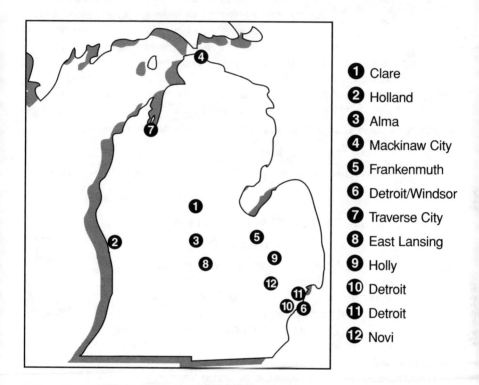

1. Clare
2. Holland
3. Alma
4. Mackinaw City
5. Frankenmuth
6. Detroit/Windsor
7. Traverse City
8. East Lansing
9. Holly
10. Detroit
11. Detroit
12. Novi

MICHIGAN'S TOP FESTIVALS

Many ethnic and heritage festivals take place throughout the state. These events celebrate the diversity of our people, exhibit our pride in the past and allow us to pass the stories and traditions of one generation to the next, ensuring their survival. From a border birthday bash in Detroit to a hearty Bavarian Fest in Frankenmuth, they honor our ancestors and the immigrant in all of us.

Here's a chronological list of some of Michigan's most popular annual ethnic events. Dates vary from year to year, so be sure to call ahead for current information. (For Detroit's series of summer ethnic festivals, see "Multicultural Detroit" chapter.)

❶ IRISH FESTIVAL
MARCH *in* CLARE

Irish eyes, along with everyone else's, are smilin' during this week-long March salute to the Emerald Isle. This town in the middle of the state was named in the 1800s by an Irish surveyor after his ancestral homeland in Ireland's County Clare.

Join in the wearin' o' the green in activities that include an hour-long parade, marching bands, an arts and crafts show, and even a leprechaun contest. If you're looking for a little exercise, you can join in a toe-tappin' Irish jig or hoof a few miles in the 5K road race.

The landmark Doherty Hotel and other city restaurants participate with authentic Irish cuisine, including corned beef and cabbage, Irish stew and, of course, green beer. *(Also see "Ireland.")*

Contact the Clare Chamber of Commerce, 609 McEwan St., Clare, MI 48617; call (517) 386-2442.

Getting there: Clare is about 70 miles north of Lansing, at the intersection of U.S. 27 and 10. From Detroit, take I-75 north to Bay City; from Bay City, take U.S. 10 west to Clare.

❷ TULIP TIME FESTIVAL
MAY *in* HOLLAND

Visit this West Michigan city in mid-May and you're in for a real Dutch treat. That's when the more than six million bulbs that make up eight miles of tulips burst into bloom to welcome spring and one of the most popular annual events in the state. A 1927 suggestion from a local high school biology teacher is responsible for what today ranks as one of the largest historic and ethnic festivals in the nation.

The city, which is 25 miles west of Grand Rapids, was settled by a group of religious dissenters from the Netherlands. Headed for Wisconsin, they were stranded during the harsh winter of 1846 and welcomed in Michigan, where they settled near Black Lake.

The 10-day festival revolves around the area's Dutch history and heritage. Three parades, more than 50 high-stepping high school bands, some 4,000 costumed street sweepers and a charming children's parade—where 5,000 of the area's youngest residents dress up in authentic Dutch costumes—are some of the highlights. There are also more than 1,700 Klompen dancers who entertain daily, big-name entertainment and ethnic cuisine such as bankets (almond-filled pastries) and metwurst (sausage).

Contact the festival at 171 Lincoln Ave., Holland, MI 49423; call 1-800-822-2770.

Getting there: From Detroit, take I-96 west to Grand Rapids; then take I-196 southwest to Holland.

(Also see "Michigan Towns" chapter.)

❸ HIGHLAND FESTIVAL & GAMES
MEMORIAL DAY WEEKEND *in* ALMA

The haunting wail of bagpipes draws visitors from all over the United States to Alma College each Memorial Day weekend. Round up the clan and head for this town about 40 miles north of Lansing. For three days, the campus is transformed into one of the largest Celtic celebrations this side of the Atlantic with music, dance, children's entertainment, athletic competitions and more.

Ever wanted to toss a caber? Here's your chance. Compete in the caber, sheaf, stone and hammer events or join in one of the most Scottish of sports in the Highland Invitational Golf Tournament at nearby Pine River Country Club.

If you prefer to be a spectator, there's plenty to look at. Check out the annual Parade of Tartans and the pipers, drummers and fiddlers from all over the world who congregate here. Watch Scottish dancers perform the traditional Highland fling, Scottish reel, sword dance or the sailor's horn-pipe. Trace your family roots at the Gathering of the Clans, and pick up a colorful tartan kilt or other Scottish-style craft. Afterward, indulge in some hearty Scottish specialties such as crusty meat pies and full-bodied ale.

Contact the Gratiot Area Chamber of Commerce
P.O. Box 516, Alma, MI 48801; call (517) 463-5525.

Getting there: From Detroit, take I-96 west to Lansing; then take U.S. 27 north to Alma.

❹ COLONIAL MICHILIMACKINAC PAGEANT
MEMORIAL DAY WEEKEND *in* MACKINAW CITY

British and Native American heritages take center stage during this popular Memorial Day weekend event at old Fort Michilimackinac by the Big Mac Bridge. The pageant commemorates the event known as Pontiac's Rebellion, in which the Ottawa, unhappy over the departure of the French, attempted (but failed) to take over the fort.

Today, participants costumed as Native Americans and British soldiers reenact the 1763 surprise attack, which was an attempt by the tribes to delay the European settlement of their lands in the Great Lakes. Guides in period dress assume the roles of those involved in the attack and explain life in the 18th century fort.

Contact the Mackinaw City Chamber of Commerce at
P.O. Box 856, Mackinaw City, MI 49701; call (616) 436-5574.

Getting there: From Detroit, take I-75 north about 250 miles.

❺ BAVARIAN FESTIVAL
JUNE *in* FRANKENMUTH

Frankenmuth, the town 80 miles north of Detroit known as Michigan's Little Bavaria, rolls out the *wilkommen* mat, and more than 600 barrels of beer, during its annual celebration of its German heritage. You're sure to come away with a feeling of warmth and friendship known as *gemeütlichkeit.*

The Franconians landed in the area in 1845 in hopes of converting the Native American Indian to the Lutheran faith. Unsuccessful, they turned to the region's rich farmland for sustenance.

Today, the town is best known for its all-you-can-eat chicken dinners and for its annual Oktoberfest-style festival celebrated each June and again in October. Conducted on the grounds of Heritage Park, it attracts thousands of spectators, many dressed in traditional dirndls and lederhosen, who meet to high-step to some of the best polka bands in the nation. In the German Show Tent, savor the German-style cuisine—including flaky pastries, plump bratwurst, homemade pretzels and locally brewed beer—or mingle with the crowds in the award-winning Bavarian Festival parade.

Other attractions include the Kinder Platz, where youngsters can watch street performers including jugglers, clowns and magicians; antique and craft shows; and what's billed as the "World's Largest Chicken Dance."

Contact the Bavarian Festival at 635 S. Main St., Frankenmuth, MI 48734; call 1-800-FUN FEST.

Getting there: From Detroit, take I-75 north to exit 136, between Flint and Saginaw. Follow signs seven miles to Frankenmuth..

(Also see "Michigan Towns" chapter.)

❻ INTERNATIONAL FREEDOM FESTIVAL
JULY *in* DETROIT/WINDSOR

The U.S.-Canadian border along the Great Lakes, set by the Rush-Bagot Agreement of 1817, is the longest unfortified frontier in the world.

Each summer, this peaceful proximity is celebrated by an estimated four million people in Detroit and its sister community of Windsor, Ontario, during an annual border bash that celebrates two birthdays: American Independence Day and Canada Day.

More than 100 free events, including the largest fireworks display in North America, are offered on both sides of the Detroit River, in Detroit's Hart Plaza and Windsor's Dieppe Park. Join in the fun by participating in a zany bed race or a tomahawk throw. Or lend a hand when the Americans take on the Canadians in a tug-of-war across the river.

Tugboat races, demonstrations by the U.S. and Canadian Coast Guards, entertainment by the Big Apple Circus and more make this one of the largest free events in the area. The festival has a serious side, too: It concludes with the swearing-in ceremonies for hundreds of new U.S. citizens.

Contact the Freedom Festival at 9600 Mt. Elliott, Detroit, MI 48211; call (313) 923-7400.

Getting there: Take I-75, U.S. 10 (Lodge Freeway) or Woodward downtown to East Jefferson. Windsor's Dieppe Park is on Riverside Drive West.

❼ NATIONAL CHERRY FESTIVAL
JULY *in* TRAVERSE CITY

A s American as...cherry pie? After visiting this All-American festival, you'll be convinced that life is just a bowl of cherries, after all. This "very cherry" event is one of the most popular attractions in the state and, with 70 years under its belt, one of its oldest. For a week in mid-July, this area known as "the cherry capital of the world" celebrates its bounty with parades, arts and crafts, fireworks, big-name entertainment and plates and plates of cherry-inspired cuisine.

Sample everything from cherry chicken casserole to cherry bran chewies, sing along at nightly concerts, shop for arts and crafts, tour cherry orchards or turn your eyes skyward during the air show featuring the U.S. Navy Blue Angels. You can participate in the cherry pie-eating contest, thrill to one of three lively parades or watch fireworks light up Grand Traverse Bay in an awe-inspiring finale.

Contact the National Cherry Festival at 108 W. Grandview Pkwy., Traverse City, MI 49684; call (616) 947-4230.

Getting there: From Detroit, take I-75 north to Grayling, then west on S.R. 72 to U.S. 31 southwest eight miles to Traverse City.

❽ MICHIGAN FESTIVAL
AUGUST *in* EAST LANSING

Spread over the campus of sprawling Michigan State University and the streets of downtown East Lansing, the 10-day Michigan Festival includes more than 200 lively events and bills itself as "Michigan's Favorite Summer Music and Fun Festival."

One highlight is the annual Festival of Michigan Folklife, the state's largest outdoor exhibition of living traditions. Since 1987, the festival has brought together storytellers, musicians, craftspeople, cooks and dancers representing the state's diverse regional, occupational and ethnic heritages. Italian American candy making, Russian and Ukrainian folk songs and Latin dance styles are a few of the diverse cultural elements featured.

One button gets you into the folklife festival, musical performances, the popular kids' parade and festival, the American Indian Heritage Pow Wow, the Festival of Michigan Foods and more.

Contact the festival at 1331 E. Grand River, Ste. 113, East Lansing, MI 48823; call 1-800-935 FEST.

Getting there: From Detroit, take I-696 to I-96, Exit 106; follow the signs to campus.

❾ RENAISSANCE FESTIVAL
AUGUST/SEPTEMBER *in* HOLLY

Step back in time to the days of Shakespeare and Merrie Ole England during more than a month of merrymaking in Hollygrove, a re-created 16th century village north of Holly. But don't look to travel back in time on weekdays; like the fictional Brigadoon, the village appears only occasionally—in this case, on weekends—each August and September.

Inside the village's turreted gates, you'll find pomp and performance. Theatergoers won't want to miss the many performances of drama and comedy; dance and music enthusiasts can thrill to performances of bawdy and courtly music, folk and classical dance, and impromptu acts by wandering troubadours, street musicians, jugglers and puppeteers.

If you want to get in on the act, you (or the kids) can learn to joust or simply savor the hearty historic cuisine, including turkey drumsticks, apple dumplings and a microbrew known as Dragon's Breath Ale. Afterward, pick up a souvenir of your 16th century visit in the arts and crafts area, which features more than 150 booths selling floral creations, pewter, glass, ceramics and more.

Contact the Renaissance Festival at 120 S. Saginaw St., Holly, MI 48442; call 1-800-601-4848.

Getting there: From Detroit, take I-75 north to the Holly exit.

⑩ ## FORD MONTREUX DETROIT JAZZ FESTIVAL
LABOR DAY WEEKEND *in* DETROIT

Tune crooners and swingin' sounds invade downtown's Hart Plaza each Labor Day weekend during one of the largest jazz festivals in North America.

This most popular musical happenings in Detroit is named for the town of Montreux, Switzerland, which helped launch the event. But most of the sounds are strictly all-American; swing, Dixieland and bebop are just a few of the styles available. Stick around for jam sessions or sit in when the stars rehearse. Performers have included big names such as Dizzy Gillespie, Wynton Marsalis and Eddie Palmieri.

After the shows, head for the food court, where you can fill up on ethnic dishes from around the world. Or consider joining the jams in one of the free clinics, where you can learn to toot your own horn or a variety of other instruments. (Also see "African American Heritage.")

Contact the Ford Montreux Detroit Jazz Festival at 350 Madison Ave., Detroit, MI 48226; call (313) 963-7622.

Getting there: Take I-75, the Lodge Freeway or Woodward downtown to East Jefferson.

⑪ DETROIT FESTIVAL OF THE ARTS
SEPTEMBER *in* DETROIT

The normally somewhat subdued University Cultural Center downtown literally overflows with "culture" during this colorful and lively annual event. Sponsored by the University Cultural Center Association (UCCA), it takes place the third weekend in September in a 15-block area. Festivities include performing, visual and literary arts. A Children's Fair is staged on Wayne State University's campus with dance, theatrical and musical performances, as well as a youth arts market, booths and demonstrations. Ethnic performers and foods are featured throughout.

Call the UCCA at (313) 577-5088.

Getting there: Warren/Forest exit from U.S. 10 (Lodge Freeway); Warren exit from I-75; Woodward/John R exit from I-94.

⑫ NATIVE AMERICAN FESTIVAL & MINI POW WOW
NOVEMBER *in* NOVI

The proud traditions of the "First Americans" are the focus of this special festival at Novi Expo Center. Each November, members of the state's Ojibwa, Chippewa, Cherokee and other tribes come together to celebrate their heritages and promote cultural understanding. The event is produced in cooperation with Southeastern Michigan Indians Inc. and the North American Indian Association of Detroit, two of the largest Native American Indian organizations in the state.

Native American Indian arts are the focus of the one-day event, which features performing arts such as drumming, dancing, story-telling and singing, as well as authentic arts and crafts and a unique Native American Indian marketplace. Continuous ceremonial music and dance take place during the day. Visitors are encouraged to join in songs and dances; learn to make sweet-grass baskets, quills and other crafts; and taste Native American Indian foods such as buffalo burgers, fry-bread, turkey wild-rice soup and buffalo stew.

Special hands-on children's events include work-shops that teach headband and totem-pole making, sand drawings, clay bead necklaces and more. (Scout troups can earn badges.)

(Also see "Native American Heritage.")

Contact the sponsor, Metro Parent Magazine, *at (248) 352-0990.*

Getting there: Take I-96 to Exit 162 (Novi/Walled Lake).

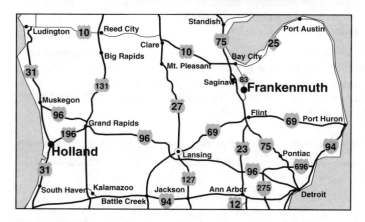

Two of Michigan's favorite towns to tour, Holland and Frankenmuth, are filled with ethnic attractions.

TOUR	HOLLAND

THE DUTCH TOUCH

Visitors to Holland, Michigan, in the early spring of 1847 would have found no semblance of the city that exists today on the western side of the state. What they would have found was an undeveloped wilderness of woods and stream and an optimistic group of Dutch immigrants who were determined to tame the area and call it home.

More than a century and a half later, the spirit of those early settlers lives on in the city. Although the annual May **Tulip Time Festival** *(see "Let's Celebrate" chapter)* is the area's best-known event, this friendly city offers a variety of activities, including museums, old-world-style cuisine and a warm *welkom* for visitors year-round. It's a great place to "go Dutch" on your next weekend getaway. *From Detroit, it's a 180-mile drive across the state on I-96.*

For an overview of the area's history, don't miss the small, but choice **Holland Museum** *on West 10th Street.* Inside this landmark building are Dutch treasures that range from early delftware and 18th-century furniture to an authentic fisherman's cottage and an 1860 Amsterdam dollhouse. Other displays highlight maritime history, area manufacturing and famous summer resorts.

Back in the 1700s, windmills dotted the Dutch countryside, providing natural energy to flax and grain growers. Today, an original windmill greets visitors to Holland's **Windmill Island Municipal Park** *at the corner of Seventh Street and Lincoln Avenue.* Transported to Michigan by special permission of the Dutch government in 1964, "De Zwaan" is as tall as a 12-story building, 200 years old and the only authentic windmill in the United States. Tour the mill with costumed guides, watch a 20-minute movie about windmills, or thrill the kids with a ride on an authentic vintage Dutch carousel.

Holland also boasts the only wooden shoe factories in the nation—just two, both *on U.S. 31.* More than 10,000 pairs of shoes fashioned from white poplar logs are created and sold at the **DeKlomp Wooden Shoe Factory** and the original **Wooden Shoe Factory.** Get fitted for a pair of *klompen,* or just watch the fascinating process as craftsmen of Dutch descent produce shoes on vintage imported machinery.

You can view the entire process, from quartered logs through final hand-decorating, on factory tours at either location. If you collect delftware, you probably already know that the DeKlomp factory is the only delft factory in the United States. It's also the site of the **Veldheer Tulip Gardens,** where millions of beautiful blooms attract thousands of visitors in spring and summer.

TULIPMANIA: THE WIND TRADE OF 1637

Originally a wildflower tamed by the Turks, cultivated tulips came to the Netherlands by way of Carolus Clusius, the director of the Royal Medicinal Garden in Vienna. Clusius successfully raised the first European tulips in the 16th century. When he fled to the Netherlands for religious sanctuary, he took his tulip bulbs with him. Both thrived in the Dutch climate, and an industry was born.

By the early 17th century, horticultural experimenting created many breeds of tulips. Available only to the rich, these exotic and expensive specimens were coveted for their beauty, rarity and status. When the middle classes began to realize how much money the upper classes spent on tulip bulbs—and how much money they made *selling* them—they sensed a foolproof get-rich-quick opportunity. "Tulipmania" soon enveloped the country.

Bulbs were sold by weight, usually while they were still in the ground. All one had to do to become rich was plant them and wait. The buying and selling of a product as invisible as unsprouted flowers came to be called the **"wind trade."**

Traders could earn as much as 60,000 florins (about $44,000 today) in a month. People were desperate to cash in on the bulb-trading frenzy. Small businesses were sold, and family jewels were traded.

Local governments tried to outlaw this commerce, but the trade wilted on its own. The bottom fell out of the market in 1637 when a gathering of bulb merchants could not get the usual inflated prices for their wares. Word spread quickly, and the market crashed.

Thousands of powerful Dutch businessmen, along with "ordinary" folk, were ruined within two months.

ANTIQUE BULBS

Michigan gardeners can grow some of the direct descendants of the infamous bulbs of 1637, thanks to Scott Kunst of Ann Arbor. The former schoolteacher now works full time as a landscape historian; he lectures to museum audiences and home owners and offers consulting services as well. His *Old House Gardens* catalog of "antique" bulbs, dating from the 1500s, features a remarkable variety, as well as useful information.

For a catalog, send $2 to:
Old House Gardens
536 Third St., Ann Arbor, MI 48103

Finally, don't miss the 15-acre **Dutch Village** *on U.S. 31 just north of downtown,* where you'll cross a bridge and travel back in time to old Holland. You'll stroll among canals, flowering gardens and Dutch-style architecture; enjoy folk dancing and musicians; and watch as craftsmen carve wooden shoes. Afterward, shop for Dutch imports in the specialty shops. Learn about the folklore of the Netherlands through a movie or historical display. Children will enjoy the wooden-shoe slide and chair swing and have fun petting the animals in the Frisian farm.

Wind down your visit with a meal at the village's **Queen's Inn,** where costumed waitresses serve Dutch and American specialties. A beamed ceiling, open-hearth fireplace and Dutch sayings add to the charm.

Along with all its Dutch attractions, Holland boasts some of the state's most beautiful beaches, bicycling paths and fishing spots; an outlet mall; a restored downtown; and other attractions—more than enough to fill a weekend or longer.

For more information on attractions, lodging and dining, contact the Holland Area Convention and Visitors Bureau, 100 E. Eighth St., Suite 120, Holland, MI 49423. Call 1-800-506-1299.

TOUR	FRANKENMUTH

MICHIGAN'S LITTLE BAVARIA

German heritage comes alive in the fairy tale-like village of Frankenmuth, *80 miles north of Detroit* in the heart of Saginaw Valley farm country. The town's 4,400 residents provide an atmosphere of congeniality, or *gemütlichkeit,* to 3 million visitors a year. Tourists flock here to indulge in all-you-can-eat chicken dinners, shop for gifts made by Black Forest craftsmen and get a dose of Christmas spirit at any time of the year.

To find Michigan's Little Bavaria, *take I-75 north about 25 miles past Flint to Birch Run (Exit 136) and follow signs seven miles to* Frankenmuth. **Manufacturers Marketplace** outlet stores at the freeway exit might be a temptation, but hold off until you're on your way back.

Make your first stop **Bronner's Christmas Wonderland,** where 50,000 holiday trims and gifts are on display year-round. The 45-acre site, modeled after an old-world European marketplace, is filled with merchandise ranging from large-scale decorations designed for cities, shopping centers and churches to tree ornaments, garlands and lights for the home. Items from Germany, where the Christmas tree is believed to have originated, figure prominently in the international selection. Collectors can choose from 500 types of nativities (miniature to life-size), as well as 500 different Hummel figurines and 200 styles of nutcrackers.

Also on the property is the **Silent Night Memorial Chapel,** a replica of the site in Oberndorf, Austria, where that most loved Christmas hymn was first played in 1818. *(For more about Bronner's, call 517-652-9931 or 1-800-ALL YEAR for recorded information.)*

When you've had your fill of Christmas cheer, head into town to "do" **Main Street.** The lot by the 19th-century-style **Holz Brucke** (covered bridge) and Visitor Center is a central place to park. Or, if you're ready for a big meal, proceed directly to the restaurant parking lots for Frankenmuth's famous family-style chicken dinners and German fare. Diners at the Alpine-style **Bavarian Inn** are served by waiters in lederhosen and waitresses in peasant blouses and dirndl skirts. The same type of menu is offered at **Zehnder's,** the expansive Colonial-style restaurant across the street.

As you stroll down Main Street and visit various shops, listen for the Bavarian Inn's 35-bell automatic carillon in the **Glockenspiel Tower,** where carved figures depict the Pied Piper of Hamelin legend. Also, **Boening's Bavarian Clock Haus** *at 250 S. Main St.* has a giant replica of the Band Player cuckoo clock, which plays every half-hour.

The **Frankenmuth Historical Museum** *(one block north of the Bavarian Inn)* tells the story of the settlement that was started by 15 German Lutheran missionaries who came to the area in 1845 to spread the gospel to the Chippewa Indians of the Saginaw Valley.

By the time you reach the north end of town, where 25 stores are tucked inside the refurbished **School Haus Square Mall,** you'll have covered the gamut of bakeries, pretzel factories, and sausage, candy, cheese and ice-cream stores, as well as woodcarving, cuckoo clock, woolen mill, leather, doll and other gift shops.

Non-shoppers may prefer to tour the **Frankenmuth Brewery** *(425 S. Main St.)* and visit the hospitality center. A **St. Julian Winery** outlet *(farther north on Main Street)* offers free tasting.

Another way to experience Frankenmuth is on a riverboat cruise on the Cass River. The ***Riverview Queen*** paddle wheeler boards passengers at the **Riverview Café** *(at the top of the hill on Main Street)* for 45-minute tours May through October.

For more information about attractions, lodging and events, contact the Frankenmuth Convention and Visitors Bureau, 635 S. Main St., Frankenmuth, MI 48734. Call (517) 652-8666 or 1-800-FUN TOWN.

For more about Frankenmuth, see "Germany."

LEDERHOSEN— leather shorts, often with suspenders— are worn especially in Bavaria. The name comes from *leder* (leather) and *hose* (trousers).

DIRNDL is a dress style with a tight bodice, short sleeves, a low neck and a gathered skirt, or simply a full skirt with a tight waistband. The name is short for *dirndlkleid—dirndl* (girl) and *kleid* (dress).

NOTES

NOTES

NOTES

NOTES

NOTES

ATTENTION TRAVELERS:

BEFORE EMBARKING ON A GLOBAL JOURNEY IN METRO DETROIT, PLEASE REMEMBER...

...the introductory pages have important information on how to make the most of this book and ensure a pleasant journey.

...imagination, flexibility, a sense of humor and an open mind will enhance every experience.

...small businesses come and go; hours of operation change; detours or highway repairs might negate some directions. Check local newspapers, radio stations and/or web sites for the latest updates.

FOR THE LATEST INFORMATION AND UPDATES CONCERNING DETROIT'S GLOBAL COMMUNITY, VISIT OUR WEB SITE:

www.globaldetroit.com

OTHER SITES:

RESTAURANTS AND ENTERTAINMENT

www.metrotimes.com
(Metro Times)

TRAVEL, EVENTS & ENTERTAINMENT

www.aaamich.com
(AAA Michigan)

www.visitdetroit.com
(Metropolitan Detroit Convention & Visitors Bureau)

ROAD CONDITIONS & WEATHER

www.mdot.state.mi.us/mits/
(Michigan Dept. of Transportation)

GENERAL INFORMATION & UPDATES

www.detnews.com
(Detroit News)
&
www.freep.com
(Detroit Free Press)

Other sites are listed at the end of each chapter. Many of the listings in this book have, or will be getting, their own web pages. You may wish to do a search or give them a call.

THESE BOOKMARKS ARE INCLUDED FOR EASY REFERENCE

BON VOYAGE!

KNOW OF A SHOP, RESTAURANT, ORGANIZATION, EVENT OR RESOURCE THAT SHOULD BE INCLUDED IN THE NEXT EDITION OF *GLOBAL JOURNEYS*?

Or if you would like to be on our mailing list, please contact us at our web site: **www.globaldetroit.com** and/or use this card.

Your name_____

Address_____

_____

City_____

State_____ Zip_____

Phone ( ) _____

❏ **Please include me on your mailing list**

The following should be included in *Global Journeys*:

Name_____

Location_____

Description_____

_____

Contact:_____

Phone ( ) _____

E-mail_____

INTERESTED IN USING *GLOBAL JOURNEYS* AS A FUNDRAISER?

Or if you would like to inquire about bulk sales, non-profit, or wholesale rates, please contact us at our web site: **www.globaldetroit.com** and/or use this card.

Please check: ❏ **bulk sales**   ❏ **non-profit rates**   ❏ **fundraiser**

Contact name (if different from above) _____

Title_____

Organization_____

Address_____

City_____ State_____ Zip_____

Phone ( ) _____ or ( ) _____

E--mail_____

Department GJ-1999

GLOBAL JOURNEYS
c/o New Detroit, Inc.
3011 West Grand Blvd.
Suite 1200
Detroit, MI 48202-3013